SECRE

OF

HEAVEN

Secrets

of

Heaven

The Portable New Century Edition

EMANUEL SWEDENBORG

Volume 4

Translated from the Latin by Lisa Hyatt Cooper

SWEDENBORG FOUNDATION
West Chester, Pennsylvania

Originally published in Latin as *Arcana Coelestia,* London, 1749–1756. The volume contents of this and the original Latin edition, along with ISBNs of the annotated version, are as follows:

Volume number in this edition	Text treated	Volume number in the Latin first edition	Section numbers	ISBN (hardcover)
1	Genesis 1–8	1	§§1–946	978-0-87785-486-9
2	Genesis 9–15	1	§§947–1885	978-0-87785-487-6
3	Genesis 16–21	2 (in 6 fascicles)	§§1886–2759	978-0-87785-488-3
4	Genesis 22–26	3	§§2760–3485	978-0-87785-489-0
5	Genesis 27–30	3	§§3486–4055	978-0-87785-490-6
6	Genesis 31–35	4	§§4056–4634	978-0-87785-491-3
7	Genesis 36–40	4	§§4635–5190	978-0-87785-492-0
8	Genesis 41–44	5	§§5191–5866	978-0-87785-493-7
9	Genesis 45–50	5	§§5867–6626	978-0-87785-494-4
10	Exodus 1–8	6	§§6627–7487	978-0-87785-495-1
11	Exodus 9–15	6	§§7488–8386	978-0-87785-496-8
12	Exodus 16–21	7	§§8387–9111	978-0-87785-497-5
13	Exodus 22–24	7	§§9112–9442	978-0-87785-498-2
14	Exodus 25–29	8	§§9443–10166	978-0-87785-499-9
15	Exodus 30–40	8	§§10167–10837	978-0-87785-500-2

ISBN (e-book of library edition)   Volume 4: 978-0-87785-722-8
ISBN (Portable)   **Volume 4: 978-0-87785-420-3**
ISBN (e-book of Portable Edition)   Volume 4: 978-0-87785-721-1

(The ISBN in the Library of Congress data shown below is that of volume 1.)

Library of Congress Cataloging-in-Publication Data

Swedenborg, Emanuel, 1688–1772.
    [Arcana coelestia. English]
    Secrets of heaven / Emanuel Swedenborg ; translated from the Latin by
Lisa Hyatt Cooper. — Portable New Century ed.
        p. cm.
    Includes bibliographical references and indexes.
    ISBN 978-0-87785-408-1 (alk. paper)
        1. New Jerusalem Church—Doctrines. 2. Bible. O.T. Genesis—Commentaries—Early works to 1800. 3. Bible. O.T. Exodus—Commentaries—Early works to 1800. I. Title.
    BX8712.A8 2010
    230'.94—dc22

                                                                        2009054171

Senior copy editor, Alicia L. Dole
Text designed by Joanna V. Hill
Typesetting by Mary M. Wachsmann and Sarah Dole
Ornaments from the first Latin edition, 1749–1756
Cover design by Karen Connor
Cover photograph by Magda Indigo

For information about the New Century Edition of the Works of Emanuel Swedenborg, contact the Swedenborg Foundation, 320 North Church Street, West Chester, PA 19380 U.S.A.
Telephone: (610) 430-3222 • Web: www.swedenborg.com • E-mail: info@swedenborg.com

Contents

Genesis Chapter 25

Genesis Chapter 26

Conventions Used in This Work

MOST of the following conventions apply generally to the translations in the New Century Edition Portable series. For introductory material on the content and history of *Secrets of Heaven,* and for annotations on the subject matter, including obscure or problematic content, and extensive indexes, the reader is referred to the Deluxe New Century Edition volumes.

Volume designation *Secrets of Heaven* was originally published in eight volumes; in this edition all but the second original volume have been divided into two. Thus Swedenborg's eight volumes now fill fifteen volumes, of which this is the fourth. It corresponds to approximately the first half of Swedenborg's volume 3.

Section numbers Following a practice common in his time, Swedenborg divided his published theological works into sections numbered in sequence from beginning to end. His original section numbers have been preserved in this edition; they appear in boxes in the outside margins. Traditionally, these sections have been referred to as "numbers" and designated by the abbreviation "n." In this edition, however, the more common section symbol (§) is used to designate the section numbers, and the sections are referred to as such.

Subsection numbers Because many sections throughout Swedenborg's works are too long for precise cross-referencing, Swedenborgian scholar John Faulkner Potts (1838–1923) further divided them into subsections; these have since become standard, though minor variations occur from one edition to another. These subsections are indicated by bracketed numbers that appear in the text itself: [2], [3], and so on. Because the beginning of the first *subsection* always coincides with the beginning of the *section* proper, it is not labeled in the text.

Citations of Swedenborg's text As is common in Swedenborgian studies, text citations of Swedenborg's works refer not to page numbers but to section numbers, which unlike page numbers are uniform in most editions. In citations the section symbol (§) is generally omitted after the title of a work by Swedenborg. Thus "*Secrets of Heaven* 29" refers to section 29 (§29) of Swedenborg's *Secrets of Heaven,* not to page 29 of any edition.

Subsection numbers are given after a colon; a reference such as "29:2" indicates subsection 2 of section 29. The reference "29:1" would indicate the first subsection of section 29, though that subsection is not in fact labeled in the text. Where section numbers stand alone without titles, their function is indicated by the prefixed section symbol; for example, "§29:2".

Citations of the Bible Biblical citations in this edition follow the accepted standard: a semicolon is used between book references and between chapter references, and a comma between verse references. Therefore "Matthew 5:11, 12; 6:1; 10:41, 42; Luke 6:23, 35" refers to Matthew chapter 5, verses 11 and 12; Matthew chapter 6, verse 1; Matthew chapter 10, verses 41 and 42; and Luke chapter 6, verses 23 and 35. Swedenborg often incorporated the numbers of verses not actually represented in his text when listing verse numbers for a passage he quoted; these apparently constitute a kind of "see also" reference to other material he felt was relevant. This edition includes these extra verses and also follows Swedenborg where he cites contiguous verses individually (for example, John 14:8, 9, 10, 11), rather than as a range (John 14:8–11). Occasionally this edition supplies a full, conventional Bible reference where Swedenborg omits one after a quotation.

Quotations in Swedenborg's works Some features of the original Latin text of *Secrets of Heaven* have been modernized in this edition. For example, Swedenborg's first edition generally relies on context or italics rather than on quotation marks to indicate passages taken from the Bible or from other works. The manner in which these conventions are used in the original suggests that Swedenborg did not belabor the distinction between direct quotation and paraphrase; but in this edition, directly quoted material is indicated by either block quotations or quotation marks, and paraphrased material is usually presented without such indicators. In passages of dialog as well, quotation marks have been introduced that were not present as such in the original. Furthermore, Swedenborg did not mark his omissions from or changes to material he quoted, a practice in which this edition generally follows him. One exception consists of those instances in which Swedenborg did not include a complete sentence at the beginning or end of a Bible quotation. The omission in such cases has been marked in this edition with added points of ellipsis.

Grammatical anomalies Swedenborg sometimes uses a singular verb with certain dual subjects such as love and wisdom, goodness and truth, and love and charity. The wider context of his works indicates that his reason for doing so is that he understands the two given subjects as forming a unity. This translation generally preserves such singular verbs.

Italicized terms Any words in indented scriptural extracts that are here set in italics reflect a similar emphasis in the first edition.

Special use of vertical rule The opening passages of the chapters treating Genesis 1–15, as well as the ends of all chapters, contain material that derives in some way from Swedenborg's experiences in the spiritual world. Swedenborg specified that the text of these passages be set in continuous italics to distinguish it from exegetical and other material. For this edition, the heavy use of italic text was felt to be antithetical to modern tastes, as well as difficult to read, and so such passages are instead marked by a vertical rule in the margin.

Changes to and insertions in the text This translation is based on the first Latin edition, published by Swedenborg himself (1749–1756); it also reflects emendations in the third Latin edition, edited by P. H. Johnson, John E. Elliott, and others, and published by the Swedenborg Society (1949–1973). It incorporates the silent correction of minor errors, not only in the text proper but in Bible verse references. The text has also been changed without notice where the verse numbering of the Latin Bible cited by Swedenborg differs from that of modern English Bibles. Throughout the translation, references or cross-references that were implied but not stated have been inserted in brackets; for example, [John 3:27]. In many cases, it is very difficult to determine what Swedenborg had in mind when he referred to other passages giving evidence for a statement or providing further discussion on a topic. Because of this difficulty, the missing references that are occasionally supplied in this edition should not be considered definitive or exhaustive. In contrast to such references in square brackets, references that occur in parentheses are those that appear in the first edition; for example, (1 Samuel 30:16), (see §42 above). Occasionally square brackets signal an insertion of other material that was not present in the first edition. These insertions fall into two classes: words likely to have been deleted through a copying or typesetting error, and words supplied by the translator as necessary for the understanding of the English text, though they have no direct parallel in the Latin. The latter device has been used sparingly, however, even at the risk of some inconsistency in its application. Unfortunately, no annotations concerning these insertions can be supplied in this Portable edition.

Biblical titles Swedenborg refers to the Hebrew Scriptures as the Old Testament and to the Greek Scriptures as the New Testament; his terminology has been adopted in this edition. As was the custom in his day, he refers to the Pentateuch (Genesis, Exodus, Leviticus, Numbers, and Deuteronomy) simply as "Moses"; for example, in §2842:7 he writes "it says in Moses" and then quotes a passage from Deuteronomy. Similarly, in sentences or phrases introducing quotations he sometimes refers to the Psalms as "David," to Lamentations as "Jeremiah," and to the Gospel of John, the Epistles of John, and the Book of Revelation as simply "John." Conventional references supplied in parentheses after such quotations specify their sources more precisely.

Problematic content Occasionally Swedenborg makes statements that, although mild by the standards of eighteenth-century theological discourse, now read as harsh, dismissive, or insensitive. The most problematic are assertions about or criticisms of various religious traditions and their adherents—including Judaism, ancient or contemporary; Roman Catholicism; Islam; and the Protestantism in which Swedenborg himself grew up. These statements are far outweighed in size and importance by other passages in Swedenborg's works earnestly maintaining the value of every individual and of all religions. This wider context is discussed in the introductions and annotations of the Deluxe edition mentioned above. In the present format, however, problematic statements must be retained without comment. The other option—to omit them—would obscure some aspects of Swedenborg's presentation and in any case compromise its historicity.

SECRETS
OF
HEAVEN

Preface

WHEN people stay with Scripture's literal meaning alone and do not seek out an inner meaning from other passages in the Word to explain it, they are delusional. The extent of their delusion can be plainly seen from the number of heresies that exist, each of which uses the Word's literal meaning to prove its own dogma. Consider especially the major heresy generated by self-love and materialism (in all their insanity and hellishness) on the basis of the Lord's words to Peter:

> I say to you that you are Peter, and on this rock I will build my church, and the gates of hell will not prevail over it. And I will give you the keys to the kingdom of the heavens; and whatever you bind on earth will be bound in the heavens, and whatever you unbind on earth will be unbound in the heavens. (Matthew 16:15, 16, 17, 18, 19)

[2] People who stress the literal meaning think that these words have to do with Peter and that he was personally given this immense power. Yet they know that Peter lived an extremely simple life, that he never exercised this kind of power, and that to do so would be an assault on God's divinity. Even so, self-love and materialism in all their insanity and hellishness prompt them to claim for themselves the highest power on earth and in heaven, and to make themselves gods. They therefore interpret the passage according to its literal meaning and vehemently defend their interpretation. In reality, the inner meaning of the words is that true faith in the Lord has this power (and such faith exists only in people who love the Lord and show kindness to their neighbor). Even at that, it is not faith but the Lord, the source of faith, who has the power. The *rock* here means this faith, just as it does everywhere else in the Word. It is on this rock that the church is built, and against it the gates of hell cannot prevail. Faith in the

Lord has the keys to the kingdom of the heavens. It closes heaven to keep out evil and falsity, and it opens heaven to what is good and true. That is the inner meaning of the words.

[3] Like the twelve tribes of Israel, the twelve apostles actually represented all aspects of faith in the Lord (§§577, 2089, 2129, 2130 at the end). Peter represented faith itself; James represented neighborly love; and John represented the good done by neighborly love (see the preface to Genesis 18). Their representation resembled that of Reuben, Simeon, and Levi (Jacob's first children in the representative Jewish and Israelite religion), as can be seen from a thousand places in the Word. The words above were addressed to Peter because he presented an image of faith.

This shows what thick darkness people plunge into—dragging others with them—by interpreting everything literally, as we see from this declaration to Peter, which they use in denying the Lord the power to save the human race and usurping it for themselves.

Genesis 22

[The Word's Inner Meaning]

THIS is how John, in the Book of Revelation, depicts the inner meaning of the Word:

> I saw heaven opened, and look! A *white horse*. And the one sitting on it
> was called faithful and true, and he judges and fights in righteousness.
> His eyes were a fiery flame. And on his head were many crowns. He had
> a name written that no one knows but him. And he was wrapped in a
> garment dyed with blood, and his name is called *God's Word*. And the
> armies in the heavens followed him on white horses, dressed in clean,
> white, fine linen. And on his garment and on his thigh he has a name
> written: *King of Kings and Lord of Lords*. (Revelation 19:11, 12, 13, 14, 16)

No one can know what the details here involve without the inner meaning. Obviously every bit of it represents and symbolizes something—the
fact that heaven was opened, the horse was white, the one sitting on it
was faithful and true and he was judging and fighting in righteousness,
his eyes were a fiery flame, he had many crowns on his head, he had a
name that no one knew but him, he was wrapped in a garment dyed
with blood, the armies in heaven followed him on white horses, they were
dressed in clean, white, fine linen, and on his garment and thigh he had a
name written. The passage states explicitly that he is the Word, and that
it is the Lord who is the Word, because it says, "His name is called God's

Word," and then, "He has on his garment and on his thigh a name written: King of Kings and Lord of Lords."

[2] An interpretation of all the different terms shows that the Word's inner meaning is being depicted here. The fact that heaven was opened represents and symbolizes the fact that the Word's inner meaning is visible only in heaven and to people for whom heaven lies open—that is, people who love and therefore believe in the Lord. The fact that the *horse* was *white* represents and symbolizes our understanding the Word's inner depths. (What follows below will make it clear that this is the meaning of the white horse.) The fact that the one sitting on it is the Word, and that it is the Lord who is the Word, is plain. It is because of his goodness that he is called faithful and is said to judge in righteousness; and because of his truth, that he is called true and is said to fight in righteousness. The many crowns on his head symbolize all facets of faith. Having a name written that no one knows but him means that no one sees what the Word's inner meaning is like except him and those he reveals it to. Being wrapped in a garment dyed with blood symbolizes the Word's literal meaning. The armies in the heavens that followed him on white horses symbolize people who understand the Word's inner content. Being dressed in clean, white, fine linen symbolizes the same people clad in love and therefore in faith. The name written on his garment and on his thigh symbolizes truth and goodness.

These words and those that come before and after them in Revelation show that around the "last time" the Word's inner meaning will be disclosed. What will happen then is also portrayed in Revelation 19, in verses 17, 18, 19, 20, 21.

2761   The fact that a white horse stands for understanding the Word's inner depths (or to put it another way, its inner meaning) can be seen from the symbolism of a horse as something related to the intellect. The prophetic parts of the Word often mention a horse or rider, but so far no one has recognized that a horse symbolizes something connected with the intellect, while a rider symbolizes an intelligent person. In the prophecy of Jacob (who by then was Israel) concerning Dan, for example:

> Dan is a snake on the path, a darting serpent on the track, biting the *horse's heels,* and its *rider* will fall off behind. Your salvation I await, Jehovah. (Genesis 49:17, 18)

A snake means a person who makes deductions about divine secrets on the basis of sensory and secular knowledge (see §195). A path or track means truth (627, 2333). A heel means whatever is lowest on the earthly level (259). A horse means understanding the Word, while a rider means a teacher. It is clear, then, what the prophecy means: people who reason about religious truth on the basis of sensory and secular knowledge cling to nothing more than the very lowest levels of the physical world. As a result they believe nothing, which is "falling off the back," and that is why the passage adds, "Your salvation I await, Jehovah." [2] In Habakkuk:

> God, you *ride* on *your horses;* your chariots are salvation. You made *your horses* tread in the sea. (Habakkuk 3:8, 15)

The horses stand for divine truth in the Word; the chariots, for teachings drawn from it; and the sea, for religious knowledge (§§28, 2120). All of these have to do with an understanding of the Word, given by God, so it says, "You made your horses tread in the sea." Here God is described as having horses, as he was above in Revelation, but he cannot be said to have horses unless they symbolize something like this. [3] In David:

> Sing to God; make music to his name! Exalt the *one riding* on the clouds by his name, Jah! (Psalms 68:4)

Riding on clouds stands for understanding the depths, or inner meaning, of the Word. A cloud is the literal meaning of the Word, which holds an inner meaning. (See the preface to Genesis 18, which explains what it means to say that the Lord will come in the clouds of the heavens with strength and glory.) [4] In the same author:

> Jehovah bent the heavens and came down, and darkness was under his feet, and he *rode* upon a guardian being. (Psalms 18:9, 10)

The darkness here takes the place of the clouds. Riding on the guardian being stands for the Lord's providence, which holds us back from prying into the religious mysteries in the Word on our own (§308). In Zechariah:

> On that day, "Holiness to Jehovah" will be on the *horse bells.* (Zechariah 14:20)

The horse bells stand for understanding the Word's spiritual contents, which are holy. [5] In Jeremiah:

> Through the gates of this city will enter monarchs and chieftains, sitting on David's throne, *riding* in a chariot and *on horses,* they and their chieftains, [each] a man of Judah, and residents of Jerusalem; and this city will be inhabited forever. (Jeremiah 17:25, 26; 22:4)

The city Jerusalem stands for the Lord's spiritual kingdom and church. Monarchs stand for truth (§§1672, 2015, 2069); chieftains, for the main things truth commands of us (1482, 2089). David stands for the Lord (1888). A man of Judah and residents of Jerusalem stand for people committed to doing good out of love, charity, and faith (2268, 2451, 2712). Riding a chariot and horses, then, stands for learning true theology from a deep understanding of the Word. [6] In Isaiah:

> Then you will take pleasure in Jehovah, and I will *make you ride* on the heights of the earth and cause you to eat the inheritance of Jacob. (Isaiah 58:14)

Riding on the heights of the earth stands for intelligence. In David:

> A love song: Strap your sword on your thigh, mighty man ([it is] your glory and finery), and in your finery advance; *ride on the word of truth* and gentle justice, and your right hand will teach you marvelous things. (Psalms 45: heading, 3, 4)

Riding on the word of truth plainly stands for an intelligent grasp of truth, while riding on the word of gentle justice stands for a wise understanding of goodness. [7] In Zechariah:

> "On that day," says Jehovah, "I will strike *every horse* with bewilderment, and *the one riding it,* with insanity. And on the house of Judah I will open my eyes, and *every horse of the peoples* I will strike with blindness." (Zechariah 12:4, 5)

Here too a horse clearly stands for the intellect, which was to be struck with bewilderment and blindness, while the rider stands for an intelligent person, who was to be struck with insanity. In Hosea:

> Remove all wickedness and accept the good, and we will repay you with the young oxen of our lips. Assyria will not save us; *on a horse we will not ride;* and we will no longer say "Our God!" to the work of our hands. (Hosea 14:2, 3)

Assyria stands for rationalization (§§119, 1186). The horse stands for intellectual arrogance.

Horses come up in many other places, too.

2762   The symbolism of a *horse* as something related to the intellect actually comes from representations in the other life. Horses often appear in the world of spirits there, in great variety, as do horseback riders. Whenever they appear, they symbolize some aspect of the intellect. (Representations like this are always presenting themselves to spirits.)

The representation of a horse as some facet of the intellect causes the spirits and angels present with us to see immediately, when horses are mentioned in the Word, that the intellect is the theme.

For the same reason, some spirits from another planet, when they have acquired understanding and wisdom and are being taken up from the world of spirits into heaven, see horses that appear to be alight with fire. I too saw the horses as the spirits were being raised up. [2] As a result I was able to tell the symbolism of the *fiery chariot* and the *fiery horses* appearing to Elisha when Elijah went up into the heavens in a whirlwind. I could also tell the symbolism of the words Elisha then shouted:

> *My father! My father! The chariots of Israel, and its horsemen!* (2 Kings 2:11, 12)

I could also see the symbolism of the same words spoken to Elisha by Joash, king of Israel, when Elisha died:

> *My father! My father! The chariots of Israel, and its horsemen!* (2 Kings 13:14)

Elijah and Elisha represented the Lord as the Word, as will be mentioned elsewhere, by the Lord's divine mercy. Specifically, the *fiery chariot* represented teachings about love and charity drawn from the Word, while *fiery horses* represented teachings about faith drawn from the Word. Teachings about faith are the same thing as an understanding of the Word's depths, or its inner meaning.

[3] You can see that chariots and horses appear among spirits and angels in the heavens from the fact that they were seen by the prophets, such as Zechariah (Zechariah 1:8, 9, 10; 6:1, 2, 3, 4, 5, 6, 7) and others. Not only the prophets saw them but also Elisha's servant, who is spoken of this way in Kings:

> Jehovah opened the eyes of Elisha's servant and he saw, and here, the mountain was full of *horses*, and *fiery chariots* were all around Elisha! (2 Kings 6:17)

In addition, where the intelligent and wise live in the world of spirits, chariots and horses constantly appear. The reason is that chariots and horses represent attributes of wisdom and understanding, as noted.

People revived from death who are entering the next life see a portrayal of a young adult astride a horse who then dismounts. This symbolizes their need to learn about truth and goodness before they can go to heaven. (See §§187, 188 in the first volume.)

The ancient church was very familiar with the fact that chariots and horses symbolized these things, as can be seen from these words in Job, a book of the ancient church:

> God made her forget *wisdom* and has not imparted a share of *understanding* to her. As in the time she rose up tall, she mocks the *horse* and *its rider.* (Job 39:17, 18, 19)

[4] The symbolism of a horse as an aspect of the intellect spread from the ancient church to the sages of neighboring lands and into Greece. That is why, when the Greeks depicted the sun (which symbolizes love; §§2441, 2495), they took to placing their god of wisdom and understanding in it and assigning him a chariot and four fiery horses. When they portrayed their sea god, they also gave him horses, because the sea symbolizes all branches of knowledge in general (28, 2120). When they wanted to depict the intellect as the source of this knowledge, they imagined a flying horse that used its hoof to break open a spring where the young women embodying the arts and sciences came to live. And the Trojan Horse actually symbolized the wall-razing techniques that came from their intellect.

Certainly, people today (who have taken the practice from those ancient people) often use a flying horse or Pegasus to depict intellectual matters, and a spring to depict scholarly learning. Hardly anyone knows, however, that in a mystical sense a horse symbolizes the intellect, and a spring, truth; still less that these symbols spread from the ancient church to people outside the church.

2763 This makes it clear, then, where the representation and symbolism in the Word come from—from the representations that emerge in the other world. The people of the earliest church, who were heavenly, and who interacted with spirits and angels while they were still alive in this world, acquired them from there. These representations they handed down to their descendants and eventually to a generation that knew little about them except that they had such and such a symbolic meaning. Because they came from earliest times and were used in these descendants' divine worship, though, they treated them reverently and considered them holy.

[2] In addition to representation, there is also correspondence. Things that correspond to one another suggest and also symbolize something completely different in the physical world than in the spiritual world. The heart, for instance, suggests and symbolizes a desire for goodness;

eyes suggest and symbolize the intellect; ears, obedience; hands, power; not to mention countless other examples. These are not exactly *represented* in the world of spirits; it is more that they *correspond,* just as the physical dimension corresponds to the spiritual. That is why every word of Scripture, down to the smallest jot of all, involves something spiritual and heavenly. It is also why the Word was inspired in such a manner that when people on earth read it, spirits and angels instantly perceive it in a spiritual way, according to its representation and correspondence.

[3] But although this branch of study was cultivated so carefully and esteemed so highly by the ancient people who lived after the Flood and enabled them to think along the same lines as spirits and angels, it has been obliterated today. So entirely has it been wiped out that hardly anyone is willing to believe it exists. Those who do believe it exists downgrade it to a mystical whimsy of no practical use. People have become altogether worldly and body-centered, to the point where if you use the words *spiritual* and *heavenly,* they feel resistance, and sometimes disgust or even nausea. What will they do in the next world, which lasts forever, and where there is nothing worldly or bodily but only the spiritual and heavenly qualities that constitute life in heaven?

Genesis 22

1. And it happened after these words that God tested Abraham and said to him, "Abraham!" And he said, "Here I am."

2. And he said, "Please take your son—your only one, whom you love, Isaac—and go your way to the land of Moriah and offer him there as a burnt offering on one of the mountains, [the one] that I say to you."

3. And Abraham got up early in the morning and saddled his donkey and took two boys of his with him, and Isaac, his son, and split the pieces of wood for the burnt offering and rose and went to the place that God had said to him.

4. On the third day, Abraham raised his eyes and saw the place from far away.

5. And Abraham said to his boys, "Stay here with the donkey, and I and the boy will go all the way there and bow down and come back to you."

6. And Abraham took the pieces of wood for the burnt offering and put them on Isaac his son. And he took in his hand the fire and the knife, and they both went together.

7. And Isaac said to Abraham his father, and he said, "My father!" And he said, "Here I am, my son." And he said, "Look: the fire and the pieces of wood, and where is the animal for the burnt offering?"

8. And Abraham said, "God will see to an animal for the burnt offering, my son," and they both went together.

9. And they came to the place that God had said to him, and there Abraham built the altar and arranged the pieces of wood and tied Isaac his son and put him on the altar on top of the pieces of wood.

10. And Abraham put out his hand and took the knife to slaughter his son.

11. And the angel of Jehovah called out to him from heaven and said, "Abraham! Abraham!" And he said, "Here I am."

12. And he said, "You are not to put your hand out to the boy nor do anything to him, because now I know that you fear God and have not held back your son—your only one—from me."

13. And Abraham raised his eyes and looked and there: a ram behind him, caught in the thicket by its horns! And Abraham went and took the ram and offered it as a burnt offering in place of his son.

14. And Abraham called the name of that place "Jehovah will see," as it is said today: "on the mountain, Jehovah will see."

15. And the angel of Jehovah called out to Abraham a second time from heaven.

16. And he said, "'Upon my life I have sworn,' says Jehovah, 'because seeing that you have done this word and have not held back your son, your only one,

17. I will surely bless you and surely multiply your seed as the stars of the heavens and as the sand that is on the seashore, and your seed will inherit the gate of your foes.

18. And in your seed all the nations of the earth will be blessed, because you heeded my voice.'"

19. And Abraham went back to his boys. And they rose and went together to Beer-sheba. And Abraham settled in Beer-sheba.

20. And it happened after these words that Abraham was told, saying, "Here, now, Milcah—she too has borne children, to Nahor your brother:

21. Uz, his firstborn, and Buz, his brother, and Kemuel (father of Aram),

22. And Chesed, and Hazo, and Pildash, and Jidlaph, and Bethuel."
23. And Bethuel fathered Rebekah. These eight, Milcah bore to Nahor, brother of Abraham.
24. And there was his concubine, and her name was Reumah, and she also bore Tebah and Gaham and Tahash and Maacah.

Summary

IN its inner meaning this chapter speaks of the Lord's heaviest, deepest | **2764** |
trials, by which he united his human nature with his divine nature.

It also talks about the way in which that union is the means of salvation for people who make up the Lord's spiritual church.

The subject matter: The Lord's heaviest, deepest trials (verses 1, 3, 4, 5, | **2765** |
6, 9, 10, 11). The uniting of his human nature with his divine nature—in other words, his glorification—through those trials (verses 2, 11, 12, 16). The way the Lord's divine humanity saves spiritual people—those inside the church who have charity and faith (verses 2, 7, 8, 13, 14, 15, 16, 17, 18, 19) and those outside the church who have goodness (verses 20, 21, 22, 23, 24).

Inner Meaning

GENESIS 22:1. *And it happened after these words that God tested Abraham* | **2766** |
and said to him, "Abraham!" And he said, "Here I am."

It happened after these words symbolizes accomplished events. *That God tested Abraham* symbolizes the Lord's heaviest, deepest trials. *And said to him, "Abraham!"* symbolizes what the Lord perceived from divine truth. *And he said, "Here I am,"* symbolizes thought and reflection.

It happened after these words symbolizes accomplished events, as can | **2767** |
be seen without explanation.

The events being talked about have to do with Abimelech and Abraham—how they struck a pact in Beer-sheba and how in the end Abraham created a grove in Beer-sheba. These things meant that human reasoning was superimposed on teachings about faith, which in themselves are divine. The current passage speaks of the trials inflicted on the

Lord's rational mind, which is symbolized by Isaac. It was through his trials that the Lord made his humanity divine. So it was through his trials that he made his rationality—the starting point of his humanity (§§2106, 2194)—divine. This he did by chastising and banishing everything in his rational mind that was merely human—in other words, everything human that he inherited from his mother. That is the connection between the events of the previous chapter and those in the current chapter, which is why it says, "It happened after these words that God tested Abraham."

2768   *That God tested Abraham* symbolizes the Lord's heaviest, deepest trials, as the discussion below shows. *Abraham* represents the Lord, and in the inner meaning he actually means the Lord, which is clear from previous remarks on all passages dealing with Abraham.

The Lord had severe, profound trials. It will become clear that they are what the inner meaning of this chapter describes.

To say that God tested Abraham, however, is to speak in harmony with the literal text, which ascribes times of trial and other hardships to God. To speak in harmony with the inner meaning, though, is to say that God never tests anyone. At such times he is constantly delivering us from our struggles, so far as he can, which is to say, so far as freeing us does no harm. At the same time he is constantly focusing on the goodness to which he can lead us when we are being tested. Otherwise he would never consent to it. Although it is fair to say he allows us to be tested, his permission does not work the way we think it does—that when he allows something, he approves of it. Humans find it impossible to grasp that any of us could permit what we do not will, but it is the evil in us that causes this. It is also the evil in us that brings on our crises, for which God is not the least bit responsible. By the same token, a monarch or judge is not to blame when a citizen commits a crime and pays the penalty for it. When we exempt ourselves from the laws of the divinely ordained plan, which all come from goodness and therefore from truth, we subject ourselves to laws that oppose the divine plan, which come from evil and falsity. This is the source of our punishments and agonies.

2769   *And said to him, "Abraham!"* symbolizes what the Lord perceived from divine truth. This can be seen from the symbolism of *saying* in the narrative books of the Word as perceiving (discussed in §§1898, 1919, 2080, 2619) and from the representation of *Abraham* as the Lord.

The perception came from divine truth, as can be seen from the fact that the verse mentions God rather than Jehovah. When the Word focuses on truth, it uses the name God, but when it focuses on goodness, it uses the name Jehovah; see §2586. As a result, this verse and those that follow, up to verse 11, speak of God, because the theme here is spiritual crisis. Verse 11 and those that follow it speak of Jehovah, because the theme there is liberation. Truth is the source of all inward trial and damnation, whereas goodness is the source of all liberation and salvation. On the point that truth condemns and goodness saves, see §§1685, 2258, 2335.

And he said, "Here I am," symbolizes thought and reflection. This can be seen from the symbolism of *saying* as perceiving (§2769), although in this case it means thinking and reflecting, since it is an answer. All thought and therefore all reflection comes from perception (1919, 2515, 2552).

2770

Genesis 22:2. *And he said, "Please take your son—your only one, whom you love, Isaac—and go your way to the land of Moriah and offer him there as a burnt offering on one of the mountains, [the one] that I say to you."*

2771

He said, "Please take your son," symbolizes the divine rationality brought forth by the Lord. *Your only one, whom you love,* means the only such rationality in all creation, through which he would save the human race. *Isaac* symbolizes its character. *And go your way to the land of Moriah* symbolizes a situation of trial, and conditions then. *And offer him there as a burnt offering* means that he would consecrate this rationality to his divine side. *On one of the mountains* symbolizes divine love. *That I say to you* means as he would perceive.

He said, "Please take your son," symbolizes the divine rationality brought forth by the Lord. This can be seen from the symbolism of a *son* as rationality (discussed in §2623). Here it symbolizes divine rationality because "your son" means Isaac, who represents the Lord's divine rationality, as shown in §§1893, 2066, 2083, 2630. Since the Lord used his own power to make his rationality divine, as noted many times before, "your son" here also means that it had been brought forth by him; see §§1893, 2093, 2625.

2772

Your only one, whom you love, means the only such rationality in all creation, through which he would save the human race. This can be seen from the meaning of *only* as unique, and in fact unique in all creation, since it is talking about the Lord. Only of the Lord can it be said that his entire humanity was God—that is, that it became divine.

2773

Isaac symbolizes its character. To be specific, that rationality is composed of the goodness that comes of truth, and the truth that comes of goodness. In other words, it is the divine marriage as embodied in the

2774

Lord's humanity. This can be seen from the naming of Isaac, which Genesis 21:6, 7 above deals with [§§2638–2644].

2775   *And go your way to the land of Moriah* symbolizes a situation of trial, and conditions then, as can be seen from the symbolism of the *land of Moriah.* Clearly the land of Moriah is a situation of trial, since Abraham was ordered to go there, offer his son as a burnt offering there, and in the process undergo a final trial.

Jerusalem—where the Lord himself endured his final trial—was in the same region. This can be seen from the fact that David built an altar on the mountain of Moriah, and Solomon afterward built the Temple there, as is clear from Chronicles:

> Solomon started to build a house for Jehovah in Jerusalem—on the *mountain of Moriah,* which had been seen by David his father—in a place that David had prepared on the threshing floor of Ornan [Araunah] the Jebusite. (2 Chronicles 3:1; compare 1 Chronicles 21:16–28 with 2 Samuel 24:16–25)

This shows fairly plainly that the things said about the sacrifice of Isaac represent the Lord. Otherwise the incident could have taken place where Abraham was staying and he would not have been ordered to travel almost a three-day journey from there.

2776   *Offer him as a burnt offering* means that he would consecrate this rationality to his divine side. This can be seen from the fact that to the Hebrew nation and the Jewish religion a *burnt offering* represented the holiest element of their worship. There were burnt offerings and there were sacrifices; for what these represented, see §§922, 923, 1823, 2180. It was by means of burnt offerings and sacrifices that they consecrated things, so *offering as a burnt offering* here symbolizes being consecrated to the Divine. The Lord consecrated himself to his divine side, which is to say that he made his humanity one with his divinity by fighting and winning in his times of trial; see §§1663, 1690, 1691 at the end, 1692, 1737, 1787, 1812, 1813, 1820.

[2] Most people today believe that the burnt offerings and sacrifices symbolized the Lord's final suffering, and that by suffering as he did, the Lord atoned for the wickedness of us all. They even think that he shifted our wickedness onto his own shoulders and in this way removed it from us. So they consider themselves absolved and saved—no matter how they have lived throughout the entire course of their life—as long as they embrace the thought, even in the last hour before death, that the Lord suffered for them. This is not the case, however. The Lord's suffering on the cross was

the final crisis by which he finished uniting his humanity with his divinity, and his divinity with his humanity, and in this way glorified himself. That union itself is the means by which people can be saved, when they believe in him because they love their neighbor. [At that time,] you see, the Supreme Divine itself was no longer able to reach through to the human race, which had so thoroughly cut itself off from the heavenly qualities of love and the spiritual qualities of faith that it no longer even acknowledged their existence, let alone perceived them. To enable the Supreme Divine to come down to such a race, then, the Lord came into the world and made humanity one with divinity in himself. The only way the two could be united was by the most intense struggles and victories in his times of trial and eventually by the final trial, which was the one on the cross.

[3] That is why the Lord in his divine humanity can now enlighten the minds even of people fairly distant from the heavenly qualities of love, as long as they have the faith that comes of charity. In the other world, the Lord appears as a sun to heavenly angels, and as a moon to spiritual angels (§§1053, 1521, 1529, 1530, 2441, 2495). That is where all of heaven's light comes from. The light of heaven by its very nature gives light to the intellect of spirits and angels at the same time it gives light to their eyes. This mental light is within the visual light, so that the more outward light anyone in heaven has, the more inner light, or understanding, that person has. It is plain, then, how heavenly light differs from worldly light. The Lord's divine humanity is what enlightens both the eyesight and the intellect of spiritual people, which would not be possible if the Lord had not made his human nature one with his divine nature. If he had not united them, people in the world (and even spiritual angels in heaven) would no longer have been able to understand or perceive goodness and truth. So they would have had no blessings or happiness and therefore no salvation. It stands to reason, then, that the human race could not have been saved had not the Lord adopted a human side and glorified it.

[4] From this you can now judge for yourself the validity of the idea that we are saved as long as some inward stirring prompts us to think that the Lord suffered for us and took away our sins, no matter how we have lived. You can compare this to the reality that heaven's light, radiating from the Lord's divine humanity, cannot shine through to any but those who live lives of religious goodness, or love for others—in other words, who have a conscience. The actual platform on which that light can operate, or the vessel that receives it, is religious goodness, or love for others, and therefore conscience.

For the idea that the salvation of spiritual people lies in the Lord's divine humanity, see §§1043, 2661, 2716, 2718.

2777   *On one of the mountains* symbolizes divine love. This can be seen from the symbolism of a *mountain* as love (discussed in §§795, 796, 1430). Here it symbolizes divine love, because it relates to the Lord. (For more on what his love is like, see §§1690, 1691 at the end, 1789, 1812, 1820, 2077, 2253, 2500, 2572.) Because it was from divine love that the Lord fought and won when he was being tested, and from divine love that he consecrated and glorified himself, it is said to Abraham here that he should offer Isaac as a burnt offering on one of the mountains in the land of Moriah.

This representation becomes clear from the fact that David built an altar on the mountain of Moriah, and Solomon built the Temple there (§2775). An altar, on which burnt offerings and sacrifices were offered, was the main object representing the Lord; and later on, the Temple was. Section 921 shows that this was true of altars, and it can be seen in David:

> They will bring me to *your holy mountain* and to your dwelling places, and I will go in to *God's altar,* to *God,* my happiness and joy. (Psalms 43:3, 4)

John makes it clear that the same thing was true of the Temple:

> Jesus said, "Take apart this *temple* and in three days I will raise it up." He was speaking about the *temple of his body.* (John 2:19, 21)

2778   *That I say to you* means as he would perceive. This can be seen from the symbolism of *saying* as perceiving (dealt with above at §2769).

2779   Genesis 22:3. *And Abraham got up early in the morning and saddled his donkey and took two boys of his with him, and Isaac, his son, and split the pieces of wood for the burnt offering and rose and went to the place that God had said to him.*

Abraham got up early in the morning symbolizes a condition of peace and innocence. *And saddled his donkey* symbolizes his earthly self, which he prepared. *And took two boys* symbolizes his earlier rationality, which he added on. *And Isaac, his son,* symbolizes the divine rationality brought forth by him. *And split the pieces of wood for the burnt offering* symbolizes a deserving righteousness. *And rose* means going higher. *And went to the place that God had said to him* symbolizes the condition he was then in and his perception of it.

Abraham got up early in the morning symbolizes a condition of peace **2780** and innocence, as can be seen from the symbolism of *morning* and of *getting up early,* when they are connected with the Lord, who is meant by Abraham here.

In a comprehensive sense, *morning,* or early day, symbolizes the Lord, and so his kingdom, and so the heavenliness of love in general and particular, as shown in §2333. Since it symbolizes these things, it also symbolizes their actual state, which is one of peace and innocence.

Peaceful conditions in the heavens resemble the mood of dawn on the earth. Everything heavenly and spiritual in the heavens exists in a state of peace, which is what gives all of it its charm, blessing, and happiness. In the same way, at the time of dawn on earth, everything displays itself to us as pleasant and cheerful. Individual details draw their character from the general mood; see §§920, 2384. The case is the same with a state of innocence. It emerges under peaceful conditions and is a general mood affecting everything involved in love and faith. Unless the various facets of love and faith have innocence within them, they lack their essential ingredient. That is why no one can go to heaven without possessing some innocence (Mark 10:15).

This shows what morning symbolizes on an inner level, especially when the text says "he got up *early* in the *morning.*" And since in the highest sense the morning is the Lord, and is a state emanating from him that produces and influences everything within his kingdom, morning and getting up early also symbolize other qualities that emerge in that state. The nuances depend on the inner meaning of whatever follows.

And saddled the donkey symbolizes his earthly self, which he prepared, **2781** as can be seen from the symbolism of a *donkey,* discussed below.

We have inside us traits of will and traits of intellect. Traits that have to do with goodness are traits of will; those that have to do with truth are traits of intellect. There are different kinds of animals that symbolize traits of will, which relate to goodness, including lambs, sheep, kids, she-goats, young cattle, and adult cattle; see §§1823, 2179, 2180. There are also animals that symbolize traits of intellect, which relate to truth, and they are horses, mules, wild donkeys, camels, and domesticated donkeys, not to mention birds. A horse symbolizes something intellectual, as shown above in §§2761, 2762. A wild donkey symbolizes truth detached from goodness; see §1949. A camel symbolizes facts in general, and a domesticated donkey, facts in particular; see §1486.

[2] There are two components to our earthly level or, putting it another way, our earthly self: earthly goodness and earthly truth. Earthly goodness is the pleasure that flows from neighborly love and faith; earthly truth is the facts about both.

Truth on the earthly level is what a donkey symbolizes, and truth on the rational level is what a mule symbolizes, as the following passages show. In Isaiah:

> An oracle of the *animals of the south:* In a land of anguish and distress, the lion and tiger—and the viper and flying fire snake from there—will bear their goods on the *shoulder of young donkeys,* and their treasures on the *hump of camels,* on a people [whom] they will not profit. And Egyptians will help futilely and in vain. (Isaiah 30:6, 7)

People who know what is good and true but treat that knowledge as a collection of facts rather than something to live by are being called animals of the south. They are said to bear their goods on the shoulder of young donkeys, and their treasures on the hump of camels, because young donkeys symbolize particular facts, while camels symbolize facts in general. Egyptians stand for different kinds of factual knowledge (see §§1164, 1165, 1186), which are said to help futilely and in vain. This oracle has an inner meaning, without which no one could understand it, as anyone can see. Without the inner meaning, no one would know what an oracle of the animals of the south is, or the lion and tiger, the viper and flying fire snake, and the fact that the animals would bear their goods on the shoulder of young donkeys and their treasures on the hump of camels. No one would know why it says directly afterward that Egyptians will help futilely and in vain. In Moses, the donkey in Israel's prophecy concerning Issachar has a similar meaning:

> Issachar is a *bony donkey* lying down between its burdens. (Genesis 49:14)

[3] In Zechariah:

> This will be the plague with which Jehovah will strike all the peoples who fight against Jerusalem. It will be a plague on *horse, mule, camel,* and *donkey,* and every animal. (Zechariah 14:12, 15)

The horse, mule, camel, and donkey symbolize the contents of the human intellect, which will be afflicted by a plague. This can be seen from everything that the verses before and after these say, because the theme is the plagues leading up to the Last Judgment, or the close of the age. John also has quite a bit to say about them in Revelation, and the rest of the prophets speak of them here and there. People who are then going to fight against Jerusalem—that is, against the Lord's spiritual church and its truth—are symbolized by the animals mentioned, and their minds are going to be afflicted with plagues. [4] In Isaiah:

> Fortunate are you who sow along all the waters, sending the foot of the *ox* and the *donkey* there. (Isaiah 32:20)

Those who sow along all the waters stand for people who let themselves be taught about spiritual things. Waters are spiritual traits, or truth in the intellect (see §§680, 739, 2702). Sending the foot of the ox and the donkey there stands for earthly qualities that will make themselves useful. The ox is goodness on the earthly plane (2180, 2566); the donkey is truth on the earthly plane. [5] In Moses:

> . . . tying *his young donkey* to the grapevine and *his jenny's foal* to the choice vine. He washed his clothing in wine, and his garment in the blood of grapes. (Genesis 49:11)

This is the oracular utterance of Jacob (who by then was Israel) concerning the Lord. The grapevine and the choice vine stand for the outward and inward aspects of a spiritual religion (§1069). The young donkey stands for truth on the earthly plane; the jenny's foal, for truth on the rational plane. The reason a jenny's foal is rational truth is that a jenny, [a female donkey,] symbolizes a desire for earthly truth (1486), and its foal is rational truth (see §§1895, 1896, 1902, 1910).

[6] Judges once rode on female donkeys, and their children on young male donkeys. The reason was that judges represented what the church values as good, while their offspring represented the truth that develops out of that goodness. Monarchs, however, rode on female mules, and their children on male mules, because monarchs and their offspring represented what the church teaches to be true (see §§1672, 1728, 2015, 2069). The Book of Judges shows that a judge rode on a female donkey:

> My heart belongs to *Israel's lawgivers,* the most willing among the people. Bless Jehovah, you who are riding on *white jennies,* sitting on middin! (Judges 5:9, 10)

Judges' offspring rode on young donkeys:

> Jair, a judge over Israel, had thirty *children riding* on thirty *young donkeys.* (Judges 10:3, 4)

And in another place:

> Abdon, a judge of Israel, had forty *children* and thirty grandchildren *riding* on seventy *young donkeys.* (Judges 12:14)

A monarch rode on a female mule:

> David said to them, "Take with you the slaves of your master, and you are to make Solomon my son *ride* on the *she-mule* that is mine." And they made Solomon *ride* on the *she-mule* of *King* David; and Zadok the priest and Nathan the prophet anointed him as king in Gihon. (1 Kings 1:33, 38, 44, 45)

A monarch's offspring rode on male mules:

> All the *sons* of *King* David got up and *rode,* each on his *he-mule,* and fled from Absalom. (2 Samuel 13:29)

[7] This shows that riding on a female donkey was the sign of a judge; riding on a female mule, the sign of a monarch; riding on a young donkey, the sign of a judge's children; and riding on a male mule, the sign of a monarch's children. The reason is that a female donkey represented and symbolized a desire for earthly goodness and truth, as just noted; a female mule, a desire for rational truth; a male donkey (young or not), earthly truth itself; and a male mule (and a jenny's foal), rational truth. This clarifies what is meant by Zechariah's prophecies about the Lord:

> Rejoice, daughter of Zion; shout for joy, daughter of Jerusalem! See: *your king* will come to you, honorable and saved, humble, and *riding on a donkey,* and on a *young donkey, the foal of jennies.* His ruling power will be from sea to sea, and from the river to the ends of the earth. (Zechariah 9:9, 10)

When the Lord went to Jerusalem, he wanted to ride on these animals, as we know from the Gospels. This is what Matthew says about it:

> Jesus sent two disciples, saying to them, "Go into the town opposite you and immediately you will find a *jenny* tied, and her *young* with her; untie them and bring them to me." This happened in order to fulfill what was said by the prophet, saying, "Say to the daughter of Zion, 'See: your king is coming to you, mild, sitting on a *jenny,* and on a *young animal, the foal of a beast of burden.'*" And they brought the *jenny* and her *young* and set their clothes on them and placed him on them. (Matthew 21:[1,] 2, 4, 5, 7)

[8] Riding on a donkey was a sign that the earthly dimension would be made subordinate, while riding on a young animal, the foal of a jenny, was a sign that the rational dimension would be. The symbolism of a foal of a jenny, as shown above at the quotation from Genesis 49:11, is the same as that of a mule. For this reason, and because it was the role of a governing judge and a monarch to ride on these animals—and also in order to fulfill the religious representation—it pleased the Lord to do so. This is what John says about it:

> The next day, when a numerous crowd that had come to the feast heard that Jesus had come to Jerusalem, they took branches of palm trees and went to meet him and shouted, "Hosanna! A blessing on the one who comes in the Lord's name, the *King of Israel!*" Jesus, however, finding a *young donkey,* sat on it. As it is written: "Don't be afraid, daughter of Zion. See: *your king* is coming, sitting on the *young of a jenny.*" These things, however, his disciples did not know at first, but when Jesus was glorified, then they remembered that these things had been written about him, and these things they had done for him. (John 12:12, 13, 14, 15, 16; Mark 11:1–12; Luke 19:28–41)

[9] From this evidence it can now be seen that everything in the church of that day represented the Lord and accordingly the heavenly and spiritual qualities of his kingdom. That includes even a jenny and a jenny's foal, which represented the goodness and truth in a person's earthly self. The reason for this representation was that the earthly self ought to serve the rational self, which ought to serve the spiritual self, which ought to serve the heavenly self, which ought to serve the Lord. That is the proper hierarchy.

[10] Since an ox and a donkey symbolized the goodness and truth of the earthly self, many laws mentioning the two animals were laid down. At first glance, these laws do not seem worthy of mention in God's Word, but when their inner meaning is unfolded, spiritual content of tremendous importance comes to view. Here are examples from Moses:

> When anyone opens a pit, or when anyone digs a pit and does not cover it, and an *ox* or a *donkey* falls in, the owner of the pit shall repay silver to the owner, and the dead animal shall be [the pit owner's]. (Exodus 21:33, 34)

> If you come across your enemy's *ox* or your enemy's *donkey* wandering, you shall most decidedly bring it back to that person. If you see the *donkey* of one who hates you lying down under its load and shrink

from removing [the load], you shall most decidedly remove it from the animal. (Exodus 23:4, 5; Deuteronomy 22:1, 3)

You shall not see your brother's *donkey* or *ox* falling down along the way and hide yourself from them; you shall certainly help it up. (Deuteronomy 22:4)

You shall not plow with an *ox* and a *donkey* jointly. You are not to clothe yourself in mixed weaving of wool and linen together. (Deuteronomy 22:10, 11)

Six days you shall do your work, and on the seventh day you shall rest, in order that *your ox* may rest, and *your donkey,* and your slave woman's child, and the immigrant. (Exodus 23:12)

In these passages, on a spiritual level, an ox and a donkey actually symbolize earthly goodness and truth.

2782 *And took two boys* symbolizes his earlier rationality, which he added on, as can be seen from the symbolism of *boys*. A boy and boys in the Word symbolize various things, because the term applies to both the sons of the household and the sons of a foreigner, and to slaves as well. Here it refers to slaves.

In the Word, slaves actually symbolize a person's earthly dimension, which needs to serve the rational mind; see §§1486, 1713, 2541, 2567. Here, though, because it says "boys" rather than "slaves," they symbolize the earlier (or merely human) rationality that was to serve divine rationality. This can be seen from the context itself, too.

2783 *And Isaac, his son,* symbolizes the divine rationality brought forth by him. This is established by the representation of *Isaac* as the Lord's divine rationality (discussed many times before). The fact that it had been brought forth by him is meant by *his son,* as above in §2772.

2784 *And split the pieces of wood for the burnt offering* symbolizes a deserving righteousness, as can be seen from the symbolism of *wood* and of *splitting* it. *Pieces of wood* symbolize both good deeds and righteous goodness. *Splitting* wood means thinking that good deeds make us deserving, but splitting the wood *for the burnt offering* symbolizes a deserving kind of righteousness. This seems too far-fetched for anyone to see unless it is revealed.

What I observed of the woodcutters described in §1110 of the second volume illustrated for me the fact that splitting wood means thinking that good deeds make someone deserving, since these were people who wanted to earn salvation for the good they had done. In addition, there are others out in front, slightly elevated, off to the right, from a certain planet, who likewise claimed all goodness for themselves and likewise seem to cut and split wood. Sometimes when they seem to themselves to be working, their faces shine with something like swamp light, which is the credit they take for being good. The reason they look this way is that wood represents goodness. All the wood in the ark and Temple represented goodness, as did all the wood on top of the altar when burnt offerings and sacrifices were being conducted. In the Word, people who attribute goodness to themselves and take credit for it are in fact said to worship wood or a carving of wood.

He rose means going higher, as can be seen from the symbolism of *rising,* wherever it occurs in the Word, as involving some kind of elevation. **2785**

And went to the place that God had said to him symbolizes the condition he was then in and his perception of it. This can be seen from the symbolism of a *place* as conditions (dealt with in §§1273–1277, 1376–1381, 2625) and from that of *God's saying* as perceiving from his divine side (dealt with in §§2769, 2778). **2786**

As for the actual condition he was in, the current verse presents a picture of it. It was the state the Lord adopted when he was undergoing times of trial—here, the one he adopted when he was undergoing his heaviest, deepest trials. His first step in preparing for that state was to clothe himself in a state of peace and innocence. Then he prepared his earthly self, and his rational self, too, so that these could serve his divine rationality. He added a deserving righteousness, and by all these means lifted himself up.

These concepts cannot possibly be explained in a way that can be grasped or pictured by anyone who does not know that many states— each different from the next—can coexist in a person. They also cannot be explained to anyone who does not know what a condition of peace and innocence is, or what the earthly self is, or the rational self, or a deserving righteousness. First you have to have a distinct idea of each of these. You also have to know that from his divine side the Lord could produce in himself any state he wished, and that he prepared himself for his crises by bringing on many different states. To human beings this information may seem as dark as night, but to angels it is as clear as day. They live in heaven's light, which comes from the Lord, so they see the countless facets of this subject and others like it in clear detail. The emotion that then flows into them inspires them with indescribable joy.

You can appreciate, then, how wide a gap separates human intellect and perception from angelic intellect and perception.

2787   Genesis 22:4. *On the third day, Abraham raised his eyes and saw the place from far away.*

On the third day symbolizes the completion and the start of a consecration. *Abraham raised his eyes and saw* symbolizes thought and insight received from his divine side. *The place from far away* means the condition that he foresaw.

2788   *On the third day* symbolizes the completion and the start of a consecration, as can be seen from the symbolism of a *third day*. In the Word, a *day* symbolizes a state (§§23, 487, 488, 493, 893). So does a year, and any period of time in general, such as an hour, day, week, month, year, or age; morning, noon, evening, or night; and spring, summer, fall, or winter. When any of these is described as the *third,* it symbolizes both the end of that state and the beginning of the next. Since the theme here is the Lord's consecration, accomplished by means of trials, the third day symbolizes both the completion of a consecration and the start of a new consecration. This meaning also follows from all that has come before.

The reason for the symbolism is that when the Lord had fulfilled everything he came to fulfill, he rose again on the third day. When it comes to representations in the church, everything the Lord did—or rather was going to do—while he lived on earth was like an accomplished event. The same is true when it comes to the Word's inner meaning. In God, to become is the same thing as to be. In fact all eternity is present to him. [2] That is why the number three had a representative meaning, not only in the ancient church and the Jewish religion but also in various nations outside the church. (See what was said about the number in §§720, 901, 1825.)

The fact that this was the origin of the symbolism can be seen in Hosea:

> We will return to Jehovah, because he has injured us and will heal us, has struck us and will bandage us. He will bring us to life after two days; *on the third day he will revive us* so that we may live before him. (Hosea 6:1, 2)

The third day stands for the Lord's Coming and his resurrection. The same thing can be seen from Jonah and his *three days* and *three nights* inside a [great] fish (Jonah 1:17), which the Lord referred to in Matthew in these words:

> Just as Jonah was in the belly of the sea monster *three days* and *three nights,* so will the Son of Humankind be in the heart of the earth *three days* and *three nights.* (Matthew 12:40)

[3] It is necessary to realize that three days and the third day symbolize the same thing in the Word's inner meaning. "Three" and "third" have the same symbolism in the passages below, too. In John:

> Jesus said to the Jews, "Take apart this temple, yet in *three days* I will raise it up." He was speaking about the temple of his body. (John 2:19, 20, 21; Matthew 26:61; Mark 14:58; 15:29)

[4] Everyone knows that the Lord rose on the third day. For the same reason, the Lord divided his life into three stages, in Luke:

> Go and say to that fox, "Look: I am casting out demons and completing cures today and tomorrow, but on the *third day* I am brought to an end." (Luke 13:32)

The Lord also endured his final crisis (the trial on the cross) at the *third hour* of the day (Mark 15:25). *Three hours* later, at the *sixth hour,* darkness fell over the whole land (Luke 23:44), and another *three hours* later, at the *ninth hour,* came the end (Mark 15:33, 34, 37). But early on the *third day* he rose again (Mark 16:1, 2, 3, 4, [6]; Luke 24:7; see Matthew 16:21; 17:22, 23; 20:18, 19; Mark 8:31; 9:31; 10:33, 34; Luke 18:33; 24:46). Because of this—and especially because of the Lord's resurrection on the third day—the number three had a representative and symbolic meaning. The following passages in the Word show that it did:

> When Jehovah came down on Mount Sinai, he told Moses to consecrate the people *"today and tomorrow,"* and that they should wash their clothes and be ready for the *third day,* "because on the *third day,* Jehovah will come down." (Exodus 19:10, 11, 15, 16)

> When they traveled from Jehovah's mountain a journey of *three days,* the ark of Jehovah traveled before them a journey of *three days* to find rest for them. (Numbers 10:33)

> In addition, there was darkness on all the land of Egypt for *three days,* and a man could not see his brother for *three days,* but the children of Israel had light. (Exodus 10:22, 23)

[5] The meat of a vow-fulfillment sacrifice and of a freewill sacrifice would be eaten on the *first and second day.* Nothing was to remain till the *third day* or it would be burned, because it was an abomination. The same was true for the meat of a thanksgiving sacrifice; and if it was eaten on the

third day, there would be no reconciliation [with Jehovah], but that soul would bear its own wickedness. (Leviticus 7:16, 17, 18; 19:6, 7, [8])

Those touching a dead body would atone for themselves on the *third day,* and on the seventh day they would be clean. If not, that soul would be cut off from Israel. And a clean person would spatter water on an unclean person on the *third day* and on the seventh day. (Numbers 19:12, 13, 19)

Those who had killed a soul in battle or touched a victim of stabbing would purify themselves on the *third day* and on the seventh day. (Numbers 31:19)

[6] When they came into the land of Canaan, for *three years* the fruit would be uncircumcised and not eaten. (Leviticus 19:23)

At the end of *three years* they would bring out all the tithes of their produce for *that year* and store it within the gates, so that the Levite, the immigrant, the orphan, and the widow could eat. (Deuteronomy 14:28, 29; 26:12)

Three times a year they would celebrate feasts to Jehovah. And *three times a year* every male would appear before the face of the Lord Jehovah. (Exodus 23:14, 17; Deuteronomy 16:16)

Joshua told the people that in *three days* they would cross the Jordan and inherit the land. (Joshua 1:11; 3:2)

[7] Jehovah called out to Samuel *three times,* and he answered the *third time.* (1 Samuel 3:8)

When Saul wanted to kill David, David hid himself in the field on the *third evening.* Jonathan said to David, "I will sound out my father at this time *the third day from now.*" Jonathan shot *three arrows* to the side of a stone. And David then fell on his face to the earth before Jonathan and bowed down *three times.* (1 Samuel 20:5, 12, 19, 20, 35, [36, 41])

David had to choose one of *three things:* seven years of famine in the land, or fleeing for *three months* before his foes, or contagion in the land for *three days.* (2 Samuel 24:12, 13)

[8] There was famine in David's days for *three years,* year after year. (2 Samuel 21:1)

Elijah stretched himself out on the dead boy *three times* and brought him to life. (1 Kings 17:21, [22])

When Elijah had built an altar to Jehovah, he said to pour water on the burnt offering and on the pieces of wood *three times*. (1 Kings 18:[32, 33,] 34)

Fire consumed the captains-of-fifty sent to Elijah *two times,* but not the one sent the *third time*. (2 Kings 1:13, [14])

This was a sign given to King Hezekiah: That year they would eat what sowed itself; in the second year, what grew out of that; but the *third year* they would sow, reap, plant vineyards, and eat the fruit. (2 Kings 19:29)

[9] Daniel entered his house, and he had the windows in his upper room opened toward Jerusalem, where *three times a day* he would bless [God] on his knees and pray. (Daniel 6:10, 13)

Daniel mourned *three weeks of days,* not eating choice bread, and not drinking wine, and not anointing himself, until the *three weeks of days* were fulfilled. (Daniel 10:2, 3)

Isaiah went naked and shoeless for *three years* as a sign and portent against Egypt and against Cush. (Isaiah 20:3)

From the lampstand there went out *three* branches on each side, and there were *three* almond-shaped *cups* on each branch. (Exodus 25:32, 33)

[10] On the Urim and Thummim there were *three precious stones* in each row. (Exodus 28:[17–18,] 19, [20])

In the new temple there will be *three* gate rooms on this side and *three* on that side, one measure for the *three of them*. On the porch of the House, the width of the gate will be *three* cubits on this side and *three* cubits on that side. (Ezekiel 40:10, 21, 48)

In the New Jerusalem there will be *three* gates to the north, *three* to the east, *three* to the south, and *three* to the west. (Ezekiel 48:31, 32, 33, 34; Revelation 21:13)

The same thing can be seen in these places:

Three times Peter denied [knowing] Jesus. (Matthew 26:34, 69, and following verses)

The Lord said to Peter *three times,* "Do you love me?" (John 21:17)

Then there is the parable in which a person who had planted a vineyard sent slaves *three times* and finally a son. (Luke 20:12; Mark 12:2, 4, 5, 6)

The people working in a vineyard were hired at the *third* hour, *sixth* hour, *ninth* hour, and eleventh hour. (Matthew 20:1–16)

And it was said of a fig tree that, since it had not borne fruit for *three years*, it would be cut down. (Luke 13:6, 7)

[11] Just as *three* and *third* had a representative meaning, so did *one third*. For instance:

Minhas were two tenths [of an ephah] of flour mixed with a *third of a hin* of oil. And the wine for a libation was a *third of a hin*. (Numbers 15:6, 7; Ezekiel 46:14)

In Ezekiel:

He was to pass a razor over his head and over his beard and then divide the hair, and a *third* he was to burn with fire, a *third* he was to strike on all sides with a sword, and a *third* he was to scatter to the wind. (Ezekiel 5:1, 2, 12)

In Zechariah:

In the whole earth, two parts would be cut off and a *third* would be left, but the *third part* would be led through fire and tested. (Zechariah 13:8, 9)

[12] In John:

When the first angel trumpeted, hail appeared, and fire mixed with blood, and it fell onto the earth, so that a *third* of the trees were burned. The second angel trumpeted, and what seemed to be a large mountain burning with fire was thrown into the sea, and a *third* of the sea became blood, for which reason a *third* of the creatures in the sea having souls died. And a *third* of the ships were ruined. The third angel trumpeted, and there fell from the sky a large star burning like a lamp, and it fell onto a *third* of the rivers; the name of the star was Wormwood. The fourth angel trumpeted, so that a *third* of the sun was struck and a *third* of the moon and a *third* of the stars, so that a *third* of them would be shadowed over and the day would not shine for a *third of it* and the night likewise. (Revelation 8:7, 8, 9, 10, 11, 12)

[13] The four angels were released to kill a *third* of all human beings. (Revelation 9:15)

By these *three* a *third* of all human beings were killed—by the fire, the smoke, and the sulfur that went out from the mouth of the horses. (Revelation 9:18)

The dragon dragged a *third* of the stars in the sky with its tail and threw them onto the earth. (Revelation 12:4)

The fraction one third, however, means some, and an amount that is not yet full, whereas a third in order and the number three mean something complete—completely evil for the evil, and completely good for the good.

Abraham raised his eyes and saw symbolizes thought and insight received **2789** from his divine side, as can be seen from the following: *Eyes* symbolize understanding (as discussed in §2701), so *raising* them means lifting one's understanding. Consequently it means thinking. And *seeing,* since it is said of the Lord, means receiving insight from his divine side.

The place from far away means the condition that he foresaw. This can **2790** be seen from the symbolism of a *place* as a state (discussed in §§1273–1277, 1376–1381, 2625), and from that of seeing *from far away* as foreseeing.

Genesis 22:5. *And Abraham said to his boys, "Stay here with the donkey,* **2791** *and I and the boy will go all the way there and bow down and come back to you."*

Abraham said to his boys, "Stay here with the donkey," means detaching his earlier rationality at this point, along with his earthly dimension. *And I and the boy will go all the way there* symbolizes divine rationality in a truth-oriented state, armed for the heaviest, most profound battles of his spiritual crisis; the *boy* is divine rationality under those circumstances. *And bow down* symbolizes submitting. *And come back to you* symbolizes reuniting afterward.

Abraham said to his boys, "Stay here with the donkey," means detaching **2792** his earlier rationality at this point, along with his earthly dimension, as can be seen from the following: *Staying here* means being detached for a while. The *boys* symbolize an earlier rationality, as mentioned above at §2782. And a *donkey* symbolizes the earthly self, or the earthly dimension, as also discussed above, in §2781.

And I and the boy will go all the way there symbolizes divine rationality **2793** in a truth-oriented state, armed for the heaviest, most profound battles of his spiritual crisis. The *boy* is divine rationality under those circumstances. This can be seen from the symbolism of Isaac as divine rationality. Here, though, since the text does not say "Isaac" or "my son," as it did before, but "the *boy,*" it means divine rationality under those circumstances, as discussed just below.

2794   *And bow down* symbolizes submitting, as can be seen without explanation.

2795   *And come back to you* symbolizes reuniting afterward, as can also be seen without explanation.

Because this chapter focuses on the Lord's heaviest, deepest struggles, it depicts all the states he took upon himself when he was undergoing those struggles. The first was portrayed in verse 3; the second is portrayed here; the third in the next verse; and the rest after that.

These states cannot be explained in a way that most people can understand until many other things are known. The reader first needs to know not only about the Lord's divinity itself (represented here by Abraham) but also about his human divinity (represented by Isaac); the state of this rationality when he underwent and endured the struggles of his inward crisis (this rationality being "the boy"); the identity and nature of the Lord's earlier rationality and of his earthly dimension; what state he was in when the two were linked together; and what state he was in when they were more or less detached from one another. Moreover, the reader needs to know many things about spiritual trials—what shallower and deeper ones are, for instance, and therefore what the very deepest, heaviest ones the Lord faced are (which this chapter describes). As long as these things are unknown, the contents of the current verse cannot possibly be described intelligibly. If they were described—even with the greatest possible clarity—they would still seem obscure. To the angels, who see them by the light the Lord radiates in heaven, these ideas are all quite plain, clear, and even blissful, since they are perfectly heavenlike.

[2] Here it needs only to be said that the Lord could never have been tested when his divinity itself was dominant, because divinity lies infinitely beyond any test or trial; but his humanity *could* be tested. This is the reason he reattached his earlier humanity—specifically, its rational and earthly aspects, as depicted in verse 3 [§2782]—when he was undergoing his most severe, profound trials. Later he detached himself from this rationality and earthliness, as the current verse says, although he still kept the element that made it possible for him to be tested. That is why the text here says not "Isaac, my son" but "the boy," which means divine rationality in that state—a state of truth armed for the most severe, profound trials and struggles (see §2793).

Neither divinity itself nor divine humanity could be tested, as anyone can see, simply from the fact that the Divine cannot be approached even by angels, much less by the spirits who inflict trials, least of all by the hells. This shows why the Lord came into the world and took on a truly human condition, with all its frailties. When he did so, you see, his human side could be tested. Through those trials, he could subdue the hells and reduce absolutely everything to obedience and to order. He could also save the human race, which had put so much distance between itself and the highest level of divinity.

In regard to the various states the Lord took on (treated of in these verses), we humans cannot help being ignorant of them, because we never reflect on changes in our own states. The changes are constant, though, and involve both our intellectual processes (or thoughts) and our volitional processes (or emotions). The reason for our failure to reflect on them is our assumption that everything that happens to us follows an earthly logic. We do not believe there is anything higher that controls events. The reality, however, is that each and every facet is arranged by the spirits and angels present with us, which is where all our states and all changes in our state come from. So the Lord directs all of them toward eternal goals, which he alone foresees. Many years of experience now have made me completely certain that this is the case. They have also enabled me to learn and see just which spirits and angels attended me, and what kinds of states they brought over me. I can also swear that all states, down to their smallest details, arise from this origin and are governed in this way by the Lord. In addition, experience has enabled me to see and observe that each state contains many other invisible ones, which coexist and therefore appear as a single, common whole. These states anticipate others that follow on in order according to their chain of progression.

In us, it is the Lord who brings all this about, but in the Lord himself when he lived in the world, it was he who was the agent, because he was divine, and the very being of his life was Jehovah.

[2] It is the part of angels to know how intellectual and volitional states change in people, what order the changes come in, what series they pass through, and accordingly how the Lord bends them toward goodness as far as he can. The wisdom of angels by its nature enables them to perceive the very smallest details of this kind. That is why this information about changes in the Lord's state, revealed in the Word's inner meaning, are clearly and distinctly perceptible to angels, who see by the light of heaven, which comes from the Lord. The same details are even somewhat intelligible to people who live a life of simple goodness. But they are merely obscure and meaningless to people who live evil lives, and also to those whose wisdom has gone mad. These people have plunged themselves into darkness in myriad ways, darkening and extinguishing the glimmer of their

2796

earthly, rational light, even though they believe themselves to be much more enlightened than others.

2797   Genesis 22:6. *And Abraham took the pieces of wood for the burnt offering and put them on Isaac his son and took in his hand the fire and the knife, and they both went together.*

Abraham took the pieces of wood for the burnt offering symbolizes a deserving righteousness. *And put them on Isaac* means that it was attached to his divine rationality. *And took in his hand the fire and the knife* symbolizes a loving goodness and religious truth. *And they both went together* symbolizes the tightest possible union.

2798   *Abraham took the pieces of wood for the burnt offering* symbolizes a deserving righteousness. This can be seen from remarks and illustrations above at §2784 and therefore needs no further explanation.

And put them on Isaac means that this deserving righteousness was attached to his divine rationality. This can be seen from the representation of *Isaac* as the Lord's divine rationality, which has been dealt with many times before, and from the symbolism of *putting* something *on him* as attaching it. The text says *his son* because the Lord's divine humanity was not only conceived but also born from Jehovah.

It is very well known from the Lord's Word that he was conceived by Jehovah. That is why he is called Son of the Highest One, Son of God, and the Only-Born of the Father (Matthew 2:15; 3:16, 17; 16:13, 14, 15, 16, 17; 17:5; 27:43, 54; Mark 1:10, [11]; 9:7, 9; 14:61, 62; Luke 1:31, 32, 35; 3:21, 22; 9:35; 10:22; John 1:14, 18, 49; 3:13, 16, 17, 18; 5:20–27; 6:69; 9:34, 35, 38; 10:35, 36; 20:30, 31). In addition, there are many other places where the Lord calls Jehovah his Father.

[2] It is also known that he was born to the Virgin Mary, but this was a birth like that of any other person. When he was born again, or in other words, was made divine, it was from Jehovah, who was in him and who was the very essence of his life. The uniting of his divine and human natures was a mutual, reciprocal process, so that he united his divine nature with his human nature and his human nature with his divine. (See §§1921, 1999, 2004, 2005, 2018, 2025, 2083, 2508, 2523, 2618, 2628, 2632, 2728, 2729.) This fact stands as evidence that, using his own power, the Lord made the humanity in himself divine and in the process became righteousness.

A deserving righteousness was what the Lord attached to his divine rationality when he was undergoing his deepest trials. It was the weapon he then fought with, and against which evil demons fought, until it too was finally glorified by him.

These are the ideas meant on an inner level by Abraham's putting the pieces of wood for the burnt offering on Isaac his son. They are also the ideas that come into angels' minds when these words are being read.

And took in his hand the fire and the knife symbolizes a loving goodness and religious truth. This can be seen from the symbolism of *fire* as a loving goodness (discussed in §934) and from that of a *knife* as religious truth.

2799

A knife, which was used on sacrificial animals, symbolized religious truth, as can be seen from the symbolism of a sword or dagger in the Word. The term *dagger* is [often] used instead of *knife*, you see. The two have the same meaning, but with the difference that a knife (used for sacrificial animals) symbolized religious truth, while a sword [or dagger] symbolized truth engaged in battle. Since the Word rarely mentions knives (for a secret reason discussed below [§2799:22]), let me show what a sword symbolizes.

On an inner level, a sword symbolizes religious truth engaged in battle, and also the devastation of truth. In a negative sense, it symbolizes falsity engaged in battle, and punishment for falsity.

[2] 1. *A sword symbolizes religious truth engaged in battle,* as can be seen from the following passages. In David:

> Gird yourself with *your sword on your thigh,* mighty man; in your glory and honor, prosper! *Ride on the word of truth,* and your right hand will teach you marvelous things. (Psalms 45:3, 4)

This is about the Lord. The sword stands for truth engaged in battle. In the same author:

> The merciful will rejoice in [Jehovah's] glory; they will sing on their beds. The exaltations of God are in their throat, and a *double-edged sword is in their hand.* (Psalms 149:5, 6)

In Isaiah:

> Jehovah called me from the womb; from my mother's belly he remembered my name and *made my mouth a sharp sword* and made me a polished arrow. (Isaiah 49:1, 2)

A sharp sword stands for truth engaged in battle. A polished arrow stands for theological truth; see §§2686, 2709. In the same author:

> Assyria will fall by a *sword that is not a man's;* a *sword that is not a human's will devour him,* and he will take his flight before the *sword,* and his young people will become tribute. (Isaiah 31:8)

Assyria stands for twisted reasoning on divine subjects (§§119, 1186). The sword that is not a man's or a human's stands for falsity. The sword before which Assyria will take flight stands for truth engaged in battle. [3] In Zechariah:

> "Turn to the stronghold, you captives with something to look forward to. Even today, as I am telling, I will return double to you—I who have stretched Judah out for myself as a bow, filled Ephraim, and stirred up your sons, Zion, over your sons, Javan—and I will *make you like the sword of a strong man.*" And Jehovah will appear over them, and like lightning will his arrow go forth. (Zechariah 9:12, 13, 14)

The sword of a strong man stands for truth engaged in battle. In John:

> In the middle of the *seven* lampstands was one like the Son of Humankind. He had in his right hand seven stars; *from his mouth a two-edged, sharp sword was issuing,* and his appearance was like the sun shining in its strength. (Revelation 1:13, 16)

Again:

> These things says the one who has the *two-edged, sharp sword:* "I will come to you quickly and *fight* with them by the *sword of my mouth.*" (Revelation 2:12, 16)

The two-edged, sharp sword plainly stands for truth engaged in fighting, which was accordingly represented as a sword coming out of the mouth. [4] In the same author:

> *From the mouth* of the one sitting on the white horse there *issued a sharp sword,* and with it he will strike the nations. And they were killed by the *sword of the one sitting on the horse, which issued from his mouth.* (Revelation 19:15, 21)

The sword coming out of his mouth, of course, means truth engaged in battle. The one sitting on the white horse is the Word and therefore is the Lord, who is the Word; see §§2760, 2761, 2762, 2763 above. That is why the Lord says in Matthew:

> Don't suppose, then, that I came to send peace onto the earth; I came not to send peace but a *sword.* (Matthew 10:34)

And in Luke:

> "Now let those who have a purse take it, likewise a bag, too; but let those who do not have them sell their clothes and *buy a sword.*" They said,

"Lord, look: *two swords here.*" But Jesus said, "That is enough." (Luke
22:36, 37, 38)

In this passage the sword has no other meaning than the truth by which
and for which they would fight. [5] In Hosea:

> I will strike a pact with them on that day—with the wild animal of
> the field, and with the bird in the heavens and the creeping animal
> of the ground. And *bow* and *sword* and *war* I will break off from the
> earth, and I will make them lie down securely. (Hosea 2:18)

This is about the Lord's kingdom. Breaking bow, sword, and war means
that no one there fights over doctrine or truth. In Joshua:

> Joshua lifted his eyes and looked, and here, now, a man standing oppo-
> site him, and *an unsheathed sword was in his hand.* He said to Joshua,
> "I am the leader of Jehovah's army." And Joshua fell on his face to the
> earth. (Joshua 5:13, 14)

This occurred when Joshua entered the land of Canaan with the children
of Israel, and by it is meant the entry of the faithful into the Lord's kingdom. Truth engaged in battle, wielded by the church, is the unsheathed
sword in the hand of the leader of Jehovah's army.

[6] Daggers or knives symbolize religious truth, as can be seen from
what was said above. It can also be seen from their use not only in sacrifices but also in circumcision. In the latter case they were made of stone
and were called "daggers of flint," as the Book of Joshua shows:

> Jehovah said to Joshua, "Make yourself *daggers of flint,* and circumcise
> the children of Israel again, a second time." And Joshua made himself
> *daggers of flint* and circumcised the children of Israel at the Hill of the
> Foreskins. (Joshua 5:2, 3)

Circumcision was an act that represented being purified of self-love and
materialism (see §§2039, 2632). Since religious truth is the means of
purification, daggers of flint were the tools (2039 at the end, 2046 at the
end).

[7] 2. *A sword symbolizes the devastation of truth,* as the following passages show. In Isaiah:

> These two things will happen to you—who is to commiserate with you?—
> *devastation* and crushing, and *famine* and the *sword.* Who is to comfort
> you? Your children fainted; they lay at the head of all the streets. (Isaiah
> 51:19, 20)

Famine stands for the devastation of what is good; the sword, for the devastation of truth. Lying at the head of all the streets stands for being bereaved of all truth, a street being truth (§2336). On what devastation is, see §§301, 302, 303, 304, 407, 408, 410, 411. In the same author:

> I will *count you with the sword*, and you will all bow yourselves to the slaughter, because I called and you did not answer; I spoke, and you did not listen. (Isaiah 65:12)

[8] In the same author:

> Jehovah will judge with *fire*, and he will judge all flesh with his *sword*; and numerous will be those stabbed by Jehovah. (Isaiah 66:16)

Those stabbed by Jehovah stand for people who have undergone devastation. In Jeremiah:

> Over all the hills in the wilderness have come *those who devastate*, because *Jehovah's sword* is devouring from the end of the earth to the end of the earth; there is no peace for any flesh. They have sown wheat and harvested thorns. (Jeremiah 12:12, 13)

Jehovah's sword clearly stands for the devastation of truth. In the same author:

> They lied against Jehovah and said, "He does not exist, and evil will not come on us, and *sword* and *famine* we will not see. And the prophets will become wind, and no message will be in them." (Jeremiah 5:12, 13)

[9] In the same author:

> I am exacting punishment on them. The young people will *die by the sword*; their sons and their daughters will *die of famine*. (Jeremiah 11:22)

In the same author:

> "When they offer burnt offering and minha, I will not be appeased by those things, because with *sword* and *famine* and *contagion* I am consuming them." And I said, "Oh no, Lord Jehovih! Here, now, the prophets are saying to them, 'You won't see the *sword*, and *famine* will not come to you.'" (Jeremiah 14:12, 13)

In the same author:

> The city has been given into the hand of the Chaldeans fighting against it, in the face of the *sword* and *famine* and *contagion*. (Jeremiah 32:24, 36)

In the same author:

> I will send against them *sword, famine,* and *contagion* to the point of consuming them off the ground that I gave to them and their ancestors. (Jeremiah 24:10)

[10] In these passages, devastation is depicted as a sword, famine, and contagion. Devastation of truth is depicted as a sword; devastation of what is good, as famine; and assault to the point of utter destruction, as contagion. In Ezekiel:

> Son of humankind, take a *sharp sword,* a barbers' razor; you are to take it for yourself and pass it over your head and over your beard and take yourself weighing scales and divide [the hair]. A third you are to burn with fire in the middle of the city. A third you are to strike on all sides with a *sword.* And a third you are to scatter to the wind, and *I will draw the sword after the people.* A third will die of *contagion* and be consumed by *famine* in your midst, and a third will *fall to the sword* on all sides, and a third I will scatter to every wind, and *I will draw the sword after them.* (Ezekiel 5:1, 2, 12, 17)

This is about the devastation of earthly truth, which is depicted in these images. In the same author:

> The *sword* outside, and *famine* and *contagion* inside! Those who are in the field will *die by the sword;* and those who are in the city—*famine* and *contagion* will consume them. (Ezekiel 7:15)

[11] In the same author:

> "You are to say to the ground of Israel, 'This is what Jehovah has said: "Look: I am against you, and I will *draw my sword out of its sheath* and cut off from you the just person and the dishonest person. Because I will cut off from you the just person and the dishonest person, therefore *my sword will come out of its sheath* against all flesh from south to north. And all flesh will know that I Jehovah have drawn *my sword out of its sheath;* it will no longer return."'" The word of Jehovah came to me, saying, "Son of humankind, prophesy, and you are to say, 'This is what Jehovah has said, "Say, '*A sword! A sword sharpened!* And even *polished;* sharpened for committing slaughter. It is *polished* to have a flash [like] lightning to it.'"' Son of humankind, prophesy, and you are to say, 'This is what the Lord Jehovih has said to the children of Ammon and to their disgrace.' And you are to say, '*A sword! A sword open* for

slaughter, and polished to consume, because of the lightning [flashing from it]. When they see visions for you, it is worthless; when they practice divination for you, it is a lie.'" (Ezekiel 21:3, 4, 5, 8, 9, 10, 28, 29)

The sword actually symbolizes devastation, as becomes clear from the individual details of the inner meaning. [12] In the same author:

> The monarch of Babylon will *destroy* your towers *with his swords*. Because of the large number of horses, their dust will cover you. Because of the noise of rider and wheel and chariot, your walls will shake. With the hooves of his horses he will trample all your streets. (Ezekiel 26:9, 10, 11)

For the symbolism of Babylon, see §1326. For the fact that it creates devastation, see §1327. In David:

> If they do not turn, *God* will sharpen *his sword*, bend his bow, and ready it. (Psalms 7:12)

In Jeremiah:

> I said, "Oh no, Lord! Without a doubt you have utterly duped this people and Jerusalem, saying, 'You will have peace'—and *a sword has reached right to their soul*." (Jeremiah 4:10)

[13] In the same author:

> Proclaim it in Egypt and make it heard in Migdol: "Stand and ready yourself, because a *sword* will devour your environs." (Jeremiah 46:14)

In the same author:

> A *sword* upon the Chaldeans and against the inhabitants of Babylon and against its rulers and against its sages! A *sword* against those who talk nonsense—and they will lose their minds. A *sword* against its mighty—and they will feel dismay. A *sword* against its horses and against its chariots and against all the rabble that is in the middle of it—and they will become women. A *sword* against its treasuries—and they will be plundered. Drought to its waters—and they will dry up. (Jeremiah 50:35, 36, 37, 38)

The sword obviously stands for the devastation of truth, because it says, "A sword against its sages, against those who talk nonsense, against its mighty, against its horses and chariots, and against its treasuries." And, "Drought to its waters—and they will dry up." [14] In the same author:

> To Egypt we gave our hand; to Assyria, to acquire enough bread. Slaves ruled over us; no one was freeing us from their hand. In [risk to] our

soul we were fetching our bread *from before the sword in the wilderness.*
(Lamentations 5:6, 8, 9)

In Hosea:

[Israel] will not return to the land of Egypt. And Assyria will be [Israel's] monarch, because they refused to return to me. And a *sword will hang over his cities* and consume the bars on his gates and devour them, because of their counsels. (Hosea 11:5, 6)

In Amos:

I sent contagion among you as in Egypt; *with the sword I killed* your young people, along with your captured horses. (Amos 4:10)

"As in Egypt" stands for secular learning that causes devastation when people engage in twisted logic about divine subjects on the basis of it. The captured horses stand for an intellect deprived of its gift.

[15] 3. *In a negative sense, a sword symbolizes falsity engaged in battle,* as can be seen in David:

As to my soul I lie down in the midst of lions, who set the children of humankind on fire. Their teeth are a javelin and arrows, *and their tongues are a sharp sword.* (Psalms 57:4)

In the same author:

Look: they bay with their mouth; *swords are on their lips,* because who is listening? (Psalms 59:7)

In Isaiah:

You were thrown out of your grave like a despicable stump, [like] the garment of the slain, those *pierced with a sword,* who drop to the stones in the pit like a trampled corpse. (Isaiah 14:19)

This quotation is about Lucifer. In Jeremiah:

In vain have I struck your children; correction they have not accepted. *Your sword ate your prophets* like a destroying lion. You [current] generation, see the Word of Jehovah! Have I been a wilderness to Israel? (Jeremiah 2:30, 31)

[16] In the same author:

You are not to go out into the field, and on the path you are not to walk, because your *enemy has a sword;* there is horror from all around. (Jeremiah 6:25, 26)

In the same author:

> Take the cup of the wine of fury, and you are to give it as drink to all the
> nations to which I am sending you, and they will drink and reel and *run
> mad before the sword* that I am sending among them. Drink and become
> drunk, and vomit and fall, and do not rise *before the sword*. (Jeremiah
> 25:15, 16, 27)

In the same author:

> Go up, horses; run mad, chariots. Let your mighty men march out,
> Cush and Put, as you grasp your shield, and Lydians as you grasp—as
> you bend—your bow. And that day belongs to the Lord Jehovih of the
> Armies—a day of vengeance. And a *sword will devour* and receive its fill
> and become drunk with their blood. (Jeremiah 46:9, 10)

[17] In Ezekiel:

> They will strip you of your clothes, and seize your splendid things, and
> leave you naked and bare, and raise a mob against you, and stone you
> with stone. *They will stab you with their swords.* (Ezekiel 16:39, 40)

This is about Jerusalem's abominations. In Zechariah:

> Doom to shepherds who are empty of worth, abandoners of the flock! *A
> sword against their arm* and *against their right eye!* Their arm will utterly
> shrivel and their right eye go utterly dim. (Zechariah 11:17)

In Hosea:

> They thought evil against me. *Their chieftains will fall by the sword because
> of the anger on their tongue.* That is their derision in the land of Egypt.
> (Hosea 7:15, 16)

[18] In Luke:

> There will be great anguish on the earth and anger on this people, *for
> they will fall by the mouth of the sword* and be taken captive among all
> the nations. In the end Jerusalem will be trampled by the nations. (Luke
> 21:23, 24)

Here the Lord talks about the close of the age. The literal meaning has to
do with the impending dispersal of the Jews and destruction of Jerusalem,
but the inner meaning describes the final stage of the [Christian] church.
Falling by the mouth of the sword means that no longer will any truth

exist, only falsity. All the nations symbolize all kinds of evil, among which they will be captives. Nations are evil qualities; see §§1259, 1260, 1849, 1868. Jerusalem is the church (2117), which is trampled by these things.

[19] 4. *A sword also symbolizes punishment for falsity,* as can be seen in Isaiah:

> On that day Jehovah, *with his steely* and *great* and *strong sword,* will exact punishment on Leviathan the stretched-out serpent and on Leviathan the coiled serpent, and he will kill the monsters that are in the sea. (Isaiah 27:1)

This is about people who pry into the mysteries of faith through sophistic arguments based on sensory evidence and secular learning. The steely, large, strong sword stands for punishment inflicted on the falsity that results.

[20] In some passages we read that both men and women, young and old, and oxen, sheep, and donkeys were exterminated or killed *by the mouth of the sword.* On an inner level this symbolizes damnation as the punishment for falsity. (Examples are Joshua 6:21; 8:24, 25; 10:28, 30, 37, 39; 11:10, 11, 12, 14; 13:22; 19:47; Judges 1:8, 25; 4:15, 16; 18:27; 20:37; 1 Samuel 15:8; 2 Kings 10:25; and other passages.) That was the reason for the command in Deuteronomy 13:12–18 that any city worshiping other gods was to be *struck with the sword,* exterminated, and burned with fire, and was to become a heap forever. The sword stands for the punishment of falsity; fire, for the punishment of evil.

The fact that the angel of Jehovah stood in the way opposing Balaam with an *unsheathed sword* (Numbers 22:22, 31) symbolized truth that would stand in the way of the falsity Balaam clung to. That is also why Balaam was *killed with a sword* (Numbers 31:8).

[21] This symbolism of a sword—in a positive sense as truth engaged in battle, in a negative sense as falsity engaged in battle, and as the devastation of truth and punishment for falsity—traces its origin to representations in the other world. There, when people say what they know to be false, daggerlike objects instantly rain down over their heads and terrify them. What is more, truth engaged in battle is represented by objects with points as sharp as swords, since that is what truth is like without goodness. *With* goodness, though, it is rounded and soft.

This being the source of the symbolism, whenever the Word mentions a knife, javelin, dagger, or sword, what springs to an angel's mind is truth engaged in battle.

[22] The reason the Word hardly ever mentions knives has to do with evil spirits in the other world called cutthroats. At their side appears a dangling knife, because by nature they are so savage that they want to slice everyone's throat with it. That is why knives are not mentioned but only daggers and swords, which, since they are used in battle, suggest the idea of war and so of truth engaged in battle.

[23] The ancients knew that a dagger, lance, and knife symbolized truth. This knowledge passed to people outside the church, so when they offered sacrifices, they frequently stabbed and cut themselves with daggers, lances, or knives to the point of drawing blood. We read about the priests of Baal:

> The priests of Baal shouted with a loud voice and *gashed themselves according to their custom, with swords and lances,* even till they bled. (1 Kings 18:28)

All weapons of war in the Word symbolize instruments of spiritual battle, and each one symbolizes something particular; see §2686.

2800   *And they both went together* symbolizes the tightest possible union, as can be seen without explanation.

2801   Genesis 22:7. *And Isaac said to Abraham his father, and he said, "My father!" And he said, "Here I am, my son." And he said, "Look: the fire and the pieces of wood, and where is the animal for the burnt offering?"*

Isaac said to Abraham his father, and he said, "My father!" And he said, "Here I am, my son." This symbolizes a dialog in which the Lord, speaking from a love for divine truth, addressed divine goodness. Divine truth is the *son;* divine goodness is the *father. And he said, "Look: the fire and the pieces of wood,"* means that love and righteousness were present. *Where is the animal for the burnt offering?* means, where are the members of the human race who are to be consecrated?

2802   *Isaac said to Abraham his father, and he said, "My father!" And he said, "Here I am, my son."* This symbolizes a dialog in which the Lord, speaking from a love for divine truth, addressed divine goodness. This can be seen from the symbolism of *Isaac,* the *son,* as divine truth, and from that of *Abraham,* the *father,* as divine goodness, which will be discussed just below. It can also be seen from the emotion in these words, which are spoken lovingly on both sides. Clearly, then, it is a conversation between the Lord and his Father.

These words hide more secrets than the human mind can perceive, as can be seen from the fact that the word *said* occurs four times in the verse.

When the Word starts on a new subject, it customarily says, "And he (or she) said" (see §§2061, 2238, 2260). The abundance of secrets hidden in the verse can also be seen from the fact that the words are words of love. When these words enter the consciousness of heavenly angels, who focus on the deepest meaning, they form from them the most sublime images in their minds. It is from the emotions in the Word that heavenly angels form light-filled ideas for themselves, whereas spiritual angels do so from the symbolism of the words and themes (§§2157, 2275). So from these words, which contain four separate clauses and four different kinds of loving feelings, they glean notions that cannot possibly be brought down to the level of human understanding or put into words. These notions form in their minds in indescribable abundance and variety. From this it can be seen what the Word's inner meaning is like, even where the literal meaning appears straightforward, as it does in the current verse.

Divine truth is the *son* and divine goodness is the *father*. This can be seen from the symbolism of a *son* as truth (discussed at §§489, 491, 533, 1147, 2623) and of a *father* as goodness. It can also be seen from the fact that truth is conceived and born from goodness. Truth cannot exist or emerge except from goodness, as shown many times.

The reason the son here is divine truth, and the father, divine goodness, is that the union of the divine nature with the human (and of the human nature with the divine) is the divine marriage of goodness with truth (and of truth with goodness). This is the source of the heavenly marriage. In Jehovah—that is, the Lord—there is nothing but infinity, and since what is in him is infinite, it cannot be grasped in any way. All we can comprehend is that he is the core reality and the manifestation of everything good and true. In other words, he is goodness itself and truth itself. Goodness itself is the Father, and truth itself is the Son. However, because the divine marriage is a marriage of goodness with truth, and of truth with goodness, as noted, the Father is in the Son, and the Son is in the Father. The Lord himself teaches this in John:

> Jesus says to Philip, "Don't you believe *that I am in the Father and the Father is in me?* Believe me *that I am in the Father and the Father is in me.*" (John 14:10, 11)

And in another passage in the same Gospel:

> Jesus said to the Jews, "Even if you do not believe me, believe my deeds, so that you may know and believe that *the Father is in me and I am in the Father.*" (John 10:36, 38)

2803

And in another passage:

> I pray for them, since *everything of mine is yours* and *of yours is mine,* and [I pray] that they may all be one, as *you, Father, are in me, and I am in you.* (John 17:9, 10, 21)

And in another passage:

> Now the Son of Humankind is glorified, and God is glorified in him. If God is glorified in him, God will also glorify him in himself. *Father, glorify your Son, so that your Son may also glorify you.* (John 13:31, 32; 17:1)

[2] This shows what the union of divinity and humanity in the Lord is like: it is a mutual interchange, or in other words, reciprocal. This union is what is called the divine marriage, and from it descends the heavenly marriage. The heavenly marriage is the Lord's own kingdom in the heavens, which he speaks of this way in John:

> On that day you will know that I am in my Father and *you are in me and I am in you.* (John 14:20)

And in another passage:

> For these I pray that they may all be one; as *you, Father, are in me, and I am in you,* that they too may be one in us—*I in them and you in me*—so that the *love* with which you loved me *can exist in them, and I in them.* (John 17:21, 22, 23, 26)

On the point that this heavenly marriage joins goodness with truth, and truth with goodness, see §§2508, 2618, 2728, 2729, and following sections.

[3] Divine goodness cannot possibly exist or emerge without divine truth, or divine truth without divine goodness. Each exists and emerges in the other, mutually and reciprocally, so the divine marriage clearly has existed from eternity. That is, the Son has been in the Father, and the Father in the Son, as the Lord himself teaches in John:

> Now glorify me—you, Father, in yourself—with the glory that I had in you before the world existed. (John 17:5, 24)

[4] However, divine humanity, which was born from eternity, was also born within time. To say that it was born within time is the same as saying that it was glorified. That is why the Lord so often said that he was going

to the Father who had sent him, or in other words, that he was returning to the Father. And in John:

> In the beginning there was the Word. [The Word is divine truth itself.] And the Word was with God, and the Word was God. This was with God in the beginning. Everything was made by him, and nothing that was made was made without him. But the Word became flesh and resided among us, and we saw his glory: glory like that of the Only-Born of the Father, who was full of grace and truth. (John 1:1, 2, 3, 14)

See also John 3:13; 6:62.

He said, "Look: the fire and the pieces of wood," means that love and righteousness were present. This is established by the symbolism of *fire* as love (discussed in §934) and by that of *pieces of wood* for the burnt offering as a deserving righteousness (discussed in §2784). **2804**

Where is the animal for the burnt offering? means, where are the members of the human race who are to be consecrated? This can be seen from the representation of sacrifices and particularly of *burnt offerings.* Burnt offerings and sacrifices were practices representing inner worship (see §§922, 923). Members of the flock and herd were used in them. When it was members of the flock that were used, it was lambs, ewes, shegoats, kids, rams, or he-goats. When it was members of the herd, it was adult cattle, young cattle, or calves. These symbolized different kinds of heavenly and spiritual qualities (see §§922, 1823, 2180) by which people could be consecrated (2776). This shows that Isaac's question, "Where is the animal for the burnt offering?" means, where are the members of the human race who are to be consecrated? What follows makes the meaning even more obvious. For one thing there is the answer of Abraham his father in verse 8, "God will see to an animal for the burnt offering," meaning that divine humanity will provide a supply of people who are to be consecrated. For another, he then saw a ram behind him, caught in the thicket by its horns, which he offered as a burnt offering (verse 13), symbolizing members of the human race who are part of the Lord's spiritual church. What follows from verses 14 to 17 also demonstrates the same meaning. **2805**

Genesis 22:8. *And Abraham said, "God will see to an animal for the burnt offering, my son." And they both went together.* **2806**

Abraham said, "God will see to an animal for the burnt offering, my son," symbolizes the answer: divine humanity will provide a supply of people who are to be consecrated. *And they both went together* symbolizes an even tighter union—the tightest possible.

2807   *Abraham said, "God will see to an animal for the burnt offering, my son,"* symbolizes the answer: divine humanity will provide a supply of people who are to be consecrated. This can be seen from the symbolism of *seeing to* (when said of God) as foreseeing and providing. *Seeing,* in its first layer of inner meaning, is understanding (§§2150, 2325). In a deeper sense it is believing (897, 2325), but in its highest sense it is foreseeing and providing.

The meaning of the verse can also be seen from the symbolism of an *animal for the burnt offering* as members of the human race who are to be consecrated (discussed just above in §2805). What follows [2828–2839] makes it clear that an animal for the burnt offering here means spiritual people.

The animals used for burnt offering and sacrifice symbolized various things. A lamb symbolized one thing, a ewe another, a kid or she-goat another, and a ram or he-goat another. The same is true of an adult ox, young ox, and calf, and also of pigeon chicks and turtledoves. Each had its own meaning, as is obvious from the fact that the rules specify just what kind of animal they were to sacrifice for each day, for each feast, for atonement, cleansing, ordination, and all the rest. The type of animal would never have been specified so exactly if each one had not symbolized something particular.

[2] Quite plainly, all the rituals, all the outward forms of worship that the ancient church and later the Jewish religion carried out, represented the Lord. The burnt offerings and sacrifices were especially important in bearing this representation, because they were the main acts of worship in the Hebrew nation. Since they represented the Lord, they also represented what is the Lord's in a person, or in other words, the heavenly qualities of love and the spiritual qualities of faith. As a result they also represented the people themselves who had these qualities, or ought to have had them. That is why the *animal* here symbolizes spiritual people—that is, people who belong to the Lord's spiritual church.

The fact that *God will see to an animal for the burnt offering, my son* means that *divine humanity* will provide can be seen from this: the text says not that Jehovah will see to it but that *God* will. When both are named, as they are in the current chapter, Jehovah means the same thing as the Father, and God means the same thing as the Son. So here, God means *divine humanity.* That is because spiritual people are the theme here, and it is divine humanity that brings salvation to the spiritual (see §§2661, 2716).

They both went together symbolizes an even tighter union—the tightest possible—as can be seen without explanation. The reason it means an even tighter union here is that the clause is a repetition; see §2800.   **2808**

Genesis 22:9. *And they came to the place that God had said to him, and there Abraham built the altar and arranged the pieces of wood and tied Isaac his son and put him on the altar on top of the pieces of wood.*   **2809**

They came to the place that God had said to him symbolizes the Lord's state at that point, as divine truth gave him to perceive it. *And there he built the altar* symbolizes preparation of the Lord's human divinity. *And arranged the pieces of wood* symbolizes the righteousness that was attached to it. *And tied Isaac his son* symbolizes the state of his divine rationality, which was now about to endure the final stages of inward struggle over the truth it possessed. *And put him on the altar on top of the pieces of wood* means within his human divinity, which was righteous.

They came to the place that God had said to him symbolizes the Lord's state at that point, as divine truth gave him to perceive it. This can be seen from the symbolism of a *place* as a state (dealt with above at §2786) and from that of *saying* in scriptural narrative as perceiving (discussed many times before). Here, *God's saying* means perceiving from divine truth, since he is called God rather than Jehovah (2586, 2807 at the end).   **2810**

And there Abraham built the altar symbolizes preparation of the Lord's human divinity, as the symbolism of an *altar* and of *building* an altar shows.   **2811**

Altars symbolized all worship in general, since they were the focal point for worship in the representative church (§921). Because they symbolized all worship in general, they also symbolized the Lord's divine humanity. The Lord's divine humanity *is* all worship and all theology—so much so that it is worship itself and theology itself. This can also be seen from the Holy Supper, which took the place of altars, or in other words, of burnt offerings and sacrifices (§§2165, 2187, 2343, 2359). It is the focal point of outward worship, because in it the Lord's divine humanity is the gift that is offered.

Building an altar is preparing the human divinity, as the above shows and as can therefore be seen without explanation.

The current verse speaks of the final preparation of the Lord's human divinity for the last stages of the trials he had to undergo. It depicts that preparation in Abraham's arranging the pieces of wood, tying Isaac his son, and putting him on the altar on top of the pieces of wood.

2812   *And arranged the pieces of wood* symbolizes the righteousness that was attached to it, as can be seen from the following: The *pieces of wood* for the burnt offering symbolize a deserving righteousness, as noted above at §§2784, 2798. And *arranging* them on the altar means attaching it to human divinity. A deserving righteousness is attached when it is present and is accompanied by true confidence that it belongs to him.

2813   *He tied Isaac his son* symbolizes the state of his divine rationality, which was now about to endure the final stages of inward struggle over the truth it possessed, as can be seen from the symbolism of *tying* and of *Isaac his son. Tying* is entering into a state in which one undergoes the *final* stages of struggle, as can be seen from the fact that a person in a state of trial is nothing if not bound and tied. *Isaac his son* is the Lord's divine rationality— here, that rationality in regard to the truth it possessed; see §§2802, 2803.

All genuine rationality consists of goodness and truth. The goodness in the Lord's divine rationality could not suffer, or undergo trial, because none of the demons and spirits who cause inner crises are capable of going anywhere near goodness that is divine. This goodness rises above any attempt to distress it. Truth that is divine and in fetters was what could be challenged. Misconceptions and especially falsehoods are the agents that batter such truth and in this way put it to the test. It is possible for people to form some thought about truth that is divine, but not about goodness that is divine, unless they have the gift of perception and are heavenly angels.

Truth that is divine is what was no longer acknowledged when the Lord came into the world and was therefore the source of the Lord's trials and the means by which he endured them.

Truth that is divine in the Lord is what is called the *Son of Humankind,* while goodness that is divine in him is what is called the *Son of God.* The Lord says many times that the Son of Humankind will suffer but never that the Son of God will. It can be seen in Matthew that he says this of the Son of Humankind, or truth that is divine:

> Look: we are going up to Jerusalem, and the *Son of Humankind* will be delivered to the chief priests and scribes, and they will condemn *him* and deliver *him* to non-Jews to mock and whip and crucify *him.* (Matthew 20:18, 19)

In the same author:

> Jesus said to his disciples, "Look: the hour is here, and the *Son of Humankind* will be delivered into the hands of sinners." (Matthew 26:45)

In Mark:

> Jesus started to teach them that the *Son of Humankind* had to suffer many things and be spurned by the elders and chief priests and scribes and be killed but after three days rise again. (Mark 8:31)

In the same author:

> It is written about the *Son of Humankind* that he will suffer many things and be despised. And the *Son of Humankind* will be delivered into the hands of humankind, who will kill *him,* but killed, he will rise again on the third day. (Mark 9:12, 31)

In the same author:

> Look: we are going up to Jerusalem, and the *Son of Humankind* will be delivered to the chief priests and scribes, who will condemn *him* to death [and] deliver *him* to non-Jews. These will mock *him* and spit on *him* and kill *him,* but on the third day he will rise again. (Mark 10:33, 34)

In the same author:

> The hour is coming. Look: the *Son of Humankind* will be delivered into the hands of sinners. (Mark 14:41)

In Luke:

> The *Son of Humankind* has to suffer many things and be spurned by the elders and chief priests and scribes and be killed and on the third day rise again. (Luke 9:22, 44)

In the same author:

> We are going up to Jerusalem, where everything that has been written by the prophets about the *Son of Humankind* will be completed; he will be delivered to non-Jews and mocked and insulted and spat on, and whipping him they will kill *him,* but on the third day he will rise again. (Luke 18:31, 32, 33)

In the same author:

> One of the angels to the women: "Remember that he spoke to you when he was still in Galilee, saying that the *Son of Humankind* had to be betrayed into the hands of people who were sinners and be crucified and on the third day rise again." (Luke 24:6, 7)

[2] In all these passages, the *Son of Humankind* means the Lord in his role as truth that is divine—that is, as the Word in its inner meaning—which the chief priests and scribes would spurn, insult, whip, spit on, and crucify. This meaning is plainly evident from the fact that Jews interpreted absolutely everything in the Word in a literal way, as applying and belonging to them. They were unwilling to learn anything about its spiritual meaning or about the heavenly kingdom, believing that the Messiah was coming to lift their kingdom up above all the kingdoms on earth, as they still believe today. Clearly, then, truth that is divine was what they spurned, insulted, whipped, and crucified. Whether you say truth that is divine, or the Lord in his role as truth that is divine, it is all the same, because the Lord is truth itself, just as he is the Word itself (§§[2010,] 2011, 2016, 2533 at the end).

[3] The Lord's resurrection on the third day involves the additional idea that truth that is divine will be revived at the close of the age, the close of the age also being the "third day" (§§1825, 2788). That is, the Word will be understood in its inner meaning, as it was by the ancient church. This is why it is said that the Son of Humankind (truth that is divine) will then appear (Matthew 24:30, 37, 39, 44; Mark 13:26; Luke 17:22, 24, 25, 26, 30; 21:27, 36).

[4] The passages quoted show that the Son of Humankind is the Lord in his role as truth that is divine, as do the following. In Matthew:

> The one who sows good seed is the *Son of Humankind;* the field is the world. At the close of the age, the *Son of Humankind* will send his angels, and they will gather out of his kingdom all the stumbling blocks. (Matthew 13:37, 41, 42)

The good seed is truth, the world is humankind, the sower is the Son of Humankind, and the stumbling blocks are falsities. In John:

> The crowd said, "We have heard from the Law that Christ remains forever, so how can you say, 'The *Son of Humankind* has to be lifted up'? Who is this *Son of Humankind?*" Jesus answered them, "For a short time, the *light* is with you. Walk, as long as you have *light,* to prevent darkness from overtaking you, because those who walk in the dark do not know where they are going. As long as you have the *light,* believe in the *light,* in order to be children of *light.*" (John 12:34, 35, [36])

In this passage, when people ask who the Son of Humankind is, Jesus gives an answer concerning light, which is truth, and says that he is the light (or truth) they should believe in. For more about the light that comes from the Lord and is divine truth, see §§1053, 1521, 1529, 1530, 1531, 1619–1632.

[5] As noted above, though, the Son of God—goodness in the Lord's human divinity—could not be tested. This is clear from the Lord's answer in the Gospels to the tempter:

> The tempter said, "If *you are the Son of God,* throw yourself down, for it is written, 'He will command his angels concerning you, to keep you from stubbing your foot against a stone.'" Jesus said to him, "Again it is written, '*You shall not test the Lord your God.*'" (Matthew 4:6, 7; Luke 4:9, 10, 11, 12)

And put him on the altar on top of the pieces of wood means within his **2814** human divinity, which was righteous. This can be seen from the symbolism of an *altar* as the Lord's divine humanity (discussed just above at §2811) and from that of *pieces of wood* for the burnt offering as a deserving righteousness (discussed in §§2784, 2798, 2812).

The divine truth in the Lord's human divinity which was put to the test, and which is the topic of discussion here, is not divine truth itself. Real divine truth lies beyond any test or trial. It is truth on the rational level that can be tested. This is the kind of truth angels have access to. It consists in *apparent* truth and is what is called the Son of Humankind, but only before he was glorified. Divine truth in the Lord's glorified divine humanity lies far above appearances. It cannot possibly be understood let alone truly grasped by people or even angels, so it cannot possibly undergo any kind of trial. It appears in the heavens as light from the Lord.

Concerning this divine truth, or the glorified Son of Humankind, the following is said in John:

> Jesus said, "Now the *Son of Humankind* is glorified, and God is glorified in him. If God is glorified in him, God will also glorify him in himself, and will glorify him immediately." (John 13:31, 32)

To enable a distinct idea of this very deep secret to be formed, let me refer to the truth in the Lord that could be tested and did in fact undergo times of trial as *truth that is divine in the Lord's human divinity.* But let me refer to the truth that could not be tested or undergo any kind of trial— because it was glorified—as *divine truth in the Lord's divine humanity.* This distinction I have observed a number of times in the preceding discussion.

Genesis 22:10. *And Abraham put out his hand and took the knife to slaugh-* **2815** *ter his son.*

Abraham put out his hand means being tested to the very limit of his strength. *And took the knife* means in regard to truth. *To slaughter his son* means until every trace of what was merely human died.

2816   *Abraham put out his hand* means being tested to the very limit of his strength. This can be seen from the sequence of ideas, since the focus is on the Lord's heaviest, deepest trials. The preceding verses dealt with the preparation of his human divinity to take on and endure these trials. The current verse depicts their actual onslaught, expressed in the text as *Abraham put out his hand*. A *hand* symbolizes strength or power (see §878), and here it symbolizes the very limit of one's strength, since all that was lacking was the act itself.

The message of the inner meaning is that the Lord's divine side led his human side into the most severe crises (*Abraham* meaning the Lord's divine side), all the way to the limits of its strength. The situation is that the Lord took these trials onto his own shoulders in order to rid himself of everything that was merely human, till nothing remained but divinity. [2] The Lord's own words in Matthew show that he did take on these trials, including the final one on the cross:

> Jesus started to show his disciples that he had to suffer many things and be killed. Then taking Jesus aside, Peter started to reproach him, saying, "Spare yourself, Lord, from letting this happen to you!" But he, having turned, said to Peter, "Go back behind me, Satan! You are a stumbling block to me, because you are wise not in the things that are God's but in those that are humankind's." (Matthew 16:21, 22, 23)

It is even more explicit in John:

> No one takes my life from me, but I lay it down by myself; I have the power to lay it down, and I have the power to take it back. (John 10:18)

And in Luke:

> Didn't Christ have to suffer these things and enter into his glory? (Luke 24:26)

2817   *And took the knife* means in regard to truth. This is established by the symbolism of a *knife* as religious truth (discussed above at §2799); and truth that is divine in the Lord was what was tested (2813, 2814).

2818   *To slaughter his son* means until every trace of what was merely human died. This can be seen from the inner meaning of these words, which symbolize the Lord's most severe, profound trials, the final one being that on the cross, in which (obviously) what was merely human died. This could not be represented by Abraham's son, Isaac, because sacrificing children was an abomination. Instead it was represented so far as it could be—that is, up to the point of the effort rather than the deed. This shows that the words *Abraham took the knife to slaughter his son* mean until everything that was merely human died.

[2] People have known from the earliest times that the Lord was to come into the world and suffer death. This can be seen quite clearly from the practice prevailing among people in non-Jewish nations of sacrificing their children, in the belief that in this way they could atone for themselves and appease God. This detestable practice they would never have viewed as their supreme act of religious devotion if they had not received from the ancients the idea that the Child of God was to come on earth for the purpose (they believed) of becoming a sacrifice. The children of Jacob were also drawn to this heinous practice, as was Abraham. After all, we are never tempted except by things that appeal to us. The prophets indicate that the children of Jacob were drawn to this abomination, but they were allowed to establish the practices of burnt offering and sacrifice in order to avoid succumbing to it; see §§922, 1128, 1241, 1343, 2180.

To speak generally of the Lord's trials, there were shallower ones and deeper ones, and the deeper they were, the more severe they were. The deepest are described in Matthew 26:37, 38, 39, 42, 44; 27:46; Mark 14:33, 34, 35, 36; 15:34; Luke 22:42, 43, 44.

See previous remarks on the Lord's trials, however: His first weapons in the battle were a goodness and truth that only appeared to be good and true: 1661. He fought the evils involved in self-love and materialism, out of divine love for the entire human race: 1690, 1691 at the end, 1789, 1812, 1813, 1820. He is the only one who has fought out of divine love: 1812, 1813. All the hells fought against the Lord's love, which was to save the whole human race: 1820. He endured the very heaviest trials of all: 1663, 1668, 1787. By struggling and winning, under his own power, the Lord became righteousness: 1813, 2025. Through his struggles and victories the Lord achieved the union of his human nature with his divine: 1737, 1813, 1921, 2025, 2026.

See also previous remarks on times of trial in general: 59, 63, 227, 847. Spiritual battles are a power struggle, determining whether good or evil, truth or falsity is to gain control: 1923. Indignation and many other emotions come up during these struggles: 1917. The trials take place on the heavenly, spiritual, and earthly planes: 847. In times of trial, evil demons and spirits attack what we love and therefore what belongs to our very life: 847, 1820. What times of trial accomplish: 1692 at the beginning, 1717, 1740. The purpose of spiritual crisis is to subdue

2819

bodily concerns: 857. Spiritual crises subdue rather than eliminate evil and falsity in an individual who is being reborn: 868. Truth is the first requirement for the battle: 1685. The good impulses and true ideas we have absorbed by learning about them are the weapons we fight with, although in and of themselves they are not good or true: 1661. Evil spirits and demons stir up falsity and evil in us, and this is what triggers our crises: 741, 751, 761. While we are being tested, we think the Lord is absent, even though he is then closer than ever: 840. We cannot possibly survive the struggles of spiritual crisis on our own, because they are struggles against all the hells: 1692 at the end. It is the Lord alone who does our fighting: 1661, 1692. Spiritual trials deprive evil demons and spirits of the power to do evil and inspire falsity in us: 1695, 1717. Trials occur in people who have conscience, and they are even more intense in people who have perception: 1668. Inward trials do not occur often these days but rather anxiety, which has a different nature and a different source: 762. People who are spiritually dead cannot survive the struggles of inward crisis: 270. All trials bring with them despair over the outcome: 1787, 1820. After their trials are over, people waver: 848, 857. Through times of trial, the good learn that they are nothing but evil and that they owe everything to mercy: 2334. Trials unite goodness more closely with truth: 2272. Our trials do not save us if we fail in them, nor if we imagine we have earned something by them: 2273. In all times of trial, a certain freedom is present—more strongly present than it is outside those times: 1937.

2820   Genesis 22:11. *And the angel of Jehovah called out to him from heaven and said, "Abraham! Abraham!" And he said, "Here I am."*

The angel of Jehovah called out to him from heaven symbolizes consolation offered by divinity itself at that time. *And said, "Abraham! Abraham!" And he said, "Here I am,"* symbolizes comfort perceived by the divine goodness in his rational mind after his trials.

2821   *The angel of Jehovah called out to him from heaven* symbolizes consolation offered by divinity itself at that time. This can be seen from the symbolism of *calling from heaven* as being consoled, a meaning that is clear from the verses directly above and below as well. It can also be seen from the symbolism of the *angel of Jehovah*. When the Word mentions angels, they mean some feature of the Lord, but just what feature they mean becomes clear from the context; see §1925. Similarly, we read that when the Lord endured a grievous struggle in Gethsemane, an *angel* appeared to him *from heaven,* comforting him (Luke 22:43). In the current verse too, on an inner level, an angel from heaven means the divinity that was in him.

And said, "Abraham! Abraham!" And he said, "Here I am," symbolizes comfort perceived by the divine goodness in his rational mind after his trials. This can be seen from the symbolism of *saying* in scriptural narrative as perceiving (mentioned many times before). The reason it means perception by the divine goodness in his rational mind here is that in the current verse *Abraham* symbolizes the divine goodness of the Lord's rational mind, or in other words, of his human side.

It is impossible to explain intelligibly the nature of perception by divine goodness in the Lord's rational mind. Before it could be explained, many different concepts would need to be taken and formed into a picture of the Lord's divine humanity. Until such a picture is formed, all the points to be explained will sink into a mind that is either empty or dark, and such a mind will either twist the truth or render it absurd.

This verse focuses on the Lord's first state after his crisis, which is a state of consolation. So the text no longer refers to God but to Jehovah, because it mentions God when it is talking about truth but Jehovah when it is talking about goodness, and truth is the weapon for battle, while goodness is the source of comfort (§2769). All comfort after trial is infused into what is good, because goodness is the source of all joy, which passes from what is good over into what is true. In the current verse, then, Abraham symbolizes divine goodness in the Lord's rational mind, as he does in other places too, especially when Jehovah is mentioned in the same verse.

Genesis 22:12. *And he said, "You are not to put your hand out to the boy nor do anything to him, because now I know that you fear God and have not held back your son—your only one—from me."*

He said, "You are not to put your hand out to the boy," means that he would not take on any further challenge to the divine truth in his rational mind. *Nor do anything to him* symbolizes liberation. *Because now I know that you fear God* means his glorification through divine love. *And have not held back your son—your only one—from me* symbolizes the uniting of his humanity with his divinity through his final trial.

And he said, "You are not to put your hand out to the boy," means that he would not take on any further challenge to the divine truth in his rational mind, as can be seen from the following: *Putting out a hand* means being tested to the very limit of his strength (discussed just above at §2816). And

2822

2823

2824

the *boy*—Isaac—symbolizes his rational mind in respect to divine truth, which is what the challenges he took on were targeting (discussed in §§2803, 2813, 2814, 2817).

2825   *Nor do anything to him* symbolizes liberation, as can be seen without explanation. When Abraham is told to do nothing to him, after all, it means that the act will be stopped and accordingly that he will be set free.

2826   *Because now I know that you fear God* means his glorification through divine love, as can be seen from the following: *Knowing,* when ascribed to the Lord's divinity, means nothing else than becoming one. To put the same thing another way, it means being glorified, since the Lord's humanity was made one with his divinity by means of his trials (§§1737, 1813). And *fearing God,* or rather fear of God, symbolizes divine love here. Because it is ascribed to truth in the Lord's divine rationality, the verse speaks of fearing God rather than Jehovah, since when the focus is on truth the name God is used, and when it is on goodness the name Jehovah is used (§§2586, 2769, 2822). Divine love is the means by which the Lord united his human nature with his divine nature and his divine nature with his human. In other words, it is the means by which he glorified himself (see §§1812, 1813, 2253).

The symbolism of *fearing God* in the Word can be seen from many passages there, understood on an inner level. Fear of God in Scripture symbolizes worship—specifically, worship based on fear, on a goodness inspired by faith, or on a loving goodness. It symbolizes worship based on fear when the subject is people who have not been reborn; worship based on a goodness inspired by faith when the subject is spiritual people who have been reborn; and worship based on a loving goodness when the subject is heavenly people who have been reborn.

[2] 1. *In a general way, fear of God symbolizes worship.* This is clear in Kings:

> The children of Israel *feared other gods* and walked in the statutes of the surrounding nations. At first the non-Jewish nations imported into Samaria *did not fear Jehovah,* so Jehovah sent lions among them. And one of the priests that they had taken captive in Samaria came and settled in Bethel and was teaching them *how to fear Jehovah.* Jehovah struck a pact with the children of Israel and commanded them, "You shall not *fear foreign gods* or bow down to them or serve them or sacrifice to them, but *Jehovah you shall fear* and to him you shall bow down and to him you shall sacrifice." (2 Kings 17:7, 8, 24, [25,] 28, 32, 33, 35, 36, 37, 41)

Fearing here clearly stands for worshiping. In Isaiah:

> Because this people approached with their mouth, and with their lips they honored me, but their heart kept far from me, *and their fear for me was* a human commandment taught [by rote], . . . (Isaiah 29:13)

"Their fear for me" stands for worship in general, because it says that this fear was a human commandment. In Luke:

> There was a certain judge in a given city who did *not fear God* or respect any human. (Luke 18:2)

Not fearing God stands for not worshiping him.

[3] 2. *When the subject is people who have not been reborn, fear of God symbolizes worship based on fear,* as is clear from the following passages. In Moses:

> When the law was being issued on Mount Sinai, the people said to Moses, "You yourself speak with us and we will listen, and do not let God speak with us or we might die." And Moses said to the people, ". . . because God has come in order to test you, and in order *that fear of him may be on your faces,* to keep you from sinning." (Exodus 20:19, 20)

And in another place:

> "Now why should we die? For this big fire consumes us. If we continue to hear the voice of Jehovah our God anymore, we will die. You yourself go near and listen to everything that Jehovah our God says, and you yourself speak to us everything that Jehovah our God says to you, and we will listen and do it." And Jehovah said to Moses, "Oh, who will grant that they may have a heart to *fear me* and to keep all my commandments all their days?" (Deuteronomy 5:25, 27, 29)

The "fear of God on your faces, to keep you from sinning" and a "heart to fear me and to keep all my commandments" symbolize fearful worship on the part of people who are like this. Those whose worship remains superficial, without depth, are moved by fear to keep the law and be obedient. Even so, they do not take up inward worship or develop holy fear unless they live good lives, know what the inner dimension is, and believe that it exists. In the same author:

> If you do not watch to do all the words of this law written in this book, to *fear this honorable and fearsome name,* "Jehovah your God," Jehovah will make your plagues and the plagues of your seed extraordinary, plagues

massive and sure, and diseases evil and sure, and he will bring back onto
you all the debility of Egypt, *which you fear,* and these things will cling to
you. (Deuteronomy 28:58, 59, 60)

Here too, fearing the honorable and fearsome name of Jehovah God is worshiping in fear; and in order for such people to worship this way, they had
to attribute all evil to Jehovah, including curses (§§592, 2335, 2395, 2447).
In Jeremiah:

> Your wickedness will chastise you, and your rebellions will convict you;
> and know and see that it is an evil and bitter thing that you desert Jehovah
> your God and that *there is no dread of me in you.* (Jeremiah 2:19)

In Luke:

> I say to you, don't *be afraid of those* who kill the body but afterward have
> nothing more they can do. But I will show you *whom you ought to fear:*
> *fear the one* who after killing has the authority to cast you into Gehenna.
> Indeed, I say to you, *fear this one.* (Luke 12:4, 5; Matthew 10:28)

Here too fearing God involves worship in some degree of fear, because fear
drove them to obedience, as just mentioned.

[4] 3. *Where the subject is spiritual people who have been reborn, fearing
God, or Jehovah, symbolizes worship based on a goodness inspired by faith,* as
is clear from the following passages. In Moses:

> Monarchs shall write themselves a copy of this law on a book in the pres-
> ence of the priest-Levites, and it shall stay with them, and they shall read
> in it all the days of their life in order that they may learn to *fear Jehovah
> their God,* to keep all the words of this law and these statutes, to do them.
> (Deuteronomy 17:18, 19)

On an inner level, monarchs stand for religious truth, because monarchy represented the Lord's spiritual kingdom (§§1672, 1728, 2015, 2069).
Fearing Jehovah their God, then, is worshiping him from truth that leads
to faith, and since this cannot be separated from good that is done out of
neighborly love, it is depicted in the keeping of the words of the law, and
the statues, to do them. In Samuel:

> Here, now, Jehovah has set a monarch over you. If you *fear Jehovah*
> and serve him and listen carefully to his voice, both you and also the
> monarch who reigns over you will follow Jehovah your God. (1 Samuel
> 12:13, 14)

Here too, in an inner sense, fearing Jehovah stands for worshiping in the goodness and truth of faith, as above, because the focus is monarchs, or monarchy. [5] In Joshua:

> Now *fear Jehovah* and serve him in integrity and truth; and take away the gods that your ancestors served. (Joshua 24:14)

Again in this passage, fearing Jehovah stands for worshiping in the goodness and truth that mark the spiritual person. Integrity has to do with the good taught by faith (§612), and truth, with the truth taught by faith. In Jeremiah:

> They will become my people, and I will become their God, and I will give them one heart and one way, *to fear me* every day, with good result to them and to their children after them. And I will strike an eternal pact with them, [pledging] that I will not turn back from doing good to them. And *fear of me* I will put into their heart to prevent them from withdrawing from me. (Jeremiah 32:38, 39, 40)

The context shows that in this passage, fearing God is worshiping in the goodness and truth of faith. So does the use of the words *people* and *God*. Those who possess religious truth are called a people (see §§1259, 1260), and God is referred to where the theme is truth (2586, 2769, 2807 at the end). In Isaiah:

> A mighty people will honor you; a city of strong nations will *fear you*. (Isaiah 25:3)

In this passage as well, fearing God stands for worshiping from spiritual truth. After all, it speaks of a people and of a city. (A city is teachings that are true; see §§402, 2268, 2449, 2451.) [6] In David:

> Who is this man *fearing Jehovah*? [Jehovah] will teach him the way that he should choose. (Psalms 25:12)

The man fearing Jehovah stands for one worshiping him. The statement that [Jehovah] will teach him the way clarifies the fact that this is about a spiritual person, a "way" being truth (see §§627, 2333). In the same author:

> Happy is everyone *fearing Jehovah,* walking in his ways. (Psalms 128:1)

Likewise in the same author:

> *Those fearing Jehovah* will glorify him. All the seed of Jacob will glorify him, and *of him* will all the seed of Israel *be afraid.* (Psalms 22:23)

Being afraid of him, in this verse, stands for worshiping in the truth of faith. The seed of Israel is the spiritual element in religion, or in other words, the goodness and truth of faith (§§1025, 1447, 1610). In Moses:

> Now, Israel, what is Jehovah your God seeking from you but to *fear Jehovah your God,* to walk in all his ways, and to love him, and to serve Jehovah your God, with all your heart and with all your soul, to keep the commandments of Jehovah and his statutes? (Deuteronomy 10:12, 13)

This defines what it is for a spiritual person ("Israel") to fear God; it is to walk in Jehovah's ways, love him, serve him, and keep his commandments and statutes. In John:

> I saw an angel flying in midair, having the eternal gospel, saying in a loud voice, "*Fear God* and give him glory, because the hour of his judgment is coming!" (Revelation 14:6, 7)

Fearing God stands for holy worship based on the goodness and truth of faith. In Luke:

> Jesus said to the crippled person, "Get up and, taking your bed, go to your house." As a result, shock seized them all, and they gave glory to God and *were filled with fear.* (Luke 5:24, 25, 26)

In this passage, fear stands for holy fear—the kind people have when religious truth is leading them to a loving goodness.

[7] 4. *When the subject is heavenly people who have been reborn, fearing God, or Jehovah, symbolizes worship based on a loving goodness.* In Malachi:

> My compact with Levi was one of life and peace; and I gave them to him along with *fear,* and he *feared me,* and for my name he was chastened. The law of truth was in his mouth, and perversion was not on his lips; in peace and uprightness he walked with me. (Malachi 2:5, 6)

This is about the Lord, who is Levi in the inner meaning here. Levi symbolizes priesthood and he symbolizes love. The fear stands for a goodness characterized by divine love. The law of truth stands for truth characterized by divine love. The peace and uprightness stand for both. [8] In Isaiah:

> A new branch will come from the trunk of Jesse, and from his roots a shoot will grow, and Jehovah's spirit will rest on him—a spirit of wisdom and understanding, a spirit of counsel and might, a spirit of knowledge

and of the *fear of Jehovah*—and he will smell [incense] in the *fear of Jehovah*. (Isaiah 11:1, 2, 3)

This too is about the Lord. The spirit of knowledge and fear of Jehovah stands for his divine love for what is true; his smelling [incense] in the fear of Jehovah stands for his divine love for what is good. [9] In David:

> The precepts of Jehovah are upright, gladdening the heart. The commandment of Jehovah is pure, illuminating the eyes. The *fear of Jehovah is clean,* standing forever. The judgments of Jehovah are truth; they embody justice, taken together. (Psalms 19:8, 9)

The cleanness of the fear of Jehovah stands for love; the truth of Jehovah's judgments, for faith. Justice is connected with the good that comes of love; judgments are connected with the truth that belongs to faith (see §2235), and they are said to embody justice, taken together, when truth becomes goodness, or when faith becomes love for others. In the same author:

> Look: Jehovah's eye is on *those fearing him,* on those waiting for his mercy. (Psalms 33:18)

[10] And in another passage:

> Not in the strength of a horse does Jehovah delight; not in the legs of a man does he take pleasure. Jehovah's pleasure is in *those fearing him* and those waiting for his mercy. (Psalms 147:10, 11)

The horse's strength stands for a person's self-sufficient power to think what is true, a horse meaning some property of intellect (see §§2760, 2761, 2762). A man's legs stand for a person's self-sufficient power to do good. Those fearing Jehovah stand for people who worship him with love for what is true; and those waiting for his mercy stand for people who worship him with love for what is good. Where the prophets speak of goodness, they also speak of truth, and where they speak of truth, they also speak of goodness. This is due to the heavenly marriage of goodness and truth in every detail (see §§683, 793, 801, 2173, 2516, 2712). [11] In the same author:

> Jehovah will bless the house of Israel; he will bless the house of Aaron; he will bless *those fearing Jehovah,* the small with the great. (Psalms 115:12, 13)

Those fearing Jehovah stand for people whose worship is based on a goodness inspired by faith (the house of Israel) and on a loving goodness (the house of Aaron). Both are mentioned because of the heavenly marriage that exists in every detail of the Word, as noted. [12] In Isaiah:

> What will be true throughout your seasons is the strength of [Jehovah's] salvation, wisdom and knowledge; and the *fear of Jehovah* is a treasure. (Isaiah 33:6)

Wisdom and knowledge here stand for religious goodness bonded to religious truth. The fear of Jehovah stands for a loving goodness. In the same author:

> Who among you is *fearing Jehovah,* is listening carefully to the voice of his servant? (Isaiah 50:10)

The person fearing Jehovah stands for one who worships with love. The person who listens carefully to the voice of his servant stands for one who worships in faith. When the one connects with the other, there is a heavenly marriage.

[13] These scriptural quotations show that the fear of God is worship based on fear, a goodness inspired by faith, or a loving goodness. The more fear there is in worship, the less faith there is, and the amount of love is even smaller. Conversely, the more faith there is in worship, and especially the more love there is, the less fear there is. Admittedly, fear is present in all worship, but under another guise and other garb. This fear is *holy fear.* Holy fear is not so much fear of hell and damnation as fear of doing or thinking anything that opposes the Lord or our neighbor. So it is fear of doing or thinking anything that opposes a loving goodness or religious truth. It is an aversion, and it forms one side of the boundary drawn around all that is holy in faith and love.

[14] Because a fear of hell and damnation is absent in people who have a goodness that grows out of faith, as noted, and even more so in those who have a goodness that grows out of love—that is, in those who are in the Lord—therefore:

5. *Fearing also means disbelieving, or lacking faith and love,* as in Isaiah:

> This is what your Creator has said, Jacob, and the one who formed you, Israel: *"Don't be afraid,* because I have redeemed you; I have called you by your name: You Are Mine." (Isaiah 43:1, 5; 44:8)

In Luke:

> . . . the oath that he swore to Abraham our father: to grant us that we— rescued *without fear* from the hand of our enemies—should serve him, in holiness and righteousness before him. (Luke 1:73, 74, 75)

In the same author:

> Don't be afraid, little flock, because it has pleased your Father to give you the kingdom. (Luke 12:32)

In Mark:

> Jesus said to the head of the synagogue, "Don't be afraid; only believe!" (Mark 5:36; Luke 8:49, 50)

In the same author:

> Jesus said, "Why are you fearful still? How can you not have faith?" (Mark 4:40)

In Luke:

> The hairs of your head have been counted, so don't be afraid! You are better than any number of sparrows. (Luke 12:7)

In these passages, fearing is disbelieving, or lacking faith and love.

And have not held back your son—your only one—from me symbolizes the uniting of his humanity with his divinity through his final trial, as can be seen from the following: *Your son,* Isaac, symbolizes divine rationality (discussed previously), or in other words, divine humanity, since humanity begins in rationality (§§2106, 2194). It is called his *only one* because it is the Only-Born; see §2773. And *not holding him back from me* means causing it to become one—specifically, one with divinity itself. This union was achieved by his final trial, as is clear from the whole previous discussion.

2827

Genesis 22:13. *And Abraham raised his eyes and looked and there: a ram behind him, caught in the thicket by its horns! And Abraham went and took the ram and offered it as a burnt offering in place of his son.*

2828

Abraham raised his eyes and looked symbolizes thought and insight received by the Lord from his divine side. *And there: a ram* symbolizes spiritual members of the human race. *Behind him, caught in the thicket* means entangled in earthly knowledge. *By its horns* means as much as possible, so far as religious truth goes. *And Abraham went and took the ram* symbolizes their liberation by the Lord's divine humanity. *And offered it as a burnt offering in place of his son* means consecrating and adopting them.

Abraham raised his eyes and looked symbolizes thought and insight received by the Lord from his divine side. See above at §2789, where the same words occur.

2829

Thought and insight received from his divine side is thought about and insight into absolutely everything that will ever happen, along with divine providence.

2830   *And there: a ram* symbolizes spiritual members of the human race, as can be seen from the symbolism of a *ram,* discussed below.

It is known in the church that the burnt offerings and sacrifices in the representative religion of Judah and Israel symbolized the Lord's divine humanity. Burnt offerings and sacrifices of lambs, though, symbolized one thing. Those of ewes and she-goats symbolized another. So did those of kids, rams, and he-goats; of adult cattle, young cattle, and calves; and of turtledoves and pigeon chicks. The same is true of minhas and libations. In general, they symbolized what was divinely heavenlike, divinely spiritual, and divinely earthly in the Lord. As a result, they symbolized everything heavenly, spiritual, and earthly from him in his kingdom and therefore in every individual who *is* a kingdom of the Lord.

This can be seen in the Holy Supper, which took the place of burnt offerings and sacrifices. In it, the bread and wine symbolize the Lord's divine humanity. The bread symbolizes his heavenly divinity, and the wine, his spiritual divinity. Accordingly, they symbolize his love for the entire human race and, in turn, the love the human race has for the Lord (§§2343, 2359). Plainly, then, the burnt offerings and sacrifices involved heavenly worship inspired by love for the Lord, and spiritual worship inspired by charity for one's neighbor and so by faith in the Lord (922, 923, 1823, 2180).

What a heavenly quality is and what a spiritual quality is—or what heavenly and spiritual people in the Lord's kingdom (or his church) are— has been said many times. See §§1155, 1577, 1824, 2048, 2088, 2184, 2227, 2669, 2708, 2715.

[2] Now, a *ram* symbolizes what is divinely spiritual in the Lord. So it symbolizes what is spiritual in us or, to put it another way, spiritual members of the human race. This can be seen from the burnt offerings and sacrifices that involved rams. For instance, when Aaron and his sons were being consecrated to perform ministry (when they were being ordained, in other words), they would offer one *young ox* as a sin offering. Some of its blood was to be spattered on the horns of the altar, and the rest was to be spattered at its base. One *ram* would also be slaughtered, and its blood was to be spattered around the altar, and then the *ram* would be burned whole *as a burnt offering.* And the blood

of the *second* slaughtered *ram* was to be spattered on Aaron's earlobe and thumb and big toe. After it was waved, it would be burned in addition to the burnt offering (Exodus 29:1–35; Leviticus 8:1–end; 9:2 and following verses). Clearly, all these rituals were holy, but the reason was that what they represented and symbolized was holy. The slaughter of the young ox; the spattering of some of its blood on the horns of the altar and of the rest at its base; the slaughter of the first ram; the spattering of its blood around the altar, and then the burning of it; the spattering of the second ram's blood on Aaron's earlobe, thumb, and big toe; the waving of it and the burning of it on the burnt offering—none of these things would have had any holiness or therefore anything to do with worship if they had not represented something holy.

What the individual details represented, though, cannot be seen by anyone except from the inner meaning. The young ox used as a sin offering symbolized what was divinely earthly in the Lord. The ram symbolized what was divinely spiritual, and also spiritual members of the human race. This can be seen from the symbolism of a young ox and a ram in the Word. Ordinations into the priesthood were conducted by spiritual means, because the spiritual dimension introduces us to the heavenly dimension. To say it another way, religious truth introduces us to a loving goodness.

Again, when Aaron entered the Holy Place, he would offer a *young ox* as a sin offering and a *ram* as a burnt offering (Leviticus 16:2, 3).

[3] When Nazirites fulfilled the days of their Naziriteship, they would offer a *male lamb*, the offspring of a year—a sound one, a single one—as a burnt offering; and a single *female lamb*, the offspring of a year—a sound one—as a sin offering; and a *single ram*—*a sound one*—as peace offerings (Numbers 6:13, 14, 16, 17). The reason was that a Nazirite represented a heavenly person, who is a likeness of the Lord (§§51, 52, 1013). By nature, a heavenly person feels heavenly love (that is, love for the Lord) and therefore knows heavenly truth (202, 337, 2069, 2715, 2718). That is why a Nazirite had to sacrifice a male lamb and a female lamb (symbolizing what was heavenly) and a ram (symbolizing what was spiritual).

During feasts, young cattle, rams, and lambs were sacrificed. On the first day of the Feast of Unleavened Bread, for example, two young oxen, *one ram,* and seven lambs, along with their minha, were sacrificed as a burnt offering (Numbers 28:18, 19, 20). Also on the day of the First Fruits, two young oxen, *one ram,* and seven lambs, along with their minha, were sacrificed as a burnt offering (Numbers 28:26, 27, 28). At new moons, two young oxen, *one ram,* and seven lambs, along with their minha, were sacrificed as a burnt offering (Numbers 28:11, 12). In the seventh month, on the first of the month, it was one young ox, *one ram,* and seven lambs, along with their minha. On the fifteenth day of the seventh month, it was thirteen young oxen, *two rams,* and fourteen lambs. And so on; see Numbers 29:1, 2, 12, 13, 14, 17, 18, 20, 21, 22, 23, 24, 26–36. Young oxen and rams symbolized spiritual qualities, but lambs symbolized heavenly qualities. In their feasts, you see, the people had to be consecrated, and introduced [to heavenly qualities] by means of spiritual qualities.

[4] Since rams symbolized what was divinely spiritual in the Lord's divine humanity, and also what was spiritual in humankind, a passage in Ezekiel concerning the new temple and the new Jerusalem (or the Lord's spiritual kingdom) says this: When they finished purging the altar there, they were to offer a *young ox* as a sin offering and a *ram* as a burnt offering. And for seven days they were to sacrifice the *he-goat* of the sin offering daily, and a *young ox* and a *ram* (Ezekiel 43:23, 24, 25). And on that day, [the Feast of Unleavened Bread,] the ruler was to sacrifice the *young ox* of the sin offering for all the people; and on the seven days of the feast, *seven young oxen* and *seven rams,* along with the minha, as a burnt offering (Ezekiel 45:22, 23, 24). And on the Sabbath day, the ruler was to sacrifice six *lambs* and a *ram* (Ezekiel 46:4, 6).

[5] In the broadest sense, the new temple and the new Jerusalem symbolize the Lord's kingdom (see §§402, 940). In particular they symbolize a new religion (2117). Neither of them will have burnt offerings or sacrifices, as anyone can recognize. Clearly, then, these rituals symbolize the heavenly qualities of love and the spiritual qualities of faith, because such qualities belong to the Lord's kingdom. So young oxen, rams, and lambs symbolize the same things. Young oxen and rams symbolize spiritual qualities, as can be seen from every particular of the inner meaning in those passages. In general it can be seen from the fact that the new temple and the new Jerusalem specifically symbolize the Lord's spiritual kingdom (Zion being his heavenly kingdom).

[6] It is also clear in Daniel that a ram symbolizes a spiritual quality or, what is the same, spiritual people. Daniel saw a *ram* with two horns standing before a stream, and then a *buck of the goats,* which struck the ram, broke its horns, and trampled it (Daniel 8:3, 4, and following verses). Here the *ram*

actually means a spiritual religion, and a *buck* of the goats means people who subscribe to a faith detached from love for others, or truth detached from goodness. Such people assert themselves with constantly increasing pride against what is good and eventually against the Lord, as the passage also portrays. In Samuel:

> Samuel said to Saul, "Does Jehovah take as much pleasure in burnt offerings and sacrifices as in attentiveness to Jehovah's voice? Look: attentiveness is better than sacrifice, and obedience *than the fat of rams.*" (1 Samuel 15:22)

Since this verse is talking about obedience, it is talking about truth, which is spiritual; and the words were addressed to the king, who also symbolizes truth (§§1672, 2015, 2069). So it says it is better than the fat of *rams* rather than the fat of cattle or of lambs. [7] In David:

> When Israel came out from Egypt—the house of Jacob, from a barbaric people—Judah became their sanctuary; Israel, their ruling power. The sea looked and fled, and the Jordan turned back. The *mountains leaped like rams;* the hills, like the offspring of the flock. What is the matter with you, O sea, that you flee? [With you,] O Jordan, that you turn back? *Mountains, you will leap like rams;* hills, like the offspring of the flock. Before the Lord you bear children, O earth—before the God of Jacob, who turned rock into a lake of water, and flint into a spring of its water. (Psalms 114:1–end)

The inner meaning here speaks of spiritual goodness after rebirth, describing its character. Its heavenly spirituality is depicted in the mountains that leaped like rams, and its heavenly earthliness, in the hills that leaped like the offspring of the flock. Mountains are the heavenly qualities of love (see §§795, 1430). Anyone can see that this passage, like the rest of David, has holy content, but only in the inner meaning. Clearly it symbolizes something when the text says that the mountains leaped like rams, and the hills, like the offspring of the flock, and that the earth bears children before the Lord. Without a deeper meaning, it is nonsense.

[8] The same is true of these words in Moses:

> He will make them ride on the heights of the earth, and make them eat the produce of the earth, and make them suck honey from a crag, and

oil from a flinty rock, the butter of the herd and the milk of the flock, together with the fat of lambs *and of rams—the sons of Bashan*—and of goats, together with the fat of the kidneys of wheat; and the blood of grapes you will drink as unmixed wine. (Deuteronomy 32:13, 14, 15)

Rams, the sons of Bashan, stand for heavenly qualities that are spiritual. For what heavenly spiritual qualities are, see §1824. In David:

Burnt offerings of marrow foods I will offer to you, *along with the incense of rams;* I will sacrifice an ox, along with he-goats. (Psalms 66:15)

Burnt offerings of marrow foods stand for the heavenly qualities of love. The incense of rams stands for the spiritual qualities of faith. [9] In Ezekiel:

Arabia and all the chiefs of Kedar were your dealers at hand for lambs, for *rams* and he-goats. (Ezekiel 27:21)

This is about Tyre, which symbolizes people who know what is good and true (§1201). Arabia stands for their wisdom; the chiefs of Kedar, for their understanding; the lambs, for heavenly attributes; the rams, for spiritual ones; and the he-goats for earthly ones—in that order. In Isaiah:

Every flock of Kedar will be gathered to you; the *rams of Nebaioth* will wait on you. They will go up for my good pleasure to my altar, and my beautiful House I will beautify. (Isaiah 60:7)

This is about the Lord's divine humanity. The flock of Kedar stands for his divinely heavenlike traits, and the rams of Nebaioth, for his divinely spiritual traits.

All this evidence now shows that on an inner level a ram symbolizes the Lord's divine spirituality and therefore the spiritual dimension in humankind or, what is the same, spiritual members of the human race.

2831   *Behind him, caught in the thicket* means entangled in earthly knowledge. This can be seen from the symbolism here of being *caught* as being entangled and from that of a *thicket* or snarled undergrowth as knowledge. A discussion follows below.

Spiritual people become caught in the tangle of earthly knowledge about religious truth, and this is why: they do not have a perception of what is good and true, the way heavenly people do. In place of perception they have conscience. Conscience is formed from the religious goodness and truth they have absorbed since their earliest years from parents and teachers, and later from the teachings of the religion they were born into. People who do not have a perception of what is good and true necessarily depend on knowledge to double-check their thinking. We each create for ourselves some picture of the things we have learned—including the things we have learned about religious goodness and truth. Without a mental picture, nothing settles in the memory, except in the form of meaningless trivia. Confirmation by other kinds of knowledge—including secular knowledge—streams in and fills out our idea of the subject. Once confirmed by a quantity of evidence, the image itself gives the idea permanence in our memory and enables it to be called forth from there into thought. Not only that, it also allows faith to be instilled into it.

[2] To turn to a general discussion of perception: It is necessary to define perception, because few know what it is. There is perception of what is good and true in heavenly and spiritual affairs; perception of what is just and fair in public life; and perception of what is honorable in private life.

As for a perception of what is good and true in heavenly and spiritual affairs, this is the type of perception the deeper angels receive from the Lord. It was also the type of perception received by the people of the very earliest church, and it is the perception received by heavenly people, who love the Lord. They know instantly, at a kind of inward glance, whether a thing is good, and whether it is true. The Lord instills this knowledge into them, because they are united to him by love.

Spiritual people, though, do not have this perception of what is good and true in heavenly and spiritual matters. Instead, they have conscience, which provides an inner dictate. But conscience, as noted, is formed from the knowledge of goodness and truth taught us by our parents and teachers, and later from our own study of theology and the Word. To this goodness and truth—even if it is not very good or true—we attach our faith. Consequently *any* kind of theology can produce a conscience. Even non-Christians can create a good substitute for conscience out of their religious persuasion.

[3] The fact that spiritual people do not have a perception of religious goodness and truth, but speak for and believe in the truth of the notions they have learned and grasped, is clear enough from the claim they each make that their own dogma is true. Heretics do so more vigorously than others. Real truth they cannot see, much less acknowledge, even if thousands of arguments support it. Examine yourself to

see whether you have any other way of telling whether something is true. Do you fail to acknowledge an idea even when its truth is made absolutely clear to you? For instance, some people consider faith rather than love the essential means to salvation. Everything the Lord said about love and charity can be read to them (see §2371), and they might know from the Word that all the Law and all the Prophets depend on love for the Lord and charity for our neighbor. Even so, they will still continue to focus their thinking on faith and claim that it alone saves us. Not so with people who have heavenly and spiritual perception.

[4] As for a perception of what is just and fair in public life, this is the type of perception received by people in the world who are rational. The same for a perception of what is honorable in private life. People differ from each other in regard to both types of perception. Neither type, though, in any way leads to a perception of religious goodness and truth, because this kind is higher, or deeper, and comes from the Lord by way of the rational mind's inmost core.

[5] Another reason spiritual people do not have a perception of religious goodness and truth is that goodness and truth are not implanted in the voluntary part of their mind, as they are in heavenly people, but in the intellectual part. (See §§863, 875, 927, 1023, 1043, 1044, 2256.) That is why the spiritual cannot even begin to experience the light that the heavenly do (2718). Instead, they live in relative dimness (1043, 2708 at the beginning, 2715). When it comes to religious truth, then, spiritual people naturally become tangled up in earthly knowledge.

[6] The idea that a *thicket*, on an inner level, symbolizes earthly knowledge (that is, knowledge that settles in the outer memory) can also be seen from passages elsewhere in the Word. In Ezekiel:

> Here, Assyria was a cedar in Lebanon, beautiful in its bough, and [forming] a shady grove, and lofty in its height; *and its branch was surrounded by thickets.* (Ezekiel 31:3)

This is about Egypt, which means secular knowledge (§§1164, 1165, 1186, 1462). Assyria stands for the rational mind (119, 1186), which in the Word is also a cedar, and Lebanon. Being surrounded by thickets stands for living among secular learning, because human rationality is founded on what it knows. [7] In the same author:

> This is what the Lord Jehovih has said: "Because you were lofty in height, and [the cedar] *set its branch among the thickets,* and its heart became

lifted up in its loftiness, foreigners will cut it off—the violent among the nations—and throw it down." (Ezekiel 31:10, 12)

This is about Egypt. Setting its branch among the thickets stands for clinging to secular knowledge and using it as a standpoint from which to view spiritual, heavenly, and divine realities. In the same author:

> . . . in order to prevent all the trees of the water from raising themselves up in their height and *setting their branch among the thickets,* and to prevent all those drinking the water from standing over them in their height, because they will all be given over to death, to the underground realm, in the midst of the children of humankind, to those going down into the pit. (Ezekiel 31:14)

This is about people who want to use sophistry based on secular knowledge to pry into the mysteries of faith. Such people are entirely blind (see §§215, 232, 233, 1072, 1911, 2196, 2203, 2568, 2588). To reason on the basis of secular knowledge is to set one's branch among the thickets. In the same author:

> She had strong saplings for rulers' scepters, and her height lifted itself *above the thickets.* (Ezekiel 19:11)

Likewise. [8] In the same author:

> Victims of stabbing in Israel lie amid their idols, around their altars, and under every green tree, and *under every tangled oak.* (Ezekiel 6:13)

The subject here is the worship that people cobble together for themselves when they put their faith in themselves and in the ideas they dream up out of the things they know. A tangled oak stands for the knowledge they use at such a time. On the point that oaks are insights based on secular facts, see §§1442, 1443, 2144. Likewise in another passage in the same author:

> They saw every high hill and every *tangled tree,* and they sacrificed their sacrifices there. (Ezekiel 20:28)

A tangled tree stands for the dictates not of the Word but of what an individual chooses to view as fact. Worship once took place in groves—symbolic worship, whose symbolism depended on the qualities of the trees; see §2722. [9] In Isaiah:

> Wickedness burns like fire; bramble patch and brier patch it will consume, and it will ignite the *thickets of the forest.* (Isaiah 9:18)

The bramble patch and brier patch stand for falsity and cravings. The thickets of the forest stand for secular knowledge. In the same author:

> Jehovah Sabaoth will cut down the *thickets of the forest* with iron, and Lebanon will be felled by the Majestic One. (Isaiah 10:34)

The thickets of the forest stand for secular knowledge; Lebanon, for thoughts on the rational plane. In Jeremiah:

> Lift a signal toward Zion, because I am bringing evil from the north, and great wreckage. The lion has gone up *from its thicket,* and the destroyer of nations, having set out, has left its place to make your land a wasteland. Your cities will be destroyed, so that there is no resident. (Jeremiah 4:6, 7)

"From its thicket" means from knowledge. Whatever goes up from secular knowledge to invade divine secrets makes the land a wasteland—that is, devastates the church.

[10] The reason the Word refers to secular facts as thickets is that they are indeed relatively convoluted, especially when they favor the cravings of self-love and materialism and promote false assumptions. Love that is heavenly and spiritual is what brings the knowledge in the outer memory into order, while self-love and materialism is what undoes the arrangement and throws it all into confusion. We do not notice, because we turn orderly patterns into disorderly ones, good into evil, and truth into falsity. That is why it is all so tangled.

Another reason is that, compared to the contents of the inner memory (which holds rational concepts), the contents of the outer memory (which holds earthly learning) are in a snarl, or in a dense forest. As long as people are living in their bodies, they cannot see how shadowy, black, and dark things are in that forest, by comparison. While on earth, they imagine that the outer memory is the fount of all wisdom and understanding, but eventually they will reach the other world and gain the use of their inner memory's contents. Then they will see that the outer memory—the memory proper to people living in the world—contains anything but the light of wisdom and understanding. They will see that its contents are relatively dark, disorganized, and tangled; see §§2469–2494.

2832 *By its horns* means as much as possible, so far as religious truth goes, as can be seen from the symbolism of *horns*. The Word mentions *horns* in many places, where they symbolize the power truth has when it comes of goodness. In a negative sense, they symbolize the power falsity has when it comes of evil. In the current verse, it means that the spiritual people symbolized by the ram become as entangled in earthly knowledge as possible, so far as [religious] truth goes. Consequently they are deprived of the possibility of perceiving truth. The more we consult earthly knowledge in regard to the tenets of religious truth, and cling to it heart and soul, the more we lose the light of truth. And when we lose its light, we also lose its life.

Anyone willing to pay attention and reflect can see this from his or her experience with people who say they cannot believe anything unless they grasp its truth through either their senses or their knowledge. If you examine their character, you will find that they believe nothing, and moreover that nothing seems wiser to them than attributing everything to nature. There is also a large number of people who claim to have belief, in spite of not understanding, but privately spend just as much time as others debating inside themselves, on the basis of sense impressions and learning, whether the truth advocated by faith is really true. Either they adopt a certain dogmatic conviction that it is so, and inflate their conviction with love for themselves and for the material world, or they actually do not believe anything at all. Their character is evident from their lives.

Both types are present in the Lord's spiritual church, admittedly, but they are not part of it. People who are part of that church live good lives and believe in what is true. Spiritual people, however, believe in other truth too, beyond the ideas impressed on them from their earliest years and later confirmed by them from theology or some other source. Such is the condition of spiritual people—a condition portrayed here by a ram caught in the thicket by its horns (see just above in §2831).

[2] The following passages show that *a horn symbolizes the power truth has when it comes of goodness.* In David:

> You are the glory of their strength, and in your good pleasure you will *lift up our horn,* because our shield belongs to Jehovah, and our monarch to the Holy One of Israel. *"My truth* and my mercy are with him, and in my name *his horn will be lifted up,* and on the sea I will put his hand, and on the rivers, his right hand." (Psalms 89:17, 18, 24, 25)

Clearly "our horn" and "his horn" stand for the power of truth. The subject of these verses is the Lord's spiritual kingdom. "Our monarch belongs to the Holy One of Israel" stands for the fact that divine truth is the Lord's. A monarch is truth, and the Lord's royal power is divine truth; see §§1672, 1728, 2015, 2069. Putting his hand on the sea and his right hand on the rivers stands for the strength to be found in secular learning and the knowledge of truth. A hand and a right hand mean strength (878), while a sea and rivers mean learning and knowledge (28, 2702). In the same author:

> I will love you, Jehovah, my strength; Jehovah is my rock and my fortress and my rescuer, my God, my towering rock in which I trust, a shield, and a *horn of salvation.* (Psalms 18:1, 2; 2 Samuel 22:2, 3)

A horn of salvation stands for truth in its power. The strength, rock, fortress, God, towering rock, and shield all symbolize the power of truth. [3] In the same author:

> In Zion I will *make the horn of David sprout;* I will arrange a lamp for my anointed. His foes I will clothe in shame. (Psalms 132:17, 18)

This is about the Lord, who is meant by David (§1888). The horn stands for the power of truth; the lamp, for the light of truth. In Samuel:

> My heart has rejoiced in Jehovah; *my horn has lifted itself* in Jehovah. My mouth has widened against my foes, because I have been glad in your salvation. Jehovah will give strength to his monarch *and lift the horn of his anointed one.* (1 Samuel 2:1, 10)

This is part of Hannah's oracular statement. The horn stands for the power of truth. [4] In Moses:

> The firstborn of his ox is an honor to him, and the *horns of the unicorn* are *his horns.* With them he will *butt* all the peoples at once, to the ends of the earth. (Deuteronomy 33:17)

This is an utterance of Moses' concerning Joseph. In it, the horns of the unicorn stand for the mighty power of truth, as is also clear from the fact that with them he was to butt the peoples to the ends of the earth. Likewise in David:

> You will *lift up my horn* like that of a unicorn. (Psalms 92:10)

And in the same author:

> Jehovah, save me from the mouth of the lion; and *from the horns of the unicorn, answer me.* (Psalms 22:21)

Divine truth is called the horns of unicorns from the idea of height. That is why horns are so often said to be lifted—because elevation symbolizes power from within. On the point that depth is expressed as height, see §§1735, 2148. [5] In Jeremiah:

> The Lord in his wrath has cut off *every horn of Israel;* he has drawn back his right hand in the face of the foe. (Lamentations 2:3)

Cutting off every horn of Israel stands for depriving people of truth and its power, which is the same as drawing back his right hand in the face of the foe. In Ezekiel:

> On that day I will *make a horn grow for the house of Israel* and enable you to open your mouth in their midst. (Ezekiel 29:21)

Making a horn grow for the house of Israel stands for increasing the amount of truth a spiritual religion has (Israel meaning a spiritual religion). Opening one's mouth stands for professing that truth. [6] In Habakkuk:

> God will come out of Teman, and the Holy One from Mount Paran; his majesty covered the heavens, and the earth was filled with his praise, and his radiance will be like the light. *He has horns coming from his hand,* and in them is the *hiding place of his strength.* (Habakkuk 3:3, 4)

This is about the Lord. "He has horns coming from his hand, and in them is the hiding place of his strength" plainly stands for the power of truth. Mount Paran is the divine spirituality of the Lord's humanity (that is, the divine truth in his humanity; see §2714), which is also the radiance and light. [7] The divine truth in the Lord's humanity is portrayed this way in John:

> I looked, when there! In the middle of the throne and the four living creatures, a Lamb, standing as if slaughtered, *having seven horns,* which are the seven spirits of God sent out into the whole earth. (Revelation 5:6)

The seven horns stand for sacred or divine truth. The number seven means what is holy; see §§716, 881. The seven spirits sent out into the whole earth are the sacred preaching of that truth.

[8] The horns on altars were also actually a symbol for truth with its power. Moses has this to say about them:

> You shall make *horns on the four corners of the altar; its horns shall extend from it.* (Exodus 27:2; 38:2)

Likewise with the altar of incense, *from which its horns were to extend* (Exodus 30:2; 37:25). The altar was the main object representing the Lord and worship of him (see §921). The altar itself represented his divine goodness, while the horns represented his divine truth. Truth comes of goodness, which was represented by the requirement that the horns "extend from it" (the altar). There is no other truth than the truth that comes of goodness; see §§654, 1162, 1176, 1608, 2063, 2261, 2417. In a positive sense, then, horns clearly symbolize the power truth has when it comes of goodness. [9] [Note] that:

> When Aaron and his sons were being initiated into the ministry, they were to take some of a young ox's blood and put it on the *horns of the altar* with their finger. (Exodus 29:12; Leviticus 8:15)

> Aaron was to make atonement *on the horns of the altar* once a year. (Exodus 30:10)

> When a priest sinned, he was to offer a young ox and put some of the blood *on the horns of the altar of incense.* (Leviticus 4:3, 7)

> And when rulers sinned, they were to offer a burnt offering, and blood would be spattered *on the horns of the altar of burnt offering* (Leviticus 4:22, 25). Likewise if a soul were to sin (Leviticus 4:27, 30, 34), and when the altar was being atoned for. (Leviticus 16:18, 19)

The horns here symbolized truth that comes of goodness. Truth was the means of all consecration, ordination, and atonement, because truth leads to goodness (§2830). The symbolism of the horns of the altar as truth that comes of goodness can also be seen in John:

> The sixth angel trumpeted. Then I heard *a voice* from the *four horns of the golden altar* that is before God. (Revelation 9:13)

The horns of the golden altar plainly stand for truth coming from goodness, because a voice issued from them. Gold stands for what is good (§§113, 1551, 1552); a golden altar, even more so. [10] In Amos:

> On the day I exact punishment on Israel for its transgressions, I will bring punishment on the altars of Bethel, and the *horns of the altar* will be cut off and fall to the earth. (Amos 3:14)

The cutting off of the horns of the altar meant that the place no longer represented the truth that grows out of goodness. Bethel means divine goodness, so in Amos 7:13 it is called a royal sanctuary and a house for the kingdom.

Monarchs were anointed with oil from a horn (1 Samuel 16:1, 13; 1 Kings 1:39), which likewise represented truth developing out of goodness. Oil meant goodness (§886), but a horn meant truth, and in an inner sense, monarchy itself means this kind of truth (1728, 2015), which has power.

[11] The following passages show that *in a negative sense, a horn symbolizes the power falsity has when it comes of evil.* In Amos:

> . . . you who rejoice at a nonentity, saying, "In our strength, haven't we taken ourselves *horns?"* (Amos 6:13)

Horns in this verse stand for the power of falsity. In Zechariah:

> I raised my eyes and looked, and here, *four horns!* And I said to the angel speaking within me, "What are these?" And he said to me, "These are the *horns* that scattered Judah, Israel, and Jerusalem." And Jehovah showed me four artisans, and I said, "What are they coming to do?" And he said, saying, "*These are the horns* that scattered Judah, so that not a man lifts his head; and they have come to terrify, to throw down the *horns of the nations* that lift their *horn* toward the land of Judah, to scatter it." (Zechariah 1:18, 19, 20, 21)

Horns here stand for the power of falsity, which devastates the church. In Ezekiel:

> With side and shoulder you push, and *with your horns you strike all the weak* till you scatter them outside. (Ezekiel 34:21)

This passage is about shepherds who use falsity to lead the flock astray. The horns stand for the power of falsity; the shoulder, for its entire power (§1085). In Jeremiah:

> Jehovah has destroyed and not spared, and he has gladdened your foe over you; he has *lifted the horn of your enemies.* (Lamentations 2:17)

In the same author:

> The *horn of Moab* has been cut off, and his arm has been broken. (Jeremiah 48:25)

The horn stands for powerful falsity. [12] In David:

> I said to the boasters, "Don't boast," and to the *ungodly,* "*Don't lift up your horn; don't lift your horn up on high!* Don't speak with a stiff neck!" I will cut off all the *horns of the ungodly;* the *horns of the upright person* will be lifted up. (Psalms 75:4, 5, 10)

The horns of the ungodly stand for the power falsity acquires from evil. The horns of the upright person stand for the power truth acquires from goodness. [13] In Daniel:

> The fourth beast appeared, terrifying and fearsome, very strong, and it had teeth of iron; it devoured and crushed, and the rest it trampled with its feet. There were *ten horns to it.* I was musing on its *horns,* and here, *another little horn* came up among them, and three of the *previous horns* were rooted out from before it, and here, eyes like the eyes of a human on *this horn,* and a mouth speaking great things! I was then looking because of the sound of the great words that the *horn was speaking.* I wanted certainty about the fourth beast, and about the *ten horns* that were on its head, and about the *other one* that came up, *before which three fell,* and about the *same horn,* that it had eyes, and a mouth speaking great things. I was seeing that the *same horn* made war with the godly, [and overpowered them, till the Ancient One came, and judgment was given for the godly]. And [a bystander] said, "As for the fourth creature, it will be a fourth kingdom on the earth, which will differ from all the kingdoms and consume all the earth and trample it and crush it. As for the *ten horns,* from the same kingdom will rise ten monarchs, and another will rise after them who will differ from the previous ones and will humble three monarchs, speak words against the Highest One, and wear down the godly; later, judgment will sit." (Daniel 7:7, 8, 11, 19, 20, 21, 22, 23, 24, 25, [26])

On an inner level, this deals with the corrupt condition of religion. What Daniel saw here—the beast, the teeth of iron, the horn with eyes on it, and the horns speaking, making war with the godly, and speaking against the Highest One—symbolize a condition of falsity and heresy within the church. The horns' symbolism as powerful, overwhelming falsity can be seen simply from the fact that they are said to have eyes, or in other words, intellect (§2701), and to have spoken even against the Highest One. The kingdoms and monarchs do not mean kingdoms and monarchs but false doctrines. This can be seen from their symbolism in the Word as true doctrines and, in a negative sense, as false doctrines; see §§1672, 2015, 2069, 2547. [14] In another place in Daniel, a ram appeared to him, standing before a river:

> And it had two *horns,* and the *horns* were *tall,* but one was taller than the other, yet the tall one had come up second. I saw a ram *butting* toward the west and toward the north and toward the south, so that

no wild animals could stand before it, and there was no one delivering others from its hand; so it acted according to its pleasure and made itself great. While I was contemplating it, look: A buck of the goats came from the west onto the face of all the earth! This buck had a *horn between its two eyes.* It came to the ram, *owner of horns,* and ran to it in the fury of its strength, struck it, and broke *its two horns,* and there was no might in the ram for standing before it. Afterward the buck of the goats made itself very great, but when it was strong, *its large horn broke,* and *four horns* came up in its place. Soon from one of them *one horn went out a bit* and grew immensely toward the south and toward the sunrise and toward the ornament [of Israel], and it grew to the army of the heavens and threw down to the ground some of the army and some of the stars and trampled them. The ram with *two horns* is the monarchs of Media and Persia; the buck is the monarch of Greece; the *four horns in place of one* are four kingdoms coming out of the nation. (Daniel 8:1–end)

In its inner meaning this passage focuses on conditions in the spiritual church, which is the ram (§2830). It illustrates how those conditions gradually deteriorate and become corrupt. The buck of the goats means people immersed in a faith detached from love for others—or truth isolated from goodness—who start to pit themselves against goodness and finally against the Lord. The ram's horns are inward and outward levels of truth in a spiritual religion. The horns on the buck of the goats are truth that gradually deteriorates into falsity. Again, the kingdoms and monarchs mentioned do not mean kingdoms and monarchs but truth and falsity, as just noted. The Lord's Word in its true essence deals not with worldly and earthly concerns but with spiritual and heavenly ones. [15] In John:

Another sign was seen in heaven. Look: a big red dragon having seven heads and *ten horns,* and on its heads, seven crowns! It dragged a third of the stars in heaven with its tail and threw them onto the earth. (Revelation 12:3, 4)

And in another place:

I saw a beast coming up out of the sea, and it had seven heads and *ten horns,* and on *its ten horns,* crowns; on its heads was the name of blasphemy. It was granted to the beast to make war with the godly and conquer them. Then I saw another beast coming up out of the earth, and it had *two horns* like [those of] a lamb. (Revelation 13:1, 2, 7, 11)

Again in the same author:

> I saw a woman, sitting on a scarlet beast, full of the names of blasphemy, and it had seven heads and *ten horns*. She was Babylon the Great. The seven heads are seven mountains, on which the woman sits, and they are seven monarchs. The *ten horns* are ten monarchs. (Revelation 17:3, 5, 7, 9, [10,] 12, 13)

The horns here, like those in Daniel, symbolize the power of falsity, as one can see.

2833   *And Abraham went and took the ram* symbolizes the liberation of [spiritual people] by the Lord's divine humanity, as can be seen from the following: *Abraham* represents the Lord—here, his divine humanity. When Jehovah or his angel speaks with Abraham, Jehovah or his angel is divinity itself, and Abraham is divine humanity. And a *ram* symbolizes spiritual people (§2830). Clearly, then, *Abraham went and took the ram caught in the thicket by its horns* symbolizes the liberation of spiritual people by the Lord's divine humanity.

Without the Lord's Coming into the world, spiritual people could never have been saved (see §§2661, 2716), and their salvation and liberation comes from the Lord's divine humanity (2716).

2834   *And offered it as a burnt offering in place of his son* means consecrating and adopting them, as can be seen from the following: *Being offered as a burnt offering* means being consecrated (discussed in §2776). And *in place of his son* means being adopted—adopted by the Lord's divine humanity, which is Abraham here (2833). The adoption of spiritual people is described in John:

> Jesus said, "I am the grapevine; you are the branches. Those who remain in me and in whom I remain bear much fruit; because without me you cannot do anything." (John 15:5)

A vine means a spiritual religion; see §1069.

2835   Genesis 22:14. *And Abraham called the name of that place "Jehovah will see," as it is said today: "on the mountain, Jehovah will see."*

And Abraham called the name of that place symbolizes the character of the state that the Lord's divine humanity brings them into. *Jehovah will see* symbolizes the Lord's providence. *As it is said today* symbolizes that which never ends. *On the mountain, Jehovah will see* symbolizes charity, which the Lord provides as a means for their salvation.

2836   *Abraham called the name of that place* symbolizes the character of the state that the Lord's divine humanity brings them—the spiritual—into, as can be seen from the following: *Calling the name* of something means recognizing what it is like, or recognizing its character, as discussed in §§144, 145, 1754, 1896, 2009. A *place* symbolizes a state, as discussed in §§1273–1277, 1376–1381, 2625. And *Abraham* represents the Lord's divine humanity, as mentioned in §2833. Clearly, then, *Abraham called the name of that place* symbolizes the character of the state that the Lord's divine humanity brings spiritual people into.

Spiritual people are saved by the Lord's Coming into the world (as shown in §§2661, 2716), and his divine humanity supplies them with enlightenment (2716). Moreover, he provides that those who have a faith born of neighborly love—that is, who have neighborly love—are saved, as the current verse goes on to say. That is the state symbolized by these words.

Jehovah will see symbolizes the Lord's providence. This is evident from the symbolism of *seeing*, when Jehovah (the Lord) is the one said to do it, as foreseeing and providing (mentioned in §2807). For the identification of Jehovah with the Lord, see §§1343, 1736, 2156, 2329.

2837

It is the naming of a place that the literal meaning speaks of here, but it is the character of a state that the inner meaning speaks of. Time and space belong exclusively to the physical world, so when the literal meaning of the Word passes from our world to heaven, the earthly idea of time and space completely disappears and becomes a corresponding spiritual idea.

As it is said today symbolizes that which never ends. This can be seen from the symbolism of *today* in the Word, as discussed below.

2838

Several times the Word says *right to this day*, or in other words, till today. Above, for instance:

> He is the father of Moab *right to this day;* the father of Ammon *right to this day.* (Genesis 19:37, 38)

Later on:

> The name of the city is Beer-sheba *right to this day.* (Genesis 26:33)

> The children of Israel do not eat the tendon of displacement that is on the hollow of the thigh *right to this day.* (Genesis 32:32)

> It is the pillar of Rachel's grave *right to this day.* (Genesis 35:20)

> Joseph made it a statute *right to this day.* (Genesis 47:26)

On the narrative level, these instances are talking about the time when Moses lived, but in an inner sense, *this day* and *today* symbolize the never-ending, eternal quality of a state. A day means a state (see §§23, 487, 488, 493, 893), so *today*, the present moment, does too. Anything in the world that has to do with time is eternal in heaven, and to symbolize this, *today* or *to this day* is added—even though it seems to people who focus on the narrative meaning as if nothing further were involved. The same words appear in other places in Scripture, such as Joshua 4:9; 6:25; 7:26; Judges 1:21, 26; and other passages.

[2] The symbolism of *today* as that which is never-ending and eternal can be seen in David:

"I will dictate a statute," Jehovah said to me. "You are my son; *today I have brought you forth.*" (Psalms 2:7)

"Today" obviously stands for eternity. In the same author:

To *eternity*, Jehovah, your Word stands firm in the heavens; for *generation after generation*, your truth. You established the earth and it stands. By your judgments, they stand *today*. (Psalms 119:89, 90, 91)

Here too "today" clearly stands for eternity. In Jeremiah:

Before I formed you in the belly, I knew you, and before you came out from the womb, I consecrated you. A prophet to the nations have I made you; I have set you *this day* [today] over nations and over kingdoms. And I have made you *today* into a fortified city and a pillar of iron and walls of bronze. (Jeremiah 1:5, 10, 18)

The literal meaning of this passage has to do with Jeremiah, but on an inner level, the Lord is meant. In the sentence "I have set you this day" (or "today") "over nations and over kingdoms, and I have made you today into a fortified city," the expression means from eternity. Only what is eternal can be ascribed to the Lord. [3] In Moses:

You are standing *today*, all of you, before Jehovah your God, to cross over into the pact of Jehovah your God, and into his oath, which Jehovah your God has made with you *today* in order to set you up *today* as his people; and he will become your God. And in fact not with you alone but [both] with those who stand here with us *today* before Jehovah our God and with those who are not with us *today*. (Deuteronomy 29:10, 12, 13, 14, 15)

In a literal sense, "today" here is a time contemporary to Moses when he was talking to the people; but plainly it still involves time to come, without end. Striking a pact with people—both with those who are present and with those who are not—implies perpetuity, and perpetuity itself is what is meant on an inner level.

[4] The symbolism of "daily" and "today" as something that never ends can also be seen from the sacrifice that took place every day. Because of the symbolism of *a day, daily,* and *today,* this sacrifice was called a perpetual or never-ending one (Numbers 28:3, 23; Daniel 8:13; 11:31; 12:11).

The same thing is even more obvious from the manna that rained down from the sky, which Moses speaks of this way:

> "Here, now, I am making bread rain down from the sky, and the people shall go out and gather the thing *from day to day,* and none of it shall be left till morning." What they left till morning produced worms and rotted, except what they gathered on the day before the Sabbath. (Exodus 16:4, 19, 20, 23)

This happened because manna symbolized the Lord's divine humanity (John 6:31, 32, 49, 50, 58). Since it symbolized the Lord's divine humanity, it symbolized heavenly bread, which is nothing but love and charity, together with the good impulses and true ideas of faith. This is the bread the Lord gives the angels in the heavens every moment, and therefore to eternity and forever; see §2493.

This is also what is meant in the Lord's Prayer by "Give our *daily* bread to us *today*" (Matthew 6:11; Luke 11:3)—that is, every instant to eternity.

On the mountain, Jehovah will see symbolizes charity, which the Lord provides as a means for spiritual people's salvation. This can be seen from the symbolism of a *mountain* as love and charity (dealt with in §§795, 796, 1430). *Jehovah will see* is the Lord's providence, or what the Lord provides for (as noted just above in §2837).

I speak of charity rather than love here because of the difference between the two, as explained in §2023. Spiritual people are saved by charity, not by faith detached from charity, as many passages in the Word show.

This is the case with charity and faith: Charity without faith is not real charity, and faith without charity is not faith. If charity is to exist, faith must exist, and if faith is to exist, charity must exist. The essential ingredient, though, is charity, because the seed of faith cannot be planted in any other soil. The union of the one with the other, mutually and reciprocally, gives rise to the heavenly marriage, or in other words, the Lord's kingdom. Unless faith is implanted in charity, it is simply knowledge. It travels no farther than the memory, because there is no desire in

2839

the heart to receive it. Faith becomes understanding and wisdom when it is implanted in charity—that is, in a person's life.

Charity without faith—the kind of charity children and upright non-Christians have—is mere soil, waiting for faith to be sown in it, which happens in the next life if not in bodily life. See §§1802, 2280, 2289–2309, 2417, 2589–2604.

2840   Genesis 22:15, 16. *And the angel of Jehovah called out to Abraham a second time from heaven. And he said, "'Upon my life I have sworn,' says Jehovah, 'because seeing that you have done this word and have not held back your son, your only one, . . .'"*

The angel of Jehovah called out to Abraham a second time from heaven symbolizes still greater consolation offered to the Lord by his divine side. *And he said, "'Upon my life I have sworn,' says Jehovah,"* symbolizes solid confirmation by his divine side. *Because seeing that you have done this word* means that the business had been completed. *And have not held back your son, your only one,* symbolizes the uniting of the Lord's humanity with his divinity through his final crisis.

2841   *The angel of Jehovah called out to Abraham a second time from heaven* symbolizes still greater consolation offered to the Lord. This can be seen from the symbolism of *calling out from heaven* as being consoled and from that of the *angel of Jehovah* as divinity itself in the Lord. These meanings are discussed above at §2821, where the same words occur.

The reason the text here says *a second time* is that the comfort was greater. Verses 12, 13, 14, which speak of divine providence, contain the Lord's first consolation: that members of the human race who are called spiritual would be adopted. His second and greater consolation is contained below in verses 17, 18, and so on to the end—namely, that the spiritual would multiply like the stars of the heavens and like the sand on the seashore, and not only they but everyone with goodness would be saved.

These goals were central to the Lord's love, which is why they gave him comfort. No one receives comfort from anything but what she or he loves.

2842   *And he said, "'Upon my life I have sworn,' says Jehovah,"* symbolizes solid confirmation by his divine side concerning the promises that follow. This can be seen from the symbolism of *saying, swearing upon my life,* and *Jehovah says,* which all involve confirmation, and in fact confirmation by the Lord's divine side—that is, by the Lord himself. Divinity cannot confirm anything except from itself, and what it confirms is irreversible, because it is eternal truth. Everything Jehovah (the Lord) says is an eternal truth (Matthew 24:35), because the vital core of truth comes from him. When he seems to confirm something with an oath, as he does here and elsewhere in the Word, it is not because the thing is more true but because he is confirming it for people who do not accept divine truth unless it is confirmed this way. These are people who do not picture Jehovah, or the Lord, as being any different from a person who can say something and then change it—which the Word often says he does; but the reality described by the inner meaning is quite different.

Jehovah, or the Lord, never confirms anything with an oath, as anyone can see. However, when divine truth itself and confirmation of it makes its way down to the type of person just described, it turns into something like an oath. The situation resembles that of the consuming fire and smoke appearing on Mount Sinai before the eyes of the people when Jehovah, or the Lord, came down (Exodus 19:18; Deuteronomy 4:11, 12; 5:22, 23, 24). This is how his glory and even his mercy, as they existed in heaven, came across to the people there, who were enmeshed in evil and falsity (see §1861). It is the same with many things Jehovah is said to have said or done, as told in the Word. It can be seen, then, that "*upon my life I have sworn,*" says Jehovah is an expression symbolizing solid confirmation by the Divine.

[2] Evidence that *swearing* means confirming something to such a person—when it is Jehovah who swears—can be found in many other scriptural passages, such as this one in David:

> Jehovah forever remembers his *pact* that he struck with Abraham—the word he commanded for a thousand generations—and his *oath* to Isaac. (Psalms 105:8, 9)

What is true of an oath is also true of a pact: Jehovah (the Lord) does not strike a pact with us, but when union through love and charity is being discussed, it is presented in concrete form as a pact; see §1864. In the same author:

> *Jehovah has sworn* and has not gone back on it: "You are a priest forever in accord with my word; [you are] Melchizedek." (Psalms 110:4)

This is about the Lord. "Jehovah has sworn" stands for solid confirmation by his divine side—that is, confirmation that the statement is eternally true.
[3] In the same author:

> I struck a pact with my chosen one; *I swore to David* my servant, "I will strengthen your seed forever and build your throne throughout generation after generation." (Psalms 89:3, 4)

This too is about the Lord. Striking a pact with his chosen one and swearing to David stands for solid confirmation, or eternal truth. David stands for the Lord (§1888). Striking a pact has to do with divine goodness; swearing, with divine truth. In the same author:

> I will not profane my compact, and the pronouncement of my lips I will not change; once for all I *swore on my holiness:* "If I lie to David, . . . !" (Psalms 89:34, 35)

Here again David stands for the Lord. The compact in this passage as well has to do with divine goodness, while the pronouncement of his lips has to do with divine truth. That is because of the marriage of goodness and truth present in individual words of Scripture, as described in §§683, 793, 801, 2516, 2712. [4] In the same author:

> *Jehovah has sworn truth to David* and will not turn back from it: "From the fruit of your belly I will fill the throne for you, if your children keep my pact and my testimony that I am teaching them." (Psalms 132:11, 12)

"Jehovah has sworn truth to David" plainly stands for confirmation of eternal truth, which is why it says he would not turn back from it. David means the Lord, as already noted. Even so, the oath really was made to David, because he was the kind of person to believe the promise was being confirmed in regard to himself and his descendants. David loved himself and his offspring, so he believed that the promise had to do with him. He believed what one of the earlier quotations says: that his seed would be strengthened forever, and his throne throughout generation after generation. In reality, though, the oath concerns the Lord. [5] In Isaiah:

> To me it is [like] the waters of Noah. I *swore* that the waters of Noah would no longer pass over the earth. So have I *sworn* that I would not rage against you. (Isaiah 54:9)

Swearing here stands for striking a pact and confirming it with an oath. Read Genesis 9:11 to see that it was a pact rather than an oath. In the same author:

> *Jehovah has sworn,* saying, "If not, . . . ! As I have thought, so it shall be." (Isaiah 14:24)

In the same author:

> *Jehovah has sworn on his right hand* and on the arm of his strength. (Isaiah 62:8)

In Jeremiah:

> Listen to the word of Jehovah, all you of Judah living in the land of Egypt! "Look: I have *sworn on my great name,*" Jehovah has said. "If my name is any longer called on in the mouth of any man of Judah, who says, 'As the Lord Jehovih lives!' in all the land of Egypt, . . . !" (Jeremiah 44:26)

In the same author:

> "*Upon my life I have sworn,*" says Jehovah, "that Bozrah will become a ruin." (Jeremiah 49:13)

In the same author:

> *Jehovah Sabaoth has sworn on his soul,* "If I do not fill you with people as with grasshoppers, . . . !" (Jeremiah 51:14)

In Amos:

> *The Lord Jehovih has sworn on his holiness,* "Look: the days are coming!" (Amos 4:2)

In the same author:

> *Jehovah has sworn on the loftiness of Jacob,* "If I ever forget all their deeds, . . . !" (Amos 8:7)

[6] In these passages, the statement that Jehovah swore by his right hand, his great name, his life, his soul, his holiness, or the loftiness of Jacob symbolizes confirmation existing within Jehovah, or the Lord. It is not possible for Jehovah to confirm anything except from himself. Jehovah's right hand, Jehovah's great name, Jehovah's soul, Jehovah's holiness, and Jacob's loftiness symbolize the Lord's divine humanity, and it was this that provided confirmation.

[7] On an inner level, Jehovah's oath—the Lord's oath—that he would give the land to Abraham, Isaac, and Jacob, or their descendants, symbolizes confirmation that he would give the heavenly kingdom to people who love and believe in him. These are the people the Word means in an inner sense by the children and grandchildren of the patriarchs Abraham, Isaac, and Jacob. The same thing was represented in a concrete way when their descendants actually *were* given the land of Canaan, and the religion they practiced served to represent the Lord's heavenly kingdom, as the land itself also did. For the idea that land and particularly the land of Canaan is the

Lord's kingdom in an inner sense, see §§1413, 1437, 1607. That is why it says in Moses:

> . . . in order that you may lengthen your days *upon the ground that Jehovah swore to your fathers* to give to them and their seed, a *land* flowing with milk and honey. . . . in order that your days and the days of your children may multiply upon the *ground that Jehovah swore to your fathers* to give to them, according to the days of the heavens on *earth*. (Deuteronomy 11:9, 21)

These passages now show that when Jehovah swore, it represented confirmation, and solid, irreversible confirmation at that, as is even more evident in Isaiah:

> *Upon my life I have sworn;* the word has issued from my righteous mouth and will not go back: to me every knee will bend down, *every tongue will swear.* (Isaiah 45:23)

[8] What is more, the people of the representative Jewish religion were directed to confirm their pacts, vows, promises, and pledges with an oath that they were swearing to these things in Jehovah's name. The reason they were directed to do so (although in truth they were only permitted to) was that in this way they would be representing confirmation by the inner self. The oaths they took in Jehovah's name under those circumstances, then, were representative, like everything else. Moses shows that these oaths were required, or rather permitted:

> Jehovah your God you shall fear and him you shall serve and *in his name you shall swear;* you shall not walk after other gods. (Deuteronomy 6:13, 14)

In another place in the same author:

> Jehovah your God you shall fear, him you shall serve, and to him you shall cling, and *in his name you shall swear.* (Deuteronomy 10:20)

In Isaiah:

> Those who bless themselves by the land will bless themselves by the God of truth, and *those who swear by the land will swear by the God of truth.* (Isaiah 65:16)

In Jeremiah:

> "If you turn back, Israel," *says Jehovah,* "you are to turn back to me; and if you take your abominations away from before me, you are not to

waver. And *swear 'As Jehovah lives!'* in truth, in judgment, and in justice." (Jeremiah 4:1, 2)

In the same author:

If they faithfully learn the ways of my people, *to swear on my name,* they will be rebuilt in the middle of my people. (Jeremiah 12:16)

They actually did swear on Jehovah's name, too, or in other words, swore to Jehovah. In Isaiah:

Listen to this, house of Jacob, you who are called by the name of Israel (and they issued from the waters of Judah), who are *swearing on the name of Jehovah* (and they have mentioned the God of Israel) but not in truth and not in justice. (Isaiah 48:1)

In the same author:

On that day there will be five cities in the land of Egypt speaking the tongues of Canaan and *swearing to Jehovah Sabaoth.* (Isaiah 19:18)

In Joshua:

The rulers of the assembly have *sworn* to the Gibeonites *by Jehovah, the God of Israel.* (Joshua 9:18, 19)

[9] Clearly, then, they were allowed to swear by Jehovah's name, or by Jehovah, but just as clearly it was simply a gesture representing confirmation by one's inner self.

Still, it is recognized that people with inner depth (that is, with conscience) do not need to confirm anything by an oath and therefore do not do so. They consider oaths shameful. They *can* assert the truth of a thing with a kind of affirmation, and they can also use rational arguments to prove the truth, but they cannot swear to it. They have internal bonds that bind them: the bonds of conscience. Requiring the additional outward bond of an oath amounts to a charge that they are not upright at heart. Moreover, people of depth by their very nature love to speak and act freely, not under force. In them, the inner dimension drives the outer dimension, not the reverse. So people with conscience do not swear. Still less do people with a perception of what is good and true—heavenly people, in other words. Such people do not even reason to themselves or prove things to each other but say only yes or no (§§202, 337, 2718). As a result, they are even further from swearing an oath.

[10] For this reason—and because oaths were among the representative acts that were to be abolished—the Lord teaches that we are not to swear at all. These are his words in Matthew:

> You have heard that it has been said, "*You shall not swear falsely* but shall fulfill *your oaths* for the Lord"; but I myself say to you, *you shall not swear at all*—neither by heaven, since it is God's throne, nor by the earth, since it is his footstool, nor by Jerusalem, since it is the city of the great monarch. *Nor shall you swear* by your head, since you cannot make one hair white or black. But let your conversation be "Yes, yes," "No, no." Anything beyond these comes from evil. (Matthew 5:33, 34, 35, 36, 37)

These words mean that we are not in any way to swear by Jehovah or by anything that belongs to Jehovah, or in other words, belongs to the Lord.

2843   *Because seeing that you have done this word* means that the business had been completed, as can be seen without explanation.

2844   *And have not held back your son, your only one,* symbolizes the uniting of the Lord's humanity with his divinity through his final crisis. This can be seen from remarks above at §2827, where the same words occur. The one difference is that the current verse does not say "from me," which means that the process of becoming one will progress still further. The Lord's human nature constantly united more closely with his divine nature, until they became fully one; see §§1864, 2033.

2845   Genesis 22:17. "'*I will surely bless you and surely multiply your seed as the stars of the heavens and as the sand that is on the seashore, and your seed will inherit the gate of your foes.*'"

I will surely bless you symbolizes fruitfulness resulting from a desire for truth. *I will surely multiply* symbolizes the truth that develops out of it. *Your seed* symbolizes spiritual people, who are saved by the Lord's divine humanity if they have a religious kind of goodness. *As the stars of the heavens* symbolizes abundant deeper knowledge of goodness and truth. *And as the sand that is on the seashore* symbolizes abundant secular facts corresponding to that deeper knowledge. *And your seed will inherit the gate of your foes* means that neighborly love and faith will replace the earlier evil and falsity.

2846   *I will surely bless you* symbolizes fruitfulness resulting from a desire for truth. This can be seen from the symbolism of *being blessed* as being enriched with heavenly and spiritual goodness (discussed in §§981, 1096, 1420, 1422). Here it symbolizes fruitfulness resulting from religious goodness or, to say the same thing another way, from a desire for truth—since it is spiritual people who are being spoken of.

Here Jehovah says to Abraham, "I will surely bless you," and Abraham represents the Lord in his divine humanity, as he does earlier in the chapter. The Lord himself could not be blessed, because he is blessing itself. He can be *described* as blessed, however, when large numbers of people are being saved—a thing he loves to see. So those people are being symbolized on an inner level here. The discussion that directly follows shows the same thing [§2848].

I use the word *fruitfulness* here because it has to do with desire, but *multiplying*, which is spoken of next, has to do with the truth that develops out of it.

I will surely multiply symbolizes the truth that develops out of it. This can be seen from the use of *multiplying*, which has to do with truth. Here, then, it means the truth that develops out of a desire for it, as just noted. On the point that being fruitful has to do with goodness, and multiplying, with truth, see §§43, 55, 913, 983.

2847

Your seed symbolizes spiritual people, who are saved by the Lord's divine humanity if they have a religious kind of goodness. This is established by the symbolism of *seed* as the faith that comes of love for others (discussed in §§1025, 1447, 1610, 1940). To put it another way, seed symbolizes those members of the human race who possess the faith that comes of love for others—that is, spiritual people. The Lord also calls them seed—and children of the kingdom—in Matthew:

2848

> The one who sows good seed is the Son of Humankind; the seeds are the children of the kingdom. (Matthew 13:37, 38)

As the stars of the heavens symbolizes abundant deeper knowledge of goodness and truth. This is established by the symbolism of *stars* as knowledge of goodness and truth (dealt with in §§1808, 2495).

2849

Spiritual people are the ones compared to *stars* in various places in the Word, and this is because they know about goodness and truth. (Heavenly people are not compared to stars, because they do not so much know about goodness and truth as perceive it.) Another reason the spiritual are called stars is that stars shine at night. Spiritual people live in a nighttime light like that of the moon and stars, by comparison with the daytime light the heavenly live in. For conditions being relatively dim for the spiritual, see §§1043, 2708 at the beginning, 2715.

And as the sand that is on the seashore symbolizes abundant secular facts corresponding to that deeper knowledge. This can be seen from the symbolism of the *sea* as knowledge in general, or a body of knowledge

2850

(treated of in §§28, 2120), and from the symbolism of *sand* as facts in particular, down to the smallest details. Facts are compared to sand because in an inner sense the tiny bits of stone that make up sand mean facts (§§643, 1298).

The verse says both—that they will multiply like the stars of the heavens and like the sand on the seashore—because stars (religious knowledge) belong to the rational mind, while the sand on the seashore (secular facts) belongs to the earthly mind. When the contents of our rational mind (concepts of goodness and truth) agree with the contents of our earthly mind (secular knowledge) so closely that they form a single unit, or confirm each other, they then correspond. The Lord brings the contents of our rational and earthly minds into this kind of correspondence when he regenerates us, or makes us spiritual. That is the reason the verse mentions both the stars of the heavens and the sand on the seashore; otherwise, one of the two would have been enough.

2851   *Your seed will inherit the gate of your foes* means that neighborly love and faith will replace the earlier evil and falsity, as can be seen from the following: *Inheriting* means receiving the Lord's life, as discussed in §2658. Here it means replacing, because when charity and faith exist where evil and falsity used to, the Lord's life takes over. *Seed* symbolizes charity and faith, as noted in §§1025, 1447, 1610, 1940. The symbolism of a *gate* appears below. And *foes* symbolize evil and falsity or, what is the same, people caught up in evil and falsity. On the Word's inner level, foes and enemies symbolize such people.

[2] As for the symbolism of a *gate*, there are two general kinds of gate in each of us. One lies open to hell and lets in the evil and falsity from there. In that gate stand hellish demons and spirits. The other lies open toward heaven and lets in the goodness and truth from there. In that gate stand angels. So there is a gate that leads to hell and a gate that leads to heaven.

The gate to hell opens to people who are consumed with evil and falsity, and only through chinks all around them overhead does any light from heaven enter, enabling them to think and reason. The gate to heaven, on the other hand, opens to people who devote themselves to the goodness and truth that come from there.

[3] There are two paths that lead to a person's rational mind: a higher or more inward path that gives access to goodness and truth from the Lord, and a lower or more outward path through which evil and falsity sneak in from hell. The rational mind itself lies at the meeting-point of the two paths. In

the Word, this level of the mind is compared to and called a city, on account of the goodness and truth present in it. Since it is compared to and called a city, gates are marked out for it, and enemies—evil demons and spirits—are described in many passages as besieging or attacking it. Angels from the Lord, which is to say, the Lord himself, are described as defending it. Hellish demons and spirits, with their evils and falsities, cannot go beyond the lower or shallower gate; they never enter the city. If they could enter the city (our rational mind), that would be the end of us. When they advance far enough that it looks to them as though they have captured the city, it is closed, so that goodness and truth can no longer flow into it from heaven. Just a small bit seeps in through cracks all around, as just mentioned.

That is why such characters no longer have any charity or any faith but view evil as good and falsity as true. That is also why they are no longer truly rational, even though they seem to themselves to be so (§§1914, 1944). And that is why they are called dead people, even though they consider themselves more alive than others (81, 290 at the end). It is because the gate to heaven is closed to them. In the other world, the closure of this gate to them is quite obvious and plain to see. By the same token, the opening of this gate to people endowed with goodness and truth is just as plain and obvious.

[4] To turn to specifics, the *gate of your foes* mentioned in the current verse is the gate we have in our earthly minds. When we are thoroughly earthbound, when we have not been reborn, evil and falsity occupy this gate. Another way to put it is that evil demons and spirits stream in through this gate with all their evil cravings and false convictions (see §§687, 697, 1692). When we become spiritual, though, or in other words, when we are being reborn, evil and falsity (or evil demons and spirits) are driven from that gate (or from that part of our mind). Once they have been driven off, goodness and truth, or neighborly love and faith, take over. That is what it means to say that *your seed will inherit the gate of their foes*. This happens to each of us individually when we are being reborn and likewise to anyone who enters the Lord's kingdom in the next life. It also happens to people in general, or in other words, to the church, which is composed of many people.

[5] This process was represented by the action the children of Israel took in driving various nations out of Canaan. That is what "your seed will inherit the gate of their foes" implies on the literal level, but on an inner level it has the symbolic meaning given.

As a result, it became customary in ancient times to say the phrase when blessing a couple about to be married. Laban's blessing on his sister Rebekah when she was about to be betrothed to Isaac makes this clear:

> You, our sister: become thousands of myriads! And *may your seed inherit the gate of those who hate you.* (Genesis 24:60)

[6] The following passages show that when the Word mentions the gate of one's foes, or of those who hate one, it symbolizes these things. In Isaiah:

> I will slay your root with famine, and your survivors I will kill. *Wail, you gate!* Shout, you city! Philistia, the whole of you has dissolved, because from the north comes smoke. (Isaiah 14:30, 31)

Slaying their root with famine and killing their survivors stands for robbing them of the good impulses and true ideas that the Lord has stored away deep within them, which is what "survivors" are (see §§468, 530, 560, 561, 562, 661, 798, 1050, 1738, 1906, 2284). A gate stands for access to one's inner depths, or in other words, to the rational mind. A city stands for that mind or, what amounts to the same thing, the goodness and truth in it (402, 2268, 2449, 2451, 2712). Philistia stands for a knowledge of the concepts involved in faith or, what is the same, for people who have that knowledge but are not committed to the goodness required by faith (1197, 1198). Smoke from the north stands for falsity from hell, smoke meaning falsity that grows out of evil (1861). [7] In the same author:

> The empty *city* will be broken; every house will be closed off to those entering. A shouting over the wine in the streets! All happiness will be abandoned, the joy of the land will go into exile, what is left in the *city* will be a ruin, and *the gate will be struck with devastation,* because so it will be in the middle of the land, in the midst of the peoples. (Isaiah 24:10, 11, 12, 13)

The empty city that will be broken stands for a human mind that has been deprived of truth. The closing of every house stands for a lack of goodness, a house meaning what is good (§2233). A shouting over the wine in the streets stands for a state of falsity. A shout is mentioned in connection with falsity (2240); wine means truth, and the shout is that none exists (1071, 1798); and streets are things that lead to truth (2336). The happiness that is abandoned has to do with truth, while the joy of the land that goes into exile has to do with goodness. This explains the symbolism of the words "What is left in the city will be a ruin, and the gate will be struck with devastation." The gate is said to be devastated when evil and falsity take complete control. [8] In Jeremiah:

> Zion's paths are mourning that none come to the appointed feast. All *its gates are abandoned,* its priests groan, its young women are troubled, and things are bitter for it. *Its foes* have become its head, *its enemies* are carefree, because Jehovah has troubled it over the abundance of its transgressions; its children have gone away captive before the *foe.* (Lamentations 1:4, 5)

The mourning of Zion's paths stands for an end to the truth that formerly grew out of goodness, since paths mean truth (§§189, 627, 2333). The abandonment of all its gates stands for the way falsity occupies all points of entry. That its foes have become its head means that evil dominates. [9] In the same author:

> Jehovah has made the bulwark and the wall of Zion's daughter mourn; together they droop. *Her gates have plunged into the earth;* he has destroyed and broken *the bars on them.* Her monarch and her chiefs are in the surrounding nations. There is no law; the prophets also have discovered no vision from Jehovah. All your enemies have opened their mouth over you; they have hissed and ground their tooth. They have said, "We have swallowed you up. Surely this is the day we have awaited! We have found it; we have seen it." (Lamentations 2:8, 9, 16)

The plunging of the gates into the earth stands for occupation of the earthly mind by evil and falsity. Having her monarch and chiefs in the surrounding nations stands for steeping truth in evils. A monarch means truth in general (§§1672, 1728, 2015, 2069); chiefs mean the most important truths (1482, 2089); and nations are evils (1259, 1260, 1849, 1868, 2588). [10] In Moses:

> A nation from far away, from the end of the earth, will *assail you in all your gates,* until the razing of your high and fortified walls (in which you will trust) in all your land. And it will *assail you in all your gates,* in your whole land; in this way will *your foe* assail you. (Deuteronomy 28:[49,] 52, 53)

This was one of the curses Moses predicted would come on the people if they did not abide by the commandments and statutes. In an inner sense, a nation from far away, from the end of the earth, stands for evil and falsity, or for people who are attached to evil and falsity. Assailing them in all their gates stands for shutting off the entry for goodness and truth. [11] In Nahum:

> Look: your people are women in the midst of you. *To your enemies the gates of your land lie wide open;* fire consumes *the bars on them.* Draw water for the siege for yourselves; shore up your strongholds; go into the clay and tread the tar; shore up the brick kiln. (Nahum 3:13, 14)

The opening of the gates of the land to their enemies stands for the fact that evil occupies the place where goodness must exist. In Judges:

> The roads disappeared, and they went on the paths; they went by crooked roads. The lanes in Israel disappeared. [Israel] chose new gods. *Then, the attacking of the gates!* Was a shield seen, or a spear, among the forty thousand of Israel? (Judges 5:6, 7, 8)

This is the oracular song of Deborah and Barak. The attacking of the gates stands for an attack on what is good and true. [12] In David:

> *Gate-squatters* think things up about me; drinkers of strong drink make up songs. (Psalms 69:12)

Gate-squatters stand for what is evil and false, and for the hellish. In Ezekiel:

> In visions of God he was brought *to the doorway of the inner gate* looking toward the north; there he saw the huge abominations of the house of Israel. He was also brought to the *doorway of the gate of Jehovah's house* looking toward the north; there too there were abominations. (Ezekiel 8:3, 6, 14, 15)

The doorway of the inner gate looking toward the north stands for a place where the deeper kinds of falsity exist. The doorway of the gate of Jehovah's house toward the north stands for a place where the deeper kinds of evil exist. Deeper kinds of falsity and evil do exist, and there is a deeper realm where the spirits and demons who possess them live; see §§2121, 2122, 2123, 2124. [13] In David:

> Here, now, children are the possession of Jehovah; the fruit of the belly is a reward. As arrows in the hand of a strong warrior, so are the children of one's first fruits; fortunate is the man who has filled his quiver with them. [His kind] will not feel shame, because they will *speak with their foes in the gate.* (Psalms 127:3, 4, 5)

Speaking with their foes in the gate stands for having no fear of evil or falsity and so of hell. In Isaiah:

On that day, Jehovah Sabaoth will serve as the spirit of judgment for one who sits in judgment, as strength *for those diverting the battle to the gate;* but these also go insane with wine and go astray with strong drink. (Isaiah 28:5, 6, 7)

In the same author:

Those who with their words make people sin will be cut off, and they *ensnare their accuser in the gate* and make an upright person turn aside to what is empty. (Isaiah 29:20, 21)

In the same author:

Elam took up his quiver in a manned chariot; [there were] riders; Kir bared his shield; and the choicest of your valleys were full of chariots and riders. They *set [themselves] firmly at the gate,* and on that day he looked toward the armory in the house of the forest. (Isaiah 22:6, 7, 8)

In Jeremiah:

Judah has mourned, and *its gates have drooped,* have been draped in black down to the earth, and Jerusalem's cry has risen up. Their nobles have sent the little ones to the water; they came to the pits and did not find water. (Jeremiah 14:1, 2, 3)

In the same author:

Elders have ceased from the gate; young people, from their music. (Lamentations 5:14)

[14] These passages show what the gate of one's foes symbolizes: hell, or hellish beings, who constantly attack what is good and true. Their seat in us, as noted, is in our earthly mind. When our character is such that we let goodness and truth in, and therefore let angels in, the Lord drives hellish spirits away from that seat, and once they are gone, the gate to heaven opens—or in other words, heaven opens. This gate the Word also mentions in many places. In Isaiah, for instance:

A song in the land of Judah: A city strong for us. Salvation will place the walls and bulwark. *Open the gates* and an upright nation keeping faith will walk in. (Isaiah 26:1, 2)

In the same author:

> This is what Jehovah has said to his anointed, Cyrus, whose right hand I
> have grasped, to make the nations go down before him, and [the sword
> belts on] the hips of monarchs I will unclasp, in order to open *double
> doors* before him, and the *gates will not be shut:* "I myself will go before
> you and straighten out the crooked places; *bronze double doors* I will shat-
> ter, and *iron bars* I will sever." (Isaiah 45:1, 2)

In the same author:

> The children of a foreigner will rebuild your walls, and their monarchs
> will tend to you. They will *open your gates permanently;* day and night
> they will not be shut. No longer will violence be heard in your land;
> devastation and shattering, in your borders. And you will call your walls,
> salvation, and *your gates,* praise. (Isaiah 60:10, 11, 18)

In the same author:

> *Pass through the gates;* pass through! Prepare a way for the people! Pave
> a path; pave it! Say to the daughter of Zion, "Watch: your salvation is
> coming!" (Isaiah 62:10, 11, 12)

In Micah:

> They will *pass through the gate* and leave through it, and their monarch
> will pass before them, and Jehovah at their forefront. (Micah 2:13)

In David:

> *Gates, raise your heads,* and be lifted up, *eternal doorways,* and a glorious
> monarch will enter. Who is this glorious monarch? Jehovah, mighty and
> a hero; Jehovah, a war hero. *Gates, raise your heads, raise your eternal door-
> ways!* (Psalms 24:7, 8, 9, 10)

In the same author:

> Jerusalem, celebrate Jehovah; praise your God, Zion, *because he strength-
> ens the bars of your gates,* he blesses your children in your midst. (Psalms
> 147:12, 13)

[15] This shows clearly that the gate of heaven is the place where angels
live in us—that is, where goodness and truth coming from the Lord touch
us. There are two gates, then, as noted above. This is what the Lord says
about them in Matthew:

> *Enter through the narrow gate,* because *wide* is the *gate* and broad is the
> way that leads off to destruction, and there are many who enter by it;

because narrow and restricted is the way that leads to life, and there are few who find it. (Matthew 7:12, 13, 14; Luke 13:23, 24)

In addition, Ezekiel has much to say about the gates to the New Jerusalem and the gates to the new temple, as does John in the Book of Revelation, and those gates actually mean access to heaven. To read about them, see Ezekiel 40:6–49; 43:1, 2, 4; 44:1, 2, 3; 46:1–9, 12; 48:31, 32, 33, 34; Revelation 21:12, 13, 21, 25; 22:14; Isaiah 54:11, 12. That is why Jerusalem is called the people's gate in Micah 1:9; Obadiah verse 13.

Genesis 22:18. *"And in your seed all the nations of the earth will be blessed, because you heeded my voice."'* **2852**

In your seed all the nations of the earth will be blessed symbolizes the salvation of everyone who has goodness. *Because you heeded my voice* means through the union of the Lord's human nature with his divine nature.

In your seed all the nations of the earth will be blessed symbolizes the salvation of everyone who has goodness, as can be seen from the following: *Being blessed* means being enriched with heavenly and spiritual goodness, as discussed in §§981, 1096, 1420, 1422, and since people with these riches are the ones who are saved, being blessed here means being saved. "Blessing" has a wide range of meanings, as people know. *Seed* symbolizes the faith that comes of love for others, as discussed in §§1025, 1447, 1610. And the *nations of the earth* symbolize people who have goodness, as mentioned in §§1159, 1258, 1259, 1260, 1416, 1849. **2853**

[2] Furthermore, the words of this verse also hold a secret: that people outside the church are saved by means of the church, which is the "earth" here (§§662, 1066, 1068, 1262). As mentioned before, "your seed" is the faith that comes of love for others. The only people who have this faith are people in the church, because the faith that comes of charity is doctrinal truth attached to the goodness in a person's life. The reality is that the Lord's kingdom on earth consists of all who are intent on goodness. Even if they are scattered over the whole globe, they are still one and, like a person's limbs, make up a single body.

The Lord's kingdom in the heavens is the same way. In that kingdom, heaven as a whole resembles a single individual, which is therefore called the universal human (§§684, 1276). What is amazing—and so far unknown—is that all the parts of the human body correspond to the different communities in heaven. So it is sometimes said that one group of communities belongs to the region of the head, another to that of the eye, another to that of the chest, and so on. More will be said about this correspondence elsewhere, by the Lord's divine mercy.

[3] The situation is similar with the Lord's church on earth. On earth the church is like a heart and lungs and people outside it resemble the parts of the body that are sustained by and live off the heart and the lungs. Plainly, then, if the church did not exist somewhere on earth, the human race would not be able to survive, just as a body cannot survive unless it contains a heart and lungs (see §§468, 637, 931, 2054). That is why a new church is always raised up, in the Lord's providence, whenever another one ends, or in other words, when it loses all charity and dwindles out. When the earliest church died out, for instance—the one called "the human"—the Lord created a new one called Noah. This was the ancient church, and it came after the Flood. Then when this one deteriorated and dwindled away, the representative religion of Judah and Israel was established. And when that was completely extinguished, the Lord came into the world and established a new one. The point was to maintain a bond between heaven and the human race through the church.

This too is meant by *in your seed all the nations of the earth will be blessed.*

2854   *Because you heeded my voice* means through the union of the Lord's human nature with his divine nature, as is established by everything that comes before, to which these words form a conclusion. *Heeding my voice* means undergoing his final crisis and in the process uniting his human nature to his divine. The Lord united his humanity to his divinity—and his divinity to his humanity—by constantly being tested and overcoming (see §§1737, 1813); and by uniting them, he saved the human race (1676 at the end, 1990, 2016, 2025). All salvation for the human race results from this union.

People generally believe that the Father sent his Son to suffer cruel hardships, including even death on the cross, and that when he observed the Son's suffering and worthiness, he therefore took pity on the human race. Anyone can see, however, that Jehovah did not become merciful as a result of observing his Son, because he is mercy itself. The secret to the Lord's Coming into the world is that in himself he was to unite divinity with humanity, and humanity with divinity, which could be accomplished only through the heaviest of trials. So as a result of this union, salvation would be able to come within the grasp of the human race, which no longer possessed any trace of heavenly, spiritual, or even earthly goodness. The union of the Lord's divinity and humanity is what saves people endowed with the faith that comes of love for others. It is the Lord himself who is merciful.

Genesis 22:19. *And Abraham went back to his boys. And they rose and went together to Beer-sheba. And Abraham settled in Beer-sheba.*   **2855**

Abraham went back to his boys means uniting again with his earlier rationality. *And they rose* means being lifted to a higher level. *And went together to Beer-sheba* means advancing in the doctrine of neighborly love and faith—a divine doctrine, to which the thoughts of his human rationality were added. *And Abraham settled in Beer-sheba* means that the Lord *is* that very doctrine.

Abraham went back to his boys means uniting again with his earlier rationality, as can be seen from the following: *Boys* symbolize his earlier or merely human rationality, which was to serve his divine rationality, as noted above in §§2782, 2792. And *going back to them* means reuniting, as also mentioned above, in §2795.   **2856**

When the Lord underwent his most severe trials, he detached his merely human rationality from himself, as shown in the explanation of verse 5 at §§2791, 2792, 2793, 2795. After the crisis was over, he reunited with that rational capacity, as previous remarks in §2795 and those on the current verse show.

And they rose means being lifted to a higher level, as can be seen from the symbolism of *rising*. When it is mentioned in the Word, it is some kind of elevation that is symbolized (§2401). Here it means the elevation of his rational mind after his trials, because after his trials, his rational mind was always lifted up. The same thing happens in us. Any time we succeed in one of these tests, it elevates our mind and everything in it, because it strengthens the goodness and truth we already possess and adds new goodness and truth (§§1692, 1717, 1740, 2272).   **2857**

And went together to Beer-sheba means advancing in the doctrine of neighborly love and faith—a divine doctrine, to which the thoughts of his human rationality were added. This is established by the symbolism of *Beer-sheba* as the doctrine of neighborly love and faith—a divine doctrine to which the thoughts of human rationality are added (dealt with in §§[2613,] 2614, 2723). Such thoughts are symbolized by boys (§§2782, 2792, 2856), and their *going together* with Abraham symbolizes the divine doctrine they were superimposed on (see §2767).   **2858**

Abraham settled in Beer-sheba means that the Lord *is* that very doctrine. This can be seen from the symbolism of *settling,* the representation of *Abraham,* and the symbolism of *Beer-sheba* (dealt with already), and also from the remarks just above.   **2859**

Settling in Beer-sheba means focusing on doctrine, but when it is the Lord who is said to settle there, it means *being* doctrine. In the same way, living in heaven—which the Lord is also said to do—does not just mean being present in heaven. It also means that he *is* heaven, since he is the all-in-all of heaven (§§551, 552).

The Lord is the Word, as people recognize, so he is doctrine (§§[2533,] 2545), because all doctrine comes from the Word. Everything theological in the Word is from the Lord and about the Lord. Its inner meaning deals only with the Lord and his kingdom, as shown many times. It is the Lord's divine humanity that the Word's inner meaning concentrates on, and any doctrinal teaching in the Word that has to do with humans tells them to worship and love him.

2860   Genesis 22:20, 21, 22, 23. *And it happened after these words that Abraham was told, saying, "Here, now, Milcah—she too has borne children, to Nahor your brother: Uz, his firstborn, and Buz, his brother, and Kemuel (father of Aram), and Chesed, and Hazo, and Pildash, and Jidlaph, and Bethuel." And Bethuel fathered Rebekah. These eight, Milcah bore to Nahor, brother of Abraham.*

It happened after these words symbolizes the end of events centering on people within the church. *That Abraham was told, saying,* symbolizes a perception the Lord had. *Here, now, Milcah—she too has borne children, to Nahor your brother* symbolizes people outside the church whose goodness makes them part of the fellowship. *Uz, the firstborn, Buz, his brother, and Kemuel (father of Aram), and Chesed, and Hazo, and Pildash, and Jidlaph, and Bethuel* symbolize different religious traditions and the worship that rises from them. *Bethuel fathered Rebekah* symbolizes a desire for truth, rising out of goodness. *These eight, Milcah bore to Nahor, brother of Abraham,* symbolizes a second category of people who are saved.

2861   *It happened after these words* symbolizes the end of events centering on people within the church. This can be seen from the symbolism of *words* as events. In the original language, events are called words, so "after these words" means after these events had been brought to a close.

So far, from verse 13 to this one, the story has had to do with the salvation of spiritual people by the Lord's divine humanity—specifically, of people within the church who have goodness. They are the ones who are capable of being truly spiritual, because they have the Word and therefore know religious truth. Doctrinal truth, united to the goodness in our lives, makes us spiritual. That is the source of all spirituality.

Because people outside the church do not have the Word, they do not learn religious truth, as long as they live in this world. Even if they devote themselves to doing good out of love for their neighbor, they are not truly spiritual until they have been taught religious truth. Most non-Christian nations cannot be taught in this world, so in the Lord's providence and mercy, those individuals who have lived lives of mutual kindness and obedience receive instruction in the other world. Then they readily accept religious truth and become spiritual. (For this as the condition and destiny of non-Christians in the other world, see §§2589–2604.)

[2] Since the message so far has had to do with people within the church saved by the Lord's divine humanity, from here to the end of the chapter it has to do with people outside the church who are saved. They are symbolized by the children born to Abraham's brother Nahor by Nahor's wife Milcah and his concubine Reumah. This also follows in order. Anyone who does not know the Word's inner meaning would imagine that this is simply a genealogy for the house of Terah, introduced because of Rebekah, who became Isaac's wife, and because of Bethuel, whose two granddaughters, Leah and Rachel, became Jacob's wives. However, as has been said and shown time and again, all names in the Word have symbolic meaning (§§1224, 1264, 1876, 1888), and if they did not, the Word would not be divine but worldly. From this too it can be seen that the verses that follow form a series dealing with the Lord's spiritual church, but specifically that church as it exists among non-Christians. The image used is Abraham's brother Nahor, and the purpose is to symbolize people whose goodness makes them part of the fellowship, as it says below in §2863.

That Abraham was told, saying, symbolizes a perception the Lord had. **2862** This can be seen from the symbolism of *being told* as thinking and reflecting, and from that of *saying* as perceiving (dealt with many times before). The Lord's reflection and perception, when the Word's inner meaning speaks of it, can be expressed in the narrative only in terms of being told and saying. In themselves, moreover, reflection and perception are an inward telling and saying.

Here, now, Milcah—she too has borne children, to Nahor your brother **2863** symbolizes people outside the church whose goodness makes them part of the fellowship. This can also be seen from earlier remarks on Milcah and Nahor (§§1363, 1369, 1370). Terah had three sons—Abraham, Nahor, and Haran—who worshiped other gods (see §1356). Milcah was the daughter of Haran and became the wife of Nahor (1369), and Haran died in the presence of Terah in Ur of the Chaldeans (1365, 1366, 1367, 1368). This shows what *Milcah* and *Nahor* symbolize: *Milcah* symbolizes the truth that those nations knew, while *Nahor* symbolizes the goodness they had.

[2] Truth exists among non-Christians, as much evidence shows. It is recognized, after all, that wisdom and understanding existed among people outside the church in times past. They acknowledged one God and wrote about him in a reverent way. They also acknowledged the immortality of the soul, life after death, the happy fate of the good, and the unhappy fate of the evil. They took as their law the Ten Commandments—that they were to worship God, honor their parents, and not kill, steal, commit adultery, or envy the possessions of others. Nor were they content to obey these commandments superficially but kept them inwardly.

Likewise in modern times the more ethical non-Christians in all parts of the globe sometimes speak more correctly about these things than Christians do; and not only do they speak about them, they also live according to them.

[3] These concepts and others are the truth that exists among non-Christians and that unites with the goodness they receive from the Lord. The union of the two puts them into a state of mind that is open to receiving even more truth, because one true thought acknowledges another and willingly forms an alliance with it. Truths share a relationship and connection. As a result, people who have lived good lives in the world gladly welcome religious truth in the next life.

With them, falsity does not form a bond with goodness but only applies itself as an added layer, and in such a way that it can be removed. That which forms a bond, stays; but that which applies itself as an added layer is removed, and it is removed when the person learns and absorbs religious truth. All religious truth detaches and removes falsity until the person finally comes to detest and shun it.

This now clearly indicates just whom the *children Milcah bore to Nahor, Abraham's brother,* symbolize: people outside the church whose goodness makes them part of the fellowship.

2864   *Uz, his firstborn, and Buz, his brother, and Kemuel (father of Aram), and Chesed, and Hazo, and Pildash, and Jidlaph, and Bethuel* symbolize different religious traditions and the worship that arises from them. From this it can be seen that names have symbolic meaning, as noted. What these names symbolize are different traditions and the worship that rises out of them, which is what the names found in Genesis 5 and 11 symbolize as well. The symbolism of each name and every son here, though, cannot be specified in the usual way, because they are simply listed. *Uz* and *Buz* come up again in Jeremiah 25:20, 23, but among many other names. *Uz* is mentioned again in Lamentations 4:21 and Job 1:1; see also Genesis 10:23, §§1233, 1234.

And Bethuel fathered Rebekah symbolizes their desire for truth, rising out of goodness, as can be seen from the representation of *Bethuel* and *Rebekah,* given in chapter 24 below.   **2865**

These eight, Milcah bore to Nahor, brother of Abraham, symbolizes a second category of people who are saved. This can be seen from the symbolism of *eight* and from the repetition of *Milcah bore children to Nahor, brother of Abraham.*   **2866**

Since the eighth day is the first day of a second week, *eight* symbolizes something new and different from what has come before (see §2044). Here, then, it symbolizes a second category. The number is added for the sake of this symbolism.

Sections 2861, 2863 above show that *Milcah bore them to Nahor, brother of Abraham,* symbolizes people outside the church whose goodness makes them part of the fellowship. Here, where it brings the story to an end, it means the same as above: that they are saved.

Genesis 22:24. *And there was his concubine, and her name was Reumah. And she also bore Tebah and Gaham and Tahash and Maacah.*   **2867**

There was his concubine, and her name was Reumah symbolizes people outside the church who worship idols and yet have goodness. *And she also bore Tebah and Gaham and Tahash and Maacah* symbolizes their different religious traditions. These constitute a third category of spiritual people who are saved.

There was his concubine, and her name was Reumah symbolizes people outside the church who worship idols and yet have goodness, as can be seen from the discussion leading up to this point.   **2868**

Non-Christians symbolized by the children born to Nahor from his wife come first; those symbolized by the children born from his *concubine* come second. As was shown, the former group—children borne by Nahor's wife—meant people outside the church whose goodness makes them part of the fellowship (§2863). The latter group meant people outside the church who worship idols and yet have goodness. The latter, then, did not have as legitimate a birth as the former, but they were still semi-legitimate, because in those days children born of slaves were adopted as legitimate. This is evident from the children of Jacob born to the slaves Bilhah and Zilpah (Genesis 30:4–12). They were just as much the originators of tribes as the children born to Leah and Rachel, without any difference. Yet there *was* a difference, as Genesis 33:1, 2, 6, 7 shows. The slave women that a wife in those days would give her

husband for the sake of producing children were called concubines, as is
evident from Bilhah, Rachel's slave, who is also called Jacob's concubine
(Genesis 35:22).

The practice of using slave women (or concubines) for producing
children was tolerated in that era in order for people outside the church—
and people of a lower order within the church as well—to be represented
by them.

When the text says *her name was Reumah,* it has to do with her character
(§§1896, 2009). Here it involves a raising up, which is what *Reumah* means.

Concerning the condition and destiny of nations and peoples outside
the church, see §§593, 932, 1032, 1059, 1327, 1328, 1366, 2049, 2051, 2284,
2589–2604.

2869 *And she also bore Tebah and Gaham and Tahash and Maacah* symbolizes their different religious traditions and the worship they gave rise to;
and these constitute a third category of spiritual people who are saved.
This can be seen from the discussion above at §§2864, 2866, 2868.

🜲🜲🜲🜲🜲🜲🜲🜲🜲🜲🜲🜲🜲🜲🜲🜲🜲🜲🜲🜲🜲🜲🜲

Human Freedom

2870 FEW know what freedom and lack of freedom are. Everything that
springs from love and its pleasure seems free, while everything that
opposes it seems nonfree. Anything that springs from love for ourselves
and worldly advantages and from the cravings they excite seems free to
us; but the freedom is hellish. On the other hand, anything that springs
from love for the Lord and love for our neighbor and therefore from a
love for what is good and true is freedom itself—the freedom of heaven.

2871 Hellish spirits have no idea there is any other kind of freedom than
freedom to follow the demands of self-love and materialism. Those
demands have to do with their craving to control everyone, persecute
and hate anyone who does not wait on them, torture everyone, destroy
the whole world (if possible) for their own ends, and steal and usurp
whatever belongs to others. When pursuing these and similar activities, they experience freedom, because they experience pleasure. Their
life consists in this kind of freedom—so much so that if it is taken
from them, they have no more life left than a newborn baby has.

Eyewitness experience has demonstrated the same thing to me. A certain evil spirit firmly believed that this kind of desire could be removed from him, so that he could go to heaven. That is to say, he believed his life could be miraculously transformed into a heavenly life. So his love and therefore his craving for these evils was taken from him. (In the next life this is accomplished by breaking a person's ties with others.) He was then clearly seen in the form of a baby making swimming motions with his hands, though he could hardly move them. In the condition he was then in, he had even less ability to think than a baby. He was completely unable to talk and knew nothing. Soon, though, he was restored to his pleasures and so to his freedom.

This incident showed that for people who have built a life out of self-love and materialism, in selfish, materialistic freedom, it is impossible to go to heaven. If this life were taken from them, they would retain no trace of thought or will.

The freedom we receive from the Lord, however, is a heavenly freedom. All the angels in the heavens enjoy this freedom. As noted, it grows out of love for the Lord and mutual love, so it grows out of the desire for goodness and truth. Here is an indication of its character: All who enjoy it share their blessings and happiness with others, out of a deep-seated desire to do so, and it is a blessing and happiness to them to be able to. **2872**

Moreover, since heaven as a whole is like this, each individual is the center of everyone else's blessings and happiness, and everyone else is the center of each individual's. The sharing itself is accomplished by the Lord, by means of the most amazing streams of inflow, which flow in a pattern that defies understanding—the pattern of heaven.

This shows what heavenly freedom is, then, and demonstrates that it comes from the Lord alone.

The size of the gap between heavenly freedom, which results from a desire for goodness and truth, and hellish freedom, which results from a desire for evil and falsity, can be seen from this: When the angels who live in the heavens merely think about the kind of freedom based on a desire for evil and falsity (that is, on the cravings of self-love and materialism), they are immediately seized with deep-seated pain. On the other hand, when evil spirits merely think about the freedom based on a desire for goodness and truth (that is, on the wishes of mutual love), they immediately suffer anguish. Astonishing to say, each kind of freedom is so dead set against the other that the freedom of self-love and materialism is hell to good spirits, and the freedom of love for the Lord and mutual love, in turn, is hell for evil spirits. **2873**

For this reason, we are all distinguished from each other in the next life according to our type of freedom. To put the same thing another way, we are distinguished according to what we love and desire. Consequently, we are distinguished according to the pleasures of our life, which is the same as saying we are distinguished according to our life. Life is equivalent to pleasure, and pleasure is nothing but the effect a thing has on us, and that effect comes of love.

2874   The preceding discussion now makes it clear what freedom is: to think and will what we want. It also clarifies the following points: The nature of our freedom reflects the nature of our desire. One kind of freedom is hellish and the other is heavenly. Hellish freedom comes from hell, but heavenly freedom comes from the Lord. People who enjoy hellish freedom cannot come into heavenly freedom—which would be to go from hell to heaven—without losing everything that gives them life. No one can come into heavenly freedom without being reformed by the Lord. After reformation we are introduced to heavenly freedom by the desire for goodness and truth, or in other words, by a living goodness in which the seed of religious truth has been sown.

2875   Living goodness, or a desire for goodness, is introduced into us by the Lord along an inner path, without our slightest awareness. Theological truth, though, or faith, is introduced by an outer path and placed in our memory. From there the Lord summons it at its proper time and in its proper sequence and unites it with the desire for goodness. This process takes our freedom into account, because human freedom, as noted, depends on desire. This, then, is the way the seed of faith is sown and takes root.

Whatever we do freely is wedded to us, but what we are forced to do is not. This fact can be seen from the consideration that nothing can become part of us unless it stirs our desire. Desire is what is actually receptive. To accept anything in violation of our desires is to accept it in violation of our life. Clearly, then, theological truth, or faith, can be accepted only out of a desire for it. The nature of our acceptance, though, depends on the nature of our desire. A desire for what is true and good is the only kind of desire that welcomes religious truth, because [this desire and this truth] harmonize, and since they harmonize, they form a bond with one another.

2876   Since no one can reform except in freedom, our freedom is never taken from us, however much it may seem to be. It is an eternal law that each of us is free on deeper levels—free in feeling and thought, that is—in order that a desire for goodness and truth can be instilled in us.

Whenever the Lord infuses a desire for truth and a desire for good- **2877** ness into us (which he does while we are completely unaware), we internalize the truth and act on the goodness—in freedom, because in a spirit of desire. Whatever we do because of wanting to do it, as noted, we do freely, and under those circumstances, the truth of the faith unites with the goodness of neighborly love.

If we were not free in everything we think and everything we will, the Lord would be wholly unable to inject into us the freedom to think what is true or will what is good. In order to be reformed, we have to think truth seemingly on our own and do good seemingly on our own. What we seem to do on our own, we do freely. If this were not so, there would be no such thing as reformation or rebirth.

Numerous causes and purposes lead us to love learning what is true **2878** and wishing what is good. Many of them have to do with worldly advantages, many with bodily concerns, and under those circumstances it is not always heaven that motivates us, let alone the Lord. It is through our own desires, then, that the Lord introduces us into truth and goodness. He introduces one person one way, another, an entirely different way, but each of us in accord with our own character, both innate and acquired. Since we are constantly being introduced into truth and goodness by means of our desires, we are constantly being introduced by means of our freedoms. Eventually we are led into a desire for spiritual truth and spiritual goodness. The timing and the states are known to the Lord alone, and he alone arranges and controls them, in accord with every individual's bent of mind and manner of life.

This makes the reason for our freedom plain.

The Lord flows into our inmost core with goodness and there unites **2879** it with truth. The two must have their root in our inmost core. Unless we are free in all our feelings and all our thoughts, deep inside, we cannot possibly undergo the changes that allow goodness and truth to take root in us.

Only what stems from freedom appears to us to be ours or, to put it **2880** another way, to be autonomous. Everything we seek, as part of what we love, is life itself to us. To act from desire is to act from life—that is, from ourselves, and therefore on our own, or (what is the same) autonomously. So to ensure that we can receive heavenly autonomy—the kind of autonomy the angels in heaven have—we are kept in freedom, and through freedom we are introduced [into truth and goodness], as noted above.

Anyone can recognize that free worship of the Lord appears to come from inside us, or from our autonomy. Compelled worship, though, does not come from inside but from an external force that makes us worship. Free worship, then, is real worship, while forced worship is no worship.

2881   If we could be reformed by force, there would not be a single soul in the universe who would not be saved. Nothing would be easier for the Lord than to make us fear, worship, and even love him, in some manner. The means are countless. But since what is done under compulsion is not wedded to us and therefore does not become part of us, it is absolutely alien to the Lord to force anything on anyone.

As long as we are in combat, or form part of the church militant, it looks as though the Lord is forcing something on us. So it looks as though we have no liberty. At such times we are constantly fighting self-love and materialism, and as a result we are fighting the freedom we were born into and grew up with. That is why we seem to lack freedom. During the battles that we win, however, our freedom is stronger than it is when we are not in combat. It is just that the freedom comes not from ourselves but from the Lord—and yet it still looks as though it is ours. See §§1937, 1947.

2882   The main reason we believe ourselves devoid of liberty [under these circumstances] is that we realize we cannot do anything good or think anything true on our own. But do not imagine that anyone anywhere has, or ever has had, the freedom to think truth and do good on his or her own— not even the people who were called the likeness and image of God on account of the perfection they lived in. The liberty to believe religious truth and do neighborly kindness all comes from the Lord. The Lord is goodness itself and truth itself and is therefore the source.

All angels have this kind of freedom and even enjoy an actual perception that it is so. The very deepest angels sense how much they receive from the Lord and how much comes from themselves. The more freedom they receive from the Lord, the happier they are, but the more it comes from themselves, the unhappier they are.

2883   If we are to receive heavenly autonomy, then, we have to do good on our own, and think truth on our own, but we still have to have the knowledge that everything good and true comes from the Lord, right down to the tiniest possible amount. After we have reformed, we need to think and believe this as well, and to do so because this is how it really is. The reason we are allowed to imagine it comes from ourselves is that truth and goodness can then come to seem our own.

2884   The freedom connected with love for ourselves and for the material world and with the cravings that come of these loves is anything but freedom. It is utter slavery. Even so, it is called freedom. In the same way, "love," "desire," and "pleasure" are used in two senses, even though love for ourselves and our material advantages is anything but love, in fact is hatred; the same goes for desire and pleasure, which are derived from love. They are given these names because of what they seem to be, not because of what they are.

No one can see what enslavement and freedom are without seeing the source of each. And no one can see the source except from the Word. In addition, no one can see the source without seeing how matters stand with human beings in regard to the desires that occupy their will and the thoughts that fill their intellect. **2885**

This is how matters stand with humans in regard to their feelings and their thoughts: No one, no matter who—human, spirit, or angel— can will and think on her or his own but only from others; and these others cannot will or think on their own but must all do so from yet others; and so on. So everyone wills and thinks from the original source of life, who is the Lord. Nothing that is disconnected comes into existence. Evil and falsity connect with the hells, and when people are immersed in evil and falsity, the hells are the source of their will and thought, their love, desire, and pleasure, and consequently their freedom. Goodness and truth, however, connect with heaven, and when people are devoted to them, heaven is the source of their will and thought, their love, desire, and pleasure, and consequently their freedom. **2886**

This shows where the one kind of freedom and the other originate.

The inhabitants of the other world know perfectly well that this is the case, but in the world today it is wholly unknown.

We always have evil spirits and angels present with us. Through the evil spirits we communicate with the hells, and through the angels, with the heavens. If these spirits and angels were taken away from us, we would instantly lose the capacity to will and the capacity to think, so we would be without life. It may seem hard to believe that this is so, but it is absolutely true. **2887**

More will be said elsewhere [§§5846–5866, 5976–5993], though, about the spirits and angels who are with us, the Lord in his divine mercy willing.

The facts about the life force in everyone—human, spirit, and angel— are that it flows in from the Lord alone (who is life itself) and permeates all of heaven, and hell too. In this way it pours into every individual, in a pattern and sequence that are beyond comprehension. The life that flows in, however, is received by each of us according to our disposition. Good people receive goodness and truth as goodness and truth, but evil people receive goodness and truth as evil and falsity, and these even turn into evil and falsity in them. **2888**

The situation here resembles that of sunlight. The sun pours into every object on earth, but each receives it in accord with its nature. The light takes on beautiful colors in beautiful forms, and ugly colors in ugly forms. This is a secret in the world, but nothing is more familiar in the other life.

In order for me to learn that this was how spiritual inflow worked, I was given the opportunity to talk with the spirits and angels accompanying me and also to feel and sense the inflow. This has happened so many times that I cannot put a number to it. I realize, though, that people will be carried away by the illusion; they will continue to believe that they will on their own, think on their own, and therefore live on their own, when nothing is further from the truth.

2889　Evil spirits are totally unable to grasp that they do not live on their own but are merely organs for receiving life. They find it even harder to comprehend that no life exists aside from the life that stems from goodness and truth. Harder still is the idea that they do not *start* to live until the life of the evil cravings and distorted convictions they are devoted to is snuffed out. They believe that if deprived of either, no trace of life could possibly remain.

The reality, though, is this: When they give up the life of their evil cravings and distorted convictions, they first start to come alive. Until that time, they do not accept the Lord or the goodness and truth in which life exclusively consists. After that time, though, understanding and wisdom—and accordingly life itself—flows into them and then increases beyond measure. It brings with it pleasure, bliss, and happiness, and therefore deep joy, with indescribable, eternal variety.

2890　The evil spirits who are with us—and through whom we communicate with hell—think of us as nothing more than contemptible slaves. They pour their appetites and delusions into us and so lead us wherever they want.

In contrast, the angels through whom we communicate with heaven consider us sisters and brothers. They instill in us a desire for what is good and true and by this means lead us in freedom, not in the direction they want but in a direction that pleases the Lord.

This shows what each is like, and that it is slavery to be led by the Devil but freedom to be led by the Lord.

2891　Spirits newly arrived [in the spiritual world] rack their brains trying to understand the idea that we cannot do what is good or think what is true on our own but only from the Lord. They believe that this would make them machines, incapable of anything, and that if so, they may as well drop their hands and let themselves be pushed around.

"No," they are told, "you really have to think, will, and do good on your own. Otherwise you wouldn't be able to develop a heavenly sense of autonomy or heavenly freedom. But you still ought to acknowledge that what is good and true comes not from you but from the Lord." All angels, they are taught, make this acknowledgment and even live in the perception that it is so. The more keenly they sense that the Lord leads them and that they therefore live in the Lord, the freer they are.

Some people live good lives and believe that the Lord governs the universe; that he alone is the source of all the good that comes of love and charity and all the truth that leads to faith; that life itself comes from him; and consequently that from him we live and move and have our being. The condition of these people is such that they can receive the gift of heavenly freedom, and peace too, because under these circumstances they trust only in the Lord and do not let anything else bother them. They are certain that under his care, everything leads forever toward what is good, blessed, and happy for them.

People who believe they control their own lives, though, constantly feel troubled. They constantly become embroiled in their appetites, in worries about the future, and so in many forms of anxiety. Because of their belief, evil cravings and distorted convictions also cling to them.

Good spirits have been astonished to learn that people in the church today do not actually believe that everything evil and false comes to them from hell, and everything good and true, from the Lord. They do not believe it even though they know from the Word, and also from what the faith teaches, that it is so. And they all say, when people do some immense evil, that they have allowed the Devil to lead them, and when people do something good, that they have allowed the Lord to lead them.

Genesis 23

[More on the Word's Inner Meaning]

2894 WE read in John:

> In the beginning there was the *Word.* And the *Word* was with God, and the *Word* was God. This was with God in the beginning. Everything was made by him, and nothing that was made was made without him. In him was life, and the life was the light of humankind; the light, however, appears in the darkness, but the darkness has not comprehended it. And the *Word* became flesh and resided among us, and we saw his glory: glory like that of the Only-Born of the Father, who was full of grace and truth. (John 1:1, 2, 3, 4, 5, 14)

Few know what "the Word" means here. It means the Lord, as the whole context shows.

The inner meaning, however, teaches that it means the Lord's divine humanity. After all, the text says that the Word became flesh and resided among us, and we saw his glory.

Moreover, since the Word means the Lord's divine humanity, it means all the truth that tells of and comes from him, in his kingdom in the heavens and in his church on earth. That is why it says that in him was life, the life was the light of humankind, and the light appears in the darkness.

Since "the Word" means truth, it means all revelation, so it also means the Word—that is, Sacred Scripture.

2895 To speak more specifically, the Word has existed at every period, though not the Word we have today. The earliest church, which came before the Flood, had one form. The ancient church, which followed the Flood, had another. In the Jewish religion there is the Word written by Moses and the prophets. And lastly in the new church there is the Word written by the Gospel writers.

The reason the Word has existed at every period is that it provides the means of communication between heaven and earth. Another reason is that it speaks of the goodness and truth that make it possible for us to live happy lives to eternity. The inner meaning treats only of the Lord, then, because everything good and true comes from him.

The earliest church, which came before the Flood, did not have a written Word but one revealed to all who were in the church. They were heavenly people, so they had a perception of goodness and truth, as do the angels, with whom they also interacted. As a result, they had the Word written on their hearts. For more about the earliest people, see §§597, 607, 895, 920, 1114–1125.

Because they were heavenly and interacted with angels, everything they saw (or sensed in any other way) represented and symbolized the heavenly and spiritual qualities of the Lord's kingdom to them. They did see worldly and earthly objects with their eyes, or perceived them with their other senses, but these were the starting point and means for thoughts about heavenly and spiritual subjects. This ability and no other enabled them to talk with angels, because what exists with angels is heavenly and spiritual, and when it is communicated to people, it is expressed in the kinds of images that are familiar to us in our world. Everything in the world represents and symbolizes something in the heavens, as has already been shown, from Genesis 1 up to here.

This was the source of their representations and symbolisms, which were gathered together by the people meant by Enoch when communication with angels started to die out. That is what is symbolized by the words of Genesis 5:24: "Enoch walked with God and was no more, because God took him." See §521.

The Word of the ancient church, which came after the Flood, grew out of this collection. Because the people of this church were spiritual rather than heavenly, they learned rather than perceived what the representations and symbolisms involved. And since what these things involved was divine, they became useful to the people of that church and were employed in their divine worship. The purpose was to allow these people a way of communicating with heaven, since everything in the world, as noted, represents and symbolizes the kinds of things that exist in heaven.

They also had a written Word, which, like the Old Testament Word, consisted of narrative and prophetic parts, but this Word was lost with the passage of time. The narrative parts were called *The Wars of Jehovah* and the prophetic parts were called *The Utterances,* as can be seen in Moses, who cites them in Numbers 21:14, 27. Their narratives were for the most part fictional, as those in Genesis 1–11 are, and were written in a prophetic mode. This can be seen from a quotation in Moses, where the following words appear:

> Therefore it is said in *The Book of the Wars of Jehovah,* "Waheb in Suphah, and the rivers of Arnon, and the downrush of the rivers that sloped toward the settling of Ar and that lean on the border of Moab." (Numbers 21:14, 15)

[2] Their prophecies were written in the same manner as the Old Testament prophecies. This too is visible in a quotation from them in Moses, where the following words appear:

> Therefore *The Utterances* [or *The Utterers of Prophecy*] say, "Come to Heshbon! The city of Sihon will be rebuilt and strengthened, because fire has issued from Heshbon, flame from the city of Sihon. It has consumed Ar of Moab, the lords of the heights of Arnon. Doom to you, Moab! You have been destroyed, people of Chemosh! He has made escapees of his sons, and delivered his daughters into captivity to Sihon king of the Amorite. And we have attacked them with arrows. Heshbon has been destroyed all the way to Dibon, and we have laid them waste all the way to Nophah—that is, all the way to Medeba." (Numbers 21:27, 28, 29, 30)

These prophecies involved secrets of heaven, just as the prophecies of the Old Testament do. This is quite plain from the fact that Moses copied them out and applied them to the state of affairs he was then describing. Not only that, but almost exactly the same words are to be read in Jeremiah as well, inserted among his prophetic sayings. Those sayings contain as many heavenly secrets as there are words, and various discussions of the Word's inner meaning demonstrate the fact. This is how the prophecy appears in Jeremiah:

> Fire has issued from Heshbon, and flame from within Sihon, and has consumed the corner of Moab and the crown of the head of the children of noise. Doom to you, Moab! The people of Chemosh have perished, because your sons have been taken into captivity and your daughters into captivity. (Jeremiah 48:45, 46)

This too shows that the Word of the ancient church also had an inner meaning.

Concerning the ancient church, which followed the Flood, see §§640, 641, 765, 1238, 1327, 2385.

This is not the only evidence that the people of that church had prophecies whose inner meaning had to do with the Lord and his kingdom. There are also the prophecies of Balaam, who was from Syria—prophecies Moses quotes in Numbers 23:7, 8, 9, 10, 18–25; 24:3–10, 15–25. These prophecies were delivered in the same mode as other prophecies in the Word. Plainly, they predict the Lord's Coming, in these words:

> I see him, but not now; I look on him, but he is not near. A star will come out of Jacob, and a scepter will spring up from Israel and break the corners of Moab and destroy all the children of Seth. (Numbers 24:17)

These prophecies are likewise called *The Utterances,* because the term is the same, as can be seen there in 23:7, 18; 24:3, 15, 20.

Later on the Word of the Jewish religion took over. It too was written in representative and symbolic language, so that it could hold within it a deeper meaning understood in heaven. In this way the Word would provide a channel of communication and a bond between the Lord's kingdom in the heavens and his kingdom on earth. The subject matter of the Word at every point has to represent the divine qualities of the Lord and therefore the heavenly and spiritual qualities of his kingdom; every word used to express that subject matter has to symbolize them. Otherwise it is not God's Word. Since this is so, it could never have been written in any other mode, because in this mode and no other, human themes and words correspond with heavenly themes and ideas, down to the tiniest jot.

For this reason, the divine contents of the Word are perceived by the angels even when it is being read by a very small child. See §1776.

As for the New Testament Word of the Gospels, the Lord spoke from divinity itself, so everything he said also represented and symbolized divine concerns and therefore the heavenly concerns of his kingdom and church. This has been shown many times before.

2898

2899

2900

Genesis 23

1. And the lives of Sarah were one hundred twenty-seven years—the years of the lives of Sarah.

2. And Sarah died in Kiriath-arba (that is, Hebron, in the land of Canaan), and Abraham came to mourn Sarah and to cry for her.

3. And Abraham rose from the presence of his dead one and spoke to the sons of Heth, saying,

4. "An immigrant and settler I am with you; give me the possession of a grave with you and I will bury my dead one out of my presence."

5. And the sons of Heth answered Abraham, saying to him,

6. "Listen to us! My lord, a chieftain of God you are in our midst. In the choicest of our graves bury your dead one. None of us will withhold our graves from you, from the burial of your dead one."

7. And Abraham rose and bowed down to the people of the land, to the sons of Heth.

8. And he spoke with them, saying, "If you have it in your soul to bury my dead one out of my presence, listen to me and plead for me with Ephron, son of Zohar.

9. And let him give me the cave of Machpelah, which is his, which is at the end of his field; for full silver let him give it to me, in your midst, for the possession of a grave."

10. And Ephron was sitting in the midst of the sons of Heth, and Ephron the Hittite answered Abraham in the ears of the sons of Heth, for the benefit of all those entering the gate of his city, saying,

11. "No, my lord; listen to me: The field I give you; and the cave that is in it—to you I give it. In the eyes of the sons of my people I give it to you. Bury your dead one."

12. And Abraham bowed down before the people of the land.

13. And he spoke to Ephron in the ears of the people of the land, saying, "Still, if you would please listen to me, I will give the silver for the field; take it from me and I will bury my dead one there."

14. And Ephron answered Abraham, saying to him,

15. "My lord, listen to me: The land is worth four hundred shekels of silver; between me and you, what is that? And bury your dead one."

16. And Abraham listened to Ephron, and Abraham weighed out to Ephron the silver that he spoke of in the ears of the sons of Heth: four hundred shekels of silver crossing [the palm of] a merchant.

17. And the field of Ephron that was in Machpelah, which is in front of Mamre—the field and the cave that was in it and every tree that was in the field, that was within its whole border all around—was established

18. for Abraham as a purchase in the eyes of the sons of Heth, in [the eyes] of all those entering the gate of his city.

19. And after this, Abraham buried Sarah his wife at the cave of the field of Machpelah on the face of Mamre (that is, Hebron, in the land of Canaan).

20. And the field and the cave that was in it was established for Abraham as the possession of a grave from the sons of Heth.

Summary

THE inner meaning here speaks of a new spiritual religion that the Lord brought to life after the previous one breathed its absolute last. It also speaks about the acceptance of faith by the people of that religion. In this chapter Sarah is truth that is divine, which died. The burial is resurrection. Ephron and the sons of Heth are people in whom religious goodness and truth find acceptance. "Machpelah, which is in front of Mamre," is rebirth. Hebron in the land of Canaan is the new religion. **2901**

The subject is truth that is divine, which breathed its last (verses 1, 2, 3), and the fact that the Lord would establish a new religion (verse 4). He was kindly received (verses 5, 6), which was a joy to him (verses 7, 12). At first, conditions for the people in that religion were dim, and they believed that charitable goodness and religious truth came from themselves (verses 8, 9, 10, 11, 14, 15). They learned, however, that goodness and truth come not from them but from the Lord (verse 13) and that in this way they would be redeemed (verse 16) and reborn (verses 17, 18). So there was a new religion (verse 19) made up of people outside the church (verse 20). **2902**

Inner Meaning

GENESIS 23:1. *And the lives of Sarah were one hundred twenty-seven years—the years of the lives of Sarah.* **2903**

The lives of Sarah were symbolizes the preceding periods and states of the church in regard to truths that are divine. *One hundred twenty-seven years* symbolizes the completion of them. *The years of the lives of Sarah* means when some truth that is divine remained in existence on the earth.

2904   *The lives of Sarah were* symbolizes the preceding periods and states of the church in regard to truths that are divine, as can be seen from the symbolism of *lives* in this instance and from the representation of *Sarah*. *Lives* here have to do with age and stages of life—childhood, young adulthood, full adulthood, and old age—so they symbolize states. That is what all periods of time in general symbolize; see §§2625, 2788, 2837. What comes afterward focuses on the church, so lives symbolize the periods and states of the church. *Sarah* is truth that is divine (see §§1468, 1901, 2063, 2172, 2173, 2198, 2507), so it follows that on an inner level *the lives of Sarah were* symbolizes the preceding periods and states of the church in regard to truths that are divine.

[2] While Sarah was alive, as Abraham's wife, she represented the Lord's divine truth united with his divine goodness, as can be seen from the sections referred to. Since she represented the Lord's divine truth, she also symbolizes the church's truth that is divine. In the church, no other truth can exist than the Lord's truth. Truth that does not come from him is not true, as the Word and teachings of faith from the Word show. An example from the Word is this in John:

> None of us can acquire anything unless it is given to us from heaven. (John 3:27)

And in another place:

> Without me you cannot do anything. (John 15:5)

As for the teachings of faith, they assert that every tenet of faith—all truth, in other words—comes from the Lord.

[3] The case with representations and symbolisms in the Word is that each and every one of them in the highest sense looks to the Lord. That is where the living force itself of the Word comes from. Since it looks to the Lord, it also looks to his kingdom, because the Lord is the all-in-all of his kingdom. Divine qualities from the Lord in his kingdom make his kingdom. Consequently, the more goodness and truth an angel, spirit, or person receives from the Lord, believing it comes from the Lord, the more that individual belongs to the Lord's kingdom. The more an angel, spirit, or person fails to receive them, however, or to believe they come from the Lord, the less that individual belongs to the Lord's kingdom. So the divine qualities that come from the Lord make his kingdom, or heaven. That is what it means to say that the Lord is the all-in-all of his kingdom.

One hundred twenty-seven years symbolizes the completion of them.   **2905**
This can be seen from the symbolism of *one hundred* as what is complete
(discussed in §2636), of *twenty,* or two tens, also as completeness (1988),
and of *seven* as what is holy (395, 433, 716, 881). So it is the completion or
end of a holy time in the church that this phrase symbolizes. (To see that
numbers in the Word all have symbolic meaning, consult §§482, 487,
647, 648, 755, 813, 1963, 1988, 2075, 2252.)

[2] The completion of them—of the states and periods of the church—
means the end of them. A church reflects the ages of a person's life, the first
being childhood, the second, young adulthood, the third, full adulthood,
and the fourth, old age. The last—old age—is called a full life, or the end
of life. A church also reflects the seasons and stages of the year, the first
being spring, the second, summer, the third, fall, and the fourth, winter,
which is the end of the year. Again, it reflects the times and stages of the
day, the first being that of dawn, the second, of midday, the third, of evening, and the fourth, of night. When night comes, it is the completion or
end of the day. In the Word, the stages of the church are also compared to
all of these and are symbolized by them, because different periods of time
symbolize different states (§§2625, 2788, 2837).

[3] Goodness and truth in the people of the church usually dwindle
in this way. When no more goodness and truth remain—or, as they say,
no more faith (that is, no more charity)—the church reaches its old age,
its winter, its nighttime. The period and state it is then in is called the
final decision, full end, and fulfillment; see §1857. It is said that the Lord
came into the world in the fullness of time, or when the time was ripe.
This means the same thing, because at that time there was no longer any
goodness—not even earthly goodness—and as a result there was also no
more truth.

This is the specific meaning of this phrase in the current verse.

The years of the lives of Sarah means when some truth that is divine   **2906**
remained in existence, as can be seen from the following: A year symbolizes a whole era in the church, from beginning to end, so *years* symbolize
different eras, as discussed just above in §2905. And the *lives of Sarah*
symbolize states in regard to truth that is divine, as also discussed just
above, in §2904. The meaning here, then, is that the end would come
when no more truth that is divine remained; and this also follows from
the remarks just above.

[2] The following passages in the Word show that a year symbolizes
the whole period of a state in the church, from beginning to end—or, to

put the same thing another way, a whole era—and that *years* therefore symbolize individual periods or eras within a major one. In Isaiah:

> Jehovah has anointed me to bring good news to the afflicted; he has sent me to bind up the broken at heart, to proclaim freedom to captives and wide-open doors to prisoners, to proclaim a *year of good pleasure for Jehovah* and a day of vengeance for our God. (Isaiah 61:[1,] 2)

This is about the Lord's Coming. The year of good pleasure for Jehovah stands for the time of the new religion. In the same author:

> The day of vengeance is in my heart, and the *year of my redeemed* has come. (Isaiah 63:4)

Again this is about the Lord's Coming. The year of the redeemed stands for the time of the new religion. In the same author:

> A day of vengeance for Jehovah, *a year of redresses* because of Zion's dispute! (Isaiah 34:8)

Likewise. [3] The same period is also called a year of divine visitation (or punishment) in Jeremiah:

> I will bring evil to the men of Anathoth in the *year of* their *visitation.* (Jeremiah 11:23)

In the same author:

> I will bring on Moab the *year of* their *visitation.* (Jeremiah 48:44)

Even more plainly in Ezekiel:

> After many days *you will be punished;* in the *aftertime of years* you will come upon a land that has returned from the sword, that has been gathered from many peoples, on Israel's mountains, which will be as a wasteland always. (Ezekiel 38:8)

The aftertime of years stands for the final days of the church. In those days the church dies out, once its former members have been rejected and others from elsewhere have been accepted. In Isaiah:

> This is what the Lord has said to me: "In one more *year* (answering to the *years of a hired servant*) all the glory of Kedar will be consumed." (Isaiah 21:16)

This too is about the final days. [4] In Ezekiel:

> In your blood that you shed you have become guilty, and in your idols that you made you have been defiled; and you have made your days approach and *have come all the way to your years.* Therefore I have made you an object of reproach to the nations and a laughingstock to all the lands. (Ezekiel 22:4)

Coming all the way to one's years stands for coming to an end, when the Lord withdraws from the church. In Isaiah:

> Now Jehovah has spoken, saying, "In *three years* (like *a hired servant's years*) the glory of Moab will grow worthless in all his vast multitude, and the remainder will be a tiny pittance." (Isaiah 16:14)

"In three years" likewise stands for the end of the previous religion, three meaning a completion and a new start (see §§1825, 2788). [5] Seven has a similar meaning, as does seventy (§§720, 728, 901), so in Isaiah:

> And it will happen on that day that Tyre will be forgotten for *seventy years,* answering to the *days of one king.* At the *end of seventy years,* it will happen to Tyre as in the harlot's song. And it will happen at the *end of seventy years* that Jehovah will visit Tyre, and it will go back to its harlot's wages. (Isaiah 23:15, 17)

Seventy years stands for a whole era, from the time when the church came into being until it passed away. These are also the days of one king, a king symbolizing the truth the church knows (see §§1672, 1728, 2015, 2069). The seventy-year captivity that the people of Judah suffered involves something similar, and Jeremiah describes it in the following words:

> "These nations will serve the king of Babylon *seventy years,* and it will happen when the *seventy years* have been fulfilled that I will inflict punishment on the king of Babylon and on this nation," says Jehovah, "for their wickedness." (Jeremiah 25:11, 12; 29:10)

[6] Still more evidence that a year and years symbolize whole eras in the church, or the length of time they last, appears in Malachi:

> "Watch: I am sending my angel, and he will prepare the way before him; and suddenly to his temple will come the Lord, whom you are seeking, and the angel of the covenant, whom you desire. Watch: He is coming!" Jehovah Sabaoth has said. "And who can endure the day of

his coming? Then the offering of Judah and Jerusalem will be sweet to Jehovah, according to the *days of old* and according to the *ancient years.*" (Malachi 3:1, 2, 4)

This is about the Lord's Coming. The days of old stand for the earliest church; the ancient years, for the ancient church. The offering of Judah stands for devotion arising from heavenly love, and that of Jerusalem, for devotion arising from spiritual love. Obviously the passage is not talking about Judah or Jerusalem. In David:

I thought about the *ancient days* and the *years of old.* (Psalms 77:5)

The ancient days and the years of old stand for the same religions. The symbolism is still clearer in Moses:

Recall the *days of old;* understand the *years of generation after generation.* Ask your father and he will point out to you; your elders and they will tell you. When the Highest One gave an inheritance to the nations, and he divided the children of humankind, . . . (Deuteronomy 32:7, 8)

[7] It is also plain in Habakkuk that a year (and years) means an entire period in the church:

Jehovah, I have heard of your fame; I have trembled, Jehovah, at your work. In the *middle of the years,* bring it to life; in the *middle of the years,* please make it known; in your merciful anger, remember. God will come out of Teman, and the Holy One from Mount Paran. (Habakkuk 3:2, 3)

This is about the Lord's Coming. "In the middle of the years" means in the fullness of time. For what the fullness of time is, see §2905 just above.

[8] When a year or years are mentioned in connection with the Lord's kingdom on earth—the church, in other words—they symbolize an entire period between its two terminations, beginning and end. As a result, when they are mentioned in connection with the Lord's kingdom in heaven, they symbolize eternity, as in David:

God, to generation after generation *your years* [continue], and you are he, and *your years* will not be used up. The children of your servants will settle down, and their seed will be strengthened before you. (Psalms 102:24, 27, 28)

In the same author:

> You will add days to the monarch's days; [you will increase] *the monarch's years* generation after generation. And the monarch will dwell forever before God. (Psalms 61:6, 7)

The years stand for eternity, because the passage is talking about the Lord and his kingdom.

[9] The lambs that were offered as burnt offerings and sacrifices were *offspring of their [first] year* (Leviticus 12:6; 14:10; Numbers 6:12; 7:15, 21, 27, 33, 39, 45, 51, 57, 63, 69, 75, 81; and other places). This symbolized the heavenly qualities of innocence in the Lord's kingdom, which are eternal. So Micah 6:6 also refers to a burnt offering of calves that were offspring of a year, describing it as very pleasing.

[10] Another indication that in an inner sense a year does not mean a year is this: Angels, whose attention is on the Word's inner meaning, cannot form any idea of a year. Instead, since a year is a full period in the world of nature, they replace the idea of a year with that of fullness or completion in regard to conditions in the church. In regard to conditions in heaven, they replace it with the idea of eternity. To them, periods of time are states (§§1274, 1382, 2625, 2788, 2837).

Genesis 23:2. *And Sarah died in Kiriath-arba (that is, Hebron, in the land of Canaan), and Abraham came to mourn Sarah and to cry for her.*

2907

Sarah died symbolizes nighttime for religious truth. *In Kiriath-arba (that is, Hebron, in the land of Canaan)* means in the church. *And Abraham came to mourn Sarah and to cry for her* symbolizes a state of grief on the part of the Lord.

Sarah died symbolizes nighttime for religious truth, as can be seen from the symbolism of *dying,* a dead person, and death. When they have to do with the church, they mean its last days, when all faith (that is, all love for others) has passed away. In many places in the Word, this time is called night (§§221, 709, 1712, 2353; for the idea that *dying* means ceasing to be what it was, see §494). And *Sarah* represents truth that is divine, as discussed above in §2904. This shows that the symbolism is as described.

2908

In Kiriath-arba (that is, Hebron, in the land of Canaan) means in the church. This can be seen from the symbolism of *Kiriath-arba* as truth in the church and from that of *Hebron, in the land of Canaan,* as goodness in the church. When the Word—especially the prophetic part—speaks of truth, it also speaks of goodness, because of the heavenly marriage

2909

present at every point in the Word. (See §§683, 793, 801, 2173, 2516, 2712.) So here, where it mentions Kiriath-arba, it also says, "that is, Hebron, in the land of Canaan." The land of Canaan is the Lord's kingdom (1413, 1437, 1607), and different places in it represented various things (1585, 1866).

[2] To identify Kiriath-arba, or Hebron, it was the area that Abraham, Isaac, and Jacob lived in. Genesis 13:18 above shows that Abraham lived there: "Abraham came and lived in Mamre (that is, in *Hebron*)." Genesis 35:27 below shows that Isaac lived there: "Jacob came to Isaac his father in Mamre, *Kiriath-arba* (that is, *Hebron*), where Abraham and Isaac stayed as immigrants." Genesis 37:14 shows that Jacob lived there: "Joseph was sent by his father Jacob to his brothers from the *valley of Hebron*." The representation of these three men (dealt with earlier) shows that Kiriath-arba, or Hebron, represented the church before Jerusalem did.

[3] Every religion withers as time passes until it has no faith or neighborly love left. At that point it is destroyed, which was also represented by Kiriath-arba, or Hebron, in that it was taken over by the Anakim, who symbolized dreadful self-deceptions (§§581, 1673). For the fact that the Anakim took possession of it, see Numbers 13:21, 22; Joshua 11:21; 14:15; 15:13, 14; Judges 1:10. The end of a religion, when it comes full circle and is destroyed, was represented by Joshua's extermination of everything there (Joshua 10:36, 37; 11:21) and by the blows struck against the Anakim by Judah and Caleb (Judges 1:10; Joshua 14:13, 14, 15; 15:13, 14). The new or renewed emergence of religion was represented by Caleb's being given the field and towns of the place as an inheritance (Joshua 21:12). The city itself became one of refuge (Joshua 20:7; 21:13) and a priestly city belonging to the children of Aaron (Joshua 21:10, 11) within Judah's inheritance (Joshua 15:54). [4] Clearly, then, Hebron represented the Lord's spiritual church in the land of Canaan. For this reason, at Jehovah's command, David was also ordered to go to Hebron, where he was anointed king over the house of Judah. After he had reigned there for seven years and six months, he went to Jerusalem and took possession of Zion (see 2 Samuel 2:1–11; 5:5; 1 Kings 2:11). That is when Jerusalem first started to represent the Lord's spiritual church, and Zion to represent his heavenly church.

2910 *And Abraham came to mourn Sarah and to cry for her* symbolizes a state of grief on the part of the Lord—grief over the night that fell on religious truth in the church. This is established by the representation of *Abraham* as the Lord (dealt with at §§1893, 1965, 1989, [2010,] 2011, 2172, 2501, 2833,

2836). *Mourning* and *crying for someone* symbolize a state of grief, as is plain without explanation. Mourning relates to grief over the night that has fallen on goodness in the church, and crying for someone, to grief over the night that has fallen on truth.

These two verses focus on the end of the church. Its end comes when no more neighborly love remains. The Word speaks of it in very many places, especially in the prophets and the Revelation of John. The Lord also describes the end of the church many times in the Gospels, where he calls it the close of the age and also the night.

[2] This is the situation with churches: In the beginning, love for others forms their foundation. At that stage, each person loves the next as a sister or brother, and they all seek what is good, not for their own sake but for the sake of their neighbor, the common welfare, the Lord's kingdom, and above all the Lord. Over time, though, neighborly love starts to cool and disappear. Later comes the hatred of one individual for another. People do not display hatred outwardly, because they live in polite society, under the rule of law, bound by outward restraints; but they still cherish it inside. The outward restraints that bind them come of self-love and materialism and consist of a love for position and prominence, for wealth and so for power, and accordingly for their own reputation. Their hatred for their neighbor hides under these types of love; by its nature it longs to control everyone and to own anything that belongs to anyone else. When their love is attacked, they store up in their heart a contempt for the neighbor who attacked it, yearn for revenge, revel in that other's ruin, and even inflict cruelty on the person, so far as they dare. This is what neighborly love eventually turns into in the church, when its end is at hand. Then it is said to have no more faith, because where love for others is lacking, so is faith, as shown many times.

[3] Numerous churches have ended this way, as people know from the Word. The earliest church died like this around the time of the Flood. The ancient church, which followed the Flood, did the same. So did the second ancient church, called the Hebrew church. Last of all, so did the Jewish religion, which never was a religion based on neighborly love. It merely represented a religion, and its purpose was to preserve a link with heaven by means of representations until the Lord should come into the world. After that, he raised up a new religion, called the church of the Gentiles. This church had depth, because the Lord revealed profound truth to it. It has now reached its end, however, because not only has love for others disappeared but hatred has replaced it. Although this

hatred does not appear on the outside, it still lies deep within and erupts whenever it can—that is, whenever outward restraints do not stop it.

[4] Besides these religions, there have been many others not chronicled this way that shriveled up and destroyed themselves in the same manner.

The reasons they shrink and perish this way are many. One is that parents heap up a mass of evil and imprint it on their very nature by frequent practice and finally by habit. As a result they pass the evil on to their offspring. What parents absorb from the repeated deeds of their lives takes root in their very nature and is passed on by heredity to their descendants. Unless their descendants reform, or are reborn, the evil continues down through the generations, constantly increasing as it goes. So the will becomes more and more inclined to evil and falsity.

When a church reaches its end and dies, though, the Lord always raises up a new one somewhere. Rarely if ever does he do so among the people of the previous religion but among the Gentiles outside it that knew nothing about it. This forms the subject of what now follows.

2911   Genesis 23:3. *And Abraham rose from the presence of his dead one and spoke to the sons of Heth, saying, . . .*

Abraham rose means being lifted up. *From the presence of his dead one* means during that nighttime. *And spoke to the sons of Heth, saying,* symbolizes the people among whom there would be a new, spiritual religion.

2912   *Abraham rose* means being lifted up. This can be seen from the symbolism of *rising* as involving some kind of elevation (discussed at §§2401, 2785). Here it means being lifted up out of grief because a new religion is to be revived, to take the place of the last one, which was destroyed.

And *from the presence of his dead one* means during that nighttime. This can be seen from the symbolism of dying, death, and a *dead one,* or dead person, as nighttime conditions in the church (dealt with above at §2908).

2913   *And spoke to the sons of Heth, saying,* symbolizes the people among whom there would be a new, spiritual religion, as can be seen from the symbolism of *Heth* and of a Hittite.

The land of Canaan had many different inhabitants, whom the Word lists in various places. Among them were the Hittites (see Genesis 15:20; Exodus 3:8, 17; 13:5; 23:23; Deuteronomy 7:1; 20:17; Joshua 3:10; 11:1, 3; 12:8; 24:11; 1 Kings 9:20; and elsewhere). Most came from the ancient church, which extended through many lands, including that of Canaan (see §§1238, 2385). All who were in that church acknowledged neighborly love as the most important thing, and all their doctrines had to do with that love, or in other words, with life. The people who instead heavily cultivated the doctrines of faith were called Canaanites and were separated from the other inhabitants of Canaan (Numbers 13:29; see §§1062, 1063, 1076).

[2] Among the better tribes in Canaan were the Hittites. This is evident from the fact that Abraham lived among them, as Isaac and Jacob did later on, and that they had graves there. It is also evident from the fact that the Hittites treated Abraham with respect and decency, as the statements about them in the current chapter make obvious, especially in verses 5, 6, 10, 11, 14, 15. In consequence, as an upright nation, they represent and symbolize a spiritual church, or truth in the church. Even so, the same thing happened to them as to the other nations that came from the ancient church: over time they fell away from love for others, or the goodness taught by faith. That is why they later symbolize falsity in the church, as in Ezekiel 16:3, 45, and other places. Still, the Hittites were among the more honorable nations, as can be seen from the fact that Hittites formed part of David's retinue. One example is Ahimelech (1 Samuel 26:6). Another is Uriah the Hittite (2 Samuel 11:3, 6, 17, 21), whose wife was Bathsheba, by whom David fathered Solomon (2 Samuel 12:24). On the point that Heth symbolizes superficial knowledge that has to do with life (which is the more superficial truth of a spiritual religion), see §1203.

[3] This verse has to do with a new religion that the Lord establishes when the previous one passes away. The verses that follow focus on the way the people of the new religion accept faith. It has nothing to do with any religion among the children of Heth but generally with the Lord's resurrection of a spiritual religion after the previous one passes away or comes to an end. The children of Heth are simply the people who represent and symbolize that religion.

See what has been said already about churches: Over time a church withers and is defiled: 494, 501, 1327, 2422. It backs away from neighborly love and produces evil and falsity: 1834, 1835. The church is then described as devastated and ruined: 407–411, 2243. A religion is established among people outside the church, and the reasons why: 1366. A vestige of religion in the devastated church is always preserved as a nucleus: 468, 637, 931, 2422. If there were not a church on earth, the human race would be destroyed: the same sections. The church is like the heart and lungs of the universal anatomy, or in other words, of the human race: 637, 931, 2054, 2853. What a spiritual religion is like: 765, 2669. It is love for others and not a detached faith that makes the church: 809, 916. The church would be unified if we all had charity, even if we had different theologies and different ways of worshiping: 1285, 1316, 1798, 1799, 1834, 1844, 2385. Although they may be scattered across the globe, all humans on earth that are part of the Lord's church still make a single whole, as they do in the heavens: 2853. Every religion has an inward part and an outward part, and both together make one church: 409, 1083, 1098, 1100, 1242. The outward church is nothing if there is no inward church: 1795. The church is compared to sunrise and sunset, to the seasons of the year, and to the times of day: 1837. The Last Judgment is the final period of the church: 900, 931, 1850, 2117, 2118.

2914   Genesis 23:4. *"An immigrant and settler I am with you; give me the possession of a grave with you and I will bury my dead one out of my presence."*

An immigrant and settler I am with you symbolizes their first stage, in which the Lord, though unknown to them, could still be present with them. *Give me the possession of a grave with you* means that they could be reborn. *And I will bury my dead one out of my presence* means that in this way the Lord would emerge from the nighttime they were experiencing and rise again.

2915   *An immigrant and settler I am with you* symbolizes their first stage, in which the Lord, though unknown to them, could still be present with them. This can be seen from the representation of Abraham as the Lord (mentioned many times before) and from the symbolism of *being an immigrant with them* and *being a settler with them* as being unknown and yet being present with them. The context above and below shows that this is the inner meaning, since the theme is a new religion. In this verse the theme is its first stage, in which the Lord is unknown to them at the very beginning but can still be present with them. Their character makes this possible because they live a life of neighborly goodness, of justice and fairness in their public dealings, and of integrity and decency in their private dealings. The Lord is present with us in our goodness, and consequently in our justice and fairness, and from this in our integrity and decency. (Integrity embraces all the moral virtues; decency is simply its outward form.) These are different types of goodness, which follow one another in order. They are also the grounds on which the Lord creates a foundation for conscience and therefore for understanding and wisdom in us.

In people who do not display these qualities—and display them from the heart, out of a devotion to them—no seed of heaven can be planted.

There is no receiving ground for it, no soil, and therefore nothing that can accept it. Since no seed of heaven can be planted in them, neither can the Lord be present there. The Lord is said to be present in us to the degree that goodness is present in us—that is, according to the kind of goodness present in us. The quality of our goodness depends on the state of innocence, love, and charity in us, which is what religious truth is planted in, or can be.

Give me the possession of a grave with you means that they can be reborn, as can be seen from the symbolism of a *grave*. On an inner level of the Word, [in a positive sense] a grave symbolizes life, or heaven, while in a negative sense it means death, or hell. The reason it symbolizes life, or heaven, is that angels (who focus on the Word's inner meaning) have no idea of graves, because they have no idea of death. In place of a grave, all they perceive is a continuation of life and therefore resurrection. After all, our spirit rises again and our body is buried (see §1854). Since burial symbolizes resurrection, it also symbolizes rebirth. Rebirth is our first resurrection, because when we are reborn our previous self dies and our new self is revived. Rebirth changes us from dead people into living ones. That is why a grave has the inner-level symbolism it does. The information on children in §2299 also shows that the thought of rebirth is what comes to mind for an angel when the image of a grave is presented.

[2] The reason a grave in a negative sense means death, or hell, is that evil people do not rise again into life. When a grave is mentioned in a discussion of the evil, then, angels just picture hell. That is why the Word also calls hell a grave.

[3] Clearly a grave symbolizes resurrection and rebirth in Ezekiel:

> Therefore prophesy, and you are to say to them, "This is what the Lord Jehovih says: 'Watch! I will *open your graves* and *make you come up out of your graves,* my people, and bring you to Israel's soil, and you will know that I am Jehovah, in my opening *your graves* and making you come up out of *your graves,* my people, and I will put my spirit into you, and you will live, and I will place you on your soil.'" (Ezekiel 37:12, 13, 14)

Here the prophet is talking about bones that have been brought to life and, in an inner sense, about rebirth. Obviously rebirth is the theme, because it says, "When I put my spirit into you, and you live, and I place you on your soil." The graves in this passage stand for the old self, with its evils

2916

and falsities. To open and come up out of them is to be reborn. The image of a grave disappears and is more or less stripped away, then, when the idea of rebirth or new life comes up.

[4] Matthew 27:52, 53 says that *graves opened* and many bodies of sleeping saints *rose again and* left *their graves after the Lord's resurrection,* entered the holy city, and appeared to many. This involves the same meaning, namely, a general resurrection because of the Lord's resurrection; and, in a deeper sense, every individual resurrection.

The Lord's resurrection of Lazarus from the dead (John 11:1 and following verses) also involves the idea that a new religion would be brought to life among people outside the church. Every miracle the Lord performed had to do with the state of his church, because all of them were divine.

The same meaning is found again in the fact that a man thrown into Elisha's grave came back to life when he touched Elisha's bones (2 Kings 13:20, 21), since Elisha represented the Lord.

[5] Because burial symbolized resurrection generally and every particular resurrection, the ancients paid the greatest possible attention to their burials and burial places. Abraham, for instance, was buried in Hebron, in the land of Canaan, as were Isaac and Jacob, along with their wives (Genesis 47:29, 30, 31; 49:30, 31, 32). Joseph's bones were brought from Egypt into Canaan (Genesis 50:25; Exodus 13:19; Joshua 24:32). David and the kings that succeeded him were buried in Zion (1 Kings 2:10; 11:43; 14:31; 15:8, 24; 22:50; 2 Kings 8:24; 12:21; 14:20; 15:7, 38; 16:20). The reason was that Canaan and Zion represented and symbolized the Lord's kingdom, and burial represented and symbolized resurrection. Anyone can see, though, that the place we are buried has no effect on our resurrection.

[6] Other representative practices also show that burial symbolizes rising again into life. Take the fact that the ungodly were not mourned or buried but cast out (Jeremiah 8:2; 14:16; 16:4, 6; 20:6; 22:19; 25:33; 2 Kings 9:10; Revelation 11:9). When the ungodly *were* buried, they were dug up out of their graves (Jeremiah 8:1, 2; 2 Kings 23:16, 17, 18).

For the symbolism of a grave, in the opposite sense, as death, or hell, see Isaiah 14:19, 20, 21; Ezekiel 32:21, 22, 23, 25, [26,] 27; Psalms 88:4, 5, 10, 11; Numbers 19:16, 18, 19.

2917   *I will bury my dead one out of my presence* means that in this way the Lord would emerge from the nighttime they were experiencing and rise again, as can be seen from the following: *Burying* means rising again, as discussed just above in §2916. And a *dead one* symbolizes a condition of shadow, or night—that is, ignorance—which is also discussed above, at §§2908, 2912. The Lord emerges from this night and rises again in us when we acknowledge him. Until then, we experience nighttime, because we cannot see him. He rises again in everyone who is reborn.

Genesis 23:5, 6. *And the sons of Heth answered Abraham, saying to him, "Listen to us! My lord, a chieftain of God you are in our midst. In the choicest of our graves bury your dead one. None of us will withhold our graves from you, from the burial of your dead one."*   **2918**

The sons of Heth answered Abraham, saying to him, symbolizes a reciprocal state in the people belonging to the new religion. *Listen to us* symbolizes acceptance. *My lord, a chieftain of God you are in our midst* symbolizes the Lord's goodness and truth that are divine in them. *In the choicest of our graves* symbolizes his pleasure in their rebirth. *Bury your dead one* means that in this way they would emerge from their nighttime and be restored to life. *None of us will withhold our graves from you* means that they were all prepared to accept rebirth. *From the burial of your dead one* means that they would emerge from their nighttime and be revived.

The sons of Heth answered Abraham, saying to him, symbolizes a reciprocal state in the people belonging to the new religion. This can be seen from the symbolism of *answering,* when the answer agrees to a request, as reciprocation, and from that of the sons of Heth as the people among whom the new, spiritual religion exists (dealt with above in §2913).   **2919**

Listen to us symbolizes acceptance, as can be seen from the meaning of *listen to us,* when it is a standard way of saying yes, as acceptance.   **2920**

My lord, a chieftain of God in our midst, symbolizes the Lord's goodness and truth that are divine in them, as can be seen from the symbolism of a *lord* and a *chieftain of God,* and from the meaning of *in our midst.*   **2921**

The term *lord* is used where the discussion focuses on what is good, as the Old Testament Word makes clear. In it, Jehovah is called "Jehovah" at one point, "God" at another, "Lord" at another, "Jehovah God" at another, "Lord Jehovih" at another, and "Jehovah Sabaoth" at another. The choice of name is due to a secret reason that can be seen only from the inner meaning. When the subject is the heavenly qualities of love, or what is good, the name used is generally Jehovah, but when the subject is the spiritual qualities of faith, or what is true, it is God. When both are dealt with simultaneously, it is Jehovah God, but when the focus is on the divine power of goodness, or omnipotence, it is Jehovah Sabaoth— that is, "Jehovah of Armies." "Lord" is also used in this last case, so that

"Jehovah Sabaoth" and "Lord" have the same meaning and symbolism. From this power—the power of goodness—people and angels are also called lords. By contrast, people are called servants if they either have no power or receive their power from those called lords. From this it can be seen that "my lord" here on an inner level symbolizes the Lord's goodness, as will be illustrated below from the Word.

A *chieftain of God,* on the other hand, symbolizes the Lord in regard to the power of truth, or in regard to truth, as can be seen from the symbolism of a *chieftain* or chieftains as primary truths (treated of in §§1482, 2089). It can also be seen from the fact that he is called God's chieftain, since the name God is used where the subject is truth, and Jehovah where the subject is goodness (§§2586, 2769, 2807, 2822).

In our midst means among them, or in them, as can be seen without explanation.

[2] The fact that Jehovah Sabaoth has the same meaning and symbolism as the Lord in the Old Testament Word can be seen in Isaiah:

> The zeal of *Jehovah Sabaoth* will do this. *The Lord* has sent word against Jacob, and it has fallen on Israel. (Isaiah 9:7, 8)

Elsewhere in the same author:

> "A strong monarch will rule them," says *the Lord, Jehovah Sabaoth.* (Isaiah 19:4)

In Malachi:

> "Watch: suddenly to his temple will come *the Lord,* whom you are seeking, and the angel of the covenant, whom you desire. Watch: He is coming!" says *Jehovah Sabaoth.* (Malachi 3:1)

Even more explicitly in Isaiah:

> I saw *the Lord* sitting on a high and lofty throne. Seraphs were standing above him, six wings, six wings to each. This one shouted to that one, "Holy, holy, holy is *Jehovah Sabaoth!*" Alas for me! Because I have been cut off, because my eyes have seen the king, *Jehovah Sabaoth;* and I heard the voice of *the Lord.* (Isaiah 6:1, [2,] 3, 5, 8)

These passages show that Jehovah Sabaoth and the Lord have the same meaning. [3] The term "Lord Jehovih," on the other hand, is usually used when people are seeking and begging for omnipotent help, as in Isaiah:

> Say to the cities of Judah, "Look: your God!" Look! The *Lord Jehovih* will come in might, and his arm will rule for him. Watch! His reward is with him and his work before him. He will pasture his flock like a shepherd. (Isaiah 40:9, 10, 11)

For further evidence that he is called the Lord Jehovih under those circumstances, see Isaiah 25:8; 40:10; 48:16; 50:4, 5, 7, 9; 61:1; Jeremiah 2:22; Ezekiel 8:1; 11:13, 17, 21; 12:10, 19, 28; 13:8, 13, 16, 18, 20; 14:4, 6, 11, 18, 20, 21; Micah 1:2; Psalms 71:5, 16; and many other passages elsewhere.

[4] What is more, "the Lord" involves the same thing as "Jehovah" in the Old Testament Word, in that "the Lord" is used when goodness is being spoken of. For this reason, "the Lord" is distinguished from "God" in the same way "Jehovah" is, as in Moses:

> Jehovah our God is *God* of gods and *Lord* of lords. (Deuteronomy 10:17)

In David:

> Acclaim the *God* of gods, because his mercy lasts forever. Acclaim the *Lord* of lords, because his mercy lasts forever. (Psalms 136:1, 2, 3)

[5] In the New Testament Word, though, the Gospels and the Book of Revelation do not mention Jehovah anywhere but use "the Lord" instead. This is for hidden reasons given below.

The use of "the Lord" for "Jehovah" in the New Testament Word is quite plain in Mark:

> Jesus said, "The first of all the commandments is, 'Hear, O Israel: *The Lord* our *God* is one *Lord.* Therefore you shall love *the Lord* your *God* with all your heart and with all your soul and with all your thought and with all your powers.'" (Mark 12:29, 30)

The same words appear in Moses in this form:

> Listen, Israel: *Jehovah* our *God* is one *Jehovah,* and you shall love *Jehovah* your *God* with all your heart and with all your soul and with all your powers. (Deuteronomy 6:4, 5)

Clearly "the Lord" is being used for "Jehovah" here. Likewise in John:

> I saw: here now, a throne was placed in heaven, and one was sitting on the throne. Around the throne were four living creatures full of eyes in

front and behind; each one had six wings for itself all around, which were
full of eyes within. They said, "Holy, holy, holy *Lord* God Almighty!"
(Revelation 4:2, 6, 8)

These words appear in Isaiah this way:

I saw the Lord sitting on a high and lofty throne. Seraphs were standing
above him, six wings, six wings to each. This one shouted to that one,
"Holy, holy, holy is *Jehovah Sabaoth!*" (Isaiah 6:1, [2,] 3, 5, 8)

John substitutes "Lord" for "Jehovah," or "Lord God Almighty" for
"Jehovah Sabaoth." It is clear from Ezekiel 1:5, 13, 14, 15, 19; 10:15 that
the four living creatures are seraphs, or guardian beings. Many other
passages also show that in the New Testament, the Lord is Jehovah, as
in Luke:

There appeared to Zechariah an *angel of the Lord.* (Luke 1:11)

An angel of the Lord stands for an angel of Jehovah. In the same author:

The angel said to Zechariah, concerning his son, "He will turn many of
the children of Israel to *the Lord* their *God."* (Luke 1:16)

"To the Lord God" means "to Jehovah God." In the same author:

Concerning Jesus, the angel said to Mary, "He will be great and will be
called the Child of the Highest One; and *the Lord God* will give him the
throne of David." (Luke 1:32)

The Lord God stands for Jehovah God. In the same author:

Mary said, "My soul exalts *the Lord,* and my spirit has exulted over God,
my Savior." (Luke 1:46, 47)

Here again the Lord stands for Jehovah. In the same author:

Zechariah prophesied, saying, "A blessing on *the Lord God* of Israel!"
(Luke 1:[67,] 68)

The Lord God stands for Jehovah God. In the same author:

An *angel of the Lord* stood near the shepherds, and the glory of *the Lord*
shone around them. (Luke 2:9)

An angel of the Lord and the glory of the Lord stand for an angel of Jehovah
and the glory of Jehovah. In Matthew:

A blessing on the one coming in *the Lord's name!* (Matthew 21:9; 23:39;
Luke 13:35; John 12:13)

"In the Lord's name" means "in Jehovah's name." Not to mention many other instances, such as Luke 1:28; 2:15, 22, 23, 24, 29, 38, 39; 5:17; Mark 12:10, 11.

[6] Among the hidden reasons why they called Jehovah the Lord were these: If it had been said at that time that the Lord was the same as Jehovah, who is mentioned so many times in the Old Testament (see §1736), people would not have accepted it, because they would not have believed it. In addition, the Lord did not become Jehovah in respect to his human side as well until he had thoroughly united his divine nature with his human, and his human nature with his divine (see §§1725, 1729, 1733, 1745, 1815, 2156, 2751). So full oneness did not occur until after his final trial, which was the one on the cross. That is why his disciples always called him Lord after his resurrection (John 20:2, 13, 15, 18, 20, 25; 21:7, 12, 15, 16, 17, 20; Mark 16:19, 20). And Thomas said:

> *My Lord* and *my God!* (John 20:28)

And since the Lord was Jehovah, whose name comes up so many times in the Old Testament, he also said to the disciples:

> You call me *Teacher* and *Lord,* and you speak correctly, because so I am. (John 13:13, 14, 16)

These words mean that he was Jehovah God. He is called Lord here in regard to his goodness, but Teacher, in regard to truth. The angel's words to the shepherds also mean that the Lord was Jehovah:

> A Savior is born to you today, and he is *Christ the Lord.* (Luke 2:11)

Christ stands for the Messiah, the Anointed, the King; the Lord stands for Jehovah. The former has to do with truth; the latter, with goodness.

People who do not examine the Word closely cannot see this. They believe that our Savior was called "Lord"—as others were—because it was a general term of respect; when in reality he was so called because he was Jehovah.

In the choicest of our graves symbolizes his pleasure in their rebirth as can be seen from the following: Choosing, choice, and that which is *choice* symbolize something having to do with preference, or good pleasure. And a *grave* symbolizes resurrection and rebirth, as noted above at §2916. **2922**

Bury your dead one means that in this way they would emerge from their nighttime and be restored to life. This is established by the symbolism of *being buried* as rising again, or being restored to life (discussed **2923** above at §2916), and from that of a *dead person* as nighttime for religious goodness and truth (discussed in §§2908, 2912, 2917).

2924   *None of us will withhold our graves from you* means that they were all prepared to accept rebirth. This can be seen from the symbolism of a *grave* as rebirth (discussed in §2916) and from that of *not withholding* as wanting to accept.

2925   *From the burial of your dead one* means that they would emerge from their nighttime and be revived. This is established by the symbolism of *being buried* and of a *dead person* as being revived from nighttime in regard to religious goodness and truth (dealt with just above in §2923, where the same words occur).

2926   Genesis 23:7, 8. *And Abraham rose and bowed down to the people of the land, to the sons of Heth. And he spoke with them, saying, "If you have it in your soul to bury my dead one out of my presence, listen to me and plead for me with Ephron, son of Zohar."*

Abraham rose and bowed down symbolizes the Lord's joy because of being kindly received. *To the people of the land, to the sons of Heth,* means by the people of the new, spiritual religion. *He spoke with them, saying,* symbolizes thought and perception about them. *If you have it in your soul* means if it is with a heartfelt desire for truth. *To bury my dead one out of my presence* means that they wanted to emerge from their nighttime and rise again. *Listen to me* means that they should submit. *And plead for me with Ephron, son of Zohar,* symbolizes those in whom religious truth and goodness could find acceptance.

2927   *Abraham rose and bowed down* symbolizes the Lord's joy because of being kindly received, as can be seen from the following: *Rising* has a symbolism that involves some form of elevation (discussed in §§2401, 2785). Gladness and joy lift the mind, so the text here says that he rose. *Abraham* represents the Lord, as noted many times before. And *bowing down* symbolizes rejoicing. Bowing is a physical action inspired by both humility and joy. The context above and below shows clearly that joy—joy because of being kindly received—was the inspiration here.

2928   *To the people of the land, to the sons of Heth,* means by the people of the spiritual religion, as is established by the following: A *people* symbolizes those dedicated to truth, so it symbolizes the spiritual, as discussed at §§1259, 1260. The *land* symbolizes a church, as discussed at §§662, 1066, 1068, 1262, 1733, 1850, 2117, 2118 at the end. And the *sons of Heth* symbolize people belonging to the new, spiritual religion, as noted above at §2913.

The Word mentions the *people of the land* in many places where it talks about Israel and Jerusalem. On an inner level, it symbolizes a spiritual religion, or those who are part of a spiritual church, because Israel and Jerusalem mean such a church or religion. When the text speaks of Judah and Zion, it then mentions nations, and a nation symbolizes a heavenly religion, because that is what Judah and Zion mean.

[2] Many passages in the Word show that where the text is talking about Israel and Jerusalem, and so about a spiritual religion, it mentions the people of the land. In Ezekiel, for instance:

> You are to say to the *people of the land,* "This is what the Lord Jehovih says to the residents of *Jerusalem,* to the soil of *Israel:* They will eat their bread in grief and drink their water in devastation, in order that the *land* of [Jerusalem] may be laid waste; the inhabited cities will be laid waste, and the *land* will be ruined." (Ezekiel 12:19, 20)

In an inner sense here, Jerusalem and the soil of Israel stand for a spiritual church, while the bread and water stand for charity and faith, or goodness and truth. The land stands for the church itself, which is said to be laid waste in respect to goodness and to be ruined in respect to truth. [3] In the same author:

> Gog and its horde the house of *Israel* will bury, to cleanse the *land* for seven months, and all the *people of the land* will bury them. (Ezekiel 39:[11,] 12, 13)

Gog stands for outward worship detached from inward, which is idolatrous (§1151). The house of Israel stands for the goodness that a spiritual church has; the people of the land, for the truth it knows. The land stands for the church itself. The reason the land means the church is that the land of Canaan represented the Lord's kingdom and consequently the church, because the Lord's kingdom on earth is the church. [4] In the same author:

> All the *people of the land* shall be at that terumah [raised offering] for the ruler of *Israel.* And on that day the ruler shall sacrifice the young ox of a sin offering for himself and for all the *people of the land.* The *people of the land* shall bow down at the doorway of the gate on Sabbaths and new moons. And the *people of the land* shall enter on the appointed feasts. (Ezekiel 45:16, 22; 46:3, 9)

This is about the New Jerusalem, or in other words, the Lord's spiritual kingdom. Its inhabitants are called the people of the land. The ruler means truth that is divine from the Lord.

[5] They are called the *sons of Heth* because sons symbolize truth (see §§489, 491, 533, 1147, 2623).

The reason truth is attributed to spiritual people is that truth is what introduces them to goodness; that is, faith is what introduces them to love for others. They do good out of a devotion to truth, and the only way they know it is good is that they have been taught that it is. As a result, their conscience is also founded on religious truth; see §§1155, 1577, 2046, 2088, 2184, 2507, 2715, 2716, 2718.

2929 *He spoke with them, saying,* symbolizes thought and perception about them. This is established by the symbolism of *speaking* and *saying* as thinking and perceiving, which was discussed at §§1898, 1919, 2080, 2271, 2287, 2506, 2515, 2552, 2619.

2930 *If you have it in your soul* means if it is with a heartfelt desire for truth, as can be seen from the inner-level symbolism of a *soul.*

The Word often speaks of doing something with one's heart and soul, or with all one's heart and all one's soul, which symbolizes doing it with all one's will and all one's intellect. Anyone can recognize that humankind has the two capacities of will and intellect. It is also clear that will is a separate capacity from intellect, since we can understand what is good and true and yet will what is evil and false.

Human beings were created in such a way from the beginning that will and intellect should form a single whole in them, meaning that they would not think something they did not will, or will something they did not think. That is how it is with heavenly people, and that is how it was in the heavenly church called Humankind, or Adam. In spiritual people, though, or in a spiritual religion, the one capacity is separated from the other; the intellect is separated from the will. The Lord reforms the former capacity (the intellect) in us, and within it he shapes a new will and a new intellect (§§863, 875, 895, 897, 927, 928, 1023, 1044, 2256). The new will in the intellect, which is from the Lord, is what is called a heart, and the new intellect is what is called a *soul.* When the text says "with all your heart and with all your soul," it means with all one's will and all one's intellect.

[2] That is what heart and soul symbolize in Moses:

> You shall love Jehovah your God with *all* your *heart* and *all* your *soul* and all your powers. (Deuteronomy 6:5)

In the same author:

> Now, Israel, what is Jehovah your God seeking from you except to fear Jehovah your God, to go in all his ways, and to love him, and to serve Jehovah your God, with *all* your *heart* and *all* your *soul?* (Deuteronomy 10:12; 11:13)

In the same author:

> This day Jehovah your God is commanding you to do these statues and judgments, and you are to keep and do them with *all* your *heart* and *all* your *soul.* (Deuteronomy 26:16)

In Kings:

> David to Solomon: "Jehovah will secure his word that he spoke concerning me, saying, 'If your children keep their way, to walk before me in truth, with *all* their *heart* and *all* their *soul,*' saying, 'not a man of you will be cut off from upon the throne of Israel.'" (1 Kings 2:4)

In Matthew:

> You shall love the Lord your God with *all* your *heart* and with *all* your *soul.* (Matthew 22:37; Mark 12:29, 30)

[3] Something similar is also said of Jehovah, or the Lord, since he is the source of the desire for goodness that exists in the will of a person in the church, and of the desire for truth that exists in the intellect of such a person. In Samuel, for example:

> I will raise up for myself a faithful priest, as is in *my heart* and in *my soul.* (1 Samuel 2:35)

And in Jeremiah:

> I will rejoice over them, to do them good, and I will plant them in this land in truth, with *all my heart* and *all my soul.* (Jeremiah 32:41)

In many other places in the Word as well, a soul symbolizes a desire for truth, as in Isaiah:

> With *my soul* I have desired you in the night; with my spirit in the midst of me I have also sought you early, because just as the earth undergoes your judgments, the inhabitants of the world learn justice. (Isaiah 26:9)

The soul stands for a desire for truth, while the spirit stands for a desire for goodness. Judgments are mentioned in connection with truth, and justice, in connection with goodness (see §2235). [4] In the same author:

> The stupid speak stupidity, to starve the *famished soul* and to cause one *thirsting for a drink* to faint. (Isaiah 32:6)

A famished soul stands for a yearning for goodness, which stupid people starve out. A soul thirsting for a drink is a yearning for truth, which the stupid cause to faint. In Jeremiah:

> Their *soul* will become like a watered garden. And I will water the *weary soul,* and every *grieving soul* I will fill. (Jeremiah 31:12, 25)

A soul stands for a desire for truth and goodness. In the same author:

> All its people are groaning, looking for bread; they have exchanged what is pleasant to them for food, to bring their *soul* back [to life]. Far away from me is one who comforts, who brings back my *soul;* my children have become desolate. They tried to find food for themselves to bring their *soul* back. (Lamentations 1:11, 16, 19)

The soul stands for the vitality of a desire for goodness and truth. The food stands for wisdom and understanding.

[5] I said that a soul symbolizes a *heartfelt* desire for truth, because it is possible to desire truth without doing so from the heart. Sometimes people desire truth out of love for themselves and their own importance, out of love for the world and its material advantages, or out of a self-righteous kind of love. These same kinds of love also generate a desire for truth, but it is not a genuine desire. It comes from the will of the flesh, not from the heart. What comes from the heart comes from the Lord.

In a comprehensive sense, a soul in the Word symbolizes all life (see §§1000, 1005, 1040, 1742), because in that sense it means something from which another thing exists and lives. The soul of the body is its spirit, because the body lives from the spirit. The soul of the spirit is its life, which lies still deeper and supplies it with wisdom and understanding.

2931   *To bury my dead one out of my presence* means that they wanted to emerge from their nighttime and rise again. This can be seen from the symbolism of *being buried* as rising again and from that of a *dead person* as nighttime in regard to religious goodness and truth (discussed above in §§2923, 2925, where the same words occur).

Listen to me means that they should submit, which can be seen from the symbolism of *listening* as obeying, or submitting, as discussed at §2542.

2932

And plead for me with Ephron, son of Zohar, symbolizes those in whom religious truth and goodness could find acceptance, as can be seen from this: The field and the cave in it where Sarah was to be buried belonged to *Ephron.* Since burial symbolizes rebirth (§2916), it follows that he symbolizes those in whom religious truth and goodness could find acceptance.

2933

The children of Heth also represent the same group, since they were from Ephron's city and were his people.

Pleading symbolizes being prepared to accept them.

Genesis 23:9. *"And let him give me the cave of Machpelah, which is his, which is at the end of his field; for full silver let him give it to me, in your midst, for the possession of a grave."*

2934

Let him give me the cave of Machpelah, which is his, symbolizes the dim sight they had of faith. *Which is at the end of the field* means where there was little of the church. *For full silver* symbolizes redemption through truth. *Let him give it to me, in your midst, for the possession of a grave* means possessing it, then, through rebirth.

Let him give me the cave of Machpelah symbolizes a dim sight of faith. This can be seen from the symbolism of a *cave* as something dark (dealt with at §2463), and from that of *Machpelah* as dimly-lit faith.

2935

The reason a *cave* symbolizes dim sight is that it is a dark place. When the cave is said to be in a mountain, what is dim is the sight of goodness, but when the cave is said to be in a field in Machpelah, what is dim is the sight of truth. Because the current verse calls it the cave of Machpelah, and Machpelah was the site of the field that had the cave at the end of it, it means a dim sight of truth. To put the same thing another way, it means a dim sight of faith. From this it is also clear that *Machpelah* means dimly-lit faith.

[2] People who are regenerating and becoming spiritual usually have tremendous difficulty seeing truth. Good coming from the Lord influences them, but the influence of truth is not as strong. So a parallelism and correspondence exists between the Lord and the goodness in us, but not between the Lord and the truth we know (see §1832). The main reason is that people regenerating do not know what is good, and even if they did know, they would not believe it at heart. As long as goodness is hard to see, truth is too, since all truth develops out of goodness. To

speak more plainly, such people know very dimly if at all that the Lord is goodness itself; that everything having to do with love for him and charity for their neighbor is good; and that everything that affirms and supports these ideas is true. In fact, they even cherish doubts about it and are willing to listen to arguments against it. As long as they are in this state, the light of truth is unable to flow in from the Lord. Indeed, they think of the Lord the way they do of any other person rather than the way they do of God. They view love for him in terms of some worldly love. What a genuine feeling of charity for their neighbor is, they have hardly any idea, or even what charity is, or what their neighbor is. Yet these things are essential. It is clear to see, then, how deep a darkness the spiritual live in, especially before they regenerate. That is the state dealt with here.

2936   *Which is at the end of the field* means where there was little of the church. This can be seen from the symbolism of an *end* or furthest part as a small amount, and from that of a *field* as the church and the church's theology (treated of in §368).

The meaning of an *end* or furthest part as a small amount can be seen from the Word's description of the earth, the ground, and fields. The middle part of any of these symbolizes a large amount, but the outer edge—also called the environs—symbolizes a small amount. Around the outer edge, the representation dies out. Here, then, the end of the field means little of the church.

2937   *For full silver* symbolizes redemption through truth, as can be seen from the following: *Silver* symbolizes truth, as noted at §1551. And *let him give it to me for silver* means buying it, and in a spiritual sense, redeeming it.

Spiritual people are said to be bought with *silver* (see §2048), or in other words, redeemed by truth, because they are reborn—that is, introduced to goodness—by religious truth. Spiritual people do not in any way perceive what is good, as a heavenly person does. It is truth that enables them to recognize and then acknowledge a thing as good. When they acknowledge and believe it, it becomes good to them, and they love it as something good. The kind of good it becomes depends on the kind of truth the person knows. That is why spiritual people are said to be redeemed by truth.

Still, the quality of the goodness does not develop and grow out of truth but out of the influence of goodness on the quality of the truth.

Let him give it to me, in your midst, for the possession of a grave means **2938** possessing it, then, through rebirth. This can be seen without explanation, since it was shown above at §2916 that a *grave* means rebirth.

Genesis 23:10. *And Ephron was sitting in the midst of the sons of Heth,* **2939** *and Ephron the Hittite answered Abraham in the ears of the sons of Heth, for the benefit of all those entering the gate of his city, saying,* . . .

Ephron was sitting in the midst of the sons of Heth symbolizes people who could accept the goodness and truth composing faith as paramount. *And Ephron the Hittite answered Abraham* symbolizes the state in which they accepted it. *In the ears of the sons of Heth* symbolizes obedience. *For the benefit of all those entering the gate of his city, saying,* means in regard to the teachings that lead to faith.

Ephron was sitting in the midst of the sons of Heth symbolizes people **2940** who could accept the goodness and truth composing faith as paramount, as can be seen from the following: *Ephron* represents those who could accept the goodness and truth that make up faith, among whom the new religion would exist, and the *sons of Heth* symbolize the same people. (This is discussed in §§2913, 2933.) And the *midst* or *in the midst* symbolizes what is paramount or most important, and also what is deepest (as discussed at §1074).

The inner-level symbolism of the *midst* or middle as what is paramount or most important, and also what is deepest, comes from representations in the other world. When something good is represented in spiritual images, the best part appears in the middle. What is less and less good appears further and further from the middle, and what is not good appears farthest away, on the circumference. That is why both the paramount (or most important) things and the deepest things occupy the center. Thoughts are represented in the same way, and so are feelings. Every alteration in the state of the thoughts and feelings is also represented this way, so that goodness and evil vary with their position relative to the middle. This phenomenon traces its source to the underlying form of spiritual and heavenly attributes, which is similar.

And Ephron the Hittite answered Abraham symbolizes the state in which **2941** they accepted it. This can be seen from the symbolism of *answering*, when the answer is affirmative, as acceptance. It is also evident from the very next words.

Ephron is called a *Hittite* here in order to represent a spiritual church in his role as its head and leader.

2942   *In the ears of the sons of Heth* symbolizes obedience. This can be seen from the symbolism of the *ear* as obedience (discussed at §2542).

2943   *For the benefit of all those entering the gate of his city, saying,* means in regard to the teachings that lead to faith, as is established by the following: A *gate* symbolizes an entry and therefore that which leads into something. A door, as discussed at §§2145, 2152, 2356, 2385, has the same symbolism. And a *city* symbolizes the truth that belongs to faith, as discussed at §§402, 2268, 2449, 2451, 2712.

The cities of the ancient church were not like later cities and modern ones. People did not gather in mixed groups in them but lived together in their individual clans. The family of a single ancestor constituted a city, such as the city of Nahor, to which Abraham's servant came when he was arranging a marriage between Rebekah and Isaac (Genesis 24:10). It was Nahor's clan that lived there. Another example is Salem, Shechem's city, in which Jacob arrived as he came from Paddan-aram (Genesis 33:18; 34). It was Hamor and Shechem's clan that lived there. The same with all other cities at that time. [2] From the very earliest people the ancients had learned that nations and clans represented the communities of heaven and therefore aspects of love and charity (§§685, 1159). When a *city* is mentioned instead of a clan, then, or a people instead of a nation, it symbolizes the truth that belongs to faith.

A further consequence is that in its genuine sense, the city of God or the holy city symbolizes faith in the Lord.

Since a city symbolized faith, a city *gate* symbolized teachings, because teachings introduce us to faith.

In the representative Jewish religion, judges and elders would sit in the city gate and pass judgment there, and this symbolized the same thing. The existence of the practice is clear in scriptural narratives and in Zechariah:

> These are the words that you shall carry out: Speak truth, a man with his companion; *pass judgment in your gates* for truth and peace-making judgment. (Zechariah 8:16)

And in Amos:

> Hate evil and love goodness, and *set judgment up in the gate.* (Amos 5:15)

A gate also symbolizes a point of entry to the rational mind, which is compared to a city; see §2851.

Genesis 23:11. *"No, my lord; listen to me: The field I give you; and the cave that is in it—to you I give it. In the eyes of the sons of my people I give it to you. Bury your dead one."*

2944

No, my lord; listen to me means the first stage, as discussed earlier. *The field I give you; and the cave that is in it, to you I give it* means preparing themselves on their own, so far as the requirements of religion and faith went. *In the eyes of the sons of my people I give it to you* means in accord with their common understanding [of those requirements]. *Bury your dead one* means in order to emerge from their nighttime and be revived.

No, my lord; listen to me means the first stage, as discussed earlier, in §§2935, 2936—specifically, the stage at which their sight of faith was dim. This can be seen from their refusal to listen to Abraham say that he would give them full silver (verse 9) or, in an inner sense, that they would be redeemed by the Lord. They wanted instead to prepare themselves, so far as the requirements of religion and faith went. In other words, they wanted to reform themselves.

2945

These words, *no, my lord; listen to me,* involve the state they were in—specifically, the state of their thinking about redemption and reformation—since directly afterward comes the proposal.

The field I give you; and the cave that is in it, to you I give it means preparing themselves on their own, so far as the requirements of religion and faith went, as can be seen from the following: A *field* symbolizes the church, as discussed at §§368, 2936. A *cave that is in it*—in the field—symbolizes a dim sight of faith, as noted above in §2935. And *giving a field* and *giving a cave* or, what is the same, turning down Abraham's silver, means wanting to be redeemed not by the Lord but by themselves, or in other words, to prepare their own selves in that regard.

2946

Such is the first state of everyone who is reforming and becoming spiritual: we do not believe we are reformed by the Lord but by ourselves. That is, we believe all our will for goodness and all our thoughts of truth come from ourselves. The Lord leaves us in that state, too, since otherwise we could not be reformed. If we were told before being reborn that we could not do anything good on our own or think anything true on our own, we would fall into one of several errors. One is that we should wait for something to touch our heart and influence our thoughts [directly], and if it does not, we should attempt nothing. Another is that no goodness or truth is credited to us or makes us righteous if it comes from somewhere other than ourselves. Another is that if it does come from elsewhere, we are like machines, without the right or ability to choose anything for ourselves. There are other errors as well. That is why we are then allowed to think that goodness and truth originate in us.

[2] After we have been reborn, though, the realization is gradually instilled in us that the case is very different. We come to know that everything good and true comes from the Lord alone. As we develop still further, we also see that anything that does not come from the Lord is evil and false. People who have been reborn receive the ability not only to see this but also to perceive it, if not during bodily life, then in the next life. Every angel senses that it is so.

See previous discussions on this topic: Everything good and true comes from the Lord (1614, 2016); all understanding and wisdom comes from him (109, 112, 121, 124); we cannot do anything good or think anything true on our own (874, 875, 876); still, we each ought to do good as if we were acting on our own, rather than drop our hands (1712); if we force ourselves to resist evil and do good, as if on our own, the Lord gives us a heavenly autonomy (1937, 1947).

2947   *In the eyes of the sons of my people I give it to you* means so far as their common understanding [of those requirements] went. This can be seen from the symbolism of *eyes* as the intellect (discussed in §2701), and from that of the *sons of a people* as all such individuals. The *sons of a people* are those who are first being introduced into truth, since a people means those who focus on truth (1259, 1260). That is why it says not "in the eyes of my people" but "in the eyes of the sons of my people."

2948   *Bury your dead one* means in order to emerge from their nighttime and be revived. This can be seen from the symbolism of *being buried* as rising again—that is, being revived—and from that of a *dead person* as nighttime in regard to what faith views as good and true (discussed above at §§2917, 2923, 2925, 2931, where the same words occur).

2949   Genesis 23:12, 13. *And Abraham bowed down before the people of the land. And he spoke to Ephron in the ears of the people of the land, saying, "Still, if you would please listen to me, I will give the silver for the field; take it from me and I will bury my dead one there."*

Abraham bowed down before the people of the land symbolizes the Lord's joy over the goodwill of the people belonging to the new, spiritual religion. *And he spoke to Ephron* symbolizes his influence on those who could accept it. *In the ears of the people of the land* means even to the point of obeying the truth known to the church. *Still, if you would please listen to me* symbolizes a deeper influence. *I will give the silver for the field; take it from me* symbolizes redemption in regard to the truth that the church knows and that comes from the Lord. *And I will bury my dead one* means that in this way they would emerge from their nighttime and come alive.

Abraham bowed down before the people of the land symbolizes the Lord's joy over the goodwill of the people belonging to the new, spiritual religion, as is established by the following: *Bowing down* here means rejoicing, as it does above at §2927. *Abraham* represents the Lord, as noted many times before. And the *people of the land* symbolize those who belong to a spiritual religion, as noted above in §2928, where the same words occur. There, however, in verse 7, it says that he bowed down to the people of the land, to the sons of Heth. The reason that verse adds the reference to the sons of Heth is that it symbolizes people in the church who are first being introduced [into truth]; and the *sons of a people* symbolize the same thing (§2947). In the current verse, on the other hand, it symbolizes people who are making progress, so it simply mentions the people of the land, without adding anything about the sons of Heth. Joy at being kindly received is symbolized there, but joy over their goodwill is symbolized here. Reception comes first, because it is a matter of the intellect, while goodwill follows, because it is a matter of the will; see §2954.   2950

And he spoke to Ephron symbolizes his influence on those who could accept it, as is established by the following: *Speaking* symbolizes thinking (§§2271, 2287) and also willing (§2626) and therefore exerting an influence, since thought and will produce the influence. And *Ephron* represents people who are capable of accepting religious goodness and truth, as noted at §2933.   2951

In the ears of the people of the land means even to the point of obeying the truth known to the church, as can be seen from the following: An *ear* symbolizes obedience, as noted in §§2542, 2942. And the *people of the land* symbolizes those who belong to a spiritual religion, as well as the truth known to that religion, as discussed in §§1259, 1260, 2928.   2952

Still, if you would please listen to me symbolizes a deeper influence, as can be seen from the train of thought in the speech. Abraham spoke to Ephron, and this symbolized the Lord's influence, as noted just above in §2951. Here, in saying, "Still, if you would please listen to me," he continues the speech and captures his listener's attention. So a deeper influence is symbolized.   2953

By nature the inner meaning is such that the words and phrases are almost unimportant. The meaning of the words, flowing from the train of thought, presents an image (a spiritual one, to the eyes of angels) for which the outward or literal meaning serves as a platform. Thoughts in our minds serve to spark angels' spiritual thoughts. The images in us that serve this way come mainly from the Word, because all the individual elements of Scripture represent something, and each and every word symbolizes something. Angels notice immediately that these images come from the Word, because they contain spiritual and heavenly messages that come one after another in their proper, most perfectly arranged order. And the spiritual and heavenly components contain a holiness that comes from the very deepest meaning, which has to do exclusively with the Lord and his kingdom.

2954   *I will give the silver for the field; take it from me* symbolizes redemption in regard to the truth that the church knows and that comes from the Lord, as can be seen from the following: *Giving silver* means redeeming someone through truth, as noted above at §2937, since *silver* is truth (§1551). A *field* symbolizes the church and its teaching of truth, as noted in §§368, 2936. And *taking from me* symbolizes reciprocation by people in the church. They reciprocate by believing that redemption comes from the Lord alone.

To take up the topic of redemption, it is the same as reformation and rebirth, so it is the same as being freed from hell and saved. For people in a spiritual religion, truth is the means of redemption, or of reformation and salvation, whereas goodness is the means for people in a heavenly religion. The reasons have been mentioned many times before: Spiritual people have no will to do what is good, but they have been endowed instead with the ability to understand what is good. An understanding of goodness is what is most often called truth—specifically, religious truth—while willing it and therefore acting on it is what is called good. So an understanding of goodness, or truth, is what introduces spiritual people to a will to do what is good, that is, to goodness. It does not introduce them into any will to do what is good that rises out of themselves, however, because they have lost any trace of a will to do good (§§895, 927, 2124). What it leads them to is a new will, which they receive from the Lord (§§863, 875, 1023, 1043, 1044), and when they receive this will, then they are specifically said to be redeemed.

I will bury my dead one means that they would emerge from their **2955**
nighttime and come alive. This is established by the symbolism of *being
buried* and of a *dead person*, which has been discussed above at §§2917,
2923, 2925, 2931, 2948. Here they are said to come alive, because they are
progressing in their acceptance of faith. It is from faith—that is, from the
good that comes of faith—that they receive life. Life does not come from
anywhere else.

Another reason *I will bury my dead one* means emerging from their
spiritual nighttime and coming alive is that when an earlier religion dies,
the Lord raises up a new one to replace it. So instead of death there is
life, and instead of night there is morning. Yet another reason is that in
anyone who is reforming and becoming spiritual the dead part is buried,
so to speak, and a new, living part rises again. So in place of the night
in such a person, or in place of the dark and cold, morning dawns with
its life and warmth. That is why angels, who live in the Lord's life, find
that the picture we have of burying a corpse is replaced with an image of
resurrection and new life.

This is the reality, too, because some kind of church always exists in
the world. When the old one passes away, and night falls, a new one rises
somewhere else, and morning dawns.

Genesis 23:14, 15. *And Ephron answered Abraham, saying to him, "My* **2956**
*lord, listen to me: The land is worth four hundred shekels of silver; between
me and you, what is that? And bury your dead one."*

Ephron answered Abraham, saying to him, symbolizes a stage of acceptance. *My lord, listen to me* symbolizes the first stage of acceptance. *The
land is worth four hundred shekels of silver* symbolizes the value of redemption through truth. *Between me and you, what is that?* means that he was
agreeing but still wanted to do it himself. *And bury your dead one* here
as before means emerging out of their nighttime and therefore being
revived.

Ephron answered Abraham, saying to him, symbolizes a stage of accep- **2957**
tance. This can be seen from the symbolism of *answering,* when the answer
is affirmative, as accepting (dealt with above at §2941). The fact that one
stage of acceptance is what *answering* and *saying* symbolize here becomes
clear from what follows [§§2958, 2960].

My lord, listen to me symbolizes the first stage of acceptance. This too **2958**
can be seen from what follows [§2960], and from the previous discussion
in §2945, where the same words occur. There, they constituted a refusal.

Here, they constitute agreement that is still tentative, since close on its heels comes "Between me and you, what is that?"—meaning that he was agreeing, yet wanted to do it for himself.

Besides, "My lord, listen to me" is simply a standard phrase designed to get the other person's attention, but it still implies a state of readiness for making a proposal.

2959   *The land is worth four hundred shekels of silver* symbolizes the value of redemption through truth. This can be seen from the symbolism of *four hundred shekels,* which is discussed below, and from that of *silver* as truth (discussed in §§1551, 2048, 2937).

The reason *four hundred shekels* symbolizes the value of redemption is that *four hundred* symbolizes devastation, while a *shekel* symbolizes the value of a thing. For a definition of devastation, see §§2455 at the end, 2682, 2694, 2699, 2702, 2704. The definition is twofold. One kind occurs when the church is completely destroyed—that is, when there is no longer any charity or faith. At that point it is said to be devastated, or laid waste. The other occurs when people in the church are reduced to a condition of ignorance and also of tribulation in order that the evils and falsities in them can be detached from them and seemingly dispelled. People who emerge from this kind of devastation are the ones who are specifically said to be redeemed, because they then learn about the good urged and the truth taught by faith, and the Lord reforms and regenerates them, as noted in the sections referred to.

Now, when the number four hundred applies to a period of time (such as four hundred years), it is a symbol for whatever length of time devastation lasts and what conditions are then like. So when the number applies to shekels, it symbolizes the value of redemption; and when *silver* is mentioned too, it symbolizes the value of redemption through truth.

[2] The words said to Abraham in Genesis 15:13 show that four hundred years is a symbol for the length of time devastation lasts and what conditions are then like: "Jehovah said to Abram, 'You must know positively that your seed will be immigrants in a land not theirs; and they will serve [the people of that land], and these will afflict them *four hundred years.*'" Look at the explanation there [§1847] to see that the four hundred years means the length of time the children of Israel spent in Egypt. Still, it is not the length of time they spent in Egypt that is meant but something else that no one can see except from the inner meaning. The

evidence is that their stay there lasted only half that amount of time, as the generations from Jacob to Moses make quite plain. From Jacob came Levi; from Levi, Kohath; from Kohath, Amram; and from Amram, Aaron and Moses (Exodus 6:16–20). Levi and his son Kohath went with Jacob to Egypt (Genesis 46:[7,] 11), and Moses belonged to the second generation after that. Moses was eighty when he spoke to Pharaoh (Exodus 7:7), so you can see that about 215 years passed between Jacob's arrival and the departure of his descendants.

[3] The words of Exodus 12:40, 41 show even more clearly that "four hundred" in Scripture means something else than what the number itself means on the narrative level: "The residence of the children of Israel during which they resided in Egypt was *four hundred thirty years.* And it happened at the end of *four hundred thirty* years—and it happened on that same day—that all the armies of Jehovah went out from the land of Egypt." In reality, the children of Israel stayed there only half that number of years. It was from Abraham's arrival in Egypt that the 430 years are dated. The statement is phrased the way it is, then, for the sake of the inner meaning lying hidden in the words. On an inner level, the stay of the children of Jacob in Egypt represents and symbolizes the devastation of the religion. What conditions were then like, and how long the devastation lasted, is depicted by the number of years: thirty and four hundred. Thirty depicts the state of devastation that Jacob's descendants experienced, which was nonexistent, since their character was such that no state of devastation could reform them. For the symbolism of the number thirty, see §2276. Four hundred years depict the state of devastation that people in the church usually experience.

[4] People who come out the other side of this devastation, then, are the ones said to be redeemed, which is clear from words addressed to Moses:

> Therefore say to the children of Israel, "I am Jehovah, and I will lead you out from under the burdens of Egypt and free you from their enslavement and *redeem* you with an outstretched arm and great judgments." (Exodus 6:6)

And in another place:

> Jehovah led you out by a mighty hand and *redeemed* you from the house of slaves, from the hand of Pharaoh, king of Egypt. (Deuteronomy 7:8; 13:5)

And in another place:

> Remember that you were a slave in the land of Egypt but Jehovah your God *redeemed* you. (Deuteronomy 15:15; 24:18)

In Samuel:

> ... your people, whom you *redeemed* for yourself from Egypt. (2 Samuel 7:23)

Since people who emerge from a state of devastation are said to be redeemed, the four hundred shekels symbolize the value of redemption.

[5] The symbolism of a *shekel* as the value of a thing can be seen from the following passages in the Word. In Moses:

> Every *appraisal* of yours shall be by the *sacred shekel*. (Leviticus 27:25)

And in another place:

> When souls have committed a transgression and sinned in error concerning Jehovah's holy things, they shall bring their guilt offering to Jehovah: a sound ram from the flock, as you *appraise* it in *silver shekels* measured by the *sacred shekel*. (Leviticus 5:15)

This shows that a shekel symbolizes the value or appraised worth of a thing. It is called the sacred shekel because value has to do with truth and goodness from the Lord. Truth and goodness from the Lord is holiness itself in the church. That is why the sacred shekel is also mentioned in many other places, such as Exodus 30:24; Leviticus 27:3; Numbers 3:47, 50; 7:13, 19, 25, 31, 37, 43, 49, 55, 61, 67, 73; 18:16.

[6] A shekel is the value of holiness, as the Book of Ezekiel makes quite plain, where it talks about the holy land and the holy city. What it says there about shekels is this:

> A *shekel* there is *twenty gerahs;* twenty *shekels* [and] twenty-five *shekels* [and] fifteen *shekels* shall be a mina [pound] to you. (Ezekiel 45:12)

Anyone can see that the shekel, the pound, and the numbers here symbolize something holy, or in other words, goodness and truth. The holy land, and the holy city in it (the new Jerusalem), which forms the subject of this verse, actually means the Lord's kingdom. In that kingdom, a shekel does not mean a shekel; gerahs, gerahs; a pound, a pound; or a numerical count, a count. Instead, the actual number, by its symbolism on an inner level, defines the value of the goodness and truth. [7] In Moses:

> A man shall give in atonement for his soul—to prevent a plague—a *half shekel* measured by the *sacred shekel (twenty gerahs a shekel);* and the half *shekel* shall be a terumah [raised offering] to Jehovah. (Exodus 30:12, 13)

The ten gerahs (a half shekel) mean the remnant we receive from the Lord. A remnant consists of traces of goodness and truth stored away inside us, and it is symbolized by the number ten (see §§576, 1738, 1906, 2284). Since a remnant consists of traces of goodness and truth stored away inside us by the Lord (§§1906, 2284), it is also called a terumah (or raised offering) to Jehovah and is said to be the means of atoning for one's soul. The statement that a shekel is twenty gerahs recurs several times, as in the passage just quoted; Leviticus 27:25; Numbers 3:47; 18:16; and other places. It recurs because "a shekel is twenty gerahs" symbolizes the value of the goodness in the remnant, twenty meaning that goodness (see §2280). For this reason, a shekel was also the weight by which people measured the value of both gold and silver (Genesis 24:22; Exodus 38:24; Ezekiel 4:10; 45:12). They used it for measuring the value of gold because gold symbolizes goodness (§§113, 1551, 1552) and for measuring the value of silver because silver symbolizes truth (1551, 2048).

Clearly, then, a piece of land worth four hundred shekels of silver symbolizes the value of redemption through truth.

This explains why the verse speaks of land, since its focal point is a spiritual religion, and the Lord reforms and regenerates a spiritual religion by means of truth (§2954). To see that land symbolizes the church, consult §§662, 1066, 1068, 1262, 1733, 1850, 2117, 2118 at the end.

Between me and you, what is that? means that he was agreeing but still wanted to do it himself—still wanted to prepare or reform himself. This **2960** can be seen when the literal meaning is applied to the inner meaning, which deals with reformation. Earlier, Ephron said, "The field I give you; and the cave that is in it—to you I give it" (verse 11). These words meant that they wanted to prepare themselves on their own, so far as the requirements of religion and faith went, or in other words, to reform themselves. This is what the first stage is like for people who are reforming (see §2946). When they learn more truth, or more about the faith, however, they reach a second stage, in which they agree [to let the Lord reform them] but still want to do it themselves. That is the stage the current verse focuses on, but a third is soon depicted, in which they really believe that the Lord reforms them.

[2] The reason they are like this at first was explained above in §2946, but the reasons why they still want to reform themselves—even when they progress in their knowledge of truth (or faith) and acknowledge that the Lord does it—are these: The cloud of ignorance breaks up only gradually. It takes time to confirm and strengthen the truth. And goodness is perfected as we absorb knowledge of the truth. Real goodness, which forms the receiving ground for truth, enables us not only to acknowledge but even to believe that the Lord is the one who reforms us. This stage is the third, and a fourth follows it: We actually perceive that the Lord does the reforming. There are not many who reach this stage during bodily life, because it is an angelic one, but people who have been reborn enter it in the other world.

This shows that the inner meaning here depicts people in a spiritual religion, illustrating what conditions are like for them before they mature, when they start to mature, and finally when they finish maturing.

2961   *And bury your dead one* means emerging out of their night and therefore being revived. This is established by the symbolism of a *dead person* as nighttime in regard to religious truth and of *being buried* as reviving. The symbolism has been dealt with several times already; see §§2917, 2923, 2925, 2931, 2948, 2955.

The reason the phrase comes up so many times in the current chapter is that it is talking about emergence from nighttime conditions for religious truth and about revival—that is, about the reformation and rebirth of a spiritual religion.

2962   Genesis 23:16. *And Abraham listened to Ephron, and Abraham weighed out to Ephron the silver that he spoke of in the ears of the sons of Heth: four hundred shekels of silver crossing [the palm of] a merchant.*

Abraham listened to Ephron symbolizes confirmation that they would obey. *And Abraham weighed out to Ephron the silver* symbolizes redemption. *That he spoke of in the ears of the sons of Heth* means so far as the people in the new religion were able. *Four hundred shekels of silver* symbolizes the value of redemption. *Crossing [the palm of] a merchant* means when it was adapted to their state.

2963   *Abraham listened to Ephron* symbolizes confirmation—by people who were capable of accepting the goodness urged and the truth taught by the religion—that they would obey. This is established by the symbolism of *listening* as obeying (discussed in §2542) and by the representation of *Ephron* as people who were capable of accepting religious goodness and truth (discussed above in §2933). The words here make it clear that they were indeed capable and did indeed confirm, since it says that Abraham listened to Ephron.

And Abraham weighed out to Ephron the silver symbolizes redemption. **2964** This can be seen from the meaning of *weighing out silver* as buying and in a spiritual sense as redeeming. The silver here is the same as the four hundred shekels, which symbolize the value of redemption, as shown above in §2959.

That he spoke of in the ears of the sons of Heth means so far as the people **2965** in the new religion were able, as can be seen from the symbolism of *speaking in the ears* and of the *sons of Heth*. On an inner level, *speaking* symbolizes both perceiving and willing. (For its symbolism as perceiving, see §2619, and for its symbolism as willing, see §2626.) *Ears,* though, symbolize obedience (§2542). So speaking in the ears means so far as one is able, since ability comes of accepting and so of obeying what we perceive and will. The meaning can also be seen from the symbolism of the *sons of Heth* as people in the new, spiritual religion (discussed above in §2913).

People in the church are reformed; in other words, the truth that belongs to faith is planted in them and unites with the goodness that belongs to love for others. This will be discussed later on in the current verse, at §2967.

Four hundred shekels of silver symbolizes the value of redemption. This **2966** was shown above at §2959, but the value or price of redemption needs to be defined. Redemption belongs to the Lord alone, so the price of redemption does too. Our acceptance of redemption is also called its price, since the value of redemption in us is equal to our acceptance of it. The price of redemption is the merit and righteousness the Lord gained through his heaviest trials, in which—using his own power—he united his human nature to his divine, and his divine nature to his human, and by uniting them saved the human race, especially those who are part of the spiritual church. On the point that the Lord became righteousness by means of his most severe trials, see §§1813, 2025, 2026, 2027. He united his human nature to his divine, and his divine nature to his human (1725, 1729, 1733, 1737, 1813, 2083) by his own power (1616, 1921, 2025, 2026, 2083, 2500, 2523, 2632). And by uniting them, he saved the human race, especially those who are part of the spiritual church (2661, 2716). All this is what the price of redemption means.

[2] The fact that our acceptance of redemption is also called its price, since the value in us is equal to our acceptance, can become clear from this explanation: The Lord's divinity is what makes the church in us. After all, nothing is considered religious if it is not the Lord's own. The goodness that comes of love and charity and the truth that comes of faith are what make the thing we call a church, and everyone knows that everything good comes from the Lord, and everything true also comes from him. No goodness or truth that comes from us is good or true. This makes it clear that the price of redemption in us is equal to our acceptance.

[3] Jews put so little value on the Lord's redemption that they considered it almost worthless, and that is why Zechariah says:

> I said to them, "If it is good in your eyes, give me my pay, and if not, decline to." And they weighed out my pay: *thirty silver [coins]*. And Jehovah said to me, "Throw it to the potter, the *grand price* at which I was appraised among them." (Zechariah 11:12, 13)

And in Matthew:

> They took the *thirty silver [coins]—the price of the one appraised*, whom they bought from the children of Israel—and gave it for the potter's field, as the Lord commanded me. (Matthew 27:9, 10)

Thirty means so small an amount as to be almost nothing; see §2276. So it means that the Jews did not value the Lord's merit or his redemption at all. On the other hand, among people who believe that everything good and everything true comes from the Lord, the value of redemption is symbolized by forty, and in a higher degree, by four hundred.

2967   *Crossing [the palm of] a merchant* means when it was adapted to their state, as can be seen from the symbolism of a *merchant* and so of *crossing [the palm of] a merchant*. In the Word, a *merchant* symbolizes people who have a knowledge of what is good and true, and merchandise symbolizes the knowledge itself. So silver *crossing [the palm of] a merchant* symbolizes the amount of truth a person can take in or, to put it another way, truth as adapted to the individual's state and ability. That this added phrase involves some hidden meaning, anyone can see. The symbolism of a merchant and merchandise is dealt with below.

[2] To address the phenomenon itself, the case is this: Everyone who is reforming and being reborn receives the gift of neighborly love and faith from the Lord, but each according to his or her ability and state.

From the time we are small, you see, we steep ourselves in evils and misconceptions that keep any one of us from receiving the same gift as another. Before we can regenerate, the evils and misconceptions have to be stripped away. The amount of heavenly and spiritual life that remains afterward determines the extent to which that remainder can be illuminated with truth and enriched with goodness. It is the remnant—the goodness and truth the Lord has stored away in us—that then receives life. These good impulses and true ideas are something we acquire from early childhood on through to the time we reform. Some of us acquire more, some less. They are preserved in our inner self and cannot be called forth from there until our outer self has been brought into correspondence [with our inner self], which mostly happens during times of trial and many other kinds of devastation. Bodily demands, which run counter to goodness and truth—demands such as those of self-love and materialism—must be put to rest first. Until then, heavenly and spiritual qualities, which relate to a desire for goodness and truth, cannot flow in. That is why we are each reformed in accord with our state and ability.

The Lord even teaches this in Matthew 25:14, 15, 16, 17, and following verses, in the parable about a man who went abroad. He called his slaves and handed his riches over to them—*five talents* to one, *two* to another, and *one* to a third, to each according to *that individual's ability.* The one that received five talents *did business* with them and made five more talents. So too did the one that received two talents, and this one also made two more. Then there is the parable in Luke 19:12, 13, and following verses about the ten slaves to whom he gave ten minas to *do business* with.

[3] These passages quoted from Matthew and Luke show that a *merchant* symbolizes people who have a knowledge of goodness and truth, and that merchandise symbolizes the knowledge itself. The following passages show the same thing. In Ezekiel:

> You are to say to Tyre, "You are one who lives at the entries to the sea, the *peoples' dealer* to many islands. Tarshish was *your merchant* for the abundance of all your riches. For silver, for iron, for tin and lead they sold *your market goods.* Javan, Tubal, and Meshech were *your dealers;* for human souls and vessels of bronze they sold *your cargo.* The children of Dedan were *your dealers.* Many islands were your *merchandise* at hand. Syria was *your merchant* for the abundance of your works. Judah and

the land of Israel were *your dealers* in wheat, minnith, and pannag; and for honey and oil and balsam they sold *your cargo*. Damascus was *your merchant* for the abundance of your works from the abundance of all your riches—for the wine of Helbon and wool of Zahar. And Dan and Javan gave you thread for *your market goods*. Dedan was *your dealer* in free-moving clothes for the chariot. The Arab and all the chiefs of Kedar were your *merchants* at hand, for lambs, for rams and he-goats; for these they were *your merchants*. The *dealers* of Sheba and Raamah were *your dealers* in the finest of every perfume. Haran and Canneh and Eden were the *dealers* of Sheba. Assyria, Chilmad were your *dealers*. These were *your dealers* in perfect things." (Ezekiel 27:[2,] 3, 12, 13, 15, 16, 17, 18, 19, 20, 21, 22, 23, 24)

This is about Tyre, which symbolizes knowledge of what is good and true, as may be seen in §1201. It also becomes clear from the details here. The trade and business and wares mentioned mean nothing else. So Tyre is called one who lives at the entries to the sea—water meaning knowledge and the sea meaning collected knowledge (§28). Tyre is also called the peoples' dealer to many islands, or in other words, even to people practicing a kind of worship that is relatively distant [from true worship]. For islands as more distant forms of worship, see §1158. For the symbolism of Tarshish, see 1156. The silver, iron, tin, and lead from Tarshish are different levels of truth in their proper order, right down to the most external kind, which is truth as we receive it through our physical senses. For the symbolism of silver, see 1551, 2048; for that of iron, 425, 426. For that of Javan, Tubal, and Meshech, see 1151, 1152, 1153, 1155. Human souls and vessels of bronze from those places are various aspects of earthly life. A soul means all the life that comes from the Lord (1000, 1040, 1436, 1742), and vessels of bronze mean earthly kinds of goodness that receive his life (425, 1551). For the symbolism of Dedan, see 1172; for that of Syria, 1232, 1234. Judah and the land of Israel as dealers in wheat, minnith and pannag, honey, oil, and balsam symbolize heavenly and spiritual messages in the Word. The rest of the nations and their merchandise, as listed, mean different general categories and specific types of truth and goodness, and therefore knowledge possessed by the people that Tyre symbolizes.

[4] Knowledge is the source of wisdom and understanding, as the same prophet makes very clear in these words:

Son of humankind, say to the ruler of Tyre, "In *your wisdom* and in *your understanding* you made yourself riches, and you made gold and silver for your treasures. In the abundance of your *wisdom,* in *your business dealings,* you multiplied your riches, and your heart is haughty in your riches. Therefore look: I am bringing on you foreigners, the violent among the nations." (Ezekiel 28:2, 4, 5, 6, 7)

Here it is very clear that the wares they dealt in mean the knowledge of what is good and true, because that and nothing else is the source of wisdom and understanding. This is why the passage says, "In your wisdom and in your understanding you made yourself riches, and you made gold and silver for your treasures." On the other hand, when people acquire knowledge for selfish reasons, in order to eclipse others and to amass either reputation or wealth, they become lifeless and lose any knowledge they had. During bodily life they embrace falsity as true, and evil as good; and in the other life they are also deprived of any true ideas. This is why the passage says, "Because your heart is haughty in your riches, therefore look: I am bringing on you foreigners"—falsity— "and the violent among the nations"—evil. [5] And elsewhere in the same prophet:

Tyre is like one cut off from the middle of the sea. In the export of *your market goods* from the seas, you satisfied many peoples; in the abundance of your riches and of *your cargo* you made the monarchs of the earth wealthy. Now you have been broken by the seas, in the depths of the water; *your cargo* and your whole assembly have fallen in the midst of it. The *merchants* among the peoples grind their teeth over you. (Ezekiel 27:32, 33, 34, 36)

And in Isaiah:

An oracle concerning Tyre: The inhabitants of the island, the *merchant* of Sidon crossing the sea, keep quiet; they have filled you up. And the seed of Sihor, the harvest of the river, its produce, came on many waters, and you were the *merchandise of the nations.* Who has proposed this over Tyre, which crowns itself, whose *merchants* are rulers? (Isaiah 23:[1,] 2, 3, 8)

This is talking about the devastation of Tyre.

[6] John says that Babylon too had merchandise and wares, which are the adulterated knowledge of what is good and the falsified knowledge of what is true:

Babylon has given some of the wine of her whoredom's fury to all the nations to drink, and the monarchs of the earth have committed whoredom with her. And the *merchants of the earth* have grown rich on her wealth of pleasures. The *merchants of the earth* will cry and mourn over her, because their *wares* no one buys anymore—*wares* of gold and silver and precious stone and pearl and fine linen and red-violet fabric and silk and scarlet fabric [and so on]. The *merchants* of these things—who have grown rich off her—will stand far away (for fear of her torment), crying and mourning. (Revelation 18:3, 11, 12, 15)

Babylon is worship whose outward expression looks holy but whose inward contents are profane (see §§1182, 1283, 1295, 1304, 1306, 1326). What its merchandise and wares mean, then, is clear.

[7] The Lord's words in Matthew show that a merchant is someone who obtains knowledge of truth and goodness and consequently understanding and wisdom:

The kingdom of the heavens is like a *merchant* looking for beautiful pearls who—when he had found a precious pearl—leaving, *sold* everything that he had and *bought* it. (Matthew 13:45, 46)

The beautiful pearl is neighborly love, or the goodness required by faith.

[8] Isaiah shows that all knowledge of what is good and true comes from the Lord:

This is what Jehovah has said: "The labor of Egypt, and the *merchandise of Cush and of Seba's inhabitants*—tall men—will pass over you and will belong to you. They will walk after you; in chains they will pass over, and to you they will bow down. To you they will pray: 'Only among you does God exist, and there is no god besides.'" (Isaiah 45:14)

This is about the Lord's divine humanity.

[9] The evidence above now shows what it means to ply the merchant's trade, or to buy and sell: it means to obtain knowledge of goodness and truth and, in the process, goodness itself. The same prophet shows that we obtain it from the Lord alone:

Oh, everyone who is thirsty, come to the water, and whoever has no silver, come, buy and eat! And come, without silver and without the price buy wine and milk! (Isaiah 55:1, 2)

The buying stands for obtaining, and the wine stands for spiritual truth (§§1071, 1798), while the milk stands for spiritual goodness (§2184). Anyone can see that going to the water does not mean going to the water, buying does not mean buying, silver does not mean silver, and wine and milk do not mean wine and milk. Instead they mean the kind of thing that is said to correspond in the inner sense. This is God's Word, and all its individual words—which rise out of the physical world and out of humankind's physical senses—have spiritual and heavenly attributes of God corresponding to them. In this way and no other was the Word divinely inspired.

Genesis 23:17, 18. *And the field of Ephron that was in Machpelah, which is in front of Mamre—the field and the cave that was in it and every tree that was in the field, that was within its whole border all around—was established for Abraham as a purchase in the eyes of the sons of Heth, in [the eyes] of all those entering the gate of his city.*

2968

The field of Ephron was established means that this is a feature of the church. *That was in Machpelah, which is in front of Mamre,* symbolizes the quality and extent of rebirth. *The field and the cave that was in it* means in respect to religious goodness and truth. *And every tree that was in the field* means relatively deep knowledge in the church. *That was within its whole border all around* symbolizes knowledge that is relatively superficial. *For Abraham as a purchase* means that these things are to the Lord's credit alone. *In the eyes of the sons of Heth* means according to the understanding of those people. *In [the eyes] of all those entering the gate of his city* means in regard to all the teachings.

The field of Ephron was established means that this is a feature of the church. This meaning is established by the symbolism of a *field* as the church and as theology (dealt with in §§368, 2936) and by the representation of *Ephron* as people capable of accepting religious goodness and truth, which are aspects of the church (dealt with in §2933). *The field of Ephron was established,* then, symbolizes a feature of the church.

2969

That was in Machpelah, which is in front of Mamre, symbolizes the quality and extent of rebirth. This can be seen from the symbolism of *Machpelah* as rebirth through religious truth, and from that of *Mamre* as its quality and extent. When a cave is connected with *Machpelah*—that is, when the text mentions a cave in Machpelah—it symbolizes faith that is dimly lit (§2935). When Machpelah is mentioned without reference to a cave, though, and the text goes on afterward to say that it held a field and cave, it means rebirth. A field and cave symbolize religious goodness and truth, which are the means of rebirth.

2970

Besides, Machpelah was also the site of a grave, and a grave symbolizes rebirth (§2916).

Mamre was Hebron, as verse 19 below says, and was in Hebron, as Genesis 13:18 says. Accordingly, it actually symbolizes the quality and extent of a thing. Here, where it is connected with Machpelah, it symbolizes the quality and extent of rebirth. When connected with Hebron, it symbolizes the quality and extent of the church. When connected with oak groves, it symbolizes the quality and extent of perception, as noted at §1616. So Mamre, a place where Abraham lived (Genesis 13:18) and where Isaac lived and Jacob visited (Genesis 35:27), simply means the measure of a thing's condition.

2971 *The field and the cave that was in it* means in respect to religious goodness and truth, as can be seen from the following: A *field* symbolizes the church and the goodness itself of the church. Heavenliness, or goodness—which has to do with love for the Lord and charity for one's neighbor—is compared to the ground, and to a field, and is even called the ground or a field. The reason for the simile and metaphor is that heavenliness, or goodness, is the soil that receives religious truth, which is compared to seed and is also called seed. And a *cave* symbolizes religious truth that is dimly lit, as noted in §2935. It is said to be dimly lit because it exists with spiritual people (§§1043, 2708 at the beginning, 2715).

2972 *And every tree that was in the field* means relatively deep knowledge in the church, as can be seen from the following: A *tree* symbolizes perceptions, when the focus is on a heavenly church (as discussed in §§103, 2163); and when the focus is on a spiritual church, it symbolizes knowledge (as discussed in §2722). Here the knowledge is relatively deep, because it says, "every tree that was in the field," and then, "that was within its whole border all around," which symbolizes knowledge that is relatively superficial. And a *field* symbolizes the church, as mentioned above.

The text mentions trees that were in the field and within its borders all around for the sake of this inner meaning. Otherwise they would not be worth mentioning in the Word, which is divine.

2973 *That was within its whole border all around* symbolizes knowledge that is relatively superficial. This can be seen from the symbolism of *borders* and *all around* as things that are relatively shallow (discussed in §2936). So the *tree that was within the border all around* symbolizes knowledge that is relatively superficial. Superficial knowledge is a knowledge of rituals, and of teachings that form the outward surface of the church. Deeper knowledge is a knowledge of teachings that form the inward heart of the church. What the outward dimension and the inward dimension of the church are has been stated several times before.

[2] In addition, the Word often mentions the middle and the environs. In respect to the land of Canaan, for instance, the region of Zion and Jerusalem was called the middle, while the nations all around were called the environs. Canaan represented the Lord's kingdom, Zion representing the heavenly part, and Jerusalem, the spiritual part. That is where Jehovah (the Lord) had his dwelling place. The surrounding parts, all the way to the edges, represented heavenly and spiritual qualities flowing and branching out from there in their proper order. At the outermost borders, the representation of heavenly and spiritual qualities ended. These representations traced their origin to phenomena in the Lord's kingdom in the heavens. The Lord as the sun is in the middle there, and from him comes all heavenly fire and spiritual light. The individuals who are closest enjoy the most light; those who are farther away have less; and the ones who are farthest receive the least. That is where the outer limits are and where hell, which is outside heaven, begins.

[3] The situation with heavenly fire and spiritual light is this: The heavenly traits of innocence and love, and the spiritual traits of charity and faith, come in the same proportions as the warmth and light the inhabitants enjoy, since these traits are the source of all warmth and light in the heavens.

That is the reason, then, why the middle symbolizes the deepest part, and the environs, the shallowest. Other parts, going in order from deepest to shallowest, have a level of innocence, love, and charity that matches their distance from the center.

The same is true with every community in heaven. The people at its center are the best of their kind, and there is less of the love and charity that characterizes their kind the more remote they are. In other words, love and charity fades in them in proportion to their distance from the core.

[4] The case is the same in people on earth. Our inmost core is where the Lord lives in us and is the site from which he governs everything in our surrounding parts. When we let him arrange the circumference in a pattern that corresponds with the inmost parts, our condition is such that we can be received into heaven. Under those circumstances, our deepest, intermediate, and outward parts act as one. When we do not let the Lord arrange the circumference in a corresponding pattern,

on the other hand, then the more we refuse, the further we pull back from heaven.

The human soul lies at a person's center, or in a person's inmost core; the body surrounds it on the outside, as is recognized. The body is what envelops and clothes the soul or its spirit.

[5] In people devoted to heavenly and spiritual kinds of love, goodness flows in from the Lord through their soul into their body and fills their body with light. In people devoted to bodily and worldly kinds of love, however, goodness cannot flow in from the Lord through their soul into their body. Their interiors are in the dark, so their body is, too, just as the Lord teaches in Matthew:

> The lamp of the body is the eye; if the eye is unclouded, the whole body is light. If the eye is bad, the whole body is dark. So if the light is darkness, how immense the darkness! (Matthew 6:22, 23)

The eye symbolizes the intellectual side of the soul (§2701). [6] The case is even worse, though, in people whose inward parts are dark shadows and whose outward parts seem full of light. They are the kind of people who mimic angels of light on the outside but are devils on the inside. They are called Babylon. When the parts that are *all around* are destroyed in them, they rush headlong into hell. This situation was portrayed in the city of Jericho when, after the priests along with the ark had *circled* it seven times and blown their horns, its walls fell and the city was exterminated (Joshua 6:1–17). The same thing is meant in Jeremiah:

> Draw yourselves up against Babylon *all around*, all you who bend the bow; trumpet over it *all around*. It has given its hand [in surrender]. Its foundations have fallen; its walls have been destroyed. (Jeremiah 50:14, 15)

This, now, shows what "all around" means.

Moreover, the Word mentions "environs" several times, such as Jeremiah 21:14; 46:14; 49:5; Ezekiel 36:3, 4, 7; 37:21; Amos 3:11; and other places, and they symbolize something on the outside. More will be said about them elsewhere, with the Lord's divine mercy.

2974   *For Abraham as a purchase* means that these things—the whole quality and extent of rebirth, in respect to religious goodness and truth, and therefore in respect to all deeper and shallower knowledge—are to the Lord's credit alone. This can be seen from the representation of *Abraham* as the Lord (dealt with many times before) and from the symbolism of a *purchase* as being his and therefore to his credit alone.

The main tenet of faith is that everything good and true is the Lord's and so comes from the Lord alone. The more deeply we acknowledge this, the deeper in heaven we are, because in heaven they perceive that it is so. In heaven, there is an atmosphere of perception that it is so, because people there live in the goodness that comes from the Lord alone, which is what is called being in the Lord. The different levels of that perception arrange themselves from the middle all the way out to the periphery, as noted just above in §2973.

In the eyes of the sons of Heth means in the understanding of those people—people in the new, spiritual religion. This can be seen from the symbolism of *eyes* as the intellect (discussed in §§212, 2701) and from that of the *sons of Heth* as people in the new, spiritual religion (discussed at §§2913, 2928). Above at verse 16 it was said that Abraham spoke in the ears of the sons of Heth, which meant according to their ability (2965, 2967). Here, though, it says "in the eyes of the sons of Heth," which means in their understanding. Above, it involves adapting to their will, but here it involves adapting to their understanding. Both parts of us are reformed. If our will and intellect do not agree in such a way that they form a single whole, we have not been reborn. That is, goodness and truth—or to say the same thing another way, love for others and faith—need to be united, love for others being a matter of the will, and faith being a matter of the intellect. That is the reason it first says "in the ears of the sons of Heth," while here it says "in the eyes of the sons of Heth."

2975

In [the eyes] of all those entering the gate of his city means in regard to all the teachings, as is established by the remarks above at §2943, where the same words occur.

2976

Genesis 23:19. *And after this, Abraham buried Sarah his wife at the cave of the field of Machpelah on the face of Mamre (that is, Hebron, in the land of Canaan).*

2977

After this means that it was so. *Abraham buried Sarah his wife* means that they would receive truth united with goodness from the Lord. *At the cave of the field of Machpelah on the face of Mamre* means that in this way they would regenerate so far as they could. *That is, Hebron* means that this is a new religion. *In the land of Canaan* means which is a single religion in the Lord's kingdom.

2978   *After this* means that it was so, as the sequence of ideas demonstrates, because this is the ending; the people have been reborn and therefore a new, spiritual religion has been established.

2979   *Abraham buried Sarah his wife* means that they would receive truth united with goodness from the Lord, as can be seen from the following: *Burying* means being reborn, as mentioned above in §§2916, 2917. We are regenerate when we have received truth united to goodness from the Lord, as will soon be discussed. *Abraham* represents the Lord, as noted many times before. And *Sarah* in her role as wife represents truth united to goodness, as dealt with at §§2063, 2065, 2507.

[2] This is how matters stand with the rebirth of spiritual people: First they learn the true ideas that belong to faith, and from then on the Lord maintains in them a desire for truth. The goodness that faith calls for, which is charity toward their neighbor, is instilled in them at the same time, but in such a way that they hardly realize it, since it hides within their desire for truth. The purpose is for truth, which belongs to faith, to unite with goodness, which belongs to charity. As time passes, their desire for the truth belonging to faith grows, and they look to truth for the sake of the goal, which is goodness, or (to put it another way) life. This they do more and more. In this way, truth is instilled into goodness, and when that happens, their life becomes steeped in goodness that accords with the truth instilled into it. So they act (or seem to themselves to act) out of goodness.

Up till this time, the truth constituting faith is the most important consideration to them, but afterward, the goodness constituting life is. [3] When the two switch, the person has been reborn. We are reborn, however, in accord with the quality and extent of the truth instilled into our goodness; and when truth and goodness act in unison, we are reborn in accord with the quality and extent of the goodness.

That is how matters stand with all rebirth.

The point of regeneration is to be capable of being welcomed into heaven. Heaven is simply a marriage between truth and goodness, and between goodness and truth. (See §§2508, 2618, 2728, 2729.) Unless truth and goodness form a marriage in us, we cannot enter into the heavenly marriage—that is, into heaven.

2980   *At the cave of the field of Machpelah on the face of Mamre* means that in this way they would regenerate so far as they could, as can be seen from the following: A cave symbolizes religious truth that is dimly lit, as noted at §2935. A field symbolizes religious goodness, as noted at §2971. Machpelah on the face of Mamre—in front of Mamre, in other words—symbolizes the quality and extent of regeneration, as noted in §2970. So the whole phrase means that they were reborn through religious truth and goodness so far as they could be. That is, they were reborn in accord with their ability and understanding (2913, 2928, 2975).

That is, Hebron means that this is a new religion, as can be seen from the symbolism of Hebron, which means a spiritual religion, as discussed earlier in the current chapter, at §2909. The verse there spoke of "Kiriath-arba, that is, Hebron," because Kiriath-arba symbolizes truth in the church, while Hebron symbolizes goodness in the church. The current verse no longer mentions Kiriath-arba but only Hebron, because the theme here is regenerate people, who no longer act at the inspiration of truth but of goodness, as noted above at §2979. **2981**

In the land of Canaan means which is a single religion in the Lord's kingdom, as can be seen from the representation of the *land of Canaan* as the Lord's kingdom, which is discussed at §§1413, 1437, 1585, 1607. **2982**

This is how matters stand with the Lord's churches: In ancient days, a large number existed simultaneously. Individual religions differed in their doctrines, as they do today, but they still made a single whole in this respect: they acknowledged love for the Lord and charity for one's neighbor as the main concern and the truly essential element. So for them, doctrine existed to show them not how to think but how to live.

When each and every person considers love for the Lord and charity for one's neighbor (living a good life, in other words) to be the essential thing, then no matter how many religions there are, they make a single religion. Each is then one in the Lord's kingdom.

Heaven is the same way. It contains numerous communities, each of them distinct from the others, and yet they constitute a single heaven, because everyone in them loves the Lord and shows charity toward the next person.

[2] The situation is entirely different with religions whose members call faith the main concern of the church, imagining they will be saved if they know this and think it, no matter what kind of life they live. When this is the case, many religions do not make a single religion; in fact they are not even religions. The goodness taught by faith—that is, an actual life of love and charity lived in accord with the tenets of faith—is what makes a church. Doctrines exist for the sake of life.

Anyone can see this. What is doctrine if it does not exist for some purpose? And what is the purpose if not life? In other words, what is the purpose if not for us to act the way doctrine teaches us to?

Such people do say that the real, true faith that saves is trust [in salvation], but this trust cannot possibly exist except in the context of a good life. Without a good life, there is no receptiveness, and where there is no receptiveness, there is no trust. An exception is the semblance that sometimes appears during emotional or physical illness, when the cravings of self-love and materialism die down. In people who live evil lives, though, this supposed trust evaporates completely when the crisis ends or is averted. Even the evil have confidence. If you want to know what kind you have, look at the feelings and goals you cherish and the way you live your life.

2983 *Genesis 23:20. And the field and the cave that was in it was established for Abraham as the possession of a grave from the sons of Heth.*

The field and the cave that was in it symbolizes the church and its faith. *Was established for Abraham as the possession of a grave* means that it would come from the Lord alone, through regeneration. *From the sons of Heth* means that it would be made up of people outside the church.

2984 *The field and the cave that was in it* symbolizes the church and its faith. This can be seen from the symbolism of a *field* as the church (discussed above at §§2969, 2971) and from that of a *cave* as faith (discussed at §§2935, 2971).

Both the church and its faith are mentioned because the church is said to exist where there is charitable goodness (and therefore practical goodness), while faith is said to exist where there is truth (which is attached to it).

2985 *Was established for Abraham as the possession of a grave* means that it would come from the Lord alone, through regeneration, as can be seen from the following: *Abraham* represents the Lord, as has been said many times before. A *possession* symbolizes what is the Lord's and therefore what belongs to him alone (see §2974 above). And a *grave* symbolizes rebirth, as also noted above, at §2916.

2986 *From the sons of Heth* means that it would be made up of people outside the church, as can be seen from the symbolism of the *sons of Heth*.

The *sons of Heth* were not the people among whom the church was established; rather they are the people who represent that church. Everything in the Word is representative. The people in it do not mean the individuals named but various aspects of the Lord's kingdom and the church.

The sons of Heth, as mentioned many times before [§§2913, 2919, 2928, 2940, 2965, 2975], symbolize the new religion or, to put it another way, the people of the new religion. The new religion, however, was to be a church of the Gentiles, or a church from among the Gentiles. This is clear from Abraham's words to the sons of Heth in verse 4, "An immigrant and settler I am with you," meaning that the Lord was unknown to them but could still be present with them (§2915). The children of Heth, then, plainly symbolize a religion made up of people outside the church. They are the only ones who can be said not to know about the Lord.

[2] In addition, it needs to be known that when any church disappears—that is, when love for others dies—and the Lord establishes a new religion, rarely if ever does this happen among the people of the old religion. Instead, it happens among people who had no church before, or in other words, among Gentiles. That is what occurred when the earliest church died; a new one, called Noah (or the ancient church that followed the Flood), was then established among Gentiles, or in other words, among people where no church had previously existed.

Likewise when this church died; a substitute for a church was then instituted among Abraham's descendants in Jacob's line. So it too was established among Gentiles. After all, when Abraham was called, he was a Gentile (see §§1356, 1992, 2559). Jacob's descendants themselves became still more gentile in Egypt, to the point where they knew absolutely nothing about Jehovah and therefore about any aspect of divine worship. After this substitute for a church came to a close, and Jews were rejected, an early [Christian] church was established among Gentiles. It will be the same with the present church, which is called Christian.

[3] The reason the Lord institutes a new religion among people outside the church is that they do not adopt falsities as premises that oppose the true tenets of the faith, since those tenets are unknown to them. When we absorb false premises from childhood on, and later confirm them, they need to be dispelled before we can regenerate and become part of the church. In fact, people outside the church cannot profane anything holy by living an evil life, because no one can profane anything holy without knowing what it is (§§593, 1008, 1010, 1059). Since people who are not in the church lack knowledge and are free of stumbling blocks, their condition is better suited to accepting truth than that of people in the church. Anyone among them who lives a good life readily

accepts truth; see more on them in §§932, 1032, 1059, 1327, 1328, 1366, 2049, 2051, 2589–2604.

Representation and Correspondence

2987   FEW know what representations and correspondences are. No one *can* know what they are without knowing there is a spiritual world that is distinctly different from the natural world. Correspondences exist between spiritual attributes and physical objects, and representations are things that emerge from spiritual phenomena in physical form.

Correspondences are so called because they correspond; representations, because they represent.

2988   To gain some idea of representations and correspondences, simply reflect on the activity of the mind and specifically the workings of thought and will. These usually shine brightly from our face and are openly visible in our expression. Our emotions gleam the brightest, the deeper ones radiating from and glowing in our eyes. When our facial features act in unison with our mental processes, they are said to correspond, and are correspondences. Our actual facial expressions represent mental activity and are representations.

The case is the same with the effects of bodily movement, and also with any action the muscles produce. Everyone recognizes that our thoughts and intentions determine them. The movements and actions of the body represent those of the mind and are representations. If they harmonize, they are correspondences.

2989   It can also be seen that the kinds of visible expressions that display themselves on the face do not occur in the mind. It is emotions that manifest themselves this way.

Again, it can be seen that the kinds of movements that present themselves in physical acts do not occur in the mind. It is thoughts that display themselves in this form.

What belongs to the mind is spiritual, but what belongs to the body is earthly.

Clearly, then, a correspondence exists between spiritual and earthly things, and a representation of spiritual entities exists in earthly entities.

To put the same thing another way, when different aspects of the inner self express themselves in the outer self, the visible expression in the outer self represents something of the inner self, and if they match, it is a correspondence.

It is also recognized—or can be—that there is a spiritual world and a natural world. Broadly speaking, the spiritual world is where angels and spirits live, and the natural world is where people live. Narrowly speaking, we each have a spiritual and natural world inside us. Our inner self is our spiritual world, and our outer self is our natural world. What flows in from our spiritual world and makes itself visible in our natural world is, in general, a representation. So far as the two conform, it is a correspondence.

2990

The fact that earthly objects represent spiritual attributes and correspond to them can also be seen from this: The earthly dimension cannot possibly come into existence except as a result of some cause prior to it. Its cause lies on the spiritual plane. No earthly object exists that does not trace its cause to that plane. Physical forms are the effect and cannot appear as causes, still less as causes of the causes, or first origins. Instead, they take a shape that suits the use they will serve in the place where they exist. Even so, the outward form of the effect represents attributes belonging to the causes, and these attributes in turn represent those of the first origins. So everything in the earthly realm represents that facet of the spiritual realm to which it corresponds, and spiritual elements in turn represent those facets of the heavenly realm from which they arise.

2991

A great deal of experience has enabled me to see that nothing exists in the physical world and its three kingdoms that does not represent something in the spiritual world, or that does not have something in the spiritual world to which it corresponds.

2992

Among many other experiences, the following one also illustrated the point: There have been times when I talked about the organs of the body and traced their links with each other, from those in the head to those in the chest and on into those of the abdomen. At those times the angels above me led my thoughts through the spiritual qualities to which the organs corresponded. This they did most precisely. They were not thinking at all about the physical organs I was considering but only about the spiritual qualities to which the organs corresponded.

The nature of angels' intelligence is such that their spiritual knowledge teaches them all there is to know about the body, even the most deeply hidden mysteries, which cannot possibly come to our knowledge. In fact, they know all about everything in the whole universe, and their knowledge is free of error, the reason being that causes come from their world, as do the first origins of those causes.

2993   The case is the same with specimens of the plant kingdom. Nothing exists in that kingdom that does not represent something in the spiritual world and correspond to it, and this I learned many times through similar interaction with angels.

The reasons for this were also told to me. The causes of all earthly phenomena come from spiritual phenomena, and the first origins of those causes come from heavenly ones. To put it another way, everything in the physical world traces its cause to something true, which is spiritual, and its first origin to something good, which is heavenly. Earthly objects spring from these causes according to all the variations in truth and goodness that exist in the Lord's kingdom. So they spring from the Lord himself, the source of everything good and true.

These ideas cannot help seeming strange, especially to people who cannot or do not want to lift their thoughts beyond the realm of nature, who do not know what spiritual reality is and therefore do not acknowledge it.

2994   As long as we are living in our body, we are incapable of sensing or perceiving much of this. With us, heavenly and spiritual entities are translated into the earthly attributes of our outer self, and there we lose the ability to sense and perceive them.

Representations and correspondences as they exist in our outer self also do not appear like the traits of our inner self that they correspond to and represent. So they cannot impinge on our awareness until we shed the outer dimension.

When we do, those of us who are in correspondence—that is, whose outer self corresponds to our inner—are very fortunate.

2995   The people of the earliest church (described in §§1114–1125) saw something spiritual and heavenly in every detail of nature, so much so that for them, physical objects merely served as springboards for thought about spiritual and heavenly subjects. In consequence, they could talk with angels and be present with them in the Lord's kingdom in the heavens and at the same time in the Lord's kingdom on earth, which is the church.

For them, then, earthly objects were connected with spiritual realities and fully corresponded to them.

The situation changed after those days, however, when evil and falsity started to take over, or when the Iron Age took up where the Golden Age had ended. Then, because the correspondence was lost, heaven closed. It closed so tightly that people hardly even wanted to know about the existence of a spiritual realm or eventually even of heaven and hell or a life after death.

In the world, it is a deeply hidden secret—although nothing is more widely known in the next life, even to all the spirits—that everything in the human body has a correspondence with something in heaven. In fact, the body has not even the smallest part to which something spiritual and heavenly does not correspond. That is, not the smallest part exists to which a heavenly community does not correspond. The communities of heaven reflect all the major categories and specific types of spiritual and heavenly properties. Taken together, they are arranged in such a pattern that they resemble a single person with all the parts that make up a human, inside and out. That is why heaven as a whole is also called the universal human. And it is why I so often say that one community belongs to this area of the body, another to that, and so on [§§956, 1385, 1525, 1977].

2996

The reason for the correspondence is that the Lord is the only human, and heaven represents him. The divine goodness and truth that comes from him is what makes heaven, and since angels are in heaven, they are said to be in the Lord.

People who are in hell, however, are outside this universal human. They correspond to excrement and also to defects.

Further evidence can also be found to some extent in the consideration that our spiritual or inner self—which is our spirit and is called our soul—has a similar correspondence with our earthly or outer self. The nature of the correspondence is such that the characteristics of our inner self are spiritual and heavenly, while those of our outer self are earthly and bodily. The remarks above at §§2988, 2989 on facial expressions and physical acts demonstrate the fact.

2997

Moreover, in regard to our inner self, we are a miniature heaven, because we were created in the Lord's image.

The existence of these correspondences has become so familiar to me over many years that hardly anything is more familiar. Yet people do not know that they exist and do not believe that we have any link with the spiritual world. The fact is that we have full connection with that world and could not survive even a moment without it—nor could anything in us survive. Our continued existence depends entirely upon it.

2998

I have also learned which angelic communities belong to each area of the body and what their nature is. For instance, I have learned which ones belong to the area of the heart and what they are like; which ones belong to the area of the lungs and what they are like; which to that of the liver and what they are like; and which to the sense organs (eye, ears, tongue, and so on) and what they are like. With the Lord's divine mercy, these will be taken up one by one.

2999   In addition, there is nothing anywhere in the created world that does not correspond to things in the spiritual world and therefore in its way represent something in the Lord's kingdom. It is from the spiritual world that everything comes into being and remains in existence.

If people knew how these matters really stand, they would never attribute everything to nature, as they so often do.

3000   That is why absolutely everything in the universe represents the Lord's kingdom. In fact, the universe with all its constellations, all its atmospheres, and its three kingdoms is actually a kind of theater representing the Lord's glory in the heavens.

In the animal kingdom, it is not just humans but all the animals as well that represent the Lord's kingdom, down to the very tiniest and lowliest of them. Take caterpillars, which creep on the ground and feed on plants. When their wedding day approaches, they turn into chrysalises, soon grow wings, and thus rise from the ground up into the air, which is their heaven. There they revel in their joy and freedom, frolicking together and taking their nourishment from the richest of the flowers, laying their eggs, and in this way providing for offspring. Because they are then in their heavenly state, they are also at their loveliest. All these particulars are representative of the Lord's kingdom, as anyone can see.

3001   There is only one life force, which is the Lord's, and it flows in and causes us to live—both those of us who are good and those of us who are evil. This can be seen from remarks and illustrations offered in explanation of the Word at §§1954, 2021, 2536, 2658, 2706, 2886–2889. To this life the recipients respond, and they are given life by the divine inflow in such a way that they seem to themselves to live on their own. That is the correspondence between life and its recipients. The life in the recipients has the same quality as their character. People who have love and charity are in correspondence, because they conform to the inflow and receive life in a fitting way. But people who have the opposite of love and charity are not in correspondence, because they do *not* receive life itself fittingly. So the kind of life they seem to have depends on their character.

This situation can be illustrated in many ways. For example, the organs of movement and sensation, which life flows into through the soul; the nature of their movements and sensations depends on the condition of the organs. Another example is objects that sunlight flows into; the colors they take on depend on the nature of the receiving forms. In the spiritual world, however, all modifications resulting from an inflow of life are spiritual. That is why there are so many different kinds of understanding and wisdom.

This also demonstrates how all earthly forms, both animate and inanimate, are representative of spiritual and heavenly forms that exist in the Lord's kingdom. In other words, it shows that each and every thing in nature represents something, and that its representation depends on the extent and nature of its correspondence. **3002**

There will be more on representations and correspondences below at the end of the next chapter [§§3213–3227]. **3003**

Genesis 24

[More on the Word's Inner Meaning]

3004 DEEP secrets lie hidden in the inner meaning, and so far they have not come to anyone's awareness, as can be seen from the remarks and examples up to this point and from those that will follow below, the Lord in his divine mercy willing.

The presence of these secrets is particularly obvious from the inner meaning of our Lord's two names, Jesus Christ. Where these names come up, most people have no idea they are anything but his proper names—almost like the names of any other person, though holier. Admittedly, the better educated realize that "Jesus" means "Savior" and that "Christ" means "Anointed," which gives their thoughts *some* depth. Still, this is not what angels in heaven perceive in the names, which is something even more divine. "Jesus" makes them think of divine goodness, when a person on earth reads it out loud from the Word, and "Christ" makes them think of divine truth. Both together give them the idea of the divine marriage between goodness and truth and between truth and goodness. So they perceive the two as meaning everything divine in the heavenly marriage, which is heaven.

For a definition of the heavenly marriage, see §§2173, 2803.

3005 Many passages in the Word show that in an inner sense, Jesus means divine goodness, and Christ, divine truth.

The reason Jesus means divine goodness is that it means safety, salvation, and the Savior. Because it means these things, it means divine goodness, since that is what they stem from. Divine goodness belongs to the Lord's love and mercy, so the only way to be saved is to accept that goodness.

The reason Christ means divine truth is that it means the Messiah, the Anointed, and the King. The meaning of the Messiah, the Anointed, and the King as divine truth will become clear below [§3009].

3006 This is what angels perceive when Jesus Christ is mentioned, and it is what is meant by the statement that there is no salvation in any other *name* [Acts 4:12]. It is also what the Lord meant by the things he said about his name so many times. In John, for instance:

Whatever you ask in *my name*, I will do it. (John 14:[13,] 14, 15, 16)

In the same author:

> These things have been written so that you can believe that *Jesus* is *Christ*, the Son of God, and so that as believers you can have life in *his name*. (John 20:31)

There are other passages, too. A *name* stands for every means of worshiping the Lord, collectively, and so for the quality of all worship and theology; see §2724. In the passages here, then, it stands for the good that love and charity inspire, united with the truth that faith teaches, which is all theology and all worship, collectively.

It can be demonstrated that Christ is the same as the Messiah, the Anointed, and the King; and that the Messiah, the Anointed, and the King is the same as divine truth. **3007**

1. Christ is the same as the Messiah, the Anointed, and the King. The following passages from the Word make this clear. In John: **3008**

> Andrew finds his own brother, Simon, and says to him, "We have found the *Messiah!*" that is (if you translate it), the *Christ*. (John 1:41)

In the same author:

> Many from the crowd, hearing this word, said, "This is truly the Prophet!" Others said, "This is the *Christ*." Others, however, said, "Is it from Galilee, then, that the *Christ* will come? Doesn't Scripture say that from the seed of David and from Bethlehem—the town where David was—the *Christ* will come?" (John 7:40, 41, 42)

Plainly Christ stands for the Messiah they were awaiting. In the same author:

> So haven't our rulers truly acknowledged that this is truly the *Christ?* But this one we know, where he is from. When the *Christ* comes, though, no one knows where he is from. (John 7:25, 26, 27)

Christ stands for the Messiah. The reason no one would know where he was from was that he was not going to be acknowledged. In the same author:

> The Jews surrounded Jesus and said to him, "How long will you keep our soul in suspense? If you are the *Christ*, tell us frankly." Jesus answered them, "I told you, but you do not believe." (John 10:24, 25)

Here too Christ stands for the Messiah they were awaiting. In the same author:

> The crowd answered, "We have heard from the Law that *Christ* remains forever." (John 12:34)

Christ stands for the Messiah. In the same author:

> Martha said, "I have believed that you are the *Christ,* the Son of God, who was to come into the world." (John 11:27)

That is, he was the Messiah. In Luke:

> There was a person in Jerusalem whose name was Simeon; he had received an answer from the Holy Spirit that he would not see death until he saw the *Lord's Christ.* (Luke 2:25, 26)

In other words, until he saw the Messiah, or Jehovah's Anointed. In the same author:

> Jesus said to his disciples, "You, though—who do you say I am?" Answering, Peter said, "*God's Christ.*" (Luke 9:20; Mark 8:29)

There are other places, too, such as Matthew 26:63, 64; John 6:68, 69; Mark 14:61, 62.

[2] Christ and the Messiah, then, are the same, "Christ" meaning "the Anointed" in Greek, and "Messiah" meaning the same thing in Hebrew. So Christ is clearly the same as the Anointed, and also the same as the King, since monarchs in general were called the anointed. This is plain from many places in the Word's narratives and also in its prophetic passages. In David, for example:

> The monarchs of the earth stood and consulted together about Jehovah and about *his anointed one.* (Psalms 2:2)

In the same author:

> Now I know that Jehovah saves *his anointed one;* [Jehovah] will answer him from his sacred heavens, in the saving powers of his right hand. (Psalms 20:6)

In the same author:

> Jehovah is strength to them, and the strength of *his anointed one's* acts of salvation. (Psalms 28:8)

In Samuel:

> Jehovah will give strength to his monarch and lift the horn of *his anointed one.* (1 Samuel 2:10)

Here and in many other places, the anointed one stands for a monarch. The word in the original language is Messiah. In an inner sense, these prophecies are talking about the Lord, who was a king, as is also plain from passages in the New Testament. In Matthew, for instance:

> The governor asked Jesus, "Aren't you the *king of the Jews?*" Jesus said to him, "You say [right]." (Matthew 27:11)

In Luke:

> Pilate questioned Jesus, saying, "Aren't you the *king of the Jews?*" [Jesus,] answering him, said, "You say [right]." (Luke 23:3; Mark 15:2)

In John:

> They shouted, "Hosanna! A blessing on the one who comes in the Lord's name, the *King of Israel!*" (John 12:13)

In the same author:

> Nathanael said, "Rabbi, you are the Son of God; you are the *King of Israel.*" (John 1:49)

2. The Messiah, the Anointed, and the King is the same as divine truth. **3009** This can be seen from many passages in the Word, and it has been demonstrated several times in various explanations, such as those in §§1672, 1728, 2015, 2069. The Lord himself also teaches it in John:

> Pilate said to Jesus, "*Aren't you* then *a king?*" Jesus answered, "You say [right], because *I am a king.* I was born for this and came into the world for this: to give testimony to the *truth.* Everyone who is on the side of *truth* hears my voice." (John 18:37)

This shows that divine truth itself is the reason the Lord was called a king.

Kings were anointed (and therefore were called the anointed) because the oil used for anointing them symbolized goodness (§§886, 2832), and the kind of truth that a monarch symbolized was the kind that comes of goodness. So it was truth marked by goodness. Among the people of that time, then, monarchy represented the divine truth in the Lord that comes of divine goodness. Accordingly, it represented the divine marriage of goodness [with and] within truth; while priesthood represented the divine marriage of truth [with and] within goodness. "Jesus" symbolizes the latter, and "Christ" symbolizes the former.

3010   This makes it clear what the [false] Christs mentioned in Matthew symbolize:

> Watch, to keep anyone from leading you astray! For many will come in my name saying, "I am the *Christ,*" and lead many astray. Then if anyone says to you, "Look: here is the *Christ!*" or "There!" do not believe it, because *false Christs* and false prophets will arise. (Matthew 24:[4,] 5, 23, 24; Mark 13:21, 22)

The false Christs symbolize truths that are not divine (falsity, in other words), while the false prophets symbolize the people who teach them (§2534). In the same author:

> Do not be called teachers, because one person is your teacher: *Christ.* (Matthew 23:10)

Christ stands for truth that *is* divine.

This shows what a Christian is: a person devoted to the truth that comes of goodness.

3011   From this it is possible to see what hidden dimensions the Word contains, which we cannot possibly become aware of without the inner meaning.

※※※※※※※※※※※※※※※※※※※※※※

Genesis 24

1. And Abraham, an old man, advanced in days; and Jehovah blessed Abraham in everything.

2. And Abraham said to his servant (the elder of his household, the one managing everything that was his), "Please put your hand under my thigh.

3. And I will put you under oath to Jehovah, God of heaven and God of earth, that you will not take a woman for my son from the daughters of the Canaanite, in whose midst I reside.

4. But to my land and to [the place of] my birth you are to go, and you shall take a woman for my son Isaac."

5. And the servant said to him, "Maybe the woman will not want to come after me to this land; am I really to take your son back to the land you came from?"

6. And Abraham said to him, "Be careful not to take my son back there!

7. Jehovah, God of heaven, who took me from my father's house and from the land of my birth, and who spoke to me, and who swore to me, saying, 'To your seed I will give this land'—he will send his angel before you, and you shall take a woman for my son from there.

8. And if the woman does not want to come after you, then you are exempt from this oath of mine; only, my son you are not to take back there."

9. And the servant put his hand under the thigh of Abraham his master and swore to him concerning this word.

10. And the servant took ten camels from his master's camels and went, and all the goods of his master were in his hand; and he got up and went to Aram-naharaim, to the city of Nahor.

11. And he made the camels kneel outside the city, at the well of water, near evening time, near the time that the women drawing water went out.

12. And he said, "Jehovah, God of my master Abraham, please make this happen before me today, and do mercy to my master Abraham.

13. Look: I am standing by at a spring of water, and the daughters of the men of the city are going out to draw water.

14. And let it be that the girl to whom I say, 'Please tilt your pitcher and let me drink,' and she says, 'Drink! And your camels I will also water'—that her you have destined for your servant Isaac; and in this I will know that you have done mercy to my master."

15. And it happened that he had hardly finished speaking when here, Rebekah comes out, who had been born to Bethuel, son of Milcah wife of Nahor brother of Abraham; and her pitcher was on her shoulder.

16. And the girl was very good to look at—a young, unmarried woman, and no man had known her; and she went down to the spring and filled her pitcher and came up.

17. And the servant ran to meet her and said, "Let me swallow, please, a little water from your pitcher."

18. And she said, "Drink, my lord!" and hurried and brought her pitcher down onto her hand and let him take a drink.

19. And she finished letting him take a drink and said, "For your camels, too, let me draw, till they have finished drinking."

20. And she hurried and emptied her pitcher at the trough and ran again to the well to draw and drew for all his camels.

21. And the man was staring dumbfounded at her, holding back to see whether Jehovah had made his path successful or not.

22. And it happened when the camels had finished drinking that the man took a gold nose-ring (half a shekel its weight) and [put] two bracelets on her hands (ten [shekels] of gold their weight).

23. And he said, "Whose daughter are you? Tell me, please, whether your father's house has a place for us to spend the night."

24. And she said to him, "I am the daughter of Bethuel, son of Milcah, whom she bore to Nahor."

25. And she said to him, "There is also hay, also much fodder with us; also a place to spend the night."

26. And the man bowed and prostrated himself to Jehovah.

27. And he said, "A blessing on Jehovah, God of my master Abraham, who has not abandoned the mercy and truth he keeps with my master! I was on my way, when Jehovah led me to the house of my master's kin."

28. And the girl ran and told her mother's household about these things.

29. And Rebekah had a brother, and his name was Laban; and Laban ran to the man outside at the spring.

30. And it happened—on seeing the nose-ring, and the bracelets on his sister's hands, and on his hearing the words of Rebekah his sister, saying, "This is what the man spoke to me"—that he came to the man; and here, the man was standing by his camels by the spring.

31. And he said, "Come, you who are blessed by Jehovah! Why are you standing outside? And I have neatened the house, and there is a place for the camels."

32. And the man came to the house and untied the camels, and [Laban] gave hay and fodder to the camels, and water to wash his feet and the feet of the men who were with him.

33. And something was put before him to eat, and he said, "I am not eating till I have spoken my words." And [Laban] said, "Speak!"

34. And he said, "I am Abraham's servant.

35. And Jehovah has blessed my master very much and enlarged him and given him flock and herd, and silver and gold, and male and female slaves, and camels and donkeys.

36. And Sarah, my master's wife, bore a son to my master after [reaching] her old age, and he has given [the son] everything he has.

37. And my master put me under oath, saying, 'You shall not take a woman for my son from the daughters of the Canaanite in whose land I reside.

38. Not except to the house of my father shall you go, and to my clan, and you shall take a woman for my son.'

39. And I said to my master, 'Maybe the woman will not come after me.'

40. And he said to me, 'Jehovah, in whose presence I have walked, will send his angel with you and make your path successful; and you are to take a woman for my son, from my clan and from my father's house.

41. Then you will be exempt from my curse, because you came to my clan. And if they do not give [her] to you, then you will be exempt from my curse.'

42. And I came today to the spring and said, 'Jehovah, God of my master Abraham, if it is your [will], please, be giving success to my path that I am walking on.

43. Look: I am standing by the spring of water; and let it be that the maiden who is going out to draw, and I say to her, "Let me take a drink, please, of a little water from your pitcher,"

44. and she says to me, "Yes, you drink, and I will also draw for your camels"—let that be the woman whom Jehovah has destined for my master's son.'

45. I had hardly finished speaking to my heart when here, Rebekah comes out, and her pitcher is on her shoulder, and she goes down to the spring and draws; and I said to her, 'Let me take a drink, please!'

46. And she hurried and brought her pitcher down from upon her and said, 'Drink! And I will also water your camels.' And I drank, and she also watered the camels.

47. And I asked her and said, 'Whose daughter are you?' And she said, 'The daughter of Bethuel, son of Nahor, whom Milcah bore to him.' And I put the ring in her nose and the bracelets on her hands.

48. And I bowed and prostrated myself to Jehovah, and I blessed Jehovah, God of my master Abraham, who led me into the way of truth, to take the daughter of my master's brother for his son.

49. And now, if you are keeping mercy and truth with my master, tell me; and if not, tell me, and I will look either to the right or to the left."

50. And Laban answered, as did Bethuel, and they said, "From Jehovah has this word come; we cannot speak evil or good to you.

51. Look: Rebekah is before you; take her and go, and let her be a woman to your master's son, as Jehovah has spoken."

52. And it happened as Abraham's servant heard their words that he bowed down to the earth to Jehovah.

53. And the servant brought out vessels of silver and vessels of gold and clothes and gave them to Rebekah, and precious gifts he gave to her brother and her mother.

54. And they ate and drank—he and the men who were with him—and spent the night and got up in the morning; and he said, "Send me to my master."

55. And her brother and her mother said, "Let the girl stay with us several days, perhaps ten; afterward, you shall go."

56. And he said to them, "Do not delay me. And Jehovah has made my path successful; send me and let me go to my master."

57. And they said, "Let's call the girl and ask of her own mouth."

58. And they called Rebekah and said to her, "Would you go with this man?" And she said, "I will go."

59. And they sent Rebekah their sister and her nursemaid and Abraham's servant and his men.

60. And they blessed Rebekah and said to her, "Our sister, may you become thousands of myriads, and may your seed inherit the gate of those who hate you!"

61. And Rebekah rose, and her girls, and they rode on camels and came after the man. And the servant took Rebekah and went.

62. And Isaac came from going to Beer-lahai-roi, and he was residing in the southland.

63. And Isaac went out to meditate in the field toward evening, and he raised his eyes and looked, and here, now, camels coming!

64. And Rebekah raised her eyes and saw Isaac and slipped off the camel.

65. And she said to the servant, "Who is that man there, walking in the field to meet us?" And the servant said, "That is my master." And she took a veil and covered herself.

66. And the servant told Isaac all the words that he had done.

67. And Isaac brought her into the tent of Sarah his mother, and he took Rebekah, and she became a woman to him, and he loved her. And Isaac was comforted after his mother.

Summary

THE inner meaning describes the entire process by which truth was
united to goodness in the Lord's divine rational mind. The current
chapter describes the process of introduction that comes before union.
Isaac is goodness in the Lord's rational mind. At this point, Rebekah is
the truth that was to be introduced to goodness. Laban is the desire for
goodness in the Lord's earthly self.

3012

This is the way the inner meaning describes the introduction process: The Lord had reduced everything in himself into a divinely heavenlike order, so that divine truth could unite with the divine goodness in
his rational mind. (The union was to come in the usual way, from his
earthly self—specifically from the secular facts, religious knowledge, and
teachings present in his earthly self.) So when it was time, and the Lord
had reduced everything to order in this way, then by means of his divine
inflow he called truth up out of his earthly self, introduced it to the goodness in his rational mind, and made it divine. Just as the Lord had made
his rational mind divine in regard to goodness, then, he also made it
divine in regard to truth.

3013

This chapter and the ones that follow show what kind of secrets the
Word's inner meaning holds.

3014

Inner Meaning

GENESIS 24:1. *And Abraham, an old man, advanced in days; and Jehovah
blessed Abraham in everything.*

3015

Abraham, an old man, advanced in days means when the stage came
for the Lord's humanity to become divine. *And Jehovah blessed Abraham
in everything* means when everything had been arranged in divine order
by the Lord.

When Abraham, an old man, advanced in days means when the stage
came for the Lord's humanity to become divine, as can be seen from the
following: *Abraham* represents the Lord, as discussed in §§1893, 1965, 1989,

3016

[2010,] 2011, 2172, 2198, 2501, 2833, 2836, and many other places. An *old man*, or old age, symbolizes shedding what is human and putting on what is heavenly, as discussed in §§1854, 2198. In the Lord's case, it means putting on divinity. And a *day* symbolizes a stage, [or state,] as discussed in §§23, 487, 488, 493, 893, 2788, so *advancing in days* means when the stage came.

The reason an *old man* and *advancing in days* symbolize these things is that angels have no notion of oldness or of the increasing age meant by "advancing in days." Instead they think of the stage of life they are in. So when the Word mentions increasing age and oldness, the angels present with a person can only picture the stage of life they have reached—the stage people reach when they finish life's different eras, including the last. In other words, they picture gradually ridding themselves of what is human and taking on what is heavenly. Human life from infancy to old age is nothing but advancement from the world to heaven; and the final part, which is death, is the actual transition. So burial means resurrection, because that is when we fully shed what is human (§§2916, 2917). Since angels think this way, advancing in days and oldness cannot symbolize anything else in the inner meaning, which exists mainly for angels, and for people whose minds are angelic.

3017   *And Jehovah blessed Abraham in everything* means when everything had been arranged in divine order by the Lord or, to say it another way, when the Lord had arranged everything in divine order. The symbolism can be seen from the fact that *Jehovah* is the Lord's divinity itself (§§1343, 1736, 1815, 2004, 2005, 2018, 2025, 2921), and in that case, *Abraham* represents the Lord's divine humanity (§§2833, 2836). So when it says *Jehovah blessed Abraham in everything,* on an inner level it means that from the divinity itself within his humanity, the Lord arranged everything in divine order. That is what *blessing* means, when applied to the Lord's humanity. When applied to us, *being blessed* means being enriched with spiritual and heavenly goodness (§§981, 1096, 1420, 1422). We are enriched with that goodness when the Lord arranges our capacities in spiritual and heavenly order and so in the image and likeness of divine order (1475). Human rebirth is nothing else.

[2] The meaning of the statement that the Lord arranged everything within his humanity in divine order will become clear from the discussion that follows in this chapter. It will show that his divine rationality (represented by Isaac), conceived by divine goodness (Abraham) and born of divine truth (Sarah), was now arranged in the divine order that enabled divine truths that were actually drawn from his human side to become part of him.

These are the mysteries that the inner meaning of the current chapter contains. Angels see them in a clear light they receive from the Lord, because in heaven's light such secrets lie open plain as day. However, in the world's light, which we see by, hardly any of it is visible, except to people who have been reborn. These people see a dim outline of it, since they also have a certain measure of heavenly light.

Genesis 24:2. *And Abraham said to his servant (the elder of his household, the one managing everything that was his), "Please put your hand under my thigh."*   **3018**

Abraham said to his servant, the elder of his household, symbolizes the way the Lord brought order to his earthly self (which is the *elder servant of his household*), and his influence on it. *The one managing everything that was his* symbolizes the duties of the earthly self. *Please put your hand under my thigh* symbolizes the earthly self's obligation regarding its power for good in relation to marriage love.

Abraham said to his servant, the elder of his household, symbolizes the way the Lord brought order to his earthly self (which is the *elder servant of his household*), and his influence on it. This can be seen from the symbolism of *saying,* here, as commanding, since a servant is being addressed. Because it is talking about the way the Lord's divine side organized the capacities of his earthly self, *saying* means bringing order, and influencing. The rational (or inward) self brings order to everything the earthly (or outward) self does, and it does so by exerting an influence on it.   **3019**

The symbolism of the *elder servant of the household* as the earthly plane, or the earthly self, can be seen from the symbolism of a *servant* as something relatively lowly that serves something higher. To say the same thing another way, it symbolizes something relatively superficial that serves something deeper. (See §§2541, 2567.) Nothing that belongs to the earthly self—including facts of any kind—is anything but a slave, because everything there serves to enable the rational mind to think fairly and form righteous intentions. The fact that the *elder of the household* is the earthly self can be seen from what follows.

The one managing everything that was his symbolizes the duties of the earthly self. This can be seen from the meaning of *managing—* and especially of managing *everything*—as carrying out one's duties or functions.   **3020**

Our earthly self, as it relates to our reasoning self (or our outward self as it relates to our inward), resembles the manager of a household, as you may see in §1795. Everything in us works the way a single household does, or in other words, the way a single family does. There is the part that functions as the head of the household and the parts that function as servants. The rational mind itself is what oversees everything as the head of the household and organizes the earthly mind by exerting an influence on it. The earthly mind is what carries out and administers orders.

[2] The earthly mind is distinct from the reasoning mind and occupies a lower level but also acts with some autonomy, so by comparison it is called the elder servant of the household and "the one managing everything that was his" there.

The contents of the earthly mind and the functions it performs show that the earthly mind is a different mind from the rational one, occupies a lower level, and has a degree of autonomy. Its contents include all facts and therefore every kind of knowledge—in short, absolutely everything in the outer or physical memory (described in §§2471, 2480). The earthly mind also contains the whole power of imagination, which is a deeper plane of the senses in us and is especially strong in youth and early adulthood. It also contains all the earthly desires we have in common with brute animals. These considerations show what its functions are.

[3] The rational mind is deeper, though. The knowledge it holds—specifically, the entire contents of the inner memory (described in §§2470, 2471, 2472, 2473, 2474, 2489, 2490)—does not lie open to us but rather is imperceptible as long as we are living in our bodies. Every thought that harbors a perception of what is fair and just or of what is true and good also belongs to the rational mind. So do all spiritual desires, which are the truly human ones that distinguish us from brute animals. The rational mind exerts the influence of such knowledge, thoughts, and desires on the earthly mind, stirs up what it finds there, casts a critical eye on it, and in this way judges and decides.

Clear evidence that these two levels of the mind are different is this: In many people, the earthly mind controls the rational mind or, to put it another way, the outer self controls the inner self. The only people in whom it does not dominate but serves are those who devote themselves to goodness inspired by neighborly love—that is, who allow the Lord to lead them.

3021   *Please put your hand under my thigh* symbolizes the earthly self's obligation regarding its power for good in relation to marriage love. This can be seen from the symbolism of a *hand* as power (discussed in §878) and from that of the *thigh* as the goodness of marriage love (discussed below).

Its symbolism as an obligation in regard to that power appears from this: In keeping with an ancient ritual, people who were undertaking any obligation connected with marriage love put their hand under the thigh of the person to whom they were obligated, which put them under oath to that person. The reason was that the *thigh* symbolized marriage love, and the *hand*, power—that is, the duty to do everything in one's power.

All parts of the human body correspond to spiritual and heavenly elements in the universal human, which is heaven, as was shown in §§2996, 2998 and will be demonstrated more fully below, with the Lord's divine mercy. The *thighs* themselves and the genital area correspond to marriage love, which the earliest people knew. That is why they had many rituals stemming from the correspondence, including that of putting one's hand under another's thigh when being bound to some good deed connected with marriage love. The knowledge of these correspondences was prized by the ancients and was one of the chief measures of learning and intelligence among them. Today, however, the knowledge has been lost, and lost so completely that people do not even realize such a thing as correspondence exists. As a consequence, they may be surprised to hear that the ritual has this symbolism.

The ritual appears here because Abraham is wanting to arrange a betrothal between his son Isaac and a woman of his own clan and tells his elder servant to perform the duty.

[2] Other passages in the Word also reveal that the thigh symbolizes marriage love, because of its correspondence, as noted. Take, for instance, the steps required when a woman was being charged with adultery by her husband, in Moses:

> The priest shall swear the woman to a curse-oath, and the priest shall say to the woman, "Jehovah will turn you into a curse and into an oath in the midst of your people, in Jehovah's making *your thigh* fall and your belly swell." When he gives her the water to drink, it shall also happen that if she has been defiled, and committed a transgression against her husband, the cursed water will come as bitterness in her, and her belly will swell, and *her thigh will fall,* and the woman will become a curse in the midst of her people. (Numbers 5:21, 27)

The falling of her thigh symbolized a negative form of marriage love: adultery. The other details of this procedure—every one of them—symbolized specific related matters. Not the least detail appears there that fails to mean *something,* then, even if people who read the Word without any idea of its holiness are destined to wonder why they come up.

Because of the thigh's symbolism as the goodness of marriage love, the Word speaks several times of people issuing from a person's thigh, as in these words concerning Jacob:

> Be fruitful and multiply! A nation and a throng of nations will exist from you, and monarchs will *come from your thighs.* (Genesis 35:11)

And in another place:

> Every soul coming with Jacob to Egypt, those *issuing from his thigh* . . . (Genesis 46:26; Exodus 1:5)

And concerning Gideon:

> Gideon had seventy children *issuing from his thigh.* (Judges 8:30)

[3] Since thighs and genitals symbolize something relating to marriage love, they also symbolize various facets of other love and of charity, because marriage love is the basis for all love (see §§686, 2733, 2737, 2738, 2739). All love comes from the same origin: the heavenly marriage, which is the marriage of what is good and true (on this subject, see §§2727–2759). The symbolism of a thigh as the goodness belonging to heavenly love and the goodness belonging to spiritual love can be seen from the following passages. In John:

> The one sitting on the white horse had a name written on his garment and *on his thigh:* King of Kings and Lord of Lords. (Revelation 19:16)

The one sitting on the white horse is the Word and is therefore the Lord, who is the Word (see §§2760, 2761, 2762). The garment is divine truth (2576), which is why he is called King of Kings (3009). It is clear, then, what a thigh is: divine goodness, which comes from the Lord's love, on account of which he is also called Lord of Lords (3004–3011). Since this is the Lord's whole nature, he is said to have had his name written on his garment and on his thigh, because a name symbolizes a person's nature (1896, 2009, 2724, 3006). [4] In David:

> Strap your sword *on your thigh,* you who are mighty in your glory and honor! (Psalms 45:3)

This is about the Lord. The sword stands for truth engaged in battle (§2799); the thigh, for a loving goodness. Strapping a sword on his thigh means that the truth he used in battle came from a loving goodness. In Isaiah:

> Justice will be the *sash around his hips,* and truth, the *sash around his thighs.* (Isaiah 11:5)

This too is about the Lord. Since justice is associated with a loving goodness (§2235), it is called the sash around his hips. Since truth comes from goodness, it is called the sash around his thighs. So the hips (or genital area) are mentioned in connection with a love for goodness, and the thighs, with a love for truth. [5] In the same author:

> He is not tired, and nothing in him is stumbling; he will not nod and will not fall asleep, and the *sash around his thighs* has not loosened, and the laces of his shoes have not been torn off. (Isaiah 5:27)

This describes the Lord. The sash around his thighs stands for the love of truth, as above. In Jeremiah:

> Jehovah told him to buy a *linen sash* and put it on his *hips* but not dip it in water. And he was to go to the Euphrates and hide it in a hole in the rock. After he had done so, when he went and took it from its place, it was ruined. (Jeremiah 13:1–7)

The linen sash stands for truth. His putting it on his hips was what represented the fact that this truth developed out of goodness. Anyone can see that these acts represented something; and their symbolism can be learned only from correspondences, which will be discussed at the end of certain chapters, by the Lord's divine mercy. [6] The same is true for the symbolism of visions seen by Ezekiel, Daniel, and Nebuchadnezzar. Ezekiel's vision:

> Above the expanse that was over the head of the guardian beings was a seeming appearance of sapphire stone, like a throne. And on the likeness of a throne was what looked like the appearance of a person on it, high above. And I saw the seeming form of an ember, like the appearance of fire within him all around. *From the appearance of his hips and up, and from the appearance of his hips and down,* I saw the seeming appearance of fire, and a brilliance to it all around, like the appearance of the rainbow that is in a cloud on a rainy day—such was the appearance of brilliance all around; such was the appearance of the likeness of Jehovah's glory. (Ezekiel 1:26, 27, 28)

You can see that this vision represented the Lord and his kingdom. The appearance of his hips and up and the appearance of his hips and down means the appearance of his love. This is plain from the symbolism of fire as love (§934) and from that of the brilliance and the rainbow as the wisdom and understanding that grow out of love (§§1042, 1043, 1053).

[7] Daniel's vision:

> Daniel saw a man clothed in linen, and *his hips were circled with the gold of Uphaz*, and his body was like tarshish, and his face, like the appearance of lightning, and his eyes, like lamps of fire, and his arms and his feet, like the radiance of burnished bronze. (Daniel 10:5, 6)

No one can tell the meaning of the individual details—such as the hips, the body, the face, eyes, arms, and feet—except by knowing their representation and the related correspondences. These reveal that it all represents the Lord's heavenly kingdom, in which divine love is the hips, and the gold of Uphaz circling them is the wise goodness that comes of love (§§113, 1551, 1552). [8] Nebuchadnezzar's vision, recorded in Daniel:

> The statue's head was fine gold; its chest and arms, silver; its belly and *thighs*, bronze; the feet, partly iron, partly clay. (Daniel 2:32, 33)

This statue represents the consecutive stages of a religion. The gold head represents its first stage, which was heavenly, because it was marked by love for the Lord. The silver chest and arms represent its second stage, which was spiritual, because it was marked by charity for others. The bronze belly and thighs represent the third stage, which was one of earthly goodness, which is bronze (§§425, 1551). Earthly goodness is marked by a love or charity for others that is a step below spiritual goodness. The iron-and-clay feet represent the fourth stage, which was one of earthly truth, which is iron (§§425, 426). It was also a stage lacking any cohesion with what is good, which is the clay.

These illustrations show what thighs and hips (or the genital area) symbolize: marriage love, first of all, and therefore all real love. The passages quoted demonstrate this, as do Genesis 32:25, 31, 32; Isaiah 20:2, 3, 4; Nahum 2:1; Psalms 69:23; Exodus 12:11; Luke 12:35, 36. Thighs and hips are also mentioned in a negative sense as meaning a love opposed to those kinds—in other words, self-love and love of the material world—in 1 Kings 2:5, 6; Isaiah 32:10, 11; Jeremiah 30:6; 48:37; Ezekiel 29:7; Amos 8:10.

3022   Genesis 24:3, 4. *"And I will put you under oath to Jehovah, God of heaven and God of earth, that you will not take a woman for my son from* *the daughters of the Canaanite, in whose midst I reside. But to my land and to [the place of] my birth you are to go, and you shall take a woman for my son Isaac."*

And I will put you under oath to Jehovah, God of heaven and God of earth, symbolizes the most sacred obligation to the divinity that exists in the highest heights and in everything that descends from them. *That you will not take a woman for my son from the daughters of the Canaanite* means that divine rationality was not to unite with any desire that clashes with truth. *In whose midst I reside* symbolizes discordant elements in the humanity he inherited from his mother that hem him in. *But to my land and to [the place of] my birth you are to go* means to the divinely heaven-like and divinely spiritual traits the Lord had acquired for himself. *And you shall take a woman for my son Isaac* means that there he would find the desire for truth that could form a bond with the desire for goodness on the rational plane.

I will put you under oath to Jehovah, God of heaven and God of earth, symbolizes the most sacred obligation to the divinity that exists in the highest heights and in everything that descends from them. This is established by the meaning of *putting someone under oath* as obligating that person by an oath. An oath, after all, is nothing but an obligation, and a very sacred one when made *to Jehovah, God of heaven and God of earth*—that is, to what is divine above and below, or in other words, to the divinity that exists in the highest heights and in everything that descends from them.

Since the words *Jehovah, God of heaven,* are being used of the Lord, they mean Jehovah himself, who is called the Father, from whom the Lord was conceived. Jehovah himself was therefore the Lord's divine essence, since conception itself provided the actual essence from which he existed. This being so, *Jehovah, God of earth,* means the Jehovah who is called the Son. So it means his human nature. His human nature came to have its being from his divine nature when the Lord made his human nature divine as well. "Jehovah, God of heaven," then, symbolizes the divinity that exists in the highest heights, while "Jehovah, God of earth" symbolizes the divinity that exists in everything descending from them.

The Lord is called Jehovah, God of heaven, because of his divinity in the heavens, and God of earth because of his divinity on earth. His divinity in the heavens is also the divinity present with us on our inner levels, while his divinity on earth is the divinity present with us on our outer levels. Our inner levels, after all, are our heaven, because through them we are connected with angels, but our outer levels are our earth

3023

because through them we are connected with other people (§§82, 913, 1411, 1733). When we have been reborn, our inner plane influences our outer plane, and our outer plane has its being from our inner plane.

This also indicates what the inner dimensions and the outer dimensions of religion are.

3024   *That you will not take a woman for my son from the daughters of the Canaanite* means that divine rationality was not to unite with any desire that clashes with truth, as can be seen from the following: *Taking a woman* means uniting in a pact of marriage. *My son,* Isaac, symbolizes the Lord's divine rationality, as noted in §§1893, 2066, 2083, 2630. *Daughters* symbolize desires, as noted in §§489, 490, 491, 568, 2362. And a *Canaanite* symbolizes evil, as noted in §§1444, 1573, 1574, so that *daughters of the Canaanite* symbolize desires that clash with truth.

The subject here is truth that is divine, which was to be linked with goodness that is divine, as it existed in the Lord's rational mind. This can be seen from the chapter's summary in §3013. The *woman* who was to be joined with Isaac in a pact of marriage means this truth itself, which was to be called up in the usual way from his earthly self. *My son* means the goodness in the Lord's rational mind that it was to link or join with. From this it can be seen that not taking a woman for Abraham's son from the daughters of the Canaanite means not uniting with any desire that clashes with truth.

Any bond between truth and goodness comes by way of desire. No type of truth ever enters our rational mind and forms a bond there except through our desire for it, because desire holds within it the good that is loved, which is all that creates a bond (§1895). Those who reflect on it can see that this is so.

[2] The fact that *daughters of the Canaanite* symbolize desires that clash with truth—that is, desires for falsity—can be seen from the symbolism of *daughters.* The Word mentions daughters in many places, and anyone can see that they do not mean daughters in those instances. Examples are the phrases *daughter of Zion, daughter of Jerusalem, daughter of Tarshish,* and *daughter of my people.* These symbolize feelings of desire for goodness and truth, as shown in the sections cited above. And since they are feelings of desire for goodness and truth, they are also religions, because these feelings are what make a religion a religion. That is why the daughter of Zion symbolizes a heavenly religion, because of its desire for goodness, while the daughter of Jerusalem symbolizes a spiritual religion, because of its desire for truth (§2362), as does the "daughter of my people" (Isaiah 22:4;

Jeremiah 6:14, 26; 8:19, 21, 22; 9:1; 14:17; Lamentations 2:11; 4:6; Ezekiel 13:17).

[3] It is clear, then, what is symbolized by the daughters of the surrounding nations, such as the daughters of the Philistines, the daughters of Egypt, the daughters of Tyre and Sidon, the daughters of Edom, the daughters of Moab, the daughters of the Chaldeans and Babylon, and the daughters of Sodom. They symbolize the desire for evil and falsity that their various religious persuasions are based on and therefore the persuasions themselves. The following passages establish this symbolism. In Ezekiel:

> The *daughters of the nations* were mourning Egypt. Lament over the throng of Egypt, and bring it—it and the *daughters of the majestic nations*—down to the underground realm, with those going down into the pit. (Ezekiel 32:16, 18)

The daughters of the majestic nations stand for a desire for evil. In Samuel:

> Do not tell it in Gath! Do not spread the news in the streets of Ashkelon, or the *daughters of the Philistines* might rejoice; the *daughters of the uncircumcised* might gloat. (2 Samuel 1:20)

In Ezekiel:

> You whored with the sons of Egypt; I delivered you to the soul of those hating you—the *daughters of the Philistines*—before your evil was exposed, as at the time of the disgrace of the *daughters of Syria* and of all its environs, of the *daughters of the Philistines* despising you from all around. (Ezekiel 16:26, 27, 57)

Anyone can see that daughters are not meant here but religiosity in the kind of people symbolized by Philistines—a religiosity that prompts them to talk a lot about faith but not to live a life of faith in any way (see §§1197, 1198). That is also why they are called uncircumcised, or in other words, lacking in love for their neighbor. [4] In Jeremiah:

> Go up to Gilead and take balsam, *virgin daughter of Egypt!* Pack baggage for deportation for yourself, inhabitant *daughter of Egypt!* The *daughter of Egypt* has been shamed, has been delivered into the hand of the people of the north. (Jeremiah 46:11, 19, 24)

The daughter of Egypt stands for the desire to debate the validity of religious truth on the basis of secular knowledge. So it stands for the belief system rising out of that desire, which by its nature refuses to accept anything that the senses cannot grasp—which means that it refuses to accept religious truth. See §§215, 232, 233, 1164, 1165, 1186, 1385, 2196, 2203, 2209, 2568, 2588. [5] In Isaiah:

> He said, "You shall no longer continue to gloat, oppressed *daughter of Sidon.*" (Isaiah 23:12)

In David:

> The *daughter of Tyre* is among your tribute; the rich among the people will entreat your favor. (Psalms 45:12)

The symbolism of the daughters of Sidon and Tyre is evident from the symbolism of Sidon and Tyre, which is dealt with at §1201. In Jeremiah:

> Rejoice and be glad, *daughter of Edom!* Your wickedness has ended, *daughter of Zion;* he will not deport you again. Your wickedness will be punished, *daughter of Edom.* (Lamentations 4:21, 22)

In Isaiah:

> Like a wandering bird, a castoff nest, will the *daughters of Moab* be. (Isaiah 16:2)

In the same author:

> Go down and sit in the dirt, *virgin daughter of Babylon;* sit on the earth. There is no throne, *daughter of the Chaldeans.* Sit silent and go into the dark, *daughter of the Chaldeans,* because you will no longer be called an overseer of kingdoms. (Isaiah 47:1, 5)

In Jeremiah:

> A people from the north, marshaled as a man is for war, is coming upon you, *daughter of Babylon.* (Jeremiah 50:41, 42)

In the same author:

> The *daughter of Babylon* is like a threshing floor; it is time to thresh her. (Jeremiah 51:33)

In Zechariah:

> Oh, Zion, escape, living as you are with the *daughter of Babylon!* (Zechariah 2:7)

In David:

> The *daughter of Babylon* has been laid waste. (Psalms 137:8)

In Ezekiel:

> Your sisters—Sodom and *her daughters*—will return to their early state. And Samaria and *her daughters* will return to their early state. (Ezekiel 16:55)

[6] In these passages, as anyone can see, daughters do not mean daughters but desires that clash with truth, and therefore the religious persuasions that grow out of them. The identity of those persuasions is clear from the symbolism of the peoples, such as the Edomites, Moabites, Chaldeans, Babylon, Sodom, and Samaria, who are discussed at various points in the explanations of earlier chapters of Genesis.

This now indicates what the daughters of the Canaanite symbolize in the current verse.

[7] The ban on marrying the daughters of the Canaanites also had to do with this spiritual reality: that goodness should not unite with falsity, or evil with truth, because such a union is the source of profanation. The same prohibition also represented the theme treated of in Deuteronomy 7:3 and in Malachi:

> Judah profaned Jehovah's holiness, because he loved and married the *daughter of a foreign god*. (Malachi 2:11)

In whose midst I reside symbolizes discordant elements in the humanity he inherited from his mother that hem him in. This can be seen from the symbolism of *residing in the midst*—the midst of the Canaanite—as the things that surround a person, or hem a person in. The things symbolized are ones that clash with truth, as can be seen from the remarks just above concerning the symbolism of the daughters of the Canaanite.

These elements are ones the Lord inherited from his mother and later rid himself of, when he made his humanity divine, as can be seen from previous remarks and explanations on the same subject at §§1414, 1444, 1573, 2159, 2574, 2649.

But to my land and to [the place of] my birth you are to go means to the divinely heavenlike and divinely spiritual traits the Lord had acquired for himself. This is established by the symbolism of the *land* as heavenly love (discussed in §§1413, 1607) and from that of *birth* as spiritual love (discussed in §§1145, 1255). The current passage is talking about the Lord,

3025

3026

so here they symbolize divinely heavenlike and divinely spiritual traits. To see that the Lord acquired these for himself by his own power, consult §§1813, 1921, 2025, 2026, 2083, 2500.

3027   *You shall take a woman for my son Isaac* means that there he would find the desire for truth that could form a bond with the desire for goodness on the rational plane. This can be seen from the discussion above in §3024.

3028   Genesis 24:5, 6. *And the servant said to him, "Maybe the woman will not want to come after me to this land; am I really to take your son back to the land you came from?" And Abraham said to him, "Be careful not to take my son back there!"*

The servant said to him symbolizes a perception the Lord had about his earthly self. *Maybe the woman will not want to come after me to this land* symbolizes the earthly self's doubt that this desire was capable of detaching. *Am I really to take your son back to the land you came from?* means, could it still unite with goodness that is divine on the rational plane? *Abraham said to him* symbolizes a perception the Lord received from his divine side. *Be careful not to take my son back there* means that it could never form the bond.

3029   *The servant said to him* symbolizes a perception the Lord had about his earthly self. This can be seen from the symbolism of *saying* as perceiving (mentioned in §§1791, 1815, 1819, 1822, 1898, 1919, 2080, 2506, 2515, 2552) and from that of the *servant* as the earthly self (discussed above in §§3019, 3020).

The rational self perceives what the earthly self is doing and what it is like, because what exists on a lower level in us is perceived by a higher level (see §2654). That is why "the servant said to him" symbolizes a perception the Lord had about his earthly self.

3030   *Maybe the woman will not want to come after me to this land* symbolizes the earthly self's doubt that this desire was capable of detaching, as can be seen from the following: A *woman* symbolizes truth—here, truth from the Lord's earthly self that was to unite with goodness that was divine in his rational mind. Since all union comes about through desire (as noted above at §3024), the woman also symbolizes a desire for that truth. And *coming after* or following *me to this land* means detaching from the earthly self and bonding with the rational self. Here as above in §3026, the *land* is a loving goodness in the rational mind. You can see that doubt is present, because the text says *maybe she will not want to.*

[2] From the discussion above, it is clear enough what these words involve, as well as those that follow (up to verse 8 and beyond). For a better understanding of them, though, a few more remarks must be made.

Real rationality *exists* from goodness and *emerges* from truth. Good flows in along an inner route, but truth, along an outer route. So goodness binds itself to truth in the rational mind, and together they cause it to be rational. Unless goodness unites with truth there, the rational mind is not rational, even if it seems to be so because the person is capable of demonstrating logically that she or he *is* rational (§1944). This is the usual route by which rationality forms in a person.

[3] Since the Lord was born like any other person and wanted to be taught like any other person, he also wanted to make his rationality divine the same way. In other words, he wanted to make the goodness in it divine by exerting his divine influence on it from the inside, and to make the truth in it divine by exerting his divine influence on it from the outside.

By now the goodness in his rational mind had taken shape so completely that it was in a condition to receive truth. That is what is understood by the words at the beginning of the chapter, "Abraham, an old man, advanced in days; and Jehovah blessed Abraham in everything"—meaning arrival at the stage in which the Lord's humanity would become divine, and everything had been arranged in divine order (see §§3016, 3017). This being so, it now follows that truth was to unite with the goodness in his rational mind, and that as noted the union was to come about in the usual way, which was by means of secular and religious knowledge from his earthly self.

[4] Genuine goodness in the rational mind, which is formed from inside, is the soil, and truth is a seed to be planted in it. Real rationality is never born in any other way.

In order for rationality to develop in the Lord in the same way and to be made divine by his own power, he came into the world and chose to be born like any other person. Otherwise he could have taken on a human nature without being born, as he did in ancient times on the many occasions when he revealed himself to people.

[5] That is what the current chapter is talking about: how truth called up out of the Lord's earthly self was to unite with the goodness in his rational mind, and how the truth was also to become divine there, just as the goodness was divine. All of this seems so terribly obscure to people on earth as to be unintelligible. It is especially murky to one who is unaware that the rational mind is something different from the earthly

mind, and who is consequently unaware that rationality is formed gradually, by means of knowledge. Even so, these ideas are relatively easy to grasp for people who know something about the rational and earthly planes in a person and are enlightened. Angels see them all as clear as day.

[6] To gain some idea of these concepts, see previous discussions and demonstrations: Truth on the rational plane is formed by an influence exerted on secular and religious knowledge (1495, 1563, 1900, 1964); rationality is born not of secular and religious knowledge but of the desire for them (1895, 1900); both kinds of knowledge are only vessels for what is good (1469, 1496); empty facts need to be destroyed (1489, 1492, 1499, 1500); on the rational plane, a desire for goodness is like the soul within a desire for truth (2072); definitions of the desire for rational truth and the desire for factual truth (2503); the outer self is united to the inner, which is to say that the rational self is united to the earthly, by means of religious knowledge, when this is grafted onto the heavenly qualities of love and charity (1450, 1451, 1453, 1616).

3031   *Am I really to take your son back to the land you came from?* means, could [this desire] still unite with goodness that is divine on the rational plane? This can be seen from previous statements regarding Abram and the land he came from; see §§1343, 1356, 1992, 2559. They make it clear that the land Abram came from was Syria, which was the land of the second ancient church, named the Hebrew church after its founder, Eber (§§1238, 1241, 1327, 1343). In Abraham's time, though, this church had fallen away from the truth. Some households in it had slipped so far that they knew absolutely nothing about Jehovah and worshiped other gods. This is the land meant here, concerning which the servant asked, "Am I to take your son back to the land you came from?" That is why the land here symbolizes a desire that does not harmonize with truth. Since it symbolizes this, leading Abraham's son back—or taking a woman of that land for him and leaving him there with her—means taking a desire not in harmony with truth and uniting it to goodness that is divine on the rational plane. This could not happen, as Abraham's answer (dealt with next) declares.

3032   *Abraham said to him* symbolizes a perception the Lord received from his divine side. This can be seen from the symbolism of *saying* as perceiving (discussed above in §3029) and from the representation of Abraham as the Lord's divine humanity, which gave him that perception.

3033   *Be careful not to take my son back there* means that it could never form the bond. This can be seen from the discussion just above in §3031, which explains the inner meaning of taking Abraham's son back to the land he came from.

A desire out of harmony with truth cannot unite with the goodness that belongs to the rational mind, as shown by earlier remarks about the bond between goodness and truth, or the heavenly marriage (§§2173, 2507, 2727–2759). The ancients therefore established [a custom of referring to] the desire for goodness and the desire for truth as partners in a marriage (see §1904). Falsity can never unite with goodness, nor truth with evil, because their character is opposite (2388, 2429, 2531). Goodness is instilled into the truths we know, which function as vessels designed to receive it; and in this way a bond develops (1469, 1496, 1832, 1900, 1950, 2063, 2189, 2261, 2269, 2429, 2434, 2697).

[2] I have been given the opportunity to sense vividly that no union can exist between falsity and goodness, or between truth and evil, but only between falsity and evil, truth and goodness. This is how I have perceived matters to stand: If we have a desire for goodness—that is, if we intend well with all our heart—then when there is anything we need to decide on and do, our goodwill flows into our thinking. There it adapts itself and inserts itself into the knowledge that is present, as into vessels designed to receive it. Through this bond, goodwill forces us to think, decide, and act in keeping with itself. It is like the grafting of goodness onto truth, or rather onto the knowledge of truth.

On the other hand, we might have a desire not for goodness but for evil; in other words, we might intend ill. For instance, we might view anything that benefits our own self—that makes us rich and important, so that we come into high rank and wealth—as good, and make it our goal. If so, then when there is anything we need to decide on and do, our will again flows into our thinking. There it stirs up knowledge that mimics truth, and forces us to think, decide, and act in keeping with itself. Its method is to misapply the knowledge and to consider certain general ideas (which we have absorbed from the literal meaning of the Word or from some other field of study) as capable of being interpreted in any way we like. So it is evil that pairs with falsity, because in such a case the truth that is present is deprived of all its truthful character.

[3] In the other world, people like this are stupider than others, no matter how much better informed they seemed in bodily life. The more convinced they are that they have the truth, the darker the cloud they draw over others' eyes. They lingered around me a while but were not open to any

feeling of desire for the goodness that grows out of truth, no matter how often I reminded them of true ideas they had known during bodily life. The reason was that they were in the grip of evil, to which truth could not be united.

They are also unable to keep company with the good. If any earthly goodness remains to them, they undergo devastation until they no longer know anything of the truth. A bit of truth is then injected into their remaining goodness, so far as that residual wisp of goodness can grasp it.

People who desired what was good with all their heart [during bodily life], though, are capable of receiving all truth, in accord with the amount and nature of the goodness that was present in them.

3034　　Genesis 24:7. *"Jehovah, God of heaven, who took me from my father's house and from the land of my birth, and who spoke to me, and who swore to me, saying, 'To your seed I will give this land'—he will send his angel before you, and you shall take a woman for my son from there."*

Jehovah, God of heaven, symbolizes divinity itself in the Lord. *Who took me from my father's house and from the land of my birth* means which gave the Lord the power to free himself from the evil and the falsity he inherited from his mother. *And who spoke to me, and who swore to me, saying,* means which gave him his divine ability to will and understand. *To your seed I will give this land* symbolizes the divine truth that the Lord's human side possessed. *He will send his angel before you* symbolizes divine providence. *And you shall take a woman for my son from there* means that his desire for truth did come from there but took a fresh start.

3035　　*Jehovah, God of heaven,* symbolizes divinity itself in the Lord, as can be seen from the discussion above at §3023 showing that *Jehovah, God of heaven,* means divinity itself in the Lord. *Jehovah,* who is mentioned so many times in the Old Testament Word, means the Lord alone, since absolutely everything in it speaks of him in its inner sense, and each and every one of the religious rites represented him (see §§1736, 2921). The earliest people, who were part of a heavenly religion, took "Jehovah" simply to mean the Lord (§1343).

In the literal meaning here and elsewhere, it looks as though "Jehovah" means some other person who is higher up, but that is what the literal meaning is like; it separates what the inner meaning unites. The reason for the separation is that people on earth, who need to learn from the literal meaning, cannot picture one unless they first picture many. With us, what is singular forms out of what is plural. To put the same thing another way, that which is simultaneous forms out of that which is sequential. Within the Lord are many different things, and they all constitute Jehovah.

So it is that the literal meaning separates the two. Heaven never separates them, however, but acknowledges one God—no other God than the Lord—under a single mental image.

Who took me from my father's house and from the land of my birth means which gave the Lord the power to free himself from the evil and falsity he inherited from his mother. This can be seen from the symbolism here of *my father's house* and *the land of my birth* as the contribution from his mother, or his maternal heredity. His maternal heredity was the source of the evil and falsity the Lord fought against and rid himself of, making his humanity divine in the process, by his own power. See the earlier remarks in §3031 about the house and land Abram came from. See those in §§1414, 1444 concerning the divinity the Lord inherited from Jehovah and the evil he inherited from his mother. To see that he fought against the evil he inherited from his mother but did not actually commit any himself, consult §§1444, 1573. To see that the Lord shed everything he inherited from his mother, so that in the end he was not her son, consult §§2159, 2574, 2649. His maternal heredity is what the house of Abraham's father and the land of his birth symbolize on an inner level. His *father's house* symbolizes the evil he inherited from her, while the *land of his birth* symbolizes the falsity he inherited from her, because where evil exists, falsity does too; they are conjoined. To see that the Lord rid himself of them by his own power, consult §§1616, 1813, 1921, 2025, 2026, 2083, 2523.

3036

And who spoke to me, and who swore to me, saying, means which gave him his divine ability to will and understand, as is established by the following: *Speaking* symbolizes perceiving (as noted in §3029) and also willing (§2626). And *swearing* symbolizes divine confirmation and has to do with truth, which belongs to the intellect (§2842).

3037

When Jehovah is said to *speak,* in an inner sense it means that he wills, because whatever Jehovah says, he wills. When Jehovah is said to *swear,* in an inner sense it means that he understands a thing to be true. So swearing means understanding, when Jehovah is the one said to do it. This can be seen from the scriptural passages quoted in §2842.

To your seed I will give this land symbolizes the divine truth that the Lord's human side possessed, as is established by the following: *Seed* symbolizes the faith that comes of love for others, and also people who have that faith (discussed in §§1025, 1447, 1610, 2848). Since everything faith values as good and true comes from the Lord, divine truth itself is what seed means in the highest sense. And *this land*—Canaan—symbolizes heaven, or the Lord's kingdom (discussed in §§1413, 1437, 1607). Because it symbolizes heaven, or the Lord's kingdom, divine humanity itself in

3038

the Lord is what the land of Canaan means in the highest sense. Divinity itself can exert an influence on heaven only through the Lord's divine humanity. The Lord revealed this in Matthew:

> Everything has been turned over to me by my Father, and no one knows the Son except the Father, nor does anyone know the Father except the Son and those to whom the Son wishes to reveal him. (Matthew 11:27)

And in John:

> God has never been seen by anyone; the only-born Son, who is in the Father's embrace, is the one who has revealed him. (John 1:18)

The Son is the Lord's divine humanity.

Those who believe that heaven worships any other Father than the Lord are very much mistaken.

3039   *He will send his angel before you* symbolizes divine providence. This can be seen from the symbolism of an *angel* in the Word as the Lord. Which aspect of the Lord it symbolizes is revealed by the context (as noted at §1925). Plainly it symbolizes divine providence here.

The reason angels in the Word mean the Lord is that everything in the Word that prophets and others say at the direction of angels comes from the Lord; in other words, it is the Lord's own message. Angels in heaven also acknowledge and sense that nothing good or true comes from them but from the Lord—so much so that they reject any implication to the contrary. That is why angels—the human race at its best—stand for the Lord, but the aspect of the Lord that they stand for is revealed by context.

3040   *You shall take a woman for my son from there* means that his desire for truth did come from there but took a fresh start. This can be seen from the symbolism of a *woman* as the desire for truth, as discussed above [§3024]. Rebekah, on whom the current chapter focuses, represents the divine truth that was to unite with divine goodness on the rational plane, this goodness being Isaac. It is not yet possible to explain how the desire for truth comes from there—from the things symbolized by the house of Abraham's father and the land of his birth—but takes a fresh start. The question is dealt with at length in what follows. To say just a little about it, all desire for truth in the earthly self arises from the inflow of a desire for goodness streaming out of the rational self—that is, streaming through the rational self from the Divine. At first the desire for truth that arises in our earthly self as a result of this inflow is not a desire for genuine truth. Genuine truth comes gradually, and gradually replaces the previous truth, which was not inherently true but was only a means to genuine truth. These few comments show what it means to say that a desire for truth does come from there but takes a fresh start.

Genesis 24:8, 9. *"And if the woman does not want to come after you, then you are exempt from this oath of mine; only, my son you are not to take back there." And the servant put his hand under the thigh of Abraham his master and swore to him concerning this word.*

3041

If the woman does not want to come after you here as before means if the desire for truth were not to detach. *Then you are exempt from my oath* symbolizes the freedom granted to the earthly self. *Only, my son you are not to take back there,* here as before means that there were no grounds for a union. *And the servant put his hand under the thigh of Abraham his master* here as before symbolizes the earthly self's obligation regarding its power for good in relation to marriage love. *And swore to him concerning this word* symbolizes a vow.

If the woman does not want to come after you means if the desire for truth were not to detach. This can be seen from the symbolism of a *woman* as the desire for truth and from that of *coming after* or following *you to this land* as detaching from the earthly dimension and uniting with the rational dimension. These meanings were discussed above at §3030, where the same words occur.

3042

Then you are exempt from my oath symbolizes the freedom granted to the earthly self, as can be seen from the following: A servant, which is what the clause is talking about, symbolizes the earthly self (§3019). And in the most directly related sense, *being exempt* if the woman does not want to follow means not having any obligation if the desire for truth would not detach. Clearly the phrase involves a freedom granted to the earthly self, since the desire for truth being discussed here—and the separation—is attributed to the earthly self, in an inner sense. On a narrative level, admittedly, the train of thought is quite different, but on an inner level, it is this.

3043

[2] See earlier statements and evidence concerning human freedom, in §§892, 905, 1937, 1947, 2744, 2870–2893, which show what the case is with freedom. Freedom is attributed more to our earthly self than to our rational self, because when the Lord creates a condition of heavenly freedom, goodness flows into our earthly self through our rational self. Our earthly self is what has to receive it. In order for our earthly self to receive it, and in the process unite with the heavenly freedom that flows in through our rational plane, our earthly self is left in freedom. Freedom, after all, is a matter of love, or desire. If our earthly self does not develop a desire for truth, under the influence of a desire for goodness, it

never unites with our rational self. That is how matters stand with human beings, who are reformed through a freedom established by the Lord; see §§1937, 1947, 2876, 2877, 2878, 2881.

[3] In his own case, the Lord also left his earthly self free, when he made the truth in his rational mind divine—that is, when he attached divine truth to the divine goodness in his rational mind—because he wanted to make his humanity divine in the usual way; the usual way is the way it is with us when we are reforming and being reborn. Our actual reformation and rebirth, then, is a kind of image [of the Lord's glorification]. Through these processes we become new people, which is why we are said to be born anew and created anew. The more we reform, the more we have a seeming divinity within us. The difference, though, is that the Lord made himself divine by his own power. We cannot do a thing under our own power, only under the Lord's. I call it a *seeming* divinity because we are merely recipients of life, whereas the Lord in regard to both his [human and divine] natures is life itself; see §§1954, 2021, 2658, 2706, 3001.

3044   *Only, my son you are not to take back there* means that there were no grounds for a union, as is established by the remarks above at §§3031, 3033, where the same words occur.

3045   *And the servant put his hand under the thigh of Abraham his master* symbolizes the earthly self's obligation regarding its power for good in relation to marriage love, as is established by the remarks above at §3021, where, again, the same words occur.

3046   *And swore to him concerning this word* symbolizes a vow. This can be seen from the symbolism of *swearing* as an obligation, and in fact as the most sacred obligation, since the servant was swearing by Jehovah, God of heaven and God of earth (as noted in §3023). Consequently it symbolizes a vow, since a vow is nothing but an obligation.

3047   Genesis 24:10. *And the servant took ten camels from his master's camels and went, and all the goods of his master were in his hand; and he got up and went to Aram-naharaim, to the city of Nahor.*

The servant took ten camels from his master's camels and went symbolizes general facts known to the earthly self that are divine. *And all the goods of his master were in his hand* symbolizes the goodness and truth associated with them that are present in that self. *And he got up* symbolizes going higher. *And went to Aram-naharaim* symbolizes a resulting knowledge of truth. *To the city of Nahor* symbolizes related teachings.

3048   *The servant took ten camels from his master's camels and went* symbolizes general facts known to the earthly self, as can be seen from the following:

The *servant* symbolizes the earthly self, as noted above at §§3019, 3020. *Ten* symbolizes a remnant, or the goodness and truth the Lord stores up inside us (see §§468, 530, 560, 561, 660, 661, 1050, 1906, 2284). When ten, or a remnant, is mentioned in connection with the Lord, it symbolizes divine possessions the Lord acquired for himself (1738, 1906). And *camels* symbolize general facts. Because they were divine, or acquired by the Lord, there were said to be ten, and to be camels from his master's camels. His *going* symbolizes being introduced by means of them, which is the theme of this chapter.

[2] The chapter talks about the process by which truth was united with goodness in the Lord's divine rationality and, to start with, the process of introduction (§§3012, 3013). What that process was like is depicted in sequence. The current passage portrays the Lord as detaching the things in his earthly self that came from himself—that were divine, in other words—from those he inherited from his mother. The things that came from himself, or were divine, were the means of introduction, and they are the ten camels from his master's camels. That is why the rest of the story has a lot to say about the camels. For instance, the servant made the camels kneel outside the city (verse 11). Rebekah also watered the camels (verses 14, 19, 20). They were led to the house and given hay and fodder (verses 31, 32). In addition, Rebekah and her girls rode on camels (verse 61). Isaac saw the camels coming, and when Rebekah saw Isaac, she slipped from her camel (verses 63, 64). The reason they are mentioned so many times is the inner meaning. In the inner meaning camels symbolize general facts known to the earthly self, these being the source of a desire for truth, which was to be introduced to a desire for goodness in the rational mind, and to be introduced in the usual way—as shown above [§§3030, 3043]. Truth can never be born or develop in the rational mind without secular and religious knowledge.

[3] Other passages in the Word mentioning camels show that they symbolize general facts. In Isaiah, for instance:

> An oracle of the animals of the south: In a land of anguish and agony, the young lion and old lion from there, the viper and flying fire snake, carry their riches on the shoulder of young donkeys, and *their treasures on the back of camels*, to a people [whom] they do not profit. And Egypt will help futilely and in vain. (Isaiah 30:6, 7)

The animals of the south stand for people who have the light of religious knowledge (in other words, who have the knowledge itself) but live lives of evil. Carrying their riches on the shoulder of young donkeys stands for carrying the knowledge that makes up their rational mind. (For the symbolism of a young donkey as truth on the rational plane, see §2781.) Carrying their treasures on the back of camels stands for carrying the knowledge that forms their earthly mind—the back of camels meaning the earthly plane. The camels themselves are the general facts on that plane, while the treasures are the knowledge such people hold dear. "Egypt will help futilely and in vain" means that secular knowledge is useless to them—Egypt meaning secular knowledge (see §§1164, 1165, 1186, 1462, 2588 at the end). Obviously the camels are not camels, because it says that the young lion and the old lion carry their treasures on the back of camels. Anyone can see that this symbolizes some theological mystery. [4] In the same author:

> An oracle of the wilderness beside the sea: This is what the Lord has said: "Go station a sentry; what he sees he will tell." And he saw a chariot, a pair of riders, a donkey chariot, a *camel chariot;* and he listened very closely. He answered and said, "Babylon has fallen, fallen!" (Isaiah 21:[1,] 6, 7, 9)

The wilderness beside the sea stands for the worthlessness of facts that do not serve a purpose. A donkey chariot stands for a mass of detailed facts; a camel chariot, for a mass of general facts in the earthly self. Empty sophistry in the people symbolized by Babylon is what is being portrayed this way. [5] In the same author:

> Your heart will expand, because the abundance of the sea will be steered toward you; the riches of the nations will come to you. *A horde of camels will blanket you,* the dromedaries of Midian and Ephah; they will all come from Sheba. Gold and frankincense they will carry, and the news of Jehovah's praises they will spread. (Isaiah 60:5, 6)

This is talking about the Lord and about the divinely heavenlike and divinely spiritual qualities of his earthly self. The abundance of the sea stands for a boundless supply of earthly truth; the riches of the nations, for a boundless supply of earthly goodness. A horde of camels stands for a wealth of general facts. Gold and frankincense stand for good impulses and true ideas, which are Jehovah's praises. "From Sheba" means from the heavenly aspects of love and faith; see §§113, 117, 1171. The queen of Sheba came to Solomon in Jerusalem with very great riches, with *camels carrying* perfumes and very much gold and precious stone (1 Kings 10:1, 2). This represented an increase in wisdom and understanding received by the Lord, who in the inner meaning here is Solomon. Camels carrying perfumes, gold, and precious stone are elements of wisdom and understanding in the earthly self. [6] In Jeremiah:

> In regard to Arabia and to the kingdoms of Hazor, which Nebuchad-nezzar, king of Babylon struck: Rise and go up to Arabia, and lay waste to the children of the east. [Others] will take their tents; [others] will take away from them their tent curtains and all their vessels and *their camels*. And *their camels will become plunder*, and I will scatter them to every wind. (Jeremiah 49:28, 29, 32)

Arabia and the kingdoms of Hazor have a negative meaning here, where they stand for people who acquire heavenly and spiritual knowledge for the sole purpose of seeming to themselves and the world to be wise and discerning. The camels that will be taken away from them, become plun-der, and be scattered to every wind are facts and the knowledge of good-ness and truth, in general. The facts and knowledge actually are taken away from them—by their belief in opposing ideas, during bodily life, and completely, in the next life. [7] In Zechariah:

> The plague with which Jehovah will strike all the peoples who fight against Jerusalem: so will be the plague on horse, mule, *camel,* and don-key, and every animal. (Zechariah 14:[12,] 15)

The plague on horse, mule, camel, and donkey stands for the withdrawal of intellectual abilities, which come one after the other in this order, going from those on the rational plane to those on the earthly plane. For the meaning of a horse, see §§2761, 2762. For that of a mule, 2781. For that of a donkey, 2781. Camels stand for general facts known to the earthly self. The contagion in Egypt on the livestock that was in the field, on horses, on donkeys, *on camels,* on herd, and on flock (Exodus 9:2, 3) symbolizes the same thing.

[8] This evidence shows that on the Word's inner level, camels sym-bolize general facts, which belong to the earthly self.

General facts are those that embrace many particular ones, which in turn embrace many details; and taken together they form the intellectual part of the earthly self.

And all the goods of his master were in his hand symbolizes the goodness and truth associated with [general facts] that are present in that self, as can be seen from the following: *All the goods of his master* symbolizes both goodness and truth, because truth in itself is goodness, since it comes

3049

from goodness. Truth is the form of goodness; that is, when something good takes form, so that the intellect can perceive it, it is then called truth. A *hand* symbolizes power, as noted in §878, so it means things that are present in that self.·

General facts are not intrinsically good or living. A desire for them makes them good and brings them alive, because they then exist for a purpose. No one loves any fact or true thought except for the use that can be made of it. Usefulness makes it good. Its goodness, though, depends on the nature of its use.

3050 *And he got up* symbolizes going higher. This can be seen from the symbolism of *getting up,* which involves some kind of elevation wherever it is mentioned, as discussed in §§2401, 2785, 2912, 2927. Here it means that divine truth, elicited from facts, was to be introduced to divine goodness in the Lord's rational mind.

3051 *And went to Aram-naharaim* symbolizes a resulting knowledge of truth. This can be seen from the symbolism of *Aram,* or Syria, as knowledge of what is good (discussed at §§1232, 1234). However, *Aram-naharaim,* or Syria of the Rivers, symbolizes knowledge of truth, on account of *naharaim* (rivers). Rivers symbolize intelligence, which has to do with a knowledge of what is true, as shown by the scriptural passages quoted in §§108, 109, 2702 and by many other passages. I will have more to say on this elsewhere, by the Lord's divine mercy.

3052 *To the city of Nahor* symbolizes related teachings. This can be seen from the symbolism of a *city* as a doctrinal teaching (discussed in §§402, 2449) and from the representation of *Nahor* as something related—since Nahor was Abram's brother and fathered Bethuel, who fathered Rebekah.

The difference between facts and teachings is that teachings grow out of facts. Teachings look to useful activity, and we compile them by reflecting on facts.

The teachings are said to be related here because they were derived from divine sources.

3053 Genesis 24:11. *And he made the camels kneel outside the city, at the well of water, near evening time, near the time that the women drawing water went out.*

He made the camels kneel symbolizes arranging general facts in a holy pattern. *Outside the city* means removing them from doctrinal teachings. *At the well of water* means in order to receive religious truth. *Near evening time* symbolizes a relatively dark stage then. *Near the time that the women drawing water went out* symbolizes a stage of instruction.

He made the camels kneel symbolizes arranging general facts in a holy pattern. This can be seen from the symbolism of *causing to kneel* as putting oneself in a holy mood, and from that of *camels* as general facts (dealt with just above in §3048).

3054

Outside the city means removing them from doctrinal teachings. This can be seen from the symbolism of a *city* as a doctrinal teaching (discussed at §§402, 2449). *Outside* it, obviously, means outside doctrine, so it means removing them from doctrinal teachings.

3055a

At the well of water means in order to receive religious truth. This can be seen from the symbolism of a *well of water* as the Word, which is the source of religious truth, and also as truth itself (discussed at §2702).

3055b

This verse speaks of a well of water, though several later verses call it a spring. For the difference in inner meaning when the text mentions a well of water and when it mentions a spring, see the passage referred to.

Near evening time symbolizes a relatively dark stage then. This can be seen from the symbolism of a *time* as a stage (treated of in §§2625, 2788, 2837) and from that of *evening* as something dim. In the Word, *evening* symbolizes the stage preceding the final one of a declining religion, which is called night. It also symbolizes [the one preceding] the first stage of a dawning religion, which is called morning; see §2323. In both senses, a dimness is what is symbolized by evening. Here, it symbolizes the darkness before morning.

3056

Near the time that the women drawing water went out symbolizes a stage of instruction. This can be seen from the symbolism of a *time* as a stage (discussed just above at §3056) and from that of a *woman* or man *drawing water* as being taught (discussed below).

3057

The things said from §3054 to this point are those symbolized on an inner level by the narrative details of the current verse. Yet the implications of each detail are not easy to see in a connected series for anyone who has not been taught about the earthly self, about the facts and teachings known to it, or about the way truth is lifted up from there into the rational mind and becomes rational. It is still harder for people who do not know what the rational plane is like, compared to the earthly plane, or what the contents of the rational mind are like, compared to those of the earthly mind. [2] Moreover, the contents of the rational mind are not visible to us as long as we are living in our bodies. It is the contents of our earthly mind that come to our attention. Rarely do we notice what is in our rational mind, except as a kind of light illuminating the material in our earthly mind, or as an inflowing ability to arrange our thoughts in order, or as an insight into some topic the mind is focusing on.

Unless these and many other things are known, it is difficult to explain intelligibly what lies behind the current verse. That includes the arrangement of general facts in a holy pattern, the consequent removal of them from doctrinal teachings in order that religious truth can be received, the dark stage that follows, and the fact that this is what a stage of instruction is like.

Still, let me express briefly whatever *can* be understood. I will put it in terms of the situation we humans face when the Lord is reforming us, since human reformation is a kind of image of events the Lord experienced while he was in the world, as noted above in §3043. [3] While we are reforming, the Lord rearranges the general attributes of our earthly self so that they correspond to the general attributes of heaven. (For an explanation of correspondence, and the fact that it exists between spiritual qualities and earthly ones, see §§2987, 2989, 2990, 2991, 3002.) The general categories are arranged first, so that the Lord can gradually fit the subcategories into them, and the individual components into these. If the general categories are not in order, the subcategories cannot be, because subcategories compose the categories and strengthen them. Still less can the individual details be in order, because they compose the subcategories (which are *their* general categories) and shed light on them. That is what is meant by arranging general facts in a holy pattern, and it is the inner-level symbolism of making camels kneel, because they accordingly yield and accept the influence.

[4] When the general facts are arranged in this manner, doctrinal teachings are then removed, because they are conclusions drawn from facts. Something like a dictate flows in through the rational mind, saying that this is true and that is not true. It says that one thing is true because it harmonizes with the pattern the general facts are arranged in, while another is untrue because it does not. No other inflow speaking to us about truth exists. Before this, teachings actually are present, but until we believe in them, they are not teachings, merely facts. Accordingly, when we think about them, we do not draw conclusions from them. Instead we draw conclusions *about* them from other facts. This is what being removed from doctrinal teachings means, and it is symbolized on an inner level here by the words *outside the city*. This stage is the one described as dark and symbolized by the evening time. When we have confirmed the teachings to the point of believing in them, though, then comes morning, or a bright stage.

The rest of the verse's contents are evident from what has now been said. The reason that *drawing water* symbolizes instruction and the resulting enlightenment (which later parts of the chapter deal with) is that on an inner level, water symbolizes religious truth (§2702). Drawing water, then, actually means learning religious truth and so being enlightened. It means the same thing in other scriptural passages, such as this one in Isaiah:

3058

> You will *draw water* in joy from springs of salvation. On that day, acclaim Jehovah! (Isaiah 12:3, 4)

Drawing water stands for learning, understanding, and being wise. In the same author:

> *Bring water* to meet the thirsty, you who live in the land of Tema! (Isaiah 21:14)

Bringing water to meet the thirsty stands for teaching them. In the same author:

> The wretched and poor are *seeking water,* and there is none; their tongue fails from thirst. (Isaiah 41:17)

Seeking water stands for wanting to be taught truth. "There is none" means that no one has any.

In the Jewish religion, furthermore, people who drew water represented individuals who constantly want to know truth but simply for the purpose of knowing it, without any interest in using it. They were considered some of the most worthless people around. The Gibeonites, discussed in Joshua 9:21, 23, 27, represented them.

Genesis 24:12, 13, 14. And he said, "Jehovah, God of my master Abraham, please make this happen before me today, and do mercy to my master Abraham. Look: I am standing by at a spring of water, and the daughters of the men of the city are going out to draw water. And let it be that the girl to whom I say, 'Please tilt your pitcher and let me drink,' and she says, 'Drink! And your camels I will also water'—that her you have destined for your servant Isaac; and in this I will know that you have done mercy to my master."

3059

He said symbolizes communication. *Jehovah, God of my master Abraham,* means between divinity itself, which is the Father, and divine humanity, which is the Son. *Please make this happen before me today* symbolizes providence from eternity. *And do mercy* symbolizes an inflow of love. *To my master Abraham* symbolizes divine humanity. *Look: I am standing by at a spring of water* symbolizes a stage at which truth that is divine unites with the Lord's humanity. *And the daughters of the men of the city are going out to draw water* symbolizes a desire for truth, and through it, instruction. *And let it be that the girl to whom I say,* symbolizes a desire that has innocence within it. *Please tilt your pitcher* symbolizes submissiveness on the part of facts. *And let me drink* means being taught truth as a result. *And she says, "Drink!"* symbolizes a reciprocal response to it. *And your camels I will also water* symbolizes the light consequently shed on all the facts known to the earthly self. *That her you have destined for your servant Isaac* symbolizes the union of truth that is divine with divine goodness in the rational mind. *And in this I will know that you have done mercy to my master* means that marriage comes from divine love.

3060   *He said* symbolizes communication. This can be seen from the symbolism of *saying* in the Word's narratives as perceiving and willing (dealt with many times before). Because it symbolizes this, it also symbolizes communicating, because perception and will leads to communication.

3061   *Jehovah, God of my master Abraham,* means between divinity itself, which is the Father, and divine humanity, which is the Son—that is, communication between them. This is established by several things said and shown above:

Jehovah God is divinity itself in the Lord, which is called the Father, while Abraham represents his divine humanity: 2833, 2836. In the Old Testament Word, Jehovah is the Lord himself (see §§1736, 1815, 2921); the earliest church (before the Flood) and the ancient church (after it) took Jehovah to be no one but the Lord (1343, 1676, 1990, 2016, 2035). In the Lord is the trinity of divinity itself, divine humanity, and their divinely holy influence, and the three are one: 1999, 2149, 2156, 2288, 2329, 2447. The whole trinity in the Lord is Jehovah (2156, 2329), and absolutely everything in the Lord is Jehovah (1902, 1921). The Lord is one with the Father; and in heaven, no one but the Lord is meant by the Father: 14, 15, 1725, 1729, 1733, 1815, 2005, 2018, 2025, 2803, 3038. The Lord is the whole of heaven, because he is everything there; from him comes every bit of innocence, peace, love, charity, mercy, and marriage love, and everything good and true; Moses and the Prophets and therefore every detail of the Word have to do with him; and all the rituals of the church represented him: 2751. The Lord is called the Son in regard to his divine humanity: 2628. His divine humanity was not only conceived but also born of his divine nature, which is Jehovah (2798), so in respect to his humanity, the Lord became Jehovah, and self-originating life (1603, 1737).

[2] The Lord has existed from eternity, as the Word makes plain (see §2803), although he was later born in time. After all, he spoke through

Moses and the prophets and appeared to many people, and it says there that he was Jehovah. This deep secret, though, cannot be revealed to anyone who does not have divine perception. As a result, it can be revealed to hardly anyone but members of the earliest church, which was heavenly and had divine perception. From them I have heard that Jehovah himself was the Lord in his divine humanity, at the times when he went down into heaven and flowed through heaven. The reason he revealed himself this way is that heaven resembles an individual human being with all the body parts, which is also why it is called the universal human (§§684, 1276, 2996, 2998, 3021). Divinity itself in heaven, or in the universal human, was the divine human, who was Jehovah himself clothed in this humanity.

[3] However, the human race eventually became such that divinity itself, clothed as divine humanity, could no longer accomplish this—that is, Jehovah could no longer reach people—because they had moved too far away from him. When that happened, Jehovah (who is the Lord in his divine essence) came down and took on a human nature. By its conception, this nature was divine, but by its birth from a young woman, it resembled that of any other person. The latter nature he banished, though, and through divine means made his earth-born humanity divine. From this divine humanity comes all his holy influence. So his divine humanity became his actual essence, which fills the whole of heaven and enables people who could not be saved before to be saved. This now is the Lord, who in his divine humanity is the only human, and from whom we have our own humanity (§§49, 288, 477, 565, 1894).

Please make this happen before me today symbolizes providence from eternity. This can be seen from the symbolism of *make this happen* as providing, and from that of *today* as being from eternity (discussed in §2838). Besides, providence is obviously what these words have to do with and what the servant is praying for.

3062

And do mercy symbolizes an inflow of love. This can be seen from the essence of *mercy,* which is love. Love itself turns into and becomes mercy when we look with love or charity on anyone who needs help, so mercy is the effect of a love for the needy and poor. Here, though, mercy in an inner sense means love, and *doing mercy* means an inflow of love, because that inflow came from the Lord's divinity itself into his divine humanity. The divine love the Lord had was what he used to make his humanity divine, because love is the true core of life; but only the Lord has divine love. See previous discussions of the Lord's love: The Lord's life was love for the entire human race (§2253), and from this love he fought his battles (1690, 1789, 1812, 1813, 1820). It surpasses all

3063

understanding (1799, 2077). The Lord is divine love itself (2077, 2500, 2572). Jehovah is love (1735). Nothing but love is alive (1589). People who share in universal love have the Lord's life in them (1799, 1802, 1803). Love and charity is heavenliness itself (1419, 1824).

3064   *To my master Abraham* symbolizes divine humanity. This can be seen from the representation of *Abraham* as the Lord's divine humanity (discussed in §§2833, 2836).

3065   *Look: I am standing by at a spring of water* symbolizes a stage at which truth that is divine unites [with and] within the Lord's humanity. This can be seen from the symbolism of a *spring* as truth (discussed in §2702)— here, truth that is divine, since the text is speaking of the Lord. The actual stage of union is symbolized by *standing by at a spring*. The fact that the union takes place within the Lord's humanity is clear from the context.

3066   *And the daughters of the men of the city are going out to draw water* symbolizes a desire for truth, and through it, instruction, as can be seen from the following: *Daughters* symbolize desires, as discussed in §§489, 490, 491, 2362. The *men of the city* symbolize truth. The Word sometimes calls a city's inhabitants the men of the city, sometimes the residents of the city. When it calls them the men of the city, they symbolize truth; when it calls them residents, they symbolize goodness. For the symbolism of men, see §§265, 749, 915, 1007, 2517. For that of residents, 2268, 2451, 2712. For that of a city, 402, 2449, 2943. And finally, *drawing water* means being taught, as discussed above at §3058. Clearly, then, *the daughters of the men of the city are going out to draw water* symbolizes a desire for truth, and through it, instruction.

Truth never teaches anyone anything; only the desire for truth does. In the absence of desire, truth does wash up against the ear like waves of sound, but it does not enter the memory. What makes it enter the memory and stay there is a desire for it. A good feeling is like the ground in which truth is planted like seed. The quality of the soil (or the desire), though, determines what grows out of the planted seed. The goal or purpose dictates the character of the soil (the desire) and therefore the character of what grows from the seed. If you prefer, love itself dictates, because love is the goal and purpose of everything; we cannot adopt anything as our goal and purpose but what we love.

3067   *And let it be that the girl to whom I say,* symbolizes a desire that has innocence within it, as can be seen from the symbolism of a *girl.* In the Word, different kinds of desire for what is good and true are called little children, girls, maidens, and daughters, but in each case there is a difference in the state of the desire. When the term *daughter* is used, it symbolizes desire in general. When the term is *maiden*, it symbolizes a desire that harbors love for others within it. When the term is *girl*, it symbolizes a desire that harbors innocence within it, and the reason is that girlhood comes next after infancy, which in the inner meaning is innocence. It is similar with a boy or little child, which symbolizes a stage at which there is innocence (see §430).

Please tilt your pitcher symbolizes submissiveness on the part of facts. This can be seen from the symbolism of *tilting* as yielding and from that of a *pitcher* as facts. The reason a water jar or pitcher symbolizes facts is that water symbolizes truth (§§680, 739, 2702), and a pitcher is a container that holds water, just as factual information is a container that holds truth. Every fact is a vessel for truth, and every truth is a vessel for goodness. A fact devoid of truth is an empty container, as is a truth devoid of goodness; but factual knowledge that holds truth, and truth that holds goodness, is a well-filled container. Desire born of love is what binds them together, each within the next in order, because love is spiritual union.

3068

And let me drink means being taught truth as a result. This can be seen from the symbolism of *drinking* as learning.

3069

Many places in the Word speak of *drinking,* and where the theme is the goodness and truth that faith encompasses, it means learning about and accepting them. In Isaiah, for example:

> The new wine will mourn; the grapevine droops; all who are rejoicing at heart will groan. *They will not drink wine with a song.* The strong drink will be bitter for *those drinking it.* (Isaiah 24:7, 9)

Not drinking wine with a song stands for not learning truth out of any desire for it or any pleasure in the activity. Strong drink that is bitter for those drinking it stands for aversion. In the same author:

> It will be as if people who are *thirsty* dream, and here, they are *drinking!* And they wake up, and here, they are faint, and their soul is longing. (Isaiah 29:8)

Being thirsty stands for wanting to learn. Drinking stands for being taught, but being taught worthless things. [2] In Jeremiah:

> Our *water we drink* at the cost of silver, our wood comes at a price. (Lamentations 5:4)

To drink water at the cost of silver stands for not being taught for free, and also for taking personal credit for the truth. A passage in Isaiah says that truth comes for free and therefore not from ourselves but from the Lord:

> Everyone who is *thirsty, come to the water,* and whoever does not have silver, *come,* buy! (Isaiah 55:1)

And in John:

> Jesus said, "If any are *thirsty,* let them come to me and *drink.* Any who believe in me, from their belly will flow *rivers of living water.*" (John 7:37, 38)

Drinking here means learning and accepting. In Luke:

> They will say, "We ate in front of you, and *drank,* and in our streets you taught." But the owner will say, "I do not know you, where you are from. Leave me, all you evildoers!" (Luke 13:26, 27)

Eating and drinking in front of the owner stands for teaching and preaching about religious goodness and truth, on the basis of knowledge gleaned from the Word, which is what "in our streets you taught" means. However, these people did it for selfish reasons—for the sake of their own prestige and enrichment—so they did it without any desire for goodness or truth. Consequently they knew truth but lived evil lives, so it says, "I do not know you, where you are from. Leave me, all you evildoers!" [3] In the same author:

> Jesus said to his disciples, ". . . so that you may eat and *drink at my table* in my kingdom." (Luke 22:30)

Anyone can see that in the Lord's kingdom they do not eat and drink and the Lord has no table there. Eating and drinking at the Lord's table in his kingdom, then, clearly means something else—namely, enjoying a perception of what is good and true. Something similar is the case with the Lord's words in Matthew:

> I say to you that from now on *I will not drink* any of this produce of the grapevine until that day when *I drink* it with you in my Father's kingdom. (Matthew 26:28, 29)

Drinking stands for teaching people about truth in a vivid way and giving them a perception of goodness and truth. The Lord said:

> Do not worry for your soul, what you are to eat or *drink,* or for your body, what you are to put on. (Matthew 6:25, 31; Luke 12:29)

These words are symbolic of spiritual things: that every ingredient of faith, whether it is something good or true, is given by the Lord. In John:

> Jesus to the Samaritan woman: "Anyone who *drinks this water will be thirsty* again. But those who *drink the water* that I give them *will never be thirsty* to eternity; instead, the water that I give them will become a spring of water gushing up in them to provide eternal life." (John 4:7–14)

Clearly, drinking stands for being taught about goodness and truth and receiving them.

And she says, "Drink!" is a reciprocal response to it, as can be seen from the fact that it is an answer, and confirmation, and therefore a reciprocal response.   **3070**

And your camels I will also water symbolizes the light consequently shed on all the facts known to the earthly self, as can be seen from the following: *Camels* symbolize general facts, and thus facts in general, or all facts, as discussed above in §3048. And *watering* means enlightening. It was shown above in §3058 that drawing water means offering instruction, so *watering* means enlightening. Enlightenment comes from instruction.   **3071**

That her you have destined for your servant Isaac symbolizes the union of truth that is divine with divine goodness in the rational mind, as can be seen from the following: *Destining*—destining someone to be someone's woman—means uniting the two in a pact of marriage. And *Isaac* represents goodness that is divine in the Lord's rational mind, as noted above at §3024. The representation of *her*, Rebekah, as truth that is divine, which is to unite with the divine goodness of the rational mind, has been mentioned several times already [§§3012, 3030, 3040] and becomes clear from the details of the chapter's inner meaning.   **3072**

In this I will know that you have done mercy to my master means that marriage comes from divine love. This can be seen from the symbolism of *mercy* on an inner level here as divine love (dealt with in §3063). Since the theme is the betrothal of Rebekah to Isaac—that is, the union of divine truth to divine goodness in the rational mind—*doing mercy to my master* simply symbolizes marriage, and therefore marriage as a result of divine love. These words also constitute the end of the servant's prayer and its whole purpose.   **3073**

The contents of the inner meaning in these three verses can be seen to some extent from the explanation. Since it is broken up, though, the   **3074** logical progression cannot appear unless we gather up the pieces and view them as one picture. At the same time, we have to turn our focus away from the literal meaning, because as long as we hold it there, it not only confuses our thoughts but also keeps us in doubt, and the more doubt we have, the darker our mind grows.

In sum, this passage depicts the process by which truth is revealed through facts, rises up into the rational self out of those facts in the earthly self, and becomes rational truth. In the Lord, it became divine truth, and this is how: His divine love flowed into his human side and stirred up an innocent desire for truth. The facts known to his earthly self were lit up by the inflowing love and various truths were revealed, which were to be raised into his rational mind and united with a loving goodness there that was divine.

The process is depicted in greater detail in what follows. However, you need to know that an inflow of love, and a resulting inflow of desires that hold innocence within them, are what organize everything in whole and in part, even in our earthly self. Otherwise, you will necessarily have a very dim idea (if any) of the matters addressed here and above.

3075   Genesis 24:15, 16. *And it happened that he had hardly finished speaking when here, Rebekah comes out, who had been born to Bethuel, son of Milcah wife of Nahor brother of Abraham; and her pitcher was on her shoulder. And the girl was very good to look at—a young, unmarried woman, and no man had known her; and she went down to the spring and filled her pitcher and came up.*

And it happened that he had hardly finished speaking symbolizes what his wishes brought about. *When here, Rebekah comes out* symbolizes a desire for truth, arising out of teachings. *Who had been born to Bethuel, son of Milcah wife of Nahor brother of Abraham,* symbolizes all the origins of that desire. *And her pitcher was on her shoulder* symbolizes receiving truth and expending effort. *And the girl was very good to look at* symbolizes the beauty of a desire for truth. *A young, unmarried woman, and no man had known her* means unsullied by any falsity. *And she went down to the spring* symbolizes truth that is divine. *And filled her pitcher* symbolizes vessels for receiving. *And came up* symbolizes a raising up.

3076   *And it happened that he had hardly finished speaking* symbolizes what his wishes brought about. This can be seen from the direct outcome: every single thing happened the way he had prayed for it to. In other words, it was brought about as he had wished. *Speaking* symbolizes willing; see §§2626, 3037.

When here, Rebekah comes out symbolizes a desire for truth, arising 3077
out of teachings. This is established by the representation of *Rebekah* as
truth that was divine, which was to unite with the divine goodness of
the rational mind. Here, though, before she became betrothed, she takes
on the representation of a desire for truth, arising out of teachings (since
they contain truth). Truth is not true unless there is life in it, and its life-
blood is the desire that comes of love.

The representation of *Rebekah* as truth that was divine, which was
to unite with goodness that was divine, existing in the rational mind,
can be seen from the individual elements of the current chapter's inner
meaning. It can also be seen from the fact that Isaac represents the Lord's
divine rationality (§§1893, 2066, 2083, 2630). So Rebekah, who became
Isaac's wife, represents the aspect of his rational mind that united with it
as a wife unites with her husband. That aspect is divine truth, as stands to
reason. By the same token, Abraham represented divine goodness itself,
while his wife Sarah represented divine truth itself united with divine
goodness (§§1468, 1901, 2063, 2065, 2904). The same holds true for Isaac
and Rebekah, but within the setting of the Lord's divine humanity, or in
other words, his rationality.

In the Word, a husband usually symbolizes goodness, and his wife,
truth (1468, 2517). In addition, the vital essence of all marriage, or all marriage love, comes from the divine marriage between goodness and truth
and between truth and goodness in the Lord (2508, 2618, 2728, 2729, 2803).

The point is made that the desire for truth arises out of teachings
because the text says Rebekah came out, meaning out of the city, and a
city symbolizes a doctrinal teaching (see §§402, 2449). Moreover, teachings contain truth.

Who had been born to Bethuel, son of Milcah wife of Nahor brother of 3078
Abraham, symbolizes all the origins of that desire, as can be seen from the
representation of Bethuel, of Milcah and Nahor, and of Abraham. The specific representation of each cannot be presented and explained intelligibly,
for this reason: The Lord's first desire for truth did trace its origin to divine
attributes acquired by him in his earthly self (§3019). But his earthly self
still possessed a maternal heredity, which could not be detached instantly,
and this too was a source of his desire. The nature of that desire in its origins is described in the inner meaning of the statement that Rebekah had
been *born to Bethuel, son of Milcah wife of Nahor brother of Abraham.*

[2] Any desire contains within itself such a boundless number of elements that it cannot possibly be grasped in any way, still less described,

even though it appears to be a single, uncomplicated entity. Every desire holds within itself the whole life we have acquired from infancy up to whatever stage we have reached when we develop the desire. In fact, it contains even more than that, since it includes what we have inherited by birth from our father and mother, our grandparents and great-grandparents. The desire is the whole person just as she or he is.

In the other world, our [dominant] desire is sometimes laid out in the open and presents a picture of us. It shows how much self-love and how much materialism we harbor, how much love for good principles, and what kind of goal and purpose we have. It reveals how much we love what is good and true, what that goodness and truth are like, and also how they are organized—the close ties, looser ties, and wide gaps between them. So it indicates how far out of tune with the design of heaven we are or how far in tune. All these things become clear from a disclosure of our [dominant] desire, as mentioned, because the desire is the whole person. It seems incredible to people on earth that this could be so, but it is still true.

3079   *And her pitcher was on her shoulder* symbolizes receiving truth and expending effort. This can be seen from the symbol of a *pitcher* as factual information and so as a holder for truth (discussed in §3068) and from that of a *shoulder* as all one's might and therefore as effort (discussed in §1085).

On an inner level, pitchers (or water jars) and containers in general symbolize that which serves to receive something else—the role facts and knowledge play in relation to truth, and the role truth itself plays in relation to goodness. Many places in the Word can illustrate this. It is exactly what the vessels of the Temple and its altar symbolized, and because they did, they too were holy. Their holiness had no other origin. [2] That is the reason for the event recorded in Daniel 5:2 and following verses: Belshazzar drank wine with his nobles and his wives out of the vessels of gold and silver that Nebuchadnezzar, his father, had brought out of the Temple at Jerusalem, and they praised the gods of gold, silver, bronze, iron, wood, and stone. Then handwriting appeared on the wall of his palace. The vessels of gold and silver stand for a knowledge of what is good and true—a knowledge that was profaned. Chaldeans, you see, symbolize people with religious knowledge, but knowledge that has been profaned by the distortions in it (§1368), so that it serves them in their worship of gold and silver gods. Belshazzar is called a Chaldean monarch in verse 30 of that chapter.

[3] The symbolism of vessels as the outward containers of spiritual qualities becomes clear from other scriptural passages as well, as in Isaiah:

> . . . as the children of Israel bring an offering in a *clean vessel* to Jehovah's house. (Isaiah 66:20)

This is about the Lord's kingdom. An offering in a clean vessel represents the relationship between the outer and inner self. The person who brings the offering is the inner self. The clean vessel is an outer self in harmony with the inner, so it is what the outer self holds, which is facts, knowledge, and teachings. [4] In Jeremiah:

> Jerusalem's cry has risen up, and its nobles have sent the young ones to the water. They came to the pits; they did not find water; they returned *with their vessels empty;* they were ashamed. (Jeremiah 14:2, 3)

Empty vessels stand for knowledge that has no truth in it, and also for truth that has no goodness in it. In the same author:

> Nebuchadnezzar, king of Babylon, has devoured me, has churned me up; he has rendered me an *empty vessel.* (Jeremiah 51:34)

An empty vessel stands for the same things here. It is Babylon that causes the devastation (see §1327 at the end). In Moses:

> They are planted as valleys are, as gardens beside the river; *the waters will flow down from buckets,* and his seed will be by many waters. (Numbers 24:6, 7)

This is Balaam's utterance concerning Jacob and Israel. "The waters will flow down from buckets" stands for the fact that truth will flow from knowledge. [5] In the parable about the ten young women, five of whom took *oil in their vessels* with their lamps, while the stupid ones did not (Matthew 25:4–[5]), the young women symbolize desires. The fact that the prudent ones took oil in their vessels means that the truth they knew had goodness in it, and so their faith had love for their neighbor in it. For the symbolism of oil as goodness, see §886. Lamps stand for love.

And the girl was very good to look at symbolizes the beauty of a desire **3080** for truth, as is established by the symbolism of a *girl* as a desire that has innocence within it (discussed in §3067).

The reason *very good to look at* symbolizes beauty—here, the beauty of a desire for truth, since it is said of a girl—is that all beauty comes from goodness that has innocence within it. When the goodness of the inner self acts on the outer self, it actually creates beauty. That is the source of all human beauty.

The same thing can also be seen from the fact that no one responds to another's face but rather to the passion that radiates from it. People with goodness are drawn to the desire for goodness they see in a face, and the more innocence there is in the goodness, the more they are affected by it. So the spiritual dimension within the physical is what appeals to them, not the physical dimension without the spiritual. People devoted to goodness respond the same way to little children; the more innocence and love for others is expressed in the face, deeds, and words of the children, the more beautiful they seem to those people. (For the idea that goodness and neighborly love is what forms and constitutes beauty, see §553.)

So it is that *the girl was very good to look at* symbolizes the beauty of a desire for truth—truth that has what is good within it.

3081 *A young, unmarried woman, and no man had known her* means unsullied by any falsity, as can be seen from the symbolism of a *young woman*. The Word mentions young women in many places, where they symbolize the Lord's kingdom and the church and therefore anyone who *is* a kingdom of the Lord, or who *is* a church. This is on account of the love for marriage that chaste young women have. In a spiritual sense, marriage love is a desire for the goodness that lies at the heart of truth and a desire for the truth that grows out of goodness. When these two wed, so to speak, they produce marriage love; see §§2508, 2618, 2727, 2728, 2729. As mentioned before, this love is found in a young woman, so the Lord's kingdom, which is compared to and actually referred to as a marriage, is called a young woman.

No man had known her means unsullied by any falsity because in the Word, a *man* symbolizes not only truth on the rational plane but also—in a negative sense—falsity; see §§265, 749, 1007. So being known by a man means being polluted by falsity, and not being known by a man means being free of falsity. In this verse a man does not mean a husband.

[2] The symbolism of a *virgin* in the Word as people who are in the Lord's kingdom (that is, who have the Lord's kingdom in them) can be seen in John:

> They are the ones who have not been defiled with women, *since they are virgins.* They are the ones who follow the Lamb where he goes, for they are spotless before God's throne. (Revelation 14:4, 5)

The people who follow the Lamb—people in the Lord's kingdom—are explicitly being called virgins, and spotless. [3] Strictly speaking, virgins are people who love the Lord, or in other words, heavenly people, and therefore people who have a desire for goodness. The term is also used for people who have charity for their neighbor, or in other words, spiritual people, and therefore people who have a desire for truth. This can be illustrated by scriptural passages. In Isaiah:

> The *virgin daughter of Zion* has despised you, mocked you. Behind you the daughter of Jerusalem shakes her head. (Isaiah 37:22)

These words are addressed to Assyria's monarch. The virgin daughter of Zion stands for a heavenly religion, and the daughter of Jerusalem, for a spiritual one. [4] In Jeremiah:

> I will build you again, and *you will be rebuilt, young woman of Israel;* you will decorate your tambourines again and go out into the dances of the merry. Their soul will become like a watered garden, and they will not continue to grieve any more; then the *young woman will rejoice in dance,* as will the young men and the old together. (Jeremiah 31:4, 12, 13)

The young woman of Israel stands for a spiritual religion. The desire such a religion has for the truth that grows out of goodness is depicted here (as it is elsewhere) by tambourines and dances. In the same author:

> Zion's paths are mourning, its priests are groaning, *its young women are sad.* The Lord has trodden the winepress for the *virgin daughter of Judah.* Look at my grief; *my young women* and my young men have gone into captivity. (Lamentations 1:4, 15, 18)

The young women stand for the desire for what is good and true. In another place in the same author:

> Women have been raped in Zion; *young women,* in the cities of Judah. (Lamentations 5:11)

The young women stand for the desire for what is good. [5] In Amos:

> They will dash about to seek Jehovah's Word and will not find it; on that day the *beautiful young women* and the young men will faint with thirst. (Amos 8:12, 13)

The beautiful young women stand for a desire for truth, and the young men, for truth—or, to say it another way, for people who have those things. It says that such people will dash about to seek Jehovah's Word and not find it and will therefore faint with thirst. [6] In Zechariah:

> Jehovah their God will save them on that day; like a flock [will he save] his people, because how great is their goodness, and how great their

beauty! Grain *will cause* young men—and new wine, *young women—to sprout.* (Zechariah 9:16, 17)

The young men stand for truth; the young women, for desire. In David:

All glorious is the king's daughter within [the palace]; her clothing is made of gold braid. In embroidery she is brought to the king; *the young women after her—her friends*—have been brought to you. (Psalms 45:13, 14)

The king's daughter stands for the Lord's spiritual kingdom. The young women after her—her friends—stand for the desire for truth. [7] In the same author:

They saw your strides, God, the strides of my God in the sanctuary; the singers went in front, the harp-players came after, *in the middle of the maidens* playing tambourines. (Psalms 68:24, 25)

Maidens playing tambourines also stand for a desire for truth.

What distinguishes "virgins" from "maidens" is innocence. Virgins are called virgins because of their love for marriage, so the term is applied to people who have innocence, because marriage love is innocence itself (see §2736). That is why they are said to follow the Lamb where he goes, in the passage quoted from John, because the Lamb means the innocence of the Lord. All in heaven are called virgins, because of the innocence that lies at the heart of their goodness. The more innocence is present in their goodness, and the purer it is, the more they follow the Lamb.

3082   *And she went down to the spring* symbolizes truth that is divine, as is established by §§2702, 3065, which showed that the symbolism of a *spring* is truth that is divine.

3083   *And filled her pitcher* symbolizes vessels for receiving, as can be seen from the symbolism of a *pitcher.* Because a pitcher is a container for water, in an inner sense it is a container for both the knowledge of truth and truth itself, which water symbolizes. On the point that in an inner sense water is knowledge and also truth, see §§28, 680, 2702, 3058.

3084   *And came up* symbolizes a raising up. This can be seen from the symbolism of going up as being raised up.

A thing is said to be raised up when it goes from a lower level to a higher, and on this account, being raised means going from a shallower level to a deeper level, since the two are the same. What humans picture as being lower and higher, angels picture as being more superficial and deeper. Heaven, for instance, seems to us to be high up, but to angels it is deep within. The same is true of our earthly plane; compared to our spiritual plane, it is relatively superficial, and our spiritual plane in turn is relatively superficial compared to our heavenly plane. Or, what is the same, the facts known to our earthly self are shallow by comparison with truth; and truth is shallow by comparison with goodness. So in relation to truth, factual knowledge is called a cloak and a garment, which is what truth is called in relation to goodness.

So it is that one is said to go "up" to Jerusalem and "down" from it, and from Jerusalem to Zion and Zion to Jerusalem. Jerusalem's surroundings symbolize the more external aspects of the church; Jerusalem itself, the more inward aspects; and Zion, the inmost.

The inner meaning here is describing the start of the process by which truth is lifted out of the earthly self up to the rational self. So first the text says that the desire for truth, represented by Rebekah, went down to the spring, and then that she came up. As noted above at §3074, divine love flows into a desire for goodness, and through this, into a desire for truth. It brings life and light to the contents of our earthly self and then organizes them. That is what *going down* means. Afterward, truth rises up out of the earthly self into the rational self, where it unites with goodness. That is what *coming up* means.

These two verses portray the origins of a desire for truth, its nature, and the stage at which it is first being introduced. **3085**

Its *origins* are described this way: "Rebekah went out, who had been born to Bethuel, son of Milcah wife of Nahor brother of Abraham." These words in their inner meaning tell about all the origins of that desire; see §§3077, 3078.

Its *nature* is described this way: "Her pitcher was on her shoulder, and the girl was very good to look at." These words depict its nature, as can be seen at §§3079, 3080, 3081.

The *stage at which it is first introduced* is described this way: "She went down to the spring and filled her pitcher and came up." This can be seen in §§3082, 3083, 3084.

[2] The problem here, as I said above [§§3057, 3078], is that the situation transcends the grasp not only of ordinary people but even of the more broadly educated. That is what the concepts of the inner meaning are like in the current chapter and some of those to follow. It dawns on hardly anyone that a divine influence is constantly being exerted on our outward self by way of our inward. In other words, heavenly and spiritual qualities are constantly flowing into our earthly self—that is,

into the earthly qualities of our outward self—by means of our rational self. Few notice this inflow or the fact that it constantly calls truth out of our earthly self, lifts it up, and grafts it onto what is good in our rational self.

Since people do not even realize that this happens, how are they to understand the entire process and its method? Because it is a product of divine activity, it is a work of such deep wisdom that we cannot possibly investigate even a millionth of it. Its most general outlines are all we can see. [3] This being so, no one should be surprised to find that the contents of the inner meaning in the current case cannot be described intelligibly, or that what *is* being described exceeds human understanding, since it focuses on and describes this process. Besides, the inner meaning exists mainly for angels, in order to establish communication between heaven and humankind by means of the Word. Angels count its contents as one of their pleasures, because heavenly food is simply any contribution to their understanding and wisdom, and what they count as the blessings of wisdom and understanding are everything having to do with the Lord.

3086   To gain any idea, however vague, about the contents of the inner meaning here, you need to know that the whole chapter is talking about truth that is divine, which was to unite with divine goodness. Specifically, it is saying this: Divine goodness acted on the Lord's earthly self, or in other words, on the facts, knowledge, and teachings there. (These three things belong to the earthly self because they reside in the earthly memory.) By means of this action, it shed light on everything there, brought it to life, and arranged it in order, since all light, life, and orderliness in the earthly self result from an inflow from the Divine (as anyone who pays attention can see). This inflow gives birth to desire—at first, a desire for general truth, which is the subject of the two current verses. Sections 3077, 3078 deal with its origins; §§3079, 3080, 3081 with its nature; and §§3082, 3083, 3084 with the stage at which it is first introduced. In their inner meaning, the upcoming verses describe the next part of the process: examining that truth, detaching the maternal heredity that had previously clung to it, and so on.

[2] I know these secrets are too deep to understand, and the reason, again, is that the subject matter is unknown. However, since the inner meaning discusses them and specifies all the circumstances associated with them, I cannot avoid bringing them out in the open, even if they end up seeming to go over the reader's head. At least the discussion can

show how many secrets the Word's inner meaning hides. By their very
nature, these secrets barely appear in the worldly light we have while living in our bodies. They constantly grow clearer and plainer, though, the
more we move from worldly light into the heavenly light we enter after
death—the light enjoyed by blissful, happy souls, or in other words, by
angels.

Genesis 24:17, 18, 19, 20. *And the servant ran to meet her and said, "Let*   **3087**
me swallow, please, a little water from your pitcher." And she said, "Drink,
my lord!" and hurried and brought her pitcher down onto her hand and let
him take a drink. And she finished letting him take a drink and said, "For
your camels, too, let me draw, till they have finished drinking." And she hur-
ried and emptied her pitcher at the trough and ran again to the well to draw
and drew for all his camels.

The servant ran to meet her and said symbolizes an examination by
divine goodness. *Let me swallow, please, a little water from your pitcher*
means to see whether any truth from [those vessels] could be united.
And she said, "Drink, my lord!" symbolizes reciprocation. *And hurried*
and brought the pitcher down onto her hand means that the receiving vessels yielded to power. *And let him take a drink* symbolizes introduction.
And she finished letting him take a drink symbolizes the result. *And said,*
"For your camels, too, let me draw, till they have finished drinking," means
responding by shedding light on all the facts known to the earthly self.
And she hurried and emptied her pitcher at the trough means removing the
desire for truth that had been introduced into goodness that was divine.
And ran again to the well symbolizes a lower plane of desire for truth.
And drew for all his camels means which shed light on general facts.

The servant ran to meet her and said symbolizes an examination by   **3088**
divine goodness, as can be seen from the following: *Running to meet her*
means testing to see whether the situation is just as he had said in his
heart. An inner level of meaning dictates this. And *saying* means perceiving, as noted many times before, so it also means examining. The reason it was done by divine goodness is that the servant is playing the
part of his master, Abraham, and also of Isaac. Messengers take on the
role of those who send them, as happens many times in the Word. For
example, when we read about angels, they are first referred to as angels
but are then called Jehovah. Take the one that appeared to Moses in the
bramble (Exodus 3:2, 4, and following verses) and the one that appeared
to Gideon (Judges 6:11, 12, 14). That is also why Rebekah says, "My
lord!" to him in the next verse.

3089   *Let me swallow, please, a little water from your pitcher* means to see whether any truth from there could be united, as can be seen from the following: *Swallowing* means the same as drinking but in smaller amounts, because the thing is to be examined or tested. Drinking means perceiving (see §3069). In an inner sense it also means being communicated and united, and is used of spiritual attributes. (Eating means the same thing and is used of heavenly attributes; 2187, 2343.) And *water* symbolizes truth (as discussed in 680, 739, 2702). So *let me swallow, please, a little water from your pitcher* symbolizes an examination to see whether any truth from there could be united. A *pitcher* is a container that stores and pours out truth (3068, 3079).

The reason for the examination was that the Lord's first desire for truth also incorporated some of his maternal heredity, which needed to be separated (3040, 3078).

In people who are being reborn, what happens is that the first desire they feel for truth is quite impure. Within it lies the goal and desire to make truth serve themselves, their worldly ambitions, their heavenly glory, and so on, and these focus on themselves rather than on the common good or the Lord's kingdom, let alone the Lord. This kind of desire necessarily comes first, but the Lord gradually purifies it, eventually shoving falsity and evil aside and banishing them to the outer limits. Nevertheless, they had served as the means to an end.

3090   *And she said, "Drink, my lord!"* symbolizes reciprocation, as stands to reason from her consent, or agreement.

The way truth reciprocates when it is to unite with goodness can be seen from marriage. Marriage is based on consent by both parties. This fact traces its origin to the marriage of goodness and truth. Forming an intention is the role played by goodness, while agreeing to it is the role played by truth, and that is what binds them together. Although this marriage is not visible in a person who is regenerating—or in other words, entering into the heavenly marriage—it does exist. By way of plainer evidence, a kind of marriage has to take place between our will and intellect when we are being reborn. Goodness belongs to the will; truth, to the intellect. That is why the ancients established [a custom of referring to] the will and the intellect, and likewise [to] each component of the will and the intellect, as partners in a marriage (§§54, 55).

3091   *And hurried and brought the pitcher down onto her hand* means that the receiving vessels yielded to power. This can be seen from the symbolism of *bringing down* as an act of submission, from that of a *pitcher* as a receiving vessel (discussed in §§3068, 3079), and from that of a *hand* as power (discussed in §878).

To say that receiving vessels yield to power is to say that teachings, knowledge, and facts (which are receiving vessels; §§3068, 3079) adapt. There is a chain of command—and so of adaptation, and so of submission—starting with the origin of life, or the Lord. Since whatever lies lower down on this chain has to serve what lies higher, it has to submit to it. Unless it submits, no bond forms.

The power mentioned here is exerted by truth; truth makes whatever lies below it subservient. Truth is the main thing to which the Word attributes power, so it is said to have hands, arms, and shoulders, which on an inner level symbolize different kinds of power (§§878, 1085). The power that appears to lie in truth actually comes from goodness by means of truth.

And let him take a drink symbolizes introduction. This can be seen from the meaning of *taking a drink,* in that it is almost the same as drinking; but taking a drink here involves more active participation on the part of the person drinking. On the point that drinking means taking in and also being united, see §§3069, 3089. So *letting someone take a drink* means giving that person the capacity to take something in, which is the first step in introducing it.

3092

And she finished letting him take a drink symbolizes the result—the result of the introduction—as can be seen from the following: *She finished,* or finishing, implies the end of a preceding action and the beginning of the next, so it means a result. And *letting someone take a drink* symbolizes introduction, as discussed just above in §3092.

3093

And said, "For your camels, too, let me draw, till they have finished drinking," means responding by shedding light on all the facts known to the earthly self. This can be seen from the symbolism of *camels* as general facts in the earthly self (dealt with in §§3048, 3071) and from that of *drawing*—drawing water—as giving instruction and also enlightening (dealt with in §§3058, 3071). Clearly it is a response, because Rebekah said she would do it and did—did draw water for the camels.

3094

The light that is being spoken of here is shed by truth, even though it comes from goodness by way of truth.

This is how matters stand with the enlightenment shed on facts known to the earthly self: All enlightenment comes from goodness, because goodness (which is a matter of love) resembles the sun's fire, which radiates warmth and light. But truth is like an object that transmits the fire's light.

So enlightenment results from the light, but the nature of the light coming from that flame determines the quality of the enlightenment.

[2] Nothing except truth receives goodness, but the character of the truth determines the character of the goodness it receives and therefore the character of the light it transmits.

When light is shed by truth, then, it seems to come *from* truth, as if it were inherent in truth, when in reality it belongs to goodness, which shines *through* truth in this way.

The light cast by goodness through truth penetrates deeply and affects us profoundly, producing a desire for truth on a lower plane (as discussed just below [§3096]).

Heaven's light comes from the Lord's divine goodness by way of his divine truth. Since it comes by way of the divine truth in his human nature, it reaches not only heavenly angels but also spiritual ones and sheds the light of wisdom and understanding on everyone there. The fact that this is the source of wisdom and understanding explains why the Word's inner meaning so often focuses on the divine goodness and the divine truth in the Lord's human nature. In the current passage it speaks of the first light of truth shed by his goodness, and of the first light of goodness shed through truth.

3095   *And she hurried and emptied her pitcher at the trough* means removing the desire for truth that had been introduced into goodness that was divine, as can be seen from the following: *Emptying a pitcher* means removing truth. Like any other container, a *pitcher* symbolizes not only facts that hold truth but also truth that holds goodness (see §§3068, 3079). Since the current passage is speaking of introduction, it symbolizes the truth that was being introduced into goodness that was divine. Truth itself is never united with goodness, though, except by means of a desire for it (3024 at the beginning, 3066), because desire contains the vital force that unites things, so here it is a desire for truth that is meant.

A *trough* or watering place symbolizes the good that comes of truth, because the water in a trough symbolizes truth (739, 2702), while the trough itself symbolizes the same thing as wood, or in other words, something good (2784, 2812). The good that comes of truth is what goodness produces by means of truth. It is like a child born of truth as its mother and goodness as its father. All real good in a person's earthly self comes from this—from the marriage of goodness and truth in the rational mind. This good is what is called the good that comes of truth, and it is symbolized in the Word by a trough or watering place.

And ran again to the well symbolizes a lower plane of desire for truth. **3096** This is established by the symbolism of a *well* as truth (discussed in §2702) but truth on a lower plane. And since the passage is speaking of the way truth is introduced, it symbolizes a desire for truth that exists on a lower plane, as noted just above at §3094.

For the difference in inner-level symbolism between a spring and a well, see the passage referred to [§2702]. The word *spring* is used when the text is dealing with a purer and higher form of truth, but *well*, when it is dealing with a less pure and lower form of truth. The current chapter, which speaks now of a spring and now of a well, provides an example. Earthly truth is a lower form of truth, and an earthly desire for truth is a lower form of the desire for truth. The latter sheds light directly on general facts, and this enlightenment penetrates deeply and affects us profoundly (see §3094).

And drew for all his camels means which shed light on general facts. **3097** This can be seen from the symbolism of *drawing* as teaching and enlightening (mentioned at §§3058, 3071) and from the symbolism of *camels* as general facts (dealt with at §3048).

The contents of the inner meaning from §3088 to this point are again **3098** by their very nature incapable of being understood except by people who have learned about a person's inner dimensions and who know what is true, because truth leads to enlightenment and determines its quality. The theme is the first stage at which truth is introduced into goodness. To repeat [§§2524, 2701], goodness itself flows into the earthly plane by way of the rational plane (and so along an inner path) and sheds light on objects there, but truth itself flows into the earthly plane by way of the senses, especially hearing and sight (and so along an outward path). That is how truth dawns, as anyone can see by reflecting on it. Goodness and truth do not unite there, however, but in the rational mind, so truth is called up from there, out of the earthly realm into the spiritual. The truth that is to unite with goodness is spiritual.

These verses, from §§3087 to 3097, tell how the case stands with truth when it has first been called up from there.

Genesis 24:21, 22. *And the man was staring dumbfounded at her, hold-* **3099** *ing back to see whether Jehovah had made his path successful or not. And it happened when the camels had finished drinking that the man took a gold* *nose-ring (half a shekel its weight) and [put] two bracelets on her hands (ten [shekels] of gold their weight).*

The man was staring dumbfounded at her, holding back symbolizes a state of perception regarding these things. *To see whether Jehovah had made his path successful or not* means regarding divine truth and its precise nature. *And it happened when the camels had finished drinking* symbolizes acknowledgment resulting from the light shed on general facts. *That the man took a gold nose-ring* symbolizes divine goodness. *Half a shekel its weight* symbolizes the amount needed for introduction. *And two bracelets* symbolizes divine truth. *On her hands* symbolizes the power of a desire for truth. *Ten of gold their weight* means fully enough for introduction.

3100   *The man was staring dumbfounded at her, holding back* symbolizes a state of perception regarding these things. This can be seen from the symbolism of *staring dumbfounded* and *holding back*—when he saw that what he had spoken in his heart was coming to pass—as involving recognition and yet suspense: was it really so? He *stared dumbfounded* because he recognized that it was happening, and he *held back* because he was waiting to see whether it was really so. This is the state of perception that is symbolized.

3101   *To see whether Jehovah had made his path successful or not* means regarding divine truth and its precise nature. This is established by the symbolism of a *path* as truth (discussed at §§627, 2333). Its divinity is symbolized by the words *whether Jehovah had made it successful.* To ask this is to ask whether it came from Jehovah, or in other words, from the Lord's divinity. So it is to ask precisely what is true, because not all truth called up out of the earthly self into the rational self is accepted. The only truth that is accepted is the truth that conforms with the goodness there and accordingly becomes one with it by being implanted in and grafted onto it.

The rest of the truth, as true as it may seem before rising up to the rational plane, is not accepted, because it is not acknowledged. Goodness is what recognizes the truth that belongs to it, and truth is what recognizes the goodness that belongs to *it.*

The fact that [the Lord] recognized precisely what was true and so accepted it also becomes clear from what now follows.

3102   *And it happened when the camels had finished drinking* symbolizes acknowledgment resulting from the light shed on general facts, as can be seen from the following: The two expressions *it happened* and *they had finished* signal a result, involving as they do the end of a preceding action and the beginning of the next, as mentioned above in §3093. So here they symbolize acknowledgment, as shown just above. *Camels* symbolize general facts, as discussed in §§3048, 3071. And *drinking* symbolizes the same thing here as drawing water (as above in §§3058, 3097) and also as watering (as above in §3071)—in other words, being enlightened. Clearly, then, the words *and it happened when the camels had finished drinking* symbolize acknowledgment—an acknowledgment of truth that was divine—resulting from the light shed on general facts.

[2] This is the situation: Whenever truth is lifted out of the earthly self—that is, out of facts, or knowledge and teachings (since these belong to the earthly self)—into the rational mind and received there, its precise nature must first be acknowledged. It must be identified as either harmonizing with the goodness there or not. If it harmonizes, it is accepted, and if it does not, it is rejected. Many apparently true ideas come in a single group, but the only ones that become attached are the ones that acknowledge the goodness present in the rational mind—and therefore that love and are loved [by goodness]. In order for those ideas to be recognized as open to goodness, though, the earthly self must have the enlightenment that enables it to see every one of them in a single glance and so allows for choice.

This enlightenment in the earthly self comes from goodness, though it comes by way of truth (see §3094). It is what is symbolized by Rebekah's drawing water for the camels and watering them, or giving them something to drink.

That the man took a gold nose-ring symbolizes divine goodness. This can be seen from the symbolism of a *gold nose-ring* as goodness, and here—since the inner meaning has to do with the Lord—as divine goodness. Because it comes from the rational mind, the word *man* is used. (For the symbolism of a man as rationality, see §§265, 749, 1007.)

In ancient times, the forms of worship in the different religions were representative, and people knew what was being symbolized. When they contracted marriage in those days, it was customary to give the bride a gold nose-ring and bracelets, because the church was represented by a bride, its goodness by a nose-ring, and its truth by bracelets. Since they knew that the marital love in a bride and wife came down to her from the marriage of the Lord's divine goodness and divine truth (§§2508, 2618, 2727, 2728, 2729), the gold ring was put in her nose. This is clear from

3103

what follows in verse 47, where the text says that the servant put the ring in Rebekah's nose. The reason was that the nose symbolized a virtuous life because of the breath in it, which in an inner sense means life, and because of its sense of smell, which means the pleasure bestowed by love—goodness being a matter of love (§§96, 97).

[2] Other passages in the Word also reveal that a nose-ring was a token symbolizing the good in a marriage. In Ezekiel, for instance:

> I decked you in finery and put *bracelets on your hands* and a necklace on your throat and put a *ring in your nose.* (Ezekiel 16:11, 12)

This is about the ancient church—Jerusalem—which is being depicted as a bride who receives bracelets, a necklace, and a nose-ring. The bracelets on her hands were a token representing truth, and the ring in her nose, a token representing goodness. [3] In Isaiah:

> Because the daughters of Zion vaunt themselves, the Lord will make the crown of their head bald and remove the rings and *nose-rings,* the ceremonial clothing, the robes. (Isaiah 3:16, 17, [18,] 21, 22)

The daughters of Zion that vaunt themselves stand for negative emotions in people within the church (§§2362, 3024). The rings and nose-rings that are going to be removed stand for goodness and its tokens, while the ceremonial clothing and the robes stand for truth and its tokens. [4] In Hosea:

> I will punish her for the days of the baals, in which she burned incense and *donned her nose-ring* and her finery and walked after her lovers. (Hosea 2:13)

This is about religion when it has been corrupted, and about a subsequent new religion. The nose-ring again stands for a token of goodness in the church.

When these rings were worn in the ear, they still symbolized goodness, but goodness in action or, in the opposite sense, evil in action, as in Genesis 35:4; Exodus 32:2, 3.

3104 *Half a shekel the weight* symbolizes the amount needed for introduction, as can be seen from the symbolism of a *shekel,* a *half shekel,* and *weight.* A *shekel* symbolizes the value of goodness and truth, and a *half shekel* symbolizes a measurement of their amount; see §2959. *Weight* symbolizes the state of goodness in a thing, as you will see. Taken together, this shows that *half a shekel the weight* symbolizes and involves the amount of goodness meant by the gold nose-ring. The fact that it is the amount needed for introduction follows from the context above and below.

[2] The symbolism of *weight* as the state of goodness in a thing is visible in the following passages from the Word: In the Book of Ezekiel, the prophet was to *eat food by weight,* twenty shekels per day, and *drink water by measure,* a sixth of a hin:

> Because watch: I am breaking the staff of bread in Jerusalem, so that they *eat bread by weight* and in anxiety, and *water by measure* and with shock they *drink,* so that they lack bread and water. (Ezekiel 4:16, 17)

This is about the devastation of goodness and truth, the portrayal of which was played out by the prophet. Eating bread and food by weight symbolizes a stage at which goodness has been devastated, while drinking water by measure symbolizes a stage at which truth has been devastated. Bread means something heavenly and therefore something good (see §§276, 680, 2165, 2177), and water means something spiritual and therefore something true (739, 2702, 3058). Plainly, then, weight is mentioned in connection with goodness, and measure in connection with truth. [3] In the same author:

> Honest *scales,* an honest *ephah,* and an honest *bath* there shall be. (Ezekiel 45:10 and following verses)

This is about the Holy Land, which symbolizes the Lord's kingdom in the heavens, as can be seen from the details in this passage of Ezekiel. Scales, an ephah, and a bath will not be used in heaven but the goodness and truth these weights and measures symbolize. In Isaiah:

> Who has measured the water in his fist and balanced the heavens in his span and encompassed the dust of the earth in a one-third measure, and *weighed out the mountains in a scale* and *the hills in balances?* (Isaiah 40:12)

Weighing out the mountains in a scale and the hills in balances means that the heavenly qualities of love and charity come from the Lord and that he alone presides over the stages of their existence. Mountains and hills, which are assigned the weights here, are the heavenly qualities of love (see §§795, 796, 1430, 2722). [4] In Daniel:

> The handwriting on the wall of Belshazzar's palace: *mene, mene, tekel, upharsin.* This is the translation. *Mene:* God has numbered your kingdom and ended it. *Tekel: you have been weighed in the balances* and found wanting. *Peres:* your kingdom has been divided and given to the Mede and the Persian. (Daniel 5:25, 26, 27, 28)

"Mene," or *"numbered,"* relates to truth, but *"tekel,"* or *"weighed in the balances,"* to goodness. The inner meaning of this passage speaks about the end [of the age].

3105   *And two bracelets* symbolizes divine truth. This can be seen from the symbolism of *bracelets* as truth and here, since the inner meaning has to do with the Lord, as divine truth. There are said to be *two* because this indicates fullness.

The bracelets were put on a bride's hands because a bride symbolized religion, and her hands symbolized the power gained from truth. (For hands being mentioned in connection with truth, see §3091.)

This symbolism of bracelets can be seen in Ezekiel 16:11, 12 (discussed above at §3103) and also in Ezekiel 23:42. Not only brides but monarchs also had bracelets, although the latter wore them on their arm, as 2 Samuel 1:10 shows. The reason monarchs wore bracelets is that monarchy was a representation and symbol of the Lord's divine truth (§§1672, 1728, 2015, 2069, 3009) and an arm was a symbol of power (878).

3106   *On her hands* symbolizes the power of a desire for truth. This can be seen from the symbolism of a *hand* as power (discussed in §§878, 3091) and from the representation of Rebekah—*her*—as the desire for truth (discussed in §§2865, 3077).

3107   *Ten of gold their weight* means fully enough for introduction, as can be seen from the symbolism of the following: Like one hundred (discussed in §§1988, 2636), *ten* symbolizes a full or complete state. *Gold* here is a kind of currency reckoned by weight. And *weight* symbolizes the state of goodness in a thing (as noted above in §3104). Plainly, then, *ten of gold the weight* symbolizes a state in which there is plenty of good in the thing being evaluated.

The fact that it is enough for introduction can be seen from the details of the current chapter, which is talking about introduction, or betrothal.

3108   These two verses are talking about the introduction of truth into goodness, but the nature of this introduction is not easy for people to picture if their enlightenment comes only from the worldly realm, and not from the heavenly realm as well, which can illuminate the worldly realm. The thinking of people who do not have goodness and therefore faith is formed solely from objects of worldly light. They do not know what spirituality is, and not even what rationality is, in a real sense. All they know is the earthly dimension, which they ascribe everything to. That is why the things the inner meaning says here about the introduction of truth into goodness seem too far-fetched to them to be worth anything. Yet these same things are some of the most precious imaginable, to people who see by heaven's light.

[2] This is how the case stands with the introduction of truth into goodness: Before truth has been introduced and properly united, it does exist in us, but it does not seem to become ours; it is not our personal property, so to speak. As soon as truth *is* introduced into what is good in us, however, we make it our own. Then it disappears from our outward memory and passes into our inward memory. To put the same thing another way, truth disappears in our earthly or outward self and passes into our rational or inward self, which it clothes. It also creates humanity in us, or in other words, determines what we are like as human beings. This is how the case stands with all truth that unites with what is good in us. Something similar happens when falsity unites with evil (which we call good). The difference is that the former process opens up our rational mind and in this way makes us rational. The latter process shuts down our rational mind and makes us irrational, even though in the darkness then surrounding us we see ourselves as more rational than others.

Genesis 24:23, 24, 25. *And he said, "Whose daughter are you? Tell me, please, whether your father's house has a place for us to spend the night." And she said to him, "I am the daughter of Bethuel, son of Milcah, whom she bore to Nahor." And she said to him, "There is also hay, also much fodder with us; also a place to spend the night."*

3109

He said, "Whose daughter are you?" symbolizes further examination regarding innocence. *Tell me, please, whether your father's house has a place for us to spend the night* symbolizes examination regarding good done out of neighborly love. *And she said to him, "I am the daughter of Bethuel, son of Milcah, whom she bore to Nahor,"* here as before symbolizes all the origins of it. *And she said to him* symbolizes a perception. *There is also hay* symbolizes factual truth. *Also much fodder with us* symbolizes the good that goes with it. *Also a place to spend the night* symbolizes conditions.

He said, "Whose daughter are you?" symbolizes further examination regarding innocence. This can be seen from the question, *Whose daughter?* which is an examination, and here, further examination, as earlier remarks in §§3088 and 3101 make plain. The focus on innocence can be seen from the symbolism of a girl as a desire that has innocence within it, as discussed in §3067. It is true that the word *girl* is not used here, but above at verses 14 and 16 Rebekah is called a girl and the current question is addressed to her, so *you* in this instance means the same thing as a girl.

3110

[2] A word about the subject itself, though—that before truth was introduced into and united with goodness, it was examined for the innocence it had in it and then for the charity it had. This idea cannot help astounding people who have no knowledge of the matter. Still, they may want to know that at the time when truth is being introduced into and united with the good in us, we each undergo a minute examination of a kind that we would be simply unable to believe.

Nothing but real, genuine truth is ever allowed to be injected into real, genuine goodness. When an idea of lesser truth draws near, it does not unite with real goodness but with a goodness that is not actually good, although it seems so. If falsity approaches, goodness takes itself indoors, while outdoors the false idea joins together with some kind of evil that we believe to be good.

[3] This divine arrangement is carried out by the Lord by means of spirits and angels and is the deepest secret in this world, although it is open knowledge in the next. Anyone of sound reason can see or at least grasp it. After all, evil and falsity is hell and flows in from hell, but goodness and truth is heaven and flows in by way of heaven from the Lord. As a consequence, evil and truth can no more join together than hell and heaven. So there is a more refined balance in all this than anyone could ever believe. This, then, is what examination means.

3111   *Tell me, please, whether your father's house has a place for us to spend the night* symbolizes examination regarding good done out of neighborly love, as is established by the following: *Tell me, please, whether* means examination. A *house* symbolizes goodness, as discussed in §§2048, 2233, 2331. The *father* here—Bethuel—symbolizes the good of neighborly love as it exists among upright people outside the church, as discussed in §§[2863,] 2865. This kind of good was the real source of the desire for truth that Rebekah represents. And a *place to spend the night* symbolizes an abiding state, as discussed below at §3115.

[2] The reason the inner meaning describes an examination into the source of the innocence and neighborly goodness present in a desire for truth is that the truth that is to be introduced and united to goodness has no other ultimate source. This fact is visible in everyone in whom truth is welcomed by goodness and marries into goodness. Within the church, people may know truth and state it out loud, but if they do not have any innocence or kindness toward their neighbor, they never acknowledge truth at heart. Outside the church, non-Christians may be called to the truth of the faith or learn about it in the other world,

but the only ones who accept it are those who have innocence and live together in mutual kindness. Innocence and love for others make a soil in which the seeds of truth can put down roots and sprout.

And she said to him, "I am the daughter of Bethuel, son of Milcah, whom **3112** *she bore to Nahor,"* symbolizes all the origins of it—of a desire for truth. This can be seen from the representation of Bethuel, Milcah, and Nahor as the source of the desire for truth that Rebekah represents; see §3078.

And she said to him symbolizes a perception. This is established by the **3113** symbolism of *saying* on an inner level of scriptural narrative as perceiving, which has been mentioned many times before.

There is also hay symbolizes factual truth. *Also much fodder* symbolizes **3114** the good that goes with it. This can be seen from the symbolism of *hay* and *fodder.*

The reason *hay* symbolizes factual truth is that it is being connected with camels, which use it for food. When camels symbolize general facts in the earthly self, its food—hay—cannot symbolize anything else, because there is no other food that sustains its life. That is what nourishes the earthly self. If it lacked the sustenance of knowledge, it could not survive. Evidence that this is so is provided by the life after death, because for spirits in that life, such things serve in place of food; see §§56, 57, 58, 680, 681, 1480, 1695, 1973, 1974.

In the earthly self, as in the rational self, there are two general kinds of things that make up its essence: traits that belong to the intellect and traits that belong to the will. True ideas are among the traits of the intellect; good impulses are among those of the will. Truth in the earthly self is factual truth, or in other words, everything in its outward memory. That is what hay symbolizes in contexts dealing with camels, and also with horses, mules, and donkeys. Good impulses in the earthly self, though, are pleasures, and especially those pleasures that go with a desire for factual truth.

Also a place to spend the night symbolizes conditions. This can be seen **3115** from the symbolism of a *place* as a state (mentioned in §§2625, 2837), and from that of *spending the night* as staying or making one's home (mentioned in §2330). In the current verse, then, it symbolizes conditions surrounding the origins of a desire for truth. Its origins are depicted as being the qualities that Bethuel, Milcah, and Nahor represent, and qualities related to it are depicted later on by Laban. Since this origin is dark and dim, the circumstances surrounding it are symbolized by a *place to spend the night,* as they also were earlier.

3116   These three verses speak about examining the truth that was to be introduced to and therefore united with goodness, with particular emphasis on its origins, because everything evolves from its source. What develops out of the source takes its form from it, as a plant or tree takes its form from its root or seed.

These things the Lord saw and examined within himself from his divine side, and by his own wisdom and understanding he introduced the one into the other—that is, truth into the goodness in his rational mind. The inner meaning here describes the actual examination, but there are not many to whom the details could be explained.

Each of us is also examined when we are reforming or receiving a remnant [of goodness and truth], but we are completely unaware of it. The examination is so dim and vague to us that we do not even believe it is happening. In reality, it is being performed all the time, but by the Lord, the only one who sees not only what conditions are like for us now but also what they will be like forever.

Examination is a very delicate balancing act that prevents the least falsity from uniting with goodness and the least truth from uniting with evil. If either occurred, we would be destroyed forever, because in the other life we would then dangle between hell and heaven. Because of the goodness in us, we would be spewed out of hell, and because of the evil in us, we would be spewed out of heaven.

3117   Genesis 24:26, 27. *And the man bowed and prostrated himself to Jehovah. And he said, "A blessing on Jehovah, God of my master Abraham, who has not abandoned the mercy and truth he keeps with my master! I was on my way, when Jehovah led me to the house of my master's kin."*

The man bowed and prostrated himself to Jehovah symbolizes gladness and joy. *And he said, "A blessing on Jehovah, God of my master Abraham!"* here as before means from divinity itself and divine humanity. *Who has not abandoned the mercy* symbolizes a perception of love's influence. *And the truth he keeps with my master* symbolizes the resulting influence of charity. *I was on my way* means at a stage in which truth unites with goodness on the rational plane. *Jehovah led me to the house of my master's kin* means [being led] to the goodness behind that truth.

3118   *The man bowed and prostrated himself to Jehovah* symbolizes gladness and joy. This can be seen from the symbolism of *bowing* and *prostrating oneself* as being glad and joyful. Bowing and prostration are acts of humility (or humility in action) at times of both sadness and joy—in sad times, when what we want does not happen, and in happy times, when it does happen. Here, for instance, Rebekah followed the wishes of the servant's heart when she gave him something to drink from her pitcher and also watered his camels. On the point that bowing can be a gesture of joy, see §§2927, 2950.

I speak of gladness and joy because the Word mentions gladness in connection with truth, and joy in connection with goodness. What is more, gladness belongs to the face, but joy lies in the heart. To say the same thing another way, gladness goes with spiritual emotion, or the desire for truth, but joy goes with heavenly emotion, or the desire for goodness. So gladness is less intense than joy, just as bowing is less extreme than prostration. The relationship between the two also becomes clear from the fact that people in a spiritual religion merely bow down to the Lord and call on his favor, while people in a heavenly religion prostrate themselves to the Lord and beg for his mercy (§§598, 981, 2423). Both come up here because of the marriage of truth and goodness in every part of the Word (§§683, 793, 801, 2516, 2712).

And he said, "A blessing on Jehovah, God of my master Abraham!" means **3119** from divinity itself and divine humanity, as is established by the remarks above at §3061, where the same words occur. Besides, these words speak of a blessing. "A blessing on Jehovah!" was a standard way of expressing gratitude and therefore joy and gladness that desired events had taken place. Moreover, for what the ancients meant when they blessed Jehovah, see §§1096, 1422.

Who has not abandoned the mercy symbolizes a perception of love's **3120** influence. This is established by the symbolism of *mercy* as love (dealt with in §§1735, 3063, 3073). The reason *he has not abandoned his mercy* means a perception of love's influence is that these are words of acknowledgment and acclaim, and all acknowledgment and acclaim of a thing come from a perception of its influence.

And the truth he keeps with my master symbolizes the resulting influ- **3121** ence of charity. This can be seen from the symbolism of *truth* as charity. Strictly speaking, truth means the same thing as faith, and Hebrew uses this kind of word for faith, so that what is called truth in the Old Testament Word is sometimes called faith in the New Testament Word. This is also the reason I have linked truth with faith, and goodness with love, so many times in what precedes [§§1577, 1809, 1824, 2173, 2435, 2619, 2975]. In an inner sense, though, faith is just charity. See numerous earlier statements and illustrations: Faith does not exist except through love (§§30, 31–38). Faith is never possible except where there is charity (654, 724, 1162, 1176, 2261). Faith is belief that comes of charity (1608, 2049, 2116, 2343, 2349, 2417). Charity makes the church, not faith isolated from charity (809, 916, 1798, 1799, 1834, 1844, 2190, 2228, 2442). Clearly, then, truth (or faith) in an inner sense is the same as charity, since all faith comes from charity and any faith that does not is not faith. To put it another way, all truth in an inner sense is goodness, since all truth comes from something good and the truth that does not is not true. After all, truth is nothing but the form of goodness (3049); nothing else gives it birth, and nothing else gives it life.

3122 More about this truth that means charity: The very earliest people, who were heavenly, understood the mercy and truth worked by the Lord in them to be simply an acceptance of the love for the Lord and the resulting charity toward others that flow into a person. The ancients, who were spiritual, understood the mercy and truth worked by the Lord in them to be charity and faith. The reason for the discrepancy is that heavenly people never thought about matters of faith, or truth, but about matters of love, or goodness. This can be seen from previous remarks about heavenly people, §§202, 337, 2669, 2715. And charity for their neighbor introduced heavenly people into love for the Lord, when they were being reformed and reborn. It is plain, then, that the mercy done by the Lord actually means a perception of an inflowing love for him, and that truth actually means a perception of an inflowing charity for our neighbor that results from it.

[2] It is different with the spiritual, though. They think about matters of faith, and when they are being reformed and reborn, matters of faith introduce them into charity for their neighbor. So when the text is speaking of them, the mercy done by the Lord means the influence charity for their neighbor exerts on them, while truth means the influence faith exerts on them. Yet when a spiritual person is reborn, this faith becomes charity, because the person then acts from charity. In fact, the ones who do not act from charity have not been reborn, but the ones who do act from charity *have* been reborn. They then lose interest in matters of faith, or of truth, because it is no longer the true ideas but the good effect of faith that gives them life. Truth has bound itself so closely together with goodness that it ceases to be visible, except as the form of goodness; in other words, faith is not visible except as the form of charity.

[3] This shows what the earliest people understood and what the ancients understood by mercy and truth, which the Word mentions so many times. In David, for instance:

> The monarch will dwell forever before God. Prepare *mercy* and *truth;* let them guard the monarch. (Psalms 61:7)

In the same author:

> *Mercy* and *truth* will meet; justice and peace will kiss. (Psalms 85:10)

In the same author:

> The Lord is a God great in *mercy* and *truth*. (Psalms 86:15)

In the same author:

> *My truth* and *my mercy* are with him. (Psalms 89:24)

In the same author:

> Jehovah has remembered *his mercy* and *his truth* toward the house of Israel. (Psalms 98:3)

In the same author:

> Jehovah, not to us but to your name give glory, because of *your mercy* and *your truth*. (Psalms 115:1)

In Micah:

> Jehovah God will give "the *truth* to Jacob, the *mercy* to Abraham, that you swore to our ancestors from days of old." (Micah 7:20)

Jacob here stands for the outer self, and Abraham for the inner self, of the Lord's human side. In Hosea:

> Jehovah has a dispute with the residents of the land, because there is no *truth,* and no *mercy,* and no knowledge of God. (Hosea 4:1)

No truth stands for no acceptance of charity's influence. No mercy stands for no acceptance of love's influence. No knowledge of God stands for no acceptance of the influence of religious truth.

I was on my way means at a stage in which truth unites with goodness on the rational plane. This can be seen from the symbolism of a *way* as truth (discussed in §§627, 2333). *On my way* means the union of truth and goodness on the rational plane, because that is the theme of the current chapter; see §§3012, 3013. People are said to be on their way when they are getting where they want to go.

Jehovah led me to the house of my master's kin means [being led] to the goodness behind that truth. This can be seen from the symbolism of his *kin's house,* from which Rebekah came, as the goodness from which truth comes.

The fact that his *kin's house* means goodness—here, the goodness from which truth comes—is established by the symbolism of a *house* as goodness (discussed in §§2233, 2559), and by that of *kin* as the source of the goodness from which comes the truth that Rebekah represents.

3125   The subject of what precedes has been an examination into the truth that was to unite with goodness on the rational plane—an examination of its innocence, its charity, and its source. Since the Lord made both the goodness and the truth in his rational mind divine by his own power, he examined the truth he united with goodness.

In humans, on the other hand, truth is never united with goodness by the person's own power but by the Lord's. You can see this clearly by considering that everything good and true flows in from the Lord, that all reformation and rebirth comes from him, and that people know absolutely nothing of the way they are reborn. In this day and age, they do not even know that they are reborn through truth and goodness, let alone that truth is introduced into goodness and unites with it. They do not know that this is accomplished by a kind of examination, or in other words, with tremendous care.

These two verses have dealt with a perception concerning the nature and source of truth and also with joy because of it. The next part, then, speaks of its introduction.

3126   Genesis 24:28, 29, 30. *And the girl ran and told her mother's household about these things. And Rebekah had a brother, and his name was Laban; and Laban ran to the man outside at the spring. And it happened—on seeing the nose-ring, and the bracelets on his sister's hands, and on his hearing the words of Rebekah his sister, saying, "This is what the man spoke to me"—that he came to the man; and here, the man was standing by his camels by the spring.*

The girl ran symbolizes the predisposition of that desire. *And told her mother's household about these things* means toward any kind of earthly goodness amenable to enlightenment. *And Rebekah had a brother* symbolizes a desire for goodness in the earthly self. *His name was Laban* symbolizes the character of that desire. *And Laban ran to the man outside at the spring* symbolizes its predisposition in favor of truth that was to be introduced into truth that is divine. *And it happened, on seeing the nose-ring, and the bracelets on his sister's hands* means when it sensed divine goodness and divine truth in the power possessed by the desire for truth (the *sister*). *And on his hearing the words of Rebekah his sister* means its inclination. *Saying, "This is what the man spoke to me,"* symbolizes the leanings of truth in the earthly self. *That he came to the man* means that it attached itself. *And here, the man was standing by his camels* symbolizes its presence in general facts. *By the spring* symbolizes the light shed on them by truth that is divine.

The girl ran symbolizes the predisposition of that desire. This can be seen from the symbolism of *running* as a sign of inclination, or of being predisposed, and from that of a *girl* as a desire that has innocence within it (discussed above at §§3067, 3110).

3127

And told her mother's household about these things means toward any kind of earthly goodness amenable to enlightenment. This can be seen from the symbolism of her *mother's household* as the goodness of the outer self, or in other words, earthly goodness. A house or *household* is goodness (see §§2233, 2559), and our outer or earthly dimension comes from our mother, while our inner dimension comes from our father (§1815).

3128

The Word compares the good in a person to a house, and on this account, a person who has goodness is called a house of God. Deep goodness is called the house of one's father; goodness on one's own level is termed the house of one's kin; but shallow goodness, which is the same as earthly goodness, is named the house of one's mother. This is also how all goodness and truth is born—by an inflow of inward goodness (the father) into outward goodness (the mother).

[2] Since this verse has to do with the source of the truth that was to unite with goodness on the rational plane, it says that Rebekah, representing that truth, ran to her mother's house, which is its source. As was said and shown above, all goodness flows in along an inner route (by way of the soul) into our rational mind and through this into the facts we know, all the way down to the facts we learn through our senses. By shedding light there, it enables us to see truth. Truth is called up from the sensory plane, puts off its earthly form, and unites with goodness along the way, in our rational mind. In doing so it makes us rational and eventually spiritual.

People have no idea at all how these things are accomplished, though, because hardly anyone today knows what goodness is, or that it is different from truth. Still less does anyone know that we are reformed by the influence goodness exerts on truth and by the bond created between the two. Nor does anyone know that the rational plane is different from the earthly. Since these very basic ideas are unknown, it is utterly impossible to see how truth is introduced into goodness and how the two unite—this being the subject matter of the chapter's inner meaning. Still, these secrets have now been revealed, and they lie open to people who have goodness, or in other words, to angelic minds. Consequently, no matter how dim such secrets are destined to appear to others, they simply must be disclosed, because they form the inner meaning.

[3] As for the light that goodness sheds in the earthly self (called her "mother's house") by means of truth: In human beings, divine goodness acts on our rational mind and through our rational mind on our earthly mind, including the facts, or in other words, the knowledge and teachings, stored there, as noted. On the earthly plane, it forms truth for itself by a process of adaptation, and by means of this truth, it brings light to everything in the earthly self. However, if the life force of our earthly self does not receive divine goodness but rejects, perverts, or smothers it, divine goodness cannot be adapted or form truth for itself. As a result, neither can light shine on our earthly part any longer. Enlightenment in our earthly self comes from goodness by way of truth, and when there is no longer any enlightenment, no reformation can occur.

That is why the inner sense often focuses on the earthly self and its nature and therefore on the source of truth in the earthly self, which is the goodness there.

3129   *And Rebekah had a brother* symbolizes a desire for goodness in the earthly self, as can be seen from the symbolism of *brother* and sister in the Word. A *brother* symbolizes the desire for goodness, and a sister, the desire for truth (as discussed in §§367, 2360, 2508, 2524). In the earthly self, as in the rational self, there are ties of blood and kinship among all the elements there (§§2556, 2739). That is why both the rational and earthly minds are called a household, or clan, with its parents, brothers, sisters, relatives, and kin in order.

3130   *His name was Laban* symbolizes the character of that desire. This can be seen from the symbolism of a *name* as the quality of a thing, as dealt with in §§144, 145, 1754, 1896, 2009, 2724. Here, then, Laban means the character of the desire being discussed.

3131   *And Laban ran to the man outside at the spring* symbolizes its predisposition—the predisposition of a desire for goodness—in favor of truth that was to be introduced into truth that is divine. This can be seen from the following meanings: *Running* is a sign of inclination or predisposition, as it is above in §3127. *Laban* represents a desire for goodness, as mentioned just above in §§3129, 3130. A *man* symbolizes truth, as discussed in §§265, 749, 1007. And a *spring* also symbolizes truth—here, truth that is divine—as discussed in §§2702, 3096, and 3137 below.

[2] From these and the other details being discussed, it can be seen what the inner meaning is like and what kinds of secrets it holds. Without deep scrutiny of the Word, and without revelation, who could tell that *Laban ran to the man outside at the spring* symbolizes the predisposition a desire for goodness has in favor of truth that is to be introduced into truth that is divine? Yet that is what angels perceive when we read the words. The correspondence between our ideas and an angel's is like this: While we are interpreting these words literally, and picturing Laban running to the man outside at the spring, an angel is thinking about the predisposition a desire for goodness has in favor of truth that is to be introduced into truth that is divine. Angels do not picture Laban or running or a spring but something spiritual corresponding to these things. That is what the correspondence between earthly and spiritual qualities—and therefore between earthly and spiritual thoughts—is like, as can also be seen from the discussion of correspondence in §§1563, 1568, 2763, 2987–3003, 3021.

[3] Let me turn now to the actual subject under discussion here, which is the fact that truth was to be introduced into truth that is divine. The first kind of truth the Lord's earthly self learned was not truth that was divine but truth that *seemed* divine. Truth in its infancy is never true but only seems true. Over time, it strips away the appearance and clothes itself in the real essence of truth. This can be illustrated by examples, for better comprehension. For the time being, here is one example of a truth that is divine: the Lord is never angry and never punishes anyone, much less does evil to anyone, and nothing ever comes from the Lord but what is good. Yet in its infancy the form this truth takes is that the Lord is angry when we sin and therefore punishes us. In some people, it even becomes the idea that evil comes from him. As we advance from childhood, though, and grow and mature in judgment, we rid ourselves of that which served as truth for us because it appeared to be true. Little by little we clothe ourselves in the real truth: that the Lord is never angry and never punishes, much less does evil. So the former truth introduces us into the latter. The thoughts that first enter are generalized, and in and of themselves they are vague. Until they are elucidated by more specific ideas, and until these more specific ideas are elucidated by the most specific, hardly anything can be seen in them. Then, when they have been clarified, their inner depths lie open.

This is how illusions and appearances—which serve as truths when we are ignorant—are scattered and dispersed.

3132   *And it happened, on seeing the nose-ring, and the bracelets on his sis-ter's hands* means when it sensed divine goodness and divine truth in the power possessed by the desire for truth (the *sister*), as is established by the following: *Seeing* means sensing, as noted in §2150. A *nose-ring* symbolizes divine goodness, as discussed in §§3103, 3105. *Bracelets* symbolize divine truth, as also discussed in §§3103, 3105. *Hands* symbolize power, as discussed in §§878, 3091. And a *sister* symbolizes a desire for truth, as discussed in §§2508, 2524, 2556. All this shows that *seeing the nose-ring and the bracelets on his sister's hands* is sensing divine goodness and divine truth in the power possessed by the desire for truth.

[2] The situation here is that the union of divine goodness and divine truth in the Lord is the divine marriage itself. The divine marriage is the source of the heavenly marriage (which is likewise a marriage of good-ness and truth) and also of marriage love (see §§2727–2759). That is why in places where the Word talks about marriage, on an inner level it sym-bolizes the heavenly marriage of goodness and truth, and on the highest level, the divine marriage within the Lord. So the marriage between Isaac and Rebekah here means nothing else.

The union of goodness and truth is marriage itself; the introduction of one into the other is betrothal, or the stage just before marriage. The stage before betrothal, however, is the one depicted here. At this stage, just as a young, unmarried woman has it in her power to become engaged and then unite with her husband as his wife, the desire for truth has it in its power to be introduced into divine truth and in this way unite with divine goodness.

Furthermore, at the core of the Lord's first desire for truth (and later in *all* his desire for truth) lay divine goodness itself and divine truth itself, because at its core lay Jehovah himself. That is where the power being spoken of here comes from.

3133   *And on his hearing the words of Rebekah his sister* means its inclination. This can be seen from the desire present in these words and the desire reflected in what leads up to them. Both testify to an inclination felt by the desire for truth, which *Rebekah his sister* represents here.

3134   *Saying, "This is what the man spoke to me,"* symbolizes the leanings of truth in the earthly self. This too can be seen from the desire expressed, and from the words that the man, Abraham's servant, spoke to Rebekah. These show that it is a leaning. The symbolism can also be seen from that of a *man* as truth (dealt with in §§265, 749, 1007). Here the man symbol-izes truth in the Lord's earthly self, received from his divine side, because he is Abraham's elder servant, who symbolizes the earthly self (see §3019).

The Word, especially the prophetic part, often mentions a man, in the phrases "man and wife," "man and woman," "man and resident," and "man and human being." In these passages, on an inner level, the man symbolizes that which belongs to the intellect, or truth. The wife, woman, resident, and human being symbolize that which belongs to the will, or goodness. In Isaiah, for instance:

> I am looking, and there is *no man,* and [seeking] among them, and there is no counselor. (Isaiah 41:28)

"No man" stands for no one with understanding, and so for no truth. In the same author:

> I came and there was *no man;* I shouted, and there was no one answering. (Isaiah 50:2)

Likewise. [2] In the same author:

> *Truthfulness* stumbled in the *street,* and uprightness could not approach, and *truthfulness* was gone, and anyone departing from evil became insane. Jehovah saw—and it was evil in his eyes—that there was *no judgment* and *no man,* and he was astounded. (Isaiah 59:14, 15, 16)

"No man" clearly stands for no one with understanding and therefore, in the broadest sense, for no truth. The focus here is on the final days of the church, when there is no longer any truth, which is why it says, "Truthfulness stumbled in the street; uprightness cannot approach; truthfulness was gone." A street also has to do with truth (see §2336), as does judgment (2235). In Jeremiah:

> Dash about through the *streets* of Jerusalem and please see and know and seek in its roads, if you find a *man,* if he is exercising *judgment,* seeking *truth.* (Jeremiah 5:1)

Again the man plainly stands for a person with understanding, and for truth. In Zephaniah:

> I will ruin their *streets,* and none will be passing through; their cities will be devastated, and there will be *no man* and no *resident.* (Zephaniah 3:6)

"No man" stands for no truth; "no resident," for no goodness (§§2268, 2451, 2712). Not to mention many other passages.

He came to the man means that it attached itself. That is, the desire for goodness represented by Laban (§§3129, 3130) attached itself to the truth symbolized by the *man* (§3134)—both of them located in the earthly self.

3135

3136   *And here, the man was standing by his camels* symbolizes its presence in general facts. This can be seen from the symbolism of *standing by* as being present, and from that of *camels* as general facts (discussed in §§3048, 3071).

3137   *By the spring* symbolizes the light shed on them by truth that is divine. This is established by the symbolism of a *spring* as truth (discussed in §§2702, 3096)—here, truth that is divine (as above in §3131). Because the Word consists in truth that is divine, it is called a spring.

The fact that the inner meaning of "standing by the spring" involves the light shed on ideas in the earthly self follows from the context. Where truth that is divine exists, enlightenment exists.

3138   These three verses are speaking about the way the earthly self is prepared and enlightened so that truth can be called up out of it in order to unite with goodness in the rational mind.

The case with preparation and enlightenment is this: There are two kinds of light that shape our intellectual gifts—the light of heaven and the light of the world. Heaven's light comes from the Lord, who is the angels' sun and moon in the other world (see §§1053, 1521, 1529, 1530). Worldly light comes from the sun and moon we see with our physical eyes. Our inner self sees and understands things by heaven's light, but our outer self sees and understands things by worldly light. The influence of heavenly light on the things we see by worldly light enlightens us and also makes it possible for us to perceive—to perceive the truth, if there is correspondence between [our outer and inner self], and to perceive the falsity that is standing in for truth, if there is not. Enlightenment and perception are not possible, however, unless there is desire, or love, which is spiritual warmth, and which gives life to the objects the light shines on. To take an example by way of comparison, it is not the sun's light that gives life to plants but warmth present in the light, as the different times of year show.

[2] The very next verses depict further preparation, as follows: Heaven's light, which is the Lord's divine light, was to act on the objects of the world's light in his earthly self, so that he could bring forth from there, in the usual way, the truth that was to unite with the goodness in his rational mind. For this reason he came into the world, in order to make his humanity divine by a common, ordinary process. That is, he chose to be born like anyone else, taught like anyone else, and reborn like anyone else. There was a difference, though, in that we are reborn from the Lord, while he not only regenerated himself but also glorified himself, or in

other words, made himself divine. Another difference was that the influence of charity and faith remakes us, but the Lord was remade by the divine love that dwelled in him and was his.

From this it can be seen that human rebirth is an image of the Lord's glorification. To say it another way, the process of the Lord's glorification can be seen reflected—though it is seen remotely—in the process of human rebirth.

Genesis 24:31, 32, 33. *And he said, "Come, you who are blessed by Jehovah! Why are you standing outside? And I have neatened the house, and there is a place for the camels." And the man came to the house and untied the camels, and [Laban] gave hay and fodder to the camels, and water to wash his feet and the feet of the men who were with him. And something was put before him to eat, and he said, "I am not eating till I have spoken my words." And [Laban] said, "Speak!"*

3139

He said, "Come, you who are blessed by Jehovah!" symbolizes an invitation to the divinity inside himself. *Why are you standing outside?* means somewhat far off. *And I have neatened the house* means that everything was ready, and filled with goodness. *And there is a place for the camels* symbolizes the conditions that existed for everything that would serve him. *And the man came to the house* symbolizes an inflow into what was good there [on the earthly plane]. *And untied the camels* symbolizes freedom for the things that were to serve. *And he gave hay and fodder to the camels* symbolizes instruction in truth and goodness. *And water to wash his feet* symbolizes purification there [on the earthly plane]. *And the feet of the men who were with him* symbolizes the purification of everything he had in his earthly self. *And something was put before him to eat* means that the goodness in his earthly self wanted (something) to be adopted. *And he said, "I am not eating,"* symbolizes refusing. *Till I have spoken my words* means until it had been instructed. *And he said, "Speak!"* symbolizes desire.

He said, "Come, you who are blessed by Jehovah!" symbolizes an invitation to the divinity inside himself. This can be seen from the meaning of *come!* as being a term of invitation, and from the symbolism of one *blessed by Jehovah* as divinity.

3140

A blessing on Jehovah symbolizes divinity itself, as may be seen in §§1096, 1420, 1422. It follows that being blessed by Jehovah means the divinity that comes from divinity itself.

Goodness is divinity itself, and truth is the divinity that comes from it. The man sent by Abraham symbolizes truth from the Lord's divine side in his earthly self (§3134). Truth that is divine is what is called one blessed by Jehovah, and it is what is being invited.

3141   *Why are you standing outside?* means somewhat far off, as can be seen without explanation.

The situation is that the Lord's divine rationality was born from divine truth itself united to divine goodness. His divine rationality is Isaac, who was born to Abraham (divine goodness, at that point) from Sarah (divine truth, at that point), as already shown [§§2010, 2063, 2093, 2172, 2621–2623]. Only the Lord had divine rationality born this way. It was born from himself, because the very being of the Lord (divine goodness itself) *was* Jehovah, while the very being of the Lord that emerged from divine goodness (divine truth itself) *belonged* to Jehovah. That is how the divine goodness in his rational mind, which is Isaac, was born. It was not goodness separated from truth but divine goodness along with divine truth, yet taken together they are called the goodness of the rational mind. This is what truth from the Lord's earthly self was to unite with, and that truth is Rebekah. If the Lord was to make both the goodness and the truth of his human side divine, and to do so in the usual way (as noted above in §3138), it could not have been accomplished by any other method. This is the divine pattern that governs all rebirth and therefore governed the Lord's glorification (§3138 at the end).

[2] That divine goodness, operating by means of divine truth on the Lord's rational plane, was what acted on his earthly self and illuminated everything there. The current passage describes the actual process, which was that divine goodness first acted at something of a distance, this being what "somewhat far off" means above. It did not want to act more directly until the Lord had been instructed. The usual path requires that instruction come first and that the inflow of goodness happen in proportion to it. From this process there constantly emerges truth, which is introduced into the goodness of the rational mind and eventually unites with it.

These remarks show what kinds of secrets the Word holds in its inner meaning. By their very nature, in their broadest outlines, they are barely comprehensible to people on earth, although to angels they seem obvious, as do countless details that could never be expressed in words.

3142   *And I have neatened the house* means that everything was ready, and filled with goodness. This can be seen from the symbolism of *neatening* as preparing and being filled (discussed just below), and from that of a *house* as goodness (discussed in §§2233, 2559), people themselves being called houses on account of the goodness in them (§3128).

The reason *neatening* means preparing and being filled is that the only thing required of us is to clean house, or in other words, to reject evil cravings and the distorted convictions they spawn. When we do, we are filled with goodness, because goodness is constantly flowing in from the Lord. What it flows into, though, is a house (a person) scoured of everything that could block it—that is, that could deflect, twist, or smother the inflowing goodness. For this reason, it was common for the ancients to speak of neatening or cleaning the house, and of clearing and preparing the way. Neatening the house meant cleansing oneself of evil and in this way preparing for goodness to enter. Clearing the way meant preparing oneself to receive truth. This was because a house symbolized goodness (§3128), and a path or way symbolized truth (627, 2333). [2] In Isaiah, for example:

> The voice of one shouting in the wilderness, "*Clear* [prepare] *the way* for Jehovah, and straighten in the desert a path for our God!" (Isaiah 40:3)

In the same author:

> Pave, pave, *clear* [prepare] *the way!* Remove the stumbling block from the way of my people! (Isaiah 57:14)

In the same author:

> Pass through into the gates; pass through! *Clear* [prepare] *the way* for the people! Pave the way; pave it! Take away the stones! (Isaiah 62:10)

In Malachi:

> Watch: I am sending my angel, and he will *clear* [prepare] *the way* before me, and suddenly to his temple will come the Lord, whom you are seeking. (Malachi 3:1)

In these passages, clearing the way stands for preparing and getting ready to receive truth. The passage is speaking of the Lord's Coming, at which time people were to prepare for receiving religious truth, and through it, neighborly goodness, and through this, eternal salvation. [3] In David:

> You have caused a grapevine to travel from Egypt; you have driven away the nations and planted it. You *cleared away* [what was] before it and rooted its root, and it filled the land. (Psalms 80:8, 9)

In its highest sense, this is about the Lord. The grapevine from Egypt means the truth that grows out of facts. Driving away the nations means cleansing himself of evil. Clearing away [what was] before it means getting himself ready to be filled with goodness.

In a negative sense, neatening a house symbolizes people who rob themselves of everything good and true and are filled with evil and falsity as a result, as in Luke:

> The unclean spirit, if it does not find a resting place, says, "Let me go back to *my house* that I left"; and if, coming, it finds it *swept* and decorated, it then goes and takes seven other spirits worse than itself and, entering, they settle there. (Luke 11:24, 25, 26; Matthew 12:43, 44, 45)

3143   *And there is a place for the camels* symbolizes the conditions that existed for everything that would serve him. This can be seen from the symbolism of a *place* as a state (discussed in §§1273–1277, 1376–1381, 2625) and from that of *camels* as general facts (discussed in §§3048, 3071). Facts are servants (see §§1486, 3019, 3020) because nothing in the earthly self has any other purpose than to serve the spiritual self. That is why on an inner level, male and female servants, camels, and donkeys mainly symbolize facets of our earthly self.

3144   *And the man came to the house* symbolizes an inflow into what was good there [on the earthly plane]. This can be seen from the symbolism here of *coming* as flowing in, and from that of a *house* as goodness (discussed in §§2233, 2559).

3145   *And untied the camels* symbolizes freedom for the things that were to serve. This can be seen from the symbolism of *untying* as freeing and from that of *camels* as general facts and therefore things that are to serve (as said just above in §3143).

This is how the matter stands: Without freedom, truth never produces anything in the earthly self, is never called up out of that self into the rational self, and never unites there with goodness. When conditions are free, all these processes take place. It is a well-motivated desire for truth that creates freedom. Unless we learn truth from a desire for it, and therefore in freedom, it does not take root, much less rise up toward more interior levels and become faith there.

See §§2870–2893 for the idea that reformation occurs only when there is freedom; that all freedom is a matter of desire; and that the Lord keeps us free so that we can feel our own, independent desire for truth and goodness and so be reborn. That is what *he untied the camels* means. If it did not, such a detail would not be worth mentioning.

And he gave hay and fodder to the camels symbolizes instruction in truth and goodness. This is established by the symbolism of *hay* as truth in the earthly self, and from that of *fodder* as the goodness there (both dealt with above at §3114). Since this is what hay and fodder symbolize, it follows that *giving* them means providing instruction in truth and goodness.

3146

What was shown about freedom at §§2870–2893 demonstrates that the point of freedom is for us to feel and be motivated by a desire for truth when we are being taught, so that truth can penetrate deeply into us—all the way to our spiritual self, or soul—and unite with goodness there. If faith (that is, the truth taught by faith) is to take root, it must be paired with goodness in the rational mind. Otherwise, it never comes to life at all or bears any fruit. What is called the fruit of faith is always the fruit of goodness (which belongs to love and charity) by means of truth (which belongs to faith). If spiritual warmth (the goodness inspired by love) was not at work within spiritual light (the truth taught by faith), we would be like ground that is hardened by frost, the way it is in winter, in which nothing grows, let alone bears fruit. Just as light produces nothing without warmth, so faith produces nothing without love.

And water to wash his feet symbolizes purification there [on the earthly plane]. This can be seen from the symbolism of *water to wash,* or washing with water, as purifying (discussed below), and from that of *feet* as earthly elements or, what is the same, attributes of the earthly self (discussed in §2162).

3147

In the representative religion, it was customary for people to wash their feet with water, which symbolized the rinsing away of filth in the earthly self. The filth of the earthly self is everything connected with self-love and materialism. Goodness and truth flow in when this filth has been rinsed away, because it is the only thing that keeps goodness and truth from flowing in from the Lord. [2] Goodness from the Lord is always acting on us, but when it passes through our inward or spiritual self to our outward or earthly self, our earthly self corrupts it, shunts it aside, or strangles it. However, when the effects of self-love and materialism are removed, goodness is welcomed by our earthly self and bears fruit, because we then do charitable deeds, as a great deal of evidence shows. For instance, when the demands of the outward or earthly self merely go to sleep, as they do during times of misfortune, distress, and sickness, we immediately start to think reverent thoughts and form good intentions. We even do pious deeds, so far as we are able. When our condition changes, though, these impulses also change.

[3] That is what washing symbolized in the ancient church and represented in the Jewish religion. The reason it symbolized that in the ancient church but represented it in the Jewish religion was that people in the ancient church considered the ritual an outward mark of worship. They did not believe they were purified by washing their bodies but by rinsing off the uncleanness of their earthly self, which, as I said, is the filth of self-love and materialism. The people of the Jewish religion, on the other hand, believed that washing purified them, not knowing (and not wanting to know) that it symbolized a purification of their inner depths.

[4] The symbolism of washing as rinsing off that filth can be seen in Isaiah:

> *Wash* yourselves; *purify* yourselves; *remove the evil of your deeds* from before my eyes; stop doing evil! (Isaiah 1:16)

Clearly washing oneself here means purifying oneself and removing evil. In the same author:

> . . . when the Lord has *washed off* the *excrement* of Zion's daughters and *rinsed away* the blood of Jerusalem from its midst, in a spirit of judgment and in a spirit of cleansing. (Isaiah 4:4)

Washing off the excrement of Zion's daughters, and rinsing away the blood of Jerusalem, in this verse, stands for purifying people of evil and falsity. In Jeremiah:

> *Scrub your heart of iniquity,* Jerusalem, in order that you may be saved; how long will your thoughts of wickedness linger in your midst? (Jeremiah 4:14)

[5] In Ezekiel:

> I *washed you with water* and *rinsed blood* off you and anointed you with oil. (Ezekiel 16:9)

This is about Jerusalem, which in this case means the ancient church. Washing it with water stands for purifying it of falsity; rinsing blood off it stands for cleansing it of evil. Anointing it with oil stands for filling it with goodness after that. In David:

> *Wash me* of my wickedness, and from my sin make me clean! You will purge me with hyssop, and I will be clean; you will *wash me,* and I will be whiter than snow. (Psalms 51:2, 7)

Being washed obviously stands for being purified of evil and the falsity it leads to.

[6] This was what washing symbolized in the representative religion. For the sake of the representation, the people of that religion were commanded to wash and be clean when their skin, hands, feet, or clothes became unclean. All of these things symbolized facets of the earthly self. In addition, bronze lavers, comprising a bronze sea and ten bronze washbowls, were placed outside the Temple (1 Kings 7:23–37, 38, 39). And a washbowl of bronze, from which Aaron and his sons washed, was placed between the meeting tent and the altar—again, outside the tent (Exodus 30:18, 19, 21). This meant that only a person's superficial or earthly parts would be purified. If they are not—that is, if the taint of self-love and materialism is not removed from them—the deeper qualities of love for the Lord and for one's neighbor can never flow in, as mentioned above.

[7] To better see how the matter stands here—why our outward aspects need to be purified—take as an example and illustration the good deeds we do, or in other words, good done out of charity, which people today call the fruits of faith. These are superficial, because they are actions. Good deeds are evil deeds if impulses of self-love and materialism are not removed. When we do good deeds before removing those impulses, the deeds do look good on the outside, but they are evil on the inside. We do them for the sake of reputation, or material advantage, or position, or to be repaid, so they are either self-righteous or hypocritical. The urges of self-love and materialism make them so. When these evils are removed, however, the deeds become good. Then they are the goodness of charity. No consideration of self, worldly advantages, reputation, or reward enters into them, so they are not self-righteous or hypocritical. Heavenly love and spiritual love then flow from the Lord into the deeds and cause them to be love and charity in action. The Lord then uses them to purify our earthly or outward self and restructure it to correspond to and receive inflowing heavenly and spiritual qualities. [8] This is quite clear from what the Lord taught in John when he washed the disciples' feet:

> He comes to Simon Peter, who says to him, "Lord, are you *washing my feet?*" Jesus answered and said to him, "What I am doing you do not know yet; but you will know after this." Peter says to him, "*You will never, ever wash my feet!*" Jesus answered him, "*If I do not wash you, you have no part with me.*" Simon Peter says to him, "Lord, not my *feet* only but also my *hands* and *head!*" Jesus says to him, "*Those who have*

bathed have no need except to have their feet washed but are all clean.
Now you are clean, but not every one of you." (John 13:4–17)

"Those who have bathed have no need except to have their feet washed"
means that people who have reformed need only to have their earthly
dimension cleaned. In other words, they need to have evil and falsity
removed from there. The Lord then restructures everything through an
inflow of spiritual qualities.

Besides, washing other people's feet was a sign of neighborly love,
which said, "I will not meditate on your faults." It was also a sign of
humility, which said, "I will clean away your faults like dirt," as can also
be seen from the Lord's words in verses 12–17 there, and in Luke 7:37, 38,
44, [45,] 46; John 11:2; 1 Samuel 25:41.

[9] Anyone can see that washing ourselves never purifies us of evil and
falsity but only of the dirt that clings to us. Since it was among the man-
datory rituals in that religion, though, it follows that the practice involves
some special meaning—specifically that of spiritual washing, or purification from the dirt that clings to a person inwardly.

Some people in the religion knew this, so they thought about purifying their heart, or removing from their earthly self the evils belonging to
love for themselves and love of the material world; and they made every
effort to do so. These people participated in ritual washing as an outward
sign of worship that had been commanded. There were others, though,
who did not know it and did not want to know. They thought that the
mere ritual of washing their clothes, skin, hands, and feet would purify
them, and that as long as they did these things, they would be allowed to
live lives of greed, hatred, vengefulness, ruthlessness, and savagery, which
are spiritual filth. These people cultivated the ritual as an idolatrous one.
Still, by means of the ritual they were able to represent something of
religion, and through the representation to present an image of it. This
allowed a measure of connection between heaven and humankind, before
the Lord arrived, but it was a kind of connection that left little or no
impression on the people of that religion. [10] Jews and Israelites were
such that they absolutely never thought about the inner self and did not
want to know anything about it, so they were completely uninterested in
learning about various heavenly and spiritual aspects of life after death.
However, in order to prevent communication with heaven and therefore
with the Lord from dying out completely, they were strictly held to external rituals that symbolized inward attributes. The general purpose of all

the captivities and plagues inflicted on them was to ensure that external observances be properly maintained for the sake of the representation. This, then, was the reason for the following:

> Moses was to *wash* Aaron and his sons *with water at the doorway of the tent* to consecrate them. (Exodus 29:4; 40:12; Leviticus 8:6)

> Aaron and his sons were to *wash their hands and feet* before they entered the meeting tent and approached the altar to minister, so as not to die; and this was to be an eternal statute for them. (Exodus 30:18, 19, 20, 21; 40:30, 31)

> Before Aaron put on the garments of his ministry, he was to *wash his flesh*. (Leviticus 16:4, 24)

> The Levites were to be purified by being spattered with atonement water and passing a razor over their flesh and *washing their clothes* and so being pure. (Numbers 8:6, 7)

> Those who ate the carcass of a clean animal, or torn flesh, were to *wash their clothes* and *rinse with water;* and if they did not *wash themselves* and *rinse their flesh,* they would carry their wickedness. (Leviticus 17:15, 16)

> Those who touched the bed of a person suffering a discharge, or who sat on a vessel on which such a person had sat, or who touched such a person's flesh, were to *wash their clothes* and *rinse with water* and be unclean till evening. (Leviticus 15:5, 6, 7, 10, 11, 12, and following verses)

> Those who released a he-goat as an azazel were to *wash their flesh*. (Leviticus 16:26)

> When the leprous had been healed, they were to *wash their clothes*, shave all their hair, and *wash with water* and be clean. (Leviticus 14:8, 9)

> In fact, even the vessels that had become unclean by contact with unclean people were to be *passed through water* and be unclean till evening. (Leviticus 11:32)

From this it can be seen that no one's inner depths would be made clean or pure by ritual washing but that [the washing] would only *represent* purity or spiritual cleanliness, for the reason given above. The Lord plainly teaches that this is so in Matthew 15:1, 2, 20; Mark 7:1–23.

And the feet of the men who were with him symbolizes the purification of everything he had in his earthly self. This can be seen from the   **3148** symbolism of *feet* as whatever belongs to the earthly self (discussed in §2162) and from that of the *men who were with him* as everything there. It was customary for wayfarers to wash their feet when they came into a house. That is what happened when Joseph's brothers were taken to Joseph's house (Genesis 43:24); when the Levite and those with him were welcomed into the old man's house (Judges 19:21); and when David ordered Uriah, arriving from his journey, to go down to his house and wash his feet (2 Samuel 11:8). The reason was that travels and journeys symbolized the things a person is taught and therefore the way a person lives (see §§1293, 1457, 1463, 2025). These would be purified, as shown just above in §3147. Another reason for the custom was to prevent dirt (understood in its spiritual sense) from being tracked into the house (that is, the person). This is clear from the requirement that [the disciples] shake off the *dust of their feet* if a town or a household would not accept peace (Matthew 10:14).

3149 *And something was put before him to eat* means that the desire for goodness in his earthly self wanted (something) to be adopted, as can be seen from the following: Laban—who did the *putting*—represents a desire in the earthly self for what is good, as mentioned in §§3129, 3130. And *eating* means being communicated and adopted, as discussed in §§2187, 2343. It is the divine qualities mentioned above in §§3140, 3141 whose adoption was sought.

3150 *And he said, "I am not eating,"* symbolizes refusing—refusing to let them be adopted yet—as can be seen without explanation.

3151 *Till I have spoken my words* means until [his earthly self] had been instructed. This can be seen from the symbolism of *speaking words* as teaching. The words that the servant spoke (and that follow in order) are indeed instructive, too.

On the point that divine attributes flow into attributes of the earthly self in proportion to the instruction it receives and the progress it makes as a result, see the end of §3141 above.

3152 *And he said, "Speak!"* symbolizes desire. This can be seen from the symbolism of speaking words as teaching, and of *"Speak!"* here as a command to teach. Obviously, the command implies desire.

3153 It is true that the contents of the inner meaning in these three verses become clear from the explanation: Everything in the earthly self was readied for receiving divine qualities; as a consequence the truth symbolized by Rebekah—which was to be introduced to goodness on the rational plane and unite with it—was made divine; and this was accomplished by an inflow into it.

Even so, unless we view it in a single sweep of thought, the inner meaning here appears by its very nature to be too obscure to understand—all the more so because the subject matter is unfamiliar. Take, for instance, the way truth is called up out of our earthly self and introduced into goodness in our rational mind when we are regenerating. Most people today know so little about the subject that they do not even realize it happens. The main reason for their ignorance is that few today regenerate. Those that do, fail to learn from doctrine that neighborly kindness is what religious truth is introduced into and unites with, or that this occurs in the rational mind. They do not learn that our state then changes radically, so that religious truth no longer directs our thoughts to neighborly kindness, but neighborly kindness leads our thoughts to the truth.

Of course the Lord was not regenerated but glorified. In other words, he made everything on both his rational and earthly planes divine. The inner meaning tells how this was done.

Genesis 24:34–48. *And he said, "I am Abraham's servant. And Jehovah* [3154] *has blessed my master very much and enlarged him and given him flock and herd, and silver and gold, and male and female slaves, and camels and donkeys. And Sarah, my master's wife, bore a son to my master after [reaching] her old age, and he has given [the son] everything he has. And my master put me under oath, saying, 'You shall not take a woman for my son from the daughters of the Canaanite in whose land I reside. Not except to the house of my father shall you go, and to my clan, and you shall take a woman for my son.' And I said to my master, 'Maybe the woman will not come after me.' And he said to me, 'Jehovah, in whose presence I have walked, will send his angel with you and make your path successful; and you are to take a woman for my son, from my clan and from my father's house. Then you will be exempt from my curse, because you came to my clan. And if they do not give [her] to you, then you will be exempt from my curse.' And I came today to the spring and said, 'Jehovah, God of my master Abraham, if it is your [will], please, be giving success to my path that I am walking on. Look: I am standing by the spring of water; and let it be that the maiden who is going out to draw, and I say to her, "Let me take a drink, please, of a little water from your pitcher," and she says to me, "Yes, you drink, and I will also draw for your camels"—let that be the woman whom Jehovah has destined for my master's son.' I had hardly finished speaking to my heart*

*when here, Rebekah comes out, and her pitcher is on her shoulder, and she
goes down to the spring and draws; and I said to her, 'Let me take a drink,
please!' And she hurried and brought her pitcher down from upon her and
said, 'Drink! And I will also water your camels.' And I drank, and she also
watered the camels. And I asked her and said, 'Whose daughter are you?'
And she said, 'The daughter of Bethuel, son of Nahor, whom Milcah bore
to him.' And I put the ring in her nose and the bracelets on her hands. And
I bowed and prostrated myself to Jehovah, and I blessed Jehovah, God of my
master Abraham, who led me into the way of truth, to take the daughter of
my master's brother for his son."*

[2] *He said, "I am Abraham's servant,"* means that it resulted from
divine goodness. *And Jehovah has blessed my master very much and enlarged
him* symbolizes the goodness and the truth in the Lord's divine humanity.
And given him flock and herd symbolizes good qualities in general. *And
silver and gold* symbolizes truth in general. *And male and female slaves,
and camels and donkeys* symbolizes particular truths. *And Sarah, my master's wife, bore a son to my master* symbolizes divine rationality arising out
of divine truth. *After [reaching] her old age* means when it was time. *And
he has given [the son] everything he has* means that everything divine was
his. [3] *And my master put me under oath* here as before symbolizes an
obligation and a vow. *Saying, "You shall not take a woman for my son from
the daughters of the Canaanite,"* here as before [§3024] means that divine
rationality was not to unite with any desire that clashes with truth. *In
whose land I reside* symbolizes discordant elements among which exists
goodness that is divine. *Not except to the house of my father shall you go*
symbolizes goodness from his divine side. *And to my clan* symbolizes truth
from his divine side. *And you shall take a woman for my son* symbolizes
the union that would result. *And I said to my master, "Maybe the woman
will not come after me,"* here as before [§3030] symbolizes the earthly self's
doubt that this desire was capable of detaching. [4] *And he said to me*
symbolizes instruction. *Jehovah, in whose presence I have walked, will send
his angel with you* here as before [§3039] symbolizes divine providence.
And make your path successful means in regard to truth. *And you are to take
a woman for my son* means that there would be a union. *From my clan and
from my father's house* means arising out of the goodness and truth from
his divine side there. *Then you will be exempt from my curse* here as before
symbolizes the freedom granted to the earthly self. *Because you came to
my clan; and if they do not give [her] to you* means in regard to detaching.

Then you will be exempt from my curse means that then the earthly self would be blameless.

The rest, up to verse 48, has the same symbolism as before.

I decline to explain the individual points, since they were already explained earlier in the chapter.   **3155**

They are repeated for the instruction of the earthly self. The introduction of truth into goodness and their union resembles the case of a young woman when she becomes engaged and then united to a husband: she needs to learn all there is to know before she gives her consent.

Although the process is not visible in people when truth is being introduced and united to the goodness in them—when they are reforming, in other words—it is taking place anyway. That is to say, goodness first learns about truth, and truth about goodness, and then both parties consent, as the next part depicts.

Genesis 24:49, 50, 51. *"And now, if you are keeping mercy and truth with*   **3156** *my master, tell me; and if not, tell me, and I will look either to the right or to the left." And Laban answered, as did Bethuel, and they said, "From Jehovah has this word come; we cannot speak evil or good to you. Look: Rebekah is before you; take her and go, and let her be a woman to your master's son, as Jehovah has spoken."*

Now, if you are keeping mercy and truth with my master means an examination into the consent by both faculties, will and intellect. *Tell me; and if not, tell me* symbolizes the atmosphere of freedom in which they deliberated. *And I will look either to the right or to the left* symbolizes an answering freedom. *And Laban answered, as did Bethuel, and they said, "From Jehovah has this word come; we cannot speak evil or good to you,"* symbolizes an acknowledgment that it was the Lord's doing alone. *Look: Rebekah is before you; take her and go, and let her be a woman to your master's son, as Jehovah has spoken* symbolizes consent inspired by the Lord.

Now, if you are keeping mercy and truth with my master means an   **3157** examination into the consent by both faculties, will and intellect. This can be seen from the symbolism of *mercy* as something related to goodness, or to love (discussed in §§3063, 3073, 3120), and from the symbolism of *truth* as something related to truth, or to faith (discussed in §§3121, 3122). The goodness inspired by love belongs to the will, and the truth taught by faith belongs to the intellect, and the request to keep mercy and truth is addressed to Laban and Bethuel, or in other words, to human beings. For this reason, it means an examination by both human faculties, will and intellect. The fact that it is an examination into the consent becomes clear both from the words here *if you are keeping* and from the words below *tell me; and if not, tell me, and I will look either to the right or to the left.*

The case with human regeneration, which is an image of the Lord's glorification (§3138), is that although we learn religious truth we do not acknowledge it (much less accept it out of goodness) unless both faculties, will and intellect, agree to it. Consent is true acknowledgment. Acknowledgment leads to acceptance, including acceptance by our will, where goodness resides.

When our will or our goodness (which is the same thing) accepts religious truth, we have been reborn, because then truth belongs to goodness. In other words, faith belongs to neighborly love, or actually becomes that love, in regard to the way we live (§3121).

3158 *Tell me; and if not, tell me* symbolizes the atmosphere of freedom in which they deliberated, as is clear from the sense of the words.

The whole discussion to this point shows that where the literal meaning of the current chapter describes Rebekah's betrothal and marriage to Isaac, the inner meaning describes the introduction of truth to goodness and their union. The introduction and union of truth to goodness is spiritual betrothal and marriage.

On both levels, deliberation demands an atmosphere of freedom. People realize that engagement and marriage require it, but they do not see very clearly that the introduction and union of goodness and truth does too. This is because the process is not visible to the earthly self and because it is one that occurs without our reflecting on it. Even so, it is taking place every second that we are being reformed and reborn; when truth is uniting with goodness, we are enjoying a condition of freedom.

Just by considering the question, anyone can see that we never have anything for our own unless it is part of our will. Nothing that belongs to our intellect alone is ours until it also becomes part of our will. What we have in our will constitutes the core reality of our life, but what we have in our intellect constitutes our life as it emerges from that core reality. Consent by our intellect alone is not consent; all consent comes from our will. So unless religious truth in the intellect is accepted by a loving goodness in the will, it is by no means an acknowledged truth, and therefore it is not faith. In order for it to be accepted by goodness in the will, an atmosphere of freedom has to exist. Everything that the will participates in appears to be free. A willing state in and of itself *is* freedom, because what I will, that I choose, that I desire, because that I love and recognize as good. From this it can be seen that we never come to have religious truth for our own until it is accepted by our will— that is, until it has been introduced into and united with the goodness there—and that this can only happen in an atmosphere of freedom.

And I will look either to the right or to the left symbolizes an answering freedom, as can be seen without explanation.

3159

This is how matters stand: Good things are always flowing from the Lord through our inner self into our outer self. In our early years, they appear in our outer self in the form of a desire for truth. The more we regard heavenly and spiritual benefit as the goal, the more truth is introduced and united to goodness or (to put it another way) the desire for truth is introduced and united to a desire for goodness. On the other hand, the more we regard our own benefit and therefore ourselves and the material world as the goal, the more heavenly and spiritual benefits withdraw. This is the answering freedom symbolized by *looking either to the right or to the left.*

And Laban answered, as did Bethuel, and they said, "From Jehovah has this word come; we cannot speak evil or good to you," symbolizes an acknowledgment that it was the Lord's doing alone. The symbolism can be seen from an explanation of the inner meaning of the individual words, but no explanation is needed to show that this is the conclusion to be drawn from the words.

3160

From Jehovah has this word come clearly means that it was from the Lord, because *Jehovah,* mentioned so many times in the Old Testament, never means anyone but the Lord (see §§1343, 1736, 1815, 2156, 2329, [2921,] 3023, 3035).

These words involve some mystery, as indicated by the fact that Laban, the young woman's brother, answered here, and then Bethuel, her father, rather than her father and mother, and that she herself did not answer till later. The explanation is that as a brother, Laban represents a desire in the earthly self for goodness (§§3129, 3130), while Bethuel represents the source of a desire for goodness.

A desire for goodness and a desire for truth in the earthly self resemble a brother and sister. When the desire for truth has been called up out of the earthly self into the rational self and has united with goodness there, it resembles a married woman.

[2] The secret reason for the response here from Laban and Bethuel— the brother first, and then the father—is that when goodness from the rational self influences the earthly self, it does not act directly on the truth

there. Instead it acts on the goodness there and through the goodness on the truth. Unless it exerts this kind of influence, no desire for truth can come into being. The earthly self's desire for goodness is what acknowledges the influence and therefore is what first agrees to it. There is direct communication between rational goodness and earthly goodness but not between rational goodness and earthly truth. On the parallelism of these things, see §§1831, 1832.

Two ancient expressions occur here—"from Jehovah has this word come," meaning that the deed had been done by Jehovah, and "we cannot speak evil or good to you," meaning that they did not dare deny or affirm.

A discussion follows of the acknowledgment that it was the Lord's doing alone.

3161   *Look: Rebekah is before you; take her and go, and let her be a woman to your master's son, as Jehovah has spoken* symbolizes consent inspired by the Lord. This too can be seen from an explanation of the individual words, but again it is the general conclusion to be drawn from their inner meaning.

As for the situation itself, when the Lord lived in the world, he made the humanity in himself divine by his own power. Humanity starts at the deepest level of the rational mind (§§2106, 2194). The current passage depicts the way he made it divine, which was now by making the truth in it divine, just as he had previously made the goodness in it divine. After all, rationality consists of both goodness and truth. The goodness in the Lord's rational mind came from his divinity itself, or in other words, from Jehovah, the Father, from whom he was conceived; but the truth there had to be amassed in the usual way, as it is in other people.

[2] It is recognized that we are not born rational but only with the potential of becoming so, and that we become so by learning facts—that is, by gathering many types and kinds of knowledge. The first kinds are the means to the next, and so on in order to the last, which are spiritual kinds concerning the Lord's kingdom and are called teachings. These are gleaned in part from the theology of the faith, in part directly from the Word, and therefore in part by our own intellectual energy, as is also recognized. As long as these teachings remain a matter of memory, they are merely factual truth; we have not yet adopted them as our own. The time when we first make them our own is when we start to love them for the role they can play in our lives, and even more so when we put them to work there. When we do that, the truth rises up out of our physical memory into our rational mind and there unites with goodness. Once

united, it is no longer a matter of knowledge but of life, because then we are no longer learning from truth how to live but are living by it. In this way we adopt truth and it becomes part of our will. So we enter into the heavenly marriage, because the heavenly marriage is the union of goodness and truth on the rational plane. This is something the Lord does in us.

[3] In himself, though, the Lord did all this by himself. From his divinity itself he brought forth not only the goodness present on his rational plane but also, by means of it, the truth present on his earthly plane, which he united with the goodness. Goodness is what chooses truth for itself and also forms truth, because goodness does not acknowledge anything to be true unless it is in harmony with it. So the goodness of a divine type that the Lord possessed created truth for itself. It refused to acknowledge anything as true that did not harmonize with divine goodness, or in other words, that was not divine truth emanating from himself. So he did absolutely all of it by his own power.

That is what is meant by the acknowledgment that it was the Lord's doing alone and came about through the consent inspired by the Lord.

Genesis 24:52, 53, 54. *And it happened as Abraham's servant heard their* **3162** *words that he bowed down to the earth to Jehovah. And the servant brought out vessels of silver and vessels of gold and clothes and gave them to Rebekah; and precious gifts he gave to her brother and her mother. And they ate and drank—he and the men who were with him—and spent the night and got up in the morning; and he said, "Send me to my master."*

It happened as Abraham's servant heard their words that he bowed down to the earth to Jehovah symbolizes a perception of joy in the earthly self. *And the servant brought out vessels of silver and vessels of gold and clothes* symbolizes truth and goodness and the beauty they add. *And gave them to Rebekah* means which now characterized the desire for truth. *And precious gifts he gave to her brother* symbolizes spiritual riches granted to earthly goodness as a result. *And her mother* means to earthly truth as well. *And they ate and drank* symbolizes adoption of the goodness and truth that had accordingly been introduced into one another. *He and the men who were with him* means as they existed in the earthly self. *And spent the night* symbolizes peace there. *And got up in the morning* symbolizes going a step higher. *And he said, "Send me to my master,"* symbolizes a desire for union.

It happened as Abraham's servant heard their words that he bowed down **3163** *to the earth to Jehovah* symbolizes a perception of joy in the earthly self, as can be seen from the following: *Hearing someone's words* symbolizes perceiving. *Abraham's servant* represents the earthly self as a whole, so far as it serves the rational self, and here, as it served the Lord's divine side, as discussed in §§3019, 3020. And *bowing down to Jehovah* symbolizes rejoicing, as discussed in §§2927, 2950, 3118.

3164   *And the servant brought out vessels of silver and vessels of gold and clothes* symbolizes truth and goodness and the beauty they add. This can be seen from the symbolism of *vessels of silver, vessels of gold,* and *clothes* on an inner level. *Silver* symbolizes truth (see §§1551, 2048), and *gold* symbolizes goodness (113, 1551, 1552). They are called *vessels* of silver and gold because they are associated with the desire for truth, which is Rebekah, at this point. Regarded in itself, truth is just a vessel or container for goodness (1496, 1832, 1900, 2063, 2261, 2269, 3068).

Vessels of silver in particular mean facts, because facts are a container for truth. *Vessels of gold* in particular mean truth, since truth is a container for goodness. *Clothes,* though, are added beauty, as can be seen without explanation.

[2] In ancient times, a young woman received gifts like these when she became betrothed, and this was for the sake of the representation and symbolism of a betrothed woman as truth in the church that is to be united with goodness. The ancient church in its earliest days is depicted in similar terms in Ezekiel:

> When it was time for love, *I clothed you with embroidery,* swathed you in fine linen, and covered you in silk, and *decked you in finery,* and put *bracelets on* your *hands* and a necklace on your throat, and put a *ring in* your *nose* and earrings in your ears and a fine crown on your head. So you were *adorned in gold and silver,* and *your clothes* were fine linen and silk and embroidery. (Ezekiel 16:8, 9, 10, 11, 12, 13)

And when the same church had fallen away from truth and goodness, it is depicted this way in the same chapter:

> You took some of *your clothes* and made yourself colorful high places. And you took the *articles* of your *finery*—made of *my gold* and of *my silver,* which I had given to you—and made yourself images of a male and took embroidered *clothes* and covered the images. (Ezekiel 16:16, 17, 18)

This shows plainly that silver, gold, and clothes are simply attributes of the church—specifically, truth and goodness themselves and all that has to do with them.

And gave them to Rebekah means which now characterized the desire **3165**
for truth. This can be seen from the representation of *Rebekah* as a
desire for truth (dealt with in §§2865, 3077). The items just above—the
vessels of silver, vessels of gold, and clothes—are used to depict the
desire for truth as a bride. So these words mean that this is what the desire
for truth was now like, or in other words, that these things now characterized the desire for truth.

And precious gifts he gave to her brother symbolizes spiritual riches granted **3166**
to earthly goodness as a result, as can be seen from the following: *Precious
things* symbolize spiritual traits, as discussed below. And a *brother* symbolizes earthly goodness, as noted in §3160, while Laban, the brother here,
is a desire for goodness in the earthly self, as noted in §§3129, 3130.

Other passages from the Word also show that *precious things* symbolize spiritual traits. Where Moses speaks of Joseph, for instance:

> A blessing from Jehovah on his land in the *precious worth of the sky,* in
> the dew, and in the underlying abyss; and in the *precious worth of the
> sun's produce;* and in the *precious worth of [many] months' yield;* and in
> the *precious worth of the eternal hills;* and in the *precious worth of the
> land* and its abundance. (Deuteronomy 33:13, 14, 15, 16)

The precious worth of the sky, of the sun's produce, of [many] months'
yield, of the eternal hills, and of the land symbolizes spiritual entities of
many different types. Other substances described as precious were precious stones, pearls, balsam, perfumes, and so on, which all symbolize
spiritual qualities.

[2] The spiritual dimension has already been defined many times. To
be specific: The Lord's kingdom contains what is heavenly and what is
spiritual. What is heavenly has to do with goodness, and what is spiritual,
with the truth that comes of goodness. There is nothing in the universe
that does not relate to goodness or to truth. Everything involved in useful
activity and life relates to goodness, while everything involved in doctrine
and knowledge—especially when it concerns useful activity and life—
relates to truth. To say it another way, what exists in the will is called
either good or evil, but what exists in the intellect is termed either truth
or falsity. So goodness, which has to do only with love and charity, and
flows in from the Lord, is heavenly, but truth, which grows out of it, is
spiritual.

The reason precious gifts were given to the brother when his sister at
her betrothal received vessels of silver, vessels of gold, and clothes was that

a *brother* symbolized goodness in the earthly self. This goodness is illuminated when truth is introduced into the goodness of the rational mind, because all the light that shines on goodness and truth in the earthly self results from that connection.

3167   *And [to her] mother* means to earthly truth as well. In other words, spiritual riches were granted to it as a result, as they had been to earthly goodness—a fact discussed just above. This can be seen from the symbolism of a *mother* as the church, which is called a mother on account of the truth it possesses, as discussed in §§289, 2717.

A few words must be said to show how it is that spiritual riches are granted to earthly goodness and earthly truth as a result of truth's being introduced into goodness on the rational plane. We each have inner depths and an outer layer. Our inner depths are called the inner self, and our outer layer is called the outer self. Few people, however, know what the inner and outer self are. The inner self is the same as the spiritual self, and the outer self is the same as the earthly self. The spiritual self is what gains intelligence and wisdom from things seen by heaven's light, but the earthly self, from things seen in worldly light. (Concerning both kinds of light, see §3138.) Heaven, after all, has nothing but spiritual objects in it, while the world has nothing but earthly objects in it. Humankind was created in such a way as to enable the spiritual and earthly dimensions in us—that is, our spiritual self and earthly self—to harmonize, or act in concert. Our spiritual self then ought to manage everything in our earthly self, and our earthly self ought to obey it, as a servant obeys a master or mistress. [2] In consequence of the Fall, though, the earthly self started to lift itself above the spiritual self, so it turned the divine hierarchy itself upside down. As a result, the earthly self separated itself from the spiritual self and lost all spiritual influence, except for what could squeeze through the cracks, so to speak, and give it the ability to think and speak.

In order for spiritual qualities to regain their influence on the earthly self, people needed to be regenerated by the Lord. That is, truth from their earthly self needed to be introduced into and united with the goodness in their rational mind. When this happens, one's earthly self gains access to the spiritual dimension, because heaven's light then flows in and shines on that which exists in the earthly self, making everything there receptive to the light. The goodness of the earthly self absorbs the warmth, or the love and charity, but truth absorbs the rays of light, or faith. So earthly goodness and earthly truth gain spiritual riches as a result.

Earthly goodness is then all the pleasure and gratification that comes from the goal of serving spiritual interests, and so of serving our neighbor, and even more so our nation, and even more so the Lord's kingdom, and above all the Lord. Earthly truth, on the other hand, is every teaching and every fact we learn for the sake of becoming wise, or in other words, for the sake of acting on what we have learned.

And they ate and drank symbolizes adoption of the goodness and truth that had accordingly been introduced into one another, as can be seen from the following: *Eating* means being communicated and united and therefore adopted, as discussed in §§2187, 2343. Since bread is what is eaten, and bread symbolizes goodness (§§276, 680, 2165, 2177, 2187), the adoption of goodness is what eating symbolizes. *Drinking* also means being communicated, united, and therefore adopted, as noted in §3089, but since it is wine that is imbibed, and wine symbolizes truth (§§1071, 1798), the adoption of truth is what drinking symbolizes. **3168**

To describe the process itself: As noted just above in §3167, when truth is being introduced into goodness on the rational plane, and especially when it is uniting with goodness there, the goodness and truth of the spiritual self (or spiritual riches) are adopted by the earthly self.

He and the men who were with him means as they existed in the earthly self. This can be seen from the representation of the servant, who is *he* in this phrase, as the earthly self (dealt with in §§3019, 3020), and from the symbolism of *the men who were with him* as everything in the earthly self (dealt with in §3148). **3169**

And spent the night symbolizes peace in the earthly self. This can be seen from the meaning of *spending the night* as resting, and on an inner level as having peace. **3170**

The situation is that when the earthly self adopts spiritual qualities, everything produced by evil cravings and false convictions—and so everything that disquiets us—goes away. Everything involved in a desire for what is good and true—and so everything that creates peace—approaches. All disquiet is the result of evil and falsity, while all peace is the result of goodness and truth. For a definition of peace and a description of a peaceful state, see §§92, 93, 1726, 2780.

And got up in the morning symbolizes going a step higher. This can be seen from the symbolism of *getting up* as a term that involves elevation (discussed in §§2401, 2785, 2912, 2927) and from that of *morning* as the Lord, his kingdom, and the peaceful conditions these inspire (discussed in §§2405, 2780). **3171**

The earthly dimension is said to go higher when it adopts spiritual traits. All elevation comes from spiritual and heavenly qualities, because these lift a person up to heaven, closer to the Lord.

3172 *And he said, "Send me to my master,"* symbolizes a desire for union. This can be seen from the general idea that results from the inner meaning of the words. The servant's wish that Laban *send him to his master* was a sign of a longing that the desire for truth—Rebekah—be united, since the betrothal (the introduction) had already been accomplished. A desire for union is what is symbolized here.

3173 Genesis 24:55, 56, 57, 58. *And her brother and her mother said, "Let the girl stay with us several days, perhaps ten; afterward, you shall go." And he said to them, "Do not delay me. And Jehovah has made my path successful; send me and let me go to my master." And they said, "Let's call the girl and ask of her own mouth." And they called Rebekah and said to her, "Would you go with this man?" And she said, "I will go."*

Her brother and her mother said symbolizes the earthly self's doubt. *Let the girl stay with us* symbolizes being held back by [goodness and truth in the earthly self]. *Several days, perhaps ten; afterward, you shall go* symbolizes a stage that seemed ripe for departure to them. *And he said to them, "Do not delay me,"* symbolizes what the desire for goodness wanted. *And Jehovah has made my path successful* means that everything had now been provided for. *Send me and let me go to my master* means in regard to the stage at which [truth] was introduced. *And they said, "Let's call the girl and ask of her own mouth,"* symbolizes consent sought only from the desire for truth. *And they called Rebekah and said to her, "Would you go with this man?" and she said, "I will go,"* symbolizes its full consent.

3174 *Her brother and her mother said* symbolizes the earthly self's doubt. This can be seen from the symbolism of a *brother* as goodness in the earthly self (discussed in §3160) and from that of a *mother* as truth there (discussed in §3167). The brother and mother, then, symbolize the earthly self, since it consists of goodness and truth. Obviously there is doubt— doubt whether the girl was to stay several days more or go with the man right away.

3175 *Let the girl stay with us* symbolizes being held back by them. This can be seen from the meaning here of *staying* as being held back, as the sequence of ideas in the inner meaning also shows.

This is how the case stands: We are never born into any truth, not even into any earthly truth, such as the idea that we should not steal, not kill, not commit adultery, and so on. Still less are we born into any spiritual truth, such as the idea that there is a God, or that we have a deeper part that will live on after death. So on our own we know nothing about eternal life. Earthly and spiritual truth are things we learn. If we did not learn them, we would be much worse than brute animals. By heredity, we love ourselves above all others and long to own everything in the world. That is why we need to be restrained by civil laws and the fear of losing our position, wealth, reputation, and life. Otherwise we would steal, kill, and commit adultery without the least twinge of conscience. This is obviously the case, because even the educated do such things without remorse and in fact defend the practice, offering many justifications for acting that way, so far as they can get away with it. What would they refrain from if they had not been educated?

It is the same in spiritual matters. Even among people who have been born in the church, possess the Word, and are constantly being taught, there are many who ascribe little or hardly anything to God but assign everything in whole and in part to nature. So at heart they do not believe that there is any God nor therefore that they will live on after death. Consequently they do not want to know anything about life after death.

[2] This shows that humankind is not born into any truth but must learn everything. We have to learn by an external route, or in other words, through hearing and sight. By this path, truth needs to be instilled and planted in our memory. As long as it confines itself to the memory, though, truth is merely knowledge. If it is to permeate us, it has to be called up from there and borne deep within. After all, our humanity lies deep within, in our rational mind. Unless we are rational, we are not human, so the kind and amount of rationality a person has determines the kind and amount of humanity the person has.

We cannot possibly be rational unless we have goodness. The goodness that sets us apart from animals is to love God and love our neighbor. This is the source of all human goodness. Such goodness is what truth needs to be introduced into and unite with, within our rational mind. Truth is introduced and united to goodness when we love God and love our neighbor, because truth then takes up residence in goodness, since goodness and truth acknowledge one another. All truth comes from goodness, and truth looks to goodness as its ultimate aim and its soul and so as the source of its life.

[3] It is hard to detach truth from the earthly self, though, and raise it from that level to the rational plane. Our earthly self contains misconceptions, cravings for evil, and a convinced belief in falsity. So long

as these are present and attach themselves to truth, so long our earthly self holds truth back, not allowing it to rise up from that level to the rational plane. That is what it means in an inner sense to say, "Let the girl stay with us several days, perhaps ten; afterward, you shall go." The process is difficult because the earthly self casts doubt on the truth and debates its validity. However, as soon as the Lord detaches our evil cravings and false convictions and therefore our misconceptions, and goodness causes us to start loathing arguments against truth and laughing at doubts about it, truth has reached the stage for leaving the earthly self. Then it is time for truth to rise up into our rational mind and clothe itself in a state of goodness, because truth then belongs with goodness and has some life.

[4] Let examples serve to make these ideas more comprehensible. It is spiritually true that everything good comes from the Lord, and everything evil from hell. This truth has to be proved and illustrated many times over before it can be raised up from our earthly self into our rational mind. What is more, it cannot possibly be raised up there till we love God, because till then, we do not acknowledge it and therefore do not believe it.

The situation is the same with other truths, such as the idea that divine providence sees to the smallest details of all, and if it did not, it could never see to the overall state of affairs.

Another example is this truth: The death of what we consider during our worldly existence to be the all-in-all of life is when we actually first start to live. The life we then take up is indescribable and unlimited, by comparison, and we are totally unaware of it as long as we are involved in evil.

These truths and others like them are completely beyond belief unless we are devoted to goodness, because goodness is what grasps them, since it is through goodness that the Lord flows in with wisdom.

3176   *Several days, perhaps ten; afterward, you shall go* symbolizes a stage that seemed ripe for departure to them, as can be seen from the following: A *day* symbolizes a stage or state, as discussed in §§23, 487, 488, 493, 893, 2788. *Ten* symbolizes fullness, as noted in §§1988, 3107—here, fullness or ripeness as it appears in the eyes of the earthly self. And *going* means departing. This shows that *several days, perhaps ten; afterward, you shall go* symbolizes a stage that seemed ripe for departure to them. As a result, there now follows the sentence, *he said to them, "Do not delay me,"* symbolizing what the desire for goodness wanted.

3177   *Jehovah has made my path successful* means that everything had now been provided for, as can be seen without explanation. After all, to say that Jehovah is *making someone's path successful* is to say that he is providing for it. Here, it means providing for the truth that was to unite with goodness, because a *path* symbolizes truth (§§627, 2333).

Send me and let me go to my master means in regard to the stage at which [truth] was introduced. This can be seen from the meaning that results from the inner sense of the words. The same words also imply a desire for union, because this desire is present in the stage at which [the desire for truth] has been introduced.

§3178

And they said, "Let's call the girl and ask of her own mouth," symbolizes consent sought only from the desire for truth, as can be seen from the following: A *girl* symbolizes a desire that has innocence within it, as noted in §§3067, 3110. Here it symbolizes a desire for truth, because it is Rebekah. Before she consents, she is called a girl, but when she consents (just below), she is called Rebekah, and Rebekah is the desire for truth (see §3077). And *asking of her mouth* means perceiving whether it consents. So consent sought only from the desire for truth is what the current verse symbolizes.

§3179

[2] The fact of the matter is that truth itself—the truth that is to be introduced into goodness—acknowledges the goodness that belongs with it, because goodness acknowledges the truth that belongs with it. This results in consent, but the consent is inspired within truth by goodness (see above at §3161).

None of this is ever visible in humankind—that there is any consent on the part of truth when it is being introduced and united to goodness, or in other words, when we are being reborn; or on the part of goodness, in that it recognizes its proper truth, which it introduces into and binds to itself. Nevertheless, this is exactly what happens. What comes about when we are being reborn is completely unknown to us. If we knew only one event out of a million, we would be dumbfounded. The secret means by which the Lord leads us at such a time are beyond counting and even beyond limit. Only a few of them shine out from the Word's inner meaning.

[3] The ancient church used marriage to create for itself a picture of this process. It used the image of a young woman's state before she became engaged, her state after she became engaged, her state when she was about to be given in marriage, then when she had married, and finally when she bore a child with her husband. The fruit produced by truth, from goodness—or by faith, from charity—they called children. And so on.

That is what the wisdom of the ancient church was like. They wrote their books in the same manner, and the custom of writing this way spread from them even to people outside the church. They wanted to use phenomena that exist in the world to express those that exist in heaven; in fact, they wanted to see spiritual qualities in earthly objects. Today, though, this wisdom has been lost entirely.

3180   *And they called Rebekah and said to her, "Would you go with this man?" and she said, "I will go,"* symbolizes its full consent. This can be seen from the meaning resulting from the inner sense of the words, because when she answers their question with *I will go,* it means that she agrees completely.

Truth's full consent occurs when truth perceives in itself an image of goodness, and perceives in goodness a likeness of itself, from which it springs.

3181   Genesis 24:59, 60, 61. *And they sent away Rebekah their sister and her nursemaid and Abraham's servant and his men. And they blessed Rebekah and said to her, "Our sister, may you become thousands of myriads, and may your seed inherit the gate of those who hate you!" And Rebekah rose, and her girls, and they rode on camels and came after the man. And the servant took Rebekah and went.*

They sent away Rebekah their sister means parting with the desire for truth that is divine. *And her nursemaid* means [parting] with the innocence in it. *And Abraham's servant and his men* means with divine qualities in the earthly self. *And they blessed Rebekah and said to her* symbolizes fervent wishes based on divine enlightenment. *Our sister, may you become thousands of myriads* symbolizes the way a desire for truth bears fruit to infinity. *And may your seed inherit the gate of those who hate you* symbolizes the Lord's spiritual kingdom, arising from the marriage of goodness and truth within his divine humanity—a kingdom endowed with neighborly love and faith, where before there had been evil and falsity. *And Rebekah rose* means that the desire for truth was lifted up and removed from there. *And her girls* symbolize subservient desires. *And they rode on camels* symbolizes an intellect raised up above earthly facts. *And came after the man* means under the watchful eye of divine truth on the earthly plane. *And the servant took Rebekah and went* means that divine goodness on the earthly plane would introduce [the desire for truth].

3182   *They sent away Rebekah their sister* means parting with the desire for truth that is divine. This can be seen from the symbolism of *sending* away as parting with, and from the representation of *Rebekah their sister* as a desire for truth that is divine (discussed above at §§3077, 3179). A *sister* means truth (see §§1495, 2508, 2524, 2556, 3160).

What is going on here can be seen from the discussion and illustrations above in the current chapter. However, a few more words need to be said to make it all clearer. When the truth that is to be introduced and united to goodness is raised up out of the earthly self, it then parts with everything in the earthly self. That parting is what *they sent away Rebekah their sister* symbolizes. The separation takes place when we no longer regard goodness from the viewpoint of truth but truth from the viewpoint of goodness. To put the same thing another way, the separation takes place when we no longer regard life from the viewpoint of doctrine but doctrine from the viewpoint of life. Doctrine teaches this truth, for example: that we should not hate anyone, because when we hate someone, we are killing that person every single second. In our early years, we hardly even admit this, but if we reform as we develop, we count it as a teaching to live by. Eventually we actually do live by it, and then we no longer think about it from doctrine but act on it in our life. When we do, the truth of this teaching is raised up out of our earthly self and even detached from it and is grafted onto the goodness in our rational mind. At that point we no longer allow our earthly self to call it into doubt by any private sophistry. In fact, we do not even allow our earthly self to argue against it.

And her nursemaid means [parting] with the innocence in it—that is, **3183** the innocence that they also sent away or parted with. This can be seen from the symbolism of a *nursemaid* or wet-nurse as innocence.

The Word sometimes mentions nursing babies and the women who nurse them, and both symbolize a baby's first state, which obviously is one of innocence. The instant we are born, we come into a state of innocence, which is to serve as a basis for all our later states and is to lie deep within them. In the Word, this state is symbolized by a nursing baby. Next we come into a state in which we feel drawn to heavenly goodness, or in other words, a state of love for our parents, which in little children takes the place of love for the Lord. This state is symbolized by a little child. Later we come into a state in which we feel drawn to spiritual goodness, or a state of mutual love, which is charity for our peers, a state symbolized by youths. When we grow even older, we come into a state of desire for truth. This state is symbolized by young adults, and following states, by full adults, and finally by the elderly. This last state, symbolized by the elderly, is one of wisdom, and it has our childhood innocence within it. So the first and last states merge, and when we are old, we enter the Lord's kingdom as a child again, but a wise one.

[2] From this it can be seen that innocence is the first state—the state of a nursing baby. Accordingly, the woman herself who is nursing the baby, or the wet nurse, also symbolizes innocence, because the state of the one giving and the one receiving (like that of one acting and one being acted upon) is seen as similar.

The point of mentioning here that they also sent away Rebekah's nursemaid, or wet nurse, is to show what the desire for truth was like, that it came from innocence. Unless it has innocence in it, a desire for truth is not a desire for truth (§§2526, 2780, 3111). It is through innocence that the Lord flows into that desire, bringing wisdom with him, because true innocence is wisdom itself (see §§2305, 2306). People who have this wisdom appear to angels' eyes as small children (154, 2306).

[3] Other passages as well show that in the Word a nursing baby symbolizes innocence. In David, for example:

Out of the mouth of *toddlers* and *nursing babies* you have founded your strength. (Psalms 8:2; Matthew 21:16)

The toddlers stand for heavenly love; the nursing babies, for innocence. In Jeremiah:

Why are you doing great evil against your own souls, in cutting off from yourselves man and woman, *toddler* and *nursing baby,* in the middle of Judah, to prevent me from leaving you a remnant? (Jeremiah 44:7)

The toddler and nursing baby here too stand for heavenly love and its innocence. When these die out, there is no longer any remnant. That is, no goodness or truth remains hidden away by the Lord in the inner self. (To see that this is what a remnant is, consult §§1906, 2284.) Everything good and true is destroyed when innocence perishes, because innocence comes directly from divinity itself, so it is the vital essence itself of goodness and truth. [4] In the same author:

The *toddler* and *nursing baby* faints in the city's streets. (Lamentations 2:11)

Likewise. In the same author:

Whales offer the breast; *they nurse their offspring.* The daughter of my people is cruel; the tongue of the *nursing baby* has stuck to the roof of its mouth for thirst. *Toddlers* have sought bread; no one is holding any out to them. (Lamentations 4:3, 4)

Again the nursing baby stands for innocence; the toddlers, for the desire for goodness. In Moses:

> Outside, the sword—and from the inner rooms, terror—will bereave both the young man and the young woman, and the *nursing baby* along with the old man. (Deuteronomy 32:25)

"The sword will bereave the young man, the young woman, and the nursing baby along with the old man" stands for the idea that falsity will destroy the desire for truth, the desire for goodness, and innocence along with wisdom. In Isaiah:

> They will bring your sons in their embrace, and your daughters will be carried here on their shoulder, and kings will be *your nourishers,* and their ladies, *your wet nurses.* (Isaiah 49:22, 23)

Kings who are nourishers stand for understanding; ladies who are wet nurses, for wisdom, which is a matter of innocence, as noted above.

And Abraham's servant and his men means [parting] with divine qualities in the earthly self. This can be seen from the symbolism of *Abraham's servant* as the earthly self (discussed in §§3019, 3020) and from that of *his men* as everything in it (discussed in §3169). The fact that there are divine qualities in the earthly self is evident, because the servant had been sent by Abraham, who represents the Lord's divinity, as shown many times before. **3184**

And they blessed Rebekah and said to her symbolizes fervent wishes based on divine enlightenment. This can be seen from the symbolism of *blessing,* in the course of a farewell to someone departing, as wishing that person all the best. The fact that those wishes come from divine enlightenment here is evident from what follows right afterward. Besides, light streams into the earthly self by way of the desire for truth (Rebekah) when it is introduced into goodness (Isaac). **3185**

Our sister, may you become thousands of myriads symbolizes the way a desire for truth bears fruit to infinity. This can be seen from the symbolism of the *sister,* Rebekah, as a desire for truth (discussed in §§3077, 3179, 3182) and from that of *may you become thousands of myriads* as bearing fruit to infinity. *Thousands of myriads* here means infinity, because the subject is the Lord, in whom absolutely everything is infinite. **3186**

In people, this is how the matter stands: Goodness does not bear fruit in us, nor does truth multiply, until truth and goodness unite in our rational mind, or in other words, until we have been reborn. At that point our fruit—the offspring we bear—springs from a lawful or heavenly marriage, which is the marriage of goodness and truth. Before then, it does look as though the good we do is good and as though the truth is true, but they are not genuine, because they lack a real soul, which is goodness filled with innocence from the Lord. As a result they do not touch our heart or make us happy. The Lord gives them a soul—a feeling of love and charity, along with happiness—when we regenerate.

[2] A large and also an infinite amount is symbolized by a *thousand* (see §2575) and even more so by a *myriad* or ten thousand and still more so by *thousands of myriads,* and this is true in other passages as well. In Moses:

> When the ark came to rest, he said, "Return, Jehovah, to the *myriads of thousands* of Israel." (Numbers 10:36)

The myriads of thousands also symbolize infinity, because they describe the Lord, who is meant by Jehovah in this verse. In the same author:

> Jehovah dawned from Seir on them; he shone out from Mount Paran and came with the holy *myriads.* (Deuteronomy 33:2)

The myriads again stand for infinity. In David:

> God's chariots: *myriads of thousands* of the peaceful. (Psalms 68:17)

God's chariots stand for the contents of the Word and of a theology drawn from it. Myriads of thousands stand for the infinite amount to be found there. In John:

> I saw and heard the voice of many angels around the throne; their number was *myriads of myriads* and thousands of thousands. (Revelation 5:11)

The myriads stand for things beyond number.

3187   *And may your seed inherit the gate of those who hate you* symbolizes the Lord's spiritual kingdom, arising from the marriage of goodness and truth within his divine humanity—a kingdom endowed with neighborly love and faith, where before there had been evil and falsity. This can be seen from the discussion and explanation above at §2851, where nearly the same words occur.

Seed means the people who are described as spiritual, so in a comprehensive sense it means everyone who makes up the Lord's spiritual kingdom or, what is the same, that kingdom itself. This is established by the symbolism of *seed* as neighborly love and faith (dealt with in §§1025, 1447, 1610, 1940) and consequently as people who have neighborly love that they have acquired through faith. Such people are spiritual (see §§2088, 2184, 2507, 2708, 2715, 2954). They receive their love for others and their faith from the marriage of goodness and truth in the Lord's divine humanity, so salvation also comes to them from that marriage (2661, 2716, 2833, 2834).

[2] In the ancient church, when a betrothed woman was about to marry, it was customary to offer her these good wishes—"May you become thousands of myriads, and may your seed inherit the gate of your foes" or "of those who hate you." The wiser people in that church, though, took these words in a spiritual sense. They understood by it that when they had entered the marriage of goodness and truth—had regenerated—goodness and truth would grow into thousands of myriads, or become fruitful beyond measure, and neighborly love and faith would replace the previous evil and falsity.

When the ancient church's wisdom had breathed its last, however, people no longer understood the words in a spiritual sense but simply in a worldly one. They took it to be a wish that the woman have countless descendants and that the descendants seize and inherit the land of the surrounding nations. Jacob's descendants more than any others took the words this way. What hardened them in their view was the fact not only that they did grow without limit but also that they did inherit the land that was the gate of their enemies. Little did they know that it was all representative, portraying the Lord's heavenly and spiritual kingdom and the substitution of goodness and truth for evil and falsity when these had been banished from it. This will become transparently clear when those representations are laid open, the Lord in his divine mercy willing.

[3] The same thing happens on the small scale, or in other words, within each individual who becomes a kingdom of the Lord. Until we *are* a kingdom of the Lord—until we regenerate—we have nothing but evil and falsity inside us. In fact, hellish and devilish spirits occupy that which is called a gate in us, as described in §2851. When we do become such a kingdom—that is, when we are reborn—evil and falsity (or the hellish and devilish spirits, to put the same thing another way) are banished from there, and goodness and truth come in and inherit the space. A conscience for what is good and true is then present.

Just as this occurs on the small scale, it occurs on the large scale as well. This now shows clearly what these words mean in a deeper sense.

3188   *And Rebekah rose* means that the desire for truth was lifted up and removed from there. That is to say, it was lifted up to the rational plane and removed from the earthly. This can be seen from the following: The symbolism of *rising* involves elevation, as noted in §§2401, 2785, 2912, 2927, 3171, and because it involves elevation, it also involves removal. And *Rebekah* represents the desire for truth, as discussed in §§3077, 3179. Plainly, then, *Rebekah rose* means that the desire for truth was lifted up and removed from the earthly plane. For a discussion of this, see §3182.

3189   *And her girls* symbolize subservient desires. This can be seen from the symbolism of a *girl*, when it refers to Rebekah, as a desire that has innocence within it (dealt with at §§3067, 3110). When "girls" refers to the women who followed Rebekah to serve her, they symbolize subservient desires.

Every desire looks as though it is one uncomplicated thing, but it actually holds an untold number of different elements (see §3078). All its contents are desires, and they are linked together into a form that defies comprehension. They are also subordinated to each other, because there are those that act as aides and those that act as household servants. Heavenly communities—in fact, the whole of heaven—display the same pattern, having been organized by the Lord according to the divine pattern inside him. The pattern governing the Lord's spiritual kingdom emerges in accord with the hierarchy of desires in his divine humanity, and this hierarchy is the theme in the inner meaning of the current and following chapters. Very little of it can be explained intelligibly, though. It is better suited to the perception of angels.

3190   *And they rode on camels* symbolizes an intellect raised up above earthly facts. This can be seen from the symbolism of *riding* as having one's intellect raised up (discussed in §§2761, 2762) and from that of *camels* as general facts in the earthly self (discussed in §§3048, 3071) and therefore as earthly facts.

Here is the situation: When truth is lifted up from the earthly level to the rational level, it is taken out of the realm of worldly light into the realm of heavenly light. So it moves from the shadow of night, so to speak, into the clear light of day. What we see by the light of the world, which illuminates everything earthly, is in relative night; but what we see by the light of heaven, which illuminates what is spiritual, is in relative day. So when truth from the earthly plane rises up toward the rational plane, we ourselves rise up into understanding and into wisdom. In fact, that is where all the understanding and wisdom in a person comes from.

That is what it means to say that the intellect is raised up above earthly facts.

And came after the man means under the watchful eye of divine truth on the earthly plane, as can be seen from this: In an inner sense, here, *going after* or following means happening by the guidance or in other words, under the watchful eye of. And a *man* symbolizes truth (discussed in §3134)—here, divine truth on the earthly plane (as above in §3184).

3191

And the servant took Rebekah and went means that divine goodness on the earthly plane would introduce [the desire for truth], as can be seen from this: A *servant* symbolizes divine goodness on the earthly plane, as above in §3184. And *taking Rebekah and going* means introducing her—specifically, to Isaac, or in other words, to divine goodness in the rational mind—as can be seen without further explanation.

3192

This is how matters stand: Truth could not be raised up from the Lord's earthly level to meet the goodness in his rational mind except by means of divine truth and divine goodness, both of them existing on the earthly plane. Divine truth on the earthly plane, which is called a man, has to show and lead the way. Divine goodness on the earthly plane, which is called a *servant,* has to bring it in and introduce it. These are the two wings, so to speak, on which it rises.

But these ideas cannot be explained any more intelligibly. First you need to know what divine truth on the earthly plane and what divine goodness on the earthly plane are. The inner meaning will deal with the subject later, when the story centers on Joseph.

Genesis 24:62, 63. *And Isaac came from going to Beer-lahai-roi, and he was residing in the southland. And Isaac went out to meditate in the field toward evening, and he raised his eyes and looked, and here, now, camels coming!*

3193

Isaac came from going to Beer-lahai-roi symbolizes divine goodness on the rational plane, born of divine truth itself. *And he was residing in the southland* means therefore in divine light. *And Isaac went out to meditate in the field* symbolizes the rational mind in a state of goodness. *Toward evening* means in relation to what is below it. *And he raised his eyes and looked* symbolizes focus. *And here, now, camels coming!* means toward general facts in the earthly self.

Isaac came from going to Beer-lahai-roi symbolizes divine goodness on the rational plane, born of divine truth itself, as can be seen from the following: *Isaac* represents the Lord's divine rationality, as noted at §§2083, 2630. Here he represents divine rationality in regard to the divine goodness in it, because truth that was divine (called up out of his earthly self and represented by Rebekah) had not yet formed a bond with it. The verses that immediately follow deal with that union. And *to come from*

3194

going to Beer-lahai-roi symbolizes what was born of divine truth. In the original tongue, *Beer-lahai-roi* means "the spring of the living one who sees me," as above in Genesis 16:13, 14, where we read, "Hagar called the name of Jehovah, the one speaking to her, 'You are a God who sees me,' because she said, 'Even in this place, did I see behind the one seeing me?' Therefore they called the spring Beer-lahai-roi ('the spring of the living one who sees me')." For the symbolism of this, see §§1952–1958. Those sections also make it clear that a spring is divine truth, and that "the living one who sees me" is divine goodness on the rational plane (there called the Lord's intermediate self) stemming from divine truth.

Here is how matters stand with this very deep secret: Divinity itself possesses goodness and truth. The Lord's divine humanity issued from divine goodness and was born from divine truth. To put it another way, his very being was divine goodness, and his emergence itself was divine truth. This was the source of the divine goodness on his rational plane, to which he united the divine truth that came out of his humanity.

3195 *And he was residing in the southland* means therefore in divine light. This can be seen from the symbolism of *residing* as living (discussed in §1293), which has to do with goodness (2268, 2451, 2712), and from that of the *southland* as divine light. The *south* symbolizes light—specifically, the light of understanding, which is wisdom (1458). The *land* of the south, for its part, means a place and state in which that light shines. In the current verse, then, "Isaac came from going to Beer-lahai-roi, and he was residing in the southland" means that because divine goodness on the rational plane was born of divine truth, it was in divine light.

[2] Light is mentioned over and over in the Word, and on an inner level it symbolizes the truth that comes of goodness. On the highest inner level it symbolizes the Lord himself, because he is goodness and truth itself.

Light does actually exist in heaven, but it is infinitely brighter than the light on earth; see §§1053, 1117, 1521–1533, 1619–1632. This light reveals spirits and angels to each other and discloses all the glory that exists in heaven. The glow of this light may indeed look like the light of the world but is not like it, because it is not earthly but spiritual. It contains wisdom, so that what streams down before the eyes of the inhabitants this way is pure wisdom. So the wiser the angels are, the more brilliant the light they enjoy (§2776). This light also illuminates the human intellect, especially in a person who has been reborn, but we do not notice it as long as we are living in our bodies, because of the worldly light that then dominates.

In the other world, evil spirits also see each other, and they see the many representative objects that emerge in the world of spirits, too. Although they see these things by heaven's light, it is a glimmer like that of a coal fire. That is what heaven's light turns into when it comes near them.

[3] As for the original source of this light, from eternity it has been the Lord alone, because the Lord *is* the divine goodness and divine truth itself from which the light comes. His divine humanity, which has existed from eternity (John 17:5), was that very light. Because this light was no longer able to affect the human race, which had moved so far away from goodness and truth and therefore from the light, and had thrown itself into the dark, the Lord wished to clothe himself in actual humanity by being born. In this way, he could shed light not only on our rational dimension but also on our earthly dimension. He made both the rational level and the earthly level in himself divine so that he could be the light also for people who sat in such thick shadow.

[4] Many passages in the Word can show that the Lord is the light, or in other words, is goodness and truth itself, so that all understanding and wisdom and consequently all salvation comes from him. In John, for instance:

> In the beginning there was the *Word,* and the Word was with God, and the Word was God. In him was life, and *the life was the light of human-kind.* John came to testify concerning the *light;* he was not that *light* but [came] to testify concerning the *light.* It was the *true light* that *shines* on every person coming into the world. (John 1:1, 4, 7, 8, 9)

The Word was divine truth, and therefore was the Lord himself in his divine humanity, of whom the text says that the Word was with God and the Word was God. [5] In the same author:

> This is the judgment: that the *light* came into the world but people loved the dark more than the *light.* (John 3:19)

The light stands for divine truth. In the same author:

> Jesus said, "*I am the light of the world;* whoever follows me will not walk in the dark but have the *light of life.*" (John 8:12)

In the same author:

> For a short time yet, the *light* is with you; walk, as long as you have *light,* to prevent the dark from overtaking you. As long as you have the *light, believe in the light,* in order to be *children of light.* (John 12:35, 36)

In the same author:

> Whoever sees me sees him who sent me; *I have come into the world as the light,* so that no one who believes in me should stay in the dark. (John 12:45, 46)

In Luke:

> My eyes have seen your means of salvation, which you have prepared before the face of all peoples: a *light for revelation to the nations* and the glory of your people Israel. (Luke 2:30, 31, 32)

This is Simeon's oracular phrase concerning the Lord when he was born. [6] In Matthew:

> The people sitting in darkness have seen a great light; and on those sitting in the vicinity and gloom of death, *light has risen.* (Matthew 4:16; Isaiah 9:2)

These passages make it obvious that the Lord is called the light in regard to the divine goodness and truth in his divine humanity. This is so in Old Testament prophecies as well. In Isaiah, for example:

> The *light of Israel* will become a fire, and its Holy One, a flame. (Isaiah 10:17)

In the same author:

> I, Jehovah, have called you in righteousness, and I will give you as a pact with the people and as a *light for the nations.* (Isaiah 42:6)

In the same author:

> I have given you as a *light of the nations,* so that you may be my salvation all the way to the end of the earth. (Isaiah 49:6)

In the same author:

> Rise, shine, because *your light* has come, and the glory of Jehovah has dawned above you! The nations will walk toward *your light,* and monarchs, toward the *radiance* of your dawn. (Isaiah 60:1, 3)

[7] John says that all of heaven's light and therefore its wisdom and understanding come from the Lord:

> The holy city New Jerusalem coming down from God out of heaven, prepared as a *bride* adorned for her husband, has no need for the sun or

the moon to *shine* in it; God's glory will *light* it, and *its lamp will be the Lamb.* (Revelation 21:2, 23)

Further on the same city:

Night will not exist there, and they will have no need for a lamp or sunlight, because *the Lord God gives them light.* (Revelation 22:5)

[8] In Isaiah, too:

The sun will no longer be for light by day for you, and not as radiance for you will the moon shine, but *Jehovah will become an eternal light to you,* and your God will become your ornament. No longer will your sun set, and your moon will not withdraw, because *Jehovah will become an eternal light to you.* (Isaiah 60:19, 20)

"There will no longer be a sun for light by day, and not as radiance will the moon shine" means that we will not see what earthly light clarifies but what spiritual light clarifies, the latter being symbolized by "Jehovah will become an eternal light." Jehovah, mentioned here and elsewhere in the Old Testament, is the Lord; see §§1343, 1736, 2156, 2329, 2921, 3023, 3035.

[9] To three of his disciples—Peter, James, and John—he revealed that he is the light of heaven. That is, when he was transfigured, *his face shone like the sun,* while his clothes became like the *light* (Matthew 17:2). A face like the sun was his divine goodness; clothes like the light were his divine truth.

This shows what [Moses'] blessing means when it says, "*Jehovah make his face shine on you* and have mercy on you" (Numbers 6:25). Jehovah's face is mercy, peace, and goodness; see §§222, 223. The sun is divine love, so the Lord's divine love is what appears as the sun in heaven (30–38, 1053, 1521, 1529, 1530, 1531, 2441, 2495).

And Isaac went out to meditate in the field symbolizes the rational mind in a state of goodness. This can be seen from the representation of *Isaac* as divine rationality (discussed many times before) and from the symbolism of *meditating in the field* as that mind in a state of goodness. *Meditation* is the state of the rational mind when it focuses, while a *field* is doctrine and all points of doctrine (§368) and therefore those that deal with goodness in the church (2971). That is why the ancients used the idiom *meditating in a field* for thoughts about something good—the kind of thoughts an unmarried man engages in when he is thinking about a wife.

3196

3197　　　*Toward evening* means in relation to what is below it. This can be seen from the symbolism of *evening* as something dim (dealt with in §3056). Since whatever is down below in us (the contents of our earthly mind) is dim compared to whatever lies above (the contents of our rational mind), *evening* symbolizes what is relatively dim. This can be seen from the series of ideas in the inner meaning. The subject is truth from the earthly self that is to unite with goodness in the rational mind. Since the theme here is union and the light this union sheds in the earthly mind, *meditating in the field toward evening* symbolizes the rational mind in a state of goodness, relative to what lies below it. A state of goodness is depicted by Isaac's residence in the southland—that is, in divine light. Compared to this, what lay below the rational mind was in a kind of evening, until the union of truth and goodness took place and the earthly plane was likewise made divine.

3198　　　*And he raised his eyes and looked* symbolizes focus. This can be seen from the symbolism of *raising one's eyes* as thinking (discussed in §§2789, 2829). Here it means focusing, since the verse says, "He raised his eyes and looked," and the words apply to goodness on the rational plane with which truth from the earthly plane had not yet united.

3199　　　*And here, now, camels coming!* means toward general facts in the earthly self. This can be seen from the symbolism of *camels* as general facts in the earthly self (discussed in §§3048, 3071). This is where the focus was directed because that is where truth was expected to come from, as numerous earlier remarks and illustrations in the current chapter have shown.

3200　　　These two verses depict the condition of goodness on the rational plane when it is waiting for the truth that is to unite with it as a bride with her husband. The next two depict the condition of truth when it comes close and perceives the goodness with which it is to unite.

It is important to know, however, that these stages did not arrive just once but constantly throughout the Lord's life in the world, up until he was glorified. The same is true in people who are regenerating, because they are not reborn all at once but constantly throughout their life and even in the other life. After all, we can never become perfect.

3201　　　Genesis 24:64, 65. *And Rebekah raised her eyes and saw Isaac and slipped off the camel. And she said to the servant, "Who is that man there, walking in the field to meet us?" And the servant said, "That is my master." And she took a veil and covered herself.*

Rebekah raised her eyes and saw Isaac symbolizes the reciprocal focus of the desire for truth. *And slipped off the camel* means that it detached from facts in the earthly self, as was perceived by goodness on the rational plane. *And she said to the servant* symbolizes examination from divine qualities on the earthly plane. *Who is that man there, walking in the field to meet us?* means concerning a rational mind concentrating only on goodness. *And the servant said, "That is my master,"* symbolizes acknowledgment. *And she took a veil and covered herself* symbolizes seeming truth.

Rebekah raised her eyes and saw Isaac symbolizes the reciprocal focus of the desire for truth, as can be seen from the following: *Raising one's eyes and seeing* symbolizes focus, as noted above in §3198. Here it symbolizes reciprocal focus because earlier the text said of Isaac that he raised his eyes and looked, and here it says of Rebekah that she raised her eyes and saw Isaac. And *Rebekah* represents the desire for truth, as noted many times before. **3202**

And slipped off the camel means that it detached from facts in the earthly self, as was perceived by goodness on the rational plane. This can be seen from the symbolism of *slipping off* as detaching and from that of *camels* as facts known to the earthly self (discussed in §§3048, 3071). The fact that this was perceived by goodness on the rational plane, which Isaac represents, is self-evident. **3203**

[2] The discussion and demonstrations above at §§3161, 3175, 3182, 3188, 3190 show what detaching from the earthly self means. To be specific, the desire for truth detaches from the earthly self when [truth] ceases to be a matter of knowledge and becomes a matter of life. When we make it a matter of life, habit causes it to permeate our being in the same way our disposition or our character does. When [truth] clothes us in this way, it spontaneously flows into activity before we even think about it from some fact or other known to us. Indeed, when it becomes a part of our life, it can take control of facts and bring forward countless numbers of them in support of itself. This happens with every true idea; when we are young, it is something we know about, but as we progress, it becomes part of our life.

The situation is like that of little children when they are learning to walk, learning to talk, learning to think, and learning to see with their mind's eye and draw intelligent conclusions. When habit makes these activities a simple matter of will, and therefore spontaneous, they vanish from the child's pool of factual knowledge, because they flow freely. [3] When people are being regenerated by the Lord, or reborn, the same thing happens in regard to their knowledge of spiritual goodness and truth. In the beginning these people are just like babies. Spiritual truth is a matter of fact to them at first, because that is all a doctrine can be when they are learning it and filing it in their memory. Gradually, though, the

Lord calls it up out of their memory and grafts it onto their life, or in other words, onto the good they do, because the good we do is our life. Once this happens, a switch occurs; they start to act on goodness—that is, on life—and no longer on knowledge, as they used to. In this respect, then, people who are being born again resemble little children. It is matters of spiritual life that they are being trained in, though, the goal being for them to act not on doctrine (or truth) but on love for others (or goodness). Once they do, they find themselves in a state of bliss and in possession of wisdom for the first time.

[4] This shows what it is to detach from facts known to the earthly self, as symbolized by Rebekah's slipping off the camel, even before she knew it was Isaac. Anyone can see that such details contain secrets within them.

3204   *And she said to the servant* symbolizes examination from divine qualities on the earthly plane, as established by the following. *Saying* means examining here, because she asked, "Who is that man there, walking in the field?" And a *servant* symbolizes divine qualities on the earthly plane, as noted above at §§3191, 3192.

3205   *Who is that man, walking in the field to meet us?* means concerning a rational mind concentrating only on goodness—that is to say, examination concerning it. This is established by remarks above concerning Isaac's going out to meditate in the field, which symbolized the rational mind in a state of goodness (see §3196). Here, *that man* symbolizes the rational mind, while *walking* (that is, meditating) *in the field* means concentrating on goodness. *To meet us* means with a view to union.

3206   *And the servant said, "That is my master,"* symbolizes acknowledgment—acknowledgment by divine qualities on the earthly level, which are the *servant*. This can be seen without explanation. See §3192 for the idea that divine qualities on the earthly level perform the introduction, and §3179 for the idea that goodness acknowledges the truth that belongs to it, while truth acknowledges the goodness that belongs to *it*.

3207   *And she took a veil and covered herself* symbolizes seeming truth. This can be seen from the symbolism of the *veil* with which a bride covered her face when she first saw her bridegroom; it symbolizes seeming truth. Among the ancients, brides represented the desire for truth, and bridegrooms, the desire for goodness. That is, they represented the church, which was called a bride because of its desire for truth. A desire for goodness, received from the Lord, was a bridegroom, so the Word calls the Lord himself a bridegroom in various places.

A bride veiled her face on first approaching the groom in order to represent seeming truth. Seeming truth is not actually true but only seems that way, as discussed below. A desire for truth cannot draw close to a desire for goodness except by means of apparent truth, and it does not shed those appearances until the two unite. At that point, truth comes to belong to goodness and to be really true—so far as the goodness is really good. [2] Real goodness is holy because it is a divine quality emanating from the Lord, and it enters us by a higher path or doorway. Truth, however, is not holy in origin, because it enters by a lower path or doorway and is first assimilated into the earthly self. When it rises up from there toward the rational plane, though, it gradually becomes purer. On first catching sight of the desire for goodness, it detaches from facts and puts on an appearance of truth, which it wears as it approaches goodness. The latter is a sign that it has this kind of origin and that it would not be able to stand its first sight of goodness that is divine, until it has entered the groom's bedroom, so to speak—the sanctuary of goodness—and the union has taken place. By then truth no longer looks at goodness from the standpoint of appearances, or through a veil of appearances, but is seen by goodness without illusion.

[3] Still, it needs to be known that in us (and even in angels) truth is never, ever pure, or in other words, free of illusion. Absolutely all of it is seeming truth. Yet the Lord still accepts it as true if there is good in it. Only in the Lord is truth pure, because in him it is divine. Just as the Lord is goodness itself, he is truth itself. See previous discussions about truth and its appearances: Veils, including those of the tabernacle, symbolized the face of truth, or the way it appears: 2576. In human beings, truth consists of appearances steeped in illusion: 2053. Our rational thinking consists of seeming truth: 2516. Truth is wrapped in appearances: 2196, 2203, 2209, 2242. Goodness that is divine has an effect on apparent [truth] and even on illusions: 2554. The Lord adapts seeming truth for use as if it were really true: 1832. The Word speaks according to appearances: 1838.

[4] What appearances are is plain to see from those passages in the Word that speak according to them. There are different grades of seeming truth, however. Most seeming truth on the earthly level is illusion—although in people who are devoted to goodness it has to be called an appearance (and even to some degree truth) rather than illusion. The goodness in them, which contains something divine, changes the essential nature of it. Seeming truth on the rational level reaches deeper and

deeper, though. This is the appearance seen by the heavens, or rather by the angels in the heavens (see §2576 concerning them).

[5] Let the following serve by way of illustration, to give some idea what apparent truth is:

1. People believe that religious truth reforms and regenerates them, but this is an appearance. It is religious goodness—charity for their neighbor and love for the Lord—that reforms and regenerates them.
2. People believe that truth, because it teaches us, enables us to perceive goodness, but this is an appearance. Goodness is what enables truth to perceive anything, because goodness is the soul or life of truth.
3. People believe that truth is introducing them into goodness when they live by the truth they have learned, but it is goodness that acts on truth and introduces truth to itself.
4. It appears to us as though truth perfects goodness, when the reality is that goodness perfects truth.
5. The good we do in our lives appears to us to be the fruit of faith, but it is the fruit of neighborly love.

These few examples to some extent show what apparent truth is. There are countless others like them.

3208   Genesis 24:66, 67. *And the servant told Isaac all the words that he had done. And Isaac brought her into the tent of Sarah his mother. And he took Rebekah, and she became a woman to him, and he loved her. And Isaac was comforted after his mother.*

The servant told Isaac all the words that he had done symbolizes a perception received from earthly divinity showing how matters stood. *And Isaac brought her into the tent of Sarah his mother* symbolizes truth's sanctuary in the Lord's divine humanity. *And he took Rebekah, and she became a woman to him, and he loved her* symbolizes union. *And Isaac was comforted after his mother* symbolizes a new stage.

3209   *The servant told Isaac all the words that he had done* symbolizes a perception received from earthly divinity showing how matters stood, as is established by the following: *Telling* symbolizes perceiving. Perception is like an internal storytelling, so scriptural narratives express perceiving in terms of telling and also saying (§§1791, 1815, 1819, 1822, 1898, 1919, 2080, 2619, 2862). The *servant* symbolizes divinity on the earthly plane, as discussed below. And *words* mean matters or affairs, as noted in §1785. These explanations show that *the servant told all the words that he had done* means that divine goodness on the rational plane perceived from earthly divinity how it was that matters stood.

[2] This is how matters stand: Rationality lies on a higher level than the earthly dimension, and the goodness in the Lord's rational mind was divine. However, the truth that was to be lifted up from the earthly plane was not divine until after it united with the divine goodness of his rational mind. If the goodness in his rational mind was to exert an influence on what was earthly, then, there needed to be a go-between, and the go-between could only be something earthly that had a divine aspect. This go-between is represented by "the elder servant of Abraham's household, the one managing everything that was his" (§§3019, 3020), who symbolizes earthly divinity (3191, 3192, 3204, 3206).

And Isaac brought her into the tent of Sarah his mother symbolizes **3210**
truth's sanctuary in the Lord's divine humanity, as can be seen from the following: A *tent* symbolizes something holy (as discussed in §§414, 1102, 2145, 2152, 2576) and therefore a sanctuary. And *Sarah his mother* symbolizes divine truth (as discussed in §§1468, 1901, 2063, 2065, 2904), from which the Lord's divine humanity was born, the rational dimension of this humanity being represented by her son Isaac. This shows that *Isaac brought her into the tent of his mother* means that goodness in his rational mind brought the truth represented by Rebekah into the sanctuary truth had within that goodness.

[2] What truth's sanctuary is can be seen from the remarks above at §3194 about the Lord's divine humanity: Divinity itself possesses goodness and truth. The Lord's divine humanity issued from divine goodness, while the divinity itself of it was born from divine truth. To put it another way, his very being was divine goodness, and his very emergence, divine truth. This was the source of divine goodness on his rational plane, to which he united the divine truth that came out of his humanity. Nothing more can be said about this very deep secret than this: The most genuinely divine goodness and truth in the Lord's divine humanity, to which the truth called up from his human side was united, is what was symbolized by the sanctuary—the Holiest Place—in the tabernacle and the Temple. Its nature was represented by the furnishings there—the golden altar, the table of showbread, the lampstand; still farther within, the appeasement cover and ark; and deepest within, the testimony, which was the law issued from Sinai. This was the real Holiest Place, or the real sanctuary of truth.

And he took Rebekah, and she became a woman to him, and he loved **3211**
her symbolizes union—the union of goodness and truth—as can be seen without explanation.

The reason I say that Rebekah became a woman to him rather than a wife is that there is no marriage between goodness on the rational plane and truth that has been called up out of the earthly plane and made divine. Instead they have a pact that resembles a marriage pact. The true divine marriage, which exists in the Lord, is the union of his divine nature with his human and of his human nature with his divine; see §2803. That is why Rebekah is called Isaac's woman rather than his wife.

3212 *And Isaac was comforted after his mother* symbolizes a new stage. This can be seen from the symbolism of *taking comfort* as a new stage. After all, a stage of comfort is a new one. The fact that it follows a previous stage is what *after his mother* symbolizes.

The new stage is a stage in which the truth on the Lord's rational plane is now glorified just as the goodness there already has been. His rational plane was glorified when it became divine in both respects.

[2] No one immersed in worldly and bodily kinds of love can possibly understand (or therefore believe) that the Lord's humanity became new, or glorified, or divine. People like this have no idea at all what spirituality and heavenliness are and do not even want to know. People who are not immersed in worldly and bodily kinds of love *can* perceive it, though, because they believe that the Lord is one with the Father and that everything holy emanates from him. So they believe that even his humanity is divine. Those who believe this also perceive it in their own way.

[3] The state of the Lord's glorification can be grasped to some extent from the state of human regeneration, since our rebirth is an image of the Lord's glorification (§§3043, 3138). When we are regenerating, we are becoming entirely different, entirely new, so when we have become regenerate, we are described as born anew and created anew. Although our face and speech remain the same, we no longer have the same kind of mind. When we have been reborn, our mind opens up toward heaven, and in it resides love for the Lord and charity for our neighbor, along with faith. Our mind is what makes us a new and different person. The change in our state cannot be detected in our body but in our spirit. The body is only a covering for the spirit. When we shed it, our spirit becomes visible, and visible in a completely different form after our rebirth. The form it then displays is one of love and charity, which is inexpressibly beautiful (§553) and replaces the previous form, which was one of hatred and cruelty, whose hideousness is equally inexpressible. This shows what a person who has been regenerated, or reborn, or created anew is: completely new and different. [4] This image gives some idea of the Lord's glorification.

He was not reborn as we are but became divine, and he became divine on the strength of divine love itself, because he *became* divine love itself. Peter, James, and John had the privilege of seeing what his form was then like, when they saw him not with their physical but with their spiritual eyes, and what they saw was that his face shone like the sun (Matthew 17:2). This was his divine humanity, as is indicated by the voice that came from the cloud on that occasion, saying, "This is my beloved son" (Matthew 17:5). On the point that the Son is the Lord's divine humanity, see §2628.

Representation and Correspondence (Continued)

I N the world of spirits, representative objects emerge in countless num- 3213 bers, almost constantly. They are the forms of spiritual and heavenly attributes and are not unlike forms found in the world.

Their origin I was allowed to learn from daily interaction with spirits and angels. They come out of heaven, from the thoughts and words of the angels there. When angels' thoughts (and the words they express them in) filter down to spirits, they present themselves in various representative forms. From them upright spirits can learn what the angels are talking to each other about. Within the representations is an angelic message whose content and also whose quality they are able to perceive because it touches their hearts.

This is the only way angelic thoughts and words can be presented to spirits, because angelic thinking contains vastly more than a spirit's thinking. If the content were not put into representative form and so presented—in visual images, that is—a spirit would understand hardly any of it. Most of it is indescribable, but when it is represented by visible shapes, it becomes comprehensible to spirits in its general outline. Amazingly, even the smallest detail of the picture that is presented embodies some spiritual and heavenly quality present in the thinking of the angelic community from which the representation descends.

Scenes representing what is spiritual and heavenly sometimes occur 3214 in a long series, lasting an hour or two, one after another, in an order that is astounding. There are certain communities in which this happens, and I was allowed to stay in them for many months. The representations are such that if I were to narrate and describe the chain of events in just one of them, it would fill many pages. The scenes are intensely pleasing, because something new and unexpected always comes next, and this keeps happening until the phenomenon being represented has been brought to perfect completion. When everything is complete, the viewer is able to take it all in at a single glance and at the same time to sense what the individual pieces of it symbolize.

This is another way good spirits are introduced into spiritual and heavenly thinking.

3215 The representative objects that present themselves to spirits come in unbelievable variety, but most of them resemble objects that exist on the earth in its three kingdoms. To learn what these representative objects are like, see previous accounts of them in §§1521, 1532, 1619–1622, 1623, 1624, 1625, 1807, 1808, 1971, 1974, 1977, 1980, 1981, 2299, 2601, 2758.

3216 To learn even more about the way matters stand with representations in the other world, and specifically with those that appear in the world of spirits, let me offer several examples here as well.

When angels are discussing teachings concerning charity and faith, an image sometimes appears in a lower realm, where there is a corresponding community of spirits. It is an image of a city, or of several cities, containing palaces of such stupendous architecture that you might describe them as the seat or the source of architecture itself; not to mention houses in various styles. Incredibly, not the smallest point or the tiniest visual detail exists in the whole or in any part that does not represent some factor in the thinking and conversation of the angels.

This shows that the elements involved are far beyond counting. To learn the symbolism of the cities that the prophets in the Word saw, such as the holy city New Jerusalem, and the cities in the prophetic part of the Word (namely, teachings concerning charity and faith), see §§402, 2449.

3217 When angels talk about the intellect, then in the world of spirits under them, or in the communities that correspond to them, horses appear. The size, shape, color, and pose of the horses matches the thoughts the angels are entertaining about the intellect; and the harnesses are decorated in various ways.

There is also a place fairly far down and a little to the right that is called the home of the intelligent, where horses are constantly appearing, because the spirits there think about the intellect. When angels who are talking about the intellect flow into such spirits' thinking, representations of horses appear.

This has shown what was symbolized by the horses that the prophets saw and the horses mentioned in the Word: aspects of the intellect (§§2760, 2761, 2762).

When angels' emotions are active, and they are talking about those emotions, their ideas are expressed among the spirits in a lower realm in representative images of animals. When the conversation is about positive emotions, animals that are beautiful, tame, and useful present themselves. These are the animals the Jewish religion used in connection with the sacrifices of its representative worship of God. They include lambs, ewes, kids, she-goats, rams, he-goats, calves, young cattle, and adult cattle. If anything ever appears sitting on one of these animals, it presents a kind of portrait of their thoughts, as upright spirits are allowed to perceive. **3218**

This shows what the animals used in the rituals of the Jewish religion symbolized and what the same animals symbolize when they are mentioned in the Word: emotions (§§1823, 2179, 2180).

However, angelic conversation about negative emotions is represented by creatures that are hideous, savage, and unable to be made useful, including tigers, bears, wolves, scorpions, snakes, rats, and so on. Negative emotions is what these animals symbolize in the Word.

When angels are talking about thought processes and about individual thoughts and the way they flow into us, what look like birds appear in the world of spirits—birds formed to match the theme of the angels' conversation. Because of this, birds in the Word symbolize rational concepts, or the products of thought (§§40, 745, 776, 991). **3219**

Once some birds came into my range of vision. One was unimpressive and ugly, but two were magnificent and beautiful. When I went to look at them, some spirits suddenly ran into me with such force that they made my muscles and bones shake. I assumed that evil spirits were assaulting me now (as they had several times before) in an effort to destroy me, but that was not it. When I stopped shaking, and the spirits who had knocked into me had been moved aside, I talked with them, asking what was going on.

"We have fallen down from a certain community of angels," they said, "where the conversation had to do with thought, and the way thought flows into people. Our opinion was that the thoughts people think come in from the outside, through the outer senses, the way they seem to. But the heavenly community we were in believed that thoughts enter us from within. Since we were wrong, we fell down from there." Not that they were thrown down, because angels never force anyone to leave or fall; but since they were wrong, they fell down from there on their own. "And that," they said, "was why."

This taught me that heavenly conversation about thoughts and the way they flow in is represented by birds—those of people stuck in falsity, by lowly, ugly birds, but those of people awake to truth, by magnificent, beautiful birds. I was also instructed that every thought we think flows in from within us, not from outside us, even if it looks that way. And I was told that it is out of order for what comes after to flow into what comes before, or for something coarser to flow into something purer, and therefore for the body to act on the soul.

3220   When angels are talking about matters of understanding and wisdom, and about perception and knowledge, their inflow into corresponding communities of spirits expresses itself in representations of things found in the plant kingdom. These include lush gardens, vineyards, forests, and flowery meadows. It also expresses itself in other beautiful sights that surpass all human imagination.

That is why the Word depicts matters of wisdom and understanding by gardens, vineyards, forests, and meadows, and why that is what is symbolized where they are mentioned.

3221   Sometimes angels' conversations are represented by clouds and the shapes, colors, motion, and changing patterns of clouds. White, rising clouds represent ideas that support truth; dark, sinking clouds represent ideas that contradict it. Inky, black clouds represent ideas that support falsity. Agreement and disagreement are represented as clouds that merge and split in various ways, in a sky of midnight blue.

3222   In addition, different kinds of love and their effect on us are represented as types of flame, with a variety that defies description. Truth, however, is represented as types of light and the countless ways light is modified. This reveals why it is that flames in the Word symbolize good that is done out of love, while light symbolizes truth that leads to faith.

3223   There are two kinds of light that shine on us: the light of the world and the light of heaven. Worldly light comes from the sun; heaven's light comes from the Lord.

Worldly light is for our earthly or outward self and so for the concerns of our earthly self. Although those concerns do not seem to have anything to do with physical light, they do. Our earthly self cannot grasp anything except in terms of objects that exist and appear in our subsolar realm and not, therefore, unless the light and shade in this world give it some shape. All ideas of time and all ideas of space—which play such an important part in our earthly self that we cannot think without them—also rely on worldly light.

Heaven's light, on the other hand, is for our spiritual or inner self. Our deeper mind, which holds the intuitive thoughts in us that are described as nonmaterial, dwells in that light. We do not know this, even though we refer to our intellect as sight and speak of it as possessing light.

The reason for our ignorance is that as long as we immerse ourselves in worldly and bodily concerns, we perceive only the sorts of things that appear in worldly light, not those that appear in heavenly light. Heaven's light comes from the Lord alone. The whole of heaven dwells in that light.

[2] That light—heaven's—is vastly more perfect than the world's. What makes one ray in the world's light makes millions of rays in heaven's light. Heavenly light contains understanding and wisdom. That light is what acts on the worldly light in our outer or earthly self and enables us to perceive objects with our senses. If it did not, we would never have any awareness, because any life present in notions that depend on worldly illumination comes from heavenly light.

A correspondence exists between the two kinds of light (or between the objects of heaven's light and the objects of worldly light) when our outer or earthly self makes common cause with our inner or spiritual self—that is, when the outer self serves the inner. What then emerges in worldly light is representative of what exists in heaven's light.

It is astonishing that people do not yet see that the intellectual part of their mind is bathed in a light that is entirely different from the world's light. The fact of the matter, though, is that heaven's light is like shadow to anyone who lives in the world's light, while the world's light is like shadow to anyone who lives in heaven's. This is mainly the result of different kinds of love, which are variations on the warmth connected with the light. People who love themselves and the world enjoy only the warmth of the world's light. They are moved only by evil and falsity, which are what extinguish the true ideas that come with heavenly light.

People who love the Lord and people who love their neighbor, on the other hand, enjoy spiritual warmth, which comes with heaven's light. They are moved by goodness and truth, which extinguish false ideas; yet a correspondence [to false ideas] still exists among these people.

[2] Spirits who restrict themselves to matters of worldly light, and consequently to the falsity that comes of evil, do receive light from heaven in the other world. The light they receive, however, is no better than swamp light, or the kind of light a burning coal or firebrand gives off. This light is immediately extinguished and turns into total darkness when heaven's light draws near, though. People who live in this kind of light hallucinate, and what they see in their hallucinations they believe to be real. This is their only truth. Their delusions are also tied to foul, obscene objects that give them intense pleasure. So they think like deranged lunatics. They do not argue over the validity of false ideas but instantly affirm them. When it comes to goodness and truth, they do nothing but argue, until their arguments end in denial.

[3] The true ideas and good impulses that come from heaven's light act on a deeper part of the mind, but this is shut off in them. So the light streams around and outside that part of their mind, which becomes resistant to any kind of modification except by falsity that appears to them to be true. The only people who can acknowledge what is true and good are those in whom the deeper mind lies open and receives the light pouring in from the Lord. The more open this level of the mind is, the greater the acknowledgment.

The inner mind lies open only in people who have innocence, love for the Lord, and charity for their neighbor—not in those who have religious truth, unless they also live a good life.

3225   From this it can now be seen what correspondence is and where it comes from, and what a representation is and where it comes from: Correspondence exists between objects of heavenly light and objects of worldly light, or in other words, between the concerns of the inner or spiritual self and those of the outer or earthly self. A representation is whatever manifests itself among the objects of worldly light (that is, whatever occupies the outer or earthly self) as it relates to the objects of heaven's light (that is, what springs from the inner or spiritual self).

3226   Among the more superb skills we possess, although we do not know it—and one we take with us to the other world, when we pass over there upon release from the body—is that of perceiving what is meant by the representative objects appearing in the other life. Another is the ability to express everything on our mind in a split second, which we were unable to do in the body even with hours of time. We do it by using ideas derived from the objects of heavenly light, ideas that are helped along and given wings, so to speak, by representative images that match the subject we are talking about. These images are such that they cannot be described.

Since we take up these abilities after death without having to be taught them in the other world, it stands to reason that we possess them (that is, they exist inside us) while we are living in our body, although we do not know it.

The reason this is so is that there is a constant inflow with us that comes from the Lord through heaven. This inflow is that of spiritual and heavenly qualities, which descend into our earthly qualities and are presented there in representative form. In heaven, angels do not think about anything but the heavenly and spiritual concerns of the Lord's kingdom. In the world, though, people think about scarcely anything but bodily and earthly concerns, which belong to the kingdom *they* live in and have to do with the necessities of life that preoccupy them. Since the spiritual and heavenly qualities of heaven that flow into us are presented in representative form in us within our earthly qualities, they remain implanted there. When we put off bodily concerns and leave behind worldly interests, we find ourselves in possession of them.

There will be more on representations and correspondences at the end of the next chapter [§§3337–3352].

3227

Genesis 25

[More on the Word's Inner Meaning]

3228 THE themes of the present chapter are: the sons Abraham had by Keturah; Ishmael's sons, by name; the birth of Esau and Jacob to Isaac and Rebekah; and the birthright Esau sold to Jacob for lentil soup. Anyone can see that material like this is useful as a religious history of the era but provides little for a person's spiritual life—and yet it is our spiritual life that the Word exists for.

What difference does it make knowing who Abraham's sons by Keturah were, or who Ishmael's were? Does it matter that Esau became worn out hunting and asked for lentil soup, or that Jacob cleverly took the opportunity to exchange it for the birthright? Likewise in the next chapter, where Abimelech's shepherds feud with Isaac's over the wells they had dug, almost the same way they had with Abraham's shepherds earlier, in chapter 21. Besides, some passages are nothing but lists of names, like the list of Esau's descendants in chapter 36. And so on.

As history, these contain so little of a divine nature that by no means can you say every expression and every jot of that Word was divinely inspired—that is, that it was sent down from the Lord through heaven to the person who wrote it out. What the Lord has sent down is divine in each and every part. So the history in it is not divine (since it is a record of human deeds) except by virtue of the content hidden deep within it, which has to do in whole and in part with the Lord and his kingdom. Scriptural narrative, more than any other history anywhere on earth, has the distinction of possessing this inner content.

3229 If the Word were the Word solely on account of its stories—that is, only on account of its outward or literal meaning—all the stories in it would be holy. More importantly, many of the people in it would be considered saintly. They would end up being worshiped as gods (as many of them are) because the holiest document ever written focuses on them. Examples are the men called patriarchs: Abraham, Isaac, and Jacob; and after them the forebears of the tribes—Jacob's twelve sons; and afterward David; and others. In reality, they were all human, and several of them had little interest in divine worship. As I can testify, their lot is nothing out of the ordinary at all. No one in the heavens knows anything about them, either. Something will be said elsewhere about them and their circumstances in the other world, by the Lord's divine mercy.

This shows starkly that the outward or literal meaning is the Word only because of the deeper or spiritual meaning that it contains and from which it arises.

Genesis 25

1. And Abraham took another woman, and her name was Keturah.

2. And she bore him Zimran and Jokshan and Medan and Midian and Ishbak and Shuah.

3. And Jokshan fathered Sheba and Dedan. And the children of Dedan were the Asshurim and the Letushim and the Leummim.

4. And the sons of Midian were Ephah and Epher and Enoch and Abida and Eldaah. All these were the sons of Keturah.

5. And Abraham gave everything he had to Isaac.

6. And to the concubines' children that Abraham had, Abraham gave gifts; and he sent them away from Isaac his son (he himself still living) eastward, to the land of the East.

7. And these are the days of the years of Abraham's lives that he lived: one hundred seventy-five years.

8. And Abraham breathed his last and died in good old age, old and full [of years]; and he was gathered to his people.

9. And Isaac and Ishmael his sons buried him at the cave of Machpelah, at the field of Ephron, son of Zohar the Hittite, which is before Mamre—

10. the field that Abraham bought from the sons of Heth. There Abraham was buried, and Sarah his wife.

11. And it happened after Abraham's death that God blessed Isaac his son; and Isaac resided near Beer-lahai-roi.

❋   ❋   ❋   ❋

12. And these are the births of Ishmael, Abraham's son, whom Hagar the Egyptian, slave of Sarah, bore to Abraham.

13. And these are the names of Ishmael's sons, by their names, according to their births: Ishmael's firstborn was Nebaioth, and [there were] Kedar, and Adbeel, and Mibsam,

14. and Mishma, and Dumah, and Massa;

15. Hadar, and Tema, Jetur, Naphish, and Kedemah.

16. And these are the sons of Ishmael, and these are their names, in their towns and in their forts, twelve chiefs of their peoples.

17. And these are the years of Ishmael's lives: one hundred thirty-seven years; and he breathed his last and died and was gathered to his people.

18. And they settled from Havilah all the way to Shur, which is before Egypt as you come to Assyria; against the face of all his brothers, [the lot] fell [to him].

✳   ✳   ✳   ✳

19. And these are the births of Isaac, Abraham's son: Abraham fathered Isaac.

20. And Isaac was a son of forty years in his taking Rebekah—daughter of Bethuel the Aramean from Paddan-aram, sister of Laban the Aramean— to himself as his woman.

21. And Isaac prayed to Jehovah because of his woman, because she was infertile, and Jehovah was prevailed on by his prayer, and Rebekah his woman conceived.

22. And the sons clashed with each other within her, and she said, "If so, why this, and [why] me?" and went to ask Jehovah.

23. And Jehovah said to her, "Two nations are in your womb, and two peoples will divide from your belly, and [one] people will be stronger than [the other] people, and the greater will serve the lesser."

24. And her days were fulfilled to give birth, and look! Twins in her womb!

25. And the first came out, ruddy, all of him, like a hairy coat, and they called his name Esau.

26. And after this, his brother came out, and his hand was grabbing onto Esau's heel, and they called his name Jacob. And Isaac was a son of sixty years in [Rebekah's] giving birth to them.

✳   ✳   ✳   ✳

27. And the boys grew up, and Esau was a man knowledgeable in game, a man of the field; and Jacob was an upright man inhabiting tents.

28. And Isaac loved Esau because there was game in his mouth; and Rebekah was loving toward Jacob.

29. And Jacob cooked soup, and Esau came from the field, and he was worn out.

30. And Esau said to Jacob, "Let me please swallow some of the red dish, this red dish, because I am worn out." Therefore they called his name Edom.

31. And Jacob said, "Sell me, as of today, your birthright."

32. And Esau said, "Look, I am on the way to dying, and what point is the birthright to me?"

33. And Jacob said, "Swear to me as of today"; and he swore to him and sold his birthright to Jacob.

34. And Jacob gave Esau bread and lentil soup, and he ate and drank and rose and went; and Esau showed contempt for his birthright.

Summary

THE inner meaning of this chapter speaks first of the Lord's spiritual kingdom and what developed out of it (verses 1, 2, 3, 4). It separated from the Lord's heavenly kingdom (verses 5, 6). Abraham's role representing the Lord came to an end (verses 7, 8), and Isaac and Ishmael took over that role (verses 9, 10, 11). **3230**

Second, the inner meaning speaks of the spiritual church (represented by Ishmael) and what developed out of it (verses 12, 13, 14, 15, 16, 17, 18). **3231**

Third, it deals with the conception and birth of [the Lord's] earthly divinity—of the goodness in it, which is Esau, and the truth in it, which is Jacob (verses 19, 20, 21, 22, 23, 24, 25). **3232**

Fourth, it deals with the question of whether goodness or truth is more important in religion (verses 26, 27, 28, 29, 30, 31, 32, 33, 34). **3233**

Inner Meaning

GENESIS 25:1. *And Abraham took another woman; and her name was Keturah.* **3234**

Abraham took another woman symbolizes a second stage for the Lord, which Abraham represents. Abraham and Sarah represented heavenly divinity in the Lord; Abraham and Keturah represent his spiritual divinity. So

Abraham here represents the Lord in regard to divine goodness on the spiritual plane, while his *woman* represents the Lord in regard to divine truth linked with that goodness. *And her name was Keturah* symbolizes the essence of this divine truth.

3235   *Abraham took another woman* symbolizes a second stage for the Lord, which Abraham represents. Abraham and Sarah represented heavenly divinity in the Lord; Abraham and Keturah represent his spiritual divinity. This can be seen from the discussion and illustrations so far concerning Abraham and his wife Sarah, and from the remarks here concerning Abraham and Keturah.

However, since I say that Abraham represents the Lord's second stage here, and that Abraham and Sarah represent heavenly divinity in the Lord, but Abraham and Keturah, his spiritual divinity, you need to know what heavenly and spiritual divinity are. [2] Heavenly and spiritual divinity have to do with the people who receive the Lord's divine qualities, because the way the Lord appears to anyone reflects that person's character. The discussion in §§1838, 1861 shows this, and it is quite plain from the fact that the Lord is seen one way by the heavenly but another way by the spiritual. The heavenly see him as the sun, but the spiritual, as the moon (§§1529, 1530, 1531, 1838). He appears as the sun to the heavenly because they give themselves over to heavenly love—that is, to love for the Lord. He appears as the moon to the spiritual, on the other hand, because they give themselves over to spiritual love—that is, to charity toward their neighbor. The difference is like that between sunlight during the day and moonlight at night, and between the warmth that comes with each of the two that would allow plants to sprout. That is what is meant in Genesis 1:16 by the words *and God made the two great lights: the greater light to rule by day and the smaller light to rule by night.*

[3] To speak in general terms, the Lord's kingdom is heavenly and spiritual. That is, it consists of heavenly individuals and spiritual ones. The Lord's divinity seems heavenly to the heavenly and spiritual to the spiritual, and that is why I say Abraham and Sarah represented the Lord's heavenly divinity, while Abraham and Keturah represented his spiritual divinity.

Hardly anyone, though, knows what heavenliness and spirituality are, or who the heavenly and the spiritual are, so see what has already been said and shown concerning them: Definitions of heavenliness and spirituality: 1155, 1577, 1824, 2048, 2184, 2227, 2507. Who the heavenly are and who the spiritual are: 2088, 2669, 2708, 2715. A heavenly person is a likeness of the Lord and is motivated by love to do good, while a spiritual person is an image of the Lord and is motivated by faith to do good: 50,

51, 52, 1013. The heavenly perceive truth from the viewpoint of goodness and never debate truth: 202, 337, 607, 895, 1121, 2715. In heavenly people, the seed of goodness is planted in their volitional side, but in spiritual people, in their intellectual side, this side being where a new will is created in spiritual people: 863, 875, 895, 897, 927, 1023, 1043, 1044, 2256. From the standpoint of real goodness, the heavenly see unlimited truth; but the spiritual, because they debate whether a thing is true, cannot reach even the outer limit of heavenly people's light: 2718. Things are relatively dim for the spiritual: 1043, 2708, 2715. The Lord came into the world to save the spiritual: 2661, 2716, 2833, 2834.

Abraham here represents the Lord in regard to divine goodness on the spiritual plane, while his *woman* represents the Lord in regard to divine truth linked with that goodness. This can be seen from previous statements about husbands and wives to the effect that a husband represents goodness, and a wife, truth. That is how it was with Abraham and Sarah (§§1468, 1901, 2063, 2065, 2172, 2173, 2198, 2904) and with Isaac and Rebekah in the previous chapter (3077). The reason a husband represents goodness, and a wife, truth, is that religion is compared to a marriage and actually is a marriage of goodness and truth. Goodness is what the husband represents, because it stands in first place, while truth is what the wife represents, because it stands in second place. That is why the Word calls the Lord a bridegroom, man, and husband, and why it calls the church a bride, woman, and wife. **3236**

[2] The sections referred to just above in §3235 show what spiritual goodness and the spiritual truth linked with that goodness are. In general, spiritual goodness in a person is the goodness described as belonging to faith, which is simply charity toward one's neighbor. To be charity, it has to arise out of the new will that the Lord gives a spiritual person. Spiritual truth linked to that goodness is the truth described as belonging to faith, which is simply truth that looks to charity as, first, the whole purpose of its existence and, second, its starting point. If religious truth (or faith) is to exist in a spiritual person, it has to arise out of the new intellect that the Lord gives such a person. The new intellect has to receive its light from the new will.

And her name was Keturah symbolizes the essence of this divine truth. This can be seen from the symbolism of a name as a quality and from that of calling someone by name as recognizing the person's character, as discussed in §§144, 145, 1754, 1896, 2009. Divinity, though, is not said to have a character but to have *being,* so the name here symbolizes an essence. **3237**

Specifically it symbolizes the essence of divine truth, divine truth being symbolized in this verse by *hers*—the woman's. To see that the woman here means divine truth, look just above at §3236. This clarifies what *Keturah* involves in general.

3238   Genesis 25:2, 3, 4. *And she bore him Zimran and Jokshan and Medan and Midian and Ishbak and Shuah. And Jokshan fathered Sheba and Dedan. And the children of Dedan were the Asshurim and the Letushim and the Leummim. And the sons of Midian were Ephah and Epher and Enoch and Abida and Eldaah. All these were the sons of Keturah.*

She bore him Zimran and Jokshan and Medan and Midian and Ishbak and Shuah represents the general types of allotment we have in the Lord's spiritual kingdom in the heavens and on earth. *And Jokshan fathered Sheba and Dedan* symbolizes further developments from the first kind of allotment. *And the children of Dedan were the Asshurim and the Letushim and the Leummim* symbolizes further developments from the second kind of allotment. *And the sons of Midian were Ephah and Epher and Enoch and Abida and Eldaah* symbolizes further developments from the third kind of allotment. *All these were the sons of Keturah* means in regard to doctrine and the worship it inspires.

3239   *She bore him Zimran and Jokshan and Medan and Midian and Ishbak and Shuah* represents the general types of allotment we have in the Lord's spiritual kingdom in the heavens and on earth. This is not easy to see from the Word, because none of the names come up elsewhere, except for Midian (discussed below [§3242]). Still, it can be seen from the fact that every figure named in the Word represents something. All those mentioned so far, starting with the first chapter of Genesis, provide sufficient evidence that on an inner level of the Word the names of people, countries, regions, and cities have symbolic meaning. (See §§768, 1224, 1264, 1876, 1888, and many other places, where this is confirmed for specific names by passages from the Word.)

The reason the others, besides Midian, do not come up elsewhere in the Word is that they are among the "children of the east" mentioned from time to time in the Word. In general they symbolize people who belong to the Lord's spiritual kingdom; see below at verse 6 of the current chapter [§3249].

[2] This representation of the sons Abraham had by Keturah can be seen from the fact that Abraham and Keturah represent divine spirituality in the Lord. Specifically, Abraham represents divine goodness on the

Lord's spiritual plane, while Keturah represents divine truth there, united to that goodness. (This is dealt with just above in §§3235, 3236.) It follows, then, that their children represent the general types of allotment we have in the kingdom that is born from the Lord's divine spirituality.

They are called general allotments because the Lord's kingdom is represented by land distributed by lot among people who receive it as an inheritance to possess, just as the land of Canaan was given to the children of Israel. There are twelve general types because twelve symbolizes every aspect of neighborly love and therefore of faith existing in the Lord's kingdom, as discussed below at verse 16 [§3272]. Here there are six, which is half the number, but half a number involves the same things as the whole number, because multiplication and division do not change the essential nature of the thing itself, as long as something similar is present in it.

And Jokshan fathered Sheba and Dedan symbolizes further developments from the first kind of allotment. This can be seen from the representation of *Jokshan* and his sons, *Sheba and Dedan,* discussed below.

3240

Because this clause consists of names alone, and because they symbolize conditions and developments in the Lord's spiritual church, it needs to be said how matters stand in general with regard to the subject.

What distinguishes a heavenly religion from a spiritual one is this: People who are part of a heavenly church and are called heavenly people are devoted to love, and specifically to the goodness and truth that come of love. People who are part of a spiritual church and are called spiritual people, on the other hand, are devoted to faith, and specifically to the goodness and truth that come of faith. The goodness that the heavenly have grows out of love for the Lord, and the truth they possess has to do with love for their neighbor. The goodness that the spiritual have grows out of charity for their neighbor, and the truth they possess has to do with faith—so far as faith is a doctrine concerning charity. Clearly, then, the Lord's spiritual kingdom, like his heavenly kingdom, possesses goodness and truth, but with major differences.

[2] Furthermore, it needs to be known that goodness and truth are what distinguish the people within these kingdoms from each other, because there are those who focus more on goodness and those who focus more on truth. From these develop new categories—new categories of goodness and of truth. The new categories of goodness in the Lord's spiritual kingdom are what Jokshan's sons (the subject of the current verse) represent. The

new categories of truth there are what Midian's sons (the subject of the next verse) represent.

Now, since the spiritual are divided into two groups—those who focus more on goodness and those who focus more on truth—they have two kinds of doctrines: doctrines concerning charity, and doctrines concerning faith. The doctrines concerning charity are for those whose faith focuses on goodness, who are symbolized by the children of Jokshan here, but the doctrines concerning faith are for those whose faith focuses on truth, who are symbolized by the children of Midian.

[3] *Sheba and Dedan* are those who make up the first group, or in other words, those in the Lord's spiritual kingdom who are involved in the goodness taught by faith and who possess doctrines concerning charity. That is why Sheba and Dedan symbolize knowledge of heavenly matters or (to say the same thing another way) people who know about heavenly matters—in other words, people who have doctrines concerning charity. (After all, doctrine is knowledge, and charity is the heavenly element in a spiritual person.) It was shown in the first two volumes (§§117, 1168, 1171, 1172) that Sheba and Dedan have these meanings. There, Sheba and Dedan are Ham's great-grandchildren and are called the sons of Raamah, but it is important to know that like Japheth and Shem, Ham never existed. Instead, the people of the church following the Flood—a church called "Noah"—were divided into three groups according to their goodness and truth, and the groups were called by those names (§§736, 1062, 1065, 1140, 1141, 1162, and several other places). Still, there *were* nations called by these names, but the names referred to other people: as the current verse makes clear, this Sheba and Dedan were born to Jokshan, son of Abraham and Keturah.

[4] The passages quoted in §§117, 1171 show that Sheba stands for people who know about heavenly concerns and so for people committed to the goodness taught by faith. Dedan has a similar meaning, as shown by the passages quoted in §1172 and also by the following. In Isaiah:

> An oracle concerning Arabia: In a forest in Arabia you will spend the night, you *troops of Dedanites*. Bring water to meet the thirsty, you who inhabit the land of Tema; approach the wanderers with bread for them; for in the face of swords they will wander, in the face of an outstretched sword. (Isaiah 21:13, 14, [15])

Spending the night in a forest in Arabia stands for being stripped of anything good, because Arabia means people with heavenly qualities, or in other words, people who do the good that faith urges. Spending the night in a forest there means no longer doing that good and therefore being stripped of it, which is also depicted by the wandering in the face of swords, in the face of an outstretched sword. The heavenly dimension— or the goodness urged by faith, or the charitable deeds—that is theirs is symbolized by bringing water to meet the thirsty and approaching wanderers with bread. [5] In Jeremiah:

> I took the goblet from Jehovah's hand and gave a drink to all the nations to which Jehovah sent me—Jerusalem and the cities of Judah and its monarchs and its chiefs—to hand them over to ruin: Pharaoh, monarch of Egypt, and his slaves and his chiefs and all his people; all the monarchs of Tyre and all the monarchs of Sidon; *Dedan* and Tema and Buz and all who have trimmed the corners [of their hair and beard]; all the monarchs of *Zimri* and all the monarchs of Elam and all the monarchs of Media; and all the monarchs of the north. (Jeremiah 25:17, 18, 19, 22, 23, 25, 26)

This too speaks about the ruination of the spiritual church, whose different forms are mentioned in order, symbolized as they are by Jerusalem, the cities of Judah, Egypt, Tyre, Sidon, *Dedan,* Tema, Buz, Zimri, Elam, and Media. [6] In Ezekiel:

> *Sheba* and *Dedan* and the traders of Tarshish and all its young lions will say to you, "Have you come to pillage pillage? Have you assembled your assembly to plunder plunder? To take away silver and gold? To seize livestock and property? To pillage immense pillage?" (Ezekiel 38:13)

This is about Gog, which symbolizes outward worship detached from inward—an idolatrous kind (§1151). Sheba and Dedan stand for the deeper aspects of worship, or the goodness that comes of faith. Tarshish stands for the corresponding outward worship. The silver, gold, livestock, property, and pillage that Gog (outward worship detached from inward) wants to take away are concepts of goodness and truth. The people represented by Sheba and Dedan fight for that knowledge and defend it, which is why they are called young lions. To speak more particularly, Sheba means people who devote themselves to the knowledge of goodness, and Dedan, people who devote themselves to knowledge of the truth that grows out of goodness.

And the children of Dedan were the Asshurim and the Letushim and the **3241** *Leummim* symbolizes further developments from the second kind of allotment. This can be seen from the representation of *Dedan* as people who are involved in religiously inspired goodness—more specifically, in religious truth that grows out of goodness (§3240 at the end). It is quite plain that this develops out of the second allotment. It is particularly the truth of faith growing out of goodness that these three symbolize. Although the symbolism of each can be given, it cannot be confirmed by other passages in the Word, because the peoples involved are never mentioned again.

[2] The Lord's kingdom contains countless varieties of goodness and truth, but they still constitute one heaven. There are so many different kinds that no community is ever exactly like another; no community possesses the same goodness and truth (see §§684, 685, 690). A single whole there is made up of many different things, arranged by the Lord in such a way that they harmonize. The Lord creates harmony or concord among them by the fact that they all relate to him (§551). The situation resembles that of the body's organs, limbs, and viscera, not one of which is exactly like another. They all differ from each other and yet make a single whole, by virtue of the fact that they all trace their origin to a single soul and through this to heaven and therefore to the Lord. After all, nothing unconnected to the Lord is anything.

This shows that there are innumerable specific kinds of truth and goodness. The general kinds and in fact the most inclusive of all, in the spiritual church, are symbolized by these sons and grandsons of Abraham.

[3] People in a spiritual religion do not perceive what is good and true, as people in a heavenly religion do. Instead, what they acknowledge as true is what they have been taught. As a result, they are always arguing about truth and debating its validity. They each stick with the theology of their own religion and call it truth, which is why there are so many differences. Besides, most of them reach conclusions about goodness and truth on the basis of appearances and illusions, this person deciding differently from that but none of them deciding from any perception. In fact, they do not know what perception is.

Because their minds are so dark on the subject of religious goodness and truth, it is no wonder there are controversies on the most vital point of all: the Lord's divinity, humanity, and holy influence. Heavenly people perceive that these are not three but one, while spiritual people stay with the idea of three, trying to think of them as one. Since there is strife over the most vital point of all, then, it is easy to see that the variety and differences in doctrine are beyond counting. This reveals the source of the new developments symbolized by the people named here.

Granted that so many variations on and differences in doctrine exist— in other words, so many new developments—they still come together to form a single church when they all acknowledge charity to be the essential ingredient of religion. To put it another way, they form a single church when they view life as the goal of theology—that is, when they ask not so much what a person in the church *thinks* as how the person *lives*. It is the good we have done in our lives that determines what lot the Lord grants us in the other world, not the truth in our theology apart from the goodness in our lives.

And the sons of Midian were Ephah and Epher and Enoch and Abida and Eldaah symbolizes further developments from the third kind of allotment. This can be seen from the representation of *Midian* as people who are involved in the truth of faith, as discussed below. Since Midian represents those who are involved in the truth of faith, it follows that his children are what grows out of it. **3242**

Here is how matters stand with a person who focuses on the truth taught by faith: None are allowed into the Lord's kingdom but those who have the goodness taught by faith, because the goodness taught by faith has to do with life. A religious life stays with us [after death], but religious doctrine does not, unless it is integrated into our life. Still, people who focus on the truth of faith (that is, who champion faith and describe it as essential, because that is how they have been taught) but live good lives (that is, are Christian at heart, not just on their lips) are in the Lord's spiritual kingdom. It is easy to be persuaded that faith is the essential thing, when that is what our teachers tell us, and when we absorb that opinion during our youth. It is also easy to be persuaded because church leaders and those considered top scholars say so—and some of them are afraid to mention the importance of a good life, because their own lives damn them. Yet another reason is that the elements of faith flow into us perceptibly but the elements of charity do not.

[2] People who concentrate on religious truth and yet live good lives are the ones called *Midian,* then, while *Midian's sons* means the truth those people live by.

Just as Midian means people who are involved in religious truth united to religious goodness, in a negative sense it also means people

who take to falsity because their lives exhibit no goodness. This will be
seen below.

In Isaiah:

> A troop of camels will blanket you, *the dromedaries of Midian and Ephah;*
> they will all come from Sheba. Gold and frankincense they will carry,
> and Jehovah's praises they will proclaim. (Isaiah 60:6)

This is about the Lord's spiritual kingdom. The dromedaries of Midian
and Ephah stand for doctrines. Gold means doctrines about goodness;
frankincense means doctrines about truth; and Jehovah's praises mean
both. This also indicates what Ephah symbolizes.

The *Midianites* who drew Joseph out of the pit and sold him to the
Ishmaelites and also sold him into Egypt to Potiphar (Genesis 37:28,
36) symbolize people who have the truth that goes with simple goodness. This will be seen later, at those verses, by the Lord's divine mercy
[§4756].

[3] What Moses says about Midian shows that Midian also symbolizes people who succumb to falsity because they do not live good lives:

> The elders of Moab and the *elders of Midian,* with sorceries in hand,
> went to Balaam and spoke to him the words of Balak. (Numbers 22:4,
> 7, and following verses)

In a positive sense, Moab stands for people who engage in an earthly kind
of goodness, although they readily allow themselves to be led astray. In
a negative sense it stands for those who adulterate what is good (§2468).
In a positive sense, Midian stands for people who possess the truth that
goes with simple goodness (as noted), although they readily let themselves be persuaded. In a negative sense, as here, it stands for those who
falsify what is true. The sorceries in their hand symbolize falsification.
Their sending for Balaam to oppose the children of Israel (who stand for
religiously inspired goodness and the religious truth that grows out of it)
symbolizes deeds based on falsity.

[4] The children of Israel whored with *Midianite women,* which brought
on a plague, and the plague abated when Phinehas stabbed the *Midianite*
and the man of Israel in a brothel (Numbers 25:6, 7, 8, and following verses).
This whoredom symbolizes the same thing, because whoredom represents
falsification of truth (§§2466, 2729). And since falsification of truth is what
it symbolizes on an inner level, twelve thousand children of Israel struck the
Midianites by command and killed their monarchs, every male, and those

women they had taken captive who had slept with a man. They also split the plunder among them (Numbers 25:16, 17; 31:1-end). The reason there were twelve thousand was that twelve symbolizes everything involved in faith (§§577, 2089, 2129 at the end, 2130 at the end), which is what destroys falsity. The monarchs they killed mean the falsity, as do the males. The women who had slept with a man mean a desire for falsity. The plunder—gold, silver, and livestock—means truth that has been falsified. Clearly, then, all the details here represent the punishment and destruction of falsity by truth.

[5] The same is the case with statements about Midianites in Judges: Because the children of Israel did evil in Jehovah's eyes, they were given into the *hand of Midian* for seven years. Because of *Midian,* the children of Israel made themselves caves in the mountains, and caverns and strongholds. And when Israel sowed, *Midian* and Amalek and the *children of the east* went up and spoiled the produce of their land. Then Gideon delivered the Israelites with the three hundred who lapped water with their tongue like a dog, and sent home those who bowed down on their knees and drank. (These stories and more appear in Judges 6, 7, 8.) Here too every single detail represents falsification of truth and punishment for it—punishment to the point where [falsity] was destroyed by the qualities symbolized by lapping water with one's tongue like a dog. It would take too long, though, to explain the inner-level symbolism of each particular here. That explanation will be given in its own place, the Lord in his divine mercy willing. In Habakkuk:

> He saw and dispersed the nations, and the timeless mountains scattered,
> and the age-old hills humbled themselves. Below Aven I saw the tents of
> Cushan; the *tent curtains of Midian's land* trembled. (Habakkuk 3:6, 7)

This is about the Lord's Coming. The tents of Cushan stand for a religiosity based on evil; the tent curtains of Midian's land, for a religiosity based on falsity.

All these were the sons of Keturah means in regard to doctrine and the worship it inspires, as can be seen from the following: *Sons* symbolize truth and doctrine (as discussed in §§489, 491, 533, 1147, 2623). And *Keturah* represents divine truth on the spiritual plane attached to divine goodness on the spiritual plane (as discussed in §§3236, 3237) and therefore qualities that mark the Lord's spiritual kingdom. Worship in that kingdom conforms with doctrine, and that is why Keturah's sons mean doctrine and the worship it inspires.

3243

3244
Genesis 25:5, 6. *And Abraham gave everything he had to Isaac. And to the concubines' children that Abraham had, Abraham gave gifts; and he sent them away from Isaac his son (he himself still living) eastward, to the land of the East.*

Abraham gave everything he had to Isaac in the highest sense means that everything in the Lord's divine rational mind became divine. In a secondary sense, it means that heavenly qualities of love belong to the Lord's heavenly kingdom. *And to the concubines' children that Abraham had, Abraham gave gifts* means that spiritual people adopted by the Lord's divine humanity have allotments in the Lord's spiritual kingdom. *And he sent them away from Isaac his son* symbolizes separating and removing spiritual people from heavenly people. *He himself still living* means to whom he could give life. *Eastward, to the land of the East* means toward the goodness taught by faith.

3245
Abraham gave everything he had to Isaac in the highest sense means that everything in the Lord's divine rational mind became divine. In a secondary sense, it means that heavenly qualities of love belong to the Lord's heavenly kingdom. This can be seen from the representation of *Abraham* as divinity itself in the Lord (dealt with before [§§1893, 1950, 2010, 2630, 3077]) and from that of *Isaac* as divine rationality in him (also dealt with before). Since Abraham and Isaac in an inner sense mean the Lord, and since the Lord made his rational mind divine from the divinity in him, *Abraham gave everything he had to Isaac* means that everything in the Lord's divine rational mind became divine.

This fact—that everything in the Lord's rational mind was made divine—is the focus of what comes before and after. Where the text deals with Abraham, Isaac, and Jacob, the inner meaning tells how the Lord's humanity became divine.

[2] Properly understood, humanity is composed of two dimensions: the rational and the earthly. The Lord's rational plane is represented by Isaac, but his earthly plane, by Jacob. He made both divine. The parts of the story that concern Isaac have told how the Lord made his rational plane divine; those below that concern Jacob tell how he made his earthly plane divine [§§3278–3306]. The latter—his earthly plane—could not become divine until his rational mind became so, because it was through his rational mind that his earthly plane was made divine. This, then, is why the words under discussion here symbolize the divinity of everything composing the Lord's divine rationality.

[3] In addition, everything that talks about the Lord in its inner meaning also talks about his kingdom and church, because the Lord's divinity makes his kingdom. For this reason, where the Lord is the subject, his kingdom is also the subject (see §1965). The level of inner meaning that treats of the Lord is the highest sense, while the level that treats of his kingdom is relative [or secondary]. The relative sense of these words—*Abraham gave everything to Isaac*—is that heavenly qualities of love belong to the Lord's heavenly kingdom. In a relative sense Isaac symbolizes the heavenly kingdom, because Abraham's other sons—the ones born to him by Keturah—symbolize the Lord's spiritual kingdom, as shown above [§§3238–3243]. Ishmael too symbolizes the Lord's spiritual kingdom, as discussed below [§§3262–3277].

And to the concubines' children that Abraham had, Abraham gave gifts means that spiritual people adopted by the Lord's divine humanity have allotments in the Lord's spiritual kingdom, as can be seen from the following: The *concubines' children* symbolize spiritual people, as discussed below. *Abraham* here represents the Lord's divine humanity, so the words *that Abraham had* mean that they (spiritual people) were adopted by the Lord's divine humanity. And the *gifts* Abraham gave them symbolize allotments in the Lord's spiritual kingdom. **3246**

[2] Descriptions in several earlier places (such as §3235 and elsewhere) of the people who constitute the Lord's spiritual kingdom and are called spiritual show that they are not offspring of the actual marriage between goodness and truth. Instead they come from a pact that is not exactly one of marriage. They do have the same father but not the same mother. In other words, they are born of the same divine goodness but not of the same divine truth.

Since heavenly people are offspring of the actual marriage of goodness and truth, they do have goodness and the truth that rises out of it. As a result, they never ask what is true but perceive it out of goodness. They say nothing more about truth than "That's true," in accord with the Lord's teaching in Matthew 5:37: "Let your conversation be 'Yes, yes,' 'No, no.' Anything beyond these comes from evil." Since spiritual people are offspring of a pact that is not exactly one of marriage, though, they do not know what is true from any perception of truth. Instead, they consider what their parents and teachers have told them is true to be true. So there is no marriage of goodness and truth in them. Even so, the truth that they believe to be true is adopted by the Lord as true if they live good lives. See what §1832 says about them.

This, now, is why the spiritual are being called *concubines' children*—meaning all Keturah's offspring named in the preceding verses and Hagar's offspring mentioned just below in verses 12–18.

[3] In order for both heavenly and spiritual people to be represented in the marriages of long ago, people were permitted to have a concubine in addition to a wife. The wife would give her husband the concubine, who was then called his woman, or who was said to be given to the man to be his woman. Sarah, for instance, gave Hagar the Egyptian to Abraham (Genesis 16:3); Rachel gave her slave Bilhah to Jacob (Genesis 30:4), and Leah gave him her slave Zilpah (Genesis 30:9). In those verses, they are called the men's women, but elsewhere they are called concubines. Hagar the Egyptian is called a concubine in the current verse; Bilhah in Genesis 35:22; and Keturah herself in 1 Chronicles 1:32.

[4] The ancient practice of taking concubines in addition to a wife was tolerated for the sake of representation. (It was not just Abraham and Jacob who did so but also their descendants, such as Gideon [Judges 8:31]; Saul [2 Samuel 3:7]; David [2 Samuel 5:13; 15:16]; and Solomon [1 Kings 11:3].) Heavenly religion was represented by a wife, and spiritual religion by a concubine. The reason it was tolerated was their character, which was such that they had no marriage love. Consequently, marriage was not marriage to them but only a physical union for the sake of producing offspring. Permission [to take concubines] could be given to people like this without damage to their love or therefore to their marriage pact, but never to people who have goodness and truth and depth (or the ability to develop depth). As soon as a person has goodness and truth and depth, such activities are cut off. That is why Christians, unlike Jews, are not allowed to take a concubine in addition to a wife, and why to do so would be adultery.

On the point that the spiritual are adopted by the Lord's divine humanity, see what was said and shown about the subject earlier, at §§2661, 2716, 2833, 2834.

3247   *And he sent them away from Isaac his son* symbolizes separating and removing spiritual people from heavenly people. This can be seen from the remarks just above saying that Abraham's offspring by Keturah and Hagar the Egyptian (called the concubines' children) are spiritual people, that *Isaac* in a secondary sense means heavenly people (§3245), and that they are separate.

3248   *He himself still living* means to whom he could give life. This can be seen from the symbolism of *he himself still living* (or *while he was still alive*) as giving life. Abraham, after all, represents the Lord—here, the Lord in his divine humanity. For the idea that life in spiritual people comes from the Lord's divine humanity, see §§2661, 2716, 2833, 2834. Since that is where they receive life from, the Lord is said (even in everyday speech) to live with them. That is why *Abraham himself still living* in an inner sense means giving life.

Life is given to spiritual people through the goodness taught by faith, which is what the words immediately following mean.

Eastward, to the land of the East means toward the goodness taught by faith. This is established by the symbolism of the *east* and the *land of the East*, as dealt with below. The goodness taught by faith, symbolized by the *land of the East*, is the same as what the Word calls charity for one's neighbor; and charity for one's neighbor is the same as a life that accords with the Lord's commandments.

3249

For this symbolism of the *land of the East*, see §1250. Because of it, people who knew about the goodness taught by faith were called "children of the east." Their land was Aram, or Syria, and Aram or Syria means a knowledge of goodness (see §§1232, 1234), while Aram-naharaim, or Syria of the Rivers, means a knowledge of truth (3051). Since Syrians, or the children of the east, symbolized people who know about goodness and truth, more than any others they were described as wise. In Kings, for example, where it talks about Solomon:

> Solomon's wisdom multiplied beyond the *wisdom of all the children of the east*. (1 Kings 4:30)

And in Matthew, concerning the visitors who came to Jesus when he was born:

> *Sages from the East* came to Jerusalem, saying, "Where is the king of the Jews who has been born? Because we have seen his *star in the East* and have come so that we can worship him." (Matthew 2:1, 2)

[2] Syria was home to the last survivors of the ancient church, so knowledge of goodness and truth still remained there. This is also evident from Balaam, who not only worshiped Jehovah but also prophesied concerning the Lord, calling him a "*star from Jacob* and a scepter from Israel" (Numbers 24:17). Clearly he was from among the children of the east in Syria, because when he uttered his pronouncement, he said of himself, "From Syria has Balak, king of Moab, brought me—from the *mountains of the East*" (Numbers 23:7). The fact that Aram, or Syria, was where the

children of the east lived can also be seen from the consideration that when Jacob went to Syria, he was said to have gone to the *land of the children of the east* (Genesis 29:1).

3250   Genesis 25:7, 8, 9, 10. *And these are the days of the years of Abraham's lives that he lived: one hundred seventy-five years. And Abraham breathed his last and died in good old age, old and full [of years]; and he was gathered to his people. And Isaac and Ishmael his sons buried him at the cave of Machpelah, at the field of Ephron, son of Zohar the Hittite, which is before Mamre—the field that Abraham bought from the sons of Heth. There Abraham was buried, and Sarah his wife.*

These are the days of the years of Abraham's lives that he lived symbolizes a stage at which Abraham represented divinity itself in the Lord. *One hundred seventy-five years* symbolizes characteristics of that stage. *And Abraham breathed his last and died* means the end of Abraham's representation. *In good old age, old and full* symbolizes a new representation. *And he was gathered to his people* means the narrative now shifts away from Abraham. *And Isaac and Ishmael his sons buried him* means that Isaac and Ishmael now took over the role of representing the Lord. *At the cave of Machpelah* symbolizes the resurrection of truth in him. *At the field of Ephron, son of Zohar the Hittite, which is before Mamre,* symbolizes the resurrection of goodness in him. As before [§2933], it also symbolizes spiritual people who receive truth and goodness from the Lord's divine humanity and are saved. *The field that Abraham bought from the sons of Heth* symbolizes a spiritual kingdom of the Lord from them. *There Abraham was buried, and Sarah his wife* symbolizes being revived.

3251   *These are the days of the years of Abraham's lives that he lived* symbolizes a stage at which Abraham represented divinity itself in the Lord. This can be seen from the symbolism of *days* and *years* as stages (discussed in §§23, 487, 488, 493, 893, 2788) and from the symbolism of *lives* too, here, as stages (discussed in §2904)—at this point, stages of Abraham's representation. His whole life, as described in the Word, was representative, and its end is the current focus.

It has been shown in these explanations that Abraham represented the Lord's divinity itself. For purposes of this representation, he was called Abraham, with the letter *h* (taken from Jehovah's name; §2010) inserted in it. Abraham represented both divinity itself (called the Father) and divine humanity (called the Son), so he represented the Lord in both respects. The divine humanity that he represented, though, was that which had existed from eternity. This was the divine humanity from which the Lord emerged, the form of divine humanity to which he restored the humanity born within time when he glorified it. Abraham is the one who represents the Lord in this regard.

One hundred seventy-five years symbolizes characteristics of that stage. This can be seen from the fact that all numbers in the Word have symbolic meaning (§§482, 487, 575, 647, 648, 1963, 1988, 2075, 2252), including this number. The fact that it symbolizes characteristics of the stage presently under discussion follows naturally.

3252

When our mind concentrates only on the story, it does not look to us as though the numbers—like those here counting Abraham's years—involve any deeper meaning, but they do. This is clear from all the explanations of numbers offered earlier. It can also be seen from the fact that a number as a number contains nothing holy, and yet the very smallest detail in the Word is holy.

And Abraham breathed his last and died means the end of Abraham's representation. This is established by the symbolism of *breathing one's last and dying* as stopping or coming to an end (§494)—here, the end of his representation. None of the description of Abraham's life in the Word is actually about Abraham, except on the narrative level. It is about the Lord and his kingdom. So when the Word says of him that he breathed his last and died, all it can mean in the genuine sense is that the stage at which Abraham represented the Lord ended.

3253

In good old age, old and full symbolizes a new representation. This can be seen from the symbolism on an inner level of *old age* as shedding the old and putting on the new (dealt with in §§1854, 2198, 3016).

3254

The reason it is newness or a new stage that old age symbolizes on an inner level is that angels (the intended audience of the Word's inner meaning) have no idea of time. So they know nothing of time-related concepts such as the different eras of a person's life—childhood, youth, young adulthood, full adulthood, and old age. Instead they replace them all with the idea of states. For the period of childhood they picture an innocent state; for the period of youth and young adulthood, a state of desire for goodness and truth; for full adulthood, a state of understanding; and for old age, a state of wisdom (§3183). In old age we pass from temporal concerns to the concerns of timeless life and therefore put on a new state. As a result, old age symbolizes newness. Here it symbolizes a new representation, because it is Abraham's representative role that is being said to have reached old age and to be *old and full,* as the remarks just above show.

3255   *And he was gathered to his people* means that the narrative now shifts away from Abraham. This can be seen from the symbolism of *being gathered to his people* as there being nothing more about him. Being gathered to his people means leaving those he had lived with and passing over to his own. Here, then, it means no longer representing anything.

When people died, the ancients customarily said they were gathered to their ancestors, or to their people, by which they meant that they literally went to their parents and other close and distant relations in the other world. This saying was one they received from the earliest people, who were a heavenly race. While the earliest people were living on earth, they were also present with angels in heaven, so they knew how matters stood. They knew that everyone who shares the same kind of goodness meets in the other life and lives together, as does everyone who shares the same truth. The former they would describe as being gathered to their ancestors, or fathers, but the latter, to their people. To them, fathers symbolized goodness (§2803) and peoples symbolized truth (1259, 1260). Those who were part of the earliest church shared a similar kind of goodness, so they live together in heaven: 1115. So do many of those who were part of the ancient church and shared similar truth: 1125, 1127. [2] What is more, while we are living in our body, our soul is always in some community of spirits in the other world: 1277, 2379. If we are evil, our soul is in a community of hellish spirits. If we are good, it is in a community of angels. So we each keep company with those whose goodness and truth or whose evil and falsity matches ours. That same community is the one we enter when we die: 687. That is what being gathered to one's ancestors or to one's people symbolized to the ancients. The current verse says it of Abraham when he breathed his last, and verse 17 of this same chapter says it of Ishmael. It is also said of Isaac (Genesis 35:29), Jacob (Genesis 49:29, 33), Aaron (Numbers 20:24, 26), Moses (Numbers 27:13; 31:2; Deuteronomy 32:50), and the first generation to enter the land of Canaan (Judges 2:10).

When the Word's inner meaning is about the representation of someone's life, then that person's being gathered to her or his people means there is nothing more about that person, as noted above.

3256   *And Isaac and Ishmael his sons buried him* means that Isaac and Ishmael now took over the role of representing the Lord, as the symbolism of *burying* shows. Being buried means reviving and rising again, as demonstrated in §§2916, 2917.

Since Abraham's representation of the Lord closes here with the idea that this state ended, and since Isaac and Ishmael now start to represent the Lord, the *burying* symbolizes a revival of this state. The symbolism varies with the symbolic item.

The fact of the matter about representation in the Word is that it is continuous, even if it seems to be interrupted by the death of the people doing the representing. In reality, their deaths do not signal an interruption but a continuation, so their burial signals a representative role revived and continued in another person.

At the cave of Machpelah symbolizes the resurrection of truth in him. *At the field of Ephron, son of Zohar the Hittite, which is before Mamre,* symbolizes the resurrection of goodness in him. As before, it also symbolizes spiritual people who receive truth and goodness from the Lord's divine humanity and are saved. *The field that Abraham bought from the sons of Heth* symbolizes a spiritual kingdom of the Lord from them. *There Abraham was buried, and Sarah his wife* symbolizes being revived. All of this is established by statements and evidence on the symbolism of each phrase above at Genesis 23 (§§2913, 2928, 2968, 2969, 2970, 2971, 2975, 2980) and on the symbolism of being buried (2916, 2917).

3257

Genesis 25:11. *And it happened after Abraham's death that God blessed Isaac his son; and Isaac resided near Beer-lahai-roi.*

3258

It happened after Abraham's death means after the condition and time in which Abraham represented the Lord. *That God blessed Isaac his son* symbolizes the start of Isaac's representing the Lord. *And Isaac resided near Beer-lahai-roi* symbolizes the Lord's divine rationality bathed in divine light.

It happened after Abraham's death means after the condition and time in which Abraham represented the Lord. This can be seen from the symbolism of *dying*, when the subject is someone's life and its representation, as the end of that representation (discussed above in §3253). So *after Abraham's death* means after the condition and time in which Abraham represented the Lord.

3259

That God blessed Isaac his son symbolizes the start of Isaac's representation, as can be seen from the symbolism of *God blessed*. When an undertaking was begun, the ancients were in the habit of saying "God bless!" which meant the same thing as the wish "Godspeed!" As a consequence, in a more extended sense, "God bless!" (like "Godspeed!") symbolizes a beginning—here, the start of Isaac's representation, because it immediately follows the end of Abraham's representation, symbolized by his death.

3260

And Isaac resided near Beer-lahai-roi symbolizes the Lord's divine rationality bathed in divine light. This can be seen from the symbolism of *residing* as living (discussed in §1293) and from that of *Beer-lahai-roi* as divine

3261

goodness on the rational plane, born from divine truth itself (discussed in §3194). So the first layer of meaning suggests that divine rationality lived or existed in the divine goodness that had been born from divine truth itself. It did *not* actually exist there, however, so the text does not say *in* Beer-lahai-roi but *near* Beer-lahai-roi—that is (when translated), near "the spring of the living one who sees me," or near that divine goodness. Isaac lived in the southland, you see, as it says in verse 62 of the last chapter: "And Isaac came from going to Beer-lahai-roi, and he was residing in the southland." In that passage the southland symbolizes the divine light resulting [from divine goodness] (§3195), so nothing else is meant here.

*　*　*　*

3262   Genesis 25:12. *And these are the births of Ishmael, Abraham's son, whom Hagar the Egyptian, slave of Sarah, bore to Abraham.*

These are the births of Ishmael, Abraham's son, symbolizes developments in the spiritual church represented by Ishmael. *Whom Hagar the Egyptian, slave of Sarah, bore to Abraham* symbolizes the birth of the spiritual self from a divine inflow into the desire for secular knowledge.

3263   *These are the births of Ishmael, Abraham's son,* symbolizes developments in the spiritual church represented by Ishmael, as can be seen from the following: *Births* symbolize the ways faith develops and accordingly the ways the church does, as discussed in §§1145, 1255, 1330. *Ishmael* represents people who are rational and are part of the Lord's spiritual church, as discussed in §§2078, 2691, 2699. And *Abraham's sons* symbolize people who focus on truth that comes from the Lord. *Sons* symbolize truth (489, 491, 533, 1147, 2623), and *Abraham* represents the Lord, including his divine humanity (3251), from which spiritual people receive truth and goodness (2661, 2716, 2833, 2834).

[2] So far as the Lord's spiritual church goes, it is important to realize that it extends throughout the globe. It is not limited to people who have the Word and therefore know the Lord and some truth taught by the faith; it also exists among people who do not have the Word, are completely ignorant of the Lord as a result, and therefore do not know any of the faith's true concepts. (All the truth of the faith has to do with the Lord.) In other words, it exists among nations far distant from the church. Many of the people in those nations have enough rational light to recognize that there is one God; that he created everything and preserves everything; that everything good and consequently everything true comes from him; and that to be like him is to be blessed. In addition,

they live according to their religion, loving that God and their neighbor. Their passion for goodness leads them to do deeds of neighborly kindness, and their passion for truth leads them to worship the Supreme Being. Non-Christians who are like this are those who are in the Lord's spiritual church. Although they do not know the Lord in this world, still, if they have goodness, they harbor a reverence for and tacit acknowledgment of him inside themselves, because the Lord is present in goodness of every kind. So they readily acknowledge him in the other life and welcome the truth that goes with a faith in him—more than those Christians who are not as focused on goodness. This can be seen from what experience reveals about the condition and lot in the other world of nations and peoples outside the church at §§2589–2604.

The earthly illumination they enjoy contains spiritual light within it, because without spiritual light from the Lord they could never acknowledge these ideas.

[3] This now shows what Ishmael and consequently Ishmaelites mean in a representative sense: people in the Lord's spiritual church who live in simple goodness and therefore possess earthly truth as their theology. They are also the kind of people symbolized by Ishmaelites later on, in the story of Joseph:

> Here, a *troop of Ishmaelites* came from Gilead, and their camels were carrying beeswax, resin, and stacte as they went to take them down into Egypt. (Genesis 37:25)

The Ishmaelites stand for people who live in simple goodness, as upright non-Christians do. The camels carrying beeswax, resin, and stacte stand for the deeper goodness of these people. The Ishmaelites in Genesis 37:28 and 39:1 have the same meaning, as do those in Judges:

> At Gideon's request, they each gave an earring from their plunder, because [the conquered] had gold earrings, *since they were Ishmaelites.* (Judges 8:24)

Gold earrings symbolized the properties of simple goodness (§3103).

Whom Hagar the Egyptian, slave of Sarah, bore to Abraham symbolizes the birth of the spiritual self from a divine inflow into the desire for secular knowledge, as can be seen from the following. *Bearing* symbolizes emerging into existence, as noted at §§2621, 2629. *Hagar the Egyptian* represents life in the outer self, as noted at §§1896, 1909. And a female *slave* symbolizes the desire the outer self has for secular and religious knowledge, as suggested at §§1895, 2691. The text says *slave of Sarah* because

3264

Sarah represents the Lord's divine truth, to which the desire for secular and religious knowledge is subordinate. Since Ishmael represents the spiritual self, clearly the words *whom Hagar the Egyptian, slave of Sarah, bore to Abraham* mean the birth of the spiritual self from a divine inflow into the desire for secular knowledge. [2] To see that this is how our rationality is born, consult §§1895, 1896, 1902, 1910, 2094, 2557, 3030, 3074. As a consequence, it is also how our spiritual dimension is born, since we have no spiritual dimension except within our rational mind. A spiritually oriented person and a rationally oriented person are almost the same. Spiritual people differ from each other only in the quality of their reason and of the life they base on their reason. On the point that their birth (or rebirth) comes from a divine inflow into their desire for knowledge, see §§1555, 1904, 2046, 2063, 2189, 2657, 2675, 2691 at the end, 2697, 2979. See previous remarks and explanations showing that Ishmael represented the Lord's first rationality, which was not yet divine (1893). Later he represented people who were truly rational, or spiritual (2078, 2691), so he represented the Lord's spiritual church (2699).

3265   Genesis 25:13, 14, 15, 16. *And these are the names of Ishmael's sons, by their names, according to their births: Ishmael's firstborn was Nebaioth, and [there were] Kedar, and Adbeel, and Mibsam, and Mishma, and Dumah, and Massa; Hadar, and Tema, Jetur, Naphish, and Kedemah. These are the sons of Ishmael, and these are their names, in their towns and in their forts, twelve chiefs of their peoples.*

These are the names of Ishmael's sons symbolizes characteristics of their doctrines. *By their names, according to their births* symbolizes deeper qualities, according to the forms of faith developed. *Ishmael's firstborn was Nebaioth, and [there were] Kedar, and Adbeel, and Mibsam, and Mishma, and Dumah, and Massa; Hadar, and Tema, Jetur, Naphish, and Kedemah* symbolizes all aspects of the spiritual church, especially among non-Christians. *These are the sons of Ishmael, and these are their names* symbolizes the doctrines and their character. *In their towns* symbolizes the outward attributes of the church. *In their forts* symbolizes the inward attributes. *Twelve chiefs of their peoples* symbolizes all the main elements of that spiritual church.

3266   *These are the names of Ishmael's sons* symbolizes characteristics of their (that is, spiritual people's) doctrines. This can be seen from the symbolism of a *name* as a quality (discussed in §§144, 145, 1754, 1896, 2009, 2724, 3006), from that of *sons* as truth and as doctrine (discussed in §§489, 491, 533, 1147, 2623), and from the representation of Ishmael as spiritual people (discussed above in §3263).

By their names, according to their births symbolizes deeper qualities, **3267** according to the forms of faith that have developed. This can be seen from the symbolism of a *name* as a quality, or of *names* as qualities (dealt with just above at §3266)—here, deeper qualities, because it says, "These are the *names* of Ishmael's sons by their *names.*" The first mention means general qualities; the second means other qualities within the general ones, or related to them, which is to say deeper ones. Consider also that these qualities accord with the forms of faith that have developed, which is what *according to their births* means. (*Births* symbolize the ways faith develops and therefore the ways the church does; see §§1145, 1255, 1330, 3263.)

[2] The case with the Lord's spiritual church is that it is scattered throughout the four corners of the earth and varies in its beliefs (the truths of its faith) everywhere it exists. Those variations are the developments meant by births, and some of them emerge simultaneously, while others follow one after another. Even the Lord's spiritual kingdom in the heavens is like this—differing in various tenets of faith. The variety is so great that not one community—not even one person in a community—views the ramifications of religious truth exactly the same way as another (§3241). The Lord's spiritual kingdom in the heavens is still one kingdom, though, because charity is everyone's primary object. Charity, not faith, forms a spiritual religion, unless by faith you mean charity. [3] People with charity love their neighbor. If their neighbor differs with them on points of faith, they overlook it, provided the person lives a life of goodness and truth. A charitable person will not condemn even upright non-Christians, despite their ignorance of the Lord and of the faith. After all, when people live in charity, or in other words, in goodness, the Lord gives them the kind of truth that harmonizes with their goodness. To non-Christians he gives the kind of truth that in the other world can be turned into real religious truth (§§2599, 2600, 2601, 2602, 2603). People who do not have charity, though, or in other words, do not lead good lives, can never accept anything true. They can *learn* truth, admittedly, but it cannot be grafted onto their life; they can carry it on their lips but not in their heart. Truth cannot unite with evil. So when people know the truth that makes up their creed but do not live lives of charity, or of goodness, they are *in* the church because they were born into it, but they do not *belong* to it. Such people have in them no trace of the church, no trace of goodness, for truth to unite with.

Ishmael's firstborn son was Nebaioth, and [there were] Kedar, and Adbeel, **3268** *and Mibsam, and Mishma, Dumah, and Massa; Hadar, and Tema, Jetur, Naphish, and Kedemah* symbolizes all aspects of the spiritual church, especially among non-Christians. This can be seen from the representation of the individuals named. Some of them (Nebaioth, Kedar, Dumah, and Tema) are mentioned elsewhere in the Word, especially the prophetic books, and in those passages they symbolize traits typical of the spiritual church, especially among non-Christians. The symbolism is also evident from the fact that there are twelve sons, and twelve symbolizes every aspect of faith and therefore of the church, as discussed below [§3272]. That is why the next verse, verse 16, says that they were twelve chiefs of their peoples.

[2] Isaiah shows that *Nebaioth* and *Kedar* represent aspects of the spiritual church, especially among non-Christians, and specifically its good qualities and consequent true ideas:

> A troop of camels will blanket you, the dromedaries of Midian and Ephah; they will all come from Sheba. Gold and frankincense they will carry, and Jehovah's praises they will proclaim. Every *flock of Kedar* will be gathered to you. The *rams of Nebaioth* will wait on you; they will go up for my good pleasure to my altar. (Isaiah 60:6, 7)

In the highest sense, this is about the Lord; in a secondary sense, it is about his kingdom. The *flock of Kedar* stands for spiritual goodness. (For the meaning of a flock as spiritual goodness, see §§343, 415, 2566.) The rams of Nebaioth stand for spiritual truth. (For the meaning of a ram as spiritual truth, §2833.)

[3] The passages below will clarify that Kedar is Arabia. Arabia was named Kedar for Ishmael's son, as is indicated by the fact that the names mentioned in these two verses are different lands, or nations, all named for Abraham's sons and grandsons. This was true, for instance, of Midian, Ephah, and Sheba, mentioned earlier, in verses 2, 3, 4, so it is also true of Kedar and Nebaioth here. [4] In Ezekiel:

> *Arabia* and all the *chiefs of Kedar* were your dealers at hand for lambs and rams and he-goats; for these they were your dealers. (Ezekiel 27:21)

This is about Tyre—that is, about people who possess knowledge of what is good and true. For this meaning of Tyre, see §1201. Arabia stands for spiritual goodness; the chiefs of Kedar, for spiritual truth. Lambs, rams, and he-goats mean spiritual goodness and truth. [5] In Jeremiah:

> Rise, go up *to Kedar* and lay waste to the children of the east. [Others] will take their tents and their flocks; [others] will take away for themselves their tent curtains and all their vessels and their camels. (Jeremiah 49:28, 29)

This is about the devastation of the spiritual church meant by Kedar and the children of the east. Tents and flocks stand for the good qualities of that church; tent curtains and vessels, for its true concepts. Sacred elements of worship are what tents and flocks, tent curtains and vessels symbolize, but all sacred elements of worship relate to goodness and truth.

[6] Arabs and Kedarites in the wilderness, on the other hand, represent people who lack truth because they lack goodness, as in Isaiah:

Babylon will be uninhabited forever; *the Arab will not stay there.* (Isaiah 13:20)

In the same author:

Let the wilderness and its cities, the *towns* that *Kedar inhabits,* lift up [their voice]. (Isaiah 42:10, 11)

In Jeremiah:

Beside the paths you have been sitting for them, like an *Arab in the wilderness.* (Jeremiah 3:2)

In David:

Alas for me! Because I am staying in Meshech, I am dwelling with the tents of *Kedar.* (Psalms 120:5)

[7] In Isaiah:

In a *forest in Arabia* you will spend the night, you troops of Dedanites. Bring water to meet the thirsty, you who inhabit the *land of Tema;* approach the wanderers with bread for them; for in the face of swords they will wander, in the face of an outstretched sword, of a strung bow, and of the weight of war. For this is what the Lord has said to me: "In one more year (corresponding to the year of a hired servant) all the *glory of Kedar* will be consumed, as will what remains of the number of bows among the mighty *sons of Kedar.*" (Isaiah 21:13, 14, [15, 16, 17])

Spending the night in a forest in Arabia stands for being stripped of truth. The troops of Dedanites stand for people with religious knowledge (§§3240, 3241). The inhabitants of the land of *Tema* stand for people with the kind of simple goodness that respectable non-Christians have—and clearly these non-Christians descended from the son of Ishmael named Tema. Kedar stands for people with simple truth. The text says they will wander in the face of swords and of the weight of war, meaning that they will not be able to stand the battles of spiritual crisis, because they no longer have goodness. [8] In Jeremiah:

> Cross the islands of the Kittim and see, and *send Kedar* and pay great attention, and see whether anything like this has ever happened, whether a nation has changed gods—and they are not even gods! (Jeremiah 2:10, 11)

The islands of the Kittim stand for people who are quite remote from [true] worship—that is, for non-Christians with simple goodness and therefore with earthly truth (§§1156, 1158). Kedar also means such people, plainly. [9] In the same author:

> I took the goblet from Jehovah's hand and gave a drink to all the nations to which Jehovah sent me: . . . and to Dedan and *Tema* and Buz and all who have trimmed the corners [of their hair and beard]; and to all the *monarchs of Arabia* and all the monarchs of the West, living in the wilderness. (Jeremiah 25:17, 23, 24)

This passage also has to do with the devastation of the spiritual church, naming Tema and Arabia, among others, which shows that Tema, like Arabia, symbolizes people in the spiritual church. Arabia is said to have monarchs and cities; Kedar, to have chiefs and towns.

[10] In addition to these, *Dumah* is mentioned in Isaiah 21:11, 12.

The reason these nations symbolize aspects of a spiritual religion is that the ancient church, a spiritual religion, existed also among them (§§1238, 2385). Their doctrines and rituals were varied, but they still formed a single church, because they made neighborly love rather than faith the essential thing. Over time, as neighborly love died out, the vestiges of the church with them disappeared too, although they continued to *represent* a church. Their representation varied, depending on what aspect of the church had existed with them. That is why it is not these nations themselves that are meant when the Word mentions them but merely the general attributes of the church that had existed among them.

3269　　*These are the sons of Ishmael, and these are their names* symbolizes the doctrines and their character. This is established by the symbolism of *sons* as truth and as doctrines, and by that of a *name* as the character. These meanings are mentioned above at §3266.

3270　　*In their towns* symbolizes the outward attributes of the church. This can be seen from the symbolism of *towns* as that which constitutes the outward attributes of faith and so of the church. Rituals are the outward attributes of a religion; and doctrines—if they are not something to know but something to live by—are its inward attributes. The outward dimension was represented by towns, because they lay outside cities, but the inward dimension was represented by the cities themselves. For the symbolism of cities as doctrines, see §§402, 2268, 2449, 2712, 2943, 3216. *In their forts* symbolizes the inward attributes. This can be seen from the symbolism of *forts* as inward aspects of faith, and in this case of the church, because the particular reference is to non-Christians, who possess rational and earthly truth rather than the truth of the faith. Rational and earthly truth are called forts when the truth of the faith is called cities.

3271

In the original language, the words that mean towns and forts also mean courtyards and palaces, and courtyards likewise mean outward attributes of the church, while palaces mean inward ones.

Twelve chiefs of their peoples symbolizes all the main elements of that spiritual church, as can be seen from the following: *Twelve* symbolizes everything involved in faith, or in religion, as noted in §§577, 2089, 2129 at the end, 2130 at the end. *Chiefs* symbolize main elements, as discussed in §§1482, 2089. And *peoples* symbolize those who are devoted to truth, as dealt with in §§1259, 1260. Therefore peoples symbolize those who are part of the spiritual church, since they are the ones properly described as being devoted to truth.

3272

All numbers in the Word have symbolic meaning, and the number *twelve*, which crops up so many times, makes this obvious. Wherever we find that number in the Word, it means all. The twelve tribes in the Old Testament, for example, and the twelve apostles in the New symbolize all aspects of faith and therefore all aspects of the church. So the twelve chiefs here symbolize all the main elements of the church that are represented by Ishmael's twelve sons.

[2] This symbolism of the number twelve can be seen from passages quoted in the sections referred to above and also from the following places in the Word. In John:

> I heard the number of those sealed from every tribe of Israel: From the tribe of Judah, *twelve thousand* sealed. From the tribe of Reuben, *twelve thousand* sealed. From the tribe of Gad, *twelve thousand* sealed. And so on. (Revelation 7:4, 5, 6, and following verses)

The twelve thousand sealed from each tribe means simply that everyone dedicated to faith (or rather to the goodness that faith teaches) is saved. In the same author:

> . . . a woman enveloped in the sun, and the moon under her feet, and on her head a crown of *twelve stars*. (Revelation 12:1)

The woman stands for the church (§§252, 253); the sun, for heavenly love; the moon, for spiritual love (30–38, 1529, 1530, 2441, 2495); the twelve stars, for everything involved in faith—stars meaning knowledge of the goodness and truth that belong to faith (2495, 2849). [3] In the same author:

> . . . the holy city New Jerusalem, having *twelve gates* and on the gates *twelve angels* and names written, which are those of the *twelve tribes* of the children of Israel. The wall of the city had *twelve foundations* and on them the names of the Lamb's *twelve apostles*. He measured the city at *twelve thousand* stadia. And he measured its wall at a *hundred forty-four* cubits [twelve times twelve], which is the measure of a human, that is, of an angel. The *twelve* gates were *twelve* pearls. (Revelation 21:12, 14, 16, 17, 21)

The holy city actually means the Lord's spiritual kingdom. The gates, wall, and foundations symbolize different facets of neighborly love and faith, and the number twelve (repeated so often) means *all* of them. Anyone can see that it is not the twelve tribes and the twelve apostles that are meant. In the same author:

> In the middle of its street and of the river, on this side and that, was the tree of life, making *twelve fruits*, offering up its fruit each month. (Revelation 22:2)

The twelve fruits mean everything involved in love for others. [4] In Matthew:

> Jesus said, "Truly, I say to you that you who have followed me—in the rebirth, when the Son of Humankind sits on his glorious throne, you too will sit on *twelve thrones* judging the *twelve tribes* of Israel." (Matthew 19:28)

The apostles in this verse do not mean the apostles, the thrones do not mean thrones, and the tribes do not mean tribes; they mean everything encompassed by faith (see §2129).

What is more, where the Old Testament Word mentions the twelve tribes, they symbolize everything connected with the church. The same is true of the *twelve stones* according to the names of the *twelve tribes* of Israel on the Urim and Thummim (Exodus 28:21); of the *twelve loaves* of showbread lined up on the table (Leviticus 24:5, 6); and likewise of all other instances [of the number twelve].

The names themselves of Jacob's (or Israel's) twelve sons also contain everything related to faith, as will be seen in upcoming chapters (Genesis 29 and 30), by the Lord's divine mercy.

Genesis 25:17, 18. These are the years of Ishmael's lives: one hundred thirty-seven years; and he breathed his last and died and was gathered to his people. And they settled from Havilah all the way to Shur, which is before Egypt as you come to Assyria; against the face of all his brothers, [the lot] fell [to him]. **3273**

These are the years of Ishmael's lives symbolizes a stage at which Ishmael represented the Lord's spiritual kingdom. *One hundred thirty-seven years* symbolizes characteristics of that stage. *And he breathed his last and died* means the end of Ishmael's representation. *And was gathered to his people* means that the narrative now shifts away from Ishmael. *And they settled from Havilah all the way to Shur, which is before Egypt as you come to Assyria,* symbolizes the extent of intelligence [in that kingdom]. *Against the face of all his brothers, [the lot] fell [to him]* means that there was strife concerning truth but [the kind represented by Ishmael] gained the upper hand.

These are the years of Ishmael's lives symbolizes a stage at which Ishmael **3274** represented the Lord's spiritual kingdom. This is established by the symbolism of *years* and *lives* here as representative stages (dealt with above at §3251) and by the representation of *Ishmael* as the Lord's spiritual kingdom (discussed in §§2699, 3263, 3268).

One hundred thirty-seven years symbolizes characteristics of that stage, **3275** as can be seen from remarks above at §3252 about Abraham's age.

And he breathed his last and died means the end of Ishmael's represen- **3276** tation. This can be seen from statements above at §3253 where the same words occur with the same inner meaning.

Likewise, *he was gathered to his people* means that the narrative now shifts away from Ishmael (see above at §3255).

And they settled from Havilah all the way to Shur, which is before Egypt **3277** *as you come to Assyria,* symbolizes the extent of intelligence [in that kingdom], and *against the face of all his brothers, [the lot] fell [to him]* means that there was strife concerning truth but [the kind represented by Ishmael] gained the upper hand. This is established by the discussion explaining these things at §§115, 1951.

*   *   *   *

Genesis 25:19, 20. And these are the births of Isaac, Abraham's son: **3278** *Abraham fathered Isaac. And Isaac was a son of forty years in his taking*

Rebekah—daughter of Bethuel the Aramean from Paddan-aram, sister of Laban the Aramean—to himself as his woman.

These are the births of Isaac, Abraham's son, symbolizes divine rationality in the Lord, which gave rise to divinity on his earthly plane. *Abraham fathered Isaac* symbolizes divine rationality acquired from divinity itself. *And Isaac was a son of forty years* means by his own power, through the struggles of spiritual trial. *In his taking Rebekah* symbolizes union with divine truth. *Daughter of Bethuel the Aramean from Paddan-aram, sister of Laban the Aramean—to himself as his woman* symbolizes its quality and condition.

3279   *These are the births of Isaac, Abraham's son,* symbolizes divine rationality in the Lord, which gave rise to divinity on his earthly plane. This can be seen from the symbolism of *births* as developments (discussed in §§1145, 1255, 1330). To be specific, when faith is the subject, birth symbolizes the ways faith develops; when the church is the subject, it symbolizes the way the church does, as above where the births of Ishmael symbolized developments in the spiritual church (§3263). In the current passage, the births are associated with the Lord, so divine births are what are meant. The text is saying that divine rationality was born from divinity itself (symbolized by Isaac's birth to Abraham), and that earthly divinity was born from divine rationality (symbolized by Esau and Jacob's birth to Isaac). Esau and Jacob represent the Lord's earthly divinity—Esau, the goodness in it, and Jacob, the truth. A discussion of these things follows directly. They are what the births symbolize here.

3280   *Abraham fathered Isaac* symbolizes divine rationality acquired from divinity itself. This can be seen from the representation of *Abraham* as divinity itself and from that of *Isaac* as divine rationality, dealt with many times before.

3281   *And Isaac was a son of forty years* means by his own power, through the struggles of spiritual trial. This is established by the representation of *Isaac* as divine rationality (dealt with many times before); by the symbolism of *forty* as trials (discussed in §§730, 862); and by that of *years* as states (discussed in §§487, 488, 493, 893, 2788). The inner meaning of these words, then, is that the Lord made even the truth in his rational mind divine through the battles of his inward trials and therefore through his own power. (It was shown before in §§1661, 1663, 1668, 1690, 1787, 2083, 2523, 2632, 2776, 3030, 3043, 3141 that the Lord made everything human in himself divine under his own power by allowing himself to be tested.)

In his taking Rebekah symbolizes union with divine truth. This can **3282** be seen from the representation of *Rebekah* as divine truth attached to divine goodness on the rational plane. The way this truth arises out of the earthly self was described in the previous chapter.

Daughter of Bethuel the Aramean from Paddan-aram, sister of Laban **3283** *the Aramean—to himself as his woman* symbolizes its quality and condition. This can be seen from the representation of *Bethuel* and *Laban* and the symbolism of Aram and *Paddan-aram* as factors in the rise of the divine truth whose quality and condition are represented by Rebekah. The representation of Bethuel and Laban and the symbolism of Aram or Syria were explained in the previous chapter.

The reason Rebekah's origins are mentioned again here is that the next verses speak of the Lord's earthly plane. His earthly plane could not be made divine until truth had been introduced into his rational thinking and had become divine. The inflow into his earthly mind had to be that of the divine goodness in his rational mind, coming by way of the divine truth there. All capacity for intelligent awareness and action in a person's earthly life comes from the rational plane. Rationality is what arranges everything on the earthly level in order and views all the material there in terms of that arrangement. Rationality is like a higher sight, and when it observes facts in the earthly self, it seems to be looking down onto a plain. The light by which our rational mind sees is the light of truth, but the source of the light belongs to goodness on the rational plane. I will have more to say on this later [§§3286, 3321, 3493, 3570, 4618].

Genesis 25:21, 22, 23. *And Isaac prayed to Jehovah because of his woman,* **3284** *because she was infertile, and Jehovah was prevailed on by his prayer, and Rebekah his woman conceived. And the sons clashed with each other within her, and she said, "If so, why me?" and went to ask Jehovah. And Jehovah said to her, "Two nations are in your womb, and two peoples will divide from your belly, and [one] people will be stronger than [the other] people, and the greater will serve the lesser."*

Isaac prayed to Jehovah symbolizes the communing of the divinity that was the Son with the divinity that was the Father. *Because of his woman, since she was infertile* means that earthly divinity did not yet exist. *And Jehovah was prevailed on by his prayer* symbolizes that [earthly divinity] was put into effect. *And Rebekah his woman conceived* means that it came from divine truth, which served as its mother. *And the sons clashed with each other within her* symbolizes the struggle that is the theme here. *And she said, "If so, why this, and [why] me?"* symbolizes anguish. *And went to ask Jehovah* symbolizes a state of communion. *And Jehovah said to her* symbolizes what he perceived from his divine side. *Two nations are in your womb* means that the Lord's earthly plane conceived inward and outward goodness. *And two peoples will divide from your belly* means that truth would result. *And [one] people will be stronger than [the other] people* means that at first truth must take precedence over goodness-from-truth. *And the greater will serve the lesser* means that goodness based on truth must be inferior for the time being.

3285   *Isaac prayed to Jehovah* symbolizes the communing of the divinity that was the Son with the divinity that was the Father. This can be seen from the symbolism of *praying* as communing (prayer being nothing but a communication) and from the representation of *Isaac* as divine rationality. *Isaac* means the divinity that was the Son, or in other words, the Lord's rational mind when truth had united with it. *Jehovah* at this point means the divinity that was the Father.

This communication took place inside the Lord, because the Father was in the Son, and the Son, in the Father (John 14:10, 11).

3286   *Because of his woman, since she was infertile* means that his earthly divinity did not yet exist, as can be seen from the following: The *woman* symbolizes divine truth united to the goodness of the rational plane, this truth being represented by Rebekah, as shown in the previous chapter. And *infertile* means that the Lord's earthly divinity did not yet exist.

The case with the Lord's earthly divinity is that it came from the divine goodness in his rational mind (its father) and from the divine truth there (its mother). Before the existence of earthly divinity, truth on the rational plane is described as infertile—here, an infertile woman.

[2] With human beings the case is this: When we are being reborn, the Lord instills goodness—benevolence toward our neighbor—into our rational mind, and into this benevolence, or goodness, he introduces truth brought up out of our earthly self. At that point our earthly level has not yet been reborn, and we can recognize the fact from our inner or rational self's frequent battles with our outward or earthly self. As long as they fight, our earthly part is not regenerate, and when it is not regenerate, the truth we have in our rational part is infertile. As in general, so in every particular: on any issue over which our rational thinking conflicts with our earthly thinking, the truth in our rational mind is said to be barren.

[3] The main thing on which the work of regeneration hinges is the effort to bring our earthly self into correspondence with our rational self, not only as a whole but also in particular, and it is through our rationality that the Lord reduces our earthly self into correspondence.

His method is to instill goodness into our rational mind, plant seeds of truth in the soil of that goodness, and then through rational truth reduce the earthly plane to obedience. When it obeys, it corresponds; and the more it corresponds, the more we are reborn.

And Jehovah was prevailed on by his prayer symbolizes that [earthly divinity] was put into effect. This is clear without explanation, because when Jehovah is prevailed on, prayer comes true, or achieves its effect.

3287

Rebekah his woman conceived means that it came from divine truth, which served as its mother. This can be seen from the representation of *Rebekah* as divine truth in the Lord's rational mind (discussed in the previous chapter) and from the symbolism of *conceiving* as the first emergence of earthly divinity from its mother, so to speak. As noted just above, the Lord's earthly divinity arose from divine goodness in his rational mind, which served as its father, and from divine truth there, which served as its mother.

3288

Hardly anyone realizes this, especially since few know that the rational plane is different from the earthly plane. The only ones who do know are those who are truly rational, and the only ones who are truly rational are those whom the Lord regenerates. People who have not been reborn do not comprehend this, because to them the rational dimension is identical with the earthly dimension.

And the sons clashed with each other within her symbolizes the struggle that is the theme here. This can be seen from the symbolism of *clashing* as fighting and from that of the *sons* as goodness and truth on the earthly level. The representation of Esau and Jacob (the *sons*) as the Lord's earthly divinity—Esau being the goodness it possessed, and Jacob, the truth—will become clear from what follows.

3289

This clash or struggle is the focus of the chapter, and it has to do with relative importance. The question is whether goodness or truth comes first—that is, whether the neighborly kindness that grows out of goodness comes first or the faith that builds on truth does. From the earliest days of the spiritual church, many people in it have fought over this. Since it is the theme of the verses that follow, the text says that the sons clashed with each other within her, which symbolizes the struggle being discussed.

And she said, "If so, why this, and [why] me?" symbolizes anguish, as can be seen from the sense of the words, which suggest anguish—anguish over the clash or struggle between the brothers.

3290

If so means if that was what they were fighting about; *why this* means it was not something to fight over. *Me* (that is, *Why me?*) means that if they fought about it, they would not accept an inflow of rational truth, which would cause anguish.

3291   *And went to ask Jehovah* symbolizes a state of communion. This can be seen from the symbolism of *asking,* when it is the Lord who is said to ask, as communing, since Jehovah—the one being asked—was within him. On the narrative level, though, this communing is expressed as praying (§3285), while a state of communion is expressed as *asking.*

3292   *And Jehovah said to her* symbolizes what he perceived from his divine side. This follows from the above, and also from the symbolism of *saying* as perceiving (discussed in §§1791, 1815, 1819, 1822, 1898, 1919, 2080, 2506, 2515, 2552). For *Jehovah* to say, then, means to perceive from his divine side.

3293   *Two nations are in your womb* means that the Lord's earthly plane conceived inward and outward goodness. This can be seen from the symbolism of *nations* as different kinds of goodness, especially those fostered by the church (discussed in §§1159, 1258, 1260, 1416, 1849). Here they plainly symbolize goodness on the earthly plane, because Esau and Jacob, who were then in Rebekah's womb, represent the Lord's earthly divinity. (Later sections dealing with them will make this clear.) Like the rational plane, the earthly plane consists of goodness and truth. Goodness on the earthly level is everything connected with earthly desire, called pleasure. Truth there is everything qualifying as secular knowledge, called fact. The earthly dimension must embrace both if it is to be itself. Facts by themselves, without the pleasure that comes from our desire for them, are nothing. The earthly level receives its life from earthly delight, since only delight makes it possible for us to learn anything. The pleasure that constitutes goodness on the earthly level *is* something without facts but not anything more than a liveliness of the kind seen in children. If the earthly dimension is to be human, then, it must consist of both; the one quality is complemented by the other. The earthly dimension receives its life, though, from goodness.

[2] As far as the goodness being discussed here goes, it is of two kinds: deep and shallow. The deeper kind communicates with our intermediate or rational self; the shallower kind, with our outer self, or our physical abilities, giving life to our bodily senses and our actions. If we did not have lines of communication in both directions, we would have no rational life or physical life.

The interior communication is what remains to us after death, and there it creates an earthlike level of existence for us. Our spirit has an earthlike existence as well, you see, since our spiritual life rests on our earthly life as its ultimate foundation. After death we cannot immediately start thinking in spiritual terms, except by analogy with concepts from our earthly existence.

The outward communication is what we have when we are living in our bodies, but it ceases when our body dies.

These considerations now show what the two nations in Rebekah's womb symbolize: goodness of both a deeper and a shallower kind on the earthly plane.

In your womb, on an inner level, symbolizes conception, which is why I say they were conceived.

And two peoples will divide from your belly means that truth would **3294** result. This can be seen from the symbolism of a *people* as truth (discussed in §§1259, 1260), and from that of *dividing from your belly,* which means arising as a result.

Where the Word talks about birth, if the point of view is the mother's, the phrase used is "issuing from the womb"; if it is the father's, the phrase is "dividing from the belly" or viscera. The womb and genital area are mentioned in connection with different aspects of love—that is, of goodness. When the text speaks of dividing from someone's belly, on the other hand, it symbolizes the rise of truth. So in the current verse, when the focus is on goodness, it says, "Two nations will come from your womb," and when the focus is on truth, it says, "Two peoples will divide from your belly," which on an inner level symbolizes the rise of truth from goodness.

The verse mentions *two* peoples because just as goodness has deeper and shallower forms (§3293), so does truth. The deeper truth on the earthly level is that which unites with the deeper goodness there, but the shallower truth is that which unites with the shallower goodness there. The deeper truth is called earthly truth, but the shallower truth is described as sense-based.

By the Lord's divine mercy, later sections concentrating on Jacob will show how matters stand with these two kinds of truth, because Jacob represents both [§§3297, 3301, 3305, 3314].

And [one] people will be stronger than [the other] people means that **3295** at first truth must take precedence over goodness-from-truth. This is established by the symbolism of a *people* as truth (discussed just above in §3294) and from that of *being stronger than* as taking precedence.

The first time *people* occurs it symbolizes truth, but the second time, it symbolizes goodness-from-truth. Goodness-from-truth is goodness that rises out of truth. It first emerges in the form of truth, but it is called goodness because it looks like goodness. That is why a people also symbolizes this kind of goodness, which is called the first form of truth-based goodness to emerge.

If you want to gain some idea of this goodness, you need to know that until we are reborn, truth motivates us to do good. After rebirth, goodness motivates us to do good. To put it more clearly, before rebirth our intellect motivates us to do good, but afterward our will does. So in itself the goodness motivated by the intellect is not goodness but truth, whereas the goodness motivated by the will *is* goodness.

For example, take people who do not honor their parents but learn from the Ten Commandments that they ought to. When they first start to honor their parents, they are responding to the commandment, but since their honor is a response to a command, it is not intrinsically good, because it does not spring from love. It grows out of either obedience to or fear of the law. It is referred to as goodness-from-truth, but as it first emerges it is actually truth, because such people are acting on truth rather than goodness. When they honor their parents from love, though, it is a form of goodness.

And so on.

3296 *And the greater will serve the lesser* means that goodness based on truth must be inferior for the time being. This can be seen from the symbolism of the *greater* as goodness; from that of *serving* as being inferior; and from that of the *lesser* as truth.

How the case stands with all this will become clear from later passages depicting the situation in terms of Esau and Jacob. As I have said, Esau represents goodness, and Jacob, truth. The existence of a clash or struggle over their relative importance and dominance is portrayed on an inner level by Jacob's taking from Esau both the birthright and the blessing. The fact that he had them only for the time being, though, is evident from Isaac's prophetic utterance concerning Esau in Genesis 27:40: "And by your sword you will live, and your brother you will serve; and it will happen when you gain the dominance that you will tear his yoke off your neck."

[2] Obviously these words—"two nations are in your womb, and two peoples will divide from your belly, and [one] people will be stronger than [the other] people, and the greater will serve the lesser"—have a deeper sense, without which we cannot see what they mean. Later sections, which deal with the subject at length, will show that the meaning is the one given here.

However, without knowing how goodness and truth interrelate, how one is born from the other, and how our state changes when we regenerate, the reader will find it difficult to believe that the words contain this kind of meaning. The inner meaning does speak of the Lord and (in this passage) of the way he made his earthly level divine, but the representative meaning deals with human rebirth. A person's rebirth mirrors the Lord's glorification (§§3043, 3138, 3212); in other words, regeneration offers an image of the process by which the Lord glorified his human side, or made it divine. Just as the Lord changed his human condition into an entirely divine one, he completely changes our condition when he regenerates us, since he makes our old self new.

Genesis 25:24, 25, 26. *And her days were fulfilled to give birth, and look! Twins in her womb! And the first came out, ruddy, all of him, like a hairy coat, and they called his name Esau. And after this, his brother came out, and his hand was grabbing onto Esau's heel, and they called his name Jacob. And Isaac was a son of sixty years in [Rebekah's] giving birth to them.*

3297

Her days were fulfilled to give birth symbolizes the first stage of [putting earthly divinity into] effect. *And look! Twins in her womb!* means that both were conceived at the same time. *And the first came out, ruddy, all of him, like a hairy coat* symbolizes the earthly goodness of life taught by truth. *And they called his name Esau* symbolizes its character. *And after this, his brother came out* symbolizes truth. *And his hand was grabbing onto Esau's heel* symbolizes the lowest type of earthly goodness, to which it clung with some power. *And they called his name Jacob* symbolizes a theology composed of earthly truth. *And Isaac was a son of sixty years in [Rebekah's] giving birth to them* symbolizes the state of the Lord's divine rationality at that time.

Her days were fulfilled to give birth symbolizes the first stage of [putting earthly divinity into] effect, which can be seen from the symbolism of *days* as states (discussed in §§23, 487, 488, 493, 893, 2788). The fact that her days were *fulfilled to give birth* symbolizes the first stage of the effect.

3298

In its spiritual sense, *giving birth* has to do with goodness and truth and means that they emerge into existence (§§2621, 2629). Goodness and truth resemble babies in that they are conceived, grow in the womb, are born, and then mature. After conception, the active agent (the implanted seed) starts to produce an effect, which takes place in the womb. When these stages are complete and the time for delivery approaches, the effect begins its own existence. This is called the start of the effect, because the newborn child then commences to act seemingly on its own and to strive for the stage that is properly called the effect.

And look! Twins in her womb! means that both were conceived at the same time. This can be seen from the symbolism of *twins* as both—both

3299

the goodness represented by Esau and the truth represented by Jacob—and from that of *in her womb* as conception (discussed above in §3293).

To say a little more about the simultaneous conception of goodness and truth on the earthly plane: Any offspring receives its vital existence from its father and its emergence into reality from its mother. It must have both if it is to become anything. Goodness on the earthly plane is conceived by goodness on the rational plane, which serves as its father, and truth on the earthly plane is conceived by truth on the rational plane, which serves as its mother (§§3286, 3288). The goodness is what gives life, but it gives life by means of truth. The combination of the two is called the soul. Mainly it is goodness that is the soul, but truth clothes goodness with the equivalent of a tender little vessel, or body, so that goodness lies within truth.

That is what *twins in her womb* symbolizes.

3300   *And the first came out, ruddy, all of him, like a hairy coat* symbolizes the earthly goodness of life taught by truth. This can be seen from the meaning of *coming out* as being born; from the symbolism of *ruddiness* as the goodness in a life (discussed below); and from that of a *hairy coat* as truth on the earthly plane (also discussed below). The fact that this child was *first* means that goodness in its essence has priority, as noted above at §3299. The verse mentions the *hairy coat* in order to symbolize the truth that clothes goodness like a tender little vessel, or a body, as also noted above in §3299. In the Word's inner sense, a *coat* simply means that which clothes something else, which is why truth is compared to a garment (§§1073, 2576).

[2] The reason *ruddiness* or redness symbolizes the goodness in a life is that everything good comes of love, and real love is heavenly, spiritual fire. [The Word] even uses fire as a simile and metaphor for love (see §§933, 934, 935, 936), and it uses blood the same way (1001). Since both are red, the good that comes of love is symbolized by ruddiness or redness. The following passages in the Word demonstrate this. In the prophecy of Jacob, who by then was Israel:

> He will wash his clothing in wine and his robe in the blood of grapes;
> he will have *eyes redder than wine* and teeth whiter than milk. (Genesis 49:11, 12)

This is about Judah, who means the Lord here, as anyone can see. The clothing and robe mean the Lord's earthly divinity. The wine and the blood of grapes mean divine goodness and divine truth on the earthly plane, the former being called *eyes redder than wine,* and the latter, *teeth whiter than milk.* It is the union of goodness and truth in the earthly dimension that is depicted this way. [3] In Isaiah:

> Who is this who comes from Edom, *red as to his garment,* and his clothes like those of one *treading in the winepress?* (Isaiah 63:[1,] 2)

In this verse, Edom stands for the divine goodness of the Lord's earthly divinity, as a later discussion will show [§3322]. "Red as to his garment" means goodness growing out of truth; "clothes like those of one treading in the winepress" means truth growing out of goodness. In Jeremiah:

> Her Nazirites were whiter than snow; they were whiter than milk. *They were redder of bone than corals;* their polish was sapphire. (Lamentations 4:7)

The Nazirites represented the Lord in his divine humanity, particularly as to its earthly divinity. The goodness in his earthly divinity was represented by their being redder of bone than corals.

[4] Everything in the Jewish religion represented the Lord and therefore his kingdom and consequently goodness and truth (this being what his kingdom consists of). So since red symbolized goodness—especially goodness on the earthly level—the people of that religion were commanded to make the tabernacle covering of *red rams' skins* (Exodus 25:5; 26:14; 35:5, 6, 7, 23; 36:19) and the atonement water from the ashes of a burned *red cow* (Numbers 19:2 and following verses). Unless the color red symbolized something heavenly in the Lord's kingdom, it never would have been commanded that the rams and cow be red. Anyone who holds the Word sacred acknowledges that these details represented something holy.

Because this was the symbolism of the color red, the tabernacle coverings had threads of scarlet, red-violet, and blue-violet interwoven and tied on (Exodus 35:[5,] 6, [7, 23]).

[5] Almost everything has a negative sense as well, as noted many times [§§1066, 1142, 1232, 1662, 1834, 2455, 2460, 2686, 2709], so red does too. When its meaning is negative, it symbolizes the evil that comes of self-love, and again this is because fire is used as a simile and metaphor for the cravings of self-love (934 at the end, 1297, 1527, 1528, 1861, 2446), as is blood (374, 954, 1005). That is what red symbolizes in a negative sense, then, as in Isaiah:

Jehovah has said, "Even if your sins are like *scarlet,* they will grow as white as snow. Even if they are as *red as crimson,* they will be like wool." (Isaiah 1:18)

In Nahum:

The shield of belial's mighty men has *turned red;* his men of strength have been *clad in crimson.* In the *fire of torches* comes the chariot on that day. (Nahum 2:3)

In John:

Another sign was seen in heaven. Look: a *big red dragon* having seven heads, and on its heads, seven crowns! (Revelation 12:3)

In the same author:

I looked; there! A white horse! And one sitting on it, having a bow, who was given a crown. He went out conquering and in order to conquer. Then *there went out another horse, red,* and the one sitting on the horse was granted to take peace away from the earth and to [make people] kill each other; so a large blade was given to this one. Later there went out a black horse, and finally a pale horse whose name was death. (Revelation 6:2–8)

3301   The symbolism of a *hairy coat* as truth on the earthly plane can be seen from the following: A *coat* symbolizes that which clothes something else, so here it symbolizes truth, which clothes goodness. Truth resembles clothing (§§1073, 2576) or—what is almost the same thing—is a vessel for receiving what is good (1469, 1496, 1832, 1900, 2063, 2261, 2269). And *hairy* means the earthly plane and its truth.

The Word mentions *hair* a number of times, and in those passages it symbolizes the earthly dimension. The reason for the symbolism is that hair grows on a person's outermost surface, just as the earthly dimension grows outside the rational and other, deeper dimensions. While we are living in our bodies, it looks to us as though the earthly part is all there is to us, but that is far from true. Rather, our earthly aspects are an outgrowth from our deeper parts, just as hair is an outgrowth from our physical parts, and it issues from below the surface in much the same way. So when people who focused exclusively on the physical world during bodily life are presented to view in the other world in regard to this mindset, hair appears to cover almost their whole face. Hair also *represents* a person's earthly level. Attractive, neatly arranged hair represents an earthly level with goodness; bad-looking, messy hair, an earthly level without goodness. [2] This representation is the reason why, in the Word, hair symbolizes the earthly plane, and particularly truth on that plane. In Zechariah, for instance:

> It will come about on that day that the prophets will be shamed, each man because of his vision, when he prophesies; and they will not *put on a hair shirt* to deceive. (Zechariah 13:4)

The prophets stand for people who teach what is true; here, for those who teach what is false (§2534). A vision stands for truth; here, for falsity. A hair shirt stands for truth on the earthly level, and since this truth was not true but false, the verse says "to deceive." Prophets wore hair shirts in order to represent such truth, because it exists on the surface.

For the same reason, Elijah the Tishbite is called a *hairy man* in 2 Kings 1:8 because of wearing this kind of attire. And John, the last of the prophets, had a garment of *camel hair* (Matthew 3:4). Camels mean facts known to the earthly self (see §§3048, 3071, 3143, 3145), and facts are the earthly self's truth (3293).

[3] The symbolism of hair as truth on the earthly plane is quite clear from Nazirites, who were commanded the following: All the days of their Naziriteship, a *razor was not to pass over their head* until the days had been fulfilled in which they were abstinent for Jehovah. Afterward they were to take off the locks of their head and *cut the hair on the head of their Naziriteship* at the doorway of the meeting tent, and their *hair* they were to put onto the fire that was under the thanksgiving sacrifice (Numbers 6:5, 18, 19). Nazirites represented the Lord's divine humanity and therefore a person in the heavenly church, who is the Lord's likeness (§51); and their hair represented such a person's earthly plane. So when they were consecrated, they would shed their old or previous earthly self—the self they were born with—and put on a new one. This was symbolized by the fact that, when the days had been fulfilled in which they were abstinent for Jehovah, they were to *take off the locks* of their *head* and put them on the fire under the sacrifice. To be a heavenly person, you see, is to devote oneself to goodness, and from goodness to know all truth. It is never from truth, let alone mere fact, that heavenly people think and talk about goodness (see §§202, 337, 2715, 2718, 3246).

In addition, before heavenly people shed their old state, their earthly self is so strong in regard to truth that they are able to battle the hells. Truth is what fights, never goodness. The hells cannot begin to approach goodness, not even from far away. To see that truth and goodness are like this, consult §§1950, 1951.

[4] This shows why Samson's strength came *from his hair,* as said here:

> The angel of Jehovah appeared to Samson's mother, saying, "Watch!
> You will conceive and deliver a son, and a *razor will not go up onto his*
> *head;* the boy *will be God's Nazirite* from the womb." (Judges 13:3, 5)

Later, he told Delilah that *if he were shaved, his strength would withdraw*
from him and he would become weak. Then *when he was indeed shaved,* his
strength withdrew and the Philistines seized him. Afterward, when "the
hair of his head began *to grow* (since he had been shaved)," his strength
returned, so that he dislodged the pillars of the house (Judges 16:1–end).
Who can fail to see that these details contain a heavenly secret? None know
the secret except those who have learned about representative meanings.
Specifically, a Nazirite presents an image of a heavenly person, and while
he has his hair, he portrays the earthly level of such a person, who possesses
all the power and might of truth mentioned earlier. All representative acts
commanded by the Lord in those days had this same force and effective-
ness, so that is where Samson's strength came from. Still, he was not a
consecrated Nazirite, like those discussed above; he did not take on a state
of goodness in place of truth. The main reason his hair gave him strength
was that he represented the Lord, who fought and subdued the hells from
the truth present in his earthly self, before he adopted divine goodness and
truth all the way down to the level of that self.

[5] This clarifies the purpose of the following commandment:

> The high priest on whose head has been poured the anointing oil, and
> whose hand has been filled so that he can put on the clothes, *shall not*
> *shave his head* and shall not tear his clothes. (Leviticus 21:10)

And likewise concerning priest-Levites, in a passage on the new temple:

> Their *head they shall not shave,* and *their locks they shall not take off.*
> (Ezekiel 44:20)

The purpose was for them to represent the truth that grows out of goodness (which is called truth-from-goodness) in the Lord's earthly divinity.

The symbolism of hair as truth on the earthly plane can also be seen
in the prophetical parts of the Word, as for instance in Ezekiel:

> I have made you a young shoot in the field, so you have grown and
> matured into [the time of] the most beautiful of ornaments; your breasts
> have become firm, and *your hair has grown.* (Ezekiel 16:7)

This describes Jerusalem. In the current case it stands for the ancient church, which became corrupt over time. Her firm breasts stand for earthly goodness; the growth of her hair, for earthly truth. [6] In Daniel:

> I was looking, until thrones were overturned, and the Ancient One sat. His clothing was like white snow, and the *hair of his head was like clean wool.* His throne was like a fiery flame. (Daniel 7:9)

And in John:

> In the middle of the seven lampstands was one like the Son of Humankind, wearing a robe, and circled at the breasts with a golden band. His head, however, and his *hair* were *white,* like white wool, like snow; but his eyes, like a fiery flame. (Revelation 1:13, 14)

White hair like clean wool stands for the truth present in the Lord's earthly divinity. In the Word and in the rituals of the Jewish religion, genuine truth was represented by white, and because it develops out of goodness, it is called clean wool. The reason white represented truth, and red, goodness, was that truth consists of light, while goodness consists of the fire that sheds the light.

[7] Like everything else in the Word, hair also has a negative sense, in which it symbolizes truth on the earthly plane that has been perverted. In Isaiah, for example:

> On that day the Lord, *by a hired razor* in the fords of the river—by Assyria's monarch—will *cut the hair on the head* and the *hair* of the feet, and the *beard* he will also devour. (Isaiah 7:20)

In Ezekiel:

> Son of humankind, take yourself a sharp sword—a *barber's razor* you are to take for yourself—which you shall *pass over your head* and *over your beard.* Then you are to take yourself weighing scales and divide [the hair]. A third you are to burn with fire in the middle of the city. A third you are to strike on all sides with a sword. And a third you are to scatter to the wind. You shall take a little of it by number and tie it on your wings. Finally, you are to take some of it again and throw it into the middle of the fire and burn it with fire, from which fire will go out to the whole house of Israel. (Ezekiel 5:1, 2, 3, 4)

This depicts through representation the fact that there was no longer any deep or shallow earthly truth (the hair and beard). What destroyed it was evil cravings (symbolized by its being burned by fire), superficial logic (being struck with a sword all around), and false premises (being scattered to the wind). This passage involves the same thing as the Lord's teaching in Matthew about the seed, which is truth: some fell among thorns; some, onto stone; and some, onto the path (Matthew 13:1–9).

[8] The symbolism of hair as truth in the earthly self that is unclean and false was also represented by the following:

> If a captive enemy woman was to be married, she was to be brought into the house, *the hair of her head was to be shaved off,* her nails were to be cut, and the clothes of her captivity were to be removed. (Deuteronomy 21:12, 13)

> When Levites were consecrated, atonement water was spattered on them, and they passed a razor over all their flesh and washed their clothes and so were pure. (Numbers 8:7)

> Nebuchadnezzar was driven away from humanity to eat grass like cattle and to have his body soaked with the dew of the heavens, *until his hair grew like eagles' [feathers]* and his nails like birds' [claws]. (Daniel 4:33)

In the presence of leprosy, the *hair and beard* were observed for their color—white, reddish, yellow, black—as were the clothes; and people who were cured of their leprosy had to shave *all the hair of their head, beard, and eyebrows* (Leviticus 13:1–end; 14:8, 9). This symbolized false ideas, rendered unclean by profanation, which is what leprosy means in an inner sense.

[9] As for baldness, it symbolized an earthly plane containing no truth at all, as in Isaiah:

> [Moab] goes up to Bayith and Dibon, the high places, to weep over Nebo; and over Medeba, Moab will wail. *On all its heads is baldness; every beard has been shaved.* (Isaiah 15:2)

In the same author:

> In place of braided work will be *baldness;* a burn in place of beauty. (Isaiah 3:24)

The youths who said, "*Go on up, you baldhead! Go on up, you baldhead!*" to Elisha and were mauled by bears from the forest (2 Kings 2:23, 24) represented people who blaspheme the Word as a work devoid of truth. Elisha represented the Lord as the Word (§2762).

From this you can also see how much power representations had at that time.

And they called his name Esau symbolizes its character—the character
of goodness on the earthly plane—as the following shows: *Calling someone's name* such and such (or calling someone by a name) means knowing what the person is like, so it symbolizes the character of a thing,
as discussed in §§144, 145, 440, 768, 1754, 1896, 2009, 2724, 3006. And
wherever names come up in the Word, in an inner sense they symbolize
something (1224, 1888), so the name Esau does too.

3302

The meaning of Esau as the Lord's earthly divinity when divine goodness was first conceived in it can be seen from prior discussion and from
what follows concerning Esau. It can also be seen from other passages in
the Word. However, Esau and Edom symbolize almost the same thing (the
difference being that Edom means the Lord's earthly divinity in regard to
goodness that has doctrinal truth linked to it). Confirmation from Scripture, by the Lord's divine mercy, will come below at verse 30 [§3322], where
Esau is called Edom.

And after this, his brother came out symbolizes truth. This can be seen
from the symbolism of a *brother* as goodness, and also as truth. These
are called brothers. Neighborly love is the brother of faith, or in other
words, goodness is the brother of truth (see §367); so faith, for its part,
is the brother of neighborly love, or in other words, truth is the brother
of goodness. Moreover on the earthly plane, a desire for goodness is called
a brother and a desire for truth a sister (§3160), and they are also called a
husband and his woman, or a man and his woman. The pairing always
relates to the conditions under discussion, however.

3303

And his hand was grabbing onto Esau's heel symbolizes the lowest type
of earthly goodness, to which it clung with some power, as can be seen
from the following: A *hand* symbolizes power (as discussed in §878) and is
ascribed to truth (3091). *Grabbing* means clinging. A *heel* symbolizes the
lowest part of the earthly level (as discussed in §259). And *Esau* represents
goodness on the earthly level (as discussed in §3302). So *his hand was grabbing onto Esau's heel* clearly symbolizes the lowest type of earthly goodness,
to which truth clung with some power.

3304

[2] Here is why truth clung with some power to the lowest kind of goodness on the earthly plane: When the earthly dimension, or the earthly self, is
being reborn, the goodness and truth in it is conceived from the rational
plane. Or rather, it is conceived through the rational plane from the spiritual, through the spiritual plane from the heavenly, and through the heavenly plane from the Divine. So the inflow progresses, starting on the divine
level and continuing in order until it comes to rest on the bottom level of
the earthly dimension—the worldly and bodily level. When the lowest part

of our earthly dimension has been flawed by the heredity we received from our mother, truth cannot become one with goodness but only cling to it with some strength. Truth does not become one with goodness until the flaw has been dealt with. That is why goodness but not truth is born into humans, with the result that babies lack any knowledge of truth. Truth has to be *learned* and then united with goodness (see §§1831, 1832). Consequently the text also says they clashed with each other within Rebekah, or in other words, struggled (§3289). As a result, truth supplants goodness from the moment of its conception, just as the text says that Jacob supplanted Esau:

> Is it because they call his name Jacob? And *he has supplanted me these two times.* (Genesis 27:36)

And in Hosea:

> . . . to bring on Jacob the consequences of his ways; according to his deeds will [Jehovah] repay him. In the *womb he supplanted his brother.* (Hosea 12:2, 3)

[3] People who focus on the narrative alone, unable to shift their minds from it, see this phrase and others leading up to it simply as foreshadowing what took place between Esau and Jacob. Subsequent parts of the story confirm them in their view. The Lord's Word, though, is such that the narratives have their logical sequence and the spiritual contents of the inner meaning have theirs. Our outer self looks at the former; our inner self, at the latter. So the two—the outer self and the inner—correspond to one another, and the Word provides the link. The Word is the union of earth and heaven, as shown many times [§§1775, 2899, 3085]. So whenever we read the Word reverently, our outer self on earth unites with our inner self in heaven.

3305 *And they called his name Jacob* symbolizes a theology composed of earthly truth. This can be seen from the symbolism of *calling someone's name* such and such (or calling someone by a name) as a characteristic, as discussed just above in §3302. The characteristic that *Jacob* represents is a theology composed of earthly truth. This can be seen from Esau's representation as the goodness of life taught by earthly truth (§3300) and from the large number of passages in the Word that mention Jacob.

There are two things that make up the earthly plane (just as there are two that make up the rational plane and in fact the entire person). One has to do with life; the other, with doctrine. The one that has to do with life is a matter of the will; the one that has to do with doctrine is a matter of the intellect. The former is called goodness; the latter, truth. That goodness is what Esau represents, but the truth is what Jacob represents. To put the same thing another way, the goodness of life taught by earthly truth is what Esau represents, and a theology composed of earthly truth is what Jacob represents.

Whether you talk about the goodness of life taught by earthly truth and a theology of earthly truth, or about people with those characteristics, it amounts to the same thing. A well-lived life and true theology cannot exist without someone to exist *in*. Without that someone, they are abstractions—and the abstractions nevertheless revolve around a person in whom they may exist. In the current verse, then, Jacob symbolizes people with a theology consisting of earthly truth.

[2] Readers who stick to the literal meaning believe that when the Word mentions Jacob, it means the whole people descended from Jacob. In consequence, they attribute to that people everything the Word says about Jacob, whether as narrative or as prophecy. The Word is divine, though—mainly because everything in it relates not to one nation or one people but to the entire human race as it is, as it was, and as it will be. Even more universally, it relates to the Lord's kingdom in the heavens; and in the highest sense it relates to the Lord himself. That is what makes the Word divine. If it applied only to one nation, it would be human, and the only divinity it would contain would be the sanctity present in that nation's worship. Anyone can recognize that the people called Jacob had no sanctity in their worship.

Another piece of evidence that Jacob does not mean Jacob and Israel does not mean Israel in the Word is that almost every prophetical passage mentioning Jacob also mentions Israel. No one can know the specific import of either except from a deeper layer of meaning that hides within it secrets of heaven.

[3] On an inner level, then, as the following passages show, Jacob symbolizes a theology consisting of earthly truth—that is, people who possess such a theology, whatever nation they belong to—and in the highest sense, he stands for the Lord. In Luke:

> The angel said to Mary, "You will conceive in your womb and deliver a son and call his name Jesus. He will be great and will be called the Child of the Highest One. And the Lord God will give him the throne of David, his father, so that he may rule over the *house of Jacob* forever; and his kingdom will have no end." (Luke 1:31, 32, 33)

As anyone can see, the house of Jacob here did not mean the Jewish nation or people, because the Lord's reign was not over that people but over everyone in the universe who has faith in him and, from that faith, love for their neighbor. The Jacob mentioned by the angel, then, clearly did not mean the people of Jacob. Consequently the seed of Jacob, children of Jacob, land of Jacob, inheritance of Jacob, monarch of Jacob, and God of Jacob mentioned so many times in the Old Testament Word do not mean those things.

[4] The same is true of Israel, as in Matthew:

An angel of the Lord appeared in a dream to Joseph, saying, "When you have woken up, take the boy and his mother and escape into Egypt"— so that there would be a fulfillment of the saying by the prophet when he said, "Out of Egypt I called my child." (Matthew 2:13, 14, 15)

The prophet himself puts it this way:

When Israel was a boy, then I doted on him, and out of Egypt I called my child. (Hosea 11:1)

Israel here is obviously the Lord, and yet the literal meaning would lead the reader to think only that the boy Israel means Jacob's first descendants, who went to Egypt and later were called up out of there.

Something similar is true in other places mentioning both Jacob and Israel, even though the literal meaning does not make it clear. In Isaiah, for instance:

Listen, *Jacob, my servant,* and *Israel, whom I have chosen:* This is what Jehovah has said, your maker and the one who formed you from the womb (he helps you): Don't be afraid, *my servant, Jacob,* and *Jeshurun,* whom I have chosen, because I will pour water out on thirsty land, and brooks on dry ground. I will pour my spirit out on your seed and my blessing on your offspring. This one will say, "I am Jehovah's," and this one will *call himself by Jacob's name,* and that one will write "Jehovah's" on his hand and *surname himself by Israel's name.* (Isaiah 44:1, 2, 3, 5)

Clearly Jacob and Israel stand for the Lord here, and Jacob's seed and offspring stand for people who believe in the Lord. [5] In the oracular statement concerning Israel's sons in Moses:

Joseph will sit in the firmness of his bow, and his arms and hands will be strengthened by the hands of *mighty Jacob,* from whom comes the Shepherd, the *Stone of Israel.* (Genesis 49:24)

In this passage, mighty Jacob and the Stone of Israel likewise plainly stand for the Lord. In Isaiah:

> My glory I will not give to another. Pay attention to me, *Jacob*, and *Israel, whom I called:* I, the same—I am first; I am also last. (Isaiah 48:11, 12)

Here too Jacob and Israel mean the Lord. In Ezekiel:

> I will take Joseph's stick, which is in the hand of Ephraim and of the tribes of Israel, his companions, and add them on top of him to Judah's stick, and make them into one stick, to be one in my hand. I will take the *children of Israel* from among the nations where they have gone and gather them from round about and lead them onto their own land and make them into one nation in the land, on the *mountains of Israel;* and one monarch will serve them all as monarch. And they will no longer be two nations, and they will no longer be split into two kingdoms again. *My servant David* will be monarch over them, and there will be a single shepherd for them all. Then they will live on the land that I gave *to my servant Jacob,* on which your ancestors lived. They will live on it—they and their children and their children's children—forever. *David my servant* will be chief over them forever. I will strike a pact of peace with them; it will be an eternal pact with them. I will place them and multiply them and put my sanctuary in their midst forever. So will my dwelling place be among them, and I will become their God, and they will become my people, so that the nations may know that I, Jehovah, consecrate *Israel* to be my sanctuary in their midst forever. (Ezekiel 37:19, 21, 22, 24, 25, 26, 27, 28)

Again it is quite plain that Joseph, Ephraim, Judah, Israel, Jacob, and David do not mean those men but (in the highest sense) divinely spiritual qualities that are in the Lord and that are the Lord's in his kingdom and church. Anyone can see that David will not be their monarch and chief forever, as it says, but that David means the Lord (§1888). Obviously it is not Israel that will be gathered from the places where it was scattered, be sanctified, and have God's sanctuary put in its midst forever, as it says. Instead it is the people that Israel symbolizes in a representative sense, which means all the faithful, as is known. [6] In Micah:

> I will unfailingly gather all of you, *Jacob;* I will unfailingly assemble the *survivors of Israel.* I will set them together like Bozrah's sheep. (Micah 2:12)

The meaning is similar. In Isaiah:

> *Jacob* will make those who are to come take root; *Israel* will bloom and flourish, and the face of the world will be filled with produce. (Isaiah 27:6)

Again the meaning is similar. In the same author:

> This is what Jehovah, who redeemed Abraham, has said to the *house of Jacob:* "No longer will *Jacob* be ashamed and no longer will his face pale. Because when he sees his children—the work of my hands—in his midst, they will revere my name and revere the *Holy One of Jacob,* and the *God of Israel* they will fear, and those wandering in spirit will know intelligence." (Isaiah 29:22, 23, 24)

In the same author:

> Jehovah has said to his anointed, Cyrus, "whose right hand I have grasped, to subdue the nations before him (and [the sword-belts on] the hips of monarchs I will loosen, in order to open doors before him, and so that the gates will not be closed): I myself will go in front of you and straighten out the crooked places; bronze doors I will shatter, and iron bars I will sever. I will give you the treasures of hideaways and the secret riches of hidden places, so that you may recognize that I am Jehovah, *the one called by your name, the God of Israel,* because of *my servant Jacob,* and *Israel* my chosen. I have called you by your name; I have surnamed you, though you did not know me." (Isaiah 45:1, 2, 3, 4)

This too is clearly about the Lord. In Micah:

> In the end of days the mountain of Jehovah's house will be set up as the head of the mountains. Many nations will go and will say, "Come, and let us go up to Jehovah's mountain, to the *house of Jacob's God,* so that he can teach us about his ways; and we will go in his paths. Because from Zion will issue instruction, and Jehovah's word from Jerusalem." (Micah 4:1, 2)

In David:

> Jehovah loves Zion's gates more than all *Jacob's dwellings;* glorious things are being proclaimed in you, city of God. (Psalms 87:1, 2, 3)

In Jeremiah:

> They will serve Jehovah their God and *David their king,* whom I will raise up for them. And you, *Jacob my servant,* don't be afraid, and

don't be terrified, *Israel*, because—look!—I am rescuing you from afar. (Jeremiah 30:9, 10)

In Isaiah:

Pay attention to me, you islands, and listen carefully, you people from far away: Jehovah called me from the womb; from my mother's belly he remembered my name and said to me, "*You are my servant, Israel*, in whom I will become glorious." (Isaiah 49:1, 3)

In the same author:

Then you will delight in Jehovah, and I will carry you to the heights of the earth and feed you with the *inheritance of Jacob*. (Isaiah 58:14)

In the same author:

From Jacob I will produce *seed*, and from Judah, the heir to my mountains, so that the ones I have chosen may own it and my servants may live there. (Isaiah 65:9)

[7] In the highest sense in all these places, Jacob and Israel mean the Lord. In a representative sense, they mean the Lord's spiritual kingdom and his church—true theology and a good life being what make the church a church. Jacob means people who involve themselves in the outward aspects of that church, while Israel means those who involve themselves in its inward aspects.

These passages and many others show that Jacob never means Jacob, Israel never means Israel, just as Isaac does not mean Isaac, nor Abraham, Abraham, anywhere they are mentioned. In Matthew, for instance:

Many will come from east and west and recline at [the table] with *Abraham* and *Isaac* and *Jacob* in the kingdom of the heavens. (Matthew 8:11)

In Luke:

You will see *Abraham, Isaac,* and *Jacob* and all the prophets in God's kingdom. (Luke 13:28)

And in the same author:

Lazarus was taken by the angels into *Abraham's embrace*. (Luke 16:22)

No one in heaven knows about Abraham, Isaac, and Jacob. When people on earth read these words, the inhabitants of heaven think only of the

Lord's divinity and divine humanity. They view the idea of reclining at the table with Abraham, Isaac, and Jacob simply as being with the Lord; being in Abraham's embrace, as being *in* the Lord. The reason it was phrased in these terms was that in those days people were cut off from deeper levels of meaning. For all they knew (or wanted to know), everything in the Word was literally true. When the Lord spoke to them in a literal way, they could believe, and the inner meaning (which unites us to him) could then be present.

These considerations, then, show what the Old Testament Word means by the God of Jacob and the Holy One of Israel: the Lord himself. To see that the God of Jacob is the Lord, read 2 Samuel 23:1; Isaiah 2:3; 41:21; Micah 4:2; Psalms 20:1; 46:7; 75:9; 76:6; 81:1, 4; 84:8; 94:7; 114:7; 132:2; 146:5. To see that the Holy One of Israel is the Lord, read Isaiah 1:4; 5:19, 24; 10:20; 12:6; 17:7; 29:19; 30:11, 12, 15; 31:1; 37:23; 41:14, 16, 20; 43:3, 14; 45:11; 47:4; 48:17; 49:7; 54:5; 55:5; 60:9, 14; Jeremiah 50:29; Ezekiel 39:7; Psalms 71:22; 78:41; 89:18.

3306   *And Isaac was a son of sixty years in [Rebekah's] giving birth to them* symbolizes the state of the Lord's divine rationality at that time, as can be seen from the discussion of numbers above in §§3252, 3275.

What the number sixty involves can be seen from its factors, five and twelve (five times twelve being sixty). For the meaning of five, see §§649, 1686; for that of twelve, §3272. It can also be seen from six and ten (six times ten being sixty). For the meaning of six, see §§720, 737, 900, and for that of ten, §§576, 2284, 3107. Again, it can be seen from two and thirty (two times thirty being sixty). For the meaning of two, see §§720, 900, 1335, 1686, and for that of thirty, §2276. Since sixty comprises these factors—all of them standing for stages of divine rationality in the Lord at that time—it encompasses them in order. The meanings are apparent to angels in the clear light they receive from the Lord, but to humans (especially those who reject the idea that secrets might be concealed in scriptural numbers) they cannot be explained, for two reasons. One is people's disbelief. The other is the impossibility of reducing the many ideas the numbers hold within them to a system people are capable of understanding.

*   *   *   *

3307   Genesis 25:27, 28. *And the boys grew up, and Esau was a man knowledgeable in game, a man of the field; and Jacob was an upright man inhabiting tents. And Isaac loved Esau because there was game in his mouth; and Rebekah was loving toward Jacob.*

The boys grew up symbolizes a first stage. *And Esau was a man knowledgeable in game* symbolizes a well-lived life resulting from sensory truth and factual truth. *A man of the field* symbolizes a well-lived life resulting from doctrine. *And Jacob was an upright man* symbolizes truth. *Inhabiting tents* symbolizes worship that goes with it. *And Isaac loved Esau because there was game in his mouth* means that divine goodness in the Lord's divine rational mind loved the goodness that grows out of truth. *And Rebekah was loving toward Jacob* means that divine truth in the Lord's divine rational mind loved a theology filled with truth.

The boys grew up symbolizes a first stage—a stage at which goodness **3308** and truth unite, as can be seen from the following: When *growing up* is connected with the rise and progress of goodness and truth, it symbolizes the first stage of that progress, as discussed below. And *boys* symbolize goodness and truth, goodness being represented by the boy Esau, and truth, by the boy Jacob, as shown above.

Goodness and truth resemble babies, in that they are conceived, grow in the womb, are born, grow up, and increase in age until they reach full maturity. Conception, gestation, and birth belong to their rise; growing up and aging till they reach full maturity belong to their progress. The stage of progress, in which goodness and truth unite, follows birth, and its start is what *growing up* symbolizes here. This stage begins right after birth and continues all the way to the end of life, and in people devoted to goodness, it continues beyond bodily life to eternity. In other words, angels are always developing.

And Esau was a man knowledgeable in game symbolizes a well-lived **3309** life resulting from sensory truth and factual truth. This can be seen from the representation of *Esau* as the goodness in a life (discussed above [§3300]) and from the symbolism of a *man knowledgeable in game* as people who love truth (discussed here). A *knowledgeable man* has to do with a desire for truth, or with people who have that desire, but *game* [or hunting] symbolizes truth itself—truth known to the earthly self that leads to goodness. Truths known to the earthly self are what are called facts (§3293), and there are two main kinds, or levels: facts gained through the senses, and facts learned as facts. Hunting, in this case, symbolizes both. Sense impressions are what children are first awake to; facts are what they focus on as they grow up. No one can possess factual truth without first acquiring sensory truth, because factual ideas are made up of sensory truth. Building on facts, people can learn and understand still deeper truth, which is called doctrine. Doctrine is what a "man of the field" symbolizes, as discussed just below.

[2] The reason hunting symbolizes sensory and factual truth, which people are taught and those who lead good lives respond to emotionally, is that in a broad sense, "hunting" means the animals hunted—rams, kids, goats, and so on—and these stand for spiritual kinds of goodness (see §§2088, 2830). Another reason is that hunting weapons, which were quivers, bows, and arrows, mean true doctrines (§§2686, 2709). The words spoken to Esau by his father Isaac in a later chapter show that such things are meant by hunting [or game]:

> Please take up *your weapons,* your *quiver* and your *bow,* and go out to the field and *hunt me game,* and make me delicacies such as I have loved. (Genesis 27:3, 4)

So do his words to Jacob (who was then playing the part of Esau) in the same chapter:

> Bring it to me and let me *eat of my son's game* so that my soul can bless you. (Genesis 27:25)

This shows what hunting means.

[3] As a result, hunting means teaching and also persuading, in either sense—either from a passion for truth or from a passion for falsity. It means teaching and persuading from a passion for truth in Jeremiah:

> I will bring them back onto their land, which I gave their ancestors. Look! I am sending for many fishers, who will fish them. And after that I will send for *many hunters,* who will *hunt them* on every mountain and on every hill and out of the openings of rocks. (Jeremiah 16:15, 16)

The fishers stand for teachers whose teaching is based on sensory truth (§§40, 991). The hunters stand for teachers whose teaching is based on factual truth and also on doctrine. Hunting on every mountain and on every hill means teaching people who love goodness and people who love truth. (For this symbolism of mountains and hills, see §§795, 796, 1430.) Hunting in the field, as in Genesis 27:3, involves something similar.

In Ezekiel, hunting means using one's powers of persuasion out of a love of falsity:

> Look now, regarding your padding, with which *you are hunting souls, there,* to [make them] fly away, and I will rip them off your arms and send away the souls *that you are hunting,* souls [that you are hunting] to [make them] fly away. I will rip up your mantles and rescue my people from your hand, and they will no longer be in your hand *for hunting.* (Ezekiel 13:18, 19, 20, 21)

For the symbolism of hunting in this sense, see §1178; but this type of hunting is usually said to be done with nets.

A man of the field symbolizes a well-lived life resulting from doctrine, as can be seen from the symbolism of a *field*. Many passages in the Word mention land, the ground, or a field, and in a good sense land symbolizes the Lord's kingdom in the heavens and on earth. So it symbolizes the church, which *is* the Lord's kingdom on earth. The symbolism of the ground is the same except for having a narrower meaning. (See §§566, 662, 1066, 1067, 1068, 1262, 1413, 1733, 1850, 2117, 2118 at the end, 2928.) A field symbolizes the same things but in a still narrower sense (368, 2971). Doctrine does not make the church a church unless it focuses on a well-lived life as its goal— that is, unless doctrine is united with living a good life—so a field mainly symbolizes that kind of life. If the goodness in a life is to be a matter of religion, it has to have doctrine from the Word planted in it. Leading a good life is possible without doctrine, but the goodness is not yet a matter of religion, so it is not truly spiritual, except in the potential it has for becoming so. That is the kind of goodness that exists in the lives of non-Christians, who do not have the Word and therefore do not know the Lord.

3310

[2] The symbolism of a field as a well-lived life that is a planting ground for tenets of faith (spiritual truth belonging to the church) is plain to see in the Lord's parable in Matthew:

> A sower went out to sow, and while he sowed, some [seeds] fell on the hard path, and the birds came and ate them. Some fell on the rocky places, where they did not have much soil, so they quickly came up, because they did not have any depth of earth, but when the sun rose they were scorched, and because they did not have any root, they withered. Some fell among the thorns, and the thorns came up and choked them. Some, however, fell on the good earth and yielded fruit—some a hundredfold, some sixtyfold, some thirtyfold. Those who have an ear to hear should listen. (Matthew 13:[3]–9; Mark 4:3–9; Luke 8:5–8)

This passage speaks of four kinds of earth or ground in a field, or in other words, in the church. Clearly the seed in the church is the Lord's Word and therefore truth, which is called religious truth, and the good earth is neighborly kindness. The good in us is what receives the Word. A hard path is falsity, stony ground is truth lacking any root in goodness, and thorns are evil urges.

[3] Here is the way things stand with a well-lived life resulting from doctrine (what a man of the field symbolizes): When we are being reborn,

we first do good from doctrine, because on our own we do not know what is good. Doctrines about love and charity are what we learn from. They teach us who the Lord is, who our neighbor is, what love is, what charity is, and consequently what goodness is. At this stage we love truth and are what are called *men of the field*. Later, when we have been reborn, we do not do good from doctrine but from love and charity, because by then we have entered into the goodness itself that we learned about from doctrine; and we are then what are called *people of the field*.

It is like people who are naturally drawn to adultery, theft, and murder but learn from the Ten Commandments that such things come from hell and so refrain from them. At that stage they are moved by the commandments because they are afraid of hell, and the commandments and the Word teach them extensively how they should structure their lives. When they do good, they do it under command. When they are governed by goodness, though, they start to loathe the adultery, theft, and murder they previously felt drawn to, and at that stage they no longer do good under command but from the goodness now present in them. In the first stage they learn from truth about goodness, but in the second, they teach truth from goodness.

[4] The case is the same with spiritual truth, which is called doctrine and consists of more inward commands. Doctrine is the earthly self's inner truth. Its first truth is sensory truth, its second truth is factual truth, and its inner truth is doctrine. Inner truth is founded on factual truth, since we are incapable of forming or retaining any idea, notion, or concept of it except through factual truth. Factual truth, in turn, is founded on sensory truth, since we cannot grasp it except through sensory truth. Both of the latter kinds, factual and sensory, are what a man knowledgeable in game symbolizes, while doctrine is what a man of the field symbolizes. That is the order in which they arise in us. Until we reach adulthood, then, and acquire doctrine through sensory and factual truth, we cannot be reborn. Only through concepts formed from facts and sense impressions can we corroborate doctrinal truth. Absolutely everything we think about—even the deepest mystery of faith—comes with some earthly, sense-based image, even though we usually have no idea of the true character of that image. In the other life, if we wish, it can be displayed for our minds or even (if we so desire) for our eyes to see. In the other world, such things can be presented to view. This seems unbelievable but is still true.

3311   *And Jacob was an upright man* symbolizes truth. This is established by Jacob's representation as a theology consisting of earthly truth (§3305) and from the symbolism of *uprightness*, which is attributed to people who focus on truth and therefore is attributed to truth itself (612).

Inhabiting tents symbolizes worship that goes with it. This is established by the symbolism of *tents* as holy love and the worship that grows out of it (§§414, 1102, 2145, 2152). Tents symbolize holy worship because religious people in the earliest times, who loved the Lord and therefore worshiped him reverently, lived and held their sacred worship in tents. At that point, holy love and the holy worship that goes with it began to be represented by tents. As a result, the people were commanded to make a tent according to the pattern shown to Moses on Mount Sinai and to start worshiping God in it [Exodus 25:[8,] 40; 26:30]. Another result was the Feast of Booths, and the purpose of living in tents during that feast was to represent the sacred worship that the people of the heavenly church had engaged in. This shows that inhabiting tents symbolizes worship.

3312

And Isaac loved Esau because there was game in his mouth means that divine goodness in the Lord's divine rational mind loved the goodness that grows out of truth, as can be seen from the following: *Isaac* represents divine goodness in the Lord's divine rationality, as noted in §§3012, 3013, 3194, 3210. *Esau* represents goodness in the Lord's earthly divinity, as noted in §§3300, 3302, and below, where Edom is discussed [§3322]. And *game* symbolizes a well-lived life resulting from earthly truth, as noted in §3309. *In his mouth* means that he responded to it with earthly desire. In the Word, whatever lies deep within and proceeds from goodness is said to be in the heart, while whatever lies on the surface and proceeds from truth is said to be in the mouth. Goodness that comes of truth (here represented by Esau and symbolized by game) is relatively shallow; it is an object of earthly desire and grows out of truth. So it is said to have been in Isaac's mouth.

3313

And Rebekah was loving toward Jacob means that divine truth in the Lord's divine rational mind loved a theology filled with truth, as can be seen from the following: *Rebekah* represents divine truth in the Lord's divine rationality, as discussed in §§3012, 3013, 3077, and throughout the previous chapter, wherever she was the focus. And *Jacob* represents a theology composed of earthly truth, and—in the highest sense—truth in the Lord's earthly divinity, as discussed in §3305.

3314

Here is why divine goodness in the Lord's rational mind loved the goodness in his earthly mind, while divine truth in his divine rationality loved the truth in his earthly mind: There are a goodness and truth that make up the rational dimension, and a goodness and truth that make up the earthly dimension. Rational goodness influences earthly goodness directly (without truth) and indirectly (by means of truth). It influences earthly truth by means of rational truth (indirectly) and by means of earthly goodness (again, indirectly). That is why goodness on the rational level has a tighter bond with goodness on the earthly level than with truth there—a bond symbolized by Isaac's love for Esau. It is also why rational truth has a tighter bond with truth on the earthly level than with goodness there—a bond symbolized by Rebekah's love for Jacob.

[2] These ideas are admittedly hard to grasp, especially since on this subject not even the most general concepts of all are known to the world, including the scholarly world. People do not realize, for instance, that the rational plane is something separate from the earthly plane, or that both consist of goodness and truth. Still less do they see that the influence the rational plane exerts on the earthly plane enables us to think and to intend to do what we are thinking about. If these broadest of notions are unfamiliar, people will hardly comprehend the kind of influence described above. Still, the subject is one that angels have light on and perceive countless things in. The perception gives them pleasure, which they become aware of when led at the same time to think about the human side of the Lord's divinity.

While they are still in the body, people with goodness and an angelic quality about them also receive some light as a gift from the Lord in these and similar matters. When people do not have goodness, though, thinking about such things bores them, and the more they think about them in relation to the divinity of the Lord's humanity, the more bored they are. It is better, then, for people like this to take their mind off it, because they understand none of it whatsoever. In fact they reject it, saying in their heart, "What does it matter to me? It's not going to bring me rank or wealth."

3315   Genesis 25:29, 30. *And Jacob cooked soup, and Esau came from the field, and he was worn out. And Esau said to Jacob, "Let me please swallow some of the red dish, this red dish, because I am worn out." Therefore they called his name Edom.*

Jacob cooked soup symbolizes a jumble of doctrines. *And Esau came from the field* means studying how to live a good life. *And he was worn out* symbolizes a state of combat. *And Esau said to Jacob* symbolizes what the Lord perceived from goodness on the earthly level. *Let me please swallow some of the red dish* symbolizes a longing for doctrine. *This red dish* means which seemed to be good. *Because I am worn out* here as before symbolizes a state of combat. *Therefore they called his name Edom* symbolizes the resulting quality of the goodness [in his earthly self] when doctrinal truth was linked to it.

Jacob cooked soup symbolizes a jumble of doctrines. This can be seen from the representation of *Jacob* as a theology composed of earthly truth (discussed in §3305) and therefore as doctrines known to the earthly self, and from the symbolism of *soup* as a confused mass of them. *Cooking* soup means jumbling them together, because in the original language the term has strictly to do with soup, as if you said "he souped a soup," or in other words, jumbled it together.

3316

The first stage of union between goodness and truth is what is depicted in this and the following verses to the end of the chapter.

[2] The first stage when we are being reborn—that is, when truth is uniting with goodness in us—is one in which we first of all amass doctrinal truth in no fixed order in our earthly self, or in the repository there called the memory. The doctrines then filling our memory can be compared to some confused, disordered hodgepodge, or a kind of chaos. The goal, though, is to reduce them to order. Anything that is later reduced to order starts out this way. That is what the soup that Jacob cooked (or jumbled together) symbolizes.

The doctrines are reduced to order not by themselves but by a goodness that acts on them. The extent and nature of the goodness acting on them determines the extent and nature of the order to which they are reduced. When goodness first wishes and longs for doctrines, with a view to uniting with them, it appears in the form of a desire for truth. That is what is meant by "Esau said to Jacob, 'Let me please swallow some of the red dish, this red dish.'"

[3] These ideas do seem rather distant from the literal meaning, but when we read the story and take it literally, the angels then present with us form no picture whatever of soup, of Jacob, of Esau, of a red dish, or of swallowing some of it. Instead they form a spiritual image, which is entirely different, and distant from the earthly one. The earthly image turns into a spiritual one instantly. The same is true with all other images in the Word. For example, when we read about bread there, angels do not picture bread but instantly think of heavenly love (love for the Lord) and its ramifications instead. When we read in the Word about wine, they do not picture wine but rather spiritual love (love for one's neighbor) and its ramifications. So when we read about soup, they do not picture soup but doctrines that have not yet been united to goodness and therefore the disorder of their arrangement.

This reveals the nature and quality of angels' thought and perception and the width of the gap between theirs and ours. If we thought this way when doing something reverent like taking Holy Supper—if we perceived love for the Lord in place of bread, and love for our neighbor in place of wine—we would be thinking and perceiving as angels do. They would then come closer and closer to us until eventually we could share thoughts with each other—but only so far as we humans also dedicated ourselves to goodness.

[4] The symbolism of *soup* as a jumble can also be seen in Kings from the story of Elisha and the sons of the prophets:

> Elisha went back to Gilgal, and there was famine in the land, and the sons of the prophets were sitting before him. And he said to his boy, "Put on the large pot and *cook soup* for the sons of the prophets." And one went out into the field to gather edible plants and found a vine of the field and gathered bitter apples of the field from it, filling his garment, and came and chopped it up into the *pot of soup,* because they did not know [what it was]. And they poured it out for the men to eat, and it came about in their eating *of the soup* that they shouted and said, "Death in the pot, man of God!" and could not eat. And he said, "Then take some meal," and he put it into the pot and said, "Pour out for the people"; and they ate, and there was nothing bad in the pot. (2 Kings 4:38, 39, 40, 41)

The inner meaning of this passage is completely different from its literal meaning. The famine in the land symbolizes a scarcity of knowledge concerning goodness and truth (§1460). The sons of the prophets symbolize people who teach (2534). The soup symbolizes a mess of facts randomly thrown together. Meal symbolizes truth that develops out of goodness, or something spiritual that develops out of something heavenly (2177). So Elisha's throwing meal into the pot, leaving nothing bad in it, means that the disarray was cured by spiritual truth from the Lord's Word—since Elisha represented the Lord and his Word (2762). Without this spiritual meaning, the story of the soup and the way the meal changed it would not have been worth mentioning in such a sacred document as the Word. The miracle occurred in order to represent these things, as did the rest of the miracles in the Word, which all conceal divine matters within them.

3317   *And Esau came from the field* means studying how to live a good life. This can be seen from the representation of *Esau* as the goodness of life taught by earthly truth (discussed at §3300) and from the symbolism of *coming from the field* as studying goodness. Meditating in a field means thinking about goodness (3196), because a *field* means the goodness in a church (2971).

And he was worn out symbolizes a state of combat. This can be seen **3318** from the symbolism of *worn out* or of weariness as the state that comes after combat. Here it means a state during combat because the theme is the state in which goodness was united with truth in [the Lord's] earthly self. The symbolism of weariness here as a state of combat can be seen only from the train of thought in the inner meaning, and mainly from the consideration that goodness cannot unite with truth in the earthly self without combat or—to say the same thing another way—without times of trial.

A few words are needed to show how matters stand here, specifically how they stand with human beings. [2] A human being is nothing else but an organ or vessel that receives life from the Lord; we do not live on our own (§§290, 1954, 2021, 2536, 2706, 2886–2889, 3001). The life that flows into us from the Lord comes from his divine love. This love, or the life that radiates from it, flows in and bestows itself on the vessels in our rational and earthly minds. Such vessels in us face away from the life force because of the evil we inherit by birth and the evil we ourselves acquire by committing it. However, so far as it can do so, the inflowing life repositions the vessels to receive itself.

The vessels in our rational and earthly selves are what are called truths. In itself, truth is nothing but a perception of the way these vessels change shape and of the alterations of state under which the various changes occur, taking place as they do in indescribable ways in the most refined substances (§2487). Goodness itself—which possesses life from the Lord, or *is* life—is what flows in and realigns the vessels.

[3] These vessels, whose shape is ever changing, face backward and upside down, away from life, as just mentioned. Clearly they need to be brought into alignment with life, or subordination to it. This can in no way be done as long as we remain in the state we were born in and reduce ourselves to, because our vessels are not subordinate to life. They stubbornly resist life and oppose the heavenly paradigm by which life acts, hardening themselves against it. The good that moves them—the good they obey—is the good sought by love for oneself and one's worldly advantage. The crude heat burning within this love gives such vessels

their character. Before they can become submissive, then, and fitted for accepting any of the life belonging to the Lord's love, they have to soften, and the only way they can be softened is through times of trial. Tribulation takes away elements of self-love, contempt for others, and therefore vain pride, and elements of a consequent hatred and vengefulness as well. So when these evils are somewhat lessened and conquered by our trials, the vessels start to become yielding and obedient to the life of the Lord's love, which is constantly flowing into us.

[4] The result is that goodness in our rational self, first, and in our earthly self, second, starts to unite with the truth there. Truth, as noted, is nothing but a perception of changes in shape that conform with constantly altering states, and perception is a function of the inflowing life force. That is why our trials (our spiritual struggles) regenerate us, or in other words, remake us and give us a different character ever after. We become gentle, humble, sincere, and chastened at heart.

This now reveals the use that times of trial serve: they enable goodness not only to flow in from the Lord but also to make the vessels in us obedient and in this way become united with them. (For truth as a vessel for receiving goodness, see §§1496, 1832, 1900, 2063, 2261, 2269.)

Since the current verse, then, deals with the union of goodness and truth in the earthly self, and the first stage of union comes about through the struggles of spiritual trial, *he was worn out* clearly symbolizes states of combat.

[5] As for the Lord, though, who is the subject in the highest sense here: through the most severe combats of spiritual trial, he reduced everything in himself to divine order, to the point that nothing whatever remained of the humanity he had received from his mother (§§1444, 1573, 2159, 2574, 2649, 3036). So he was not made new, as other people are, but was made completely divine. When we become new through rebirth, we still keep in us an inclination to evil and even actual evil, but the influence of the vital force in the Lord's love withholds us from it with tremendous power. The Lord, however, entirely rid himself of all the evil he had inherited from his mother and made himself divine, even down to these vessels called truth. That is what the Word calls his glorification.

3319   *And Esau said to Jacob* symbolizes what the Lord perceived from goodness on the earthly level, as is established by the following: *Saying* means perceiving, as noted in §§1791, 1815, 1819, 1822, 1898, 1919, 2080, 2862. *Esau* represents goodness on the Lord's earthly level, as noted in §§3300,

3302, and just below [3322], where Edom is the subject. And *Jacob* represents truth on the earthly level, as noted in §3305, which is what the perception was about.

Let me please swallow some of the red dish symbolizes a longing for doctrine, and *this red dish* means which seemed to be good, as the following shows: *Swallowing* means being communicated and united, as noted in §3089, so *let me please swallow* means longing to unite with truth, or doctrine. And *red* symbolizes something good, as noted in §3300—here, something that seemed to be good. Even though the doctrines appear in their outward form to be organized as something good, inside they are still a jumble (3316).

Another reason these details are mentioned is that they are the reason Esau had the name Edom. The word for "red" in the original language is *edom,* and the idea was for Edom to symbolize the goodness to which doctrinal truth was joined.

Because I am worn out symbolizes a state of combat. This can be seen from the symbolism of *worn out* or weariness as a state of combat, discussed above at §3318. The reason *worn out* is repeated is to confirm that spiritual combat—inward trial—is what unites goodness to truth in the earthly self.

The way the union of goodness and truth in the earthly self generally works is that our rational mind accepts truth before our earthly mind does. The point is to enable life from the Lord (which is composed of love, as just mentioned [§3318]) to flow in through the rational level into the earthly level, organize it, and reduce it to obedience. The rational dimension is purer; the earthly dimension, coarser. In other words, the rational is deeper, and the earthly, shallower. It is orderly for the rational to flow into the earthly but not the reverse, as anyone can learn. [2] As a result, our rational part can adapt to truth and accept it before our earthly part can, as is plain from the fact that in a person who is regenerating, the rational self fights a lot with the earthly self, or in other words, the inner self fights with the outer. The inner self can see truth and also form an intent to act on it while the outer self refuses and resists, as people also recognize.

Our earthly self contains facts that for the most part trace their origin to sensory illusions, and although they are false, we believe them to be true. What is more, there are countless concepts that our earthly self does not grasp, because it lives in relative shadow and darkness, and what it does not grasp it believes to be either nonexistent or contrary to fact.

3320

3321

We have cravings that develop out of self-love and materialism, and whatever justifies those cravings we describe as truth. When we allow them to control us, everything that grows out of them is contrary to spiritual truth.

We base our logic on falsities that have been stamped on us from our earliest years.

Until we shed our bodies, moreover, we have a very clear picture of what is in our earthly self but not of what is in our rational self. This also convinces us to believe that the earthly dimension is all there is and to dismiss anything that does not fall within our earthly awareness.

[3] As a consequence of these facts and others, our earthly self accepts truth much later and with much more difficulty than our rational self does. The result is combat, which lasts quite a long time and does not end until the vessels in our earthly self for receiving goodness have been softened by inward trial, as shown above in §3318. Truth is just a vessel for receiving goodness (§§1496, 1832, 1900, 2063, 2261, 2269), and the vessel becomes harder the more rigid we are about truth, as described [in §3318]. The more rigid we are, the heavier the battle, if we are to be reborn.

Accordingly, since this is what happens in the earthly self to unite truth with goodness there, and it is accomplished through the struggles of inward trial, the text repeats *I am worn out*.

3322   *Therefore they called his name Edom* symbolizes the resulting quality of the goodness [in his earthly self] when doctrinal truth was linked to it. This can be seen from the symbolism of *calling someone's name* such and such (or calling someone by a name) as a quality (discussed in §§144, 145, 1754, 1896, 2009, 2724, 3006) and from the representation of *Edom*. The Word mentions Esau and Edom in many places, and in those places Esau symbolizes goodness on the earthly plane before doctrinal truth has been fully united to it. Esau also symbolizes a good life resulting from the influence of the rational mind. Edom, on the other hand, symbolizes goodness on the earthly plane when doctrinal truth *has* been attached to it. In a negative sense, Esau symbolizes the evil of self-love before falsity has been fully attached to it, while Edom symbolizes the evil of that love when falsity *has* been attached to it. Most names in the Word also have a negative meaning, as shown many times before [§§1066, 1142, 1232, 1662, 1834, 2455, 2460, 2686, 2709, 3300], because through various types of adulteration, the same things that started out good and true in different religions degenerated with the passage of time into evil and falsity.

[2] This symbolism of Esau and Edom can be seen from the following passages. In Isaiah:

> Who is this who *comes from Edom*, spattered in his clothes, from *Bozrah*, honorable in his apparel, marching in the abundance of his strength? Why is his garment *red* and why are his clothes like those of one treading in the winepress? "The winepress I have trodden alone, and from among the peoples no man was with me; I looked around, but none was helping, and I was astounded that no one was supporting me, and my arm saved me." (Isaiah 63:1, 2, 3, 5)

In this passage, Edom is obviously the Lord. It is also clear that Edom is the divine goodness in the Lord's earthly divinity, because the theme is the union of goodness and truth in the Lord's humanity and the struggles and trials through which he united them. The clothes mean truth known to his earthly self, or truth on a relatively low plane (see §2576), and their redness means the goodness in his earthly self (3300). *The winepress I have trodden alone, and from among the peoples no man was with me; I looked around, but none was helping; I was astounded that no one was supporting me, and my arm saved me,* depicts the way the Lord united truth on that level with goodness, by his own might, through the battles of inward crisis. An arm means power (§878). [3] In Judges:

> Jehovah, when you *came out from Seir,* when you *marched from the field of Edom,* the earth trembled, the heavens also showered; yes, the clouds showered, mountains streamed down. (Judges 5:4, 5)

Marching from the field of Edom symbolizes almost the same thing as coming from Edom—the phrasing we just saw in Isaiah. Likewise in Moses:

> Jehovah came from Sinai and *dawned from Seir on them.* (Deuteronomy 33:2)

In the same author:

> I see him, but not yet; I view him, but he is not near. A star will rise out of Jacob and a scepter will spring up from Israel, and *Edom will be an inheritance,* and an *inheritance* will *Seir* be for its enemies, and Israel

will be doing mightily and will rule from Jacob and destroy the rest of the city. (Numbers 24:17, 18, 19)

This is about the Lord's Coming into the world. His human nature is being called a star out of Jacob and a scepter from Israel. As an inheritance, Edom and Seir stand for divine goodness in the Lord's earthly divinity. The prophecy that it would become an inheritance for its enemies means that this goodness would take the place of whatever was present on the earthly plane before. Its subsequent dominion over truth on that plane is meant by its ruling over Jacob and destroying the rest of the city. Jacob is truth on the earthly level (§3305), and a city is doctrine (402, 2268, 2449, 2712, 2943, 3216). Goodness is said to rule over both when they become secondary and subordinate to it. Until then they are called enemies, because they constantly fight back, as shown above in §3321. [4] In Amos:

> On that day I will raise up David's fallen tent, and wall up their breaches, and its wreckage I will restore; and I will rebuild [the city] as in the days of old, so that they may possess the *survivors of Edom* and all the nations on whom my name has been put. (Amos 9:11, 12)

David's tent stands for the church and its worship of the Lord. The survivors of Edom stand for people in the church who have goodness. The nations on whom his name has been put stand for people outside the church who have goodness—nations meaning people with goodness (§§1259, 1260, 1416, 1849). In David:

> *On Edom* I will set my shoe. Who will bring me to the stronghold city? Who will lead me *right to Edom?* Will not you, God? (Psalms 60:8, 9, 10)

Edom stands for goodness on the earthly level. The fact that the goodness is on that level is clear from the symbolism of a shoe as the lowest part of the earthly dimension (§1748). [5] In Daniel:

> At the time of the end, the king of the south will clash with [the king of the north]; therefore the king of the north will storm onto him with chariot, and flood in and invade. And when he comes into the beautiful land, many will cave in. Still, they will be snatched from his hand: *Edom* and Moab and the first fruits of the children of Ammon. (Daniel 11:40, 41)

The subject here is the final stage of the church. The king of the north stands for falsity or, alternatively, for people in falsity. Edom stands for people who possess simple goodness, which is the kind of goodness that exists in people who make up the Lord's more superficial church. So do Moab and the children of Ammon (§2468), and since both Edom and Moab symbolize people with goodness, many passages mention both. The difference is that Edom means goodness on the earthly plane with doctrinal truth linked to it, while Moab is earthly goodness of a kind that also exists with people in whom they are not linked. The former and the latter look the same on the outside but not on the inside.

[6] From this it is now evident why Deuteronomy 23:7 says, "You shall *not treat Edomites as an abomination,* because they are your kin, nor Egyptians, because you were immigrants in their land." An Edomite symbolizes goodness on the earthly plane, and an Egyptian symbolizes truth on the earthly plane, or in other words, facts (§§1164, 1165, 1186, 1462), so both are referred to in a good sense here. It is also evident why Jehovah told Moses that they were *not to join battle with the children of Esau,* and that the children of Jacob would not be given any of their land, down to the print of the sole of a foot (Deuteronomy 2:4, 5, 6).

[7] In an opposite sense, though, Esau and Edom represent people who turn away from goodness because they wholly despise truth and resist the introduction of any religious truth—usually as a result of self-love. These people, then, are the ones Esau and Edom symbolize in a negative sense. The same phenomenon was represented by the episode in which the king of Edom went out with many people and a strong hand and refused to let Israel pass through his border (Numbers 20:14–22). In various scriptural passages, Esau and Edom depict the way this evil—the evil of self-love—closes the door to the truths of the faith and consequently to teachings of truth. They also depict the condition of the church when it acts the same way. In Jeremiah, for instance:

> Against *Edom:* Is there no more wisdom in Teman? Has counsel perished from the intelligent? Has their wisdom become rank? Run away! Dedan's inhabitants turned their backs; they took themselves into the depths to live, *because Esau's calamity* I will bring over him. I myself will *strip Esau naked,* I will expose his secret places, so that he cannot hide. His seed has been laid waste, and his kin, and his neighbors. Leave your orphans (I myself will keep them alive) and your widows; let them trust in me. *Edom* will become a wasteland; everyone who passes through it will be dumbfounded and hiss over all its plagues. (Jeremiah 49:7, 8, 10, 11, 17, and following verses)

[8] In David:

> They say, "Let the name of Israel be mentioned no more." For they consult in their hearts together; the *tents of Edom,* and the Ishmaelites, and Moab and the Hagarites are striking a pact over you. (Psalms 83:4, 5, 6)

In Obadiah:

> This is what the Lord Jehovih has said to *Edom:* "Here, I have made you small among the nations; you have been greatly despised. The *pride of your heart* has deceived you; you are living in crevices of rock, in the height of your seat, who say in your heart, 'Who will pull me down to the earth?' *If you exalt yourself* like an eagle, and if you put your nest among the stars, from there I will pull you down." How are [the people of] *Esau sought out,* their hidden treasures tracked down? On that day, won't I destroy the *sages from Edom,* and the intelligent *from the mountain of Esau,* so that your mighty ones will be dismayed, Teman, and a man be cut off *from the mountain of Esau* by slaughter? Because of the violence against your brother Jacob, shame will cover you, and you will be cut off forever. The house of Jacob will be a fire and the house of Joseph a flame, and the *house of Esau* will serve as stubble, and they will ignite them and consume them, and nothing will be left to the *house of Esau,* and southerners will inherit the *mountain of Esau.* (Obadiah verses 1, 2, 3, 4, 6, 8, 9, 10, 18, 19, 21)

Edom and Esau here stand for evil in the earthly self, rising out of self-love, which despises and rejects all truth, bringing about its own destruction. [9] In Ezekiel:

> Son of humankind, set your face against *Mount Seir* and prophesy against it and say to it, "This is what the Lord Jehovih has said: 'I am against you, *Mount Seir,* and I will stretch my hand out against you and make you a wasteland and a devastation, because you hold eternal enmity and pour the children of Israel out on the hands of a sword, in the time of their destruction, in the time of the end of their wickedness, because you have said of two nations and of two lands, "They are mine, and we will inherit it," although Jehovah is there. And you will know that I, Jehovah, have heard all your insults that you have spoken against the mountains of Israel. A wasteland *Mount Seir* will be, and all *the whole of Edom.*'" (Ezekiel 35:2, 3, 4, 5, 8, 9, 10, 12, 15)

In an obvious negative sense here, Edom means people who despise, reject, and insult spiritual goodness and truth (the mountains of Israel). [10] In the same author:

> This is what the Lord Jehovih has said: "If I do not speak in my fiery zeal over the survivors of the nations and *over all Edom,* who have given my land to themselves as an inheritance with the joy of all their heart, with contempt of soul, . . . !" (Ezekiel 36:5)

The meaning is similar. Giving themselves the land as an inheritance stands for destroying the church—that is, the goodness and truth that belong to the church. [11] In Malachi:

> The word of Jehovah against Israel: "I loved you," Jehovah has said, "and you say, 'In what way have you loved us?' Isn't *Esau brother to Jacob?* And I love Jacob, and *Esau* I hate, and I make its mountain a wasteland." (Malachi 1:1, 2, 3)

In this instance Esau stands for evil in the earthly self, which does not open up to spiritual truth (Israel; see §3305) or doctrinal truth (Jacob; see §3305) and is therefore laid waste (that is, hated; this is exactly what hating means, as the scriptural quotations above concerning Esau and Edom in a good sense show). Conversely, when truth does not allow itself to be linked with goodness, the criticism goes against Jacob, as in Hosea:

> . . . to bring on Jacob the consequences of his ways; according to his deeds will [Jehovah] repay him. *In the womb he supplanted his brother.* (Hosea 12:2, 3)

Genesis 25:31, 32, 33. *And Jacob said, "Sell me, as of today, your birth-right." And Esau said, "Look, I am on the way to dying, and what point is the birthright to me?" And Jacob said, "Swear to me as of today"; and he swore to him and sold his birthright to Jacob.*   **3323**

Jacob said symbolizes a true theology. *Sell me, as of today, the birthright* means that for the time being, a truthful theology was apparently more important. *And Esau said, "Look, I am on the way to dying,"* means that [goodness on the earthly level] would rise again after that. *And what point is the birthright to me?* means that [this goodness] had no need for first place at that point. *And Jacob said* symbolizes a true theology. *"Swear to me as of today"; and he swore to him* symbolizes confirmation. *And sold his birthright to Jacob* means that [goodness] yielded priority meanwhile.

3324   *Jacob said* symbolizes a true theology. This can be seen from the representation of *Jacob* as a theology composed of earthly truth (discussed in §3305) or, what is the same, as people who adopt a true theology.

These verses, to the end of the chapter, deal with the right of priority. They ask whether that right belongs to truth or to goodness, or in other words, to a true theology or to a good life, or again to faith so far as it consists of true theology or to neighborly love so far as it consists in a good life. When we draw conclusions on the basis of earthly perception, we believe that faith so far as it consists of true theology is more important than neighborly love so far as it consists in a good life. This is because we can see how we take in truth, which is a matter of theology, but not how we take in goodness, which is a matter of life. After all, truth enters along an outward path (the path of the senses), but goodness enters along an inward path. What is more, we cannot help viewing truth—which teaches us what goodness is—as more important than goodness. In addition, truth is the means and the guide to our reformation. In fact, the goodness in us is perfected to the degree that truth can unite with it, which means that goodness is perfected by truth. An even larger factor is this: We can dedicate ourselves to truth, thinking and speaking from truth and doing so with apparent fervor, even though we do not also dedicate ourselves to goodness, trusting that truth will save us.

These considerations and many others cause those of us who judge by our sensory and earthly self to imagine that truth, which is a matter of faith, is more important than goodness, which is a matter of love for others. However, every one of those considerations is an argument based on illusions that we adopt because of the way things seem to our sensory and earthly self. [2] Goodness, which belongs to life, really comes first. Goodness in life is the actual soil in which truth needs to be sown, and the quality of the soil determines how the seed—religious truth—is received. Truth can first be stored away in the memory, admittedly, like seed in its hull or in the crop of a tiny bird, but it does not become part of us unless the ground has been prepared. The quality of the ground (the goodness) determines how it sprouts and bears fruit.

However, see the many previous explanations of this topic, which I cite here to indicate what goodness and truth are, and to show that the priority goes to goodness and not to truth:

[3] Why people do not distinguish clearly between goodness and truth: 634. Goodness flows in along an inner route unknown to us, but truth is acquired by an outer route that we know about: 3030, 3098. Truth is a

vessel for receiving what is good: 1496, 1832, 1900, 2063, 2261, 2269, 3068, 3318. Goodness recognizes its proper truth, to which it is united (3101, 3102, 3179); painstaking examination is made and great care taken to prevent falsity from uniting with goodness, or truth with evil (3033, 3101, 3102). Goodness creates its own truth to unite with, because it does not acknowledge anything as true that does not harmonize with it: 3161. Truth is simply the product of goodness: 2434. Truth is the form of goodness: 3049. [4] Truth holds inside itself an image of goodness, and [perceives] in goodness a likeness of itself, from which it springs: 3180.

The seed of truth takes root in the goodness that characterizes charity: 880. Faith cannot possibly exist except within a life of faith, or in other words, within love and charity: 379, 389, 654, 724, 1608, 2343, 2349. It is possible to view the truth that composes religious doctrine from the standpoint of love and charity but not the reverse (2454); to view things from the standpoint of faith and not of love and charity is to look behind and turn backward (2454). Truth comes alive in accord with the goodness an individual has and therefore in accord with the state of innocence and charity that exists in a person: 1776, 3111. Religious truth can be accepted only by people who devote themselves to goodness: 2343, 2349. People who have no love for others cannot acknowledge the Lord, so they cannot acknowledge religious truth. If they claim to believe, they are being either superficial or hypocritical: 2354. There is absolutely no faith without neighborly love: 654, 1162, 1176, 2417.

Wisdom, understanding, and knowledge are the offspring of love for others: 1226. Angels have understanding and wisdom because they have love: 2500, 2572. [5] Angelic life consists in charitable deeds, and angels are forms of charity: 454, 553. Love for the Lord is the Lord's likeness, and charity for our neighbor is his image: 1013. It is through love for the Lord that angels perceive everything involved in faith: 202.

Nothing but love and desire is alive: 1589. People who possess mutual love, or charity, possess the Lord's life: 1799, 1803. Love for the Lord and for one's neighbor is heaven itself: 1802, 1824, 2057, 2130, 2131. The state of love and charity in us determines the extent of the Lord's presence with us: 904. The whole of the Ten Commandments and all tenets of faith are contained in neighborly love: 1121, 1798. If we do not love our neighbor, a knowledge of religious doctrine makes no difference, because doctrine looks to neighborly love as its goal: 2049, 2116. We cannot acknowledge truth or have faith if we do not possess goodness: 2261. The holiness of our worship depends on the type and amount of religious truth grafted onto our charity: 2190.

[6] There is no salvation through faith, only through a life of faith, which is charity: 2228, 2261. The kingdom of heaven is for those who have the faith that comes of love for others: 1608. All in heaven are viewed in terms of their love for others and the faith that grows out of that love: 1258. People do not get to heaven except through heartfelt goodwill: 2401. People with faith are saved, as long as there is goodness in their faith: 2261, 2442. Faith that is not rooted in a good life dies away completely in the other world: 2228. If a purely intellectual faith saved us, we would all go to heaven, but since our life stands in the way, we cannot: 2363. People who hold it as a principle that faith alone saves us pollute the truth with their false premise: 2383, 2385. The fruit of faith is good deeds, which is charity, which is love for the Lord, which is the Lord: 1873. The fruit of faith is the fruit of goodness, which is the fruit of love and charity: 3146. [7] Confidence or trust—which is called the faith that saves us—cannot exist except in people who live good lives: 2982. Goodness is the vital energy of truth: 1589. At what point truth is said to come alive: 1928. Goodness flows from the Lord into every kind of truth, but it is extremely important that the truth be genuine: 2531. The more we push evil and falsity off to the side, the more influence goodness and truth from the Lord have on us: 2411, 3142, 3147. Goodness cannot exert an influence on truth as long as we engage in evil: 2388. Truth is not true until we receive it from goodness: 2429. There is a marriage of goodness and truth in absolutely everything: 2173, 2508. We desire goodness as part of our life; we desire truth as a guide to life: 2455 at the end. Truth leads to goodness, and truth originates in goodness: 2063.

[8] A [divine] inflow calls truth up out of the earthly self, lifts it up, and grafts it onto the goodness in the rational self: 3085, 3086. When truth unites with goodness, it becomes our own: 3108. If truth is to unite with goodness, the intellect and the will must consent, and when the will consents, there is union: 3157, 3158. The rational mind acquires truth by means of knowledge, but truth becomes our own when it unites with goodness, at which point it becomes part of our will and focuses on life as its goal: 3161. Truth is introduced and united to goodness not just once but throughout life and beyond: 3200.

Just as light produces nothing without warmth, the truth that leads to faith produces nothing without goodness inspired by love: 3146. What the idea of truth without goodness is like, and what kind of light that idea sheds in the other world: 2388. A detached faith resembles winter light, while the faith that comes of love for others resembles the light of spring: 2231. People who detach religious truth from charity in their actions cannot have conscience: 1076, 1077. The reasons why people started to isolate faith from charity and to say that faith saves us: 2231.

[9] When we are being reborn, the Lord instills goodness into the truth we know: 2063, 2189. It is not truth but goodness that regenerates us: 989, 2063, 2189, 2697. When we are being reborn, the Lord meets us halfway and fills the truth we know with charitable kindness: 2063. People who live good lives but do not know the truth of the faith—non-Christians and children, for instance—welcome that truth in the other life and are reborn (989; concerning non-Christians, 932, 1032, 2049, 2284, 2589–2604; concerning children, 2290, 2291, 2292, 2293, 2302, 2303, 2304). We are reborn through a desire for truth, but once reborn, we act on a desire for goodness: 1904. In a person who is regenerating, seed can take root only in goodness: 880, 989. The light of a person reborn radiates from neighborly love: 854. The same truth is true in one person, less true in another, and even false in others. It all depends on the goodness in their lives: 2439. Differences among childhood goodness, uninstructed goodness, and a knowing goodness: 2280. Just who can come to know truth and gain faith, and who cannot: 2689.

[10] Religion does not exist unless a well-lived life has doctrinal truth planted in it: 3310. It is not doctrine but neighborly love that makes the church: 809, 916, 1798, 1799, 1834, 1844. The church's doctrines are worthless if people do not live according to them: 1515. A theology of faith is a theology of charity: 2571. Charity makes the church, not faith detached from charity: 916. By looking at the love we have for others, we can see whether our worship has any depth: 1102, 1151, 1153. The Lord's church varies throughout the world in regard to truth, but charity unites it: 3267. The church would be one if we all loved each other, even though we differ on ritual and doctrine: 809, 1285, 1316, 1798, 1799, 1834, 1844. Out of many religions we would have one if we all viewed charity rather than faith as the most important element of religion: 2982. There are two doctrines: the doctrine of charity and the doctrine of faith. The ancient church possessed doctrines concerning charity, but today they are among the knowledge that has been lost: 2417. [11] How little truth people know when they do not live by the doctrines concerning charity: 2435. And since people today consider faith the essential ingredient of religion, they do not even see or notice what the Lord so often said about love and charity: 1017, 2371. Goodness,

which is a matter of love for the Lord and charity for our neighbor, comes above and before truth, which is a matter of faith—not the other way around: 363, 364.

3325   *Sell me, as of today, your birthright* means that for the time being, a truthful theology was apparently more important, as can be seen from the following: *Selling* means claiming as one's own. *As of today* means for the time being. On an inner level of the Word, *today* symbolizes that which is never-ending and eternal (§2838), and to avoid that meaning, the text says *as of* today. So *as of* also means apparently. And the *birthright* symbolizes priority—specifically, priority for the true theology that Jacob represents (§3305).

[2] Having the priority of the birthright means being first not only in time but also in supremacy. The question is which will dominate, goodness or truth. Until truth unites with goodness or (to say the same thing another way) until people under the sway of truth have been reborn, they always believe that truth comes before goodness and outranks it, and at the time that appears to be the case. However, when truth unites with goodness in them—that is, when they have been reborn—they see and perceive that truth is later and lower. Then goodness has dominion over truth in them. This is symbolized by the words of his father Isaac to Esau:

> Watch: of the fatness of the earth your dwelling will consist, and of the dew of the sky from above. And by your sword you will live, and your brother you will serve; and it will happen *when you gain the dominance that you will tear his yoke off your neck*. (Genesis 27:39, 40)

[3] In the church, though, there are more people who are not regenerating than who are, and people who are not regenerating draw conclusions on the basis of appearances. So there was a controversy going back to ancient times about the relative priority of truth and goodness. The prevailing opinion among people who had not been reborn (and among people who had not been *fully* reborn) was that truth came first. They were not yet able to perceive what was good, and as long as we cannot perceive goodness, we live in shadows of ignorance on the subject.

People who *have* been reborn, though, are actually immersed in goodness, which brings them understanding and wisdom, so they are able to discern what is good. They can also tell that what is good comes from the Lord, that it flows in by way of the inner self into the outer, that it flows in constantly, without any awareness on our part, that it links up with doctrinal truth in the memory, and consequently that goodness by its very nature is prior, even though it had not seemed so before.

This, then, is the origin of the quarrel over which of the two came first and which was uppermost—a quarrel represented by Esau and Jacob, by Perez and Zerah (Judah's sons by Tamar; Genesis 38:28, 29, 30), and later by Ephraim and Manasseh (Joseph's sons; Genesis 48:13, 14, 17, 18, 19, 20). The reason was that a spiritual church by its very nature needs to be introduced to goodness by truth. At that introductory point it lacks any intuitive awareness of goodness, except the amount and kind of goodness that lies at the heart of a desire for truth. At the time, this goodness cannot be distinguished from the pleasure of self-love and materialism, which also lurks within the desire for truth and is believed to be good.

[4] The status of goodness—meaning the good that comes of love for the Lord and of love for our neighbor (since only the good that rises out of these is genuinely good)—as firstborn can be seen from the fact that goodness contains life. Truth does not, except for the life that comes from goodness, and goodness flows into truth to bring it alive, as is fairly clear from statements and explanations above in §3324 concerning goodness and truth. So everyone who loves the Lord and exhibits charity toward others is called a firstborn. People like this were also represented by firstborns in the Jewish religion, or at least were meant by firstborns in a secondary sense, since [in the highest sense] the Lord is the firstborn and they are his likenesses and images.

[5] The fact that the Lord in his divine humanity is the firstborn can be seen in David:

> The name he will give me is "You are my Father, my God, and the Rock of my salvation." Indeed, I will *make him the firstborn,* high above the monarchs of the earth. I preserve my mercy toward him forever, and my pact will be firm for him, and I will make his seed everlasting and his throne like the days of the heavens. (Psalms 89:26, 27, 28, 29)

This is about the Lord. And in John:

> . . . from Jesus Christ, who is the faithful witness, the *firstborn of mortals,* and chief of the earth's monarchs. (Revelation 1:5)

To fulfill what had been written about him and represented, he really was born as a *firstborn* (Luke 2:7, 22, 23).

[6] The Lord also refers to people who love him and show charity for their neighbor as firstborn, because they are his likenesses and images. This can be seen in John:

> The hundred forty-four thousand bought from the earth—they are the ones who have not been defiled with women, since they are virgins. They are the ones who follow the Lamb where he goes. They were bought from among humankind, *first fruits [the firstborn]* to God and to the Lamb. And in their mouth deceit was not found, because they are spotless before God's throne. (Revelation 14:[3,] 4, 5)

The hundred forty-four (twelve times twelve) stands for people who have a faith born of neighborly love (§3272). The thousands stand for a countless number (or in other words, all) of them (2575). Virgins stand for the goodness belonging to love for the Lord and charity for one's neighbor (2362, 3081) and therefore for people with innocence. Following the Lamb also symbolizes innocence, since the Lord is called the Lamb because of his innocence. That is why they are called first fruits, or the firstborn.

[7] These quotations show that the Lord in his divine humanity was represented in the Jewish religion by firstborns, as were people who love him, since they are in the Lord. Firstborns in the Word represent two things, though: the Lord's divine love in its heavenly form, and his divine love in its spiritual form. His divine love in its heavenly form is his love relative to a heavenly religion, or to the people in such a religion, who are called heavenly because of their love for him. The Lord's divine love in its spiritual form is his love relative to a spiritual religion, or to the people in such a religion, who are called spiritual because of their love for their neighbor. The Lord's divine love extends to everyone, but since we receive it in different ways—one way if we are heavenly, and another if we are spiritual—it is described as relative.

[8] This is what Moses says about firstborns that represented the Lord's divine love in its heavenly form and, in a secondary sense, people in a heavenly religion:

> The firstborn of your male offspring you shall give to me; so shall you do with your ox and your flock. Seven days it shall be with its mother; on the eighth you shall give it to me. And men of holiness you shall be to me. (Exodus 22:29, 30, 31)

The reason a firstborn would stay with its mother seven days was that the seventh day symbolized a heavenly person (§§84, 85, 86, 87), and seven accordingly symbolizes something holy (395, 433, 716, 881). The reason firstborns were given to Jehovah on the eighth day was that the eighth day symbolized what continued after a new beginning, and specifically, an extension of love (2044). In the same author:

A *firstborn* that is *given as a firstborn to Jehovah* among the animals—a man shall not consecrate it, whether it is an ox or member of the flock; it is Jehovah's. (Leviticus 27:26, 27)

In the same author:

The *first fruits* of everything that is in the land, which they bring to Jehovah, shall be yours [Aaron's]. *Everything that opens the womb* among all flesh that they offer to Jehovah, among human and among animal, shall be yours. Nevertheless you shall *redeem the firstborn of a person.* And the *firstborn* of an unclean animal you shall redeem. The *firstborn of an ox* or the *firstborn of a sheep* or the *firstborn of a goat* you shall not redeem; they are a holy thing. Their blood you shall spatter on the altar and their fat you shall burn: a fire offering as a restful smell to Jehovah. (Numbers 18:13, 15, 16, 17, 18)

In the same author:

Every firstborn that will be born in your herd and in your flock—the male—you shall *consecrate to Jehovah your God;* you shall not do work with the *firstborn of your ox.* And you shall not shear the *firstborn of your flock.* If there is a blemish in it, lameness or blindness, any evil blemish, you shall not sacrifice it to Jehovah your God. (Deuteronomy 15:19, 20, 21, 22)

[9] Since a firstborn represented the Lord and also people who are the Lord's because they love him, the tribe of Levi was taken in place of all firstborns, the reason being that Levi represented the Lord's love. Levi also symbolized love, because the name means closeness and union, and closeness and union in an inner sense mean love. By the Lord's divine mercy, this will be discussed later, at Genesis 29:34 [§3875]. Here is what Moses says about the Levites:

Jehovah spoke to Moses, saying, "Look, I myself shall *take the Levites* from the midst of the children of Israel *in place of every firstborn, those who open the womb* from among the children of Israel, and *the Levites shall be mine.* For *every firstborn was mine* on the day I struck every *firstborn* in the land of Egypt; *I consecrated every firstborn in Israel to myself.* From human to animal they shall be mine." (Numbers 3:11, 12, 13)

In the same author:

> Jehovah said to Moses, "Count *every firstborn male* to the children of Israel, from the son of a month and above, and take up the number of their names. And you are to *take the Levites for me*—I am Jehovah!—*in place of every firstborn among the children of Israel,* and the animals of the Levites *in place of every firstborn* among the animals of the children of Israel." (Numbers 3:40, 41, and following verses; 8:14, 16, 17, 18)

The Levites were given to Aaron (Numbers 8:19) because Aaron represented the priestliness of the Lord, or in other words, his divine love. (For the priesthood as representing the Lord's divine love, see §§1728, 2015 at the end.)

[10] Concerning firstborns that represented the Lord's divine love in its spiritual form and, in a secondary sense, people of a spiritual religion, Jeremiah says this:

> They will come with weeping, and I will bring them with prayers; I will lead them to springs of water on the path of uprightness; they will not stumble on it. And I will be as a father to Israel, *and Ephraim is my firstborn.* (Jeremiah 31:9)

This is about a new spiritual religion. Israel stands for spiritual goodness. Ephraim stands for spiritual truth, which is called the firstborn because the verse speaks to the planting of a religion in which the intellect (which focuses on truth) seems to be the firstborn. After all, Ephraim took Reuben's place and became the firstborn (Genesis 48:5, 20; 1 Chronicles 5:1), the reason being that Joseph, father to Ephraim and Manasseh, represented the Lord's divine love in its spiritual form. Israel, though, or spiritual goodness, is the real firstborn, as Moses reveals:

> Jehovah said to Moses, "You shall say to Pharaoh, 'This is what Jehovah has said: "*My firstborn child is Israel,* and I say to you, 'Send my child to serve me,' and you refused to send him. Watch: I am killing your own *firstborn* child!"'" (Exodus 4:22, 23)

In this passage, in the highest sense, Israel means the Lord's divine love in its spiritual form, but in a secondary sense it means people with spiritual love—that is, people who display charity toward their neighbor.

[11] In the first stages of a spiritual religion, while it is being planted, a true theology is the firstborn in the outward part of it, and the truth of that theology is the firstborn in the inward part. To put it another way, a theology concerning faith is the firstborn in the outward part, while faith itself is the firstborn in the inward part. When a religion has been planted, though, or actually exists in people, the goodness of neighborly love is the firstborn in the outward part, while that love itself is the firstborn in the inward part. When a religion refuses to be planted—which takes place when the people in it can no longer be reborn—it gradually withdraws from neighborly love and turns aside toward faith; it no longer applies its energies to life but to theology. When this happens, it plunges into shadow, falls into falsity and evil, and in this way disintegrates and brings about its own extinction. This state of affairs was represented by Cain's murder of his brother Abel. (To see that Cain means faith detached from charity, while Abel means the charity it destroyed, consult §§340, 342, 357, 362, and following sections.) It was also represented by the ridicule to which Ham and his son Canaan exposed Ham's father, Noah (1062, 1063, 1076, 1140, 1141, 1162, 1179). Later it was represented by the actions of Reuben, Jacob's firstborn, in defiling his father's bed (Genesis 35:22). And finally it was represented by Pharaoh and the Egyptians' abuse of the children of Israel. All these perpetrators were cursed, as the Word reveals. Cain's curse:

Jehovah said, "What have you done? The voice of your brother's blood is crying out to me from the ground. And now, a curse on you from the ground, which opened its mouth, receiving your brother's blood from your hand!" (Genesis 4:10, 11)

Ham and Canaan's curse:

Ham, father of Canaan, saw his father's nakedness and pointed it out to his two brothers, and Noah, when he had woken up from his wine, said, "A curse on Canaan! A slave of slaves he will be to his brothers." (Genesis 9:22, 24, [25])

Reuben's curse:

Reuben, my firstborn, you are my strength and the beginning of my power, excelling in honor and excelling in might. Light as water, do not be excelling! For you climbed onto your father's beds, then you defiled them; my pallet he climbed onto. (Genesis 49:3, 4)

That is why he was deprived of the birthright (1 Chronicles 5:1). [12] Pharaoh and the Egyptians represented something similar, and that is why their firstborn children and animals were killed. This can be seen from their representation as facts (§§1164, 1165, 1186). When we use facts to pry into the hidden wisdom of faith and fail to believe in anything more than we can grasp by our senses and our science, we pervert and obliterate the teachings of faith, especially those concerning love for our neighbor. That is what is represented on an inner level by the killing of the firstborn in Egypt, which Moses describes this way:

> I will pass through the land of Egypt this night and strike *every firstborn in the land of Egypt,* from human to animal, and on all the gods of Egypt I will pass judgment; I am Jehovah! And the blood will serve as a sign on your houses, [to show] where you are, and when I see the blood I will pass by you, and the plague will not come onto you as a destroyer, in striking the land of Egypt. (Exodus 12:12, 13)

The firstborn of Egypt is the doctrine of faith and charity, which is corrupted by the use of facts, as mentioned. The gods of Egypt, on which judgment was to be passed, are falsities. The fact that the plague was not inflicted by the destroyer where there was blood on the houses means, in the highest sense, where the Lord was present with the spiritual form of his divine love. In a secondary sense it means where there was spiritual love, or charity for one's neighbor (§1001). [13] The same author has this further point to make about Pharaoh and the Egyptians:

> Moses said, "This is what Jehovah has said: 'As of the middle of the night, I myself will go out into the middle of Egypt, and *every firstborn in the land of Egypt will die,* from the *firstborn of Pharaoh* destined to sit on his throne to the *firstborn of the slave woman* who is behind the millstones, and every *firstborn of the animals.* And toward all the children of Israel, from man to animal, not a dog will move its tongue.'" (Exodus 11:4, 5, 6, 7)

And still further:

> It came about in the middle of the night that Jehovah struck *every firstborn* in the land of Egypt, from the *firstborn of Pharaoh* destined to sit on his throne to the *firstborn of the prisoner* who was in the house of the pit, and *every firstborn of the animals.* (Exodus 12:29)

The reason it came about in the middle of the night was that night symbolizes the final stage of the church, when it no longer has any faith because it no longer has any neighborly love (§§221, 709, 1712, 2353). In David:

He struck every firstborn in Egypt, the beginning of their powers in the tents of Ham. (Psalms 78:51)

In the same author:

Then Israel came to Egypt, and Jacob became an immigrant in the land of Ham; God *struck every firstborn in their land,* the beginning of all their powers. (Psalms 105:23, 36)

The Egyptian forms of worship are called tents of Ham because of their false premises, rising out of truth separated from goodness, or in other words, out of faith separated from charity. (For tents meaning forms of worship, see §§414, 1102, 1566, 2145, 2152, 3312. For Ham being faith divided from charity, §§1062, 1063, 1076, 1140, 1141, 1162, 1179.) [14] This confirms that the firstborn of Egypt that were killed symbolized nothing else. And since every one of them was killed, [the Israelites] were commanded as soon as they left Egypt to consecrate every firstborn, so that the Lord's divinely spiritual love (and people who have that love) would still be represented by the firstborn. Moses speaks of it this way:

Jehovah spoke to Moses, saying, "*Consecrate to me every firstborn, that which opens every womb* among the children of Israel. Among human and among animal, let them be mine!" You shall hand *everything that opens the womb* over to Jehovah, and every *offspring of an animal that opens [the womb]*—the males that you have—to Jehovah. And everything that opens [the womb] of a donkey you shall redeem with a member of the flock; if you do not redeem it, you shall break its neck. And every *firstborn* among your sons you shall redeem. And it will happen that your son will ask you tomorrow, saying, "What is this?" And you shall say to him, "With a mighty hand Jehovah brought us out of Egypt, out of the house of slaves, and it happened that Pharaoh hardened himself against sending us, and Jehovah killed *every firstborn in the land of Egypt,* from the *firstborn* of human to the *firstborn* of animal. Therefore I sacrifice to Jehovah *everything that opens the womb* (the males); and *every firstborn* of my children I redeem." (Exodus 13:2, 12, 13, 14, 15; 34:19, 20; Numbers 33:3, 4)

All this now shows what the birthright symbolizes in a spiritual sense. *Esau said, "Look, I am on the way to dying,"* means that [goodness on the earthly level] would rise again after that. This is established by the representation of *Esau* as goodness on the earthly level (discussed in §§3302, 3322) and from the symbolism of *dying* as a final stage, when

3326

something comes to an end (discussed in §§2908, 2912, 2917, 2923). Since the end of a previous stage is the start of the next, being *on the way to dying* means rising again after that—just as being buried does. (On the point that being buried means rising again, see §§2916, 2917, 3256.)

That it would rise again afterward means that goodness would gain priority or control over truth, after truth's apparent, temporary priority, which is discussed above [§3325].

3327   *And what point is the birthright to me?* means that [this goodness] had no need for first place at that point, as can be seen without explanation.

3328   *And Jacob said* symbolizes a true theology. This can be seen from the representation of *Jacob* as a true theology, as above at §3324.

3329   *"Swear to me as of today"; and he swore to him* symbolizes confirmation. This is established by the symbolism of *swearing* as confirming (discussed at §2842), and since the confirmation was only for the time being, it says not *today* but *as of today* (see §3325 at the beginning).

3330   *And sold his birthright to Jacob* means that [goodness] yielded priority meanwhile—to the true theology that *Jacob* stands for. This can be seen from the symbolism of the *birthright* as priority, which is dealt with above at §3325. The fact that it yielded priority in the meantime becomes clear from remarks and evidence above at §§3324, 3325.

The main reason truth initially dominates in spiritual people is that at this first stage the pleasures of self-love and materialism (which they believe to be virtues) are what link up with the truth they know and for the most part compose their desire for truth. At this point they think truth can serve to bring them position, affluence, worldly prestige, or even credit in the other life. All these possibilities stir up their desire for truth and set it on fire; yet these are not virtues but evils. Still, the Lord allows such things to carry them away at this first stage, because otherwise they could not regenerate. Understanding and wisdom come with time. Meanwhile such pleasures introduce them to goodness, or love for their neighbor, and when they have that love, they first start to perceive what goodness is and to act from it. Then they make judgments and draw conclusions about truth on the basis of that goodness. Whatever does not harmonize with it, they label as false and reject. So they gain control over truth, as a master or mistress gains control over domestic servants.

3331   Genesis 25:34. *And Jacob gave Esau bread and lentil soup, and he ate and drank and rose and went; and Esau showed contempt for his birthright.*

Jacob gave Esau bread and lentil soup symbolizes the goodness in our life when it has benefited from the good effects of truth and the good effects of doctrine. *And he ate and drank* means adopting them as our own. *And rose* means being lifted up from there. *And went* means living by them. *And Esau showed contempt for his birthright* means that in the interim the goodness in our life dismisses the question of priority.

Jacob gave Esau bread and lentil soup symbolizes the goodness in our life when it has benefited from the good effects of truth and the good effects of doctrine, as can be seen from the following: *Esau* represents the goodness in our life, as discussed at §§3300, 3322. In general, *bread* symbolizes the good that comes of love—both heavenly good and spiritual good—as noted in §§276, 680, 2165, 2177. Accordingly, it also symbolizes the good effects of truth, since this is spiritual goodness. And *lentil soup* symbolizes the good effects of doctrine, because *soup* symbolizes a jumble of doctrines (3316), but *lentils* symbolize the goodness in them. The fact that *Jacob* gave the food to Esau means in an inner sense that the way to those forms of goodness lies through the true theology that Jacob represents (3305).

[2] These words and the ones that follow in this final verse portray the way truth and goodness develop in spiritual people who are being reborn: First they learn doctrinal truth. Then they develop a desire for it, which is the good effect of doctrine. Next, as they gain insight into the doctrine, they respond to the truth it contains, which is the good effect of truth. And finally they choose to live according to it, which is the goodness in their lives. So when spiritual people are regenerating, they proceed from a theology composed of truth to a life composed of goodness.

Once their lives are filled with goodness, though, the pattern reverses. The goodness in their lives shapes their views on the good effect of truth, which shapes their views on the good effect of doctrine, which shapes their views on doctrinal truth. These details show how people grow from sense-oriented beings into spiritual ones, and what they are like once they have become spiritual.

[3] These three kinds of goodness—the good we do in life, the good we find in truth, and the good we see in doctrine—differ from one another, as those who mull it over can see. The good we do in life is what flows from our will; the good we find in truth is what flows from our understanding of it; and the good we see in doctrine is what flows from our knowledge of it. Doctrine contains all three.

[4] The symbolism of *lentils* as the good to be found in doctrine can be seen from this: Wheat, barley, beans, lentils, millet, and spelt are words related to bread, but of different kinds. Bread in general means goodness, as the statements and explanations at §§276, 680, 2165, 2177 make clear. So the different kinds of produce mentioned symbolize different kinds of goodness—wheat and barley symbolizing the loftier types of goodness, beans and lentils the lowlier types. This also becomes clear from the following words in Ezekiel:

> You, take yourself wheat and barleycorns, and bean and *lentils,* and millet and spelt, and you are to put them into a single vessel and make them into bread for yourself. (Ezekiel 4:9, 12, 13)

3333   *And he ate and drank* means adopting them as our own. This is established by the symbolism of *eating* as making what is good our own (discussed in §§2187, 2343, 3168) and from that of *drinking* as making what is true our own (discussed in §§3069, 3089, 3168).

3334   *And rose* means being lifted up from there. This can be seen from the symbolism of *rising* as involving some kind of elevation wherever it is mentioned (discussed in §§2401, 2785, 2912, 2927). We are said to be lifted up when we are perfected in spiritual and heavenly ways, or in regard to the truth that belongs to faith and the goodness that belongs to love and charity (3171).

3335   *And went* means living by them. This can be seen from the symbolism of *going* as advancing into different aspects of goodness, or into different aspects of life (since all goodness is a matter of life)—almost the same meaning as that of traveling, emigrating, and advancing (discussed in §§1293, 1457).

3336   *And Esau showed contempt for his birthright* means that in the interim the goodness in our life dismisses the question of priority. This can be seen from the symbolism of *showing contempt* as dismissing, from the representation of *Esau* as the goodness in a life (dealt with in §§3300, 3322), and from the symbolism of a *birthright* as priority (dealt with in §3325). This was for the interim, or the time being, as may be seen in §§3324, 3325, 3330. *Esau showed contempt for his birthright,* then, plainly means that in the interim the goodness in our life dismisses the question of priority.

In order to grasp what this chapter has said about Esau and Jacob on its inner level of meaning, you have to stop thinking at all about narrative details and therefore about the people Esau and Jacob. Instead you have to substitute the things they represent: truth and goodness on the earthly level or (what amounts to the same thing) a spiritual person who is being regenerated by truth and goodness. Names have a purely symbolic meaning in the Word's inner sense. When you mentally replace Esau and Jacob with goodness and truth on the earthly level, you discover how matters stand with a person's rebirth through truth and goodness. In the beginning, truth seems to come first in time and in supremacy with that person, even though goodness is intrinsically prior and higher.

[2] In order to clarify the subject of this priority and supremacy further, I need to add a few more words. It is possible to recognize that absolutely nothing can enter our memory and stay there unless some desire, some form of love, introduces it. If there were no desire—that is, no love—for it there would not be any awareness of it. That desire, or that love, is what couples with the information as it enters and, once coupled, keeps it there. This stands to reason if you consider that when a similar desire or love returns, the information reappears, bringing with it many other pieces of information memorized earlier at the call of a similar desire or love, and so on in a chain. That is the source of our thoughts and, from our thought, of our speech. By the same token, when we remember the information, whether prompted by objects of the senses, or objects of thought, or another's words, the desire that introduced it into our memory also returns. Such is the lesson of experience; and anybody can confirm it by reflecting on it.

[3] One of the things we memorize this way is doctrinal truth, and what introduces it into our memory in the early stages is the desires produced by various kinds of love, as noted above at §3330. Real desire, which results from charitable kindness, is imperceptible at that point, but it is still present. To the extent that it can be present, the Lord attaches it to doctrinal truth, and it stays attached.

When the time comes that we can be reborn, then, the Lord inspires in us a desire for what is good, and through this desire he stirs up information linked to it by him (information that the Word refers to as a remnant). Then he uses that desire for goodness to remove gradually the desires produced by other kinds of love and accordingly the information coupled with them. In this way the desire for goodness (that is, the goodness in a person's life) starts to dominate. This desire had the upper hand all along, but its dominance was invisible to us, because the more we love ourselves and the material world, the less visible is the goodness that comes of a genuine love.

This now shows what the story told about Esau and Jacob symbolizes on an inner level.

Correspondence and Representation (Continued)

3337 EARLIER statements and explanations [§§2987–3002, 3213–3226] show what correspondences and representations are. To repeat: between objects of heavenly light and objects of worldly light there is correspondence, and what manifests itself among the objects of worldly light is a representation (§3225). We cannot see very clearly what the nature and quality of heaven's light is, though, because we are immersed in the realm of worldly light, and the more we immerse ourselves in it, the more the objects of heavenly light seem shadowy and worthless to us.

These two kinds of light give us all our understanding, when life flows in.

Our imagination consists solely of the things we have grasped with our physical sight—in different forms and shapes, varying in marvelous ways—and have, so to speak, modified. Our inner imagination or thought, though, consists solely of the things we have taken in through the eyes of our mind—in different forms and shapes, varying in even more marvelous ways—and have, so to speak, modified.

What results is lifeless of itself, but the inflow of life from the Lord animates it.

3338 In addition to these two types of light, there is also warmth that flows from two origins. Heavenly warmth comes from heaven's sun, which is the Lord, while worldly warmth comes from the world's sun, which is the light source we see with our eyes. Heavenly warmth reveals itself to our inner self as spiritual kinds of love and emotion, while worldly warmth reveals itself to our outer self as earthly kinds of love and emotion. The former kind composes the life force of our inner self; the latter, the life force of our outer self. Without love and desire, we could not possibly survive.

These two kinds of warmth also correspond to one another.

When the Lord's life flows in, it turns the two kinds of warmth into love and emotion, so it does not appear to us to be warmth, but it is. If we did not receive warmth from those sources in both our inner and our outer self, we would instantly fall down dead.

These things are plain to anyone who considers that the more we burn with love, the warmer we grow, and the more love dies away, the more sluggish we grow.

This warmth is what our will lives on; the light mentioned earlier is what our intellect lives on.

The two kinds of light and warmth are vividly experienced in the other world. Angels live in heaven's light and in the warmth just described. The light supplies them with understanding; the warmth, with a desire for what is good. The varieties of light, which are visible to their outward sight, originate in the Lord's divine wisdom, while the varieties of warmth, which they also sense, originate in the Lord's divine love. So the more fully spirits and angels understand truth and the more strongly they seek goodness, the closer to the Lord they are. **3339**

That light has its opposite in darkness, and that warmth, in cold. Hellish spirits live in both. Their darkness results from the falsities they adopt, and their coldness from the evils they indulge in. The further they stray from truth, the greater their darkness; and the further they stray from goodness, the greater their coldness. **3340**

When a glimpse is given into hell, where such spirits live, a dark cloud in which they spend their lives appears. If a gust of air escapes, it gives off the smell of insanity wafting from falsity and of hatred wafting from evil.

Sometimes they do receive illumination, but it resembles swamp light, and it is extinguished and turns into darkness for them as soon as they gaze on the light of truth. Sometimes they are also given warmth, but the warmth of a dirty bath. This changes to cold for them as soon as they sense anything good.

A man was once sent into the dark cloud the hellish spirits inhabit to learn how the situation stands with them, but angels from the Lord were protecting him. Addressing me from there he said that the place was filled with an insane fury against everything good and true and especially against the Lord. The fury was so strong that it astounded him to think it could ever be resisted. The spirits sought only hatred, revenge, and murder, with such intensity that they wanted to destroy everyone in the universe. Unless the Lord constantly repelled their fury, the entire human race would perish.

3341   Representations can be created in the other world only through distinctions of light and shadow, so it is important to know that all light (and therefore all understanding and wisdom) comes from the Lord, while all shadow (and therefore all insanity and stupidity) comes from a person's, spirit's, or angel's selfhood. From these two sources flow and stream all variations of light and shadow in the other life.

3342   In fact, spirits and angels always employ representations when they speak. They use amazing changes in light and shadow to present their ideas in a lifelike way to the inner and outer eyes of the one they are talking to, and matching changes in emotional state to instill the ideas in the other's mind.

The representations that accompany speech differ from those described earlier [§§2987–3003, 3213–3227, 3337–3341], being as rapid and fleeting as the thoughts expressed. It is as if something were being described at length and at the same time displayed as a visual image. Surprising to say, any spiritual subject, no matter what it is, can be portrayed in a representative way by different kinds of images, all of which are incomprehensible to people on earth. Within them these images contain perceptions of truth and, even more deeply, perceptions of goodness.

[2] Such things exist in people on earth too, because we are spirits clothed in a body, and this is the evidence: Whenever we take words in with our ears, and they rise up into our inner reaches, they transform into ideas that share some similarity with visual images. From visual images they transform into intellectual ideas, and as a result we perceive the words' meaning.

If you think properly about this, you can grasp that you have inside you a spirit, which is your inner self, and that your spirit talks in a representative way after separating from your body, since it does so while you are still alive. We do not see plainly that it possesses this kind of speech, though, because of the dimness and even darkness that earthly, bodily, and worldly factors produce.

3343   The speech of angels in the next deeper heaven is still more beautiful, and its representations are still more appealing, but the thoughts that take this representative shape cannot be expressed in words. If they were so expressed, they would pass not only all comprehension but even all belief. Spiritual entities, which are forms of truth, are generated by modifications of heavenly light, in which the emotions change in countless miraculous ways. Heavenly phenomena, which are forms of goodness, are generated by modifications of heavenly fire, or warmth. So they stir all the emotions.

We too take up this deeper style of speech when we separate from our body, but only if we have devoted ourselves to spiritual goodness—which is goodness born of faith, or charity for our neighbor—while still alive in the world. It is a language we have inside us, even if we are unaware of it.

Angels of a still deeper heaven, the third heaven, also use representations when they speak, but the speech cannot possibly be grasped by any kind of [earthly] thought, so it cannot be described. **3344**

We have this kind of language in us, too, but only if we devote ourselves to heavenly love, or love for the Lord. Again, we take it up after separating from our body, as if born into it, even though we were unable to form any conception of it as long as we were alive in our body, as noted.

In short, representative images attached to thoughts bring speech to life. In us, language is least alive of all, since our speech is verbal; it is more alive in angels of the first heaven; still more alive in angels of the second heaven; and most of all in angels of the third heaven, since they are most directly steeped in the Lord's life. Whatever comes from the Lord is inherently alive.

This reveals that the different kinds of speech go deeper and deeper in order, in such a way that each springs from the next in order, and each nests within the last in order. We know what our own speech and the thinking that produces it is like. The analytical processes it entails can never be thoroughly explored. The speech of good spirits (or angels) in the first heaven, and the thinking that produces it, is deeper and contains even more marvels that defy examination. The speech of angels in the second heaven, and the thinking that in turn produces this kind of speech, is still deeper and contains still more indescribable perfections. But the speech of angels in the third heaven, and the thinking that in turn produces it, is the deepest and contains what is absolutely indescribable. Even though these types of speech seem varied and different, they compose a single language, because each type forms the next, and each lies within the last. The form of speech that emerges on the outside represents what exists inside it. **3345**

These things cannot be believed by people who do not think beyond what belongs to the world and the body. They view anything deeper as nothing, when in reality their deeper levels are everything, and shallower concerns rising out of the world and the body, which seem like everything to them, are hardly anything by comparison.

3346 In order for me to learn all this and know it for certain, the Lord in his divine mercy has allowed me to talk with spirits and angels almost continually for many years now. With spirits or angels of the first heaven I have been granted to use their own language, and sometimes with angels of the second heaven I have been granted to use theirs. The speech of angels in the third heaven, though, only presented itself to me as a burst of light in which perception radiated from a blaze of goodness at its core.

3347 I once heard some angels talking about the human mind and the thought and consequent speech the human mind produces. They compared it to a person's outward form, which, though outward, owes its whole existence to countless internal structures such as the brains, medulla oblongata and spinal cord, lungs, heart, liver, pancreas, spleen, stomach, and intestines, not to mention many others, such as the reproductive organs in both sexes. Then there are the countless muscles that surround them and ultimately the tissues covering them. All these forms are woven together out of blood vessels and nerve fibers and in fact out of vessels and fibers within those vessels and fibers, which form the ducts and the smaller structures. There are components without number, then, all of which still contribute, each in its own way, to the composition of the outward form, in which none of the internal elements are visible. To this external form the angels compared the human mind, its thoughts, and the resulting speech, but the angelic mind they compared to the internal components, which are comparatively unlimited in number, and mystifying.

In addition, they compared the capacity for thought to the capacity organs have for action, in accord with the anatomy of nerve fibers. "The ability lies not in the fibers," they said, "but in the vital energy the fibers contain, just as the ability to think belongs not to the mind but to the vital energy flowing into it from the Lord."

When comparisons like these are drawn by angels, they also show up as representations, in which the inner structures mentioned appear to both the eyes and the intellect, instantly, down to their smallest, most mysterious parts.

Comparisons that use spiritual and heavenly images—the kind of comparison heavenly angels draw—far outstrip in beauty and wisdom those that use earthly images.

Some spirits from another planet were with me for a fairly long time, **3348** and I told them about the wisdom on our earth. "The studies that give people here a reputation for scholarship include investigation and analysis of the ways the mind and its thinking work—studies that they call metaphysics and logic," I said. "But they've made little progress beyond terminology and a few inconsistent rules. They quarrel over the terms, such as *form, substance, mind,* and *soul,* and they use their broad, inconsistent rules to engage in bitter disputes over the truth."

When I told the spirits this, they saw that when people become bogged down in terms as terms and use made-up rules to govern their thinking about those terms, it drains away all meaning and comprehension. [2] "Those are just little black clouds that block the eyes of the mind and drag the intellect down into the dust," they said. "That's not how it is with us. Our thoughts on these subjects are all the clearer for our total ignorance of such methodologies."

I was also given the opportunity to see how wise these spirits were. They created a representation of the human mind as a marvelous heavenly object, and of its moods as auras moving in answer to it. The job they did was so skillful that angels applauded them.

They also used representation to show how the Lord takes inherently unpleasant emotions and turns them into pleasant ones.

[3] Some of our own planet's best-educated were on hand, and they could not understand a bit of it, even though they had spent a lot of time in philosophical discussion on these subjects during bodily life. When the spirits again perceived the way the scholars' thoughts fastened on terms alone and the way they tended to argue the validity of every last detail, the spirits described such activities as frothy dregs.

The discussion so far reveals what correspondences are and what rep- **3349** resentations are. However, in addition to everything that has been said and shown at the end of the previous chapters (§§2987–3003, 3213–3227), see remarks on the topic in other sections, as follows:

Everything in the Word's literal meaning represents and symbolizes the elements present in the inner meaning: 1404, 1408, 1409, 2763. Moses and the prophets used representation and symbolism in writing the Word, and it could not have been written in any other mode if it was to have an inner meaning through which heaven and earth could communicate: 2899. For this reason, and because he spoke from divinity itself, the Lord's words were also representative: 2900. That was the source of representative and symbolic objects that appeared in the Word and in various kinds of ritual: 2179. The use of representation grew out of the ancient church's use of symbolism, which in turn grew out of the earliest church's perceptions: 920, 1409, 2896, 2897. The earliest people also took their representations from dreams: 1977. Enoch stands for those who gathered the perceptive knowledge of the earliest people: 2896. In heaven one sees constant representations of the Lord and his kingdom: 1619. The heavens are full of representations: 1521, 1532. In the world of spirits, angels' thoughts turn into various representative images: 1971, 1980, 1981. The representations that lead children into intelligence: 2299. Representations in the realm of nature result from an inflow from the Lord: 1632, 1881. Everything throughout nature represents the Lord's kingdom: 2758. Our outer self contains traits that do and traits that do not correspond to our inner self: 1563, 1568.

3350   Let me cite one more example to show what representations are like. I heard a large number of angels in the middle heaven who were working together, in concert, to create a representation. The spirits around me could perceive the representation only when they were touched by an inflow of relatively deep emotion. The angels formed a choir whose many members were all thinking and saying the same thing. Using representation, they formed a gold crown set with diamonds on the Lord's head. This required a series of representations as rapid as thought and speech, as described above in §§3342, 3343, 3344.

Remarkably, although there were so many of them, they all still thought and spoke in unison and accordingly created their representation in unison. This was because none of them wanted to do anything on their own, let alone set themselves up over the others and lead the choir. Anyone who does that instantly and spontaneously splits away from the group. Instead, they allow themselves to be led by each other, so that all of them, individually and collectively, are led by the Lord.

All good people who enter the other life are brought into like-minded groups of this kind.

[2] Then I heard numerous choirs putting forth various representations, and even though there were many choirs and many in each choir, they acted as one. The forms of the various contributions combined into a single whole filled with heavenly beauty.

The same effect can be produced by the entirety of heaven, populated as it is by millions and millions, who act in unison because they love each other, since as a result they allow the Lord to lead them. Amazingly, the more there are—the more *millions* there are—to populate heaven, the more distinct and perfect everything becomes. The deeper the heaven an angel inhabits, too, the more distinct and perfect everything becomes, since all perfection increases as it deepens.

The angels who were forming the choirs at that time were from the area  of the lungs (and therefore from the Lord's spiritual kingdom); I could tell because they were flowing gently into my breathing. The choirs involved in voluntary breathing, though, were different from those involved in involuntary breathing.

There is more on correspondences and representations—especially those in the Word—at the end of the next chapter [§§3472–3485].

3351

3352

Genesis 26

[Matthew 24:3–8]

3353 MOST people believe that when the Last Judgment comes, everything in the visible universe will be destroyed—the earth will burn up, the sun and moon will dissolve, the stars will vanish—and then a new heaven and new earth will materialize. Revelation and prophecy describing such events have given them this view, but the real case is quite different, as shown by previous remarks concerning the Last Judgment, at §§900, 931, 1850, 2117–2133. These sections show that the Last Judgment is in fact the end of the church in one nation and its beginning in another. This end and beginning take place when no one acknowledges the Lord any longer—that is, when faith no longer exists. Acknowledgment or faith comes to an end when neighborly love does, because faith can exist only in people who love their neighbor. Under those circumstances the church dies out and is transferred to other people, as is quite plain from everything the Lord himself taught and prophesied concerning that final era, the close of the age, in the Gospels (Matthew 24; Mark 13; Luke 21).

[2] Since no one can understand his words there without the key of the inner meaning, let me reveal their contents bit by bit, starting here with the following words in Matthew:

> The disciples came up to Jesus, saying, "Tell us when these things will happen and what the sign of your coming and of the close of the age will be." And answering, Jesus said to them, "Watch, to keep anyone from leading you astray! For many will come in my name saying, 'I am the Christ,' and lead many astray. But you are sure to hear of wars and rumors of wars. See that you are not troubled! Because it all has to happen, but it is not yet the end. For nation will be roused against nation, and kingdom against kingdom; and there will be famines and plagues and earthquakes in various places. But all these things will be the beginning of woes." (Matthew 24:3, 4, 5, 6, 7, 8)

People who cling to the literal meaning cannot tell whether these verses and the ones that follow in Matthew 24 have to do with the destruction of Jerusalem and the scattering of the Jewish nation or with the cataclysm called the Last Judgment. People who focus on the inner meaning, on the other hand, see clearly that the passage is talking about the end of the church, which is referred to here and elsewhere as the Lord's Coming and the close of the age.

Since the end of the church is meant, you can see that all the elements symbolize aspects of religion. The specific symbolism is indicated by the particulars of the inner meaning:

In the sentence *Many will come in my name saying, "I am the Christ," and lead many astray,* the *name* does not mean a name, nor does *Christ* mean Christ. The *name* symbolizes a means of worshiping the Lord (§§2724, 3006), and *Christ* symbolizes truth itself (3009, 3010). So it means that people will come saying, "This is what faith teaches"—or "This is true"—when it is neither a tenet of faith nor true but false.

You are sure to hear wars and rumors of wars means that arguments and disputes over truth will arise, these being wars in a spiritual sense.

Nation will be roused against nation, and kingdom against kingdom means that evil will fight with evil, and falsity with falsity. On the point that a *nation* means goodness and, in an opposite sense, evil, see §§1259, 1260, 1416, 1849; and that a *kingdom* means truth and, in an opposite sense, falsity, see §§1672, 2547.

There will be famines and plagues and earthquakes in various places means that no one will know about goodness and truth any longer and the state of religion will therefore change, this change being the earthquakes.

These remarks show what the Lord's words refer to: the first stage in the corruption of the church, when people start to forget what is good and true and quarrel about it, which gives rise to falsity.

3354

Since this is the first stage, the text says *it is not yet the end* and *these are the beginning of woes.* It calls this stage *earthquakes in various places,* which on an inner level symbolizes a partial or initial change in the church's condition.

The fact that the message is addressed to the disciples means that it is addressed to all who are in the church, because those are the ones the twelve disciples represented (§§2089, 2129, 2130). That is why it says [in the plural], *"Watch, to keep anyone from leading you astray,"* and *"You are sure to hear of wars and rumors of wars; see that you are not troubled!"*

The inner meaning of an *earthquake* as a change in the church's condition stands out from the symbolism of the *earth* as the church (discussed in §§566, 662, 1066, 1068, 1262, 1733, 1850, 2117, 2118, 2928) and from that

3355

of a *quaking* as a change in state—here, a change in regard to traits of the church, or goodness and truth. The same thing becomes clear from other places in the Word, such as Isaiah:

> It will happen that one fleeing from a horrifying sound will fall into the pit, and one climbing out of the middle of the pit will be caught in the snare. For the floodgates in the heights opened, and *the earth's foundations shook; the earth was shattered* utterly; *the earth quaked* violently; *the earth totters* helplessly like a drunkard. It *sways* like a shack, and its transgression weighs on *it,* and it will fall and never rise again. And it will happen on that day that Jehovah will punish the army of the heights on high, and the monarchs of the *ground* down on the *ground.* (Isaiah 24:18, 19, 20, [21])

Obviously the earth here means the church, because the passage is talking about the church. Its foundations are said to shake and the church itself is said to shatter, quake, totter, and sway when people no longer recognize goodness and truth. The monarchs of the ground are true ideas, although here they are false ideas, which will incur punishment. For the meaning of kings as truth and in an opposite sense falsity, see §§1672, 2015. Like the earth, the ground means the church, but with a difference; see §§566, 1068. [2] In the same author:

> I will render humankind more rare than pure gold, and humanity [more rare] than Ophir's gold. Therefore I will shake heaven, and *the earth will quake out of its place,* in the outrage of Jehovah Sabaoth and on the day when his anger blazes up. (Isaiah 13:12, 13)

This is about Judgment Day. Here too the earth clearly stands for the church, which is said to quake out of its place when its state changes. On the point that a place means a state, see §§1273, 1274, 1275, 1377, 2625, 2837. In the same author:

> Is this the man *shaking* the earth, shaking *kingdoms?* He makes the world a wilderness, and its cities he destroys. (Isaiah 14:16, 17)

The subject here is Lucifer. The earth stands for the church, which he is said to shake when he claims all its attributes as his own. Kingdoms are the truth known to the church; see §§1672, 2547. [3] In Ezekiel:

> It will happen on that day, [on the day] Gog comes over the *land of Israel,* that my wrath will rise up in my anger; and in my zeal, in the fire of my outrage I will speak: "If on that day there is not a big *earthquake* on Israel's *soil . . . !*" (Ezekiel 38:18, 19, 20)

Gog stands for outward worship separated from inward and so made idolatrous (§1151). Israel's land and soil stand for a spiritual religion. The earthquake stands for a change in its state. In Joel:

> Before him *the earth quaked,* the heavens trembled, the sun and moon
> turned black, and the stars withdrew their rays. (Joel 2:10)

This too is about the day of the Last Judgment. The quaking earth stands
for changed conditions in the church. The sun and moon stand for a loving goodness and the truth it leads to (§§1529, 1530, 2441, 2495), which
are said to turn black when people no longer acknowledge goodness or
truth. Stars stand for a knowledge of what is good and true (2495, 2849).
In David:

> *The earth shook and quaked,* and the foundations of the mountains quiv-
> ered and shook, because [anger] blazed in him. (Psalms 18:7, 8)

The shaking, quaking earth stands for the church's state when it has been
corrupted. [4] In John:

> Furthermore, I looked as [the Lamb] opened the sixth seal, when sud-
> denly a *huge earthquake occurred!* And the sun turned black as sackcloth
> made of hair, and the whole moon became like blood, and the stars of
> the sky fell onto the earth. (Revelation 6:12, 13)

The earthquake, sun, moon, and stars symbolize the same thing they do
above in Joel. In the same author:

> In that hour, *a huge earthquake occurred,* and a tenth of the city fell,
> and in the *earthquake* the names of seven thousand people fell dead.
> (Revelation 11:13)

All these passages show that an earthquake actually means a change in the
church's condition and that in an inner sense the land means the church.
Since it does, plainly the new heaven and new earth that were to take the
place of the old ones (Isaiah 65:17; 66:22; Revelation 21:1) mean nothing but
a new church on inner and outer planes (§§1733, 1850, 2117, 2118 at the end).

   A quake means a change in condition because it occurs within space   **3356**
and time, and in the other world there is no concept of space or time but
of state instead. Everything in the next life does appear to occupy space
and to progress in time, but in and of themselves these are changes in
state, because they result from such changes. All spirits are well aware
of this fact—even evil ones, who impose changes of state on others to

make it look as though they are present in places where they are not. People on earth can recognize the same thing by considering that the more joy we have from being in our element, and the more absentminded we are because of being absorbed in thought, the more slender our connection with time. Many hours then seem like barely one. Our inner self, or spirit, experiences states, to which the space and time of our outer self correspond. So a quake, since it moves forward through space and time, in an inner sense means changed conditions.

Genesis 26

1. And there was famine in the land, besides the earlier famine that was in Abraham's days. And Isaac went to Abimelech, king of the Philistines, to Gerar.

2. And Jehovah appeared to him and said, "Do not go down to Egypt; live in the land that I tell you.

3. Stay as an immigrant in this land, and I will be with you and bless you; because to you and your seed I will give all these lands, and I will set up the oath that I swore to Abraham your father.

4. And I will make your seed multiply like the stars of the heavens and will give your seed all these lands; and in your seed all the nations of the earth will be blessed,

5. because Abraham heeded my voice and observed my observances, my commandments, my statutes, and my laws."

6. And Isaac settled in Gerar.

7. And the men of the place questioned [him in regard] to his woman. And he said, "She is my sister," because he was afraid to say "my woman." "Perhaps the men of the place will kill me because of Rebekah, because she is good to look at."

8. And it happened, because his days there lengthened, that Abimelech, king of the Philistines, looked out through a window and saw, and look: Isaac laughing with Rebekah, his woman!

9. And Abimelech called Isaac and said, "But look: she is your woman! So how could you say, 'She is my sister'?" And Isaac said to him, "Because I said, 'Perhaps I might die because of her.'"

10. And Abimelech said, "What is this you have done to us? At the least, one of the people might have lain with your woman, and you would have brought guilt on us."

11. And Abimelech commanded all the people, saying, "The one touching that man and his woman will surely die."

12. And Isaac sowed in that land and found a hundred measures in that year, and Jehovah blessed him.

13. And the man grew and went—went, and grew!—until he became very great.

14. And he had property in flock and property in herd and large slaveholdings; and the Philistines envied him.

15. And all the wells that the slaves of his father dug in the days of Abraham his father—the Philistines kept stopping them up and filled them with dirt.

16. And Abimelech said to Isaac, "Go away from us, because you far overpower us."

17. And Isaac went from there and camped in the valley of Gerar and settled there.

18. And Isaac went back and redug the wells of water that they dug in the days of Abraham his father, which the Philistines kept stopping up after Abraham's death. And he called them by name according to the names by which his father called them.

19. And Isaac's slaves dug in the valley and found there a well of living water.

20. And the shepherds of Gerar feuded with the shepherds of Isaac, saying, "The water is ours!" And he called the name of the well Esek, because they quarreled with him.

21. And they dug another well, and they feuded over it, too, and he called its name Sitnah.

22. And he moved on from there and dug another well, and they did not feud over it; and he called its name Rehoboth and said, "Because now Jehovah has broadened us, and we will be fruitful in the land."

23. And he went up from there to Beer-sheba.

24. And Jehovah appeared to him that night and said, "I am the God of Abraham your father. Do not be afraid, because I am with you and will bless you and make your seed multiply because of Abraham my servant."

25. And he built an altar there and called on Jehovah's name and stretched his tent there, and Isaac's slaves hollowed out a well there.

26. And Abimelech went to him from Gerar, and Ahuzzath his comrade, and Phicol, leader of his army.

27. And Isaac said to them, "Why have you come to me, when you hated me and sent me from you?"

28. And they said, "We saw unmistakably that Jehovah was with you, and we said, 'Please let there be a vow between us, between us and you, and let us cut a pact with you:

29. If you do evil with us . . . ! Just as we did not touch you, and just as we did only good to you and sent you off in peace. Now, Jehovah's blessing on you!'"

30. And he made them a banquet, and they ate and drank.

31. And they got up early in the morning and swore an oath, a man to his brother. And Isaac sent them off, and they went from him in peace.

32. And it happened on that day that Isaac's slaves came and told him the account of the well that they had dug and said to him, "We have found water."

33. And he called it Sheba. Therefore the name of the city is Beer-sheba up to this day.

❋   ❋   ❋   ❋

34. And Esau was a son of forty years, and he took a woman: Judith, daughter of Beeri the Hittite, and Basemath, daughter of Elon the Hittite.

35. And they were a bitterness of spirit to Isaac and to Rebekah.

Summary

3357   IN an inner sense this chapter deals with appearances of truth on three levels, showing how they are joined to divine truth so that truth and its doctrinal formulation can be accepted and the church can exist.

3358   Appearances of truth on the highest level exist in the Word's inner meaning. Angels live amid these appearances, which contain divine truth and goodness (verses 1, 2, 3, 4, 5, 6). Divine goodness and truth cannot be comprehended or accepted unless they are couched in appearances (verses 7, 8, 9, 10, 11, 12, 13).

3359   Appearances of truth on a lower level exist in a meaning of the Word that is quite deep. People whose religion has depth can tap into these appearances (verses 14, 15, 16, 17).

3360   Lastly, appearances of truth on a still lower level exist in the Word's literal meaning, and people in a shallower religion can access them (verses

18, 19, 20, 21, 22, 23, 24, 25). These still provide a close connection with the Lord (verses 26, 27, 28, 29, 30, 31, 32, 33).

See verses 34 and 35 for the factual truths that are attached to good- **3361** ness on that level.

Inner Meaning

CHAPTER 21 spoke of Abimelech, the pact he struck with Abraham, **3362** and Abraham's denunciation of him at that time for a well of water that Abimelech's slaves had stolen. Almost the same thing recurs here between Abimelech and Isaac—including Isaac's claim, like Abraham's, that his wife was his sister. Clearly some divine secret lies behind and explains the repetition of the events and of their telling, and the mention of wells in both cases. It would not be very important to know about any of these things if something divine did not lie hidden in them. The inner meaning teaches us what it is: a treatment of the Lord's union with inhabitants of his kingdom in the heavens and on earth through truth— specifically, through appearances of truth. A higher level of appearances enables him to unite with angels, and a lower level, with people on earth. So the means of union is the Word, whose inner and outer meanings contain those appearances.

In itself, by its very nature, divine truth cannot possibly be grasped by any angel, let alone a person on earth. It completely transcends their intellectual abilities. In order for a union between them and the Lord to exist anyway, divine truth is cloaked in appearances as it flows in, and so cloaked, it can be both received and acknowledged by them. This process adapts to the intellect of each person undergoing it. Appearances, then (or angelic and human truth), come on three levels.

These are the divine secrets contained in an inner sense in the events recounted earlier concerning Abimelech and Abraham and here concern- ing Abimelech and Isaac.

Genesis 26:1. And there was famine in the land, besides the earlier fam- **3363** *ine that was in Abraham's days. And Isaac went to Abimelech, king of the Philistines, to Gerar.*

There was famine in the land, besides the earlier famine that was in Abraham's days symbolizes a lack of knowledge concerning faith. *And Isaac went to Abimelech, king of the Philistines, to Gerar* symbolizes doctrines about faith; *Abimelech* means a theology that describes faith in rational terms; *king of the Philistines* means doctrines; *Gerar* means faith.

3364   *There was famine in the land, besides the earlier famine in Abraham's days* symbolizes a lack of knowledge concerning faith, which can be seen from the symbolism of *famine* as a lack of knowledge (discussed in §1460). That the knowledge concerns faith can be seen from what comes next: the representation of Abimelech and symbolism of Gerar as aspects of faith. The famine in Abraham's days, as recorded in Genesis 12:10 and discussed in §1460, was a deficiency of knowledge in the earthly self, but the famine depicted here is a deficiency of knowledge in the rational mind. So it says that there was famine in the land *besides the earlier famine that was in Abraham's days.*

In an inner sense this tells about the Lord, indicating that everything he learned about faith came from his divine side. No doctrine exists, not even the smallest bit, that does not come from the Lord. The Lord is theology itself, which is why he is called the Word, the Word being theology.

Everything in the Lord is divine, however, and nothing divine can be understood by any created being. As a result, when the doctrines coming from the Lord are presented to created beings, they are not true in a purely divine way but consist of appearances of truth. Still, divine truth resides within the appearances. Because it does, the appearances too are considered to be truth.

These are the themes of the current chapter.

3365   *And Isaac went to Abimelech, king of the Philistines, to Gerar* symbolizes doctrines about faith, as is established by the following: *Isaac* represents the Lord's divine rationality, as noted in §§1893, 2066, 2072, 2083, 2630. Isaac is divine goodness in the Lord's divine rationality (3012, 3194, 3210) and also divine truth there, which is represented by Isaac's marriage to Rebekah (3012, 3013, 3077). In the current passage, then, since Rebekah accompanied him and was called his sister, Isaac represents divine truth united to divine goodness in the Lord's rational mind. *Abimelech* represents a theology that describes faith in rational terms, as noted in §§2504, 2509, 2510, 2533. *King of the Philistines* symbolizes doctrines. In an inner sense, a *king* means the truth contained in doctrine (see §§1672, 2015, 2069), and *Philistines* mean a knowledge of religious concepts, which is also a knowledge of doctrine (1197, 1198). And *Gerar* symbolizes faith (1209, 2504). This shows what is meant by Isaac's going to Abimelech, king of the Philistines, to Gerar: that the Lord is the source of a theology that describes faith in rational terms, or in other words, of doctrines concerning faith.

All theological teachings are called doctrines, and so far as they can be received and acknowledged in heaven by angels and on earth by people, they are said to be rationally oriented. One's rationality is what receives and acknowledges them. However, the rational mind can never comprehend divine ideas, because it is finite, and what is finite cannot grasp what comes from the Infinite, so the Lord presents divine truth to one's rational dimension in the form of appearances. That is why doctrine is simply the way divine truth appears, or simply a heavenly or spiritual vessel containing something divine. Since it holds something divine—the Lord—it touches the heart, which leads to the union of the Lord with angels and people.

Genesis 26:2, 3. *And Jehovah appeared to him and said, "Do not go down to Egypt; live in the land that I tell you. Stay as an immigrant in this land, and I will be with you and bless you; because to you and your seed I will give all these lands, and I will set up the oath that I swore to Abraham your father."* **3366**

Jehovah appeared to him and said symbolizes a thought [the Lord] received from his divine side. *Do not go down to Egypt; live in the land that I tell you* means that he was not to resort to secular facts but to rational ideas, which are appearances of truth when the Divine illuminates them. *Stay as an immigrant in this land* symbolizes being taught. *And I will be with you* symbolizes divinity. *And bless you* symbolizes a consequent increase. *Because to you* symbolizes goodness. *And your seed* symbolizes truth. *I will give all these lands* symbolizes spiritual qualities. *And I will set up the oath that I swore to Abraham your father* symbolizes a resulting confirmation.

Jehovah appeared to him and said symbolizes a thought [the Lord] received from his divine side, as can be seen from the symbolism of *appearing.* When the Lord as *Jehovah* is the one said to appear, it symbolizes the divinity itself within him. Jehovah was within the Lord, and the Lord himself *was* Jehovah, as pointed out many times before (see §§1343, 1725, 1729, 1733, 1736, 1791, 1815, 1819, 1822, 1902, 1921, 1999, 2004, 2005, 2018, 2025, 2156, 2329, 2447, 2921, 3023, 3035, 3061). The more the Lord united his human with his divine nature, the more he **3367** talked to Jehovah as identical with himself (1745, 1999). So in an inner sense Jehovah's appearing to him means that the message came from his divinity. The symbolism of *saying* as perceiving and also thinking (shown many times) indicates that a thought is what he received.

3368   *Do not go down to Egypt; live in the land that I tell you* means that he was not to resort to secular facts but to rational ideas, which are appearances of truth when the Divine illuminates them. This can be seen from the symbolism of *Egypt* as secular facts (discussed in §§1164, 1165, 1186, 1462) and from that of the *land* in this instance as rational ideas that are appearances of truth when the Divine illuminates them. The land meant here is Gerar, where Abimelech king of the Philistines lived. Gerar symbolizes faith, while Abimelech symbolizes a theology that describes faith in rational terms, and the king of the Philistines symbolizes doctrines (see §§3363, 3365). So that is exactly what the land—the land of Gerar, with Abimelech in it—symbolizes on an inner level.

[2] The symbolism of the *land* varies (see §§620, 636, 1066) according to the character of the nation it refers to (1262). Strictly speaking, it symbolizes the church (3355), and because it does, it also symbolizes that which makes the church, or which creates the church in us. As a result, it symbolizes doctrines concerning neighborly love and faith, and therefore rational ideas as well, which are appearances of truth when illuminated by the Divine. These are the church's truths and consequently its doctrines (see above in §§3364, 3365). It is all the same whether you say rational ideas illuminated by the Divine, or appearances of truth, or heavenly and spiritual truth as it exists in the Lord's kingdom in the heavens (heaven) and in the Lord's kingdom on earth (the church). These same ideas are also called doctrines, but that is because of the truths they contain. Angelic and human rationality is rational—and is called rational—because of appearances of truth illuminated by the Divine. Without these appearances there is no rationality, so rational ideas are those appearances.

[3] The verse forbids a journey down to Egypt, or recourse to secular facts, because such facts were dealt with earlier. Abraham's stay in Egypt represented the Lord's education in facts during his youth (see §1502).

Let me explain the secret behind the command not to go down into Egypt but to stay as an immigrant in the land of Gerar—that is, not to focus on facts but on rational thinking: All appearances of truth containing something divine belong to the rational level—so much so that rational ideas are the same as appearances of truth. Facts, though, belong to the earthly level—so much so that earthly ideas are the same as factual truth. Rational truth, or appearances of truth, can exist and emerge only from an inflow from the Divine into the rational dimension and through rational ideas into the facts occupying the earthly dimension. The resulting activity on the rational level shows up on the earthly level like the image of a busy scene reflected in a mirror. That is how it presents itself to us and also to angels. The earthly image is not as conspicuous to an angel as it is to those in the world of spirits and those on a spiritual-earthly level. So the latter two groups have truth *represented* to them. [4] It is the same with everyone on earth; as noted before [§§644, 684, 911, 978, 1733, 1900, 1928, 2634, 2997], any person devoted to goodness is a miniature heaven, an image of heaven as a whole. Again, divine truth cannot flow into the facts known to that person's earthly self directly but only by way of rational ideas, so the current verse says not to go down to Egypt but to live in the land of Gerar.

But we cannot gain a clear picture of these things without knowing the nature of inflow and of mental images, so by the Lord's divine mercy, these two topics will be discussed at the end of several chapters, where I recount some experiences of mine [§§6053–6058, 6189–6215, 6307–6327, 6466–6496, 6598–6626].

Stay as an immigrant in this land symbolizes being taught. This can be seen from the symbolism of *staying as an immigrant* as teaching (discussed in §§1463, 2025) and from that of the *land* here as rational ideas, which are appearances of truth when illuminated by the Divine (discussed just above in §3368). *Staying as an immigrant in this land,* then, means being taught them.   **3369**

And I will be with you symbolizes divinity, as is indicated by the consideration that Jehovah, and therefore divinity itself, is the one speaking. When divinity itself says in a given context, "I will be with you," it means that divinity will be in that thing.   **3370**

And bless you symbolizes a consequent increase. This is established by the symbolism of *blessing* as a fruitfulness of what is good and a multiplication of what is true (discussed at §§981, 1420, 1422, 1731, 2846, 3140) and therefore as an increase.   **3371**

Because to you symbolizes goodness, as can be seen from the fact that *to you* means to Isaac, who represents the Lord's divine rationality (as shown often), the Lord's divine rationality being nothing but goodness. Even the truth there is goodness, because it is divine.   **3372**

3373   *And your seed* symbolizes truth, as can be seen from the symbolism of *seed* as truth (dealt with in §§29, 255, 1025, 1447, 1610, 1940, 2848, 3310) and therefore as truth from the Lord's divine side—"*your* seed."

People who take the Word only according to its literal meaning have no idea that seed is anything but offspring. In this case, they take it to mean the descendants of Isaac through Esau and Jacob—mainly Jacob, since that nation had the Word, which tells so many stories about them. In an inner sense, though, seed does not mean any descendants of Isaac but all who are the Lord's children and are therefore the children of his kingdom, or in other words, who are devoted to the goodness and truth that come from the Lord. Since these are the seed, it follows that the goodness and truth coming from the Lord is itself the seed, since that is what makes people his children. Accordingly, true concepts from the Lord are also called the children of the kingdom in Matthew:

> The one who sows *good seed* is the Son of Humankind; the field is the world; *the seeds are the children of the kingdom.* (Matthew 13:37, 38)

So sons in general also symbolize truth (§§489, 491, 533, 1147, 2623).

[2] The seed of Abraham, Isaac, and Jacob is mentioned many times in the Word of God, which repeatedly says their seed would be blessed—blessed above all nations and peoples in the entire world. Anyone who thinks at all deeply or inwardly can see that this seed cannot mean the off-spring of those men, because among all nations they were the least active in doing the good called for by love for the Lord and charity toward their neighbor. They did not even possess any of faith's truth. The nature of the Lord, his kingdom, heaven, and life after death was completely unknown to them, partly because they did not want to know about it, and partly because if they had found out, they would have denied it at heart. In doing so, they would have profaned deeper goodness and truth the same way they profaned shallower goodness and truth by their repeated blatant idolatry. (That is why the deeper contents of the Old Testament Word so rarely disclose themselves in the literal meaning.) Seeing that they were like this, the Lord said of them, quoting from Isaiah:

> He has blinded their eyes and closed off their heart to prevent them from seeing with their eyes and understanding at heart and turning and being healed by me. (John 12:40)

When they called themselves Abraham's seed, he spoke of them as follows:

> They said, "We are Abraham's seed. Abraham is our father." Jesus says to them, "If you were children of Abraham, you would do the deeds of

Abraham. You are from your father, the Devil, and your father's desires
you wish to do." (John 8:33, 39, 44)

Abraham means the Lord here, as he does throughout the Word. The Lord
explicitly says they were not his seed or children but from the Devil.

This shows plainly that the seed of Abraham, Isaac, and Jacob does
not in any way mean those people in either the narrative or the prophetic
part of the Word, because the Word is divine throughout. Instead it means
everyone who is the Lord's seed—that is, everyone committed to the goodness and truth that comes of faith in him.

The Lord alone produces heavenly seed, or everything good and true;
see §§1438, 1614, 2016, 2803, 2882, 2883, 2891, 2892, 2904, 3195.

I will give all these lands symbolizes spiritual qualities, which is established by the symbolism of *lands* here as rational ideas that constitute
appearances of truth when illuminated by the Divine (dealt with above
at §3368). These appearances are truths (also shown above, in §§3364,
3365), so they are spiritual qualities, spiritual things being nothing but
truth from the Divine, as numerous remarks on their meaning have
demonstrated.

In its genuine sense, spirituality means the actual light of truth from
the Lord, just as heavenliness means all the fire of goodness from the
Lord. This light flows from the Lord into our rational and earthly levels,
so spirituality obviously relates to both levels, and divinity in the form of
truth is what flows in.

From this you can see what spirituality means in its genuine sense,
and that there is spiritual rationality and spiritual earthliness.

And I will set up the oath that I swore to Abraham your father symbolizes confirmation. This can be seen from the symbolism of an *oath* or the
act of swearing as confirmation (discussed at §2842). The current verse
does not speak of setting up the pact with Abraham but of setting up
the oath. A pact has to do with something heavenly, or goodness, but
an oath, with something spiritual, or truth (see §3037), and truth is the
subject here. A consequence of this is that verse 31 below does not mention Isaac when it speaks of the pact he struck with Abimelech but says,
"A man swore an oath to his brother." In contrast, Genesis 21:32 says of
Abraham that he and Abimelech struck a pact (see Psalms 105:[9,] 10).

The confirmation symbolized here by the oath means the Lord's union
with the inhabitants of his kingdom, because an oath is confirmation of
a pact, and a pact symbolizes union (§§665, 666, 1023, 1038, 1864, 1996,
2003, 2021).

3374

3375

3376   The inner meaning of the last two verses is this: When divine truth flows in through rational ideas, it creates appearances of truth. In the process it causes goodness and truth to become fruitful and multiply—specifically, the goodness and truth through which the Lord unites with angels and people.

The reader cannot tell that this is the meaning from the first presentation of it in §3366, where it appears disconnected, as follows: *From his divine side [the Lord] received the thought that he should not resort to secular facts but to rational ideas, which are appearances of truth when the Divine illuminates them. This resulted in instruction by his divine side and an increase, thus a goodness and truth, which are spiritual and are the means of union between the Lord and the inhabitants of his kingdom.* Although these ideas seem disjointed to people on earth, they connect in perfect order in the inner meaning. To angels, or in heaven, they appear and are perceived in a very beautiful series, accompanied by angelic portrayals presented in a heavenly form with indescribable variety.

This is what the Word is like throughout its inner meaning.

3377   Genesis 26:4, 5. *"And I will make your seed multiply like the stars of the heavens and will give your seed all these lands; and in your seed all the nations of the earth will be blessed, because Abraham heeded my voice and observed my observances, my commandments, my statutes, and my laws."*

I will make your seed multiply like the stars of the heavens symbolizes religious truth and religious knowledge. *And will give your seed all these lands* symbolizes the resulting churches. *And in your seed all the nations of the earth will be blessed* symbolizes everyone devoted to goodness, both inside and outside the church. *Because Abraham heeded my voice* symbolizes the uniting of the Lord's divine nature with his human nature through times of trial. *And observed my observances, my commandments, my statutes, and my laws* means through constant revelations from himself.

3378   *I will make your seed multiply like the stars of the heavens* symbolizes religious truth and religious knowledge. This is established by the symbolism of *seed* as truth (treated of above in §3373) and by that of *stars* as religious knowledge (treated of at §§2495, 2849).

3379   *And will give your seed all these lands* symbolizes the resulting churches, as can be seen from the following: *Seed* symbolizes truth and therefore people who know truth, for which reason they are called children of the kingdom (as discussed above in §3373). And *lands* symbolize rational ideas that are appearances of truth when illuminated by the Divine (as also discussed above, in §3368). So they symbolize people who think rational thoughts illuminated by the Divine—in other words, people who enjoy heavenly light. The only ones who have the use of that light are those in the Lord's heavenly kingdom (heaven) and in the Lord's earthly kingdom (churches), so clearly *these lands* means churches. Churches are churches not because they are so called and because they publicly avow the Lord's name but because they dedicate themselves to the goodness and truth involved in faith. This goodness and truth itself is what makes the church—in fact, what *is* the church—because the Lord is in it, and where the Lord is, there the church is.

And in your seed all the nations of the earth will be blessed symbolizes everyone devoted to goodness, both inside and outside the church, as can be seen from the following: *Being blessed* means seeing one's goodness bear fruit and one's truth multiply, as discussed above at §§981, 1422, 1731, 2846, 3140. *Seed* symbolizes goodness and truth from the Lord, as noted above at §3373. And the *nations of the earth* symbolize everyone with goodness. For the meaning of nations as goodness, or in other words, people with goodness, see §§1259, 1260, 1416, 1849. So *in your seed all the nations of the earth will be blessed* means that goodness and truth from the Lord will save everyone who lives a life of mutual neighborly love, whether inside or outside the church. Those people in nations outside the church who live good lives are also saved; see §§593, 932, 1032, 1059, 1327, 1328, 2049, 2051, 2284, 2589–2604, 2861, 2986, 3263.   **3380**

Because Abraham heeded my voice symbolizes the uniting of the Lord's divine nature with his human nature through times of trial, as can be seen from the following: *Abraham* represents the Lord's divine humanity as well [as his divinity] (dealt with in §§2833, 2836, 3251). And when the Lord is said to *heed my voice,* it symbolizes the uniting of his divine with his human nature through trials. Trials are what the Word is referring to when it speaks of obedience on the part of the Lord. The text is pointing to the story of Abraham in Genesis 22, in which God *tested him,* telling him to take his son and offer him as a burnt offering (verses 1, 2). When Abraham heeded his voice, it says, "Now I know that you fear God and have not held back your only son from me. Upon my life I have sworn (says Jehovah), because seeing that you have done this word and have not held back your son, your only one, I will surely bless you and surely multiply your seed as the stars of the heavens" (verses 12, 16, 17). "Not holding back your only son from me" was Abraham's heeding of God's voice,   **3381** and it symbolizes the uniting of the Lord's humanity with his divinity through his final trial; see §§2827, 2844. What he said in Gethsemane also demonstrates that this is what heeding Jehovah's (or the Father's) voice means. In Matthew:

> "My Father, if it is possible, let this cup pass me by; *yet not as I wish but as you do."* Again a second time: "My Father, if this cup cannot pass me by unless I drink it, *let your will be done."* (Matthew 26:39, 42; Mark 14:36; Luke 22:42)

Since Jehovah, or the Father, was in him—or rather he was in the Father, and the Father, in him (John 14:10, 11)—his heeding Jehovah's voice means he made his divinity one with his humanity by his own power through his inward trials. The Lord's own words in John show the same thing:

> As the Father knows me and I know the Father, and *I lay down my soul for my sheep*—because of this the Father loves me: that *I lay my soul down* so that I can take it back. No one takes it from me, but *I lay it down by myself. I have the power to lay it down, and I have the power to take it back.* This commandment I received from my Father. (John 10:15, 17, 18)

To see that the Lord made his divine nature one with his human nature by his own power through times of trial, consult §§1663, 1668, 1690, 1691 at the end, 1725, 1729, 1733, 1737, 1787, 1789, 1812, 1820, 2776, 3318 at the end.

3382   *And observed my observances, my commandments, my statutes, and my laws* means through constant revelations from himself—that is, the Lord also united his divine with his human nature through revelations, just as he had through times of trial. The evidence for this is that *observing observances, commandments, statutes, and laws* involves everything in the Word. *Observances* mean everything in it in general; *commandments* mean its inner contents; *statutes* mean its outer contents; and *laws* mean everything in it in particular. The Lord is the one said to have observed them, and he has been the Word from eternity, the source of everything in it. The inner meaning, then, cannot be that he observed them but that he revealed them to himself during the times when his humanity was at one with his divinity.

[2] At first glance this does seem rather distant from the literal meaning and even from the first layer of inner meaning, but when people on earth read these words, that is how they are understood in heaven. As noted several times before (and as the examples in §§1873, 1874 show),

the literal meaning is sloughed off as it rises toward heaven, and a different, heavenly meaning takes its place—so different and so heavenly that the literal meaning can hardly be recognized as its source. Heaven's inhabitants live in the thought that the Word's whole inner meaning has to do with the Lord, and that everything in the Word comes from him. Even when he was in the world, they realize, his thinking came from the Divine and therefore from himself, and he acquired all understanding and wisdom for himself through constant revelations from his divine side. Consequently that is exactly the meaning they perceive in these words. The Lord cannot be said to observe the observances, commandments, statutes, and laws, because he *was* the Word, so *he* was the one to be observed; *he* was the commandment; *he* was the statute; *he* was the law. All these types of rules focus on him as their first source and final goal. The clause on its highest level therefore actually symbolizes the uniting of the Lord's divinity with his humanity through constant revelations from himself.

The Lord's thinking, unlike other people's, originated in the Divine and so in himself; see §§1904, 1914, 1935. He acquired understanding and wisdom for himself through constant revelations from his divine side; §§1616, 2500, 2523, 2632.

[3] Many passages viewed in their inner meaning can illustrate that in their proper sense the observances to be observed are everything in the Word in general; the commandments, its inner contents; the statutes, its outer contents; and the laws, everything in the Word in particular. Let me quote some of them here, such as the following in David:

> Fortunate are those who are upright in their path, walking in *Jehovah's law.* Fortunate are those keeping *his testimonies.* If only my paths were directed toward keeping *your statutes! Your statutes* I will keep. Do not desert me so utterly! With my whole heart I have sought you; do not make me stray from *your commandments.* In my heart have I hidden *your word,* to prevent my sinning against you. A blessing on you, Jehovah; teach me *your statutes.* With my lips I have recounted all the *judgments of your mouth.* In the path of *your testimonies* I am glad. On *your requirements* I meditate, and I pay regard to *your paths.* In *your statutes* I take pleasure. I do not forget *your word.* Repay your servant, so that I may live and keep *your word;* uncover my eyes, so that I may see marvels from *your law.* Do not hide *your commandments* from me. Give me life according to *your word.* Teach me *your statutes.* Make me understand the *way of your requirements.* (Psalms 119:1–27)

This whole psalm talks about the Word and different elements of the Word, which are plainly meant by the commandments, statutes, judgments, testimonies, requirements, and paths. However, their individual meanings cannot be detected at all in the literal sense, where they are hardly anything more than redundancies. The meaning can be seen only from the inner sense, in which commandments symbolize one thing; statutes, something completely different; and judgments, testimonies, requirements, and paths, other things again. [4] Likewise elsewhere in the same author:

> The *law of Jehovah* is perfect, bringing back the soul. The *testimony of Jehovah* is firm, making the simple wise. The *requirements of Jehovah* are upright, gladdening the heart. The *commandment of Jehovah* is pure, illuminating the eyes. The fear of Jehovah is clean, standing forever. The *judgments of Jehovah* are truth. (Psalms 19:7, 8, 9)

And in Kings, David tells Solomon:

> You shall *observe the observances* of your God, to walk in *his paths,* to keep *his statutes* and *his commandments* and *his judgments* and *his testimonies* according to what is written in *Moses' law.* (1 Kings 2:3)

The observances to be observed stand for everything in the Word in general, because they are mentioned first and point to the items that follow as less general. After all, observing what should be observed is the same as keeping what should be kept. In Moses:

> You shall love Jehovah your God and *observe his observances* and *[his] statutes* and *his judgments* and *his commandments* all your days. (Deuteronomy 11:1)

The observances to be observed (or kept) again stand for everything in the Word in general. The statutes stand for the external demands of Scripture, such as ritual and other acts that represent and symbolize the inner meaning. The commandments stand for the Word's inner dimensions, such as those having to do with life and doctrine and particularly with the inner meaning. However, more will be said elsewhere about the symbolism of commandments and statutes, the Lord in his divine mercy willing.

3383   Genesis 26:6, 7. *And Isaac settled in Gerar. And the men of the place questioned [him in regard] to his woman, and he said, "She is my sister," because he was afraid to say "my woman." "Perhaps the men of the place will kill me because of Rebekah, because she is good to look at."*

Isaac settled in Gerar symbolizes the Lord's state in regard to different aspects of faith as they related to the rational ideas that were to be attached to them. *And the men of the place questioned [him in regard] to his woman* symbolizes the investigations people make into divine truth. *And he said, "She is my sister,"* symbolizes rational truth. *Because he was afraid to say "my woman." "Perhaps the men of the place will kill me because of Rebekah"* means that he could not divulge real divine truth, because then divine goodness would not be accepted. *Because she is good to look at* means that people could easily accept that it was called divine.

Isaac settled in Gerar symbolizes the Lord's state in regard to different aspects of faith as they related to the rational ideas that were to be attached to them. This can be seen from the following: *Settling in Gerar* means being involved in the different aspects of faith, so it symbolizes the state of them. *Settling* means living (§1293), while *Gerar* symbolizes aspects of faith (1209, 2504, 3365). And *Isaac* represents the Lord's divine rationality (as discussed in §§1893, 2066, 2072, 2083, 2630). The theme is the way these states relate to the rational ideas to be attached to them, as the preceding and following verses suggest, because the whole chapter focuses on rational ideas that are appearances of truth when the Lord's divinity illuminates them.

[2] *Settling* or dwelling means existing and living, so it means a state, and many passages in the Word clarify this. In David, for instance:

> *I will dwell in Jehovah's house* to a great length of days. (Psalms 23:6)

> One thing have I asked of Jehovah; this I will seek: *May I dwell in Jehovah's house* all the days of my life! (Psalms 27:4)

> Someone working deceit *will not dwell in the middle of my house.* (Psalms 101:7)

Dwelling in Jehovah's house stands for existing and living in the goodness that love inspires, because a loving goodness is Jehovah's house. In Isaiah:

> *Those settling in the land of death's shadow*—light has shone on them. (Isaiah 9:2)

Those settling in death's shadow stand for the condition of people who know nothing about goodness and truth. In the same author:

> Babylon will be *uninhabited* forever. (Isaiah 13:20)

This stands for the state of damnation that the people meant by Babylon are in. [3] In the same author:

> Jehovah, God of Israel, *inhabiting the guardian beings.* (Isaiah 37:16)

3384

Shepherd of Israel, *inhabiting the guardian beings,* shine out! (Psalms 80:1)

The one inhabiting the guardian beings is the Lord as regards a state in which his providence prevents anyone from entering into the sacred experience of love and faith without first being prepared by him (§308). In David:

In peace I both lie down and sleep, because you, Jehovah, alone *make me dwell securely.* (Psalms 4:8)

Making someone dwell securely stands for peaceful conditions. In Jeremiah:

You who dwell on many waters, great in treasures—your end has come, the full measure of your gain. (Jeremiah 51:13)

This is about Babylon. Dwelling on many waters stands for knowing about truth. [4] In Daniel:

God himself reveals deep and hidden things; he knows what is in the dark, and *light dwells with him.* (Daniel 2:22)

Dwelling stands for existing. In the same author:

Under the tree the animal of the field found shade, and *in its branches dwelled the birds of the sky.* (Daniel 4:12)

And in Ezekiel:

Under its branches every wild animal of the field gave birth, and *in its shade all the great nations settled.* (Ezekiel 31:6)

Dwelling [or settling] stands for existing and living. In Hosea:

Threshing floor and winepress will not feed them, and the new wine will prove false to [that land]; *they will not settle in Jehovah's land,* and Ephraim will return to Egypt. (Hosea 9:2, 3)

Not settling in Jehovah's land stands for not being in a state of loving goodness and consequently not in the Lord's kingdom.

3385   *And the men of the place questioned [him in regard] to his woman* symbolizes the investigations people make into divine truth, as can be seen from the following: *Questioning* means investigating. The *men of the place*—Gerar—symbolize people engrossed in doctrines concerning faith. Gerar means aspects of faith (see §§1209, 2504), so the men of the place mean people in that state. And the *woman*—Rebekah—symbolizes divine truth in the Lord's divine rational mind (as discussed in §§3012, 3013, 3077).

The preceding verses described the way appearances of truth arise through a divine inflow from the Lord into a person's rational thinking. The current verse deals with the acceptance of those appearances, first of all by people taken up with doctrines about faith—the ones meant by the men of the place (Gerar). They belong to the first category of those called spiritual. Because they do not have the perception of heavenly people and live in relative darkness (§§1043, 2088, 2669, 2708 at the beginning, 2715, 2718, 2831, 3235, 3241, 3246), they investigate whether the appearances are right and whether they constitute divine truth. Unable to perceive whether things are so, they are given an idea that looks like truth and that suits their rational capacity, or their ability to grasp it, because then they can accept it. We are all free to believe the truth as we understand it; if we were not, we would not accept it, because we would never acknowledge it.

That is the theme here.

And he said, "She is my sister," symbolizes rational truth. The symbolism of a *sister* as rational truth (discussed in §§1495, 2508, 2524, 2556) shows this. "Rational truth" means that which looks like truth to our rational mind, or so far as we can grasp it, as noted just above.

Isaac's claim that Rebekah was his sister involves a secret similar to the one involved in Abraham's earlier claim that Sarah was his sister, in Egypt (Genesis 12:11, 12, 13, 19 [§§1465–1477, 1494–1497]) and afterward in Gerar (Genesis 20:2, 5, 12 [§§2505–2511, 2521–2526, 2555–2558]). This can be seen from the explanation in those places. Since the same thing happened three times, all of them recorded in the Word, the secret that is involved obviously has tremendous importance, and no one can see it without the inner meaning. What it is will become clear from the remarks that follow.

Because he was afraid to say "my woman." "Perhaps the men of the place will kill me because of Rebekah" means that he could not divulge real divine truth, because then divine goodness would not be accepted, as can be seen from the following: *Being afraid to say* means being unable to reveal something. The *woman,* Rebekah, symbolizes divine truth in the Lord's divine rationality, as noted at §§3012, 3013, 3077. *Killing me* means a failure to accept goodness, because Isaac—*me*—represents divine goodness in the Lord's rational mind (3012, 3194, 3210). Goodness is said to be killed or to die out when it is not accepted, because it disappears in that person. And the *men of the place* symbolize people focusing on doctrines about faith, as explained just above in §3385.

From this the inner meaning of the words can now be seen: If real divine truth were brought into the open, people who devote themselves to doctrines concerning faith would not accept it, because that truth lies beyond any ability these people have to comprehend it rationally and therefore any ability they have to believe it. No goodness from the Lord would be able to influence them, because goodness from the Lord, divine goodness, can flow only into truth. Truth is a vessel for goodness, as shown many times. [2] We are given truth, or appearances of truth, to enable divine goodness to form our intellect and therefore our actual self. The whole point of truth is to allow goodness to inflow. Without vessels or containers to receive it, good cannot find a spot for itself, because it cannot find suitable conditions. Where truth is missing, then, or where it is not accepted, rational or human goodness is also absent, and we lack spiritual life. So to insure that we still have truth and therefore some spiritual life, we are given appearances of truth, each of us according to our intellectual ability. These appearances are recognized as truth because they are capable of holding what is divine.

[3] To learn about appearances and the role they play among humankind as divine truth, take this example as an illustration: Suppose I said that no idea of place and distance exists in heaven but that the idea of state replaces it. People would never be able to understand this. They would think that nothing was distinct, everything was jumbled together, people were all combined into one; when in reality everything there is as distinct as it could possibly be. In heaven, the places, distances, and space characteristic of the physical world are states (see §3356). Clearly, then, whatever the Word says about places and space (or in terms of them) is an appearance of truth. If it were not expressed in terms of appearances, it would never be accepted, which means that hardly anything in the Word would be accepted. The notion of space and time enters into virtually all our thinking as long as we are in the world, subject to space and time.

[4] Almost everything in the Word shows that it speaks in harmony with the appearance of space. In Matthew, for instance:

> Jesus said, "How can David say, 'The Lord said to my Lord: "Sit *on my right* till I have placed your enemies as your *footstool*"?'" (Matthew 22:43, 44)

"Sitting on the right" draws on the idea of position and consequently harmonizes with appearances, but the passage is actually depicting a state of divine power in the Lord. In the same author:

> Jesus said, "From now on you will see the Son of Humankind *sitting to the right of power* and coming *on the clouds of heaven.*" (Matthew 26:64)

"Sitting on the right" (again) and "coming on the clouds" makes people think of position, but it makes angels think of the Lord's power. In Mark:

> The sons of Zebedee said to Jesus, "Grant us to sit one *on your right* and the other *on your left* in your glory." Jesus answered, "To sit on *my right* and on *my left* is not mine to give but belongs to those for whom it has been prepared." (Mark 10:37, 40)

This illustrates what the disciples' picture of the Lord's kingdom was, namely, sitting on his right and left. Because they thought this way, the Lord answered in terms they could understand and so in accord with appearances as they saw them. [5] In David:

> Like a bridegroom *leaving his room,* he rejoices as a hero does to run a path; from [one] *end of the heavens* is his departure, and *his circuit* is to their [other] *end.* (Psalms 19:5, 6)

This is about the Lord. The state of his divine power is being depicted through images involving space. In Isaiah:

> How you have *fallen from the sky,* Lucifer, son of the dawn! You said in your heart, "*I will climb* into *the heavens;* I will *raise* my *throne* above the stars of the sky; *I will climb onto the loftiest parts of the cloud.*" (Isaiah 14:12, 13, 14)

Falling from the sky, climbing into the heavens, raising a throne above the stars of the sky, and climbing onto the loftiest parts of the cloud all draw on the image and appearance of space or place to depict self-love as it profanes what is holy.

Since heavenly and spiritual concepts are presented to people on earth by means of appearances and in keeping with them, heaven itself is portrayed this way. It is described as being high up, for instance, when it is not high up but deep inside (§§450, 1380, 2148).

Because she is good to look at means that people could easily accept it because it was called divine. This can be seen from the symbolism of

3388

good to look at as something whose form is pleasing and which is therefore readily accepted.

The people being spoken of here concentrate on doctrines concerning faith. They have no ability to perceive truth from goodness, only a conscientious awareness of truth based on their parents' and teachers' say-so. They are the ones called the men of the place—that is, of Gerar (§§3385, 3387). The first confirmation of truth for them is the assertion that a thing is divine, because that immediately rouses the idea of holiness in them. The thought that it is holy provides them with universal corroboration for everything that is being said, even if they do not understand it. Even so, what they are hearing has to be adapted to their comprehension. It is not enough for people to know *that* a thing is; they also want to know *what* it is, and what it is *like*. This provides a measure of confirmation to their intellectual side and elicits further confirmation in return. If not, the concept can still be forced into their memory, but it does not stay except in a dead form, as something they recall hearing about. Unless supporting ideas—wherever they come from—fasten it there, it dissolves like the recollection of a thought that merely echoed in the mind.

3389   Genesis 26:8, 9. *And it happened, because his days there lengthened, that Abimelech, king of the Philistines, looked out through a window and saw, and look: Isaac laughing with Rebekah, his woman! And Abimelech called Isaac and said, "But look: she is your woman! So how could you say, 'She is my sister'?" And Isaac said to him, "Because I said, 'Perhaps I might die because of her.'"*

It happened, because his days there lengthened symbolizes a receptive state. *That Abimelech, king of the Philistines, looked out through a window and saw* symbolizes the doctrine of faith viewed in terms of the rational ideas embedded in religious knowledge. *And look: Isaac laughing with Rebekah, his woman!* means that divine goodness was present in divine truth. *And Abimelech called Isaac and said* symbolizes what the Lord perceived from doctrine. *But look: she is your woman! So how could you say, "She is my sister"?* means if it were divine truth, it would not also be rational truth. *And Isaac said to him, "Because I said, 'Perhaps I might die because of her,'"* means that it would not be accepted.

3390   *It happened, because his days there lengthened* symbolizes a receptive state, as can be seen from the following: *His [days] there lengthened*— Isaac's—means that when the divine goodness represented by Isaac had been there a while, truth would be accepted (the focus of the inner sense being the acceptance of truth by spiritual people). And *days* symbolize states, as noted at §§23, 487, 488, 493, 893, 2788.

That Abimelech, king of the Philistines, looked out through a window **3391**
and saw symbolizes the doctrine of faith viewed in terms of the rational
ideas embedded in religious knowledge, as is established by the following: *Abimelech* represents the doctrine of faith viewed in rational terms, as discussed in §§2504, 2509, 2510, 2533, while *king of the Philistines* symbolizes doctrines, as noted at §3365. And a *window* symbolizes an intellectual capacity, as noted in §§655, 658, so it symbolizes inner sight, since that is what people once meant by "windows." *Looking out through* a window, then, means perceiving what is visible through the inner eye—that is, religious knowledge, broadly speaking, which belongs to the outer self. Rational ideas (or appearances of truth, or spiritual truth) are not religious knowledge but are present within that knowledge, because they belong to the rational mind and so to the inner self. The inner self is what observes things in the outer self, so it sees the truth embedded in religious concepts. Because they belong to the earthly self, these concepts are vessels designed to receive rational ideas. Divine truth flows into the rational mind and through this into the earthly mind, where it resembles the image of a busy scene reflected in a mirror; see §3368.

[2] The scriptural passages quoted in §655 show that *windows* symbolize the abilities of the inner eye, or of the intellect, which are all included in the term "intellectual." The following quotations make it even clearer. In Joel:

> In the city they will dash about; on the wall they will run; onto houses they will climb; *through windows they will enter* like a thief. (Joel 2:9)

This is about evil and falsity during the church's last days. Climbing onto houses stands for destroying what is good in the will (houses meaning what is good; see §§710, 2233), and entering through windows stands for destroying truth and the knowledge of it in the intellect. In Zephaniah:

> Jehovah will stretch his hand out over the north and destroy Assyria. Packs [of animals] will lie down in its midst, every wild animal of that nation; the spoonbill and the harrier will also spend the night among its pomegranates. *A voice will sing in the window.* Drought is at the threshold, because he has stripped its cedar bare. (Zephaniah 2:[13,] 14)

The subject here is the destruction of religious truth through twisted reasoning (meant by Assyria; §§119, 1186). "A voice will sing in the window" stands for the abandonment of truth, which ruins any ability to understand it. [3] In Judges:

> *Through the window* Sisera's mother *looked out,* and she cried aloud through the *lattice,* "Why is his chariot slow to come?" (Judges 5:28)

Deborah and Barak's oracular song concerns the revival of spiritual religion. To look out through a window stands for the skewed logic of people who deny truth, destroying what religion has to offer. Such reasoning is a negative use of intellectual powers. In Jeremiah:

> Doom to those who build their house without justice and their upper rooms without judgment; who say, "I will build myself a house of [large] dimensions, and upper rooms that are spacious," and *cut windows out for themselves* (and it is paneled in cedar) and paint it with vermilion. (Jeremiah 22:13, 14)

Building a house without justice and upper rooms without judgment stands for constructing a sham religion out of what is not good or true. For the meaning of justice and judgment as goodness and truth, see §2235. Cutting windows out for themselves, using cedar paneling, and painting with vermilion stands for falsifying intuitive, spiritual truth.

The windows of the Jerusalem temple represented the intellectual and therefore the spiritual dimension. The symbolism is the same for the windows of the new temple, described in Ezekiel 40:16, 22, 25, 33, 36; 41:16, 26. Anyone can see that the new temple, new Jerusalem, and new land depicted by that prophet actually mean the Lord's kingdom, so that any details mentioned mean different aspects of his kingdom.

3392   *And look: Isaac laughing with Rebekah, his woman!* means that divine goodness was present in divine truth (in other words, divine truth was attached to divine goodness), as can be seen from the following: *Isaac* represents the divine goodness of the Lord's rationality, as discussed in §§3012, 3194, 3210. *Laughing* symbolizes a love or desire for truth, as discussed in §§2072, 2216. And *Rebekah* represents divine truth in the Lord's rational mind, as discussed in §§3012, 3013, 3077. Clearly, then, *Isaac was laughing with Rebekah, his woman,* means that divine goodness was present in divine truth.

The meaning of the clause in context is this: At first people accept spiritual truth because someone tells them it is divine, but later they accept it because something divine is present in it. Those who are being reborn and are coming to be part of a spiritual religion are able to see through to the divinity within. Abimelech stands for these people—that is, for those dedicated to the doctrine of faith who focus on the truth to be found within religious knowledge, as described just above in §3391.

And Abimelech called Isaac and said symbolizes what the Lord perceived from doctrine. This is established by the representation of *Abimelech* as a theology that focuses on rational ideas (discussed in §§2504, 2509, 2510, 2533, 3391); by that of *Isaac* as the Lord's divine rationality (mentioned above); and by the symbolism of *saying* as perceiving (dealt with in §§1898, 1919, 2080, 2862). Since Abimelech symbolizes that kind of theology (in which something divine was now perceived; 3392), he also represents the Lord in relation to it. In its highest sense, everything in the Word relates to the Lord. The Lord is doctrine itself—that is, the Word. He is not only the Word in its highest sense but also in its inward sense and in its literal sense, because the literal sense represents and symbolizes the inward sense, which represents and symbolizes the highest sense. In its essence, a representation or symbolism in the Word actually is the thing that it represents or symbolizes, so it is a divine facet of the Lord. A representation is just an image of the thing it represents, and the one who is being portrayed is present in the image. Human speech and gestures illustrate this plainly. Our words and actions are only tokens of what is happening inside us, within our mind and heart, so that speech and gestures are thought and will in a form. If you took away thought and will, what remained would be only a lifeless trifle, completely nonhuman. This shows that the Word is divine, even in its literal meaning.

But look: she is your woman! So how could you say, "She is my sister"? means if it were divine truth, it would not also be rational truth. This can be seen from the symbolism of the *woman*, Rebekah, as divine truth known to the Lord's divine rationality (discussed in §§3012, 3013, 3077) and from that of a *sister* as truth on the rational plane (mentioned in §3386). So *Look: she is your woman! So how could you say, "She is my sister"?* means that because it is divine truth, it cannot be rational truth.

[2] Here is the situation with this secret: Because spiritual people do not have perception, as the heavenly do, they do not realize that divine truth becomes rational truth in us when we are reborn. They do say that everything good and everything true comes from the Lord, but when goodness or truth emerges in their rational mind, they imagine that it is theirs, as if it originated with them. They cannot detach from their sense

of autonomy, which wants this to be the case. Heavenly people, however, perceive divine goodness and truth on the rational plane, or within rational ideas, which are appearances of truth when illuminated by the Lord's divinity (§3368). They also perceive divine goodness and truth on the earthly plane, or within facts and sense impressions. As a result of these circumstances, they can acknowledge that everything good and true flows in from the Lord. They can also recognize that their ability to perceive goodness and truth is something the Lord imparts to them as their own, creating pleasure, bliss, and happiness for them. That was why the earliest people, who were heavenly, perceived only what was heavenly and spiritual in any object they saw with their eyes (§1409).

[3] The current verse is talking about spiritual people who have been reborn. Through rebirth they have received divine goodness from the Lord in their new power of will, and divine truth in their new intellect. As I said above, though, they cannot help thinking that if such truth were reasoned, it could not be divine, so that if it were divine, it could not share any common ground with rational thinking. That is the reason for the phrasing "if it were divine truth, it would not also be rational truth."

For the same reason, people demand that tenets of faith simply be believed, without rational examination. They do not realize that we never grasp any article of faith, even the most arcane, without some rational and even earthly idea of it, although we are unaware of the true character of that idea (§3310 at the end). Admittedly this attitude does enable people to protect themselves against others who argue from a negative standpoint over the validity of absolutely everything (2568, 2588). Still, to people who approach the Word affirmatively, as something they ought to believe, such a position is damaging. Those who adopt it are likely to take away others' freedom of thought and shackle others' consciences, perhaps under obligation to some egregious heresy, controlling people's inner and outer life.

All this is meant by "Abimelech said to Isaac, 'Look: she is your woman! So how could you say, "She is my sister"?'"

3395   *And Isaac said to him, "Because I said, 'Perhaps I might die because of her,'"* means that it would not be accepted, as can be seen from the discussion above in §3387 at the words *Because he was afraid to say "my woman." "Perhaps the men of the place will kill me because of Rebekah."*

The fact that *saying* means perceiving and thinking is more obvious here than elsewhere.

Genesis 26:10, 11. *And Abimelech said, "What is this you have done to us? At the least, one of the people might have lain with your woman, and you would have brought guilt on us." And Abimelech commanded all the people, saying, "The one touching that man and his woman will surely die."*

Abimelech said, "What is this you have done to us?" symbolizes outrage. *At the least, one of the people might have lain with your woman, and you would have brought guilt on us* means that [divine truth] could have been adulterated and therefore profaned. *And Abimelech commanded all the people, saying,* symbolizes a decree. *The one touching that man and his woman will surely die* means that divine truth and goodness was not to be divulged, that faith was not to reach all the way to it, because there was danger of eternal damnation if it were profaned.

Abimelech said, "What is this you have done to us?" symbolizes outrage, as stands to reason without explanation.

At the least, one of the people might have lain with your woman, and you would have brought guilt on us means that [divine truth] could have been adulterated and therefore profaned, as can be seen from the following: *Lying [with]* means being perverted or adulterated. *One of the people* symbolizes anyone in the church—the spiritual church—as noted in §2928. The *woman,* Rebekah, symbolizes divine truth, as noted above. And *guilt* symbolizes responsibility for profaning truth. This shows that *At the least, one of the people might have lain with your wife, and you would have brought guilt on us* means that anyone in the church could easily have adulterated divine truth and incurred guilt for profaning it.

Above at §3386, I pointed out that there must be a very secret reason why Abraham twice referred to his wife Sarah as his sister (first in Egypt, then in Gerar with Abimelech); why Isaac too told Abimelech that Rebekah his woman was his sister; and why the Word mentions all three instances. The secret involved becomes clear in the inner meaning: A sister symbolizes what is rational, and a woman [attached to a man], divine truth. Divine truth (Isaac's woman, Rebekah) was described as rational (a sister) to keep it from being adulterated and therefore profaned.

[2] To turn to the topic of truth's profanation: Divine truth can be profaned only by people who have already acknowledged it. After all, they first entered on the truth by acknowledging and believing in it, which means they were initiated into it. Later, if they back away from it, a trace remains permanently imprinted on them deep inside, and it returns when falsity and evil are recalled. The truth clinging to the falsity

3396

3397

3398

and evil is then profaned. So the people in whom this happens always have something in them that damns them—a private hell. When hellish beings go near an environment in which goodness and truth exist, they instantly become aware of their hell, because they are entering what they hate and therefore what tortures them. So people who profane truth live constantly with a source of torment, according to the magnitude of their profanation.

Because of this, the Lord takes the greatest care to prevent divine goodness and truth from being profaned. With people who cannot help profaning what is true and good his main method is to keep them as far as possible from acknowledging and believing in it. Again, the only people who can profane something are those who once acknowledged and believed it.

[3] That was why deep truth was not revealed to Jacob's descendants in Israel and Judah. It was not even said to them explicitly that people have a deeper level or that such a thing as inward worship exists. They were barely told anything about life after death or about the heavenly kingdom of the Lord—that is, of the Messiah they were waiting for. The reason was their character. It was foreseen that if these concepts had been revealed to them, they could not have helped profaning them, because all they were interested in were earthly concerns. That was the character of that generation, and it is the same today, so even now they are still allowed to be complete nonbelievers. If they had ever acknowledged these things and then recanted, they would necessarily have brought the very heaviest hell of all upon themselves.

[4] Furthermore, that was why the Lord did not come into the world and disclose the inner contents of the Word until nothing good whatever remained to those people, not even earthly goodness. At that point they were no longer able to accept truth to the point of acknowledging it internally (since goodness is what accepts truth), so they could not profane it. Those are the conditions meant by the fullness of time, the close of the age, and the last day, mentioned many times in the prophets.

The reason the secrets of the Word's inner meaning are now being disclosed is the same: there is hardly any faith today because there is no neighborly love, so the era has reached its close. When this happens, secrets can be revealed without danger of profanation, because they are not inwardly acknowledged.

[5] This bit of hidden wisdom explains why the Word recounts the times in Gerar when Abraham and Isaac told Abimelech that their wives were their sisters.

In addition, see previous remarks and explanations on the same subject: People who acknowledge something can profane it, but not those who do not acknowledge it, let alone those who do not know about it: 593, 1008, 1010, 1059. What the danger is in profaning holy qualities and in profaning the Word: 571, 582. People who are inside the church can profane what is holy, but not those who are outside it: 2051. The Lord takes great care to prevent our committing profanation: 1001, 2426. Worship is made superficial to prevent a deeper form of it from being profaned: 1327, 1328. People are kept in ignorance so that they will not profane religious truth: 301, 302, 303.

Lying with [another man's] woman in an inner sense means twisting and adulterating truth—in this case, truth that is divine, since divine truth is what the woman, Rebekah, represents, as shown above [§3398]. This can be seen from the fact that in the Word, lying with someone, adultery, and prostitution actually mean corruption of what is good and falsification of what is true, as shown in §§2466, 2729. Adultery is diametrically opposed to the love in marriage (to the point of destroying it), and marriage love originates in the marriage of goodness and truth (2508, 2618, 2727–2759, 3132). So anything that opposes goodness and truth or destroys them is called adultery in the Word.

3399

[2] It is important to realize that people in a spiritual religion cannot adulterate goodness enough to profane it because they are not open enough to it to perceive it, as the heavenly can. The spiritual *can* profane truth, because they can acknowledge it, but in the church's final days, they cannot do even that. At that stage, disbelief in the Lord, in life after death, and in the inner self pervades their whole being, and when it does, it keeps religious truth from penetrating their surface. What is all-pervasive in an individual restrains and prohibits such things from entering more deeply, although the people in whom this is happening do not realize it and even imagine that they are believers.

[3] The people who can profane what is good are those in a heavenly religion, because they *can* let goodness in far enough to perceive it. That is what happened among the people living before the Flood, and they are therefore kept in complete isolation, in a hell detached from others' hells. For more about them, see §§1265–1272. The fact that after Jehovah threw

the humans out he caused guardian beings to live on the east of the Garden of Eden, and the flame of a sword turning itself, to guard the way to the tree of lives (Genesis 3:24), symbolizes an intent to prevent anything good from ever being profaned again; see §§308, 310.

3400 The symbolism of *guilt* as responsibility or assignment of blame for sinning and transgressing against what is good and true can be seen from passages in the Word that mention guilt and also describe it. In Isaiah, for instance:

> Jehovah wishes to crush him and has weakened him. *If you make his soul a guilt [offering],* he will see his seed, he will lengthen his days, and the will of Jehovah will prosper through his hand. (Isaiah 53:10)

This is about the Lord. Making his soul a guilt [offering] stands for sin imputed to him and so for blame cast by those who hate him. It is not saying that he shouldered any sin himself in order to remove it. In Ezekiel:

> By the blood that you shed *you have incurred guilt,* and by your idols that you made you have been defiled. (Ezekiel 22:4)

Shedding blood stands for inflicting violence on what is good (§§374, 376, 1005), which results in guilt. In David:

> Those who hate the righteous individual will *incur guilt.* Jehovah is redeeming the soul of his servants, and *none* of those trusting in him *will incur guilt.* (Psalms 34:21, 22)

So guilt stands for any sin that remains. [2] Redemption is removal of sin through goodness from the Lord, which was also represented by atonement by a priest when people offered a guilt sacrifice, as described in Leviticus 5:1–19; 6:1–7; 7:1–10; 19:20, 21, 22; Numbers 5:1–8. These passages also list different types of guilt: hearing the voice of a curse and not telling; touching anything unclean; swearing to do evil; sinning by mistake concerning Jehovah's holy things; doing one of the things it is commanded should not be done; denying [receipt of] a neighbor's deposit; finding a lost item, denying it, and swearing falsely; lying with a woman who was a slave owned by [another] man, not redeemed or freed; and doing any of the sins against a person, committing a transgression against Jehovah.

3401 *And Abimelech commanded all the people, saying,* symbolizes a decree, as can be seen from the following: *Commanding* means making a decree. *Abimelech* represents people whose attention is on the doctrine of faith (as noted in §3392), and in the highest sense represents the Lord (3393).

And a *people* symbolizes those in a spiritual religion (as discussed at §3398). Clearly, then, *Abimelech commanded all the people* symbolizes a decree from the Lord in a spiritual religion. The decree itself is what follows: that divine truth and goodness is not to be divulged, that faith is not to reach that far, because there is danger of eternal damnation if it is profaned. See the next section.

The one touching that man and his woman will surely die means that divine truth and goodness is not to be divulged, that faith is not to reach all the way to it, because there is danger of eternal damnation if it is profaned, as can be seen from the following: *Touching that man and his woman* means approaching divine truth and goodness, represented by Isaac and Rebekah. Truth is mentioned first here, and goodness second, because the text is talking about people in a spiritual church, who are capable of adulterating and even profaning truth but not goodness. On that account it says "man and woman" (see §§915, 2517). And *surely dying* symbolizes eternal damnation, which is spiritual death, in this case resulting from profanation, which I will now discuss. **3402**

[2] The Lord in his providence sees to it that we not enter into goodness and truth—into acknowledging and being touched by them—past a level we can sustain, because of the danger of eternal damnation (see above at §3398).

As has been said and shown several times before [§§50, 571, 573, 798, 1740, 2284], the more we indulge in evil and falsity, the more deeply goodness and truth bury themselves inside us, which means that the angels from heaven around us withdraw and devilish spirits from hell come close; and the reverse. If we are involved in evil and falsity, we do not notice the removal of goodness and truth and so of the angels. We are convinced that evil is good and falsity is true, because we like them and take pleasure in them, and under those circumstances, we cannot possibly be aware that goodness and truth have been taken from us.

Goodness and truth (angels, in other words) are said to leave us when we are not affected by them—that is, when they no longer delight us. On the contrary, self-love and materialism call to us; they alone delight us.

[3] To possess goodness and truth is not merely to know them, or hold them in our memory and carry them on our lips, but to respond to them from the heart. Nor are they ours when we seek them for the sake of amassing prestige and wealth. In that case it is not goodness and truth we seek but position and riches; we view goodness and truth as the means of acquiring them. With people like this in the other world, the good and true things they knew and even preached are taken from them; the love

for themselves and for worldly advantages on which they based their lives remains.

This evidence shows how matters stand with goodness and truth. We are not allowed to approach them with desire or belief unless we can remain in them to the end of our life; but people who profane them cannot be stopped.

3403 Genesis 26:12, 13, 14. *And Isaac sowed in that land and found a hundred measures in that year, and Jehovah blessed him. And the man grew and went—went, and grew!—until he became very great. And he had property in flock and property in herd and large slaveholdings; and the Philistines envied him.*

Isaac sowed in that land symbolizes deep truth coming from the Lord, as that truth appears to the rational mind. *And found a hundred measures in that year* symbolizes abundance. *And Jehovah blessed him* means in regard to the loving goodness within that truth. *And the man grew and went—went, and grew!—until he became very great* symbolizes increases. *And he had property in flock and property in herd* means in regard to inward goodness and outward goodness. *And large slaveholdings* symbolizes the resulting truth. *And the Philistines envied him* means that people who merely know the concepts cannot comprehend.

3404 *Isaac sowed in that land* symbolizes deep truth coming from the Lord, as that truth appears to the rational mind, as is established by the following: On the highest level, *sowing* symbolizes divine truth from the Lord, who is the sower (§3038). On an inward level it symbolizes the resulting truth and goodness in people (3373). And the *land* symbolizes rational ideas that are appearances of truth, when the Divine illuminates them (3368), or (to put the same thing another way) deep truth coming from the Lord, as that truth appears to the rational mind. These appearances or truths exist on a very high level, since they are the focus of the inner meaning up to verse 14. Angels live amid these appearances of truth, which immeasurably transcend our grasp as long as we are living in the world.

[2] To clarify further what appearances of truth are, here is another example: It is known that the divine existence is infinite, and the divine emergence is eternal; and that what is finite does not have the capacity to comprehend the infinite, or even the eternal (since eternity is an infinite emerging). Because divinity itself is infinite and eternal, the things it produces are all infinite and eternal as well, and being infinite, they cannot possibly be grasped by angels, who are finite. As a result, things

that are infinite and eternal are presented to them in appearances, which are finite, although they still lie far above the reach of human comprehension. For instance, humans cannot form any concept at all of eternity except in terms of time, and consequently they cannot understand what "from eternity" means. They cannot imagine how the Divine could exist before time, before the world was created. As long as any notion of time remains in their thinking, they cannot help falling into inescapable errors whenever they contemplate the subject. Angels, on the other hand, who think in terms not of time but of state, are given the ability to see it quite clearly. Their eternity is not one of time but one of state without time. [3] This indicates how angels' appearances of truth compare to people's and how much loftier theirs are. We on earth cannot have even the slightest [stirring] of thought without some impetus from time and space. In contrast, angels gain nothing from time and space but rather from a state's core being and its emergence.

These brief remarks show what the higher-level appearances of truth depicted here are like. What follows deals in order with appearances of truth on lower levels suited to the human race.

And found a hundred measures in that year symbolizes abundance. **3405** This can be seen from the symbolism of a *year* as the whole state being portrayed (discussed in §§487, 488, 493, 893); from that of a *hundred* as a large and complete amount (discussed in §2636); and from that of a *measure* as the state of a thing in regard to truth (discussed in §3104). Put these together and the symbolism is an abundance of truth.

The highest sense here has to do with the Lord (as it does everywhere). It says that he too was subject to appearances of truth when the humanity he received from his mother was dominant, but as he shed that humanity, he shed the appearances and put on infinite and eternal divinity itself.

In a secondary, inward sense, the theme is appearances on quite a high level, which exist among angels, as noted. "He found a hundred measures in that year" symbolizes the abundance of these appearances. [2] This is how matters stand with appearances of truth, or with truths coming from the Divine: Those on a higher level immeasurably surpass those on a lower level in number and perfection. Where individuals on a higher level distinctly perceive tens of thousands and even hundreds of millions of details, those on a lower level see only a single whole. Lower things are simply composites of higher things. This can be concluded from the two types of human memory. The deeper kind is on a higher level, so it is vastly superior to the more superficial kind, which is on a lower level (see §§2473, 2474).

This shows how angels' wisdom compares to the wisdom of people on earth. In fact, angels of the third heaven are on the fourth step above us, so the only way to characterize their wisdom to us is to say that it is incomprehensible and even indescribable.

3406   *And Jehovah blessed him* means in regard to the loving goodness within that truth. This can be seen from the symbolism of being *blessed* as being enriched with all kinds of heavenly and spiritual goodness (discussed in §§981, 1731, 2846). Being blessed by *Jehovah,* then, means being blessed with heavenly goodness, which is a loving goodness, because Jehovah is the essence itself of love, or goodness (1735). So where the text is dealing with goodness, it names Jehovah, but where it is dealing with truth, it speaks of God (2586, 2769).

3407   *And the man grew and went—went, and grew!—until he became very great* symbolizes increases. This can be seen from the symbolism of *growing,* of the repeated *go,* and of *becoming very great* as increases of goodness and truth in their proper order, which is from truth to goodness, and from goodness to truth.

3408   *And he had property in flock and property in herd* means in regard to inward goodness and outward goodness—that is, in regard to goodness on the rational plane and on the earthly plane. This is established by the symbolism of a *flock* as inward or rational goodness (discussed in §§343, 2566) and by that of a *herd* as outward or earthly goodness (discussed in §2566).

The earthly goodness symbolized by a herd is not the goodness we are born with but the goodness we acquire through an education in truth joined to a desire for what is good. The earthly goodness we are born with is essentially just an animal instinct, since animals also exhibit it. The earthly goodness that we acquire (or that the Lord gives us as a gift) has something spiritual within it, so that a spiritual goodness is within the earthly. This goodness is the real earthly, human kind. The other (the inborn kind) looks good but it can be less than good and even evil, because it can also accept falsity and can believe that vice is virtue. This kind of earthly goodness exists among nations whose lives and beliefs are among the worst.

3409   *And large slaveholdings* symbolizes the resulting truth. This can be seen from the symbolism of *servitude* as everything below, everything that is subordinate and obeys (as discussed in §§1713, 2541, 3019, 3020), and therefore as truth, since truth grows out of goodness and serves it. This subject has been treated of many times before.

The Philistines envied him means that people who merely know the concepts cannot comprehend. This can be seen from the symbolism of *envying* here as not grasping (which becomes clear from what follows [§§3412, 3413, 3417, 3419, 3420]) and from that of Philistia as a knowledge of religious concepts. *Philistines,* then, symbolize people who know religious concepts, as noted at §§1197, 1198. **3410**

Genesis 26:15, 16, 17. *And all the wells that the slaves of his father dug in the days of Abraham his father—the Philistines kept stopping them up and filled them with dirt. And Abimelech said to Isaac, "Go away from us, because you far overpower us." And Isaac went from there and camped in the valley of Gerar and settled there.* **3411**

All the wells that the slaves of his father dug in the days of Abraham his father—the Philistines kept stopping them up means that people who knew religious concepts did not want to learn the deeper truth that comes from the Divine, so they obliterated it. *And filled them with dirt* means by means of earthly traits. *And Abimelech said to Isaac* symbolizes what the Lord perceived about the doctrine [of faith]. *Go away from us, because you far overpower us* means that they could not stand that truth because of the divinity in it. *And Isaac went from there* means that the Lord abandoned deeper doctrines. *And camped in the valley of Gerar and settled there* means that he moved toward lower rational ideas, or in other words, from deeper appearances to shallower ones.

All the wells that the slaves of his father dug in the days of his father— the Philistines kept stopping them up means that people who knew religious concepts did not want to learn the deeper truth that comes from the Divine, so they obliterated it. This can be seen from the following: *Wells* symbolize true ideas, as noted in §§2702, 3096. Here they are the deep truth that comes from the Divine, because the wells symbolizing that truth are said to have been *dug by the slaves of his father in the days of Abraham his father. Abraham* represents the Lord's divinity itself (§§2010, 2833, 2836, 3251, 3305 at the end). *Stopping them up* means not wanting to know [truth] and therefore obliterating it. And the *Philistines* represent people who merely know about religious concepts, as discussed in §§1197, 1198. **3412**

[2] The text is now describing appearances of truth on a lower level, which can be attributed to the people meant by the Philistines here: people devoted to the knowledge of religious concepts.

Here is the situation with deep truth that comes from the Divine and is wiped out by the people called Philistines: In the ancient church and after its time, "Philistines" referred to people who had little energy for learning how to live but a great deal of energy for learning theology. Eventually they even rejected life issues and acknowledged belief issues as the essence of the church, detaching them from life. So they dismissed and erased doctrines concerning neighborly love, which formed the whole of the ancient church's theology. Instead they touted doctrines focusing on faith, which they considered to be the whole of religion. Since this drew them away from life, which is a matter of charity—or from charity, which is a matter of life—they more than others were called the uncircumcised. The uncircumcised symbolized all those who lacked neighborly love, no matter how well versed in doctrine they were (§2049 at the end).

[3] The ones who withdrew from love for others also removed themselves from wisdom and understanding. No one has the wisdom or intelligence to see what the truth is except those who are involved in what is good, or in neighborly love, because all truth grows out of goodness and focuses on it. People without goodness cannot understand truth and do not even want to know about it.

In the other world, when people like this are distant from heaven, the light they see is sometimes bright, but it is the kind that shines in winter—sterile, because it lacks warmth. When such people go near heaven, their light changes into pure darkness, and their mind also enters the shadows, or in other words, a stupor.

This shows what is meant by the statement that people who merely knew religious concepts did not want to know the deep truth that comes from the Divine and therefore obliterated it.

3413   *And filled them with dirt* means by means of earthly traits, or by means of love for themselves and love of wealth. This can be seen from the symbolism of *dirt* as something earthly (discussed in §249). The meaning is that the people called Philistines—those interested in theology but not in living by it—destroyed deep truth through earthly kinds of love, or love for themselves and love of gain. Owing to these kinds of love, they are called the uncircumcised (§§2039, 2049, 2056, 2632). People with these loves can only fill Abraham's wells with dirt; they cannot help annihilating the deep truth of the Word through what is earthly, because such love does not enable them to see anything spiritual, anything visible by the light of truth from the Lord. Self-love and love of wealth generate darkness, which extinguishes that light. As noted just above in §3412, people who concentrate on doctrine alone, not on life, go blank and completely blind when the light of truth from the Lord approaches. In fact, they grow angry and try every way they can to get rid of truth. Love for oneself and for riches do not allow any truth from the Divine to come near them.

Still, they can boast and crow about the fact that they know the truth and even preach it with apparent zeal; but it is the fire of those loves that kindles and stirs them. The zeal is merely the resulting fervor. This is fairly obvious from their ability to preach with the same zeal or ardor against the life they themselves are leading.

These are the earthly traits that block up the Word itself, the wellspring of all truth.

And Abimelech said to Isaac symbolizes what the Lord perceived about the doctrine [of faith]. This is established by the symbolism of *saying* as perceiving (dealt with many times before); from the representation of *Abimelech* (king of the Philistines here) as that doctrine (dealt with in §§3365, 3391); and from the representation of *Isaac* as the Lord's divine rationality.

3414

Go away from us, because you far overpower us means that they could not stand that truth because of the divinity in it. This can be seen from the symbolism of *going away from us* as not being able to stand its presence, and from that of *far overpowering* as the fact that it was due to the riches— in this case, to the divinity that lay within deep truth. People referred to as Philistines cannot stand the presence of goodness, so they cannot stand the presence of divinity; see just above at §3413.

3415

And Isaac went from there means that the Lord abandoned deeper truth. This can be seen from the symbolism of *going from there* as abandoning— abandoning deep truth, since that is the current subject—and from the representation of *Isaac* as the Lord's divine rationality.

3416

That the Lord abandons deep truth means that he does not reveal it to people. Inward truth is present throughout the Word, but we do not even see it when we read the Word if we are the type that knows religious concepts without living by them. This becomes clear from the fact that people who consider faith the key to salvation do not notice what the Lord repeatedly said about love and charity (§§1017, 2371). Any who do notice call [good deeds] the fruits of faith, distinguishing and even separating them from charity, whose nature they do not know. So they see the Word from the back, not the front; in other words, they see its surface, not what is inside it. To see the back, or the outside, without the front, or the inside, is not to see anything divine in it.

That is what it means to say that the Lord abandoned deep truth, symbolized by Isaac's going from there. Not that the Lord abandons it, but that people remove themselves from the Lord, because they remove themselves from anything that affects their life.

3417   *And camped in the valley of Gerar and settled there* means that he moved toward lower rational ideas, or in other words, from deeper appearances to shallower ones, as can be seen from the following: *Camping* means arranging something in order. The *valley of Gerar* symbolizes lower rational ideas, or shallower appearances of truth. A *valley* symbolizes something lower or, what is the same, something shallower (§1723), and *Gerar* symbolizes aspects of faith and so of truth (1209, 2504, 3365, 3384, 3385). And *settling* means existing and living (dealt with at §3384). It stands to reason, then, that *he camped in the valley of Gerar and settled there* means that the Lord arranged truth in a pattern that would also suit the mental grasp and character of people attracted more to teachings about faith than to living by them. This can be seen from the Word, in which truth is arranged the same way.

[2] For instance, people who focus more on doctrines than on life are absolutely convinced that the heavenly kingdom resembles earthly kingdoms in conferring status on people who wield power over others. The pleasure that results is the only pleasure they know, and they exalt it above any other kind, so the Lord spoke in accord with this appearance as well in the Word. In Matthew, for example:

> Those who do and teach [the commandments] *will be called great in the kingdom of the heavens.* (Matthew 5:19)

And in David:

> I have said, "*You are gods,* and you are all children of the Highest One." (Psalms 82:6; John 10:34, 35)

Even the disciples at first viewed the heavenly kingdom solely as a matter of importance and prestige like that on earth (as is evident in Matthew 18:1; Mark 9:34; Luke 9:46) and pictured sitting on the King's right and left (Matthew 20:20, 21, 24; Mark 10:37). So when a quarrel rose among them over which of them would be the greatest, the Lord again answered in a way that met their level of understanding and temperament, saying:

> You will eat and drink at my table in my kingdom and *sit on thrones* judging the twelve tribes of Israel. (Luke 22:24, 30; Matthew 19:28)

At that point they did not realize that heavenly gratification was not to be found in importance and prestige but in humility and the desire to serve others, and therefore in wanting not to be greatest but least. As the Lord teaches in Luke:

> Whoever emerges as *least* among you all, *that one will be great.* (Luke 9:48)

[3] So people who know religious concepts but do not live a life of love for others cannot see that any pleasure exists besides that which results from supremacy. It monopolizes their minds and constitutes their whole life. Consequently they are completely unacquainted with the heavenly satisfaction that comes of humility and the desire to help others—that is, with the joy of love for the Lord and charity for their neighbor—and with the bliss and happiness these produce. For that reason, the Lord accommodated to their weaknesses when he spoke, so that by this means they could be stirred up and led to learn, teach, and do good. All the same, he teaches what importance and prestige in heaven really are, as in Matthew 19:30; 20:16, 25, 26, 27, 28; Mark 10:31, 42, 43, 44, 45; Luke 9:48; 13:30; 22:25, 26, 27, 28.

These and similar examples are appearances of truth on a lower level. We do admittedly become relatively great, important, powerful, and imperial, since a single angel is stronger than many thousands of hellish spirits. But the power comes from the Lord, not ourselves. We receive it from him in proportion to our belief that we are incapable of anything on our own and are therefore least. And we believe this in proportion to our humility and desire to serve others, or in other words, in proportion to the good we do out of love for the Lord and charity for our neighbor.

Genesis 26:18. *And Isaac went back and redug the wells of water that* **3418** *they dug in the days of Abraham his father, which the Philistines kept stopping up after Abraham's death. And he called them by name according to the names by which his father called them.*

Isaac went back and redug the wells of water that they dug in the days of Abraham his father means that the Lord revealed the truth the ancients had known. *Which the Philistines kept stopping up after Abraham's death* means that people with nothing more than a knowledge of religious concepts denied that truth. *And he called them by name* symbolizes its character. *Like the names by which his father called them* means symbols of truth.

3419   *Isaac went back and redug the wells of water that they dug in the days of Abraham his father* means that the Lord revealed the truth the ancients had known, as is established by the following: *Isaac* represents the Lord's divine rationality, as noted before. *Going back and redigging* means reopening. *Wells of water* symbolize the truth within religious knowledge, *wells* symbolizing truth (see §§2702, 3096), and *water,* religious knowledge (28, 2702, 3058). And the *days of Abraham his father* symbolize an earlier period and state in regard to the truth symbolized by the wells *that they dug* then— in other words, truth known to the ancients. For the symbolism of *days* as a period and state, see §§23, 487, 488, 493, 893. When they symbolize a state, Abraham as father represents the Lord's divinity itself before he joined his humanity to it; see §§2833, 2836, 3251. When they symbolize a period of time, Abraham as father symbolizes the goodness and truth coming from the Lord's divinity before he joined his humanity to it, which is the goodness and truth known to the ancients.

[2] The truth known to the ancients has been obliterated today—so much so that hardly anyone knows it existed, or that it could have been different from the kind now taught. It was entirely different. They had *representative images and symbols* that stood for the heavenly and spiritual qualities of the Lord's kingdom and so for the Lord himself. People who understood them were called sages, and sage they were, because they could talk with spirits and angels. Angelic speech is incomprehensible to humankind because it is spiritual and heavenly, and when it filters down to people in the earthly realm it expresses itself in the kind of representations and symbols that appear in the Word. That is why the Word is a sacred volume. It is the only way anything divine can be presented to an earthly person and retain its full correspondence.

[3] Since the ancients used representative images and symbols to stand for the Lord's kingdom, where nothing but heavenly and spiritual love exists, they also had *doctrines* that dealt exclusively with *love for God* and *charity for their neighbor.* These doctrines too gave them a reputation for wisdom. From the doctrines they knew that the Lord would come into the world, Jehovah would be in him, he would make the humanity in himself divine and in the process would save the human race. It also showed them what charity was (a desire to serve others without any thought of repayment) and what the neighbor they were to treat charitably was (everyone everywhere—although in a different way for each neighbor). These doctrines have vanished completely today, to

be replaced by teachings concerning faith, which the ancients deemed comparatively unimportant.

Teachings about love for the Lord and charity for our neighbor have been rejected these days partly by people whom the Word calls Babylonians and Chaldeans and partly by people whom it calls Philistines and Egyptians. The loss has been so complete that hardly a trace remains. Does anyone today know a kind of charity that is completely forgetful of self and rejects all selfish motivation? Does anyone know what the neighbor is? Everyone is our neighbor, with differences, depending on the nature and amount of good in her or him, so goodness itself is our neighbor. In the highest sense, the Lord himself is our neighbor, because he dwells within goodness and is its source. Any good that is not from him is not good no matter how it looks. Who knows any of this? And since people do not know what charity is or what their neighbor is, they do not know whom the Word means when it mentions the poor, wretched, needy, sick, hungry, thirsty, oppressed, widowed, orphaned, imprisoned, naked, foreign-born, blind, deaf, lame, maimed, and so on. Yet the ancients' doctrines taught them just who these people were, what category of neighbor they belonged to, and so what kind of charity applied. The Word's whole literal meaning accords with these doctrines, so anyone who does not know them cannot have any idea of its inner meaning. [4] In Isaiah, for example:

> Isn't [this my fast:] to break bread for the *hungry*, and that you bring *afflicted refugees* into your house, when you see the *naked* and cover them and do not hide yourself from your flesh? Then your light will burst forth like the dawn, and your health will quickly sprout, and your righteousness will walk before you; the glory of Jehovah will gather you in. (Isaiah 58:7, 8)

People who emphasize the literal meaning believe that if they only give bread to the hungry, bring afflicted refugees or vagrants into their house, and cover the naked, they will come into "the glory of Jehovah"—heaven—on that account. In reality, these are merely outward acts, and even the ungodly can perform them to earn credit. No, the hungry, afflicted, and naked symbolize people who are spiritually so, and accordingly they symbolize different wretched states plaguing the neighbor whom we are to treat with charity. [5] In David:

> He is passing judgment for the *oppressed*, giving bread to the *hungry*; Jehovah is releasing the *imprisoned*; Jehovah is opening [the eyes of] the

blind; Jehovah is straightening up the *bowed;* Jehovah is loving the fair-minded; Jehovah is guarding the *foreign-born;* the *orphan* and *widow* he sustains. (Psalms 146:7, 8, 9)

The oppressed, hungry, imprisoned, blind, bowed, foreign-born, orphan, and widow do not mean people known to be such but people who are such spiritually, in their souls. The doctrines of the ancients taught who they each were, what condition and degree of neighbor they were, and what kind of charity they should be shown. The same applies everywhere else in the Old Testament. Certainly when divinity comes down onto our earthly plane, it descends into acts of kindness, differentiating by category and subcategory.

[6] The Lord also spoke in similar terms, because he spoke from divinity itself, as in Matthew:

The king will say to those on the right, "Come, you who are blessed by my Father! Take possession of the kingdom prepared for you. For I was *hungry* and you gave me something to eat; I was *thirsty* and you gave me a drink; I was a *foreigner* and you gathered me in; I was *naked* and you dressed me; I was *sick* and you visited me; I was *in prison* and you came to me." (Matthew 25:34, 35, 36)

The actions listed here symbolize the most general types of charity and the different levels of good deed, or of good people who are the neighbor we are to exercise charity toward. In the highest sense the Lord is our neighbor, seeing that he says, "so far as you did it for one of these least consequential brothers and sisters of mine, you did it for me" (Matthew 25:40).

These brief remarks show what "truth known to the ancients" means. This truth is obliterated by the people whom the Word refers to as Philistines—people who devote themselves to doctrines concerning faith but fail to live a life of neighborly love. That is what the stopping up of the wells by the Philistines after Abraham's death symbolizes, as I will discuss next.

3420   *Which the Philistines kept stopping up after Abraham's death* means that people with nothing more than a knowledge of religious concepts denied that truth. This is established by the symbolism of *stopping up* as not wanting to know, or denying, and in this way obliterating (discussed above at §3412), and from the representation of the *Philistines* as people who merely know religious concepts (discussed in §§1197, 1198, 3412, 3413).

A mere knowledge of religious concepts is what people have when they give their attention to doctrines about faith and do not want to know the truth within those concepts, or within those doctrines. Anything that has to do with life, anything that focuses on charity for our neighbor and love for the Lord, constitutes the truth within religious knowledge, or within doctrines. The theology that comprises those doctrines and concepts merely teaches such truth. People who teach others what to do but do not do it themselves do not want to know truth, because it opposes their life, and when something opposes their life, they deny it. These are the reasons why the doctrines of love and charity that composed the whole of the ancient church's theology were wiped out.

And he called them by name symbolizes the character of [that truth]. This is established by the symbolism of *calling* things *by name* as their character (discussed in §§144, 145, 1754, 1896, 2009, 2724, 3006, 3237). Since calling things by name, or the name itself, means their character, *calling* without the addition of the word *name* in the Word's inner sense means *having that character.* In Isaiah, for instance:

> Listen to this, house of Jacob, you who are called by the name of Israel (and they issued from the waters of Judah), because *after the holy city they are called,* and on the God of Israel they lean. (Isaiah 48:1, 2)

Being called after the holy city stands for being holy. And in Luke:

> See: you will conceive in your womb and deliver a son and call his name Jesus. He will be great and *will be called the Son of the Highest One.* (Luke 1:31, 32)

Being called the Son of the Highest One stands for being just that.

Like the names by which his father called them means symbols of truth. This can be seen from the fact that in ancient times the names given to people, places, and things were always symbolic of something (see §§340, 1946, 2643). So the names given to springs and wells symbolized the kinds of things that people once meant by springs and wells. These had to do with truth, as shown in §§2702, 3096. Since names had symbolic meaning, a name and calling a thing by name symbolized the general character of some entity or some state, as noted just above in §3421. And since this was so, in the Word's inner meaning a name does not refer to any person, nation, kingdom, or city but always to some phenomenon.

Anyone can conclude that the wells here have some heavenly meaning. If they did not, it would not be worthy of the Word of God to mention so

3421

3422

many particulars connected with them, because there is no use in know-ing such things: that Philistines stopped up wells that Abraham's slaves had dug; that Isaac redug them and called them by names like their ear-lier names; that Isaac's slaves dug a well in a valley, which the shepherds feuded over; that they dug another, which they also feuded over, and then another, which they did not feud over; that they dug yet another; and that they told Isaac about the new well (verses 15, 18, 19, 20, 21, 22, 25, 32, 33). The identity of the heavenly phenomenon that the wells symbolize now becomes clear from the inner meaning.

3423   Genesis 26:19, 20, 21. *And Isaac's slaves dug in the valley and found there a well of living water. And the shepherds of Gerar feuded with the shepherds of Isaac, saying, "The water is ours!" And he called the name of the well Esek, because they quarreled with him. And they dug another well, and they feuded over it, too, and he called its name Sitnah.*

Isaac's slaves dug in the valley and found there a well of living water sym-bolizes the Word's literal meaning, which holds an inner meaning. *And the shepherds of Gerar feuded with the shepherds of Isaac* means that teach-ers of doctrine did not see any inner meaning in it because the two seem opposed. *Saying, "The water is ours,"* means that they have the truth. *And he called the name of the well Esek, because they quarreled with him* symbol-izes denial for those reasons, and for other reasons that work against those people, and so on. *And they dug another well, and they feuded over it, too* means whether the Word has an inner sense. *And he called its name Sitnah* symbolizes the nature of their [arguments].

3424   *Isaac's slaves dug in the valley and found there a well of living water* symbolizes the Word's literal meaning, which holds an inner meaning, as can be seen from the following: *Digging in the valley* means looking down below to find out where truth is, because *digging* means seeking, and a *valley* means a lower level (§§1723, 3417). And a *well of living water* sym-bolizes the Word, which holds divine truth, so it symbolizes the Word's literal meaning, which holds an inner meaning. People know that the Word is called a spring and in fact a spring of living water. It is also called a well because that is what the literal meaning is like by comparison, and because the Word is a well rather than a spring for spiritual people (see §§2702, 3096). Because a valley stands for something lower, or more superficial, and the well was found in a valley, it means the Word's literal sense, since the literal sense is lower, or more superficial. However, the lit-eral sense does contain an inner sense—a heavenly and a divine sense—so its water is described as living. The water that went out under the doorsill of the new House is described the same way in Ezekiel:

> And it will come about that every wild soul of an animal that creeps— *every soul the river reaches there—lives.* And the fish will be very numerous, because that water goes there and is cured, and *everything lives, wherever the river goes.* (Ezekiel 47:8, 9)

The river is the Word; the water that makes everything live is the divine truth in it; and the fish are facts (§§40, 991).

[2] The Lord's Word by its very nature gives life to the thirsty (people who desire life), and it is a spring whose water is living, as the Lord also teaches in John:

> To the woman from Samaria at *Jacob's well* Jesus said, "If you knew God's gift, and who it is that says to you, 'Give me something to drink,' you would ask him, and he would give you *living water.* Those who drink the water that I give them will never be thirsty to eternity; instead, the *water* that I give them will become a *spring of water gushing up* in them *to provide eternal life.*" (John 4:10, 14)

The Word is living and therefore life-giving because in its highest sense it talks about the Lord, and in its inward sense it talks about his kingdom, where he is everything. This being so, life itself is what fills the Word and flows into the minds of those who read it with reverence. That is why the Lord, in referring to the Word that comes from him, calls himself a spring of water gushing up to provide eternal life. See also §2702.

[3] It can be seen in Moses that just as the Lord's Word is called a spring, it is also called a well:

> Israel sang a song: "Gush up, you *well!* Answer it! A *well:* the chieftains *dug,* the nobles of the people *excavated,* for the Lawgiver, with their staffs." (Numbers 21:17, 18)

The place this occurred was Beer, that is, the place of a well. This well symbolizes the ancient church's Word (discussed at §2897), as the preceding verses there show. Chieftains mean the main truths that composed it (for the meaning of chieftains as main truths, see §§1482, 2089); the nobles of the people mean the lowlier kind of truth that appears in the literal sense (1259, 1260, 2928, 3295). The Lawgiver is the Lord, obviously. The staffs are the power of those truths.

3425   *The shepherds of Gerar feuded with the shepherds of Isaac* means that teachers of doctrine did not see any inner meaning in it because the two seem opposed. This is established by the symbolism of *feuding*, when it has to do with the Word's inner meaning, as denying that such a thing exists, saying they could not see it; by that of *shepherds* as teachers of doctrine (discussed in §343); and by that of *Gerar* as faith (discussed in §§1209, 2504, 3365, 3384). So the *shepherds* of the valley *of Gerar* mean people who acknowledge only the Word's literal meaning.

The reason they do not see any inner meaning is that the two—the thrust of the inner meaning and that of the literal meaning—seem opposed. Just because the two seem opposed does not mean they are; on the contrary, they fully correspond with one another. They seem opposed because people who view the Word this way are in a state of opposition.

[2] The situation resembles that of people at odds with themselves, people whose outward, earthly self totally disagrees with their inward, spiritual self. They see the values of their inward, spiritual self as standing against them, when it is their own outer, earthly self that puts up the opposition. If their outer, earthly self obeyed their inner, spiritual self instead of defying it, the two would be in complete correspondence.

For example, oppositional people believe that they have to give up their riches and all the sensual pleasures of bodily and worldly gratification—everything that makes life sweet—if they want to receive eternal life. They believe such things run counter to spiritual life, but in and of themselves they correspond rather than conflict. They are means to the end of an inner, spiritual self that enjoys using them to do deeds of neighborly kindness and that lives content in a healthy body. The aims alone are what determine whether the inner and outer self oppose or correspond to one another. They oppose one another when the riches, pleasures, and sweetness mentioned become our goal, because we then despise, mock, and reject the spiritual and heavenly qualities of our inner self. They correspond to one another when we make them not ends in themselves but the means to higher ends—life after death, the heavenly kingdom, and the Lord himself. Under those circumstances, bodily and worldly gratifications strike us as trifling by comparison, and when we do think about them, we regard them only as means to an end.

[3] Clearly, then, what look like opposites are not inherently so. They appear opposite only because people are in a state of opposition.

Those who are not defiant act, talk, seek wealth, and indulge in pleasure in the same ways as those who are—so much so that in external appearance they can hardly be told apart. Only their aims differentiate them; to put it another way, only what they love differentiates them (since what we love is our aim). Yet although they look the same in their outward form, or body, they have nothing in common in their inner form, or spirit. People who are in correspondence—whose outer self harmonizes with their inner self—have a spirit that is radiant and beautiful, as heavenly love is when embodied. People who are in opposition—whose outer self resists their inner self—may look the same on the outside, but their spirit is dark and ugly, as self-love and materialism are, or as contempt and hatred are, when embodied.

[4] The case is the same with much in the Word: statements in the literal meaning look contrary to the ideas of the inner meaning, when they are never contrary but completely in correspondence. The Word often says, for example, that Jehovah (the Lord) grows angry, blazes up, lays waste, and throws people into hell, when in reality he never feels anger, let alone throws anyone into hell. The one is what the literal meaning says; the other is what the inner meaning says. They seem to clash, but only because of humankind's state of opposition. By the same token, the Lord appears to angels in heaven as a sun and therefore as the warmth of spring and the light of dawn, while to the hellish he appears as utter blackness and therefore as the cold of winter and the dark of night. Angels view him with love and charity; the hellish view him with hatred and enmity. So he appears to the hellish the way he does in the literal meaning, as being angry, blazing up, laying things waste, and throwing people into hell, but he appears to angels the way he does in the inner meaning, as never being angry or blazing up, let alone laying things waste or throwing people into hell. [5] When the Word speaks of things that are contrary to the divine nature, then, that is the only way they can be presented: according to appearances.

Furthermore, God's work is what evil people turn into the Devil's work, so that the effect of the Divine on them is devilish. As a result, the closer they come to the Divine, the more they subject themselves to hell's torments.

It is the same with the Lord's words in his Prayer: "Do not lead us into trials." The meaning that accords with the literal text is that the Lord leads us into trials, but the inner sense is that he never does; and people

realize this. (See §1875.) The same holds true for the rest of the Word's
literal meaning.

3426   *Saying, "The water is ours,"* means that they have the truth, or the
truth is theirs. This can be seen from the symbolism of *water* as religious concepts, and as truth—a symbolism discussed at §§28, 680, 739,
2702, 3058.

3427   *And he called the name of the well Esek, because they quarreled with him*
symbolizes denial for those reasons, and for other reasons that work against
those people, and so on. This can be seen from the fact that the names people gave in ancient times symbolized some entity or state (§3422), which
enabled them to remember many things about it, especially its character.
Here, the name given to the well resulted from the dispute between the
shepherds of Gerar and Isaac's shepherds.

Feuding, or quarreling, also means denying (see §3425). Hence the
name *Esek,* which means strife or a feud in the original language and
comes from a related word for oppression or a wrong. Since the well here
symbolizes the Word's literal meaning, which holds an inner meaning,
Esek or "strife" symbolizes denial of the Word's inner meaning. The reasons for the denial are also present in the same word, including (obviously) the fact that the two levels appear opposed, as discussed just above
in §3425, and other considerations as well.

[2] This is how matters stand with the Word's inner meaning: People who merely know religious concepts ("Philistines") and those who
restrict themselves to doctrines concerning faith ("shepherds of the valley of Gerar") and show no love for their neighbor inevitably deny that
the Word has an inner meaning. The main reason is that they do not
acknowledge the Lord at heart, even though they proclaim him with
their lips. Neither do they love their neighbor at heart, even though they
declare to the contrary that they do. People who do not acknowledge
the Lord or love their neighbor at heart cannot possibly do otherwise
than deny the Word's inner meaning, because the Word in its inner sense
speaks of nothing but love for the Lord and love for our neighbor. That
is why the Lord says that on these two commandments depend the Law
and the Prophets, or the whole of the Word (Matthew 22:37, 38, 39, 40).
I was permitted to see how much they deny the Word's inner meaning
by observing their like in the other world. If you so much as mention
in their presence that the Word has an inner meaning, not apparent in
its literal meaning, which has to do with love for the Lord and for one's

neighbor, you sense from them not only denial but also rejection and even nausea. This is the primary reason.

[3] A second reason is that they turn the Word completely upside down, putting what is at the bottom on top—that is, putting what is last first. They declare the principle that faith is the crucial factor in religion and that acts of love for the Lord and for our neighbor are the fruits of faith, when the reality is this: If love for the Lord is the tree of life in the Garden of Eden, charity and charitable deeds are the fruit it yields, but faith and all its ins and outs are merely leaves. So considering the way they invert the Word to derive the fruit not from the tree but from the leaves, it is no wonder they deny its inner meaning, acknowledging only its literal meaning. The literal sense is capable of supporting any dogma whatever, even the most heretical, as people recognize.

[4] What is more, people who restrict themselves to the doctrines concerning faith, ignoring goodness in life, cannot help forming dogmatic beliefs, or seizing on principles without regard to their falsity or truth. As a result they are stupider than others, because the firmer our hold on these beliefs, the stupider we are. Conversely, the more we devote ourselves to goodness in life, or to love for the Lord and charity for our neighbor, the more intelligent we are, which is to say, the more faith we have in the Lord. As a further result, the former necessarily have a negative attitude toward the Word's inner meaning, but the latter necessarily have an affirmative one. The deeper dimensions of people interested only in doctrine and not in a good life are closed so tightly that the light of truth cannot flow into them from the Lord or enable them to sense that there is an inner meaning. The deeper dimensions of people dedicated to loving the Lord, however, are open wide enough to let the light of truth flow in from the Lord and touch their minds, giving them an awareness that there is an inner meaning.

[5] This also explains why such people take no pleasure in reading the Word except as a way of acquiring position and wealth and therefore prestige—a self-centered, grasping kind of pleasure. In fact, if they could not gain any material advantage from it, they would absolutely reject the Word. People like that deny at heart not only the inner meaning of the Word, when they hear about it, but even its literal meaning, no matter how firmly they imagine they believe in it. If we set the pleasures of self-love and materialism as our goal, our heart completely rejects anything about eternal life. Only our earthly, body-oriented self then promotes

eternal ideas, whose truth we grant not for the sake of the Lord and his kingdom but for the sake of ourselves and those closest to us.

These factors and many others cause the people called shepherds of the valley of Gerar and those called Philistines to deny the Word's inner meaning.

3428   *And they dug another well, and they feuded over it, too* means whether the Word has an inner sense. This can be seen from the symbolism of *another well* and of *feuding*, dealt with above [§§3419, 3422, 3424, 3425], and therefore from the train of thought. When people who deny a thing like the Word's inner sense feud or quarrel a second time, the dispute cannot take up any question but whether such a thing exists.

Most disputes today go no further, as is generally recognized, but as long as the debate bogs down over whether a thing exists and whether it is such and such, the participants cannot advance into any measure of wisdom. The topic under discussion involves countless issues they can never see until they acknowledge the thing itself, because till then they know nothing about any of them. [2] Modern scholarship hardly ventures beyond the bounds of those questions, of whether a thing exists, and whether it is such and such, so when it comes to understanding truth, modern scholars stand outside a locked door.

Anyone who disputes whether the Word has an inner meaning, for instance, can never see the countless and even endless contents of the inner meaning. For another example, anyone who debates whether charity has any importance in religion, or whether matters of charity are all matters of faith instead, cannot know the countless and even endless elements composing charity. In fact, such a person remains in total ignorance of what charity is.

[3] The same is true of life after death, the resurrection of the dead, the Last Judgment, and heaven and hell: people who simply argue over their existence are standing outside the doors of wisdom. They are like a person who only knocks at wisdom's magnificent palace and cannot even peek in. Oddly enough, the ones who do this believe themselves wiser than others. The more skilled they are at wrangling over an entity's existence and (better yet) proving that it is not such and such, the wiser they consider themselves. Yet naive people governed by goodness, to whom they feel superior, can tell instantly that a thing exists and what it is like, without any arguing, let alone learned debate. They have a commonsense insight into truth, whereas the others snuff out that sense in themselves by their desire to stop first and decide whether a thing even exists. The Lord refers to these

two groups when he says that things have been hidden from the wise and understanding and revealed to children (Matthew 11:25; Luke 10:21).

And he called its name Sitnah symbolizes the nature of their [arguments]. This can be seen from the symbolism of *calling something's name* as its nature (discussed in §§144, 145, 1754, 1896, 2009, 2724, 3006, 3421) and from the meaning of *Sitnah* in the original tongue as hostility—a further level of denial. **3429**

Genesis 26:22, 23. *And he moved on from there and dug another well, and they did not feud over it; and he called its name Rehoboth and said, "Because now Jehovah is broadening us, and we will be fruitful in the land." And he went up from there to Beer-sheba.* **3430**

He moved on from there means to a still lower level. *And he dug another well, and they did not feud over it* symbolizes the Word's literal meaning. *And he called its name Rehoboth* symbolizes the nature of its truth. *And said, "Because now Jehovah is broadening us,"* symbolizes increases in truth as a result [of descent to a lower level]. *And we will be fruitful in the land* symbolizes increases in goodness as a result. *And he went up from there to Beer-sheba* symbolizes divine teachings on faith acquired from [the literal meaning].

He moved on from there means to a still lower level. This can be seen from the symbolism of *moving on* as proceeding to the next part of the series. Here it means to lower or shallower truth, because higher or deeper levels of truth have been dealt with in order up to this point. Lower or shallower truth is the truth visible in the Word's literal sense, which suits the mental grasp of our earthly self. This truth now becomes the topic of discussion. **3431**

And he dug another well, and they did not feud over it symbolizes the Word's literal meaning. This is established by the symbolism of a *well* as the Word, which is discussed in §§2702, 3096, 3424. Here it symbolizes the Word's literal meaning, because the text says Isaac moved on from there and dug another well that they did not feud over. This symbolizes the superficial meaning of the Word, which they do not deny—the meaning referred to as literal. **3432**

The literal meaning has three aspects: narrative, prophetic, and doctrinal. Each is capable of being understood by people who stay on the surface of things.

[2] Concerning the Word: In earliest times, when the church was heavenly, there was no Word, because the people of that church had the Word written on their hearts. The Lord taught them directly through heaven

what was good and therefore what was true, enabling them to perceive both concepts from love and charity and to learn both concepts from revelation. For them, the real Word was the Lord.

After this church came another that was spiritual rather than heavenly. At first its only Word was something collected from the earliest people that contained representations of the Lord and symbols of his kingdom. For the people of this spiritual church, the inner meaning was the actual Word. They also had a written Word, containing both narrative and prophecy, which no longer exists and which likewise had an inner meaning relating to the Lord; see §2686. The wisdom of that era consisted in the use of representation and symbolism in oral and written communication on divine themes (within the church) and other topics (outside the church), as is clear from the surviving manuscripts of those ancient people.

Over time this wisdom faded until people finally forgot there *was* any inner meaning, even in the books of the Word. An example is the Jewish and Israelite nation, which considered scriptural prophecy holy because it sounded old and they heard Jehovah's name in the literal text. They did not believe anything divine lay any more deeply hidden in it than that. Neither does the Christian world view the Word as any more sacred.

[3] This evidence shows how wisdom receded with the passage of time from the inmost depths to the outermost surface. Humankind removed itself from heaven and finally sank all the way down to the dust of the earth, where it now places its wisdom.

Since that is what happened to the Word, the current chapter depicts the stages of gradual decline, the progressive obliteration of the inner meaning until people today do not know it exists, although that meaning actually is the real Word, where divinity is most directly present.

3433 *And he called its name Rehoboth* symbolizes the nature of its truth. This can be seen from the symbolism of *calling something's name* as its nature (discussed in §§144, 145, 1754, 1896, 2009, 2724, 3006, 3421) and from that of *Rehoboth* as truth. In the original language, *Rehoboth* means broad places, which in the Word's inner sense stand for truth, as shown in §1613.

3434 *And said, "Because now Jehovah is broadening us,"* symbolizes increases in truth as a result [of descent to a lower level]. This can be seen from the symbolism of breadth as truth, mentioned just above in §3433. *Broadening* consequently means receiving increases in truth.

And we will be fruitful in the land symbolizes increases in goodness **3435** as a result, as can be seen from the following: *Being fruitful* symbolizes increases in goodness, since fruitfulness is mentioned in connection with goodness, and multiplication, with truth (see §§43, 55, 913, 983, 2846, 2847). And the *land* symbolizes religion in all its facets (dealt with in §§662, 1066, 1068, 1262, 1733, 1850, 2928, 3355).

And he went up from there to Beer-sheba symbolizes divine teachings **3436** on faith acquired from [the literal meaning]. This can be seen from the symbolism of *Beer-sheba* as divine teachings on faith (discussed at §§2723, 2858, 2859).

The doctrine of faith symbolized here by *Beer-sheba* is actually the literal sense of the Word, because the Word is doctrine itself. Although the nature of the Word's literal meaning enables people to draw truth from it, it can also provide proof for ideas that are not true, as various heresies demonstrate.

Those who read the Word in order to become wise—that is, to do good and understand truth—receive instruction matched to their goals and desires. The Lord flows into them unawares, enlightening their minds. When they become stuck on a problem, he helps them understand it from other passages. [2] Then again, those with simple goodness who believe the Word naively, according to its literal meaning, receive the gift of being able to perceive truth when they are taught by angels in the other life. Meanwhile, the small store of truth they do possess is brought to life by neighborly love and innocence. When these qualities are present, the falsity that has also poured in under the shadow of their ignorance does no harm, because it does not attach to anything good but is kept on the outer edges, where it can easily be removed.

The case is quite different with people who do not live good lives. In them, the falsities they concoct by misinterpreting the Word occupy the middle, or center, while truth stays on the outer bounds, or circumference. Falsity is what unites with the evil in their life, and truth is driven off.

Genesis 26:24, 25. *And Jehovah appeared to him that night and said, "I* **3437** *am the God of Abraham your father. Do not be afraid, because I am with you and will bless you and make your seed multiply because of Abraham my servant." And he built an altar there and called on Jehovah's name and stretched his tent there, and Isaac's slaves hollowed out a well there.*

Jehovah appeared to him that night and said symbolizes the Lord's perception about that darkness. *I am the God of Abraham your father; do not be afraid, because I am with you* means that his divine side was also there. *And will bless you and make your seed multiply* means that an increase in goodness and truth comes out of it. *Because of Abraham my servant* means from the Lord's divine humanity. *And he built an altar there* means something that symbolized and represented the Lord. *And called on Jehovah's name* symbolizes the worship that grew out of it. *And stretched his tent there* symbolizes what was holy there. *And Isaac's slaves hollowed out a well there* symbolizes the doctrine that grew out of it.

3438   *Jehovah appeared to him that night and said* symbolizes the Lord's perception about that darkness, as can be seen from the following: When *Jehovah's appearing and saying* has to do with the Lord, it means his perceiving from his divine side. *Jehovah's appearing to him* means that it came from his divine side (see §3367), and *saying* means perceiving (2862, 3395). Jehovah was in the Lord, so until his human side was glorified, Jehovah's appearance was a divine perception, or a perception from his divine side, and that is what *Jehovah appeared to him and said* symbolizes. The *night* symbolizes a condition of shadow or darkness, as noted in §1712. "That darkness" means the Word's literal sense, because it compares to the inner sense as shadow compares to light.

[2] I must say a few words to explain more clearly what the case is with the Word's literal meaning. The inner meaning relates to the literal meaning the way our deeper levels (our heavenly and spiritual planes) relate to our outer levels (our earthly and bodily planes). Our deeper levels bask in heaven's light, but our outer levels live in worldly light. For the difference between heavenly and worldly light and therefore between what heavenly light and what earthly light illuminate, see §§1521–1533, 1619–1632, 1783, 1880, 2776, 3138, 3167, 3190, 3195, 3222, 3223, 3225, 3337, 3339, 3341, 3413. The difference is like that between the light of day and the shadow of night. Since we live in this shadow and do not want to know that truth from the Lord contains light, we cannot help believing that our shadow is the light and conversely that the light is shadow. We are like owls flying through the shadows of night thinking they are in the light, but when they encounter daylight, they think they are in shadow. In people like this, the inner eye, the eye of the intellect, by which we see inside, is not formed for any other purpose, because such people themselves have formed it this way. They open it when they look down to worldly and bodily concerns and close it when they look up to spiritual

and heavenly concerns. For them the Word is similar; what appears in its literal sense they consider full of light, but what appears in its inner sense they consider full of shadow. We each see the Word according to our nature. In reality, though, the Word's inner meaning compares to its literal meaning the way heaven's light compares to the world's light (§§3086, 3108), or as daylight compares to the light of night.

[3] The inner meaning contains subtle details, many thousands of which together make a single particular as presented in the literal meaning. To say it another way, the inner meaning contains particulars, many thousands of which together make a single generality in the literal meaning. This generality is what we see, rather than the particulars that fill and compose it. Even so, the orderly pattern of particulars within the general idea appears to us, but we see it according to our character. That pattern is the holy element that touches our heart.

I am the God of Abraham your father; do not be afraid, because I am with you means that his divine side was also there, in the Word's literal meaning, as can be seen from the representation of *Abraham.* Abraham represents the Lord's divinity (as noted in §§2833, 2836, 3251, 3305 at the end), so Jehovah, *God of Abraham,* symbolizes the divinity of the Lord's that Abraham represents. The theme here is the Word, which is also the Lord (since the whole Word is from him and everything in it is about him), so *I am the God of Abraham; do not be afraid, because I am with you* means that his divinity is also there. **3439**

To take up the subject of divinity in the Word: divinity itself lies in the Word's very highest meaning, because that is where the Lord is. There is also divinity in its inward meaning, because that is where the Lord's kingdom in the heavens is. Accordingly, the deep meaning is called heavenly and spiritual. Divinity also exists in the Word's literal meaning, because that is where the Lord's kingdom on earth is, and that meaning is accordingly called outward and earthly. It contains coarse appearances, quite far removed from divinity, but everything in it is still divine.

These three layers of meaning resemble the tabernacle. Its inmost room, behind the veil, where the ark holding the testimony stood, was extremely holy, or a holy of holies. Its intermediate room, right outside the veil, where the golden table and the lampstand stood, was holy. Its outer part, the courtyard, was also holy. That was where the assembly met, so it was called the meeting tent.

And will bless you and make your seed multiply means that an increase in goodness and truth comes out of it. This can be seen from the symbolism **3440** of *blessing you* as an increase in goodness (dealt with in §3406) and from that of the *multiplying of your seed* as an increase in truth (dealt with in §§43, 55, 913, 983, 2846, 2847). On the point that *seed* means truth, which is what is said to *multiply,* see §§1025, 1447, 1610, 2848, 3038, 3373, 3380.

Even the Word's literal meaning provides us with an increase in goodness and truth because in it too each and every thing is divine (as noted just above at §3439) and because the inner meaning often lies open in the literal meaning. The Old Testament prophets, for instance, said that the Lord was coming and would be the salvation of the human race. Then there are the statements that all the Law and the Prophets consist in loving God and our neighbor, and that killing means hating. After all, anyone who hates another is killing that other all the time; murder lurks in such people's will and forms the central pleasure of their life. These and many other statements in the literal meaning belong to the inner meaning.

3441 *Because of Abraham my servant* means from the Lord's divine humanity. This can be seen from the representation of *Abraham* as the Lord's divinity and also as his divine humanity (discussed in §§2833, 2836, 3251) and from the symbolism of *my servant,* where it describes the Lord, as his divine humanity. Not that his divine humanity is a servant, because it too is Jehovah (1736, 2156, 2329, 2921, 3023, 3035), but that the Lord served the human race through it. By it we are saved, as we never could have been had the Lord not united his humanity with his divinity, enabling us to mentally gaze on and worship his human side and in this way approach his divine side. Our union with divinity itself, called the Father, takes place through the divine humanity, called the Son. So it takes place through the Lord, whom spiritual people take to mean his humanity but heavenly people take to mean divinity itself. Clearly, then, the Lord's divine humanity is called a servant because it serves his divinity by providing us with access to it and because it serves the human race by saving us. [2] That is what *Abraham my servant* symbolizes, as it also does in David:

> Recall his marvels that he has done, the portents and judgments of his mouth, you seed of *Abraham his servant,* you children of Jacob his chosen. He sent Moses, *his servant;* Aaron, whom he chose. He remembered his holy word with *Abraham his servant.* (Psalms 105:5, 6, 26, 42)

Abraham his servant means the Lord's divine humanity.

That is also what Israel his servant, Jacob his servant, and David his servant mean in the highest sense.

The Lord's divine humanity is meant by Israel his servant in Isaiah:

> *You are Israel, my servant;* Jacob, whom I have chosen; the seed of Abraham, my friend, whom I snatched from the ends of the earth. And from its edges I called you, and I said to you, "*You are my servant; I have chosen you.*" (Isaiah 41:8, 9)

"Israel my servant" in its highest sense means the Lord in relation to a spiritual religion's inner dimensions, and Jacob, in relation to its outer dimensions. In the same author:

> He said to me, "*You are my servant, Israel,* in whom I will become glorious. It is too trifling *that you should be a servant to me,* to raise up the tribes of Jacob and to bring back those in Israel who have been saved from harm, so I have made you a light for the nations, so that you may be my salvation to the end of the earth." (Isaiah 49:3, 6)

In this passage, Israel "in whom I will become glorious" plainly stands for the Lord's divine humanity. He is called a servant because of how he served people, of course, since it says, "That you should be a servant to me, to raise up the tribes of Jacob and to bring back those in Israel who have been saved from harm."

[3] The Lord's divine humanity is also meant by Jacob his servant in Isaiah:

> I will give you the treasures of the dark and the secret riches of hiding places, because of *my servant Jacob,* and Israel my chosen. (Isaiah 45:3, 4)

His servant Jacob, and Israel his chosen, mean the Lord—his servant Jacob, in relation to the church's outer dimensions, and Israel his chosen, in relation to its inner dimensions.

[4] It is also meant by David his servant in Ezekiel:

> I will gather the children of Israel from round about; *my servant David will be king over them,* and there will be a single shepherd for them all. They will live on the land that I gave *to my servant Jacob,* and they will live on it—they and their children and their children's children— forever. And *David my servant* will be chief over them forever. (Ezekiel 37:21, 24, 25)

His servant David clearly stands for the Lord's divine humanity (§1888) because of the divine truth symbolized by a king (David, in this case; 1728, 2015, 3009). Truth actually is a comparative slave (see §3409), and since it is, the Lord refers to himself in Mark as one who serves others:

> Anyone who wants to be great among you must be your attendant. And whichever of you wants to be first must be everyone's slave, since even *the Son of Humankind did not come to be served but to serve others.* (Mark 10:43, 44, 45; Matthew 20:26, 27, 28)

And in Luke:

> Which is greater: the one who reclines [at table] or the one who serves? Isn't it the one who reclines? *Yet I am in your midst as one who serves.* (Luke 22:27)

3442   *And he built an altar there* means something that symbolized and represented the Lord. This can be seen from the symbolism of an *altar* as the main item representing the Lord (discussed in §§921, 2777, 2811).

3443   *And called on Jehovah's name* symbolizes the worship that grew out of it. This can be seen from the symbolism of *calling on Jehovah's name* as worship (discussed in §§440, 2724). *Jehovah's name* means every method of worshiping God, collectively (2628, 2724, 3006).

3444   *And stretched his tent there* symbolizes what was holy there. This can be seen from the symbolism of a *tent* as the holiness in worship (discussed in §§414, 1102, 2145, 2152, 3312).

3445   *And Isaac's slaves hollowed out a well there* symbolizes the doctrine that grew out of it. This can be seen from the symbolism of a *well* as the Word (discussed in §§2702, 3424). Since the Word is the true doctrine and therefore the source of the church's whole theology, *hollowing out a well* symbolizes the doctrine that grows out of it—out of the Word's literal meaning, since that is the theme here.

There is only one true doctrine that comes from the Word's literal meaning: that of charity and love—charity for our neighbor and love for the Lord. This doctrine and a life according to it are the whole Word, as the Lord teaches in Matthew 22:37, 38, 39, 40.

3446   Genesis 26:26, 27. *And Abimelech went to him from Gerar, and Ahuzzath his comrade, and Phicol, leader of his army. And Isaac said to them, "Why have you come to me, when you hated me and sent me from you?"*

And Abimelech went to him from Gerar symbolizes the doctrine of faith viewed in rational terms. *And Ahuzzath his comrade, and Phicol, leader of his army* symbolizes the main teachings in their doctrine of faith. *And Isaac said to them, "Why have you come to me, when you hated me and sent me from you?"* means, why were they looking for something divine, when they denied the divinity of the Word's inner meaning and showed hostility toward it?

Abimelech went to him from Gerar symbolizes the doctrine of faith viewed in rational terms. This can be seen from the representation of *Abimelech* as the doctrine of faith viewed in rational terms (discussed in §§2504, 2509, 2510, 3391, 3392, 3393) and from the symbolism of *Gerar* as faith (discussed in §§1209, 2504, 3365, 3384, 3385). Read §3368 to see what it is to view doctrine in rational terms.   **3447**

From here to verse 33 the subject matter has to do with people interested in the Word's literal meaning and in doctrines concerning faith, and with the harmony that exists between the inner meaning and these doctrines, so far as they come from the literal meaning. Abimelech, Ahuzzath his comrade, and Phicol leader of his army represent those doctrines. They stand for people who make faith the real essential and who do not reject neighborly love but make it secondary, promoting doctrine over life. Almost everyone in our religion today belongs to this category, not counting the part of it that exists in the world of Christian paganism, where people are allowed to worship saints and the idols portraying them.

[2] Every church of the Lord's has people with depth and people without. The deeper people are those who respond to what is good; the shallower ones respond to truth. Likewise with the people represented here by Abimelech, his comrade, and the leader of his army: The deeper ones were the theme of Genesis 21:22–33 above, which says that Abimelech and Phicol, the leader of his army, came to Abraham and struck a pact with him in Beer-sheba (for a discussion, see §§2719, 2720). The shallower people are the theme here.

And Ahuzzath his comrade, and Phicol, leader of his army symbolizes the main teachings in their doctrine of faith. This can be seen from the representation of *Abimelech* as the doctrine of faith viewed in rational terms. *His comrade* and the *leader of his army*, then, stand for the teachings of doctrine, and in fact the main ones. Like a chieftain, a *leader* means the most important parts (§§1482, 2089), and an *army* means the actual teachings. The reason an army symbolizes doctrinal teachings (which relate to truth, or are lower forms of truth) is that in the Word, military service and war symbolize aspects of spiritual military   **3448** service and war (1664, 1788, 2686). So do weapons like spears, shields, bows, arrows, swords, and so on, as shown in various places [309, 1664, 1788, 2686, 2709, 2799]. It is true ideas, or doctrines, that wage spiritual warfare, so they are what armies symbolize. In an opposite sense, they symbolize false ideas, or heresies.

[2] Many passages can illustrate both the positive and negative symbolism of armies in the Word. In Daniel, for instance:

> One horn of the buck of the goats grew immensely toward the south and toward the sunrise and toward the ornament [of Israel], and it grew *right to the army of the heavens* and threw down to the ground some of the army and some of the stars. And it trampled them. In fact, [the horn] exalted itself *right to the chief of the army. Its army* was handed over, along with the perpetual offering, for transgression, and it *cast truth* to the ground. I heard a holy one speaking. He said, "How long will the vision, the perpetual offering, and the devastating transgression continue, so that both the Holy Place and the *army* are given over for trampling?" (Daniel 8:9, 10, 11, 12, 13)

The horn that grew toward the south, the sunrise, and the ornament [of Israel] means the power falsity acquires from evil (§2832). The army of the heavens means truth. The chief of the army is the Lord in regard to his divine truth. Since in a good sense an army means truth, the text says that the horn threw some of it down to the ground, and that the horn cast truth to the ground. [3] In the same author:

> The king of the north will marshal a great throng—more than before—and at the end of the times—years!—he will unquestionably come *with his large army* and with many resources. Then he will stir up his forces and his heart against the king of the south *with a large army*. And the king of the south will engage in war with a *large and very strong army* but will not stand. For those eating his food will break him, and *his army* will drain away, and many will fall down stabbed. (Daniel 11:13, 25, 26)

That whole chapter is about the war between the kings of the north and south, the northern king and therefore his army meaning falsity, and the southern king and his army meaning truth. It is a prophecy of the church's devastation. [4] In John:

> I saw heaven opened, when look! A white horse. And the one sitting on it was called *faithful* and *true;* he was dressed in a garment dyed with blood, and *his armies in heaven* followed him on white horses, dressed

in fine linen, white and clean. I saw the beast and the monarchs of the earth and *their armies* gathered to make war with the one sitting on the horse and *with his army*. (Revelation 19:[11, 13,] 14, 19)

The one sitting on the white horse stands for the Lord's Word, or the Lord in regard to his Word (§§2760, 2761, 2762). His armies in heaven that followed him stand for truth from the Word and so for heaven's inhabitants, who have that truth. The beast stands for the evils that come of self-love; the monarchs of the earth and their armies, for falsities. Falsity's battle with truth is what the passage portrays. [5] In David:

By Jehovah's word were the heavens made; and by the spirit of his mouth, *their army*. (Psalms 33:6)

The army of the heavens stands for truth. Since an army symbolizes truth, angels and the children of the kingdom are called the armies of the heavens because of the truth they know, as in Luke:

Suddenly there was with the angel a *throng of the heavenly army*, praising God. (Luke 2:13)

In David:

Bless Jehovah, *all you his armies*, his attendants doing his will. (Psalms 103:21)

In the same author:

Praise Jehovah, all you angels of his; praise him, all you *armies of his*. (Psalms 148:2)

In Isaiah:

Raise your eyes up high and see who has created these things, *who leads their army out by number*. He calls them all by name; from the throng of the powerful and mighty, not a man will go missing. (Isaiah 40:26)

In the same author:

I made the earth, and the human being on it I created. Myself, my hands spread out the heavens, and *to their whole army I gave commands*. (Isaiah 45:12)

The army of the heavens stands for truth and so for angels, who possess truth, as mentioned. [6] In 1 Kings:

I saw Jehovah sitting on his throne, and the *entire army of the heavens* standing next to him, on his right and on his left. (1 Kings 22:19)

In Joel:

> Jehovah uttered his voice *before his army* because his camp is very large, because those who do his word are numerous. (Joel 2:11)

In Zechariah:

> *I will set up a camp from the army* for my house, as [the army] passes through and returns, to keep a despot from passing over them anymore. Rejoice immensely, daughter of Zion; cheer aloud, daughter of Jerusalem! See: your king comes to you! (Zechariah 9:8, 9)

This is about the Lord's Coming; his army stands for divine truth. For this reason, and because the Lord alone fights for us against the hells, which are constantly trying to invade, very often the Word refers to him as Jehovah Sabaoth, God Sabaoth, the Lord Sabaoth—that is, Jehovah, God, or Lord of Armies. In Isaiah, for example:

> The voice of tumult of the kingdoms of the gathered nations! *Jehovah Sabaoth is leading an army ready for war.* (Isaiah 13:4)

The kingdoms of the nations stand for falsity that grows out of evil. Leading an army ready for war stands for fighting on humanity's behalf.

[7] The twelve tribes of Israel represented the Lord's heavenly kingdom, and tribes and the number twelve both symbolized all aspects of faith—all truth in that kingdom—taken as a whole (§§577, 2089, 2129, 2130, 3272). For this reason they were also called *the armies of Jehovah* (Exodus 7:4; 12:17, 41, 51); were commanded to be led out of Egypt *according to their armies* (Exodus 6:26); camped *according to their armies* (Numbers 1:52); and were divided *into armies* (Numbers 2:1–end).

[8] The symbolism of an army as truth can also be seen in Ezekiel:

> Persia and Lud and Put, *in your army,* were your men of war. Shield and helmet they hung on you; they themselves gave honor to you. The sons of Arvad and *your army* were on your walls all around, and the Gammadians were in your towers. (Ezekiel 27:10, 11)

This is about Tyre, which symbolizes a deep knowledge of goodness and truth and accordingly people with that knowledge (§1201); the army stands for the truth itself. Lud and Put too mean people with religious knowledge (see §§1163, 1164, 1166, 1195, 1231). The shield and helmet mean the accoutrements of spiritual battle or war.

[9] The meaning of an army in a negative sense as falsity is evident in Isaiah:

> It will happen on that day that Jehovah will punish *the army of the heights* on high, and the monarchs of the earth down on the earth. (Isaiah 24:21)

The army of the height stands for falsity springing from self-love. In Ezekiel:

> I will bring you back and put hooks in your jaws and lead you and *your whole army* out—horses and riders, all of them dressed perfectly, a great assembly with shield and buckler, all grasping swords. You will come from your place, from the flanks of the north, you and many peoples with you, all riding on horses, a great assembly, a *large army*. (Ezekiel 38:4, 15)

The reference here is to Gog, which symbolizes an outward show of worship that has been detached from any inward worship and so has become idolatrous (§1151). Its army stands for falsity. [10] In Jeremiah:

> I will send against Babylon one who bends, bending his bow and vaunting himself in his armor. Do not spare the young people; exterminate *its whole army*. (Jeremiah 51:2, 3)

Babylon stands for worship that appears pious on the outside but is inwardly profane (§§1182, 1283, 1295, 1304, 1306, 1307, 1308, 1321, 1322, 1326). Its army means the falsities of people whose worship is like that. Babylon's army has the same meaning in other places too, such as Jeremiah 32:2; 34:1, 21; 39:1. In Ezekiel:

> Pharaoh will see them and comfort himself over his whole throng; [they will be] stabbed by the sword—Pharaoh and *his whole army*—because I will put terror of me in the land of the living. (Ezekiel 32:31, 32)

This is about Egypt, which symbolizes people who twist truth by reasoning about it on the basis of secular facts (§§1164, 1165). Pharaoh's army stands for the falsity that results, as it does in other passages as well, such as Jeremiah 37:5, 7, 11; 46:2; Ezekiel 17:17. In Luke:

> When you see Jerusalem surrounded *by armies*, then know that devastation is near. (Luke 21:20)

This is about the close of the age, or the church's final days, when faith no longer exists. Jerusalem symbolizes the church (see §2117), which is surrounded by armies when besieged by falsities.

[11] From this it can be seen that falsity is symbolized on an inner level by "the armies of the heavens" that Jews and idolaters worshiped, as described in 2 Kings:

> They abandoned all the commandments of their God and had made themselves a cast image—two calves—and made a grove and *bowed down to the whole army of the heavens.* (2 Kings 17:16)

The Israelites are depicted here; Manasseh, in a different verse:

> They built altars to the *whole army of the heavens.* (2 Kings 21:5)

Second Kings 23:4 says that King Josiah brought out of the Temple all the vessels made for Baal and for the grove and for the *whole army of the heavens.* And in Jeremiah:

> They will spread out the bones of chieftains, priests, and prophets before the sun, the moon, and the *whole army of the heavens,* [bones] that they loved and that they served and that they walked after. (Jeremiah 8:[1,] 2)

And in another place:

> The houses of Jerusalem and the houses of Judah's monarch will be like Topheth—unclean—in regard to all the houses on whose roofs they burned incense to the *whole army of the heavens* and poured abundant libations to other gods. (Jeremiah 19:13)

And in Zephaniah:

> I will stretch my hand out against those worshiping the *army of the heavens* on roofs. (Zephaniah 1:[4,] 5)

It is mainly the stars that are called the army of the heavens, but stars symbolize truth and, in a negative sense, falsity; see §§1128, 1808.

3449   *And Isaac said to them, "Why have you come to me, when you hated me and sent me from you?"* means, why were they looking for something divine, when they denied the divinity of the Word's inner meaning and showed hostility toward it? This is established by remarks above at verses 15, 16, 19, 20, 21 [§§3412–3415, 3424–3429].

3450   Genesis 26:28, 29. *And they said, "We saw unmistakably that Jehovah was with you, and we said, 'Please let there be a vow between us, between us*

and you, and let us cut a pact with you: If you do evil with us . . . ! Just as
we did not touch you, and just as we did only good to you and sent you off in
peace. Now, Jehovah's blessing on you!'"

They said, "We saw unmistakably that Jehovah was with you," means
that they knew something divine was in [the Word's literal meaning].
And we said, "Please let there be a vow between us, between us and you, and
let us cut a pact with you," means that their doctrines concerning faith in
and of themselves would not be denied. *If you do evil with us . . . ! Just as*
we did not touch you, and just as we did only good to you and sent you off
in peace means that they had not harmed the Word's inner meaning and
would not do so. *Now, Jehovah's blessing on you!* means that it was from
the Divine.

They said, "We saw unmistakably that Jehovah was with you," means
that they knew something divine was in it. This can be seen from the
symbolism of *seeing unmistakably* as discerning and therefore knowing for
certain, and from that of *Jehovah's being with you* as the inward presence
of something divine. As noted above at §3447, the subject here is the harmony of the Word's inner meaning with its literal meaning and therefore
with the doctrines concerning faith symbolized by Abimelech, Ahuzzath,
and Phicol, so far as they come from the Word's literal meaning. So the
subject is the union of the Lord's kingdom on earth with the Lord's kingdom in the heavens—and with the Lord—through the Word. In its very
highest sense, the Word is the Lord himself. In its deep or inner sense the
Word is the Lord's kingdom in the heavens, and in its literal sense it is the
Lord's kingdom on earth. This has also been said before.

[2] The Lord's kingdom on earth—his church—draws its doctrines
from the Word's literal meaning, so those doctrines cannot help but be
varied and conflicting. One congregation describes one thing as the truth
of the faith because it is what the Word says; another describes something
else as true, again because it is what the Word says; and so on. So the
Lord's church, since it draws its doctrines from the Word's literal meaning, always varies from place to place. Not only congregations but sometimes even the individuals in a congregation differ. Yet disagreement over
the doctrines concerning faith does not prevent the church from being
united, as long as everyone feels the same about wishing and doing well.

[3] Take, for instance, people who acknowledge as doctrine the idea
that neighborly love results from faith, and yet live a life of charity toward
their neighbor. Although their theology lacks truth, their lives do not, so
they have the church, or the Lord's kingdom, in them.

There are also people who say that we should do good deeds in order to earn a reward in heaven (according to the Word's literal meaning in Matthew 10:41, 42; 25:34–46; and elsewhere) but never think about their own merit when they are doing good. They too are in the Lord's kingdom, because they live the truth. Since they do, they readily allow themselves to be taught that no one can earn heaven and that deeds we take credit for are not good.

The same is true with all other fallacies. The literal meaning by its very nature appears self-contradictory in many passages, but that is because it contains appearances of truth accommodated to people who focus on the surface and are therefore caught up in worldly and also bodily kinds of love.

[4] Consequently the text here, under the figure of Abimelech, treats of people dedicated to the doctrines concerning faith (who consider faith essential to salvation, as noted before [§3447]) and of the harmony between those doctrines and the inner meaning. These people also form a bond [with the Lord], obviously, but only if they are ruled by goodness—that is, only if they consider love for others the essential element in life, even though they consider faith the essential element of theology. When they place their confidence or trust (which is what they call faith) in the Lord, they are being affected by love for him. As a result, they live good lives.

However, see previous discussions and demonstrations on this topic: It is not doctrine but neighborly love that makes the church: 809, 916, 1798, 1799, 1834, 1844. Doctrine is worthless if people do not live by it: 1515. The church varies in regard to truth, but love for others makes it one church: 3267. A parallelism exists between the Lord and humankind in heavenly matters, which have to do with goodness, but not in spiritual matters, which have to do with truth: 1831, 1832. There is only one doctrine: that of love for the Lord and charity toward our neighbor: 3445. The church would be united if all the people in it had charity, even if they differed in their worship and doctrine: 809, 1285, 1316, 1798, 1799, 1834, 1844, 2982. The church would resemble the Lord's kingdom in the heavens if everyone had charity: 2385. Heaven contains countless variations on goodness and truth, but through harmony they still make a single whole, just as the body's organs and limbs do: 684, 690, 3241.

3452   *And we said, "Please let there be a vow between us, between us and you, and let us cut a pact with you,"* means that their doctrines concerning faith in and of themselves would not be denied—so far as they came from the Word's literal meaning. This can be seen from the following: A *vow* *between us* symbolizes agreement between doctrine and the Word's literal meaning. *Between us and you* symbolizes harmony with its inner meaning. And *cutting a pact* symbolizes the resulting possibility of a bond. For the symbolism of a *pact* as union, see §§665, 666, 1023, 1038, 1864, 2003, 2021. The idea flowing from all this is that as a result, the doctrines of their faith in and of themselves would not be denied. To repeat, doctrinal teachings are never denied, as long as they come from the Word. The Lord accepts them, provided the person who adopts them lives a life of neighborly love, because everything in the Word can form common cause with such a life. The deeper contents of the Word, though, are joined to a life marked by charity's deeper goodness. See the statements and references at §3324.

If you do evil with us . . . ! Just as we did not touch you, and just as we did only good to you and sent you off in peace means that they had not harmed the Word's inner meaning and would not do so. This is established by the train of thought in the inner meaning and from the remarks above at verses 11, 22, 23 [§§3402, 3432, 3436].

3453

Now, Jehovah's blessing on you! means that it was from the Divine. This can be seen from the symbolism of one *blessed by Jehovah,* when it describes the Lord (that is, the Word's inner meaning, since the Lord is the Word) as divine truth (dealt with in §3140). So it means that it was from the Divine and consequently that they had not harmed the inner meaning and would not do so because it was from the Divine.

3454

To hurt the inner meaning is to deny its main principles, which constitute the actual holiness of the Word: the Lord's divine humanity, love for the Lord, and love for one's neighbor. These three are the main principles of the inner meaning and constitute the holiness of the Word. They are the deepest and most sacred of all the doctrines that come from the Word and the deepest and most sacred aspects of all worship, because they hold within them the kingdom of the Lord itself.

A fourth is that absolutely everything in the Word is divine, down to the smallest tip of a letter; in other words, that the Lord is in the Word. Everyone who possesses doctrine from the Word admits and acknowledges this. Still, people actually deny it at heart when the only sanctity they acknowledge in the Word is that which appears in its literal text. They cannot discern any holiness in the narratives—or in the prophecies—aside from a certain superficial luster the text receives from being characterized as holy. Nevertheless, the Word must be profoundly sacred if it is divine down to the smallest tip of a letter in it.

3455   Genesis 26:30, 31. *And he made them a banquet, and they ate and drank. And they got up early in the morning and swore an oath, a man to his brother. And Isaac sent them off, and they went from him in peace.*

He made them a banquet symbolizes coexistence. *And they ate and drank* symbolizes sharing. *And they got up early in the morning* symbolizes an enlightened state. *And swore an oath, a man to his brother* symbolizes confirmation among people who practice the goodness that comes of truth. *And Isaac sent them off, and they went from him in peace* means that they were content.

3456   *He made them a banquet* symbolizes coexistence. This can be seen from the symbolism of a *banquet* as living together (discussed in §2341).

3457   *And they ate and drank* symbolizes sharing. This can be seen from the symbolism of *eating* as sharing what is good (discussed in §§2187, 2343, 3168) and from that of *drinking* as sharing what is true (discussed in §§3089, 3168).

3458   *And they got up early in the morning* symbolizes an enlightened state. This can be seen from the symbolism of *morning* and of *getting up early* as an enlightened state. In their very highest sense, *morning* and dawn mean the Lord. In an inward sense they mean the heavenly quality of his love and therefore a state of peace as well (see §§2333, 2405, 2540, 2780). And in that inward sense, *getting up* means being lifted (2401, 2785, 2912, 2927, 3171). This shows that *they got up early in the morning* symbolizes an enlightened state.

3459   *And swore an oath, a man to his brother* symbolizes confirmation among people who practice the goodness that comes of truth. This can be seen from the symbolism of *swearing an oath* and of the oath itself as confirmation (discussed in §§2842, 3037, 3375) and from that of *a man with his brother* as the goodness that comes of truth or, equally, people who practice that goodness. On the point that a *man* means truth, see §§265, 749, 1007, 3134, 3309 at the beginning; and that a *brother* means goodness, §2360. For a definition of the goodness that comes from truth, see §§3295, 3332. That kind of goodness characterizes the people represented here by Abimelech, or by the Philistines, whose king he was—people who consider faith the vital component of religion, placing it ahead of neighborly love. The only goodness people like this adopt is the kind that results from truth. All they glean and gather from the Word has to do with faith and so with truth. If anything has to do with goodness and so with life, they hardly even see it. As a consequence, they reinforce in themselves the doctrines concerning faith but not any of those concerning charity. When they do good, they do it because of doctrinal teachings about faith. The goodness that results is called the goodness that comes of truth.

[2] The Lord binds himself to people with this kind of goodness but not as closely as he does to those with the goodness that comes of charity. Love and charity is spiritual connectedness, but faith is not, unless it operates through love and charity. That is why the text says not that they struck a pact with Isaac but that they swore an oath, a man to his brother. A pact relates to goodness, which is an aspect of love and charity, but an oath relates to truth, which is an aspect of faith (§3375). People with the goodness that comes of truth are also said to coexist, as symbolized by the banquet (§3456).

From people like them in the other world I have been granted to see that they are separated from the ones who practice the goodness that comes of charity. The latter are more closely united to the Lord than the former, because the goodness of the former is, so to speak, rigid, unyielding, and ungenerous. It stands not in heaven but on the threshold to heaven.

And Isaac sent them off, and they went from him in peace means that they were content, as can be seen without explanation. **3460**

This too shows that they achieved coexistence rather than closeness, as noted just above in §3459.

Genesis 26:32, 33. *And it happened on that day that Isaac's slaves came and told him the account of the well that they had dug. And they said to him, "We have found water." And he called it Sheba. Therefore the name of the city is Beer-sheba up to this day.* **3461**

It happened on that day symbolizes that state. *That Isaac's slaves came* symbolizes rational ideas. *And told him the account of the well that they had dug and said, "We have found water,"* means inner truth through [doctrines]. *And he called it Sheba* symbolizes the union and confirmation of truth through them. *Therefore the name of the city is Beer-sheba* symbolizes the character of the resulting theology. *Up to this day* symbolizes a permanent state.

It happened on that day symbolizes a state. This is established by the symbolism of a *day* as a state (dealt with in §§23, 487, 488, 493, 893, 2788)—here, the state of the theology under discussion. **3462**

That Isaac's slaves came symbolizes rational ideas. This is established by the symbolism of *slaves* as rational ideas and as facts (dealt with in §2567) and from the representation of *Isaac* as the Lord's divine rationality (dealt with in §§1893, 2066, 2072, 2083, 2630, 3012, 3194, 3210). **3463**

The preceding context indicates which aspect of the Lord Isaac represents here: the Word's inner meaning. Abimelech, Ahuzzath, and Phicol symbolize doctrines about faith drawn from the Word's literal meaning. That is the kind of doctrine that exists with the people called Philistines in a positive sense—those who focus exclusively on the doctrines concerning faith and whose lives are indeed marked by goodness, but the goodness that comes from truth. Their doctrines have some measure of connection with the inner meaning and so with the Lord. [2] People who restrict themselves to teachings about faith and live according to them do form a connection, but a distant one, because they do not learn what charity for their neighbor is—let alone what love for the Lord is—from any desire for it but only from some religious concept. They do not have any perception of what is good but a kind of persuasion that what their doctrine dictates is true and therefore good. When they prove the validity of these doctrines to themselves, they are as likely to be wrong as right, because the only thing that confirms the truth of an idea to us is its goodness. Truth does teach us to recognize goodness, but not to do so perceptively. Goodness, however, teaches us to recognize truth from a perception of it.

[3] Anyone can see how the case stands, and what the nature and identity of the difference is, simply from this general rule concerning neighborly love: "Everything whatever that you want people to do for you, you do likewise for them" (Matthew 7:12). People who do this by command do good to others but only because it has been ordered, not because their heart seeks it. Whenever they do, they start with themselves, and in doing good they are thinking of their own merit. On the other hand, people who do it not by command but out of neighborly love, or because they want to, are operating from the heart, in freedom. Whenever they act, they start with goodwill itself and therefore with something that gives them pleasure. Since this pleasure is their reward, they do not think of taking credit. [4] From this you can see what the difference is between doing good from faith and doing good from charity. You can also see that people who act on faith are further from real goodness—or the Lord—than people who act on charity. It is not easy to introduce them into charitable goodness to the point where they perceive it, because they have little truth. We cannot be brought into charitable goodness until things that are not true have been rooted out of us, which cannot happen as long as their roots reach all the way to conviction.

And told him the account of the well that they had dug and said, "We **3464**
have found water," means inner truth through [doctrines]. This can be
seen from the symbolism of a *well* as the Word (dealt with in §3424) and
from that of *water* as truth (dealt with in §2702)—truth from the Word.
So *telling him the account of the well that they had dug* means [telling]
about the Word, the source of doctrine; and *they said, "We have found
water,"* means that the doctrines contained inner truth. As noted above
[§§3451–3452], all doctrines taken from the Word's literal meaning contain deep truth. The Word's literal meaning is like a well holding water,
because absolutely everything in it has an inner meaning, and this inner
meaning is also present in doctrines that come from the Word.

[2] When we devote ourselves to doctrinal teachings from the Word's
literal text and at the same time to a life matching them, there is correspondence in us. The angels with us are awake to the inner truth, while
we are awake to the outer truth, so we communicate with heaven through
those teachings, but only in proportion to the goodness in our lives.

For instance, while taking Holy Supper, when we simply think about
the Lord because of the words *this is my body* and *this is my blood,* the
angels with us think about love for the Lord and charity for one's neighbor. Love for the Lord corresponds to the Lord's body and the bread, while
charity for one's neighbor corresponds to his blood and the wine (§§1798,
2165, 2177, 2187). On account of this correspondence, desire flows from
heaven through the angels into the reverence we are then experiencing,
and we receive it in proportion to the goodness in our lives.

[3] Angels dwell with each of us in our life's desires and so in our
liking for doctrines we live by, never in a liking for doctrines at odds
with our life. If our life departs from doctrine—say we aim to win status
and wealth through doctrinal knowledge—the angels leave, and hellish
beings take up residence in that desire. These evil beings do one of two
things. One is to flood us with confirmation of those doctrines for selfish
and worldly reasons—in other words, with a dogmatic faith. (When our
beliefs are dogmatic, we are indifferent to their truth or falsity, as long as
they win us allies.) The other is to rob us of all belief. Then the doctrine
on our lips is merely noise sparked and tempered by the fire of love for
ourselves and for worldly gain.

And he called it Sheba symbolizes the union and confirmation of truth **3465**
through them. This can be seen from the symbolism of *calling* something
by a name as its quality (discussed in §§144, 145, 1754, 1896, 2009, 3421), so

that names symbolize some entity or some state (1946, 2643, 3422). Here the name symbolizes the union of confirmed truth through them—that is, through doctrinal teachings. In the original language, *Sheba* means an oath, which symbolizes confirmation (2842, 3375).

Confirmed truth is said to be united when inner truth joins with the outer truth of doctrine from the literal sense of the Word. In the people under discussion, the union is achieved more through truth (matters of faith) than goodness (matters of charity), as noted above at §3463.

3466   *Therefore the name of the city is Beer-sheba* symbolizes the character of the resulting theology. This can be seen from the symbolism of a *name* as the quality (mentioned just above in §3465) and from that of a *city* as doctrine (dealt with in §§402, 2449, 2712, 2943, 3216). So *Beer-sheba,* which in the original language means "well of the oath," symbolizes a theology whose truth has been confirmed. (For the meaning of Beer-sheba as theology, see §§2723, 2858, 2859.)

Genesis 21:30, 31 above says, "'Because you must take seven lambs from my hand; therefore let it serve as a witness for me that I dug this well.' Therefore he called the *place Beer-sheba,* because there they both *swore.*" In that passage Beer-sheba symbolized the state and nature of a theology that came from the Divine and the fact that it was a means of union. Since the subject there was the inner depths of that religion, it says the *place* was called Beer-sheba; but here, since it is talking about the outer surface of this religion, it says the *city* was called that. The term *state* applies to inner depths, and a place symbolizes a state (§§2625, 2837, 3356, 3387), but *doctrine* applies to the outer surface, and a city symbolizes doctrine. All doctrine acquires its state and nature from its inner depths.

3467   *Up to this day* symbolizes a permanent state. This can be seen from the symbolism of *to this day* as a permanent state (dealt with in §2838).

3468   Genesis 26:34, 35. *And Esau was a son of forty years, and he took a woman: Judith, daughter of Beeri the Hittite, and Basemath, daughter of Elon the Hittite. And they were a bitterness of spirit to Isaac and to Rebekah.*

Esau was a son of forty years symbolizes a stage at which the earthly goodness that comes of truth was tested. *And he took a woman: Judith, daughter of Beeri the Hittite, and Basemath, daughter of Elon the Hittite* symbolizes the adding on of earthly truth from other sources than the genuine one. *And they were a bitterness of spirit to Isaac and to Rebekah* means that at first it caused pain.

3469   *Esau was a son of forty years* symbolizes a stage at which the earthly goodness that comes of truth was tested. This can be seen from the representation of *Esau* as the earthly goodness that comes of truth (discussed at §§3300, 3302, 3322) and from that of *forty years* as a state of trial. *Forty* means times of trial (see §§730, 862, 2272), and *years* mean states (487, 488, 493, 893).

The reason this information about Esau is tacked on right after the story of Abimelech and Isaac is that the theme has been people who do the good that grows out of truth—people who live according to doctrines taken from the Word's literal meaning—and they are symbolized by Abimelech, Ahuzzath, and Phicol, as noted repeatedly above [§§3447, 3448, 3451, 3463]. [2] The inner levels, or rational dimension, have been reborn in people with the goodness that comes of truth (that is, people who live according to doctrine), but not yet their outer levels, or earthly dimension. Our rationality is reborn before our earthly part (§§3286, 3288), because our earthly part lives entirely in the world and acts as a base on which our thought and will are founded. That is why we sense conflict between our rational, inner self and our earthly, outer self when we are regenerating. Our outer part regenerates much later and much more reluctantly than our inner part. Nothing that is close to the world and the body can easily be pressured into offering obedience to the inner self, only over a long period of time. The process also requires us to be introduced by the struggles of spiritual trial into many new stages of acknowledgment about ourselves and the Lord—that we ourselves are pitiful, and the Lord, merciful. So it requires many new stages of humility. This situation is the reason for the current addendum concerning Esau and his two wives, who symbolize such things on an inner level.

[3] Anyone can see that earthly goodness is the goodness we are born with, but few if any know what the earthly goodness that comes of truth is. Earthly goodness, the goodness we are born with, comes in four kinds, which are produced by a love of goodness, a love of truth, a love of evil, or a love of falsity. The goodness we are born with takes this nature from our parents, mother and father alike. All the customs and habits that our parents acquire or develop from the way they actually live—eventually becoming so used to them that they seem inborn—pass on to their children and become hereditary. If parents live good lives because they love what is good, finding their pleasure and bliss in such a life, and in that state conceive offspring, the offspring inherit a tendency to similar goodness. If parents live good lives because they love truth (to read about this kind of goodness, see §§3459, 3463), finding their pleasure in such a life, and in that state conceive offspring, the offspring inherit a tendency to similar goodness. [4] Likewise with those who inherit the goodness of a

love for evil or a love for falsity. (These are called good because they look good on the surface to the people who possess them, even though they are anything but.) The vast majority of people in whom earthly goodness appears have this kind.

People with the earthly goodness produced by a love of evil lean and incline toward every type of evil, because they readily allow themselves to be led astray. That goodness makes them especially servile to foul lusts, adultery, and cruelty. People with the earthly goodness produced by a love of falsity lean toward every type of falsity. That goodness makes them seize on dogmatism, especially as advocated by hypocrites and liars who know how to captivate another's mind, worm their way into the other's feelings, and feign innocence.

It is into these kinds of "good"—the goodness of evil and the goodness of falsity—that most people with earthly goodness in the Christian world today are born. Their parents developed a pleasure in evil and in falsity through their actual lives and implanted it in their children and through them in future generations.

3470   *And he took a woman: Judith, daughter of Beeri the Hittite, and Basemath, daughter of Elon the Hittite,* symbolizes the adding on of earthly truth from other sources than the genuine one, as can be seen from the following: A *woman* [attached to a man] symbolizes truth linked to goodness; this is discussed where Sarah and Rebekah form the subject, in §§1468, 1901, 2063, 2065, 2172, 2173, 2198, 2507, 2904, 3012, 3013, 3077. Here it symbolizes earthly truth attached to the earthly goodness currently being dealt with. And *Judith, daughter of Beeri the Hittite, and Basemath, daughter of Elon the Hittite,* represents truth from other sources than the genuine one. The Hittites were among the honest nations in Canaan among which Abraham lived, and from them he bought the cave of Machpelah as a grave (Genesis 23:3–end). Those nations represent a spiritual religion among non-Christians (see §§2913, 2986), but because it does not have truth from the Word, the same people symbolize truth that does not come from a genuine source. A nation representing a religion also symbolizes the type of truth and goodness that exist in that religion, because truth and goodness are what cause a religion to be a religion. So when I speak of a religion, I mean its goodness and truth, and when I speak of these, I mean the religion.

[2] The earthly goodness that comes of truth is not spiritual goodness— not a goodness that embodies faith or neighborly love—until it has been reformed. Earthly goodness comes from our parents, as noted just above at

§3469, but spiritual goodness comes from the Lord. So if we are to welcome spiritual goodness, we have to be reborn. When we are being reborn, truth from other sources than the genuine one attaches to us at first. It naturally fails to stick; all it does is serve as a means for introducing real truth. When real truth has been introduced, truths that are not genuine are removed.

The case resembles that with the young. At first they learn many things, some of them frivolous, like games and so on. The point of these is not to make them wise but to *prepare* them for receiving the useful knowledge that goes with wisdom. When they have acquired this kind of knowledge, they set aside and even discard the knowledge of childhood. The case also resembles the situation with fruit. At first, before it can develop sweet juice, it is filled with bitterness. The bitter juice, which is not its real juice, is a means of introducing the sweet. When the latter enters, the former disappears.

[3] The situation is the same with our earthly self when it is being reborn. Earthly goodness does not naturally want to obey and serve our rational self the way servants serve the person they work for; it would rather wield the power itself. In order for it to be forcibly subdued and tamed, it is plagued by various states of purging and testing until its cravings weaken. Then it is tempered by an inflow of the goodness belonging to faith and charity, coming from the Lord by way of our inner self. Bit by bit the goodness we inherit is rooted out and a new goodness is planted in its place. Religious truth works its way into this goodness like new fibers reaching into a human heart, bringing it fresh fluid, until a new heart gradually grows. [4] The first truth to enter cannot spring from a genuine source because the prior, earthly goodness contains evil and falsity. Instead, the first truth is the seeming truth or appearance of truth that bears a sort of resemblance to real truth. Little by little it creates the capacity and opportunity for genuine truth to instill itself. Real goodness is like the blood in blood vessels or like the fluid in fibers; it guides and molds truth into a form. The goodness formed this way in our earthly, outer self is comprehensive, as if it had been woven together or assembled out of smaller and smaller impulses of spiritual goodness. It is formed through the instrument of our rational, inner self by the agency of the Lord, the only one who forms anything or creates it anew—which is why the Word so often calls the Lord the one who formed you, and the Creator.

They were a bitterness of spirit to Isaac and to Rebekah means that at first it caused pain. This can be seen from the symbolism of *bitterness of spirit* as pain, and from the representation of *Isaac and Rebekah* as the

3471

divine goodness and divine truth in the Lord's divine rationality. In the highest sense this is about the Lord, but in a representative sense it is about people who are his likenesses or images. In the highest sense it tells how the Lord made the humanity in himself divine; in a representative sense it tells how the Lord regenerates us, or makes us heavenly and spiritual. Human regeneration is an image of the Lord's glorification (see §§3043, 3138, 3212, 3296).

There was pain at first because when truth is being incorporated into earthly goodness, it hurts to begin with. It weighs on our conscience and worries us, since we have cravings that spiritual truth fights against. But this initial pain slowly lessens and finally disappears. It is like a sick and feeble body that can be restored to health only by a painful cure; in that state, it has pain at first.

Correspondence and Representation (Continued), Particularly in the Word

3472   THE whole and every part of the Word's literal meaning represents the spiritual and heavenly elements of the Lord's kingdom in the heavens, and in the highest sense it represents the Lord himself. This can be seen from various points made so far and others yet to be made, the Lord in his divine mercy willing.

However, people have put a great distance between themselves and heaven and have immersed themselves in the lowest level of the material world, right down to the dirt. So they find it completely distasteful when you tell them that the Word hides deeper thoughts than they grasp from the literal meaning. They react even more strongly when you say that it contains opaque mysteries suited only to angels' wisdom, and still more strongly when you say it actually holds divine ideas that infinitely transcend an angel's ability to understand.

The Christian world does acknowledge that the Word is divine, but it denies at heart, if not out loud, that the Word is divine in this way. This is not surprising, considering that the earthbound level to which human-kind has currently sunk does not comprehend or want to comprehend anything more elevated.

Spirits or souls entering the other world often receive a visual dem-onstration of the fact that the Word hides secrets like this in its text. Several times when this has happened I have had the opportunity to be present, as can be seen from experiences related in the second volume, in "Sacred Scripture, or the Word, Which Conceals a Divine Message That Lies Open to the View of Good Spirits and Angels" §§1767–1776, 1869–1879. Let me repeat from it the following account, offered by way of confirmation.

3473

A spirit came to me not long after he had left his body. (This I could tell from the fact that he did not yet realize he was in the other life but believed he was still living in the world.) I sensed that he had devoted his time to intellectual pursuits, which I discussed with him, but then to my amazement he suddenly soared into the air. I decided he was the type of person whose ambitions had been lofty (since people like this usually rise into the air) or that he thought heaven was high in the sky. (This kind of person too is usually raised aloft, in order to learn that heaven is not up high but deep within.) I soon perceived, though, that he had been lifted up to a group of angelic spirits positioned a little out in front and to the right, on the first threshold of heaven. He then spoke to me from there, saying that he was seeing sights grander than the human mind could ever conceive. While this was happening, I was reading in the first chapter of Deuteronomy about the Jewish people, specifically the ones sent to scout out the land of Canaan and all that it held. As I was reading it, he said that he caught none of the literal meaning but only the contents of the spiritual meaning, which were too astounding to describe. This occurred on the very threshold of the angelic spirits' heaven. What would it be like in their heaven proper, or in the heaven of true angels?

3474

[2] Then certain spirits present with me, who had previously doubted that the Lord's Word was like this, began to regret their disbelief. In their present state, they said they believed, because they had heard from the spirit that he heard, saw, and perceived it to be so.

Other spirits, however, stood by their disbelief and kept saying it was not true, it was all imagination. So they too were suddenly swept up high. They talked to me from there and confessed that it was anything but imagination, because they really perceived that it was true. In fact, they perceived it more keenly than would ever be possible with any of the senses available during physical life.

[3] Soon others too were raised into the same heaven, including someone known to me in his bodily life. He gave the same testimony, saying among other things that he was too dumbfounded to describe the glory of the Word in its inner sense. Speaking with a kind of pity, he expressed astonishment that humans were completely unaware of such things.

[4] On two later occasions I saw yet others raised into the second heaven to be with angelic spirits, and they talked to me from there. At the time, I was reading Deuteronomy 3 from start to finish. They said they focused only on the deeper sense of the Word and stated positively that not one tip of a letter in it failed to contain something spiritual that harmonized in the most beautiful way with all the other parts. They added that the names symbolize something deeper. This proved to them as well that each and every particular in the Word had been inspired by the Lord, which they had not believed earlier. They also wanted to swear to the truth of this in the presence of others but were not allowed.

3475   Representations like those in the Word are constantly presenting themselves in the heavens, as I have already said and shown several times. One characteristic of these representations is that spirits and angels see them in much clearer light than the noonday light of the world. Another is that when spirits and angels look at the outward appearance, they perceive what it symbolizes on an inward level and on further levels within that one.

There are three heavens. In the first heaven, they see the superficial appearance of an object and perceive what it means on an inner plane. In the second heaven, they see the object as it is in its inner form and perceive what it is like on a still deeper plane. In the third heaven, they see that still deeper form, which is the inmost.

The phenomena that appear in the first heaven are composites of those that appear in the second heaven, which are composites of those that appear in the third. Accordingly, the images seen in the first heaven contain within them those seen in the second, and within these, those seen in the third. Since they are presented according to their different layers this way, you can see how complete, how full of wisdom, and how blissful the images in the deepest heaven are. They are utterly indescribable, because millions of them present themselves as one particular piece of the composite whole.

Each and every representation involves attributes of the Lord's kingdom, which involve attributes of the Lord himself. Inhabitants of the first heaven see within their representations the kinds of things that exist in a deeper realm of the kingdom, within which they see those that exist in a still deeper realm. In this way they see those that represent the Lord, but distantly. Inhabitants of the second heaven see within their representations the kinds of things that exist in the deepest realm of the kingdom, within which they see those that represent the Lord more directly. But inhabitants of the third heaven see the Lord himself.

This reveals how matters stand with the Word. The Lord gave the Word to people and angels so that through it they could be present with him. The Word is a means of uniting earth with heaven and through heaven with the Lord. Its literal sense is what ties us to the first heaven. The literal sense holds an inner sense treating of the Lord's kingdom, which holds a highest sense treating of the Lord, and these senses are nested within each other in order. You can see, then, what the union with the Lord through the Word is like. **3476**

I said that representations are constantly appearing in the heavens and that they involve wisdom's deepest secrets. The ones that people on earth are able to see in the Word's literal meaning are as meager by comparison as the water of a tiny pond is to the water of the ocean. What the representations appearing in the heavens are like can be seen from a number of my earlier eyewitness reports and also from the following. **3477**

As I watched, several individuals were presented with a portrayal of the broad way and the narrow way mentioned in the Word [Matthew 7:12–14; Luke 13:24], the broad way leading to hell, and the narrow way, to heaven. The broad way was planted with trees, flowers, and other plants that looked pretty and pleasant on the outside, but hidden among them lay different kinds of snakes and serpents, which the people did not see. The narrow way did not look as well adorned with trees and flower beds, instead appearing austere and dark, but along it were little angel children beautifully dressed, in the most charming possible parks and gardens—although these too the people did not see. They were then asked which way they wanted to go. They said the broad way, but immediately their eyes were opened, and they saw snakes on the wide path but angels on the narrow. Then they were asked again which way they wanted to go, and this time they silently hesitated. The more open their sight was, the more they said they wanted to go the narrow way, but the more closed it was, the more they said they wanted to go the broad way.

3478 Also represented before several individuals was the tabernacle with the ark. People whose highest pleasure when they lived in the world was the Word have sights like these presented before their eyes. So in this case they saw the tabernacle with all its paraphernalia—its courts, its surrounding curtains, the inner veils, the golden altar of incense, the table with its loaves, the lampstand, the appeasement cover with its guardian beings. Some upright spirits were then granted a perception of the symbolism of the individual parts. The tabernacle represented the three heavens. The testimony in the ark, topped with the appeasement cover, represented the Lord himself. The more their eyes were opened, the more they saw within these objects something heavenly and divine, of which they had had no knowledge during bodily life. Amazing to say, the scene had not the smallest element that was not representative, even down to the hooks and rings [on the curtains].

[2] To take just the bread on the table: Within this bread as a representation and symbol they saw the food on which angels live—heavenly and spiritual love, with all its joy and happiness. Within the bread and within the love they saw the Lord himself as the bread or manna from heaven. In the shape, placement, and number of the loaves they saw still more, as they did in the surrounding gold and the lampstand shedding light on all these things, revealing a representative meaning even more ineffable. And so on in regard to everything else there.

From this it was clear that the rituals or representative acts of the Jewish religion contained within them all the secret wisdom of the Christian religion. It was also evident that people to whom the representation and symbolism of the Old Testament Word is opened up are capable of learning and perceiving the secrets of the Lord's church on earth, when they live in the world. When they enter the other life, they can learn and perceive the secrets of secrets known to the Lord's kingdom in the heavens.

3479 The opinion of Jews living before and after the Lord's Coming concerning the rituals of their religion has been that worship of God consists only in outward acts. They never cared what those acts represented or symbolized. They did not know—and did not want to know—that there was an inner content to their worship or the Word, or consequently that life continued after death, or therefore that heaven existed. They were oriented entirely toward their senses and their bodies. Because they were involved in outward acts devoid of inward content, their worship was actually idolatrous, so far as the worshipers themselves were concerned. They inclined heavily to worshiping any gods that came along, as long as they were persuaded that those gods could make them successful.

[2] That nation was such that it could maintain a superficial piety, performing sacred rituals that represented the heavenly qualities of the Lord's kingdom. Its people were able to sustain a reverence for Abraham, Isaac, and Jacob, for Moses and Aaron, and for David, all of whom represented the Lord. Their highest veneration was for the Word, in which everything in general and particular represented and symbolized something divine. As a result, a representative religion was established among that nation, but if it had learned enough about inner things to acknowledge them, it would have defiled them. It would have engaged simultaneously in outward holiness and inward profanation, so no communication between the representative acts and heaven through that nation would have been at all possible. That is why nothing deep was revealed to that nation—not even the Lord's presence within to save their souls.

[3] The tribe of Judah had more of this character than any other. Jews today, like those of long ago, consider the traditions that they can observe outside Jerusalem to be sacred. They venerate their ancestors and especially the Old Testament Word. Moreover, it was foreseen that Christians would practically reject the Word and befoul their own inner depths with profane practices. For all these reasons, the Jewish nation has been preserved up to the present day, according to the Lord's words in Matthew 24:34. It would have been different if Christians, in addition to possessing deep knowledge, had also lived as deep people. If they had, that nation would have been cut off before too many centuries, as other nations have been.

[4] However, the fact of the matter in regard to that nation is that their reverent exterior, or their holy worship, had no effect at all on their inner dimensions. Their inner depths were sullied with the taint of self-love and the taint of materialism and with the idolatrous habit of worshiping the outer surface devoid of any inner content. Since they have nothing of heaven inside them, they also cannot take any of heaven with them into the other world, except for the few who live a life of mutual love, free of contempt for others.

I have also been shown how the impurities staining that nation did **3480** not prevent the inward, spiritual and heavenly contents of the Word from being displayed in heaven. The dirt was always pushed to the side, where it could not be seen, and the evil was turned into something good, so that only the reverent exterior served as a base. The inner depths of the Word were exhibited to angels without the intrusion of any barriers. This made it clear to me how that people, which was inwardly idolatrous, could represent anything holy, especially the Lord himself. So I could see how the Lord was able to reside in the midst of their uncleanness (Leviticus 16:16) and therefore how they could have something like a religion. A merely representative religion is not a religion but resembles one.

[2] The same thing is impossible for Christians, because although they do not believe in the inner dimension of worship, they know about it, so they cannot have an external piety detached from any inward reverence. For the ones who live their faith, their good qualities provide a means of communication, during which their evil and falsity is put aside. Under those circumstances, surprisingly, everything they read in the Word lies open to angels, even if the reader does not pay attention to the meaning. Abundant experience has shown this to me, because the inner part of such people, which is not very perceptible to them, serves as a basis [for the communication].

3481   I have spent a lot of time talking with Jews in the next world—they appear out in front, in an underground region below the level of the left foot—and one time the conversation had to do with the Word, the land of Canaan, and the Lord.

About the Word, I said that it holds very deep secrets that we on earth cannot see, and they agreed. Then I said that all the secrets there have to do with the Messiah and his kingdom; this too they liked. But when I said that *Messiah* in Hebrew is the same as *Christ* in Greek, they refused to listen.

"The Messiah is absolutely holy," I also said. "Jehovah is in him; and the Holy One of Israel and the God of Jacob mean no one else. Since he is absolutely holy, the only people who can live in his kingdom are those who are godly, not on the outside but on the inside—those without a sordid love of worldly advantages, arrogance toward other nations, or hatred for each other." Again they could not listen.

[2] "As was prophesied," I then said, "the Messiah's kingdom will last forever, and anyone who is with the Messiah will inherit the land eternally. If his kingdom belonged to the world, and its heirs were brought into the land of Canaan, it would last only the short years of human life. What is

more, anyone who died after the exile from Canaan would miss out on the blessing. So you should have realized that Canaan represented and symbolized the kingdom of heaven, especially now that you know you are in the other world and will live forever. Clearly the Messiah has his kingdom here, and if you have the chance to talk to some angels, you will learn that the whole angelic heaven is his kingdom. [3] Besides, the new land, New Jerusalem, and new temple in Ezekiel actually mean the Messiah's kingdom."

The only answer they could give was that the people whom the Messiah was to bring into Canaan who would die after so few years, losing the blessing they were to have there, would cry bitterly.

Although the language of Scripture seems to us so plainspoken and **3482** sometimes unpolished, it is the angelic language itself in its outermost form. When angelic language, which is spiritual, descends into human words, this is the only kind of diction in which it can express itself, because all of its content represents something, and every word symbolizes something. The ancients had no other language, interacting as they did with spirits and angels. It was full of representation and every element of it held spiritual meaning. Their books were written in the same language, because to speak and write this way was the pursuit of their wisdom.

You can see from this how far humankind has since alienated itself from heaven. Currently people do not recognize that the Word contains anything besides what appears in the literal text, not even that a spiritual meaning lies inside it. If anything is described as transcending the literal meaning, they call it mystical and on that account alone reject it. That is why communication with heaven has now broken off so completely that few believe heaven even exists. Strange to say, far fewer of the scholarly and educated than of the uneducated believe in it.

Everything that appears in the universe represents the Lord's king- **3483** dom. In fact, nothing can exist anywhere in the atmosphere and in outer space, or on the earth and in its three kingdoms, that does not represent something in its own way. Anything and everything in the material world is an outermost image. From the Divine come heavenly forms of goodness; from these come spiritual forms of truth; and from both come what is earthly.

This shows how dull, how earthly, and how upside-down human intelligence is, seeing that it attributes everything to nature detached from or rather devoid of any prior influence (its efficient cause). People who think and speak along these lines seem to themselves to be wiser than anyone else in ascribing everything to nature. Angelic intelligence, in contrast, is to attribute nothing to nature but everything to the Lord's divinity—to life, that is, rather than to some dead thing. The experts realize that to remain in existence is constantly to come into existence. However, it violates the passion they have for falsity and the reputation they have for erudition to say that nature continues to remain in existence—as it once came into existence—from the Lord's divinity.

The Divine, then, keeps every single thing in existence, or constantly brings it into existence, and nothing whatever that comes from the Divine can help representing the qualities through which it came into existence. So it follows that the visible universe is actually a theater representing the Lord's kingdom, which is a theater representing the Lord himself.

3484   A great deal of experience has taught me that there is only one life force, which is the Lord's. It flows into us and causes us to live—both those of us who are good and those of us who are evil. Forms consisting of substance respond to this life, and they are given life by a constant divine inflow in such a way that they seem to themselves to live on their own. That is the correspondence between organisms and life. But the nature of the receiving organism determines what kind of life it has. People who have love and charity are in correspondence, because they receive life itself in a fitting way. But people who have the opposite of love and charity are not in correspondence, because they do *not* receive life itself fittingly. So the kind of life that emerges in them depends on their character.

This situation can be illustrated by physical forms that the sun's light flows into; the way light is modified in them depends on the nature of the forms receiving it. In the spiritual world, modifications are spiritual, so the nature of the recipient forms there determines what kind of understanding and wisdom the inhabitants have.

So it is that good spirits and angels appear as forms of genuine neighborly love, but evil and hellish spirits appear as forms of hatred.

3485   The representations that occur in the other life are appearances, but vivid ones, because they are produced by the light of life. The light of life is divine wisdom, which comes from the Lord alone. So everything that becomes manifest in that light is something real, unlike what appears in the world's light. People in the other life have sometimes said that what they see there is real, while the things we on earth see are comparatively unreal. What they see is alive and directly affects their life. What we see is not alive and does not directly affect our life, except so far and so well as the things we see by the world's light unite in a fitting and correspondential way with those we see by heaven's light.

This now shows what representation and correspondence are.